THE AVIFAUNA OF BRITISH INDIA AND ITS DEPENDENCIES

THE AVIFAUNA OF BRITISH INDIA AND ITS DEPENDENCIES

A SYSTEMATIC ACCOUNT, WITH DESCRIPTIONS OF ALL THE KNOWN SPECIES OF BIRDS INHABITING

JAMES A. MURRAY

IN TWO VOLUMES

VOL. I

Published by

Gyan Publishing House
5, Ansari Road
Daryaganj, New Delhi-110002
Phone: 011-47034999, 9811692060
E-mail: books@gyanbooks.com

Distribution Network
gyanbooks.com
India, USA, Canada, UK, Australia

ISBN: 978-93-7447-269-9 (Set)
978-93-7447-377-1 (PB)

First Published, 1887

2nd Impression 2025

Printed at: Gyan Press, Delhi.

THE AVIFAUNA OF BRITISH INDIA AND ITS DEPENDENCIES (VOL. I)
Author: JAMES A. MURRAY

THE
AVIFAUNA OF BRITISH INDIA
AND ITS DEPENDENCIES.

A SYSTEMATIC ACCOUNT,
WITH DESCRIPTIONS OF ALL THE KNOWN
SPECIES OF BIRDS INHABITING BRITISH INDIA,
OBSERVATIONS ON THEIR HABITS, NIDIFICATION, &c.,
TABLES OF THEIR GEOGRAPHICAL
DISTRIBUTION IN PERSIA, BELOOCHISTAN,
AFGHANISTAN, SIND, PUNJAB, N. W. PROVINCES,
AND THE PENINSULA OF INDIA GENERALLY,

WITH

WOODCUTS, LITHOGRAPHS, AND COLOURED ILLUSTRATIONS.

BY

JAMES A. MURRAY,

MEM. NAT. HIST. SOC. AND OF THE ANTHROP. SOC., BOMBAY;
MANAGER, VICT. NAT. HIST. INSTITUTE; LATE CURATOR KURRACHEE MUNICIPAL
LIBRARY AND MUSEUM; AUTHOR OF "A HAND-BOOK TO THE GEOLOGY,
BOTANY, AND ZOOLOGY OF SIND;" "THE PLANTS AND DRUGS OF SIND;"
"KURRACHEE TO KANDAHAR;" "THE VERTEBRATE ZOOLOGY OF SIND;"
"THE REPTILES OF SIND," &c.

VOLUME I.

LONDON:—Trübner & Co., Ludgate Hill.
BOMBAY:—Education Society's Press, Byculla.

1888.

ERRATA.

(*Slips for pasting in Vol.* I.)

At end of page 25—

Sub-family.—CORVINÆ.

Bill stout, long and straight; culmen arched; tarsi stout, scutellate.

At top of page 169—

FAMILY.—CAMPOPHAGIDÆ.

Bill short, a few bristles at the base; nostrils rounded; wings moderate, 3rd to 5th quills longest; tarsi transversely scutellate.

Correct the top heading of alternate pages from 170 to 180 to read Campophagidæ instead of Prionopidæ.

CAMPOPHAGIDÆ.

CAMPOPHAGIDÆ.

CAMPOPHAGIDÆ.

CAMPOPHAGIDÆ.

CAMPOPHAGIDÆ.

CAMPOPHAGIDÆ.

PREFACE.

LED on by friends, correspondents and working field and cabinet Ornithologists, as well as by the successes of all my previously published books, I began this work, which, it is hoped, will be found a useful Manual to the student and to those interested enquirers to whom hitherto a descriptive monograph of all the Birds known to inhabit British India and its dependencies was a desideratum. It is purely intended as a means to the acquirement of a better knowledge of the Avian inhabitants of British India and its dependencies, by furnishing under a generally accepted classification, and within a moderate compass, the ordinal, generic and specific descriptions of all the known species, including all the discoveries made subsequent to the publication of the late Dr. Jerdon's work, and thus rendering greater facilities to the student of the Ornis of the British Indian Empire.

In every instance where a sufficiently large series of specimens was not available to me for description, and where the species had been already so fully described as to leave nothing to be desired, I have by preference given the original descriptions. These are chiefly from Sharpe, Seebohm and Gadow's valuable monographs.

To facilitate the study and identification of species, I have given diagrams illustrating the different parts of Birds, with the corresponding terms used in their description. These, it is hoped, will be found useful to the student, the collector and the would-be enquirer; while numerous woodcuts and coloured illustrations of structural, specific, generic and other characters have been added to simplify identification. The scientific and trivial English names are given of every species described, as well as the different synonyms by which a species has been known. Habits, resorts and distribution have also been given as far as the materials within my reach would permit.

J. A. M.

INTRODUCTION.

Birds form one of the most marked and grand divisions of vertebrated animals, as well as the most lovely group in creation. They are oviparous, red and warm-blooded, feathered bipeds breathing by lungs which are bound by cellular tissue to the inside of the ribs and the sides of the dorsal vertebræ, there is therefore no distinct thoracic cavity, nor free muscular diaphragm. The cells open directly from the bronchial trunks and, though minute, are large compared with the cells of the lungs of quadrupeds. The interior of the bones, by communicating with the cells of the lungs, are respiratory organs, which communicate circuitously with the trachea. The cells which are continued from the lungs into the cavity of the abdomen, extend to the interior of the trunk, appear in the axillæ, in the neck, and in the region of the pelvis. In fact, every part is impregnated with the air in which they are destined to move. The young of birds, however, have the interior of their bones filled with a thin serous fluid or marrow, but this is soon displaced by air from the air-cells of the lungs which gains access at the proximal extremities, to the extent necessary for the various species according to their habits and modes of life. Being intended for flight, their external anatomy or those parts generally visible are specially organized for the purpose. The body is covered with feathers, instead of hair or wool, and the two forefeet of mammals are transformed into wings. As in other classes the form of structure of the body and all its various members as well as the modifications which these parts assume are discriminating characters which enable the Ornithologist to form conceptions of their respective peculiarities. The primary parts of birds, as of all vertebrates, are the head, body and limbs, under which subordinate members may be classed. The head is composed of the bill and the skull. The latter is joined to the body by a neck. The skull is formed of a thin, nearly diaphanous and continuous plate of bone above, with all the cranial bones anchylosed. The occipital is not separated from the parietal bones by a lambdoidal suture, nor is there a sagittal suture to separate the parietals from the frontal. All these have anchylosed at a very early period. The first cranial vertebræ at the base of the occipital bone is short. The sphenoid bone and the parts in front which form the face are lengthened, while the pterygoid portions of the former are detached. The basilar part of the occipital bone ends in a single condyle, and its position at the lower margin of the foramen as well as its rotundity afford mobility to the connection of the occipital (*A*) bone with the slender circular atlas and the vertebral column generally. The neck being composed of numerous bones (*K*) is rendered flexible, and this enables a bird to preen its feathers both on the upper and lower surface of the body and to sleep with its head turned round and placed under the wing. The face of a bird is moveable upon the rest of the skull,—whether articulated as in parrots or not,—the thin nasal (*F*) bones being elastic to a certain extent. The orbits and organs of vision are large, the former being separated only by a thin translucent plate or membrane, while the latter are largely developed in lieu, to a great extent, to the want of the sense of touch. The lower jaw (*P*) moves freely and widens the gape very sensibly. The palatine bones are much developed in length and breadth, and these have between them a large fissure. The nostrils are very various in position, shape, and size, and the upper and lower jaws are also very variable and suited to their habits. In some the mandibles are compressed and lengthened, and terminate in a hook; in others they terminate in a point as in woodpeckers; others again are broad, sharp-pointed, hooked, rounded and hard, or as in ducks long, flat, spoon-shaped, and toothed; while birds of prey have a dense horny bill with the edges sharp, strong, and cutting, and the tip hooked. The bill is composed of two pieces corresponding to the jaws of quadrupeds; the upper portion (*a*) is called the upper mandible, which is either continued far back on the forehead and there dilated as to form a casque or helmet, or there is a soft naked skin at the base as in rapacious birds, which is the cere (8); the lower portion (*b*) is the lower mandible. At the base of the upper mandible, concealed or not, and of various shapes, are the nostrils (*c*), while the high medial keel of the bill is the culmen (*d*) and the corresponding keel of the lower mandible is the gonys (*e*). The margins of both mandibles (*f*), commonly called the commissure, is either arched, straight, curved, or festooned, or the upper overlaps the lower; the forehead (*g*) is the region lying close to the nostrils. The body commences with or joins the breast (*o*) and extends the whole length of the sternum or breast-bone. It is succeeded by the abdomen (*q*) and terminated by the vent (*r*) and the under-tail coverts (*s*).

On the upper part of the body are the wings, the interscapularies or back (*t*), lower back (*v*), the rump (*w*), where the upper tail coverts (*w*2) are situated, and last the tail (*x*). The leg, as in quadrupeds, is composed of the thigh (*gg*), tarsus (*hh*), the toes (*ii*), and the claws.

It is scarcely necessary to give a detailed sketch of the internal anatomy of birds, since a knowledge of what is visible to the eye is almost sufficient to determine or classify them generally, or even closely allied groups—though it would no doubt be of much service to the ornithologist to know the various parts or rather the osteology of birds, in order that comparisons may be made of the bones of different groups and species. Professor C. J. Sundevall, in an article "On the Wings of Birds," translated for the "Ibis" of 1886, by W. S. Dallas, F.L.S., considers the feather covering of the wings of birds to be of the greatest significance in their systematic arrangement. He says, "It is a truth that every external part of an animal can furnish equally certain indications of affinity or distinction between species as an internal part of the body, and that in this respect no order of precedence can be established *à priori* * * * *." From a physiological point of view, indeed, the internal parts may be regarded as more important than the external, but zoographically we must regard the external parts as possessing an equal, if not greater value, because the characters derived from them can be easily recognized and examined.

Birds have much in common with mammals, and it cannot be denied that there are striking resemblances between individuals of both classes, especially in their habits. The Eagle and the Owl may be said to represent the feline tribe; the Vulture, the Hyæna; the Hawk, the Fox; the Parrots, the Monkeys feeding on fruit; the Ostrich, the Camel; the Cassowary, the Llama; and so on, so far as habits and character are concerned. With a few exceptions, they are essentially creatures of the air, and their organization has been fitted for the purpose; the larger birds, as the Pelican and others, are specially organized for carrying their weight by air sacs under their breasts, besides the bones in their body being filled with air, which makes them more buoyant, and facilitate respiration under various pressures of the atmosphere.

Just as is the hair or fur of a mammal or the scales of a snake the feather is a horny production of the epidermis. According to Professor Huxley, it is devolved within sacs from the surface of a conical papilla of the dermis. The external surface of the dermal papilla, whence a feather is to be developed, is provided upon its dorsal surface with a median groove which becomes shallower towards the apex of the papilla. From this median groove lateral furrows proceed at an open angle, and passing round upon the under surface of the papilla, become shallower until, in the middle line opposite the dorsal median groove, they become obsolete. Minor grooves run at right angles to the lateral furrows. Hence the surface of the papilla has the character of a kind of mould, and if it were repeatedly dipped in such a substance as a solution of gelatine and withdrawn to cool until its whole surface was covered with an even coat of that substance, it is clear that the gelatine would be thickest at the basal or anterior end of the median groove, at the median ends of the lateral furrows, and those ends of the minor grooves which open into them; whilst it would be very thin at the apices of the median and lateral grooves and between the ends of the minor grooves. If, therefore, the hollow cone of gelatine, removed from its mould, were stretched from within, or if its thinnest part became weak by drying, it would tend to give way along the inferior median line opposite the rod-like casts of the median groove and between the ends of the casts of the lateral furrows as well as between each of the minor grooves, and the hollow cone would expand into a flat feather-like structure with a median shaft as a "vane" formed of barbs and barbules. In point of fact, in the development of a feather, such a cast of the dermal papilla is formed, though not in gelatine, but in the horny epidermic layer developed upon the mould, and as this is thrust outwards it opens out in the manner just described. After a certain period of growth, the papilla of the feather ceases to be grooved and a continuous horny cylinder is formed which constitutes the quill. Shortly, a feather may be said to consist of a tube or quill (calamus), a shaft, and two webs. The tube or quill is horny and transparent, varies in length according to the species, and is fixed in the skin. The shaft or *rhachis* is that part above the quill which is filled with an elastic, corky, white buoyant pith-like substance which bears the vane or web. It is coated on the outer or generally convex side with a horny lamella not unlike the tube, and on the inner or pithy side (also coated, though slightly) is a well-defined groove along its length up to the umbilicus or the small opening into the interior of the tube, which is closed inside by dry membrane. On the side of the shaft, from above the quill or tube, are vane rays or webs. These latter are, in general, fine, filiform, and nearly cylindrical in the smaller feathers, and flattened in the larger ones, as the quills. These, again, are furnished with barbs, barbules and barbicels, which help to give coherency to the entire web.

Then there are the plumules or accessory plumes which, constructed like the larger feathers issue from the margin of the quill tube below the opening into the interior of the tube, which is regarded as an appendage checked in its growth. This is inconspicuous in gallinaceous birds, as pheasants. The plumules, unlike other feathers, have the vane rays very delicate and fibre-like; two series of barbs issue from them and from the barbs barbicels, extremely fine, entirely disunited, and loose. In the Cassowary and the Emu this *plumula accessoria* is as large as the outer shaft and vane; in others as Grouse and Falcons, about three-fourths the length, downy and incoherent. In the most well-developed feathers, as the quill feathers, the plumule is not present, and in other altogether wanting throughout the whole of their plumage, as in *Strix*, *Columba*, and *Anas*, while in song-birds it is very minute and downy.

Feathers may be divided into those which protect the bird from extreme cold, and those specially intended for flight. Those which are next the body, and commonly known as down, are analagous to the underfur of quadrupeds. These keep the body in an equal temperature, and may be said to resist cold or wet.

Birds which lead an aquatic life have these feathers generally more developed than in others, for the manifest intention of affording additional warmth.

The feathers intended for flight are, first, the wing quills, which may be divided into primaries (4), secondaries (5), and tertiaries (6). The primaries may be distinguished from all the others by their greater size and stiffness. These arise from the bones of the hand. In number they are usually 10; the first of which is on the second finger joint, the 2nd, 3rd and 4th upon the first finger joint, and the other 6 upon the metacarpus. In some songbirds, however, the number is only 9, and the first feather is either rudimentary or wanting, but never the longest. Secondaries are those which arise from the forearm and are inserted in the skin on the posterior side of the ulna. They are not so stiff and strong as the primaries, usually shorter than them, more curved and more mobile. The tertiaries are those attached to the proximal end of the forearm, while the scapulars lie over the humerus and scapula.

The feathers on the upper surface of the wing are mostly developed on the cubitus and commonly designated wing coverts. The greater series (3) cover the base or root of the quills, and in general resemble the quill feathers or primaries, and, like them, are destitute of plumules. The second series, or median coverts (2), are also seated in the fold of the skin behind the arm. The smaller feathers behind this series are the lesser coverts (1).

Next is the tail, the feathers of which in the majority of birds are 12 in number, but there are others with as many as 14 to 18; these act in unison with the wing, during flight, and when expanded act as a rudder. The tail is longest in the Rasorial types and shortest in the natatorial and grallatorials. The tail feathers are covered at the base by the upper and under tail coverts. The tail, as the wing, in its structure shows a peculiar organization specially adapted for various purposes. An even tail is very uncommon; rounded tails are the most prevalent, while the racket tail is exhibited in 2 or 3 groups only as *Edolius*, or *Dissemurus* and *Dissemuroides*, and the lyre-shaped tail exclusively in the Rasorial order.

Of the osteology of birds much will not be said. In the composition of the frame of the body, birds may be said to have false ribs anterior and posterior to the true ribs. These cover nearly the whole short body or trunk, terminate anteriorly in a single articulation with the sternal ribs, and pass forwards to be fixed on the sternal appendices on the middle of the trunk. The false ribs do not at all touch the sternum (TT) or breast bone. In the act of respiration the sternum in birds plays a very important part. It is one of the most remarkable and characteristic bones of the skeleton—first, for its great development; next, for the extent to which it covers the trunk, enveloping, as it does, all the internal organs, and by the median carina in front, giving it solidity, as well as strength and power to the pectoral muscles, the limits of attachment of which latter are marked on the external surface. The surface presented by the sternum or breast-bone bears the permanent and powerful muscles of the humerus; the trunk is solid, and the scapula, situated as it is along the side of the vertebral column, gives attachment to the powerful muscles of flight, while the chief support and means of resistance is the coracoid-bone (*c*). The sternum is not of one shape or form throughout the class, but is variable in consonance with the habits of the different orders, and these different shapes, forms, and varieties of appearance lend considerable aid to the anatomist and systematist in working out perplexed affinities. In ducks and geese the posterior margin is replaced by membrane. In gallinaceous birds it terminates in narrow, separate bones; this is on account of their habit of running and feeding on the ground; while the high-flying rapacious birds have it solidly anchylosed and ossified. There are no parts of animals which vary so much in form and structure as the atlantal and sacral (*f*) extremities; the parts remotest from the centre of the skeleton are the most mutable in form; and the organs of progressive motion conform most to the medium in which animals reside. These parts vary so much in the same class of animals, that we might almost be induced to imagine that in organs so different as the human hand, and the fin of the porpoise or the wing of the bat, or the forefoot of the mole, all unity of composition was lost; and in passing to different classes we should scarcely expect to find the same element of structure which compose the fin of a fish or the foot of a turtle metamorphosed into the wing of the bird. But these very diversities of form of the same organ, when carefully examined, present the best proofs of the unity and simplicity of the plan upon which all organic forms are constructed.

Anterior to the sternum are the clavicles which unite below and form the furcula or merry-thought bone. These are joined to the sternum by ligament or cartilage—and the width of these serve to keep apart the shoulders, in opposition to the strong exertions of the muscles of the wing in flight.

In most birds—arboreal birds especially—the legs are slender and as light as the wings. These have the long tendons of the flexors and extensors continued to the foot. By the long flexor of the toes passing over the knee and behind the heel, the bending of these joints forces them to grasp mechanically the branches on which they are perched.

The leg bones consist of a short femur, long tibia with an imperfect fibula anchylosed to it; a patella; an anchylosed tarso-metatarsal bone (the tarsus) and the toes. The pelvis is much extended longitudinally, and being anchylosed with the vertebral column, affords a large surface for the attachment of the muscles which support the trunk upon the thighs. The long iliac bones are excavated below and receive the kidneys. The ischia and pubic bones are wide and develope in their cavity the eggs, from which they are also expelled.

The muscular system of this class is also adapted for their aërial life and to carry them through the atmosphere. According to Professor Grant, of the Edinburgh College, their irritability or power of contraction is the greatest in the living state, and is the most quickly lost after death, its tenacity after death being generally in the inverse ratio of the degree of activity of that power during life. The muscles are generally more firm and vascular, tougher, stronger, and of a darker colour than in the cold-blooded vertebrates. These properties are most exhibited in the high-flying rapacious birds, and less so in granivorous birds. This muscular force becomes necessary in birds in order that they may fly, either for safety or to pursue their prey through the air, as well as to follow the seasons from latitude to latitude and to perform their migrations over mountain chains, continents, or the trackless ocean. Though the muscles of the extremities of birds are generally short and thick, the tendons are longer and slender, dense, and often ossified. The form and movements of birds being nearly the same, there is a great uniformity in the disposition of their muscles. Their arms and hands being appropriated for flight, their progressive motion through the air depends chiefly on the action of the *pectoralis major* or the *humerus,* a muscle surpassing in magnitude all the rest in the body and covering nearly the whole of the forepart of the trunk. The muscles of the arm, the forearm, and the hand are inserted high up, and their fleshy portions confined to near their orifice, so that only the long tendons are sent down to the points which are to be moved. There is very little motion in the phalanges of the fingers.

It is not within the scope of this introduction to give an exhaustive or detailed classification of the organs of birds. The osseous system or the organs of support has been touched upon, also the tegumentary organs and those of motion. To detail the organs of connexion, sensibility and sensation as well as of nutrition and generation would go far beyond the intended limits of this introduction, while the proper treatment of these would need a more competent writer. *En passant,* however, a few remarks may not be out of place, especially in reference to those organs which the ornithologist and the student must necessarily examine—for instance, the testes. These, it is generally known, lie in front of, and in close proximity to, the kidneys, and although there are certain external characters which would enable the determination of the sex of a bird, yet nothing would be more satisfactory than an examination of this organ of generation—testes or ovaries decide the question beyond doubt. During the breeding or pairing season the testes of all male birds are much developed, while the female sex exhibit in the same situation well-developed ovaries which at other times though present, are small and granular. External sexual differences are more marked in birds than in mammals and other vertebrates; but these are not always reliable, especially in the case of birds, the young and the males of which assume the plumage of the female, or *vice versâ,* at different seasons of the year. The males, with some exceptions, are as a rule larger and more highly coloured.

The voice organs are placed in a glottis, at the bifurcation at the end of the wind-pipe, which is formed of entire rings of cartilage, and the call of each bird is produced by peculiar sets of muscles called the larynx. It is here, that that peculiar gift of Nature, the voice of birds, is formed, and this one of all other attributes distinguishes the class from all others in the animal kingdom. The air contained in the cells of the lungs is the force used, while the wind-pipe and the larynx with their contractions, or expansion or movements in the gullet, contribute to the modulations and modifications of the voice. By their song one knows of their happy and cheerful life, and by it the male woos its mate. It is a language which is not even known whether belonging to one family only, or generally intelligible among the class.

The nervous system in birds and the organs of the senses run rapidly to high development.

The sense of sight is also very highly developed in birds, and each class and each family and sub-family will be found to be fitted with organs developed to the extent of their wants and to suit their living condition. The eagle and the raptores generally soar out of human sight, and yet they can see their prey notwithstanding the immense distance. The owl is consigned as a night watchman, and its organs of sight are so adapted that it can only distinguish objects with greater facility in the dusk and when all nature is desirous of repose. It is, however, compensated by a larger or more highly developed sense of hearing. The sense of sight is certainly extremely keen and piercing, and this fact no doubt is an important factor in the solution of the question of the manner in which thousands of miles are traversed by birds in their annual migrations. This must assist them.

It is doubtful whether there is any special development of the sense of taste in birds; while that of smell, in the absence of any reliable data, may be said to be, if at all, very little developed, except in carrion feeders.

Like quadrupeds, birds may be classified as granivorous, carnivorous, and mixed feeders, or those that partake of both. Granivorous birds are furnished with larger and proportionally longer intestines than carnivorous species. Their food first enters a craw where it reaches entire, but soon undergoes partial dilution by a peculiar liquor secreted from the glands—thence enters another stomach, and eventually the gizzard or true stomach, where, with the aid of powerful muscles, thick and powerful membrane and stones it is triturated and becomes fit for the action of the gastric juices.

In their habits birds are either monogamous or polygamous, the latter exists generally among the Rasores or Gallinacea. Some again live a solitary life till the breeding season, when they begin their courtship and live in pairs, whilst their united efforts are necessary in forming their temporary habitation and in rearing their offsprings. There are also some, as the cuckoo, which leave their eggs to the care of a foster parent. Birds generally evince great affection for their young, and do not leave them till they can feed themselves. A great number or the majority of those known to inhabit India and its dependencies quit the country for the purpose of breeding. Each species associate in flocks and aided by their keen sight, together with the advantage they possess of flying at considerable heights in the air, they are enabled with their instinctive knowledge to discover the route they are to take to migrate—taking, probably, as a guide, the appearance of the atmosphere, direction of winds, &c.; so that without recourse to improbable modes it is not difficult to form an idea of the speed at which they go in transporting themselves to far countries by crossing vast ocean tracts. Without the means of conveying themselves from one place to another they could scarcely subsist for the reason that climatic influences affect their food-supply. This may also be said to be one of the reasons for migrating. Besides the want of food, other causes of migration are, the want of a proper temperature of air and a convenient situation for the great work of breeding and rearing their offspring. They either remove from one country or climate to another—or from the inland districts to hills, forest regions or to sequestered rocks or islands in the sea, or to vast sandy plains far removed from, or in the vicinity of, the sea or river. And all this is conducted with the greatest punctuality, and the same may be said of their reappearance a few months later. It is also a noteworthy fact, proved by experiments, that birds which affect a certain station or district usually return to it year after year. The question as to how they subsist during their migrations is readily solved, when we consider the velocity of their flight together with the considerable length of time the majority continue on the wing. If we estimate the speed of a bird's flight at a mile in two minutes it would need but 24 hours to carry it as many as seven hundred miles without taking into consideration favourable wind currents which would probably nearly double the distance. Red-starts and other short-winged birds pass by gradual and slow movements—as is evidenced by their appearance in different countries at different times of the year—but these seldom go further than the inaccessible heights of mountain ranges. Many journey during the night to avoid the dangers of daylight or for the purpose of taking advantage of favourable air currents. What the true reason for migrating is, has yet to be learnt. We see their punctuality of departure and return, we note the dates very carefully, the time of their nidification, the composition of the various structures they build for the rearing of their young, also the number of eggs they lay, their colour, size and shape as well as the changes of their plumage during the breeding season, but beyond this, and conjecture, we have not gone. The nidification of birds is indeed very various, but in consonance with their habits. The high-flying rapacious birds have their eyries on the ledges of high mountains in the most inaccessible parts or on the tops of high trees; the larger ones, including the Vulturinæ, lay but one, and seldom two eggs. The lesser ones, as the Accipitrinæ, build generally on trees, or on steeple tops, and lay 2—4 eggs, and seldom do more than repair their nests annually. All true vultures lay but a single egg, and their nests, as are those of eagles, are built entirely of stout sticks and twigs with a hollow receptacle lined with coarse grass or fine twigs and any soft material. Bones also form a part of the structure. Many birds build in society—occupying trees, mountain ledges, plains, and the eaves of roofs—as sparrows, crows, herons, gulls, terns; and some when robbed of their eggs lay others very shortly after. The situation of the nests, too, are quite in consonance with their habits of life. Owls build in holes in wells, caverns, and in old decayed trees; Woodpeckers in holes in trees; Kingfishers in the banks of streams; the Swallow tribe build nests composed of mud plaster and feathers against the face of a wall, or under a roof or bridge, while others again, as the Byah or Weaver-bird, Honeysuckers, &c., build pensile nests, and all songsters nearly, of the Timeliinæ, group make small nests in bushes or shrubs; and with an instinctive knowledge endeavour to hide their nests by various artifices, as covering them with cobwebs, lichen, or plaster to give them the appearance of the surroundings of the nest.

Of the Avian inhabitants of India nearly one-half are known to breed in the country. A great number go no further than the Himalayan range, while the rest may be said to be resident members, and to breed on the plains.

It is not necessary to refer to the geographical distribution of species, nor to divide the country into geographical regions, as the table at the end of the volume will sufficiently show the first, and the text the latter, while it is patent to all that humid countries comprise birds of bright plumage, and those of the plains of duller plumage, and in consonance with the nature of the surroundings. The geographical distribution of species has been worked out from all the materials available.

It is above half a century since Major Franklin, who was the first writer on Indian Ornithology, published a paper on the Ornithology of India. This paper appeared in the Proceedings of the Zoological Society of London. Colonel Tickell soon followed by publishing in the Asiatic Society's Journal a list of the Birds of Bhorabum and Dholbum. Another equally energetic naturalist was Col. Sykes, who in 1832 began his Catalogue of the Birds of the Deccan, and continued his studies and publications for some years, not only of birds but of the mammals and fish of the Mahratta Country so designated, while Mr. Brian Hodgson, who was attached as Resident at the Court of Nepaul, added largely to the store of knowledge of the avian inhabitants of the Himalayas. His contributions are spread both in the Indian and Home scientific periodicals, and his valuable MSS. and drawings, so largely referred to in every Ornithological work, are zealousy watched over and consulted at the British Museum. Assam was next worked out by MacClelland, and his papers,—also published in the Zoological Society's Proceedings in 1839,—are full of interest, and particularly as showing the geographical distribution of the Himalayan birds.

Dr. Adam collected in Cashmere, as well as in the North-West Provinces of India; Colonel Tytler in Barrackpore and Dacca; while the names of Hutton and numerous other observers and collectors are prominent in the earlier journals as contributors of interesting notes on habits, nidification, &c., of species in various parts of India.

Mr. Blyth, who is rightly called the Father of Indian Ornithology, "was by far the most important contributor to our knowledge of the Birds of India." Seated, as the head of the Asiatic Society's Museum, he, by intercourse and through correspondents, not only formed a large collection for the Society, but also enriched the pages of the Society's Journal with the results of his study, and thus did more for the extension of the study of the Avifauna of India than all previous writers. There can be no work on Indian Ornithology without reference to his voluminous contributions. The most recent authority, however, is Mr. Allen O. Hume, C.B., who, like Blyth and Jerdon, got around him numerous workers, and did so much for Ornithology, that without his Journal "Stray Feathers,"—no accurate knowledge could be gained of the distribution of Indian birds. His large museum, so liberally made over to the nation, is ample evidence of his zeal and the purpose to which he worked. Ever saddled with his official work, he yet found time for carrying out a most noble object. His "Nests and Eggs," "Scrap Book," and numerous articles on birds of various parts of India, the Andamans and the Malay Peninsula, are standing monuments of his fame throughout the length and breadth of the civilized world. His writings and the field notes of his curator, contributors and collectors are the pith of every book on Indian Birds, and his vast collection is the ground upon which all Indian Naturalists must work. Though differing from him on some points, yet the palm is his as an authority above the rest in regard to the

Ornis of India. Amongst the hundred and one contributors to the Science in the pages of "Stray Feathers," there are some who may be ranked as specialists in this department, and their labors need a record. These are Mr. W. T. Blanford, late of the Geological Survey, an ever watchful and zealous Naturalist of some eminence. Mr. Theobald, also of the Geological Survey, Mr. Ball of the same Department, and Mr. W. E. Brooks. All these worked in Northern India, while for work in the Western portion must stand the names of Major Butler, of the 66th Regiment, Mr. W. F. Sinclair, Collector of Colaba, Mr. G. Vidal, the Collector of Bombay, Mr. J. Davidson, Collector of Khandeish, and Mr. Fairbank, each one having respectively worked the Avifauna of Sind, the Concan, the Deccan and Khandeish.

The country referred to in the following volumes embraces the whole of India, including those recently acquired possessions in (now British) Burmah. Of this latter and most interesting portion of the Indian Empire, Mr. Eugene Oates, of the Public Works Department, has written a connected and detailed account, and it is from the pages of his valuable work I have been able to add much to the knowledge of the Avifauna of the Indian Empire as it now stands. In his Introduction he gives a *resumé* of the Ornithological explorations in that country. Colonel Tickell, whose contributions in the early numbers (1833) of the Asiatic Society's Journal are of much interest, is said to be the first Ornithologist who attempted to work Burmah. His field of work was in Tenasserim, chiefly among the higher hills and mountains to the east of Moulmein, culminating in the peak of Mooleyit, which rises about 6,000 feet above sea level. The late Mr. Blyth, after assuming charge of the Asiatic Society's Museum, found willing contributors in Captain (now Sir Arthur) Phayre, also the late Major Berdmore, Dr. Mason and others. Mr. Blyth's contributions of the birds of this country also swell the pages of the Asiatic Society's Journal, as well as those of the "Ibis," His valuable Catalogue of Burmese Birds was his last contribution, and this was published in 1875 by the late Lord Tweeddale as a posthumous work. The latter, recently known as Lord Walden, also interested himself in the

Ornithology of Burmah, and his valuable papers have also been published as a posthumous work, edited by Captain R. G. Wardlaw-Ramsay, who explored a considerable portion of Pegu.

The following are other particulars given by Mr. Oates of the work done in Pegu. He says: "Turning now (1883) to those who are engaged in active work in connection with Burmese Ornithology, I come to a small band of hardworking field naturalists. Mr. A. O. Hume in his study and Mr. W. Davison in the field have for many years past actively worked Tennaserim." The notes of these Naturalists enrich the pages of Oates' work, as well as of this, culled from both sources.

Other workers in the field of Burmese Ornithology are Mr. W. T. Blanford, Captain Fielden, Dr. Armstrong, Captain Bingham, the late Colonel Lloyd, the late Captain Beavan, Mr. Oliver and Mr. DeWet; also Mr. Hough and Mr. Shopland. The contributions of all these gentlemen are to be found in the pages of "Stray Feathers."

British Burmah, according to Oates, is an irregular, narrow, maritime country, hardly any portion being more than 200 miles from the sea. It lies entirely within the tropics, the most northern portion of Arrakan being at a short distance from the Northern tropic, and the most Southern point of Tennasserim lying on the 10th degree of North Latitude. The general character of the country may be said to be mountainous, the only flat portions being strips of land along the banks of the larger rivers, and considerable areas at the mouths of these rivers.

The whole of British Burmah where not cultivated is covered with dense growth of vegetation. On the elevated portions, the vegetation is composed of large forest trees and bamboos, and on the low alluvial plains, elephant grass of great height. The climate, owing to a heavy rain-fall, is said to be humid, and its effects, to cause the plumage of birds to be of great brilliancy. The same may be said of that portion of the Zoological region which comprises the Himalayas, also Eastern Bengal, and Malabar.

Southern India has been practically worked out by the late Dr. Jerdon. His admirable manual shows the energy he spent in bringing to perfection a system of classification to this day admitted as practically good though not very natural; but, yet the foundation for the past quarter of a century of every work on the Avifauna of India, and if there are any who differ from him in certain views, it is because they live in later times, and follow, though not quite, those who base their classifications on internal as well as external structure.

Classification—according to Jerdon—may be said to be the grouping of objects according to their affinities, and their arrangement into divisions of various degrees of magnitude. Its object is to bring together those beings that most resemble each other, and to separate those that differ. By some it has been regarded simply as a convenient method of arrangement for shortening the labour of the naturalist, who, by its means, instead of studying all the characters which each specimen presents, is enabled, by knowing its general position, to confine his attention to a few of the minor details of structure. His labour is thus simplified by the union into one group of all the animals which agree in the most important and essential characters. The Philosophic naturalist has, however, a higher aim, and his object is to discover the natural system, or in other words, to endeavour to develop the general plan on which the Creator has formed and arranged the numberless species of natural objects.

On comparing certain species with others, we find various degrees of resemblance of structure and general appearance. Those, which are nearest and most close, are called affinities, and the more distant resemblances, analogies; and these are of every degree of nearness or remoteness. The affinities of species may be said to point out their order of succession in nature, and are easily understood and appreciable. Not so, however, the analogies exhibited by many species and groups to others, perhaps very distantly related. These may be resemblances of structure, or of colour, or of habits. Some naturalists explain them by expressing their belief that in every group, great or small, there are certain types of structure, offering fixed characteristic marks, and that analogies are, simply, the representation in one group of a certain type in another or, to put it in other words, that analogous groups or species simply occupy a corresponding place in their respective classes, orders, or families. This theory of representation has, perhaps, been carried out, to too great an extent, by certain writers, but, nevertheless, it appears to be founded on nature; and the existence of these, often unexpected analogies between distant groups and species, clearly manifests the unity of the plan of the animal creation. According to Mr. Darwin's views, such analogies might be explained on the supposition that the resemblances were due to some remote ancestral origin. The colours and markings of some birds appear to be repeated in other groups; and, in most natural divisions, great variety of form of bills, and also of other parts is exhibited, representing several distinct types; and, in some, more distantly related groups, analogy is shown by habits, by the colour of the eggs, by seasonal change of plumage, &c., &c. Many examples of analogy will be pointed out in the present work.

On beginning at any point in any series of beings, and tracing step by step, the scale of affinities, we soon find that the supposed chain is interrupted, and that branches strike off in various directions. That a linear arrangement is quite impossible has long been conceded universally; but what directions the divergencies take, is not agreed on; nor, indeed, have Zoologists of the present day decided, that there is a fixed plan for any one class, still less that the same system extends through all. Strickland, and quite recently, Wallace, have attempted to show the affinites of some families and orders of birds by means of diagrams.

Certain English Naturalists, and simultaneously, one or more German Botanists, have maintained that, in arranging any series of animated beings, according to their affinities, the tendency is to revert to the point whence they set out, not indeed in an unbroken line, but in a series of circles. Thus, the circular system, as it has been termed, has been strained, perhaps, too far by its exponents, but there is no doubt that in many instances this tendency to a quasi-circular arrangement appears to exist in nature, and even Wallace's diagrams show this. It appears, however, according to some, that the affinities of the species of any group are various, and cannot be expressed by figures, every natural group and species being connected not with two only, but with several; and it is possible that any natural group, if we possessed all the forms which it comprised, would present links of transition towards all the other groups of the same family or order. Many examples might be given to show the tendency to a circular arrangement, but I shall content myself by pointing out to the student this supposed feature, to verify, or otherwise, in any group he may be studying. Many gaps of course occur in following the chain of affinities, some very great, others easily bridged over. These of course are stumbling blocks in the way of such as believe in a complete chain or circle; and the fossil remains of birds, hitherto discovered, have not been sufficiently numerous to make these intervals much less.

That a special design is exhibited in Creation there can, I think, be but little doubt. It is admitted by almost all, and most fully and unequivocally, in the best known and most highly organized group, the Vertebrata; in all the classes of which a certain archetype of form is preserved, marked and recognizable, however disguised for special ends. It is surely more consonant to our ideas of a Creator to believe that He formed His numberless creatures with certain relations to each other, than to conceive that each was brought to life independently. Indeed, a follower of Darwin might fairly argue that the evidence of design is as clearly shown by the theory of the transmutation of species, as by that of separate individual creation; but Darwin himself, perhaps, lays too much stress on external and fortuitous circumstances as producing varieties, and not enough on the inherent power of change, which, as he clearly shows, is now and then exhibited by various organic bodies.

That species were created at hap-hazard, without any reference to others, either of the same group or more distant ones, is a doctrine so opposed to all the affinities and analogies observed throughout the animated world, that the mind refuses to accept it, and intuitively acknowledges the evidence of design.

That a certain system has been followed, if we allow design at all, must be admitted, but the exponent of the *natural* system—Sharpe, Gadow, Seebohm and others too numerous to mention notwithstanding—has yet to appear. "The tendency of the present age is to accumulate facts, and not to generalize, but we have now a sufficiency of facts, and want our Lyell to explain them."

By the consent of most naturalists, all objects of nature are divided into kingdoms, sub-kingdoms, classes, orders, families, and genera, and, in some cases, where the families are numerous, tribes, sub-families, and sub-genera are added. Birds are a class of the sub-kingdom Vertebrata, of the Animal kingdom. The Orders of birds are founded chiefly on the form of the bill, and more especially of the feet. Families are characterized by more minute distinctions of the bill and feet, together with characters drawn from the wings, tail, and certain habits, more or less common to all. A genus comprises one or many species closely resembling one another in the structure of bill, feet, wings and tail, and in habits, yet differing, it may be, in colour, size, or some minute differences of structure. To give a familiar example, the European Kite and the common Kite of India are species of the same genus, *Milvus;* and the English Kingfisher and the little Indian Kingfisher, are separate species of the same genus Alcedo, each of these genera containing several species. Of late years genera have been greatly divided and multiplied, some of them being classed as sub-genera; but, in practice, and till the whole realm of Ornithology is presided over by a master hand, no distinction can be satisfactorily pointed out, or acted on. When the families of any order are very numerous, they are classed in tribes; and when the genera of any family are numerous, or comprise several distinct forms, they are grouped into sub-families.

In every natural assemblage of forms, whether it be genus, family or order, there is some one form which presents the characters that are common to all, in a more remarkable and complete manner than the rest; and this is called the type of the group. Thus each genus has its typical species; each family its typical genus, and so on; the type being, in each instance, that form to which our minds naturally revert as best exhibiting the characters that belong to the entire group. Some are very close to the type, others differ from it to such a degree that we might have failed to recognise the connection, were it not for the presence of intermediate links. These are called aberrant forms.

It may be asked, are the divisions, which are here indicated, natural, *i.e.*, marked out by nature, or, in other words, designed? That some of them are so, we may, I think, safely infer from the example already quoted of the Vertebrata. Here we have at least four, some say five, great divisions marked out by nature so broadly that the distinctions are in most cases recognizable and patent to all; and, in each of these classes so clearly marked, that there are certain divisions apparent even to the uninstructed; such, for example, among birds, are the Birds of Prey, Owls, Finches, Game birds. Ducks, &c., &c. Many genera, too, are undoubtedly exceedingly natural and clearly defined; and on the whole, I think, we may conclude that Nature herself (could we but correctly read her lessons) has pointed out most of the divisions; or, in other words, has varied each group, small as well as great, in a certain and definite method. Many natural divisions however appear to grade into each other, and have no definite limits; yet, for purpose of study, we must assign limits and characters; and the affinities, by which they are grouped, must be judged of by as many and as constant characters as possible, derived from all parts; but certain typical characters must be assigned.

There are at present above 8,000 species of birds known and described, though much of the civilized world has yet to be explored. When this has been done, what the number may be it is difficult to conjecture, but this large number has been arranged by Naturalists into six large orders, founded entirely on the organs of manducation and prehension. These are :—

I.—Raptores, or birds of prey.
II.—Insessores, or perching birds.
III.—Gemitores, or pigeons.
IV.—Rassores, or game birds.
V.—Grallatores, or waders.
VI.—Natatores, or swimming birds.

Though this is the basis of classification, there is a tendency in the present day to split and divide these, and to upset the order of arrangement, owing to structural and external characters combined, being made the basis, hence we see the Raptores placed after the Parrots, and the Passeres holding the first place, as in the following rather mixed arrangement :—

I. Passeres ; II. Macrochires ; III. Pici ; IV. Coccyges ; V. Psittaci ; VI. Striges ; VII. Accipitres ; VIII. Steganopodes ; IX. Herodiones ; X Anseres ; XI. Columbæ ; XII. Gallinæ ; XIII. Geranomorphæ ; XIV. Limicolæ ; XV. Gaviæ ; XVI. Tubinares ; XVII. Pygopodes. It is needless to defend this system ; it cannot be done ; the oldest system must survive.

Raptores, or birds of prey, are distinguished by their crooked bill and claws, by means of which they are enabled to overcome, and in the order of nature to prey upon other birds and small quadrupeds, to keep that necessary balance so needful. They hold the same rank among birds as the *Carnivora* among the quadrupeds. They are divided into two families, the diurnal and nocturnal, the latter being the owls, which issue at dusk. The diurnal species are the eagles, vultures, kites, falcons, hawks, &c. They are readily distinguished by having their nostrils placed in a naked skin or cere, and their feet bearing three toes before and one behind and their eyes placed laterally ; while the *Striges*, or nocturnal species, have their nostrils covered with stiff hairs, the outer toe reversible ; eyes large, and directed forwards. The Passerine birds form the largest class. They are all very nearly alike in structure, and are divided according to the position of their exterior toe, those having the midtoe united to the middle by one or two joints only ; and those with the exterior toe united to the middle one as far as the last joint but one. The next order is that of the Climbers or Scansores, with both the outer and great toe directed backwards. Following this are the Gallinaceous birds, or Rasores of some : birds of heavy gait, short, rounded wings, heavy flight, such as peafowls, game jungle cock, &c. The Waders or Grallatores, comprising the 5th order, are distinguished by the naked tarsus and a portion of their thighs also, their long legs, which they lay back under the tail feathers in flight. The last are the web-footed birds, as the ducks, characterized by their webbed feet, and generally broad, spathulate bills. A more detailed account of the orders, sub-orders, families and sub-families into which these have been divided will be found under the respective headings in the body of the work, which cannot from its nature have much pretensions to originality.

It is only as a descriptive handbook of the birds of British India, that this work should be regarded. The idea of writing it did not originate wholly with myself, but besides the trouble and inconvenience experienced by me in my official capacity when Curator of the Kurrachee Museum in looking up literature for determining species, there was a general conviction among all my correspondents and numerous working cabinet and field naturalists that a work of this kind in a moderate compass would be welcomed as supplying a desideratum, especially if all the knowledge extant of the birds of British India were put together under one consecutive serial number, so as to remedy the present existing confusion, and simplify identification. Numerous valuable works have been laid under contribution in preparing the work, especially Sharpe, Seebohm and Gadow's Catalogues; Jerdon's valuable Manual; Oates' Birds of British Burmah; Stray Feathers; Ibis; Hume's Nests and Eggs, &c., &c., all of which have been referred to under the synonyms of species, and thus avoiding the use of inverted commas wherever they may have been required. In doing this latter I would crave the indulgence of all authors for the privilege I have taken, of in this way, so largely adding from their valuable works, to the existing knowledge of the Avifauna of British India. I only trust that this small effort will find public favour. It will be made as complete as possible. As the work progresses, everything new to the Ornithology of India will be added, so that future labourers will no longer have to search far and wide, and consult large libraries of books, often too vainly, for what has been already recorded; but in using this work will find it an unpretending manual to guide them in adding to the present accumulation of facts, much which is at present hidden and unknown to science.

In concluding this Introduction, it only remains for me to acknowledge the valuable assistance received in this attempt to collate the scattered information regarding the Avifauna of British India, into a systematic account, and, as stated in the Prospectus, arranged according to the most modern and generally accepted classification. Though seemingly simple, even this little of the 1st volume has involved considerable labour and research. The whole of it cannot well be successfully accomplished without aid. Up to the present very little of this has been received, though the calls have been unceasing, and it has been left for me to work single-handed, assisted by only a few to the best of their abilities, when freed from the weighty cares of their office. Among those to whom I am under special obligation I would mention Mr. W. F. Sinclair, the Collector of Colaba, and Mr. J. Davidson, the Collector of Khandeish, both of whom very kindly furnished me with such specimens as they could obtain from their respective districts. To Lieutenant Henry E. Barnes, D.A.C., I am also indebted for many valuable notes in regard to nidification, &c., while the kindness of Mr. A. O. Hume, C.B., in sending me, some little time ago, a large collection of birds from British Burmah and the Himalayas generally, has helped me considerably in more accurately describing and comparing birds, which till very recently were almost unknown. I have also to acknowledge the assistance received from Mr. Charles Taylor, Superintendent of the Education Society's Press, in generally getting this work through the press with that care and neatness which is evident on every page, and in continuing the publication of the work in anticipation of better results, the total amount of subscription to date being, —including the coloured plates—far less than the cost of production.

Lastly, I have to tender my acknowledgements to Dr. Gerson da Cunha, F.R.A.L., &c., and to Mr. Thomas Lidbetter for assistance given in precisely the most important direction, viz., introduction to the library of the Bombay Branch of the Royal Asiatic Society, where I have the opportunity of consulting several important works which would have been otherwise inaccessible to me.

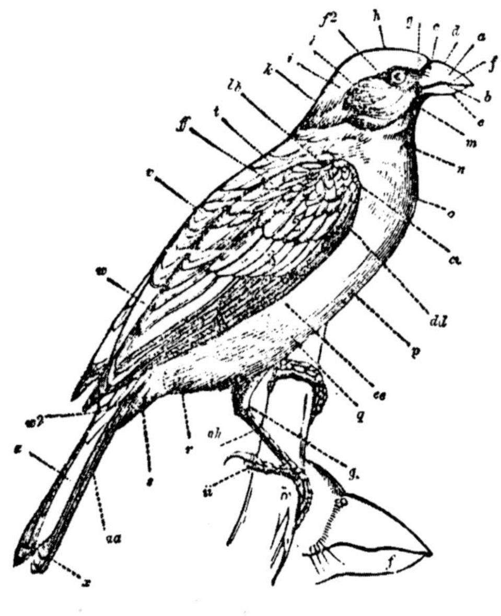

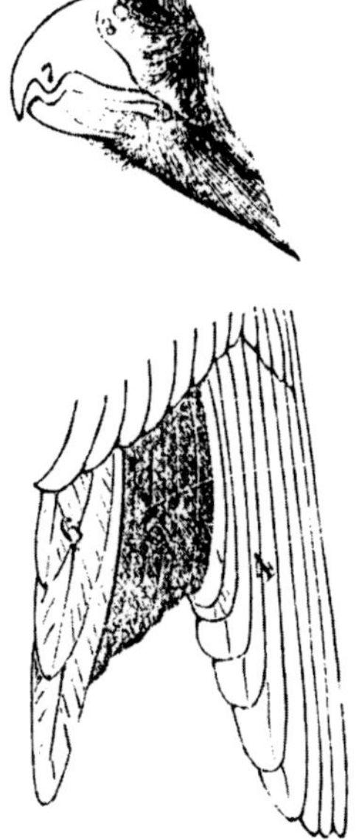

a Upper mandible.

b Lower mandible.

c Nostrils.

d Culmen or keel.

e Gonys.

f Margins of mandibles or commissure.

f2 Ophthalmic region, or orbit.

g Forehead.

h Crown.

i Sinciput or hind head.

k Nape.

l Ear-coverts.

m Chin or mentum.

n Throat.

o Breast.

p The body.

q Belly or abdomen.

r Vent.

s Under-tail coverts.

t Insterscapularies or back.

v Lower back.

w Rump.

w2 Upper-tail coverts.

x Tail feathers.

z Central or median tail feathers.

aa Lateral tail feathers.

bb Shoulder of wing.

cc Shoulder joint (lesser wing coverts).

dd Axilla, or edge of wing.

ee Spurious wing or primary coverts.

ff Scapulars.

gg Thigh or tibia.

hh Tarsus.

ii Toes.

1 Lesser coverts.

2 Median coverts.

3 Greater coverts.

4 Primaries.

5 Secondaries.

6 Tertiaries.

7 Festoon.

8 Cere.

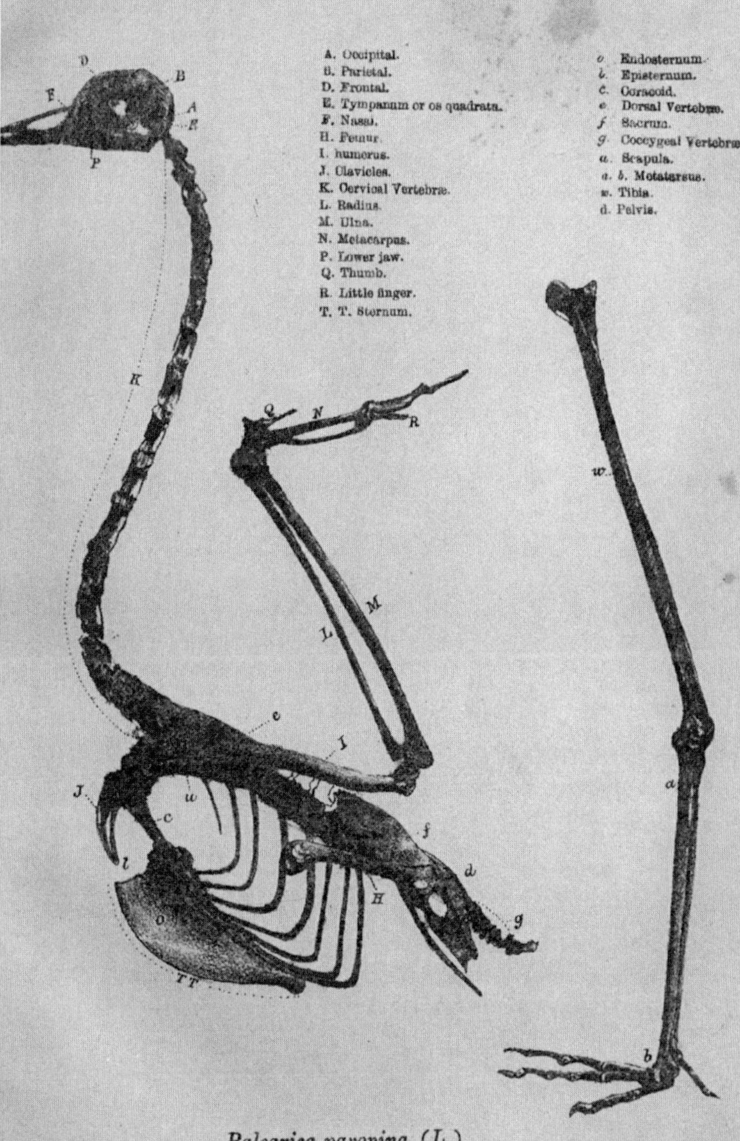

Balearica pavonina (L.).

CONTENTS OF VOLUME I.

ORDER—ACCIPITRES.

SUB-ORDER—FALCONES.

Family—VULTURIDÆ.

Sub-family—VULTURINÆ.

Family—FALCONIDE.

Sub-family—ACCIPITRINÆ.

Sub-family—BUTEONINÆ.

Sub-family—AQUILINÆ.

ORDER II.—PASSERIFORMES.

SUB-ORDER—PASSERES.

DIVISION—ACROMYODI.

GROUP—COLIOMORPHÆ.

Family—CORVIDÆ.

Sub-family—CORVINÆ.

PAGE

Sub-family—FREGILINÆ.

PAGE

Family—ORIOLIDÆ.

Family—DICRURIDÆ.

Family—PRIONOPIDÆ.

Sub-family—PRIONOPINÆ.

LIST OF ILLUSTRATIONS.

THE

AVIFAUNA OF BRITISH INDIA

AND

ITS DEPENDENCIES.

ORDER—ACCIPITRES.

Bill short, strong, stout, covered at the base with a cere or naked skin and strongly curved; the tip perpendicular; nostrils open. Legs and feet muscular and strong, the latter armed with powerful curved, sharp, elongated talons capable of being bent under the feet. Toes four, three in front and one behind.

The Accipitres or Raptores vary greatly in size. The Vultures and Eagles comprise some of the largest of the feathered tribes, while the Falcons are small. The order comprising these is analogous to the feline quadrupeds, and forms a distinct and primary one in the class of birds. They are readily recognized by their strong hooked bill, the upper mandible of which is longer than the lower. The edges in some are festooned or toothed to assist in the operation of tearing their prey. They are notoriously the most muscular and powerful. The muscles of their legs and feet are of great strength to enable them to strike down or hold their prey. The greater number are suited for rapid flight and live on prey got by their own courage and exertions. The Vultures however are slothful, large bodied, and, not unlike the Hyæna, feed upon carrion and act the part of scavengers.

The males are always smaller than the females, and owing to this difference in size of the sexes, and the almost totally different plumage of the various stages of growth of the members, from the young to the adult, they are difficult to determine, even with large series of specimens. In number and species they are not many—taking them world wide—compared with the Insessores or perching birds. For special reasons in the economy of nature they are not prolific, but propagate slowly. Many lay but one egg, others two, and none of the order are known to lay more than four, nor to breed more than once a year.

The order is divided by Sharpe (*Cat. Acc. Br. Mus.*) into three sub-orders, viz., Falcones, Pandiones, and Striges; four families, viz.:—Vulturidæ, Falconidæ, Bubonidæ and Strigidæ, and these again into nine sub-families. The members of 7 (seven) only occur in India, the exceptions being the Polyborinæ and Sarcoramphinæ.

The following is the division of the Accipitres:—

SUB-ORDER—Falcones.
Family—Vulturidæ.
Sub-Family—Vulturinæ.
Family—Falconidæ.
Sub-Family—Accipitrinæ.
„ Buteoninæ.
„ Aquilinæ.
„ Falconinæ.
SUB-ORDER—Pandiones.
SUB-ORDER.—Striges.
Family—Bubonidæ.
Sub-Family—Buboninæ.
„ Syrniinæ.
Family—Strigidæ.

These comprise the Vultures, the Falcons, and the Owls, the two former are diurnal, and the latter nocturnal birds of prey.

SUB-ORDER—FALCONES.

Toes without feathers; outer toe not reversible; eyes lateral; cere soft and fleshy, generally not hidden by bristles. Facial disk none. Plumage compact.

Family—VULTURIDÆ—VULTURES.

Upper mandible not toothed, sometimes sinuate. Head and neck more or less bare or clothed only with short down. No true feathers on crown of head.

Sub-Family—VULTURINÆ,—VULTURES PROPER.

Nostrils not perforated. 1st quill short, 3rd and 4th subequal, 4th longest; tarsi reticulate.

These are the scavengers of nature wherever they occur, especially in hot countries where putrefaction is rapid. Their food imparts to them a fœtid odour, which, according to some writers, is a means of defence, for, if seized during the torpid inactivity which succeeds their meals, they disgorge the nauseous contents of their craw over the luckless captor in order that he may quickly and loathingly relinquish his hold.

Gen. **Vultur.**—*Linn.*

Bill higher than broad. Cere large. Nostrils rounded, naked. A neck ruff present.

1. Vultur monachus, *Linn. S. N.* i., p. 122; *Jerd. B. of Ind.* vol. i. p. 6; *Hume, Str. F.*, vol. vii., p. 321; *Murray, Hdbk. Zool., &c., Sind; id. Vert. Zool. Sind*, p. 61; *Sharpe, Cat. Acc. Br. Mus.* p. 3.—The CRESTED OR GREAT BROWN VULTURE.

Adult.—Colour rich dark chocolate brown throughout, including the crop patch, darker on the wings, tail, and under parts. Feathers of the nape lengthened, lanceolate, and forming a ruff. Lores, cheeks, and throat downy, also a patch on the occiput; rest of head and neck both behind and laterally bare, and of a livid flesh colour in life. Bill black; feet yellowish; iris dark brown.

Length.—42 to 45 inches; expanse 96 to 118; wing 29·5 to 32; culmen 3·3; tarsus 4-25.

Hab.—A native of Europe. Found on the lofty mountains of Italy, the Tyrol, and also in Africa. In India it affects the hilly ranges of Central India, Guzerat, Sind, Beloochistan, Persia, Afghanistan, Punjab, N.-W. Provinces, Oudh, Bengal, Rajpootana, Central India, Kutch, Tennaserim, and the Nepal Valley. In the Himalayas it is fairly abundant; also in Assam and Bhootan.

There is no positive information as to the breeding of this Vulture in India, but from facts collected by Mr. A. O. Hume and recorded in his "Rough Notes on Indian Ornithology and Oology," it is probable that it breeds in the Himalayas from January to March. The Rev. H. B. Tristram, "Ibis," 1865, and Mr. C. Farman give interesting particulars of its nidification in Central Bulgaria and Palestine. In the Pyrenees it is said to lay two eggs, varying from a more or less pure white with scarcely any trace of markings, to a reddish or fulvous white, richly marked with reddish brown; in shape a very blunt slightly pyriform oval; texture coarse and rough; size 3·48 × 2·75 inches.

Gen. **Gyps**.—*Savigny*.

Tarsus shorter than middle toe; 14 tail feathers; nostrils perpendicular, rather oval.

2. Gyps fulvescens, *Hume, Rough Notes*, p. 19; *Str. F.*, vol. vii. p. 322; i., p. 149; *Ibis* 1869; *Sharpe, Cat. Acc. Br. Mus.* (Sub-Sp. B.), p. 7;

Murray, Hdbk. Zool, &c., Sind, p. 102; *id. Vert. Zool. Sind,* p. 63.—The BAY VULTURE.

Adult.—Top of head, cheeks, chin, and throat covered with dingy, yellowish-white hair-like feathers. Nape and whole of neck (except the back and basal one-fifth or less) also covered, but with dense, fur-like yellowish-white down. Crop patch pale wood brown, or dark brown; rest of under surface rufous or fulvous brown, with conspicuous whitish central stripes, the under wing coverts darker. Upper back, whole of upper wing coverts, and all but the longest scapulars, rufous ashy, or brownish rufous fawn. Secondaries, tertials, and longer scapulars umber brown. Lower back and rump brown, with distinct central streaks of fulvous white, the upper tail coverts more rufescent. Quills brownish black, the primaries shaded with ashy grey, the secondaries externally washed and tipped with rufous ashy. Tail black, the feathers somewhat shaded with brown on their margins. Feathers of the ruff lanceolate, brown or rufous fawn, mesially streaked with whitish.

Length.—41 to 47 inches; expanse 94 to 106; wing 27 to 30; tail 12·5 to 13·5; culmen 3·7; tarsus 3·88 to 4.

Hab.—Sind, Beloochistan, Persia, Afghanistan, Punjab, N.-W. Provinces, Oudh, Rajpootana, Central India, Kutch, and Guzerat. Breeds during January and February on lofty trees, laying a single white egg usually soiled and discoloured by the droppings of the parent bird. Size 3·5 × 2·8 inches.

3. **Gyps himalayensis,** *Hume, Rough Notes,* i. p. 14 (1869); *Jerdon, Ibis,* 1871, p. 235; *Sharpe, Cat. Acc. Br. Mus.* p. 8. Otogyps fulvus, *Tytler, Ibis,* 1868, p. 194.—The HIMALAYAN GRIFFON.

Adult.—Head, cheeks, chin, and throat closely covered with yellowish white filamentous feathers; nape, upper two-thirds of back, and sides of the neck covered with a similar coloured down; basal third of back and sides of neck bare, the front sparsely studded with star-like tufts of down. Crop patch whitish fawn. Ruff round the neck whitish, the feathers linear, lanceolate, about 3 inches long with filamentous webs. Upper back, shorter scapulars, and wing coverts (except the larger row) a nearly unichromous pale brown, or whitey brown, many of the feathers inconspicuously paler centred. Lower back pure white, shading into pale creamy fawn colour on the rump and upper tail coverts. Longer scapulars and largest wing coverts deep umber brown, tipped broadly on the scapulars with fulvous fawn, and externally washed with ashy. Quills black, the secondaries brownish, the innermost inclining to fulvous towards the tip. Tail black, or a deep chocolate brown. Under surface, including wing lining and lower tail coverts white, or fulvous white, some of the feathers on the flanks with ill-defined paler centres. Bill very pale horny green, dusky at tip; cere pale brown; legs and feet dingy greenish grey or greyish white; claws pale brown.

Length.—46 to 49 inches (Hume), 42 inches (Sharpe); expanse 106 to 110; wing 28 to 31; tail 15 to 17, tarsus 4·25 to 4·8.

Young.—Entire plumage dark chocolate brown, with central streaks of paler brown, those on the ruff and under surface being lighter and more fulvescent, and consequently more distinct.

Hab.—Himalayas, Bhootan, Afghanistan, Nepal.

Breeds in January, February, and March. Mr. Hume says, the nest is a huge platform of sticks placed on a rocky ledge of some bold precipice in the Himalayas at least 3,000 feet above the sea. It lays a single egg, larger than that of any of the other Indian Vultures, oval, or a broad oval, the ground colour being of the usual greenish or greyish white of all the true Vultures, unspotted or richly blotched and mottled chiefly towards the small end with brownish red. Size 3·78 × 2·8 inches to 3·98 × 2·85 inches.

4. **Gyps indicus,** *Blyth, Cat. B. Mus. As. Soc. Beng.* p. 33, 1849; *Jerd. B. Ind.* i. p. 9, No. 4; *Gray, Cat. Mam. and B. Hodgson,* p. 16; *Sharpe, Cat. Acc. Br. M.* p. 10; *Hume, Stray F.* vii. 165. Gyps tenuirostris, *Hodgs.*; *Scully, Stray F.* viii. 219.—The Long-billed Vulture.

Adult.—Head bare, also the nape, neck, cheeks, and throat, but very thinly sprinkled with brownish white hair-like feathers; ruff and upper surface of body dark brown, the feathers mesially streaked with fulvous; the wing coverts slightly paler with the streaks more distinct. Lower back and rump creamy white, the feathers washed with brown on their edges. Quills and tail black or deep chocolate brown. Crop patch brown. Under surface of body light brown, the feathers broadly streaked with creamy white; abdomen and under tail coverts slightly paler. Under wing coverts whitish, the marginal ones dark brown with pale shaft stripes. Bill dark horn brown, yellowish on culmen and towards tip. Irides brown.

Length.—36 to 40 inches; wing 24; tail 11; tarsus 4·5; bill from gape 2·85.

Hab.—The Indian Peninsula, Burmah, Nepal, Siam and the Malayan Peninsula. Ajmere and Mount Aboo are places where this species has been known to breed from December to March on inaccessible and precipitous cliffs. Eggs vary in length from 3·48 to 3·9 inches in length and from 2·62 to 2·85 in breadth, larger than those of *G. Bengalensis;* texture finer, as a rule unspotted pale greyish or greenish white, thinly spotted or blotched with pale reddish brown and purplish brown.

5. Gyps pallescens, *Hume, Stray F.* i. p. 150; *id.* vol. iii. p. 442; *id.* vol. ii. p. 325, vol. ix. p. 369; *Swinhoe and Barnes, B. of Central India, Ibis,* vol. 1885, p. 54; *Barnes, Birds of Bombay,* p. 5. Gyps indicus, *Hume, Rough Notes,* i. p. 21.—The LONG-BILLED PALE BROWN VULTURE.

Adult.—Head, nape, cheeks, and throat bare, but sprinkled with brownish white hair-like feathers; lower half of the back and sides of the neck bare. Crop patch covered with silky dark brown feathers; ruff composed of soft, white, much disintegrated feathers. Mantle pale earthy brown, the centres of the lesser and all but the tips and margins of the larger scapulars dark hair brown. The whole of the lower surface of the body pale whitey brown, vent and lower tail coverts nearly pure white. Lower back, rump, and upper tail coverts white, tinged with pale earthy brown. Some of the longer tail coverts brown at the base. Primaries and tail feathers deep chocolate brown; secondaries and tertiaries hair brown, more or less suffused on their outer webs with pale dingy earthy or fulvous brown.

A quite young bird, has the top and back of the head and upper part of the back of the neck thickly covered with white down, rest of the head and neck as in the adult; crop patch covered with pale dove-coloured brown feathers, lower surface pale brown, albescent towards the vent, each feather broadly centred with dingy white, sides and breast the same; ruff feathers long, lanceolate, pale fulvous white, faintly margined with brown; mantle pale hair brown, the feathers with fulvous white centres mesially. Primaries chocolate brown; tail feathers the same; rump and upper tail coverts white, in some specimens very slightly tinged with brown. *Rectrices of 14 feathers.*

Adult.—Length 36 to 39 inches; expanse 85 to 90; wing 23 to 25·5; tail from vent 10 to 11; tarsus 3·5 to 4; bill from gape 2·65 to 2·95. Bill and cere pale greenish yellow, horny on culmen; irides brown; legs and feet dusky plumbeous. (Hume, *Rough Notes.*)

Hab.—Sind, Kutch, Jodhpur, Kattiawar, Northern Guzerat, Mount Aboo, the Concan, Deccan, the Southern Mahratta country, and Central India.

Gen. **Pseudogyps**.—*Sharpe.*

Tarsus shorter than middle toe. Tail of 12 feathers.

6. Pseudogyps bengalensis, *Sharpe, Ann. Nat. Hist.* (4) xi., p. 133; *Cat. Acc. Br. Mus.* p. 11. Gyps bengalensis, *G. R. Gray, Gen. of B.* i. p. 6; *Jerd. B. of Ind.* vol. i. p. 90; *Hume, Str. F.* vol. v. p. 245; *Murray, Hdbk., Zool. &c., Sind,* p. 104; *Gidh.*; Hind and Sind.—THE BENGAL OR COMMON BROWN VULTURE.

Adult.—Cinerous black above, beneath dark brown, the shafts narrowly streaked with fulvous. Lower back and rump white. Ruff scanty, whitish. Head and neck bare with a few dull brown bristles on the crown and nape. Quills, tail, and crop patch black. Under wing coverts white. Cere horny black; legs dusky black; iris red brown.

Length.—30 to 35 inches; wing 23 to 23·5; tail 10 to 11; tarsus 4·2; culmen 3·1.

Hab.—Throughout India. It is a permanent resident in Sind, and breeds from November to February or later, laying ordinarily one or two glossless white eggs, at times with rusty markings at the larger end.

Gen. **Otogyps.**—*Gray.*

Tarsus longer than middle toe; head and neck bare, with fleshy folds and a neck lappet or wattle of skin.

7. Otogyps calvus, *G. R. Grav, Gen. B.* i. p. 4; *Jerd. B. of Ind.* vol. i. p. 7, No. 2; *Hume, Str. F.* vol. viii. p. 370; *Sharpe, Cat. Acc. Br. Mus.* p. 14; *Murray, Hdbk. Zool. &c. Sind; Murray, Vert. Zool. Sind,* p. 62. Vultur calvus, *Scorp. Del. Faun. et Flor. Insbur.* vol. ii. p. 85. V. pondicerianus, *Lath. Ind. Orn.* i. p. 7; *Ran-Gidh, Bhaonra,* Hind.; *Wudda Gidh,* Sind.—The BLACK VULTURE.

Adult.—Glossy black, inclining to brown on lower back and rump, some of the scapulars also washed with brown. Quills black, the shafts white, becoming brownish towards the tips. Secondaries whitey brown, blackish towards their tips. Tail black, shaded with brown, the shafts brownish. Crop patch black. A circlet of white down across the breast, and a patch of white above the thigh joint. Under parts of body deep black. Inner face of thighs bare. A small black ruff round the neck, the feathers impending and partially concealing the bare patches on each side of the breast. Bill black; legs dull red; iris reddish brown.

Length.—31 to 33 inches; culmen 2·5; wing 24·5; tail 10 to 11; tarsus 4·1.

Hab.—This is spread nearly all over the continent of India and not unlike *V. monachus* affects the hilly districts in Sind. It is a permanent resident wherever it occurs. Nest varies from 2½ to 4 feet in length and breadth, with usually a lining of leaves. It lays a single egg, pale greenish white, spotted or unspotted with purplish; generally a round oval, varying in size from 3·2 inches to 3·5 in length, and from 2·45 to 2·8 inches in breadth. It is said to breed on inaccessible cliffs from January to April.

Sub-Family—NEOPHRONINÆ, SCAVENGERS.

Bill lengthened, slender; nostrils longitudinal, nearly in the middle of the bill, perforated, and without bony septum.

Gen. Neophron.—*Savigny.*

Characters, same as those of the family.

8. Neophron ginginianus, *Lath. Ind. Orn.* i. p. 7; *Blyth, Ibis,* 1866; *Jerd. B. of Ind.* i. p. 12, No. 6; *Sharpe, Cat. Acc. Br. Mus.* p. 18; *Hume, Str. F.* vol. i. p. 150; *Rough Notes,* i. p. 39; *Murray, Hbdk. Zool. &c. Sind,* p. 105; *id. Vert. Zool., Sind,* p. 64.—The WHITE SCAVENGER VULTURE or PHARAOH'S HEN OF BRUCE.

Adult.—Yellowish or creamy white. Quills black, neck hackles long, lanceolate, tinged somewhat rusty; secondaries dark brown and, like the quills, internally ashy white at base. Head bare, throat with a little scanty down; a few white feathers in front of the eye. Irides reddish brown; cere and face turmeric yellow; bill pale horny brown; feet and legs yellowish white.

Length.—21 to 22 inches; wing 15·5 (not reaching the tip of the tail); tail 9·5; tarsus 3·4; culmen 2·9.

Hab.—Throughout India and a permanent resident. Breeds from February to April on cliffs, old mosques, &c., seldom on trees, making a rude nest of twigs, lined with rags, &c. Eggs variously coloured, the ground colour usually a dirty white, blotched and smeared with reddish brown, or marked all over with deep red, with blotches at the larger end.

Family—FALCONIDÆ, Falcons.

Bill usually short and compressed; tip elongated, curved and sharp. Commissure of upper mandible distinctly toothed or festooned. Head always covered with true feathers.

Sub-Family—BUTEONINÆ.

Bill small, moderate, tip hooked. Wings moderate; tail generally short; tarsus with scutæ in front and behind; tibia longer than tarsus. Outer toe connected to middle toe by interdigital membrane.

Gen. Circus.—*Lacep.*

Upper mandible slightly festooned; lower emarginate. Nostrils round, with no bony excrescence. Tarsi long and slender, naked; wings long; the first quill not so long as the fifth, the third and fourth longest; cere large, surrounded with a ruff of setaceous curved plumes.

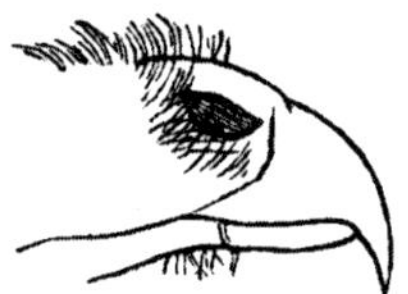

9. Circus cyaneus, *Linn. Sys. Nat.* i. p. 126; *Yarrell, Br. B.* i. p. 94; *Sharpe, Cat. Acc.* p. 52; *Boie, Isis*, 1822; *Gould. B. Eur.* i. pl. 33; *Jerd. B. Ind.* i. p. 95; *Gould. B. Gt. Bt.* 1867; *Hume, Rough Notes*, ii. p. 93, No. 50; *Str. F.* i. p. 160, 418; *Reid, Cat. B. Prov. Mus. N. W. P. and Oudh.*—The Hen Harrier.

Adult Male.—Upper parts, chin, throat, cheeks, ear-coverts, sides of the neck, and breast bluish ashy, paler on the wing coverts and tail, the former also slightly margined with whitish and the scapulars slightly tinged with fuscous. Frontal plumes and lores whitish; feathers of the nape pure white. Forehead and supercilium whitish. 1st 6 primaries blackish both above and below, the outer webs, towards the tips, more or less suffused with silvery grey; the inner webs white at the bases. Secondaries silvery grey on the outer webs and tips, with black shafts and an indistinct subterminal band. Tail ashy grey, tipped with white, the middle tail feathers entirely uniform pale ashy grey, white-shafted, the lateral ones becoming less grey and white on the inner webs, with from 6 to 8 imperfect, and sometimes almost obsolete transverse ashy bars. *Upper tail coverts white. Under surface from below the breast, including the thighs, the axillary plumes, and under wing coverts white,* (in the adolescent stage slightly suffused with very pale bluish grey). Cere yellow; bill bluish black; irides yellow; legs and feet bright yellow; claws black.

Length.—17 to 19 inches; wing 12·2 to 13·8; tail 8·1 to 9·0; tarsus 2·5 to 2·9; bill from gape 1·16.

Young Male.—Above brown; bright rufous on the head and neck. Upper tail coverts white with rufous brown mesial lanceolate streaks. Tail tawny, fulvous at tip, with four broad black cross bands. Young females with rufous cross bars on the tail.

Adult Female.—Crown of the head, hind neck, and nape reddish fawn or pale tawny fulvous, the feathers broadly streaked mesially with dark brown. Forehead, a narrow supercilium, lores, and cheeks, and a streak over the ear coverts fulvous white; basal two-thirds of feathers of the nape white; ear coverts and cheeks rufous, streaked with brown. Quills brown, tipped with whitish, and with 3—5 dark brown transverse bars on the inner webs. *2nd, 3rd, 4th, and 5th primaries emarginated on the outer web.* Scapulars, interscapulary region, lower back and rump, also wing coverts brown, spotted with large oval tawny buff marks. Upper tail coverts pure white with sometimes lanceolate rufous brown spots on the shafts. Tail white at the extreme base, the central feathers grey brown, narrowly tipped with white or rufescent white, and crossed with 4—5 broad transverse bars of darker brown; lateral tail feathers similar but with broader white tips, and the interspaces on the outer webs creamy buff, the outermost tinged with rufous; sides of neck and under surface of body yellowish white, brown-shafted, and with more or less conspicuous ovate rufous-brown spots. Irides reddish brown.

Length.—19·5 to 21·6 inches; wing 14·5 to 15·6; tail 10 to 10·9; tarsus 3·1 to 3·17.

Hab.—Throughout Europe. Occurs also in all countries bordering the Mediterranean and extending in winter to N. India (Sharpe). In India the Hen Harrier is common about the outer ranges of the Himalayas; from Abbottabad to Kumaon, in the Punjab; Sind, N.-W. Provinces, and Oudh, also the Central Provinces. It has been obtained in Meerut, Bareilly, Etawah, Saugor, Nagpoor, Chanda, and Goona (Hume); also in Beloochistan, S. Afghanistan, Nepal, Eastern Turkestan, and Gilgit.

This species is not known to breed in India. Dr. Scully in his contribution to the Ornithology of Eastern Turkestan says it is a permanent resident in the plains of Kashgaria and breeds there. The nest, he says, is placed in long grass jungle; and adds that he often observed the bird sailing low over rush-grown marshes and bare fields with a wonderfully long sustained flight. It never seems to tire and always appears keenly intent on looking for its prey, every now and then suddenly dropping down among the reeds as if shot, but soon rising again to resume its hunting. He does not however give any particulars of its nidification, except as to the position of the nest. In Europe it is said to be placed on the ground and the materials used are small sticks and coarse grass. Eggs 4—5; in colour pale white or skimmed milk-blue; 1·67 × 1·33 inches.

10. Circus melanoleucos, *Forst. Ind. Zool.* p. 12, pl. 11; *Vieill, N. Dict. d' Hist. Nat.* vi. p. 465; *Jerd. B. Ind.* i. p. 98, No. 53; *Sharpe, Cat. Acc. B. M.* p. 61; *Stray F.* i. p. 98; *id.* iii. p. 33; vi. p. 11; *id.* vii. p. 250; *Hume, Rough Notes,* ii. p. 307; *Holdsw. P. Z. S.* 1872, p. 414.—The PIED HARRIER.

Adult Male.—The whole head, chin, *throat*, neck all round, *upper breast*, nearly two-thirds of the back, scapulars (except the undermost one or two), primaries, and a broad band across the wing black. Wing coverts silvery grey, often broadly tipped with brown. Primary coverts and secondaries silvery grey, except the innermost which are black. Lower portion of back, rump, and upper tail coverts white, the latter with two or three broad cross bars of black or ashy grey. Tail pale, silvery dove colour or silvery grey, narrowly tipped with white; below and the inner webs also broadly margined with white. Under surface from lower breast, including wing lining and axillaries, pure white. Bill and cere black. Irides and feet yellow.

Length.—16 to 17·15 inches; wing 13·70 to 14·4; tail 8·5 to 10; tarsus 2·98 to 3·13; culmen 1.

The young male as described by Mr. Hume has the whole head, neck, and back of neck clove brown, each feather broadly margined with pale rufous. Upper back and scapulars uniform clove brown; lower back and wings of a slightly lighter shade. Some of the longest feathers of the back with two obscure, terminal, rufous spots, one on each web; edge of the wing rufous white and many of the lesser coverts faintly or boldly margined with fulvous or rufescent. Upper tail coverts pure white, dark shafted, and with a conspicuous oval, rufous brown subterminal spot. Tail feathers a somewhat greyish pale-brown, narrowly tipped with fulvous white and with broad, rather dark brown transverse bars. Lower parts buffy or rufous white, with central rufous brown stripes, broad on the lower breast and abdomen, almost obsolete on the chin and the thigh coverts. Inner webs of primaries pale rufous white, barred with darker brown, the bars wider and more conspicuous on the under surface. Wing lining rufous buff; axillaries the same, with darker shafts and two or more broad, irregular transverse red brown bars. Winglet, greater primary coverts, and bases of the outer webs of the later primaries grey, with broad transverse brown bars.

The adult female is larger than the male and has a slatey grey wash on the back. Wing 15·4; tail 10; tarsus 3·13 inches.

Hab.—Mr. Sharpe gives Eastern Asia, eastern side of the Indian Peninsula and Burma, northwards to Mongolia, Amoor land and Northern China. It occurs in Ceylon, Nepal, Burma, Assam, and Eastern Bengal generally, (extending westward to Mirzapoor), also almost throughout the Himalayas, from the valley of the Burhampooter to Afghanistan. It has been noted from Bengal, Rajputana, Central India, the Central Provinces, the Concan, Deccan, South India, British Burma, and Nepal.

Nothing is known of the nidification of this species. Dr. Jerdon however remarks in his appendix, that he has every reason to believe it breeds in Northern India.

11. Circus pygargus, *Linn. S. N.* i. p 48; *Sharpe, Cat. Acc. B. M.* p. 64. Circus cineraceus, *Cuv. Regne. An.* i. p. 338; *Jerdon, B. of India,* i. p. 97, No. 52; *Hume, Rough Notes,* ii. p. 303; *Shelley, B. Egypt,* p. 184; *Murray, Hdbk. Zool. &c. Sind; id. Vert. Zool. Sind,* p. 88.—MONTAGUE'S HARRIER.

Adult Male.—Above blue grey; throat, breast, and wing coverts darker, the latter slightly mottled, and with a terminal spot of a dark ash colour. Primary coverts and secondaries silvery grey, tipped with white, and with two bands of black, one of which is hidden by the greater wing coverts. Primaries black, the inner ones greyish at the tips and on the inner web. Secondaries grey with a black band. Tail grey or greyish white, the two outer feathers banded on their inner webs with rufous, the others dusky, with fine ashy black bands. Upper tail coverts white, shading into ashy grey. Lores whitish. *Abdomen, flanks, thighs, and under wing coverts white, streaked with fawn;* the axillaries with spots of the same colour. Cere greenish yellow. Feet and irides yellow.

Length.—18 inches; wing 14 to 15; tail 9·5; tarsus 2·3.

The adult female differs from the male in being nearly uniform brown with scarcely any fulvous margins to the feathers. The hind head and neck are streaked with fulvous, as also the sides of the neck and facial ruff. Feathers under the eye whitish. *Outer margin of 5th primary entire; notch in second primary, an inch or more distant from tip of coverts.* Upper tail coverts white; tail brown, tipped with paler brown and banded with five bars of darker brown. Under surface of body buffy white, the feathers with rufous centres; legs yellow; irides hazel.

Length.—19 to 19·5 inches; wing 15·3; tail 8·7; tarsus 1·4; culmen 1·1 to 1·2.

Hab.—In India it has been found in Sind, Punjab, N. W. Provinces, Oudh, Bengal, Rajpootana, Central India, the Central Provinces, Kutch, Behar, Guzerat, the Concans, Deccan, South India, and British Burmah. Occurs also in Ceylon, Beloochistan, Afghanistan, and Nepaul. Sharpe gives its distribution as Europe generally, ranging in winter through Palestine and along the Nile to Abyssinia and South Africa, India, and Ceylon.

It is, like the last, a winter visitant to India generally. Like the last, it flies low, skimming along the surface of the ground in search of prey. It frequents open jungle and cultivated fields, preying on birds, reptiles, insects, &c. It has not been known to breed in India. In England it is said to make its nest on the ground, generally among furze. The eggs are white, sometimes faintly spotted 1·58 × 1·33 inches, and seldom above four in number.

12. Circus macrurus, *S. G. Gmel. N. Comm. Petrop.* xv. p. 439; *Sharpe, Cat. Acc. B. M.* p. 67; *Murray, Hdbk. Zool. &c. Sind,* p. 115. Circus swainsonii, *Smith, S. Afr. Q. Journ.* i. p. 384; *Gray, Gen. B.* i. p. 32; *Jerd. Birds of Ind.* p. 96, No. 51; *Hume, Rough Notes,* ii. p. 298. Circus pallidus, *Sykes, P. Z. S.* 1832, p. 80; *Shelley, B. Egypt,* p. 183; *Hume, S. F.* i. p. 160; *Murray, Vert. Zool. Sind.* p. 88; *Reid, Cat. B. Mus. N. W. P. and Oudh.*—The Pale Harrier.

Adult Male.—Above pale bluish grey, scapulars slightly darker; eyebrow and sides of face white; under surface of body greyish white. Quills blackish brown; the secondaries ashy grey, tipped with white, and the primaries washed with ashy grey, white at base of inner web; other quills white underneath. ***Upper tail coverts white, banded with ashy grey.*** Tail feathers—except the two middle ones, which are uniform ashy grey—banded grey and white; the tips and under surface of all the feathers white. Bill black; feet and irides yellow.

Length.—17·5 to 18·5 inches; culmen 1·15; wing 13·5 to 14; tail 8·8 to 9·5; tarsus 2·75.

Adult Female.—Above brown, the feathers of the head and hind neck streaked, and of the upper surface and lesser wing coverts margined and tipped with rufous. Forehead, supercilium, and a spot below the eye white. Cheeks and ear coverts dark brown, slightly streaked with tawny. Quills dusky brown, the primaries externally shaded with ashy grey, and like the secondaries obsoletely barred darker and tipped with buffy white. ***Outer margin of 5th primary entire; notch in second primary nearly or quite hidden by coverts;*** upper tail coverts white, banded or spotted with dark brown. Tail with the two centre feathers ashy brown and with six blackish brown bands, the rest with four bands, those on the outer feathers being pale rufous. Under tail coverts rufescent. Under wing coverts buffy white, spotted and streaked with brown. Cere greenish yellow; feet yellow; irides brownish.

The young, in the livery of which Mr. Hume says he has numerous specimens, is shortly described by Mr. Sharpe as being brown, like the old female, but not so much variegated above, with tawny margins to the feathers; under surface entirely pale fawn colour (rufous buff—*Hume*), the facial ruff of this same colour, and therefore contrasting in marked prominence with the dark brown cheeks and ear coverts, the flank feathers and axillaries with indistinct brown central streaks; frontal feathers, superciliary streak and spot under the eye whitish; upper tail coverts white, spotted with pale rufous; tail much as in the female, but the dark bars only five in number.

Length.—20·5 to 21 inches; wing 14 to 14·5; tail 10 to 10·5; tarsus 2·8 to 3.

Hab.—Europe, Africa, and throughout India, Ceylon, China, and Burmah. Has been noted from the N.-W. and Central Provinces, Punjab, Sind, Beloochistan, Afghanistan, Persia, Mesopotamia, S. India, Kutch, the Concans and Deccan, Kattiawar, Behar, Nepaul. In India it is a winter visitant, arriving about the middle of September and leaving again in March.

Nothing is known of its nidification anywhere in India, no birds having ever been seen in India after March or the middle of April.

13. Circus æruginosus, *Linn. S. N.* i. p. 130; *Savigny, Syst. Ois. Egypt*, p. 90; *Hume, Rough Notes*, p. 314; *Shelley, Birds Egypt*, p. 181; *Jerd. Birds of Ind.* p. 99, No. 54; *Sharpe, Cat. Acc. B. M.* p. 69; *Murray, Hdbk. Zool., &c., Sind*, p. 116; *Hume, S. F.* i. p. 100; *Murray, Vert. Zool., Sind*, p. 89; *Reid, Cat. B. Mus. N.W. P. and Oudh.*— The MARSH HARRIER.

Adult Male.—Above dark brown, the feathers of the upper surface edged with rufous; the smaller wing coverts buffy and centred brown; primary, coverts, and secondaries bluish ashy, tipped very slightly with pale white. Primaries blackish brown, paler at the tips, whitish at base of inner web. Upper tail coverts greyish white and tinged with rufous. Tail bluish ash or uniform grey, slightly fulvescent beneath. Head, neck, and breast pale rufous or creamy buff, with dark brown streaks; under parts reddish brown or pale rufous, as also are the thigh coverts, the latter in some spotted or margined with white; under wing coverts buffy white, the axillaries with brown shaft stripes. Cere greenish yellow; legs and irides yellow; claws black.

Length.—19 to 22·5 inches; wing 16; tail 9 to 10; tarsus 3·25; culmen 1·55.

Adult Female.—Larger; length 23 inches; wing 17; tail 10 to 11; tarsus 3·8.

The young bird is uniform reddish brown, the head, neck, and cheeks in some stages being yellowish, rufous white, or white with brown stripes on the crown; upper tail coverts rufous brown.

Hab.—Europe generally, China, Japan, N. E. and S. Africa, and throughout India, Burmah, and Ceylon. In Sind and the Punjab it occurs in great numbers, frequenting the maritime districts, rivers, marshes, lakes, and inundated fields, feeding on rats, mice, frogs, fish, &c. It occurs also in the N.-W. Provinces, Oudh, Bengal, Rajpootana, Kutch, Kattiawar, Jodhpore, North Guzerat, Central and Southern India, the Deccan and Concans, and in fact throughout India; also in Beloochistan, Persia, Mesopotamia, Afghanistan, Eastern Turkestan, Gilgit, Nepaul, Malacca, and Upper Pegu.

Gen. **Astur**.—*Gm.*

Bill broad at base, compressed to tip, festooned in the middle. Nostrils oval, situated anteriorly in the cere. Wings long; 3rd, 4th, and 5th quills longest. Tarsi long, scutate.

14. Astur palumbarius, *Linn. S. N.* i. p. 130; *Temm. Man. d'Orn.* i. p. 55; *Yarr. B. Birds*, i. p. 57; *Cuv. Regne. An.* i. p. 320; *Gray, Gen. B.* i. p. 27; *Jerd. B. Ind.* i. p. 45, No. 21; *Hume, Rough Notes*, i. p. 112; *Jerd. Ibis.* 1871, p. 243; *Sharpe, Cat. Acc. Br. Mus.* vol. i. p. 95.—The GOSHAWK.

PLATE.

Crown of the head, ear coverts and sides of neck dark brownish black; hind neck slightly mottled with white; lores, cheeks, and supercilium white.

ASTUR PALUMBARIUS.

Ignatius Siqueira, Lith. *B. E. S. Press.*

spotted with blackish. Chin and throat white streaked with dusky; breast greyish white, transversely waved with small bars of greyish black; rest of the under surface white covered with transverse bars of greyish or ashy brown; under tail coverts white; upper tail coverts and back dark bluish grey tinged with brown. Tail ashy brown, tipped with white and with four broad transverse bands of dark brown. Primaries brown, barred with darker brown; shafts reddish, the inner webs whitish towards the base; lower surface of the wing ashy grey; secondaries, tertiaries, and the greater and lesser wing coverts as the back; under wing coverts barred transversely with dusky. Cere yellow; bill bluish horn; irides bright yellow; legs and feet yellow; claws black.

Length.—18 to 19·5 inches; culmen 1·5; wing 12·2 to 12·5; expanse 43 to 45 inches; tail 9·0; tarsus 3·0.

Adult Female.—Similar to the male, but a little larger, and the back is of a browner tint, except in very old birds when there is scarcely any difference between them.

Length.—22 to 23 inches; wing 14; tarsus 3·4.

Hab.—Europe generally, wintering in E. Turkestan, Algeria, Palestine, Egypt, the Himalayas, and Northern China. In India it has been found in the Punjab and in the forests of Gurhwal in the N.-W. Provinces. Hodgson has collected specimens in Nepal. Mr. Hume says that Dr. Jerdon mentioned to him that it is occasionally taken in the plains of the Punjab during winter, and adds that he saw a pair in July that evidently had their nest in a wood in the Asrang Valley above Chini about 12,000 feet. Nothing certain is known of its breeding in India. Mr. Hume (*Rough Notes*) says, it breeds so far as he has been able to ascertain only in the higher regions of the Himalayas. He says a pair of young birds were brought to him late in July from near the Chor and the shikari asserted that he had taken them from a nest. Mr. Thomson too tells him that they breed from March to June, building on trees and laying 3—4 nearly pure white eggs, confining themselves to the interior of the deep precipitous valleys lying close to the snowy peak.

15. Astur trivirgatus, *Tem. Pl. Col.* i. pl. 303; *Cuv. Regne An.* p. 332; *Jerd. B. Ind.* i. p. 47, No. 22; *Wallace, Ibis*, 1868, p. 6; *Sharpe, Cat. Acc. B. M.* p. 95. Astur palumbarius, *Jerd. Madras Journal*, p. 85. Lophospizia trivirgatus, *Kaup. Contr. Orn.* 1850, p. 65; *Hume, Rough Notes*, p. 116; *Stray F.* v. p. 8, 502.—The Crested Goshawk.

Adult Male.—Above slatey grey, the upper tail coverts blackish and tipped with white. Head and neck clearer slatey grey, including a conspicuous occipital crest, the sides of the neck somewhat tinged with rufous; quills browner than the back; primaries with rufescent shafts, barred above with dark brown, much plainer underneath where the quills are white at the base of the inner web. Tail ashy brown, paler at tip, crossed with four bands of dark brown; throat white with a distinct black moustachial streak on each side and a broad medial line; chest clear tawny rufous; rest of under surface white, broadly banded with pale rufous, each bar of this colour having a conterminous brown bar; the thighs thickly barred with ashy brown without any rufous tinge. Under tail coverts white; under wing coverts white, spotted with brown or rufous brown; axillaries similarly barred. Bill black, plumbeous at base. Cere orange yellow. Cheeks and orbits orange; feet yellow; irides orange yellow.

Length.—14 to 16 inches; wing 7·8 to 8·5; tail 6·3 to 7; tarsus 2·1 to 2·2.

Adult Female.—Much larger. Length 17·5 to 18 inches; wing 9·5 to 9·7; tail 8·0; tarsus 2·5 to 2·7.

Young.—Brown above, with a fully developed occipital crest. Upper tail coverts banded with darker brown and tipped with white. Tail with five cross bands of darker brown. Under surface of body white, throat as in the adult; breast broadly streaked with pale rufous or dark brown; lower breast, thighs, and abdomen barred with pale rufous, darker on the thighs; under tail coverts white, with a few narrow rather indistinct cross bars; under wing coverts buff, spotted and barred with dark brown.

Hab.—Southern India and Ceylon, Assam, Burmah, Java, Borneo, Sumatra, and the Phillipine Islands. Nothing is known of its nidification in India. The larger Nepalese race is provisionally separated by Mr. Sharpe as *A. indicus.*

16. Astur badius, *Kaup. Isis*, 1847; *Sharpe, Cat. Acc. Br. Mus.* p. 109, (Sub-Sp. A.). Micronisus badius, *Bp. Consp.* i. p. 33; *Jerd. B. Ind.* i. p. 48, No. 23; *Blyth, Ibis*, 1863; *Hume, Rough Notes*, p. 117; *Murray, Hdbk. Zool., &c., Sind; id. Vert. Zool. Sind*, p. 108. Accipiter badius, *Strickl. Ann. Mag. N. H.* xiii. p. 33.—The SHIKRA or BROWN HAWK.

Young.—Head, nape, neck behind, back, scapulars, wing and upper tail coverts ashy, dusky, or pale earthy brown, the feathers on the head slightly darker, and all edged with pale rufous, the feathers of the neck with their white bases showing through. Lores and eyebrow white; sides of the face and ear coverts pale brown, tinged with rufescent and mesially streaked with darker; chin and throat white, with a mesial dark brown throat stripe; breast and abdomen whitish with large longitudinal drops—oval on the upper breast—of a pale rufous colour. Vent and under tail coverts white; under wing coverts buff, streaked and barred with dark brown; thigh coverts also barred. Primaries brown, their inner webs buffy, and barred with dark brown; secondaries brown, barred darker on both webs and margined and tipped with buffy. tail ashy brown with 5—6 broad dark brown bands; narrower and about nine on the outermost feathers, the interspaces and tips of all buffy white. Cere yellow; bill dusky with a bluish tinge. Iris pale yellow; feet yellow.

In the adult plumage the upper parts are bluish grey; the nape is mottled with white, and the white bases of the scapular feathers show through in some specimens; the primaries are dusky black, with their inner webs of a buff colour and barred darker brown, nearly black; the secondaries are bluish grey and also barred. The tail is ashy grey, and tipped with white, the bars on the lateral tail feathers 9 – 11 in number, and of a dark brown colour. The throat stripe is less distinct than in the young, and the entire lower surface is barred with white and rufescent brown. The abdomen, thighs, and under tail coverts unspotted white; rest as in the young. The adult female is like the male but larger.

Length.—Adult male 13·5 inches; wing 7·9; tail 6·3; tarsus 2.

Adult Female.—Length 14·5; wing 8·3; tail 6·4; tarsus 2·15.

Hab.—The Indian Peninsula generally, and Ceylon, extending to Assam and Burmah, and also to Beloochistan, Persia, and Afghanistan. Occurs in Oudh, Bengal, Central Provinces, Rajpootana, Central India, Kutch, Kattiawar, Guzerat, Concan, Deccan, and Southern India. Breeds in April and May in Sind, Punjab, and N.-W. Provinces on large lofty trees on the edges of streams or lakes, laying usually three or four eggs, oval or pyriform in shape, smooth, fine, glossless shells of a pure, delicate bluish white, as a rule without markings or at most thinly sprinkled all over with very faint greyish specks and spots. In size the eggs vary from 1·5 to 1·63 inches in length and from 1·2 to 1·26 in breadth. It is commonly trained by natives, being easily reclaimed and expert in striking a quarry.

17. Astur poliopsis, *Hume, Stray Feathers*, vol. ii. p. 325 (1874); *id.* vol. iii. p. 24; *id. Hume and Davison, Birds of Tennaserim*, vol. vi. p. 7; *Sharpe, Cat. Acc. Br. Mus.* Sub.-Sp. B, vol. i. p. 110. Micronisus badius, *Sel. Ibis*, 1864, p. 246; *Swinhoe, Ibis*, 1870, p. 84; *id. P. Z. S.* 1871, p. 411.—The GREY-FACED SHIKRA.

Adult.—Very similar to *A. badius* which it replaces to the eastward of Bengal. Much paler blue above and below, banded with broader and brighter vinous bands than its near ally; wanting the nuchal rufescent collar and the central throat stripe and with the cheeks and ear coverts unicolorous with the crown. Legs and feet yellow; claws black; base of upper and lower mandible, except tips, plumbeous; rest of bill black; cere greenish yellow.

Length.—11 inches; culmen 6·7; wing 7·3; tail 6·1; tarsus 1·95.

In the *Birds of Tennaserim* Hume and Davison give the following measurements:—

	Length.	Expanse.	Tail.	Wing.	Tarsus.	Bill from gape
Males.	12·0 to 12·75	24·0 to 26·0	5·9 to 6·62	7·3 to 8·12	1·9 to 2·0	0·8 to 0·85.
Females.	13·9 to 14·62	26·75 to 28·37	6·7 to 7·37	8·3 to 9·0	1·8 to 2·05	0·9 to 1·0

Hab.—Tennaserim, Burmah, Siam, and Camboga; Formosa, Hainan (Hume and Sharpe). Occurs throughout Tennaserim, but Hume and Davison say it is nowhere common. The species is excessively shy, seldom allowing of even a moderately near approach. Feeds entirely on insects and small reptiles.

18. Astur soloensis, *Horsf. apud Lath, Gen. Hist.* i. p. 209; *Sharpe, Cat. Acc. Br. Mus.* vol. i. p. 114; *Str. F.* vol. v. 124; *id.* vi. p. 8. Dœdalion soloensis, *Horsf. Tr. Linn. Socy.* xiii. p. 137. Micronisus soloensis, *Gray, Cat. Acc. B. M.* p. 75; *Wallace, Ibis,* 1868, p. 12. Nisus soloensis, *Schleg. Mus. P. B. Astures; Blyth, Ibis,* 1863, p. 16.—The Sooloo Falcon.

The following is Sharpe's description of the adult plumage of this species:—The adult plumage appears to be gained by a gradual mersion of the rufous stripes on the breast. Above light bluish grey, some of the feathers margined with darker grey; sides of face and neck grey like the head but a little more dingy; under surface of the body pale buffy vinous, the throat, flanks, and thighs, as well as the under wing and tail coverts white with a slightly greyish shade on the sides of the breast; quills black, externally shaded with ashy grey; under surface white at base of inner web, but having no distinct bars above or below; tail dull bluish grey above, ashy white beneath, with four or five indistinct cross bands of dark brown, a little plainer underneath, but these not strictly continuous. Cere yellow; gape and orbits yellowish; bill black, lead colour at base; feet and irides yellow. Total length 11·8 inches; culmen 0·75; wing 7·9; tail 5·4; tarsus 1·9.

Young.—Above brown, with rufous edgings to the feathers, a little broader on the upper tail coverts; the sides of the neck washed with rufous, the nape mottled with white; crown blackish; an ill-defined eyebrow and fore part of the cheeks white, narrowly lined with blackish brown. Ear coverts brown, slightly washed with dull rufous; throat buffy white with a moustachial line on each side and a median streak of brown; rest of under surface buffy white, the chest broadly streaked and the breast and flanks barred with pale rufous. Under tail coverts white; under wing coverts clear buff, the lowest, spotted with blackish. Quills dark brown, slightly tipped with whitish very indistinctly barred above with darker brown; underneath buffy white at the base of the inner web, indistinctly barred with dark brown, visible only on the inner webs; tail ashy brown, whitish at tip, crossed with five bars of darker brown; the under surface whitish ashy, the cross bars more distinct, except on the outer web, where they are almost obsolete.

Hab.—Tennaserim (Malewoon, Mergui district), Java, Malacca, Sumatra, Phillipine Islands; Batchian, Celebes, New Guinea.

ASTUR SOLOENSIS

Mintern Bros lith.

Gen. **Accipiter**.—*Briss.*

Bill short, much compressed, festooned. Nostrils oval, rather oblique, situated on the forepart of the cere, and partly hidden by setæ. Wings moderate, rounded, and with the 4th and 5th quills longest. Tarsi long.

19. Accipiter nisus, *Lin. Syst. Nat.* i. p. 130; *Pall. Zoogr. Rosso As.* i. p. 370; *Gray, Gen. B.* i. p. 29; *Jerd. B. Ind.* i. p. 51, No. 24; *Hume, Rough Notes,* i. p. 124; *Sharpe, Cat. Acc. Br. Mus.* p. 132; *Murray, Hdbk. Zool. &c., Sind,* p. 110; *id. Vert. Zool. Sind;* (*Basha,* the female; *Bashin,* the male, Hind).—The European Sparrow-Hawk.

Young.—Head, nape, neck behind, back, scapulars, and wing coverts dusky brown, darker on the upper back, the feathers margined with rufous, the occiput and nape with white mottlings, caused by the broad white bases of the feathers showing through. Lores and eyebrow white; chin and throat and sides of the neck white, the feathers with mesial dark streaks. Ear coverts the same. Rump and upper tail coverts like the back, the feathers with dark shafts and tipped rufous. Primaries and secondaries dusky brown, basally rufescent white on their inner webs and barred with dark brown. The tips of the secondaries rufous or rufescent white; inner web of the tertiaries subterminally white, and margined at the tips with pale rufous. Tail ashy brown above, greyish white on the under surface, tipped whitish and with five dark brown bands; breast, abdomen, flanks, and thigh coverts barred with rufous brown and white. Under tail coverts white. Under wing lining buff, with spots and transverse dark brown bars.

Adult Male.—Head, nape, hind neck, wing coverts, back, and scapulars slatey, with a bluish tinge, the nape mottled white, and some of the tertials basally white. Upper tail coverts and scapulars with indistinct dark shafts. Tail, like the back, tipped white, and with four dark brown bands. Primaries dark brown, their inner webs rufescent white, and crossed with darker brown, nearly black bars; secondaries slatey, also rufescent white on their inner webs and barred across with dark brown. Chin and throat white, with a rufous tinge;

breast, flanks, and abdomen barred with bright rufous and white. Thigh coverts the same. Under tail coverts white. Under wing coverts barred with rufous and dark brown. Bill horny or dark horn blue; cere, base of lower mandible, and legs yellow; iris orange.

Length.—13 inches; wing 8·15; tail 6·3; tarsus 2·3. Females larger and of a duller tint. Length 15·5; wing 9·3 to 9·5; tail 7; tarsus 2·5.

Hab.—The whole of Europe and Northern Asia, extending in winter into Algeria, N. E. Africa, the Indian Peninsula, and China (Sharpe). Occurs throughout Sind, Punjab, N.-W. Provinces, Oudh, and Bengal; also throughout the Western Presidency, in Rajpootana, Central India, Kutch, Guzerat, Concan, Deccan, Southern India, and in Beloochistan, Persia, Mesopotamia, and Afghanistan; also British Burmah, Upper Pegu, Tennaserim, and Nepal. Affects gardens and cultivation. It is much used for hawking, and is said to be easily tamed, and owing to its courage, a better bird than the Shikra for the quarry.

Mr. Hume in his "Rough Notes," p. 128, describes in detail the Dove-Hawk (*Accipiter melaschistos*) from Simla as a new species which Mr. Sharpe thinks is only a dark race of this species.

20. Accipiter virgatus, *Temm. Pl. Col.* i. pl. 109; *Vig. Zool. Journ.* i. p. 338; *Gray, Gen. B.* i. p. 29; *Jerd. B. Ind.* i. p. 52, No. 25; *Hume, Rough Notes,* i. p. 132; *Jerd. Ibis,* 1871, p. 243; *Sharpe, Cat. Acc. Br. Mus.* vol. i. p. 150; *Stray F.* vol. ii. p. 141.—The BESRA SPARROW-HAWK.

Adult Male.—Head and neck dusky black, sides of the neck washed with rufous, nape mottled with white; ear coverts and face light dusky, throat buffy white; wing coverts blackish slate colour. Quills dark brown, unbarred above; under surface ashy, pale rufous near the base of the inner web and barred with blackish. Tail ashy grey above, much paler below, with three transverse bands of slatey black. Abdomen and under tail coverts white, rest of under surface bright ferruginous or vinous chestnut, paler on the thighs; under wing coverts yellowish ochry; axillaries barred with brownish. Cere pale lemon yellow; bill black, plumbeous at base. Legs and feet pale orange yellow. Irides yellow.

Length.—11 to 11·25 inches; wing 6·5 to 6·6; tail 15·75 to 6·6; tarsus 1·9 to 2·2.

Adult Female.—A little larger than the male.

Length.—13 inches; wing 7·4 to 8; tarsus 1·9 to 2·2.

The plumage of the various stages of the young of this species is so very variable, that it is not possible to give a description which would suit, but the following from *Rough Notes* is the usual type of colouration of specimens from the Punjab, in the Kurrachee Museum. Head, nape, back, mantle, and upper tail coverts dusky cyaneous, darkest on the head. Nape mottled with white. Tail slatey grey, brownish on lateral feathers, and with seven narrow transverse bars on the inner webs and four broad blackish bars on both webs of the other ten feathers. Sides of neck and coverts dusky, the latter with traces of rufous striæ. Chin and throat white with one central blackish stripe; a streak of white over the eye. Breast deep ferruginous at the sides, the central portion having the feathers a mixture of blackish, deep ferruginous and white. Sides, flanks, and upper abdomen ferruginous, imperfectly barred with white; lower abdomen white, barred with pale ferruginous. Tibial plumes white, closely barred with rusty grey; under tail coverts white.

Hab.—Throughout the Indian Peninsula nearly. Occurs in the Concan and Deccan, Rajpootana, in South and Central India; also in the Punjab, N.-W. and Central Provinces, the Himalayas, and S. Andamans. Mr. Wallace gives it from Malacca, Timor, and Java, and Dr. Jerdon says extends to Assam, Burmah, and Malayana. Mr. Thompson (*Rough Notes*) is confident that it breeds in the forests of Gurhwal from March to May, but nothing certain is known. It is caught wherever fairly numerous and much used by falconers for the quarry. It is said however to be a difficult bird to train, but when trained fetches a considerable price, being speedy and active, especially at partridges, quails, doves and snipe.

Sub-Family—BUTEONINÆ.

Bill small, moderate, tip hooked. Wings moderate; tail generally short; tarsi with scutæ in front and behind; tibia longer than tarsus. Outer toe connected to middle toe by interdigital membrane.

Gen. **Buteo**.—*Cuv.*

Bill short with hooked tip; margin of upper mandible slightly festooned; nostrils oval. Lores clothed with bristle-like feathers. Wings long; 3rd, 4th, and 5th quills sub-equal and longest; inner webs of 1st four quills strongly notched. Tarsus bare or feathered on the upper third only.

21. Buteo ferox, *S. G. Gmelin, N. Comm. Ac. Petrop.* xv. p 442; *Hume, Rough Notes,* ii. p. 274; *Stray Feathers,* iv. p. 362 (1873); *Sharpe, Cat. Acc.* p. 176. Buteo canescens, *Hodgs. Beng. Sport. Mag.* 1836, p. 180; *Jerd. B. of Ind.* p. 88, No. 45. Buteo longipes, *Jerd. Madr. Journ.* x. p. 75. B. aquilinus, *Hodgs. J. A. S. B.* xiv. p. 176; *Jerd. B. of Ind.* i. p. 90, No. 46.—The Long-legged Buzzard.

The plumage of this large and handsome Buzzard varies considerably in all its different stages. This circumstance has led to its being described as *canescens*, Hodgs; *longipes*, Jerdon; *rufinus*, Rupp.; *leucurus*, Naum.; and *fuliginosus*, Hume. Mr. Hume in his scrap book goes very minutely into the differences observed in the plumage of its various stages, and states at page 281, that "the great difficulty we meet with in assigning any chronological value to these changes is that the changes on the upper surface do not correspond with those on the lower. It is easy enough, he says, to arrange any number of specimens, in what, looking at the upper or under surface only, appears a very perfect series in which no links are wanting, but directly we turn the specimens over, all traces of any arrangement seem to vanish." The question as to which is the adult plumage seems yet a vexed one, the Buzzard being known to breed in plumage which has been described as immature, but it is probable that the fuliginous plumage (*B. fuliginosus*) of Hume is that of very old birds, in which the whole head, neck, ear coverts, cheeks, throat, and breast is a deep umber brown, indistinctly margined with rufous.

Male.—Feathers of the forehead and crown of the head rufescent brown with stiff dark shafts. A narrow dark line in front of the superciliary edge of the eye. Lores whitish, with numerous elongated stiff bristle-like feathers which extend to the base of the cere, partially cover the nostrils and turn up on to the front of the forehead above the base of the cere. Cheeks rufescent brown, the feathers dark shafted. Ear coverts yellowish or a soiled white, the feathers dark shafted. Chin and throat white, some of the feathers with dark shafts. All round the edges of the lower mandible there are stiff bristle-like hairs, which are ½ an inch or more long. A rufous brown line behind the eye, and another from the gape forming a fairly distinct moustachial stripe. Sides of the neck rufous, the feathers dark shafted and edged lighter. Breast rufescent, the feathers dark shafted and edged buffy. Nape and back of the neck rufous brown, mottled with white, the basal portion of the feathers showing through. Abdomen deep chestnut brown, the feathers edged fulvous and with dark shafts. Thigh coverts deep brown, the feathers edged reddish fulvous; upper back, scapulars, and lesser wing coverts brown, edged with rufous; lower back and rump uniform brown, the lateral feathers of the upper tail coverts bright rufous and irregularly barred with brown. Lower tail coverts white. Tail (except the two lateral feathers, which are shaded with ashy grey) pale rufous, with a broad terminal band of slightly deeper rufous; the shafts and inner webs white, with traces of brown cross bars. Outer webs of quills ashy grey, the inner webs blackish from the tip to the emargination or sinuosity and white beyond, forming on the under surface of the wing a large white patch. Except the first three, all the other primaries are barred on both webs; the 3rd, 4th, and 5th quills emarginate on the outer webs, and all five primaries emarginate on their inner webs.

Legs and feet pale lemon yellow. Irides brownish yellow; orbital ridge dusky greenish. Bill brownish plumbeous, gape yellow, tip black. Cere yellowish green.

Length.—24 inches; wing 16·75; tail from vent 9·75; tarsus 3·20.

Female obtained at Sehwan, 5th February, similar to the male. Length 25 inches; wing 19·75; tail from vent 10·75; tarsus 2·75.

Hab.—Winter visitant in Sind. Found throughout India. It is recorded from Northern, Southern, and Central India, N.-W. Provinces, the Punjab, the Gangetic Valley, N.-W. Himalayas, Kashmir, Nepal, Oudh, and Behar; also from Beloochistan, Persia, Afghanistan, Eastern Turkestan, and Palestine. In Palestine Mr. Tristram (*Ibis*, 1865) took its eggs from a rocky ledge on Mount Carmel. The plumage of his Palestine specimen, he says, is very rufous, and he shot breeding birds with and without the bar on the tail.

22. Buteo desertorum, *Daud. Traite*, ii. p. 164; *Vieill. N. Dic. d' Hist. Nat.* iv. p. 478; *Hume, Rough Notes*, ii. p. 268; *Jerd. Ibis*, 1871, p. 338. Buteo rufiventer, *Jerd. Ill. Ind. Orn.* pl. 27. Buteo vulgaris, *Jerd. B. Ind.* i. p. 87.—The AFRICAN BUZZARD.

Adult.—Above brown, all the feathers except on the lower back and rump margined with rufous. Head and neck tawny rufous, the feathers mesially streaked with dark brown; sides of face whitish, washed with rufous and narrowly shafted with dark brown. Under surface of body tawny rufous, some of the feathers of the lower breast tipped with creamy buff, the under tail coverts inclining to this colour, as also the middle of the breast; thighs and flanks rufous, shaded with ashy brown; under wing coverts creamy buff with rufous central streaks, the outermost and greater series inclining to ashy brown; upper wing coverts dark brown, the feathers margined with rufous. Primaries black, externally shaded with ashy grey, the secondaries lighter brown, tipped with whitey brown. Under surface of quills white at base of inner webs, shading into ashy white gradually towards the tips.

Upper tail coverts rufous at tip and on outer web; tail rufous, yellowish at tip, with an indistinctly indicated subterminal bar of brown, the shafts white. Cere lemon yellow. Bill dark plumbeous, lighter near the cere; feet lemon yellow; iris light hazel, or yellowish. Length 21 inches; culmen 1·55; wing 13·4; tail 7·8; tarsus 3. (Sharpe.)

Hab.—The whole of Africa, S.-E. Europe, and the Indian Peninsula generally. Common in the Himalayas. Recorded from the Neilgherries, and from Murree to Darjeeling. Nothing is known of the nidification of this species, except what Dr. Bree says, that, according to M. Fairer, it nests among the rocks and the male takes its turn in sitting.

23. Buteo plumipes, *Hodgs. in Gray's Zool. Misc.* p. 81; *id. P. Z. S.* 1845, p. 37; *Jerd. B. Ind.* p. 91 No.; *Hume, Rough Notes*, p. 285; *Jerd. Ibis*, 1871, p. 340; *Str. F.* iv. pp. 358-371; *Sharpe, Cat. Acc. B. M.* p. 180. Buteo japonicus, *Bp. Consp.* i. p. 18; *Jerd. Ibis*, 1871, p. 337. Buteo vulgaris, *Blyth, Ibis*, 1863, p. 20.—The HARRIER BUZZARD.

PLATE.

Adult.—Above dark purplish brown, the feathers rufescent on their margins; sides of face and neck rufous, the feathers mesially streaked with brown; lores whitish. Upper margin of ear coverts dark brown; cheeks blackish, forming a strongly pronounced moustache. Under surface of body rufous, streaked with blackish on the chin and less distinctly on the throat; chest almost uniform rufous with a black shaft stripe; lower breast fulvous white, irregularly barred with rufous brown; thighs rufous with fulvous margins to the feathers; lower abdomen, vent, and under tail coverts creamy buff. Primaries blackish; secondaries paler with whitish tips and irregularly mottled or barred with brown; tail brown with an indistinct purplish subterminal band, a white tip, and 3—4 other distinguishable bars of darker brown.

Length.—21·5 inches; wing 15·7; tail 9; tarsus 3; culmen 1·35.

Aged specimens are everywhere dull smoky brown, the wing coverts and scapulars lighter; primaries dark brown, inclining to purplish brown near the tips; the inner web buffy white, barred with brown; shafts whitish; secondaries like the back; tail uniform smoky brown with whitish shafts and pale whitey brown tips with obsolete remains of cross bars. Sides of face and neck and entire under parts uniform smoky brown.

Length.—20 inches; wing 15·4; tail 9; tarsus 3.

Hab.—The Travancore Hills of Southern India, the Himalayas, the Northern portions of the Tennaserim province of British Burmah, Nepal and Sikkim and eastwards to China and Japan.

Mr. Bourdillon in *Str. F.* states that this is a winter visitor in Travancore during December, January, and February, preferring high open country, where two or three may be seen steadily quartering the ground and occasionally pouncing on some mouse or lizard. As to the identity of this species with *plumipes* there is still a set controversy owing to the very variable plumage of the Buzzard in all their different stages. Messrs. Hume, Blyth, Sharpe, Dresser, and Gurney have worked hard to find out the points of distinction between the Indian species of Buzzards, but no satisfactory conclusion has yet been come to. Mr. Sharpe has, however, in his Catalogue fairly well given a key to seventeen species of *Buteo* from all parts of the world. I doubt whether anything could be made of the Indian species.

Gen. **Archibuteo.**—*Brehm.*

Characters of Buteo. Tarsi lengthened and feathered to the toes.

24. Archibuteo strophiatus, *Hodgs.; Gray, Cat. Mam. and B. Nepal; Jerdon, Ibis,* 1871, p. 340; *Sharpe, Cat. Acc. B. M.* p. 199. Archibuteo hemiptilopus. *Bly. J. A. S. B.* xv. p. 1; *Jerd. B. Ind.* i. p. 94, No. 49; *Hume, Rough Notes,* p. 232; *id. Str. F.* i. p. 315. Archibuteo leucoptera, *Hume, Str. F.* i. p. 318.—The BROWN EAGLE BUZZARD.

PLATE.

Adult.—Above rich deep fuscous brown, slightly glossed with pinkish; interscapulary region slightly darker; scapulars and wing coverts margined paler; lores whitish; sides of face and neck brown. Entire under parts brown; also the tarsal feathers, which extend to the root of the toes; a broad irregular band of white across the breast. Quills dark brown; primaries shaded greyish

1/5.

ARCHIBUTEO STROPHIATUS. BUTEO PLUMIPES.

Mintern Bros. lith.

externally and white at base of inner web. Tail brown above, ashy white beneath; the shafts and tips white or albescent and the feathers crossed with traces of 7—8 bars of dark brown.

Length.—27 inches; wing 19·4; tail 11; tarsus 3·6; bill 1·9.

Hab.—Sikkim, Nepal, and Tibet. Nothing is known of the habits and nidification of this Buzzard, of which there are only 3 or 4 specimens in existence.

Sub-Family.—AQUILINÆ, Eagles.

Bill strong, more or less lengthened, festooned but not toothed; tarsus reticulate behind, more than half the length of the tibia. Outer toe only connected to middle toe by membrane. Wings moderate. 4th quill usually longest.

Gen.—Gypætus.

Bill strong, lengthened, compressed, straight; tip of upper mandible much hooked. Nostrils oval, hidden by stiff bristles. Chin with a tuft of black rigid hairs.

Gypætus barbatus.

25. Gypætus barbatus, *Storr. Alpenreisse*, p. 69; *Jerd. B. of Ind.* p. 13; *Hume, Rough Notes*, vol. i. p. 35; *Murray, Hdbk. Zool., &c., Sind*, p. 105; *id. Vert. Zool. Sind*, p. 64. Falco barbatus, *Gm. S. N.* vol. i. p. 252. Gypætus hemalachanus, *Hutton, Jour. As. Soc. Ben.* vol. vii. p. 22. Gypætus orientalis, *Blyth, Ibis*, 1863.—The BEARDED VULTURE or LAMMERGEYER.

Adult.—Above black, a few brown feathers on the rump; quills brown, externally washed with ashy, the secondaries with ochreous brown, the shafts of all the feathers white, feathers of the back also white shafted, tinged with buffy, especially on the wing coverts. Head white, with dark streaks; nape feathers lanceolate, elongate, tinged with bright tawny; cheek stripe and supercilium black; bristles over the nostrils and tuft of hairs under the chin black. Entire lower parts rich tawny, dull orange, or ferruginous; a dark pectoral collar (not always present) more or less distinct. Under wing coverts dark brown with pale shaft streaks. Bill bluish horn, the tip darker; feet plumbeous; iris pale orange; sclerotic membrane blood red.

Length.—45 to 46 inches; expanse 108 to 112; wing 29·5; tail 20; tarsus 4; culmen 3·7.

Hab.—The highest mountains of Europe, Asia, and Africa, principally the the most inaccessible parts; also the Himalayas from Nepal to Cashmere, and the Salt and Sooliman Ranges; not uncommon in the Bolan (Beloochistan) and South Afghanistan.

The Lammergeyer is not common in any part of Sind, except the northern country, at and beyond Jacobabad, affecting the hilly districts. Whether it is a permanent resident of those parts or only a winter visitant, is not known. Mr. Hume, in his contributions to the Ornithology of India, &c., in *Stray Feathers* states that he observed it on two occasions in the hills dividing Sind from Khelat. Dr. Day observed it in Durryah, and it is said to be well known to sportsmen who have shot ibex in those ranges.

It does not possess the carrion-eating propensities of the other vultures, but kills its own game, comprising ibex, hares, &c.

Breeds in the Himalayas during December, January, and part of February. The nest is a large heap of sticks about 3 × 5 feet, lined with hair, rags, feathers and bones and commonly placed in almost inaccessible situations. Captain Cock took a nest in December 1868, two marches from Rawulpindee on the Peshawur side. There were two eggs in it which Mr. Hume says are excessively like one of the common types of the eggs of *Neophron ginginianus*, but much larger, a rather broad oval, somewhat pointed towards one end. Texture coarse, but the shell more compact and less chalky than those of the Neophrons. In colour a nearly uniform pale salmon buff, here and there mottled paler. They measure 3·43 to 3·05 × 2·68 to 2·52 inches.

Gen. **Aquila**.—*Briss.*

Bill straight at the base, very much curved at the tip. Sides compressed. Wings, 4th and 5th quills longest and equal. Tarsi feathered to base of toes.

26 Aquila chrysætos, *Lin.; Dumont, Dict. Sci. Nat.* i. p. 339; *Gould. B. Eur.* i. pl. 6; *McGill. Brit. B.* iii. p. 204; *Jerd. B. Ind.* i. p. 55, No. 26; *Stray Feathers,* i. p. 157; *Hume, Rough Notes,* i. p. 139; *Murray, Vert. Zool. Sind,* p. 74; *Sharpe, Cat. Acc.* p. 236. Aquila fulva, *Sav. Descr. Ois. De Egypt*; *Shelley, B. Egypt.*—The Golden Eagle.

Adult Male.—Crown of the head brown; nape and hind neck pale orange brown, the feathers lanceolate, with brown bases; sides of the face paler. Lores greyish white. Cheeks blackish. Back, scapulars, and wing coverts dark brown, the latter and scapulars margined slightly paler. Greater wing coverts with brownish mottlings. Primaries dark brown, blackish towards their tips, basally white on their inner webs and clouded or mottled with brown. Tail nearly square, the middle feathers slightly elongated. At the tip it is dark brown or nearly black, greyish basally; the intervening space brown and much mottled. Under surface of body dark brown; the thigh, leg and under wing coverts pale brown, tinged or washed with tawny. Cere yellow. Bill bluish horn colour, darker at the tip. Legs yellow. Irides hazel.

Length.—35·5 to 40 inches; wing 24·5 to 28; tail 14 to 17; tarsus 3·8 to 4·5. The young has the plumage of a lighter shade. The feathers of the back, scapulars, and tertials brown, basally broadly white and showing through. The tail broadly black terminally, white or ashy at the base, and mottled with brown. Under surface of body light brown, the feathers basally white. The thigh and under tail coverts tawny rufous. Adult female is larger than the male.

Hab.—The whole of Europe and N. Asia, extending into India and N. China. Has been found in the Punjab and in the Himalayas. In Sind it occurs on the hills dividing Sind from Khelat; also in the Bolan, Beloochistan, and probably extends into Persia and Afghanistan.

Nothing is known as to the breeding of this noble and majestic eagle in India. Of its breeding in Europe, Yarrell and Morris give long accounts. The former says it makes a large platform of sticks on high and inaccessible rocks and precipices, occupying a space of several square feet. Morris (*B. Birds*) says, or on the stump of some tree projecting from them or on the lofty trees of the forest. The nest is usually lined with roots, dry grass, heather, moss, or other vegetable materials. The usual number of eggs is two, but sometimes three are found. They are usually of a dirty white colour and either richly blotched and spotted or thickly mottled, streaked, and clouded with varying shades of red or reddish brown. Some are pure white. The eggs according to Mr. Hume are broad, very perfect ovals, slightly compressed towards one end. Mr. Hewitson's figures of three eggs measure 3 × 2·35 inches; 3·13 × 2·3; 2·95 × 2·35.

Of the habits of this noble bird much has been written, to compile which would take pages of print. In Central Asia it is said to be trained to kill antelopes, foxes, &c., and to be held in much esteem by all the tribes. Its food consists principally of sheep, lambs, rabbits, and such like small animals, but it does not hesitate to attack larger game, fixing itself on the head of the victim and flapping its wings in the animal's eyes; the smaller animals it is said to seize with one foot and drag the other on the ground.

27. Aquila heliaca, *Savign. Desc. Egyp.* p. 459; *Gould. B. Eur.* pl. 5; *Gray, Gen. B.* i. p. 13; *Sharpe, Cat. Acc.* p. 238; *Murray, Vert. Zool. Sind,* p. 74. Aquila imperialis, *Cuv. Regne. Anim.* i. p. 325; *Gray, Ill. Ind. Zool.* ii. p. 28; *Jerd. B. of Ind.* i. p. 57, No. 27; *Hume, Rough Notes,* i. p. 142; *Stray Feathers,* i. p. 157; *Murray, Hdbk. Zool. &c. Sind,* p. 109. Aquila mogilnik, *Strickl. Orn. Syn.* p. 57 (*S. G. Gmel.*). Aquila bifasciata, *Saund. P. Z. S.* 1871—The Imperial Eagle.

Young.—Above rather light brown, the back feathers mostly shaded down the middle with ashy and on the margins with purplish; all the feathers of the upper surface pointed with buffy fawn colour, giving a spotted character to the plumage; head and neck tawny buff, the feathers with clear brown bases, which show through more or less and impart a streaked appearance; the plumes of the hind neck long and lanceolate, brown like the back, with tawny streaks down the centre; wing coverts brown, pointed with fulvous like the back; the greater and median coverts with broad buffy white terminal spots, widening up the shafts of the feathers; quills blackish; the secondaries rather browner, and broadly tipped with buffy white; feathers of hinder back and rump tawny fulvous, with dark brown lateral margins, spreading more over the plumes of the latter part; upper tail coverts buffy white, in strong contrast to the tail, which is uniform brown, tipped with buffy white; under surface of tail light tawny fulvous, nearly uniform on the throat, abdomen, thighs, tarsus, and under tail coverts; the whole of the breast feathers laterally margined with brown, producing a distinctly streaked appearance; under wing coverts rufous fawn colour, streaked with brown; the lower series ashy brown, like the inner lining of the wing.

Adult Male.—Blackish brown above, much lighter brown on the hinder part of the back and on the upper tail coverts, which are mottled with white near the base, and broadly tipped with the same; many of the scapulars pure white, forming a conspicuous patch, which, however, is confined to the scapulars themselves; the least wing coverts slightly mottled with brown, but not with white near the carpal bend; rest of wing coverts blackish brown, uniform with interscapulary region; quills blackish; the primaries externally shaded with ashy grey; the secondaries browner, the innermost slightly tipped with buffy white; the lower surface of wing ashy brown; the primaries mottled with whitish at base of inner web. Tail ashy grey for a little more than the basal two-thirds, shaded with silvery grey, and mottled with blackish brown, forming indistinct and broken bars on some of the feathers; the terminal third blackish brown with a narrow tip of fulvous; head and neck light fulvous with fawn-coloured bases to some of the feathers of the nape. Hind neck dark. fawn brown with light buff tips and dark brown centres; forehead and anterior part of crown blackish, as well as the feathers over the eye; sides of face and of neck light fulvous like the crown, the feathers under the eyes inclining to brown. Cheeks and entire under parts blackish; the under tail coverts tawny buff with dark brown shaft lines and whitish tips to the feathers; under wing coverts and axillaries blackish, like the breast. Cere pale yellow. Bill bluish, darker at tip. Feet pale yellow. Iris brownish yellow.

Length.—Male 31 inches; culmen 2·6; wing 22·6; tail 11·3; tarsus 2·9. (Sharpe, *Cat. Acc.*)

Adult Female.—Larger. Length 32·34 inches; wing 23·75—24 inches; tail 11·5; tarsus 3·85. (Sharpe, *Cat. Acc.*)

Hab.—South, Eastern and Central Europe, and throughout India nearly. Occurs in Sind, the Punjab, Beloochistan, Afghanistan, Persia, Concan, and Deccan; Nepal, Behar, Central and Southern India, and the Himalayas.

Mr. Hume (*Rough Notes*) has collected all the information possible in regard to the nidification of the Imperial Eagle. A few, he says, remain to breed in the upper Punjab and possibly in the Dhoon; the rest breed in the Himalayas. They lay (in the plains) in February, March, and possibly April, building a large platform of sticks on or near the top of trees; Peepul trees generally, and also at times on Babool (Acacia) and other thorny trees. The nests were from 2 to 2·5 feet in diameter and some 6 to 8 inches thick, lined with a few green leaves. Mr. Blewitt took a nest near Hansie which was only 18 inches in diameter, without any lining and also from on top of an Acacia tree. The eggs, Mr. Hume adds, vary much in size and shape—2·6 to 3 inches in length and from 1·95 to 2·15 in breadth. The average of nine eggs is given as 2·7 × 2·09 inches. The figure in Bree measures 2·05 × 2·88, normally the eggs seem a broad oval, but one or two are a good deal lengthened. The Kurrachee Museum specimens are all broad ovals, white or greyish white, and one only has the faint spots and streaks of pale brown with purplish brown blotches. The number of eggs is generally two, and sometimes three. Mr. C. Farman (*Ibis*, 1869; and *Rough Notes*) notes that it is a very shy bird and difficult to approach, and is very daring during the breeding season. The male, he says, is always on the watch circling gracefully in the air above the nest or seated on some neighbouring tree, whence on the slightest approach of danger he comes swooping down towards his eyrie, uttering a hoarse, croaking noise as a warning to the female who instantly leaves the nest and joins her partner.

This is not however Mr. Hume's experience, he looks upon the "Konigsadler" as no better than a great hulking kite. He has taken their eggs before their eyes without the parents flapping a pinion to defend what a Shrike would swoop to save. The Imperial Eagle, though preying on quails, rats, and sometimes hares, does not disdain carrion.

28. Aquila mogilnik, *Gm. N. Comm. Petrop,* xv. p. 445, pl. xi. b. (1770). Aquila bifasciata, *J. E. Gray in Gray & Hardw. Ill. Ind. Zool.* i. pl. 17; *Anderson, P. Z. S.* 1871, p. 621. Aquila nipalensis, *Hodgs. Asiatic Researches,* xviii. pt. 2, p. 13, pl. 1.—The Russian Eagle.

Adult Male.—Head darker brown than the back, which is a pale brown, as also the lesser and median wing coverts; lower back, and rump, the under surface of the body and some of the median wing coverts tipped with fulvous; the greater wing coverts dark brown, also tipped with fulvous. Lores whitish. Primaries and their coverts deep brown, tipped broadly in some with buffy or ashy grey with buffish tips. Under surface of the wing blackish brown, mottled with greyish at the base of the inner web; under wing coverts brown, the lesser series pure white. Upper tail coverts white, tail brown with indistinct ashy bars and fulvous tips. Cere, gape, base of lower mandible, and feet deep yellow; bill blackish; irides dark brown.

Length.—30 inches; wing 22; tail 11·7; tarsus 4. (Sharpe.)

The adult female is not very much larger. The length as given by Sharpe in his Catalogue of the Accipitres in the British Museum is 30 inches; wing 23·2; tail 11·5; tarsus 4. The young male is described as ashy brown on the upper surface, shaded with glossy purplish black on the back, scapulars, and wing coverts. Median and greater coverts blackish, shaded with ashy grey and broadly tipped with bright ochraceous fawn colour, paling into fulvous on the extreme tip and forming a triple band across the wing. Primaries and their coverts blackish, broadly tipped with fawn colour; both webs, like the wing coverts, distinctly but irregularly barred with silvery grey, distinctly so on the under surface of the secondaries. Primaries black below, greyish on the inner web, and thickly mottled with brownish; lower back and rump ashy brown like the head, the lower feathers of the latter part more or less marked with fawn colour; the upper tail coverts entirely fawn colour, paling into fulvous on their tips; tail dark brown with a broad terminal band of fawn colour mottled conspicuously with ashy grey on the outer feathers and taking the form of imperfect bars on the middle ones, sometimes 8 or 9 being distinguishable. Sides of face and neck as well as entire under surface of the body ashy brown, paler on the tarsal feathers. Under tail coverts pale buffy fawn, some of the under wing coverts also marked with a terminal triangular spot of the same colour. Bill, feet, and gape yellow. Cere greenish.

Hab.—South-Eastern Europe, N.-W. India, and the Himalayas, extending into Siberia.

It has been found in Nepal and in Kumaon and Gurhwal in the N.-W. Provinces. Of its nidification nothing certain is known, and this is owing chiefly to the vexed question whether or not, Radde's *Imperialis*, Gray's *bifasciata nævia*, and *punctata* are not identical with this species. There are marked differences, but the various stages and colouration of plumage of this order and the present uncertainty of the validity of the typical specimens of the various stages compel me to accept Mr. Sharpe's description of this Russian Eagle as distinct from those above referred to.

29. Aquila vindhiana, *Frankl. P. Z. S.* 1831, p. 114; *Strickl, Orn. Syn.* p. 59; *Sharpe, Cat. Acc.* p. 244. Aquila punctata, *Gray, in Gr. & Hard. Ill. Ind. Zool.* i. pl. 16. Aquila fusca, *id. Op. Cit.* ii. pl. 26. Aquila fulvescens, *id. Op. Cit.* ii. pl. 29; *Jerd. B. of Ind.* i. p. 60, No. 29; *Hume, Rough Notes*, i. p. 173; *Stray Feathers*, i. p. 158; *Murray, Hdbk. Zool. &c. Sind*, p. 109; *id. Vert. Zool. Sind*, p. 76. *Wokhab*, Hind; *Ukab* Sind.—The Tawny Eagle.

Young.—Above glossy purplish brown with distinct fulvous tips to the feathers, broader on lower back, rump and upper tail coverts; head and neck all round and entire under parts greyish mouse colour, with distinct points to all the feathers of the head and neck, absent on the under surface, excepting a few remains on the tips of the abdominal and lower throat feathers; lores and chin whitish, with narrow black shaft lines, the latter also apparent on the cheeks and ear coverts, which are mouse grey, like the breast; tarsal feathers and under tail coverts more fulvescent; under wing coverts mouse grey with pale fulvous tips; upper wing coverts ashy brown, with a very slight purplish gloss, but not so dark as the back, nor so grey as the head, though tipped like the latter with fulvous; greater and primary coverts, as well as the secondaries, deep brown, with whitish ends; primaries black, slightly shaded with brown near the base; lower surface of wing ashy brown, blackish towards tips of primaries; the inner webs of all slightly mottled with greyish. Tail purplish brown, tipped with buffy white; all the feathers shaded with ashy grey, forming indistinct bars on the centre feathers, on which remains of eleven or twelve can be counted.

Length.—28 inches; wing 20·75; tail 11; tarsus 3·2.

Adult Female.—General colour fulvous or tawny brown, most of the feathers with lighter margins, especially on the least wing coverts; the median coverts darker brown, but not so glossy as the back, with fulvous margins; greater and primary coverts, as well as secondaries, tipped with fulvous;

primaries blackish, externally shaded with ashy grey, forming distinct bands on both webs, these bands more vermiculated on the lower surface, the inner webs of the quills being ashy brown, shading into deep brown towards the tips of the primaries; tail dark brown, tipped with fulvous, the feathers shaded with ashy grey, forming 8—9 distinct bars on centre feathers; head and neck rather paler than the back, the feathers of the latter part margined with fulvous, giving a very mealy appearance; sides of face also light fulvous; under surface of body pale fulvous brown, lighter on the throat, thighs, and under tail coverts; under wing coverts with many of the feathers whitey brown on their margins, and near the base, the lower series ashy brown like the inner lining of the wing. Cere and gape deep yellow; feet yellow. Iris hazel brown. (Sharpe, *Cat. Acc.*)

Length.—27—28 inches; expanse 67—69 inches; wing 19·75—21·75; 4th and 5th primaries longest; tail 11·25—11·5; tarsus 3·8.

Adult Male.—28 inches; wing 20·5; tail 11; tarsus 3·4. (Sharpe, *Cat. Acc.*)

Hab.—Sind, Punjab, N.-W. Provinces, Bengal, Rajpootana, Kattiawar, the Deccan, Concan, Behar, the Carnatic, Central and Southern India, Nepal and Darjeeling.

A permanent resident in Sind and most parts of India. In Sind it breeds in January, making a large nest of sticks lined wtth straw, leaves, &c., on high trees, laying normally 2 broad oval or spherical eggs; the ground colour is greyish white, either unspotted or with blotches and patches of yellowish brown. In upper India it breeds from the middle of November to the middle of June, but the majority, according to Hume, lay in January. In size the eggs vary from 2·35 to 3·25 inches × 1·8 to 2·25.

30. Aquila hastata, *Less. Voy. Belang.* p. 217; *Blyth. J. A. S. B.* xv. p. 7; *Jerd. B. Ind.* i. p. 62 No.; *Hume, Rough Notes*, i. p. 180; *Anderson, P. Z. S.* 1871, p. 622. Aquila nævia, *Brooks, Str. F.* i. p. 293.—The LONG-LEGGED EAGLE.

Adult.—Glossy hair brown above, most of the feathers tipped with white. Quills glossy purplish black; tail the same, but obsoletely barred with dusky grey and tipped white; upper tail coverts barred with white. Breast, abdomen, feathers of the leg, lower wing coverts, and under tail coverts yellowish white, closely barred with brown. Quills and tail beneath grey, mottled and barred with dusky. In some only the feathers of the hind head and neck are tipped with white, the tertials are broadly tipped with white and there are three distinct rows of spots on the wings; *lesser wing coverts with small white spots; nostrils rounded.*

The young and adolescents are much lighter in colour, the lower parts from the breast are streaked longitudinally with fulvous white and the secondaries and tertials barred and clouded with whitish and brown.

Adult ♂.—Length 23 to 25 inches; wing 19 to 19·15; tail 9·5; tarsus 3·9 to 4; culmen 2·3.

Males are smaller.

Hab.—Upper India. Recorded from Behar, Darjeeling, and Nepal.

Nothing is known of the nidification of this handsome eagle, regarding which there is a set controversy as to its being distinct from *A. nævia.* Mr. Sharpe however remarks that the small white spots on the least wing coverts which frequently occur in this species may perhaps present a character of importance in distinguishing it from *A. nævia.*

31. Aquila clanga, *Pall. Zoogr. Rosso. Asiat.* i. p. 351; *Gray, Hand List.* i. p. 28; *Sharpe, Cat. Acc.* p. 248; *Murray, Hdbk. Zool. &c. Sind.* Aquila vittata, *Hodgs. in Gray's Zool. Miscellany,* 1844. Aquila nævia, *Schrenck. Reis. Amurl. Vog.* p. 220; *Jerd. B. of Ind.* i. p. 29, No 28; *Hume, Rough Notes,* i. p. 162; *Stray Feathers,* i. p. 158; *Andr. P. Z. S.* 1871; *Murray, Vert. Zool. Sind,* pp. 75, 76.—The SPOTTED EAGLE.

Young Male.—Above brilliant purplish brown; head and neck rather duller with lanceolate apical streaks of dingy buff on the nape and hind neck; wing coverts purplish brown like back, with a few dull white longitudinal streaks on the median coverts, much larger and forming distinct oval spots on the primary and greater coverts and tips of the scapulars. Quills blackish; secondaries browner with obsolete blackish bars and oval markings as the scapulars; lower back and rump with distinct triangular spots of ochraceous buff; the upper tail coverts almost uniform buffy white; tail feathers blackish, shading into brown towards the end, and tipped with whitey brown with 3—4 black bars near the tips; under surface of body blackish; the chin browner; breast feathers with pale brown mesial streaks, more ochraceous on the abdomen and leg feathers. Under tail coverts ochraceous buff; under wing coverts uniform blackish; axillaries browner.

Length.—26—28 inches; wing 20—21; tail 10—10·5; tarsus 3·9.

Adult Male.—Smaller than female. Length 26—27; wings 20—20·5; tail 10; tarsus 3·6. The female is a powerful bird, and is 29 inches in length, the wing being 21·4, tail 11·8, tarsus 4·2. (Sharpe, *Cat. Acc.*)

Hab.—Sind, Persia, Punjab, N.-W. Provinces, Bengal, Kutch, and Guzerat; also the Concan and Deccan, Malabar, and Southern India. Breeds in Sind, the Punjab, N.-W. Provinces and Oudh; also in Bengal and Central India. Capt. Marshall's note on the nidification of this species in the Sharunpur district gives May and June as the period of breeding. He says the nest was placed in a fork near the top of a large tree along the bank of the Eastern Jumna canal. It was a large circular platform-like structure of sticks with a few dead leaves in the egg receptacle but no other lining. The diameter of the whole nest was about 20 inches with an interior depth of two inches. Eggs one and sometimes two—a very blunt oval of a slightly yellowish white ground, somewhat profusely spotted and blotched with rather faint yellowish brown and a pale washed out purplish brown, which latter colour greatly predominates. In size the eggs vary from 2·5 to 2·7 inches × 1·96 to 2·5.

Gen. **Nisætus**.—*Hodgs.*

Bill much hooked at tip; cere large; nostrils large, elliptic; upper mandible festooned; tarsus feathered to the toes. No elongated occipital crest.

32 Nisætus fasciatus, *Vieill* (*Aquila apud Vieill*) *Mem. Lin. Soc. Paris*, p. 152; *Sharpe, Cat. Acc.* p. 250; *Strickl. Orn. Syn.* p. 61; *Murray, Vert. Zool. Sind*, p. 77. Falco bonelli, *Tem. Pl. Col.* i. pl. 288. Aquilla bonelli, *Less. Man. Orn.* i. p. 83; *Gould. B. Eur.* i. p. 7; *Shelley, Birds of Egypt*, p. 206. Eutolmætus bonelli, *Blyth, J. A. S. B.* xix. 174; *Hume, Rough Notes*, i. p. 189. Pseudætus bonelli, *Bp. Cat. Ois. Eur. Parzud.* p. 1; *Hume, Stray Feathers*, i. p. 158. Nisætus bonelli, *Jerd. B. of Ind.* i. p. 67, No. 33; *Murray, Hdbk. Zool. &c. Sind*, p. 100.—The CRESTLESS HAWK EAGLE.

Adult Female.—Above deep brown, the feathers white at base, some of them paler margined; eyebrow and sides of neck streaked with white. Sides of the face white; cheeks streaked with brown, ear coverts inclining to rufous. Under surface white with dark shaft stripes; flanks irregularly barred and marked with dark brown arrow-head markings. Feathers of the tarsus more or less pale brown, varied with dark brown and irregularly spotted with white; under wing coverts white, streaked with black; the lower ones entirely black with white tips; axillaries white, barred and streaked with blackish. Quills deep brown, mottled on the inner web with white. Tail ashy brown, inclining to grey, with 5—6 indistinct bars of brown near the base, and a broad subterminal band of dark brown; the tips of the feathers fulvous; cere and gape dingy yellow, bluish about the nostrils. Bill horn black. Feet whitish brown, tinged with yellow. Iris yellow.

Length.—26 inches; culmen 2·5; wing 21; tail 11·5; tarsus 4.

Adult Male.—Length 27—29 inches; wing 18—19·6; tail 11; tarsus 3·5. (Sharpe, *Cat. Acc.*)

Hab.—Found in Southern Europe and the Mediterranean. Breeds nearly throughout India. In Sind and the Punjab during December and January and in the Himalayas according to Hume in April and May. It occurs in the N.-W. Provinces, also in Persia, Beloochistan, and Southern Afghanistan, Kutch, Guzerat, the Deccan, Concan, Central and Southern India, Kattiawar, the Carnatic, Nepal, Assam, and in fact the entire Indian Peninsula.

This Eagle breeds on trees, or on ledges of precipitous rocky cliffs. The nest is from 4 to 6 feet in diameter, made of sticks, with scarcely any depression, except in the middle for the reception of the eggs. The lining of the nest is usually of green twigs and leaves. The number of eggs is usually two, but three have occasionally been found. They vary in shape and size, also in colouring; generally they are oval, unspotted pale greyish or faintly streaked and blotched with pale yellowish or reddish brown. In size they vary from 2·56 to 3 inches in length and from 1·95 to 2·22 in breadth.

33. Nisætus pennatus, *Gm. Sys. Nat.* i. p. 272; *Tem. Pl. Col.* i. pl. 33; *Sharpe, Cat. Acc.* p. 253; *Murray, Vert. Zool. Sind*, p. 78. Aquila pennata, *Vig. Zool. Journ.*; *Gray, Gen. B.* i. p. 14; *Jerdon, B. of Ind.* p. 63, No. 31; *Layard, B. S. Afr.* p. 10; *Murray, Hdbk. Zool. &c. Sind.* Hieratus pennatus, *Kaup. Mus. Senck.* iii. p. 260; *Blyth, J. A. S. B.* xv. p. 7; *Hume, Rough Notes*, i. p. 182; *S. F.* vol. vii. pp. 74, 198; viii. 162.—The Dwarf or Booted Eagle.

Head and neck behind, and on the sides, rufous or pale orange brown, the feathers lanceolate and streaked mesially with dark brown; some of the lengthened feathers entirely dark brown and forming a not very apparent crest. A narrow superciliary stripe; a band from the angle of the mouth below the ear coverts, and a central chin stripe dark brown. Ear coverts rufescent brown; back, scapulars, and wing coverts sepia brown; the median wing coverts and some of the scapulars broadly edged with fulvous white, forming a conspicuous wing band; rump and upper tail coverts like the back, the latter shading from dull fawn brown to buffy white on their margins and tips. Tail dull sepia brown, shaded with ashy, tipped with fulvous white, and with 4—5 indistinct bars of darker brown, more distinct on the under surface. Primaries dark brown, inclining to ashy white basally on their inner webs; secondaries indistinctly barred with dull brownish white. Under surface of body rufous, buffy, or fulvous white, deeper on the breast, and streaked with dark brown, the streaks disappearing on the abdomen, thighs, and under tail-coverts, which are white. Under wing coverts white with a few narrow shaft streaks. Cere and gape bright wax yellow; bill bluish black, pale blue at the base; feet pale wax yellow; iris pale brown.

Length.—Female 19—24 inches; wing 15·5 to 16; tail 9 to 9·25; tarsus 2·8. The young bird is paler beneath, the breast rufous or fulvous with a white shoulder spot, and white lores and forehead. The upper tail coverts are whitish, and the tail distinctly barred on both webs.

Adult Male.—Smaller than the female. Length 19 inches; wings 13·7; tarsus 2·4.

Hab.—Sind, the Punjab, N.-W. Provinces, Oudh, Beloochistan (Quetta), Persia, and Afghanistan; also the Concan, Deccan, and throughout the Indian Peninsula and Ceylon. Hume says it breeds in Spain in April and May, and that Mr. Theobald found a nest in the Salem district at Huroor. The eggs were two in number; one which reached him, he says, was a very broad oval. Ground colour dead white, devoid of gloss, and thickly blotched and streaked throughout with reddish brown. Size 2·13 × 1·78 inches.

Gen. **Lophotriorchis.**

Nostrils visible; no chin tuft; crest long and wedge-shaped; bill short, high at the base, with a prominent festoon; tarsi feathered to the base.

34. Lophotriorchis kieneri, *Geoff. St. Hil. Rev. Zool.* 1845, pl. 35; *Sharpe, Cat. Acc. Br. Mus.* p. 255. Spizaetus kieneri, *Gray, Gen. B.* i. p. 14; *Hume, Rough Notes,* i. p. 216; *id. Str. F.* i. p. 311. Limnaetus kieneri, *Strickl. Ann. Nat. Hist.* xiii. p. 33; *Jerd. B. Ind.* i. p. 74, No. 37.—The RUFOUS-BELLIED HAWK EAGLE.

Above black, slightly shaded with brown. Occipital crest 2·4 to 2·5 inches long; feathers of the nape white at the base. Ear coverts mixed white, black and rufous; cheeks, throat and breast pure white with a few narrow black shaft lines; rest of under surface including under wing and tail coverts tawny rufous, streaked with black shaft stripes, broader on the flanks; wings black, some of the feathers externally brownish, the inner lining of quills whitish ashy with a few blackish bars on the inner webs of the primaries; secondaries narrowly tipped with white; tail black, very narrowly tipped with whitey brown and with 6—7 indistinct bars of dark brown; lower surface of tail ashy white with a subterminal brown bar. Cere and feet yellow; bill plumbeous; irides brown.

Length.—21 to 25 inches; wing 14 to 16; tail 8·5 to 9·5; tarsus 2·9 to 3; culmen 1·5.

Hab.—The Indian Peninsula, Burma to Borneo and Sumatra, Travancore. Not uncommon in Lower Bengal, extending to the Himalayas. Mr. Inglis gives it from N.-E. Cachar and Wallace from the Phillippines. Nothing is known of its nidification. It is said to have a rapid and elegant flight and to mount and soar well.

Gen. **Neopus.**—*Hodgs.*

Bill moderate, bending from the base, much hooked at the tip, with a slight festoon in the upper mandible; cere large; nostrils ovoid oblique; wings exceeding the tail, which is long and slightly rounded; primaries emarginate; claws nearly straight.

35. Neopus malayensis, *Tem. Pl. Col.* i. pl. 117; *Horsf. and Moore, Cat. B. M. E. I. Co.* i. p. 381; *Jerd. B. Ind.* i. p. 65, No. 32; *Hume, Rough Notes,* i. p. 187; *Sharpe, Cat. Acc. B. M.* p. 257.—The BLACK EAGLE.

Uniform brown black, paler and duller beneath. Upper tail coverts barred with white, feathers of the tail more or less distinctly barred with ashy; quills mottled with white or greyish white near the base and faintly barred on their inner webs. Cere, gape, and feet deep yellow; bill greenish horny, black at the tip; iris dark brown.

Male.—Length 27·5 to 29·5 inches; wing 22 to 22·7; tail 12·8 to 14; culmen 2·05; tarsus 3·4.

Female.—30·5 to 31·5; wing 23 to 25·5; tail 14 to 14·75; tarsus 3·62 to 3·75.

Hab.—The Indian Peninsula, Ceylon, Burmah, the Malayan Peninsula to Java and Sumatra. It occurs in Malabar, in the Wynaad, Coorg, the Western Ghats, Travancore, Central India, the Punjab, N.-W. Provinces, throughout the Himalayas, Nepal, and Ceylon.

Jerdon says it is a bird of easy, graceful, and elegant flight, always soaring and circling about at no great height, with hardly any flapping of its wings. It lives chiefly on eggs of birds and nestlings.

Gen. **Spizaetus**—*Vieil.*

Form aquiline; bill short, high at the base, curved, hooked at the tip; upper mandible with a festoon; wing short, tail long and square; tarsi moderate, feathered to the base; inner toe without the claw, shorter than the outer.

36. Spizaetus nipalensis, *Hodgs. J. A. S. B.* v. p. 229, pl. 7; *Gray, Cat. Acc.* p. 8; *Blyth, J. A S. B.* xix. p. 333; *Hume, Rough Notes,* i. p. 210; *Sharpe, Cat. Acc. B. M.* p. 267. Limnaetus nipalensis, *Jerd. B. Ind.* i. p. 73, No. 36; *Holdsw. P. Z. S.* 1872, p. 411.—The SPOTTED or HODGSON'S HAWK EAGLE.

Adult Male.—Crown of the head, occipital crest, ear coverts, cheeks, sides of the neck and nape blackish brown; the occipital crest, which is usually from 2·5 to 4 inches in length, is tipped with white, and the feathers on the nape, cheeks, and sides of neck edged with tawny; chin and throat white or fulvous white with a broad streak of black down the centre; back, scapulars, wing coverts and secondaries deep brown, the feathers with darker transverse bars; upper tail coverts a lighter brown than the back, narrowly tipped with white, and with broad transverse white bars; tail pale brown, narrowly tipped with white, and with 4—5 broad transverse, deep brown bands broader than the interspaces; neck in front and upper breast a mixture of brownish and fulvous white, the feathers broadly centred with blackish brown; rest of under surface including tarsal feathers which reach to between the inner and middle toes brown, barred transversely with white or fulvous white; under wing coverts white or fulvous white, also barred or spotted with brown; cere and bill black; feet dirty yellowish white; iris yellow.

Length.—28 to 29 inches; wing 18·5 to 19; tail 13 to 13·2; tarsus 3·9 to 4; culmen 1·9.

The adult female is larger than the male. Length 29·25 to 32 inches; wing 18·5 to 18·7; tail 12·6 to 13; tarsus 4·2 to 4·4.

Mr. Hume in *Rough Notes* describes a young male as having the whole of the head, back, and sides of the neck and ear coverts rufous buff, each feather with a narrow dark brown central stripe, a long conspicuous occipital crest black and narrowly tipped with white; scapulars and interscapulary region hair brown, the feathers paling at the margins and towards their bases to a pale wood brown; rump and upper tail coverts dingy, somewhat rufous wood brown; central tail feathers a sort of olive brown, very narrowly tipped with white with a one inch subterminal and four other half inch broad transverse dark brown bands; wing coverts, except the greater primary coverts, a rather pale wood brown with dark brown centres, paling into the margins; secondary greater coverts almost wholly white on their inner webs; quills and primary coverts umber brown; 2nd to 5th primaries emarginate on their outer webs and obscurely barred with dingy buff; chin and throat pure white, also the base of neck in front, breast and abdomen—the feathers tipped with rufous buff and black shafted near the tip; lower tail coverts, flanks, and tibial plumes pale rufous brown, barred obscurely with white; axillaries the same, with spots forming imperfect bars; under wing coverts barred with dingy rufous or hair brown.

Hab.—Punjab, N.-W. Provinces, the Himalayas, Khasia, Southern India, Travancore, and Ceylon.

This species as far as is at present known breeds in the Himalayas during March, April, and May. Its nest, not unlike other eagles, is made of sticks and is said to be either hidden in a dense forest or projecting from the face of some inaccessible cliff. The normal number of eggs is two, in shape a broad regular oval, almost symmetrical at both ends. Shell coarse, dull, and glossless; the ground colour a slightly greenish white spotted thinly with reddish brown and with numerous large blotches and streaks of very pale inky purple. Size 3·78 by 2·23 inches. (Hume.) Hodgson's Hawk Eagle is a shy forest bird and confines itself to deep wooded hills ascending far into the interior of the Himalayas, where it feeds on pheasants, hares, and partridges.

37. Spizaetus cirrhatus, *Gmel. S. N.* i. p. 274; *Bp. Consp.* i. p. 29; *Hume, Rough Notes*, i. p. 206; *Sharpe, Cat. Acc. B. M.* p. 269. Limnaetus cristatellus, *Jerd. B. Ind.* i. p. 71, No. 35; *Holdsworth, P. Z. S.* 1872, p. 411; *Stray F.* vol. iv. 356; *id.* vol. vii. p. 33.—The Crested Hawk Eagle.

Adult Male.—Head, nape, and upper back brown, the feathers with a mesial dark brown shaft streak; occipital crest 3·9 to 4·9 inches, black, with or without white tips, and with white bases. Cheeks and ear coverts pale brown the feathers with a very narrow mesial dark brown stripe; throat white, with a broad white central streak and with a distinct moustachial stripe on each side; breast and upper abdomen pure white inclining to rufous, the feathers with a broad dark brown central stripe on the terminal half; lower abdomen, vent, under tail coverts, and tibial plumes uniform brown, also the lower back, rump, and upper tail coverts. Under wing coverts rufous brown, with dark shaft stripes; the lower series white, centred or barred with blackish brown. Axillaries a paler brown. Quills brown, barred with darker brown. Secondaries tipped with buff or buffy white, the innermost paler than the back, and the barrings very conspicuous. Wing coverts dark brown, the greater series margined paler. Tail pale brown with three and a broad sub-terminal dark brown band, broader than the interspace between it and the next. Cere pale yellow, feet and iris yellow.

Length.—Male 25 to 26 inches; wing 16; tail 11; tarsus 3·9 to 4.

Female.—Length 29 to 32 inches; wing 17·5 to 17·8; tail 12·51 to 12·57; tarsus 4·1.

Hab.—Central and Southern India, the Central Provinces, Guzerat, Ceylon and Nepal. It has been found in Travancore, the Western Ghauts, Madras, the Neilgherries, Seone, Raepoor, Etawah, Mundla and other localities in the Central Provinces; also at Mount Aboo, in Guzerat and South Concan.

Mr. Bourdillon in *Stray Feathers*, iv. 356, says of it, that it is very daring, frequently making a dash amongst chickens, when, if it misses, it retires to some neighbouring tree to concert a fresh plan of attack. It usually keeps to well-wooded tracts and feeds generally upon small birds as quail and pigeons, and at times on snakes and lizards; and Mr. Vidal in *Stray Feathers*, vol. vii. p. 31, adds that he had heard of one having been seen attacking a mongoose. Mr. Vidal has taken the eggs of this Hawk Eagle in the South Concan. He says it breeds during December and January and as late as April. The nests he says are large and comparatively deep stick structures loosely put together with the twigs hanging down untidily, built very high up, as a rule, in fork of trees. They are always profusely lined with green mango leaves. The old birds make no attempt to defend their nests. Out of 32 nests examined by Mr. Vidal, none contained more than one egg or one young bird. The largest egg measured 3 inches × 2·1 and the smallest 2·25 × 1·85. In shape they vary greatly, but the usual type is a moderate oval pointed at the smaller end. Colour a dull greenish white, sometimes unspotted and sometimes faintly streaked at the larger end with reddish brown. It is unglossed and has a pale green lining.

38. Spizaetus alboniger, *Blyth, J. A. S. B.* xiv. p. 173; *id.* xix. p. 335; *Wall. Ibis,* 1868, p. 215; *Sharpe, Cat. Acc. B. M.* p. 271. Limnaetus alboniger, *Hume and Davison, Stray F.* vi. p. 12. Spizaetus nanus, *Wall. Ibis.* 1868, pl. 1.—The PIED-CRESTED HAWK EAGLE.

PLATE.

Adult.—Crown, occiput, sides of the face and a broad throat stripe black. Occipital crest black, 2·25 to 2·75 inches in length and tipped with white; lores white. Chin and throat white. Breast white, tinged in some with ferruginous, each feather with a broad central spot. Rest of under surface of body, including tarsal and tibial plumes, also the flanks and lower tail coverts, white, barred transversely with blackish brown, narrowly on the flanks and tibial plumes and a little more broadly on the abdomen and lower tail coverts. Back, wing, scapulars, and upper tail coverts black. Quills paler, banded with black, tipped white, and with a subterminal black band. Under wing coverts white, barred or spotted with black. Tail ashy brown, tipped very slightly paler and with a subterminal and three other bands of black; the basal or third band hidden under the upper tail coverts.

Length.—21 to 22·5 inches; wing 12·13; tail 9·5; tarsus 3·3; culmen 1·4.

The young is paler brown above; the head and neck is a fawn brown; the occipital crest from 1·8 to 1·9 inch in length with white tips, and the scapulars, tertiaries, wing, and upper tail coverts tipped with white. The entire under surface is white or tinged with fawn colour, most marked on the breast. Under wing coverts pure white, and unspotted. Primaries blackish brown with transverse darker bands. Tail brown, tipped with white and with three broad transverse dark bands.

Length.—19·5 to 20 inches; wing 11·2 to 12; tail 9 to 9·5; tarsus 2·85 to 3.

Hab.—Tennaserim, Malacca, Borneo, and the Sunda Islands.

The Pied-crested Hawk Eagle is an inhabitant of dense forests near the foot of the hills at the extreme south of the Province of Tennaserim. Nothing is on record in regard to its habits and nidification.

39. Spizaetus limnaetus, *Horsf. Tr. Lin. Soc.* xiii. p. 138. Spizaetus niveus, *Blyth. Ann. Mag. N. Hist.* xii. p. 91; *Sharpe, Cat. Acc.* p. 272. Spizaetus caligatus, *Gray, Cat. Acc.*; *Wall. Ibis,* 1868, p. 13; *Hume, Rough Notes,* i. p. 198. Spizaetus nipalensis, *Bly. J. A. S. B.* xiv. p. 174. Limnaetus niveus, *Tem. Pl. Col.* i. pl. 127, *Jerd. B. Ind.* i. p. 70, No. 34; *Stray F.* vi. 11, n; vii. p. 94, 198, 246; viii. p. 44; ix. p. 373.—The CHANGEABLE HAWK-EAGLE.

Adult.—Above and below deep chocolate brown, the head, back, quills, and tail darker, the shafts of the latter brownish and the inner webs of the quills ashy. Tail the same as the back, the under surface ashy white, brownish towards the tips and with irregular dark transverse bars. Occipital crest rudimentary, or none. Tarsi shorter than in *Cirrhatus.* Cere, feet, and the iris yellow. The young is described by Sharpe (*Cat. Acc. B. M.*) as being clear brown above with faint terminal margins of fulvous brown, the buff coloured bases showing very conspicuously on all the upper parts but especially distinct on the wing coverts, which are also broadly margined with buffy white. Quills deep brown, the secondaries lighter and more purplish brown, broadly tipped with buffy white and indistinctly barred with darker brown, plainer on the inner web, especially underneath where it is ashy white on the primaries and greyish on the secondaries; lower back and rump pale brown; upper tail coverts brownish buff; tail brown, tipped with buffy white and crossed with 6—8 bars of darker brown. Under surface of body buffy white, washed with pale fawn colour on the sides of the body and thighs, with a few indistinct spots of the same on the breast. Head and neck whitish buff, washed with sandy rufous, and centred dark brown. Under wing coverts white, spotted with dark brown; tarsal plumes white, not extending beyond the point of the toes.

Adult.—Length 25 inches; wing 16; tail 11; tarsus 4·1; culmen 1·7.

Young.—Length 24 inches; wing 15·5; tail 9·5; tarsus 3·7. Irides brownish.

Hab.—The Concan, Deccan (rare), Central Provinces, N.-E. Cachar, Gurhwal, Lower Bengal, the Malayan Peninsula, Tennaserim, Java, Sumatra, Borneo, Ceylon and the Eastern Himalayas. According to Mr. Thompson, in Hume's *Rough Notes*, p. 198, the breeding season of this eagle commences in March and lasts till the end of June. The nest is usually placed on a high tree in a locality good for game, but in dense woods. Eggs usually two. In Gurhwal it is commonly known as Moorhaitah or Peacock-killer.

Gen. **Circaetus.**—*Vieill.*

Bill short, gradually curving from the base, much hooked at tip. Nostrils oval, oblique. Wing long, more than once and a half the length of the tail. 3rd quill longest. First three quills emarginate. Tarsi plumed below the heel. Toes scutellate at base of the claws.

40. Circaetus gallicus. *Gmel. Syst. Nat.* i. p. 295; *Vieill. Nat. Hist. Dict.* vii. p. 137; *Gray, Gen. Birds,* i. pl. 16; *Jerdon, B. Ind.* i. p. 76, No. 38; *Hume, Rough Notes,* i. p. 217; *Shelley, Birds of Egypt,* p. 202; *Sharpe, Cat. Acc.* p. 280; *Hume, Str. Feathers,* vii. 74, 199, 503; *Murray, Hdbk. Zool. &c. Sind,* p. 110; *id. Vert. Zool. Sind,* p. 79.—The COMMON SERPENT-EAGLE.

Adult Male.—Above dark brown with a purplish gloss; the wing coverts rather paler, especially on their margins; head rather more ashy brown; the forehead, lores, sides of face, and chin whitish with narrow hair-like lines of black, a streak of which overhangs the eyebrow. Cheeks, hinder ear coverts, and sides of the neck brown. Under surface of body white; the throat narrowly streaked with brown, and with a distinct central dark shaft stripe; chest white, streaked with brown; flanks barred brown at wide intervals, the bars disappearing on the thighs and under tail coverts, which are almost entirely white; under tail coverts and axillaries white with irregular spots or bars of brown. Quills black; secondaries browner, the outer ones glossed with purplish and narrowly tipped with white. Inner lining of quills white, excepting the tips and inner margins of primaries, which are deep brown; secondaries barred with dark brown, the subterminal band broad. Some of the upper tail coverts notched externally and tipped with white. Tail brown, tipped with white and crossed with three dark or blackish brown bars. Cere whitish, tinged bluish grey. Bill pale bluish grey at base, blackish horny at tip. Iris bright or orange yellow.

Length.—Male 26 inches; culmen 2·15; wing 19·65; tail 11·5; tarsus 3·7.

Adult Female.—Larger. *Length* 31 inches; wing 21·3; tail 12·5; tarsus 4.

Hab.—Sind, Punjab, N.-W. Provinces, Bengal, the Concans, Deccan, Kutch, Kattiawar, Behar, Nepal, and Rajputana. Said to be found throughout the Indian Peninsula and all the countries bordering the Mediterranean, extending into South-Eastern Europe. Breeds in Upper India (Gurhwal, Etawah, *Hume*); also in Palestine (*Tristram*) during January, February, March, April and May on high trees. Hume (*Rough Notes*) says, that from between forty and fifty nests, taken by himself and friends, never more than a single egg was obtained from any one. The eggs are typically broad ovals, with a slightly pyriform tendency, of a bluish white colour and invariably spotless. Mr. Tristram, in his *Ornithology of Palestine* (*Ibis*, 1865), remarks that of the eggs he took at Carmel and Heshbon, east of the Dead Sea, one was prettily spotted and the others were white.

Gen. **Spilornis**, *Gray*. Hæmatornis, *Vigors*.

Bill straightened at the base; wings short; head crested, crest feathers rounded. Other characters as in *Circaetus*.

41. Spilornis cheela, *Lath. Ind. Orn.* i. p. 14; *Bp. Consp.* i. p. 17; *Strickl. Orn. Syn.* p. 17; *Jerd. Birds of Ind.* i. p. 77, No. 39; *Hume, Rough Notes*, i. p. 222; *Hume, S. F.* i. p. 306; *Sharpe, Cat. Acc.* p. 287; *Murray, Hdbk. Zool. &c. Sind*, p. 110; *id. Vert. Zool. Sind*, p. 80. Circaetus cheela, *Gray, Cat. Acc.* p. 18.—The CRESTED SERPENT-EAGLE.

Young.—Above brown, with large spots of dark brown near the end of each feather, which is slightly tipped with fulvous, the bases of the feathers white; the upper tail coverts tipped and barred on the outer web with the same; wing coverts blackish brown, the least ones apically margined with white; the greater series whitey brown, more or less entirely white on inner web, mesially streaked with dark brown, widening into a spatulate apical spot. Quills dark brown, tipped with white; the secondaries more broadly barred across with blackish brown, very distinct underneath, where the inner webs are for the most part white. Tail ashy brown, tipped with white, and crossed with three broad bands of darker brown. Head and neck all round white, with a narrow shaft stripe and a diamond-shaped apical spot of dark brown. Ear coverts and cheeks nearly uniform brown. Under surface of body white, with broad streaks of brown on the breast, becoming very narrow and linear on the flanks; thighs narrowly barred with brown. Under wing coverts white, with large oval spots of rufous brown on the innermost, and having bars of brown on the lower series.

Adult Female.—Head much crested, jet black, with conspicuous white bases to the feathers, those of the nape tipped with dull ochraceous; rest of upper surface of body purplish brown, paler on the interscapulary region; the wing coverts blacker, with remains of white tips, which are less distinct on the scapulars, but very broad on the upper tail coverts. Quills brown, tipped with white and mottled slightly on the outer web, but more on the inner with the same; all the quills dark brown at base and having a broad subterminal band of blackish brown, the primaries showing a second dark brown band near the base; the inner web of the quills below whitish, showing the bands very distinctly. Tail black, narrowly tipped with whitish and crossed with a very broad median band of pale whitey brown; sides of face and chin blackish with a distinct greyish band, the latter showing slight tips of fulvous to the feathers; rest of under surface pale ochraceous brown, with distinct but irregular transverse lines of dark brown; the rest of the under surface with large white spots, rather oblong in shape, mostly margined above and below with black, changing to bars on the thighs and under tail coverts. Under wing coverts and axillaries light rufous with very distinct oval spots of white.

Length.—30 inches; culmen 2·25; wing 20·5; tail 13; tarsus 4·5.

Adult Male.—Smaller. Length 28 inches; wing 18·5; tail 12; tarsus 4·5. Chest perfectly uniform brown with no traces of cross barrings on the under surface; breast and lower parts very largely and distinctly spotted with white; cere, loral skin, and gape bright yellow; bill slatey plumbeous at base, bluish black at tip and on culmen; feet pale dingy yellow; iris intense yellow. (Sharpe).

Hab.—Sind, in the Narra Districts, and in well-wooded situations; also the Concan, Lower Bengal, Himalayas, Nepal, Assam, and Burmah; not uncommon in the Panjab (Shaharunpur District). Breeds throughout the sub-Himalayan ranges and regions as far west as Kangra at heights from 2,500 to 5,500 feet above the sea level, laying in March, April and May. Nest usually in the vicinity of water, built in the fork of a tree, circular, loosely made of sticks and twigs lined with fresh leaves and roots of grass. Eggs usually one in number, mottled and streaked with dingy brick-red and blood-red; ground colour white. Size 2·8 × 2·25 inches. Mr. Hume, in his *Rough Notes*, gives a good compiled account of the nidification of this species.

42. Spilornis melanotis, *Jerd. Madras Journ.* xiii. p. 165; *Sharpe, Cat. Acc. B. M.* p. 289, Sub-sp. a; *Davison and Wenden, Stray F.* vol. vii. sp. 74; *Ball. id.* p. 199; *Vidal, Stray F.* ix. p. 33; *Butler, id.* ix. p. 373 Hæmatornis spilogaster, *Bly. J. A. S. B.* xvi. p. 351. Spilornis spilogaster, *Blanf. J. A. S. B.* 1871, p. 270. Spilornis davisoni, *Hume, Stray F.* i. pp. 305, 422; *id.* iv. pp. 281, 358. Spilornis rutherfordi, *Swinh. Ibis*, 1870, p. 85; *id. P. Z. S.* 1871; *Wald. Ibis*, 1870, p. 298. Spilornis bacha, *Holds.* (*non Le Vaill*) *P. Z. S.* 1872, p. 412.—The SOUTHERN or LESSER HARRIER EAGLE.

Similar to *Spilornis cheela*, but smaller.

Cere, orbital skin, and legs yellow; irides orange; bill bluish, black at the tip. The following are comparative measurements of this species and *S. cheela* in inches.

	S. cheela. Adult.	S. melanotis. Adult.
Length	28 to 30	24 to 26.
Wing	18·5 to 20·5	15 to 16·8
Tail	12 to 13	10·8 to 12·5
Tarsus	4·15 to 4·5	3·65 to 3·75

Hab.—Central and Southern India, the Andamans to Ceylon and China. Occurs in both Northern and Southern Concans, the Deccan, Travancore, Raipoor, and other localities in the Central Provinces from the Ganges to the Godavery, Orissa, and also in Lower Bengal.

The Lesser Harrier Eagle affects marshy and hilly forest tracts, especially where there are rice and other cereal cultivations. It feeds chiefly on frogs, mice, and small birds. The only record of its nidification is in a paper in *S. F.* by Mr. Vidal on the Birds of the South Concan. Two nests were taken by him during March, and the eggs in his possession measured respectively 2·75 × 2·25 inches and 2·65 × 2·12 inches. They are said to be broad ovals, slightly pointed at the smaller end, white, streaked all over with reddish brown, and with a confluent cap of the same shade at the large end.

43. Spilornis pallidus, *Wald. Ibis*, 1872. p. 363. Spilornis cheela, *Wall. Ibis*, 1868, p. 15; *Hume, Stray F.* iv. 281; *id.* vii. p. 513; *id.* viii. p. 44.—The PALE HARRIER EAGLE.

Adult Male.—Crown of the head black with an elongate occipital crest, which is black with white bases to the feathers. Feathers of the nape with slightly rufous tips; sides of the face and throat clear bluish grey, of the neck and chest uniform pale brown. Above pale brown with indistinct margins of fulvous brown to the feathers, the scapulars slightly tipped with white, the upper tail coverts broadly so, and the wing coverts with two white spots at the tip of each feather. Quills ashy brown, tipped with buffy white, and with a broad subterminal and basal blackish brown band. Tail dark brown, tipped with buffy white, and crossed with a broad median band of pale whitey brown shaded with ashy. Under surface of body pale brown spotted with white; on the thighs and under tail coverts the spots take the form of bars; under wing coverts the same, but paler and more rufescent.

Length.—21 inches; culmen 1·8; wing 14; tail 8·8; tarsus 3·25 (*Cat. Acc. B. M.*)

The young female is described by Sharpe as pale brown above, with lighter margins. Crown of the head white with a black terminal spot; the body below pale brown; the throat and chest vermiculated with cross lines of dark brown, with a few white spots on the abdomen, turning to bars on the thighs and under tail coverts. Tail brown at base with two broad black bands, the basal one with slight indications of a whitish band immediately preceding the lower of the two and a broad subterminal whitey brown band.

Length.—24·5 inches; wing 14·3; tail 9·4; tarsus 3.

Hab.—The Malay Peninsula, Tennaserim, British Burmah, Borneo, Sarawak. This is a doubtful Indian species, but I have given a description of it owing to two skins, received from Mr. E. Whimper, being labelled Tennaserim and British Burmah.

Gen. **Butastur**, *Hodgs. J. A. S. B.* xii. p. 311.

Bill short. Edge of mandible scarcely festooned; nostrils small, oval, with a superior membrane. Wings reaching nearly to end of tail; 3rd and 4th quills subequal and longest; the first four emarginate.

44. Butastur teesa, *Hodgs. J. A. S. B.* xii. p. 311 (1843); *Sharpe, Cat. Acc.* p. 295; *Murray, Vert. Zool. Sind*, p. 87. Poliornis teesa, *Kaup. Classif. Saug. u. Vog.* p. 122; *Gray, Gen. Bird*, i. p. 30; *Jerd. B. of Ind.* i. p. 92, No. 48; *Hume, Rough Notes*, ii. p. 286; *id. Stray Feathers*, p. 159; *Murray, Hdbk. Zool. &c. Sind*, p. 115 (1873).—The ZUGGUN FALCON or WHITE-EYED BUZZARD.

Adult Male.—Above umber or pale rufous brown, the feathers margined paler, and with dark shaft stripes. Forehead and a nuchal mark white. Ear coverts light brown, the feathers very lax. Lores white, with elongate stiff hair-like feathers, the edges of the under mandible also with stiff bristles. Rump and upper tail coverts rufous brown, the rump with dark shaft stripes, and the upper tail coverts with dark cross bars. Tail pale rufous, tipped with buffy white and crossed with 6—7 indistinct bars, the subterminal one black, and broadest; wing coverts like the back, the median series mottled light brown and whitish. Primary coverts dark brown, externally shaded greyish. Outer webs of primaries dark brown, frosted over with ashy grey, and broadly tipped with darker brown. Inner web pale brown between the black tip and emargination of the first four quills, and white beyond, with a few faint dark incomplete bars. The secondaries pale brown, half the inner webs, with 4—5 bars of dark brown and tipped darker; outer web of the secondaries pale brown with a rufous tinge, tipped blackish, and with faint traces of transverse bars. Chin and throat white or yellowish white, bordered on each side with a black moustachial stripe from the base of the lower mandible, and one of the same colour down the centre of the chin and throat. Breast pale rufous brown, with yellowish white or fulvous spots, the feathers dark shafted. Rest of under surface buffy white, barred with rufescent brown. Under wing coverts white, some of the feathers streaked and spotted with rufous brown. Thigh coverts pale fulvous or buffy white, most of the feathers with a subterminal triangular patch of rufous brown. Vent and lower tail coverts white, some of the feathers with a subterminal band or triangular patch of rufous brown; under surface of tail feathers greyish white, the transverse band showing through in all but the exterior feather.

Legs and feet dingy orange yellow. Iris pale yellowish white. Eyelids orange yellow.

Length.—16·75 to 18·5 inches; culmen 1·4; wing 11 to 12·5; tail 6·56 to 7·8; tarsus 2 to 2·55.

Hab.—Throughout India to British Burmah and Malaya to Assam and Nepal. Recorded from Sind, Beloochistan, Persia, Punjab, N.-W. Provinces, Oudh, Bengal, Nepal, Behar, Kattiawar, Deccan, Concans, Cutch, Rajputana, and N. Guzerat.

The White-eyed Buzzard is plentiful in all the places where it is known to occur. Not unlike the Kestrel its flight is very rapid, and living as it does on rats, lizards, frogs, crabs, and insects, it is always seen flying low, skimming along just above the ground. It affects bare plains, low jungle, cultivated ground, and marshy tracts.

Breeds nearly throughout India from January to April, nesting on high trees and laying three eggs of a pale bluish colour, a broad oval in shape and varying in size from 1·4 to 1·9 inches. Mr. Hume says the parent birds are much attached to their nests and hang about them for many days after they have been robbed, and at times will lay in them a second time.

45. Butastur liventer, *Tem. Pl. Col.* i. pl. 438. Buteo liventer, *Cuv. Regne. Anim.* i. p. 37. Poliornis liventer, *Kaup. Classif. Saug. u. Vog.* p. 122; *Wall. Ibis*, 1868, 11; *Hume, Stray F.* i. 319; iii. p. 31; iv. 299; vi. p. 21.

Adult Male.—Whole head and neck all round are a pale earthy or grey brown, the feathers darker shafted; lores whitish; chin and throat more or less faintly streaked with white; breast like the neck, but with faint traces of obscure rufescent bars, all the feathers darker shafted; sides and abdomen the same; tibial plumes, vent, lower tail coverts and the whole lower surface of the wing, except the primaries beyond the notches on the inner web, pure white; axillaries white, with close-set transverse bars of brown and rufous. Quills, primary greater coverts, and winglet a rich chestnut red, tipped more or less broadly with brown, darkest on the primaries; the outer webs of the second to the 5th primaries from above the emarginations pure white, the red portions of the inner webs with a few widely distant narrow dark brown transverse bars, the outer webs with traces of similar bars. The first four primaries conspicuously notched on their inner webs; the 3rd, 4th, and 5th somewhat emarginate on their outer webs. Rump and upper tail coverts a rich more or less rufous brown, each feather darker shafted; *tail bright chestnut*, tipped white or rufous white and with a moderately broad transverse subterminal black band on both webs; the central and outer feathers exhibit two or three narrow transverse dark brown bars and a few black spots, traces apparently of these, the one about an inch and the other about two inches above the band just described, and the third just below the tips of the coverts; mantle a more or less rufous brown, some of the coverts faintly margined paler, and all the feathers darker shafted; lesser and median coverts browner and less rufous and more or less fringed with albescent. Longest scapulars brownish at the tips, bright chestnut above, and with traces of grey brown bars; primaries and secondaries narrowly margined towards the tips with dull white. Edge of the wing white; lower surface of the tail white, tinged purplish (*S. F.* iii. 31). The adult female (type of species) is described by Sharpe (*Cat. Acc. B. M.*). I have not seen a specimen, nor is one recorded in *Stray Feathers* as having been obtained by any one of Mr. Hume's numerous correspondents. The shaft stripes of the male is everywhere indicated in the female, but the coloration is paler. Tail rufous instead of bright chestnut, margined and tipped with ashy grey and *crossed with six blackish bars*, the subterminal one a little broader.

Length.—Male 14 to 14·5; expanse 35 to 37·5; tail 5·8 to 6·5; wing 10·7 to 11·5; tarsus 2·3 to 2·6; bill 1·2 to 1·4. Female larger. Bill pale orange yellow, the tip black. Cere, orbits, and feet yellow. Irides pale yellow.

Hab.—British Burmah and Siam to Celebes; occurring in Java (Sharpe), the Continent of India (Tem.). Dr. Armstrong has had it in the vicinity of Elephant Point, in the Rangoon district of the Irrawady Delta, where he says it is by no means common and frequents the extensive paddy fields, coursing along with a graceful swooping flight from one field to another. Messrs. Hume and Davison say that it is confined to the northern and central portions of the province of Tennaserim, and rare in the northernmost districts. Tonghoo (Lloyd and Ramsay), Kankaryit, Hongthraw, R. Thyetmoo, and Amherst are also given as localities.

It is said by Mr. Oates, (*S. F.* v. 141) to breed in British Burmah during March, laying 2 eggs of a pale greenish white colour without gloss. Size 1·81 x 1·45 inches. A second egg measured 1·86 x 1·47 inches.

46. Butastur indicus, *Gm. S. N.* I. p. 264 (*ex Lath*). Buteo pygmæus, *Blyth, J. A. S. B.* iv. p. 177. Poliornis indicus, *Gray, Cat. Acc.* 1848, p. 68. Poliornis poliogenys, *Gray, Gen. B.* i. p. 30; *Wall. Ibis*, 1868, p. 19; *Hume, Rough Notes*, p. 290; *Stray F.* vi. 19.—The GREY-CHEEKED BUZZARD.

Adult.—Above uniform hair brown, inclining to ashy on the head and upper back, and to rufous on the lower back, rump and upper tail-coverts, the *latter barred and broadly tipped with white;* forehead white; *sides of the face clear grey;* sides of the neck ashy brown; wing coverts and scapulars slightly tipped with rufous white, or rufous brown, and mottled with clearer rufous. Primary coverts rufous, broadly tipped with black. Quills rufous, narrowly tipped with buffy white; primaries brown externally and towards their tips, also barred with dark brown on their inner webs; the secondaries ashy brown, inclining gradually to whitey brown at their tips, washed with rufous and barred with dark brown; the lower surface of the wing creamy white on the inner webs of the quills, somewhat washed with rufous; tail ashy brown, whitey brown at tips, and crossed with three or four broad bars of blackish brown; the lower surface ashy white, the bars showing more plainly except on the outermost feathers, where they are obsolete. Throat white, with a mesial line of ashy brown, as well as two not very distinct moustachial stripes. Upper breast ashy brown, washed with rufous; the lower breast and abdomen barred with white and rufous brown, the rufous bars decreasing towards the vent and thighs and absent on the under tail .coverts. Bill blue black, pale on the gonys and lower portion of the base of the upper mandible. Cere, irides, and feet yellow. (Sharpe.)

Length.—17 to 18·5 inches; wing 13·12 to 13·15; tail 7·9 to 8; tarsus 2·4; bill from gape 1·3.

The adult female is larger than the male. Length 18·5 to 18·8 inches; wing 13·6 to 13·8; tail 8·4; tarsus 2·45; bill from gape 1·45.

The young is considerably different from the adult. The crown, occiput, nape and sides of the neck are brown; the feathers of the crown and hind neck margined with creamy white and slightly washed with rufous. Forehead and eyebrow creamy white, also the fore part of the cheeks. Breast buffy white, with lanceolate rufous brown shaft stripes and spots. Under tail coverts creamy buff; also the under wing coverts, but with a few rufous brown markings. Axillaries barred. Tail ashy brown, tipped with pale rufous brown, and crossed with five bars of darker brown. Throat with a central dark streak.

HALIAETUS ALBICILLA.

Hab.—Borneo, Sumatra, and the Phillipine Islands, also Tennaserim. Recorded localities from the latter are Amherst, Mergui, Pakchan and Bankasoon. Hume and Davison (*Str. F.* vol. vi. p. 19) state that it seemed to be of a confiding and somewhat indolent disposition, preferring to seat itself on some dry tree or other point of vantage from whence it keeps a look out for lizards and locusts, &c., of which its food seems principally to consist.

Gen. **Haliætus**, *Savigny*.

Bill straight at the base, longish, compressed, curved towards the tip, which is much hooked; margin of upper mandible sinuate; wings long; 4th and 5th quills sub-equal, longest; tarsus plumed for nearly half its length; lower half of tarsus scutellate.

47. Haliætus albicillus, *Linn. Syst. Nat.* i. p. 123; *Sharpe, Cat. Acc.* p. 302. H. albicilla, *Leach. Syst. Cat. Mam. &c., B. M.* p. 9; *Gould. Birds Eur.* p. 10; *McGillivray, Brit. B.* iii. p. 221; *Shelley, Birds of Egypt,* p. 204; *Hume, S. Feathers,* i. p. 159; *id. Rough Notes, p.* 257; *S. Feathers,* vii. 341 467; *Murray, Hdbk. Zool. &c. Sind,* p. 111. Falco albicilla, *Gm. Syst. Nat.* i. p. 253. Aquila albicilla, *Pall. Zoogr. Rosso. As.* i. p. 345. Haliætus pelagicus, *Hume, Rough Notes,* ii. p. 252. Haliætus brooksi, *Hume, Ibis,* 1870, p. 438; *Murray, Vert. Zool. Sind,* p. 83,—The European White-tailed Sea Eagle.

Male.—The legs and feet bright orange yellow. Gape and portion of cere yellow, the upper portion being yellowish brown. Bill blackish horny; head, nape, cheeks, ear-coverts and sides of the neck hair brown, all the feathers white at their bases, in some for the basal half, in others for fully the basal two-thirds, but very little of the white showing through, the feathers being densely set; all the feathers of these parts long and linear, those of the occiput especially; the back of the neck, the whole of the back and rump, scapulars and wing coverts, except the greater primary coverts, as well as the feathers of the breast and abdomen a warm buffy fawn colour, changing to white at their bases, and more or less broadly tipped with hair brown; the longer scapulars and the upper tail coverts,—which latter are very broad and come down to within some four inches of the tip of the tail,—a mixture of yellowish and hair brown, mottled and freckled with white and yellowish white; tail, which is very wedge-shaped, dark brown, mottled all over with dingy yellowish white, which colour predominates on the inner webs; the quills, winglet, and greater primary coverts chocolate brown; the second to the 5th primaries conspicuously emarginate on the outer web, and with a grey silvery tinge above the emarginations; the 1st to the 5th primaries conspicuoucly notched on the inner webs; the chin and throat pale buffy brown, the feathers whitish at the base and darker at the tips; the flanks and thigh coverts pale yellowish brown, the feathers tipped darker; the lower tail coverts dingy white, broadly tipped with brown, which in the longer ones is a dark hair brown: in the shorter a dull yellowish brown; wing lining a sort of umber brown, the bases of all the feathers paler, some of them fawn-coloured and some white.

Female.—The legs, feet, cere and gape a sort of brownish yellow; the upper mandible and claws blackish horny; the tip of the lower mandible yellowish horny; the whole of the head, nape, sides of the neck, cheeks, chin and throat pale yellowish brown; the feathers white, tipped with yellowish brown, which, owing to the feathers being closely set, is the predominant colour, especially on the top of the head; the ear coverts a darker brown; the whole of the back of the neck, back, rump and upper tail coverts, breast, sides, abdomen, vent, and lower tail coverts white, comparatively narrowly tipped with yellowish brown, and many of the feathers, with a narrow, linear, ovate, hair brown shaft spot near the tip. As in the male, the upper tail coverts are ovate lanceolate, very broad and long, and reach to within less than six inches of the end of the long wedge-shaped tail; most of the scapulars and the tail feathers are a mixture of dull dark and pale dingy yellowish brown, everywhere mottled and freckled with dirty white, which occupies almost the whole of the inner webs of the lateral tail feathers; the wing coverts, except the greater primary coverts, are wood brown, showing little or nothing of the white bases; most of the tertiaries are mottled white and dingy yellowish brown, like the tail; the secondaries are a dull, slightly rufous brown, much mottled on the inner webs with white, and the primaries are dark chocolate brown, greyish above the emarginations; some of the primary greater coverts are dark chocolate brown and others are a pale rufous brown. (*Str. F.* vii. 341.)

The following is McGillivray's description quoted in *Stray Feathers*:—

Male.—The cere and bill are pale yellow; the iris bright yellow; the tarsi and toes gamboge; the claws black with a tinge of greyish blue; the plumage of the head, neck, forepart of the back and breast with the upper wing coverts greyish yellow, the feathers all greyish brown at the base; of the other parts greyish brown, edged with yellowish grey; scapulars and feathers of the rump glossed with purple; those of the abdomen, tibia and subcaudal region inclining to chocolate brown; the quills and alular feathers brownish black, with a tinge of grey, the inner secondaries inclining to chocolate brown; the shafts of all white towards the base; the lower surface of the quills and the large coverts tinged with greyish blue; the upper tail coverts and the tail are white (generally freckled with dusky grey at the base); the down on the breast pale grey, that on the sides darker.

Length, to end of tail, 36 inches; extent of wing 72 inches; bill along the ridge 3·41, along the edge of lower mandible 3; its height 1·41; wing from flexure 24 inches; tail 11·4; tarsus 4.

The female does not differ from the male in colour, and her superiority in size is often not very remarkable. Length, to end of tail, 40 inches; extent of wing 10; bill along the ridge 3·91; along the edge of lower mandible 3·33; its height 1·66; wing from flexure 27·5; tail 12 inches; tarsus 4·5 inches.

Hab.—Sind, Punjab, N.-W. Provinces, Oudh, Beloochistan Coast, and Persia. On the Indus and the larger lakes or dhunds throughout Sind, especially on the Munchur Lake it is very common; also on the Jhelum, Chenab and Sutlej rivers. Sharpe gives its habitat as Greenland, Iceland, Faroe Islands, the whole of Europe and Northern Asia, Kamschatka and Japan, extending into China as far as Amoy.

The Erne or European White-tailed Sea Eagle is a bird of a very imposing aspect. It often assumes many elegant attitudes, especially when excited. Its habitat is always either near the sea on rocky prominences, or inland on the larger lakes, where it feeds upon fish, plunging into the water after the manner of the osprey. Aquatic birds also form part of its food. Of its breeding in India there is no information. Morris in his *British Birds* says it builds in March and sits very close, but is by no means so courageous as the Golden Eagle in defending its brood. The nest is about five feet wide, flat, and has only a slight hollow in the middle. It is a mass of stick, heather or seaweed, as the case may be, and lined with any soft material as grass, wool or feathers. It is placed on some precipice, or in the hollow of a crag or rock overhanging the sea, or else in some inland fastness. The eggs, one or two in number, are about 3 × 2¼ inches, white or yellowish white, thickly sprinkled over with reddish spots.

48. Haliætus leucogaster, *Gm. S. N.* i. p. 257; *Vig. Zool. Journ.* i. p. 336; *Jerd. B. Ind.* i. p. 85; *Sharpe, Cat. Acc. B. M.* p. 307; *Str. F.* ii. 149; iii. 324-335; iv. 422-461; vi. 17; vii. 199; ix. 32. Cuncuma leucogaster, *Hume Rough Notes*, i. p. 259; *Wall. Ibis*, 1868, p. 15.—The WHITE-BELLIED SEA EAGLE.

Adult.—Head, neck all round, breast, abdomen, under tail and wing coverts white; the outermost of the latter shaded with grey; the greater series ashy grey with white bases; body above ashy grey, shaded with brown. Primaries cinereous black; also the secondaries, but tipped narrowly with white; tail black, broadly tipped with white. Cere and orbital ridge bluish lead tinged with green; legs and feet yellowish. Irides olive brown.

Length.—28 to 30 inches; wing 22 to 24; tail 9 to 9·5; tarsus 3·1 to 4; bill from gape 2·25.

The adult female is larger. The young is described by Mr. Sharpe (*Cat. Acc.*) Head and neck dark brown, streaked with buffy white; throat sandy buff, the feathers paler centred; rest of under surface rufescent brown with distinct buffy shaft streaks widening towards the apex; under tail coverts for the most part white, irregularly mottled with reddish brown. Above brown, the feathers margined paler, and with dull whitish shaft stripes; lower back and rump rather darker than the rest of the back, and with distinct white streaks; quills deep brown; secondaries paler and tipped with buffy white; the quills with more or less distinct darker brown bars; tip of inner web whitish below for the greater part of its length; tail dark brown, tipped with whitish and crossed with three ill-defined bars of paler brown, much mottled with darker brown and shaded with whitish.

Hab.—The whole of India, including British Burmah and the Tennaserim province, also Assam and the Malay Archipelago, the Andamans and Nicobars. Occurs in the Concan, Deccan, Central, Northern and Southern India, Punjab, N.-W. P. and Bengal. A permanent resident in most parts, breeding on lofty trees.

Mr. Vidal has taken the eggs, in October, November and December, in the Southern Concan. The nests are gigantic platforms, built of strong, thick sticks, and are fully 5 feet in diameter. The normal number of eggs is one, and sometimes two have been found; they are greenish white, unspotted and glossless, from 2·7 × 2·04 to 3· × 2·06 inches. Mr. Vidal's experience is that the same nests are used year after year, after being repaired, and that they build on large trees in cocoanut and other gardens. As its English name implies, it feeds chiefly upon fish.

49. Haliætus leucoryphus, *Pallas, Reis. Russ. Reichs.* i. p. 454; *Keys. and Blas. Wirb. Eur.* p. xxx.; *Strick. Orn. Syn.* p. 52; *Hume, Rough Notes*, ii. p. 242; *Stray Feathers*, i. pp. 102-159; *Hume and Henderson, Lahore to Yarkand*, p. 173; *Blanford, Eastern Persia*, p. 112; *Sharpe, Cat. Acc. B.M.* p. 309; *Murray, Hdbk. Zool. &c. Sind*; *id. Vert. Zool. Sind*, p. 111. H. fulviventer, *Jerd. B. Ind.* i. p. 82, No. 42. Ichthyætus leucoryphus, *Blyth, Ann. and M. N. H.* xv. p. 37. Cuncuma macei, *Gray, Cat. Acc.* p. 23.—The RING-TAILED SEA EAGLE.

Adult Male.—Above dark brown, with a slight purplish gloss; some of the greater coverts slightly margined with paler brown; quills blackish; the secondaries rather browner like the scapulars; the lower surface of the quills brown, inclining to bluish ash colour on the inner web of the primaries; some of the secondaries mottled with white near the base of the inner web; lower back, rump, and upper tail coverts purplish brown, some of the outermost of the latter whitish at base; tail white, blackish at base, with a broad black terminal band. Head, hind neck and interscapulary region sandy-brown, the feathers of the head and hind neck streaked with fulvous. Sides of face and throat buffy white, the latter with narrow whitish streaks down the centre of the feathers; rest of under surface of body dull fulvous brown, lighter on the chest, where the feathers are paler centered and deeper brown also on the flanks, thighs and under tail coverts. Under wing coverts and axillaries blackish brown, slightly mottled with white. Cere pale bluish green. Nostrils, gape, and base of lower mandible bluish. Upper mandible greenish horn colour, dusky at tip; feet greyish white; iris pale brownish yellow.

Length.—30 inches; culmen 2·6; wing 22·2; tail 12·2; tarsus 3·6.

Adult Female.—Length, 33 inches; wing 24·4; tail 11·7; tarsus 4·3.

Young.—Above dark brown, the feathers of the back deeper brown towards their bases; the wing coverts lighter than the back, and the upper tail-coverts plainly margined with whitey-brown; greater coverts dark brown with whitey-brown tips; quills blackish, externally shaded with ashy; the innermost secondaries dark brown like the back; lower surface of quills ashy brown, some of the innermost primaries inclining to whitish on inner web; tail dark brown, shaded with ashy above and below; head, neck, and under parts fulvous brown, deeper on the head and varied with white bases to the abdominal plumes and under tail coverts; the head and neck rather darker than the under parts and streaked with sandy brown; the chest and breast feathers with broad whitey-brown margins and tips; under wing coverts dull brown, margined with paler brown; the median series streaked with whitey-brown, the greater ones ashy white at the base and mottled along the shaft towards the tip, which is also white; feet clear lemon yellow. (Sharpe.)

Mr. Hume (*R. N.* p. 245) describes a nestling female nearly able to fly as a nearly uniform dark brown above and lighter below; the legs and feet a clear pale lemon yellow.

Hab.—Sind, Punjab, N.-W. Provinces, Oudh and Bengal; Kutch, Rajputana, the Western Coast and the Concan; also Beloochistan, Persia and Afghanistan. Ascends the Ganges and other large rivers; found also in Nepal and Cashmere. In the Concan and along the Sind, Kutch and Kattiawar Coasts, it is known as the ***Mutchee Mar*** or ***Mutchlee Mung***.

The Ring-tailed Sea Eagle is found throughout the year in Sind, along the Indus, and on the larger lakes. It breeds in the winter months (November, December and January), building a nest of twigs, &c., from 4 to 5 feet in diameter, inclusive of the outer thin layer, usually on high trees in the vicinity of water. Eggs usually 2, but I have found a third and fourth laid by the same bird a fortnight after taking the two first ones. In colour they are white or greyish white and unspotted, and measure $2\frac{3}{4}$—3 inches × $2\frac{1}{4}$ to $2\frac{1}{2}$.

Gen. **Haliastur.**—*Selby.*

Bill stout, curved and hooked. Nostrils circular with bony margin all round. Wings very long, the 4th quill longest; tail slightly rounded; tarsi plumed at the knee, and covered with scutæ.

50. Haliastur Indus, *Bodd. Tabl. Pl. Enl.* 25; *Gray, Gen. Birds*, i. p. 18; *Jerdon, B. of Ind.* i. p. 101, No. 55; *Hume, Rough Notes*, ii. p. 316; *S. F.* vii. 251, i. p. 160; *Murray, Hdbk. Zool. &c. Sind*, p. 116; *Gray, Cat. Acc. B. M.* p. 313. Haliætus indus, *Sch. Mus. P. B.* p. 19.—The Maroon-backed Kite.

Adult.—Head, neck, throat, entire breast, and as far as the middle of the abdomen white, with dark brown shaft stripes; rest of the plumage maroon. or rufous chestnut, paler on the secondaries, the tail paling into a fulvous white at the tip. Quills black, rufescent at the base of inner web; under wing coverts deep maroon, with dark shaft stripes; cere brownish; feet greenish yellow; irides brown.

Length.—20 to 21 inches; wing 14·75 to 16; tail 7 to 8.

The young bird is a rather deep brown above, the feathers tipped with rufous. Head, neck, and lower parts pale rufous, streaked paler.

Hab.—India and Ceylon. Recorded from Sind, the Punjab, N.-W. Provinces, Kutch, Kattiawar, Ajmere, Concan, Deccan, Tranvancore, Upper Pegu, Nepal. Breeds wherever it occurs from the middle of February to the beginning of April. The nest is always on a tree near by water, and is not unlike that of *Milvus govinda.* The normal number of eggs is two, but it is not uncommon to find three. In shape they vary much; but typically they are very perfect, moderately broad ovals, slightly compressed towards one end; in colour greyish white, speckled or spotted with pale dingy brown or reddish brown. Size 1·89 to 2·28 × 1·5 to 1·79.

Gen. **Milvus.**—*Cuv.*

Bill short, straight at the base, well curved and hooked at tip. Upper mandible with a rounded festoon. Nostrils oval, oblique. Wings long. Tail forked or emarginate. Tarsi short, plumed at the knees, and with scutæ in front below.

51. Milvus govinda, *Sykes, P. Z. S.* 1832, p. 81; *Jerd. B. of Ind.* p. 104, *No.* 56; *Hume, Rough Notes*, ii. p. 320; *Sharpe, Cat. Acc. B. M.* p. 325; *Stray Feathers*, i. p. 160; *Murray, Hdbk. Zool. &c. Sind*, p. 116; *id. Vert. Zool. Sind*, p. 90.—The COMMON PARIAH KITE.

Adult Male.—Above brown or rufous brown, the head and neck rufescent with dark central stripes. Scapulars and wing coverts edged with buff, the wing coverts with dark central stripes. Quills and greater coverts dark brown, the quills albescent near the base and mottled with brown. Tail ashy brown, tipped with buffy white and barred with brown; the under surface pale brown or whitish, and also mottled and barred. Throat albescent with brown shaft stripes. Under parts dull rufous brown, buffy on the vent and under tail coverts, and with brown shaft stripes. The feathers of the breast somewhat fulvescent. Under wing coverts rufous brown, with dark brown centres to the feathers. Cere and gape yellow. Bill horny black. Feet yellowish. Irides yellowish.

Length.—20 to 23 inches; wing 18·5 to 19; tail 13; tarsus 2·25.

Hab.—Throughout India. A resident scavenger. Breeds on house tops, old mosques, and flat-roofed buildings,—seldom on trees,—during January, February, and March. It occurs also in Beloochistan, Afghanistan, and Nepal.

52. Milvus melanotis, *Tem. et Schleg. Faun. Jap.*; *Blanford, J. A. S. B.* 1872, p. 153; *Gray, Gen. Birds*, i p. 24; *S. F.* i. p. 160; *id.* iii. 229; *Sharpe, Cat. Acc. Br. Mus.* p. 324; *Murray, Zool. &c. Sind*, p. 116. Milvus major, *Hume, Rough Notes*, ii. p. 326; *Murray, Vert. Zool. Sind*, p. 91.—The LARGE PARIAH KITE.

Adult Male.—Above dark chocolate brown, all the feathers distinctly streaked down the centre with black; the wing coverts a little paler brown, the lesser series washed with rufous, all with distinct black shaft stripes. Greater coverts and quills dark brown, the secondaries paler brown, the primaries blackish, all the quills distinctly white at the base of the inner web, and sometimes mottled with brown. Tail rather pale brown, the centre feathers with a slight rufous tinge and distinctly barred with darker brown; these bars are distinct on the inner web only of the outer feathers Under surface of tail brownish ashy, the bars more or less distinct. Lores, forehead, cheeks and throat white, with distinct shaft lines of dark brown; ear coverts dark brown; throat white, tinged with rufous on the lower part. Breast deep rufous brown, shading into clear rufous on the abdomen and under tail coverts; the feathers on the breast margined lighter and with broad central dark streaks. Under wing coverts dark brown, dashed with rufous; the lower ones ashy brown, notched or barred with white on their inner webs. Cere pale greenish yellow. Bill horn black. Feet dull yellow. Irides reddish brown.

Length.—25·5 inches; wing 21; tail 13·2; tarsus 2·5.

There is yet a set controversy in regard to the distinctness of this species from *M. govinda.* Mr. Edwin Brooks, in vol. iv. *S. F.*, says that from an examination of the type of *M. govinda* in the South Kensington Museum, he concludes that *M. melanotis* (T. and S.) and *M. major* (Hume) must be considered as synonyms of *M. govinda* (Sykes). Schlegel again unites *melanotis* and *govinda,* but Mr. Hume holds that the pure white wing patch of *major* distinguishes it equally from *melanotis, govinda* and *affinis,* a third species found in India, also by its larger size.

The following comparative measurements are given by Mr. Hume:—

	Wing, Male.	Wing, Female.
M. govinda.........	17·5 to 18	18 to 19·5
M. major......	19 to 20·5.........	19·45 to 21
M. affinis	16 to 17·5.........	17 to 17·75

Hab.—Throughont India, Japan, and China; also Nepal and Eastern Turkistan.

53. Milvus affinis, *Gould. P. Z. S.* 1837, p. 140; *id. B. Austr* i. pl. 21; *Wall. Ibis,* 1868, p. 13; *Jerd. Ibis,* 1871, p. 343; *Sharpe, Cat. Acc. B. M.* p. 323; *Str. F.* i. p. 160; vii. 44-200; *Murray, Vert. Zool. Sind,* p. 91.—The MALAYAN or LESSER INDIAN KITE.

Head pale brown, or rufescent brown, the feathers darker streaked; lores and ear coverts blackish; chin whitish, with distinct black shaft stripes, under surface of body dull rufous brown, inclining to dusky on the chest and flanks—all the feathers distinctly but narrowly streaked with black along the shaft; back blackish brown, the wing coverts paler, and with distinct shaft stripes; primaries blackish; secondaries paler; under surface of wing pale brown, ashy near the base; tail dark brown, ashy beneath, with remains of dark bars on the centre feathers; under wing coverts rufous brown with blackish shaft stripes; cere and feet yellow; bill blackish; irides brown.

Length.—20 inches; wing 16 to 17·5; tail 10·7; tarsus 2·05; culmen 1·55. *Females* larger.

Hab.—Sind, Punjab, N.-W. Provinces, Central and Southern India, Ajmere, Bengal, the Deccan, British Burma (Upper Pegu); Maccassar, Celebes, Timor, Chusan, and Australia.

Common throughout India nearly; habits the same as *M. govinda.*

54. Milvus korschun, *Gm. N. Com. Petrop.* xv. p. 444; *Strickl. Orn. Syn.* p. 133; *Blf. Geol. Zool. Abyss.* p. 300; *Shelley, Birds Egypt; Sharpe, Cat. Acc.* p. 322. Falco ater, *Gm. Syn. N.* i. p. 262; *Bree. B. Europe,* i. p. 101. Milvus niger, *Bp. Comp. List. B. Eur. and N. Am.* p. 4.

Adult Male.—Crown, sides of the head and nape white; the forehead narrowly and the other parts broadly striped with blackish brown; upper parts dark hair brown, with a metallic gloss on the back; the feathers on the hind neck with dark central stripes, those of the wing coverts and a few of the scapulars with lighter edges; primaries black, excepting some of the inner ones, which are deep brown; secondaries blackish brown, the inner ones assimilating in colour to the back; tail like the back, but slightly duller and a trifle grey in tinge, and with scarcely perceptible darker bars, being also but slightly forked; throat dull white, striped with blackish brown; breast clove brown with blackish stripes; rest of the under parts deep ferruginous, each feather with a dark shaft line; under wing coverts rufous, varied with deep brown; bill blackish horn, yellowish at the base of the lower mandible; cere pale yellow; iris greyish, with a yellow tinge surrounded by a black line; legs pale yellow; claws black. Total length about 32 inches; culmen 1·6; wing 17-0; tail 11·2; tarsus 2·25.

Female.—Resembles the male, but is somewhat larger in size, rather darker, and a trifle more rufous in general colouration.

Young.—Upper parts of a much duller brown than the adult; the feathers tipped with yellowish white, which gives it a very spotted appearance; crown and nape with these terminal spots much larger, so as almost to hide the rest of the feathers; throat brownish white, the feathers with dark shafts; rest of the under parts dull dark brown, becoming dull reddish brown on the abdomen, every feather with the terminal portion, except on the edge, dull horny colour, which gives the under parts the appearance of being marked with elongated oval spots of this latter colour; quills and tail as in the adult; but the latter is tipped with dull brownish white, and the bars are more conspicuous.—(Dresser, *Birds of Europe.*)

Hab.—Upper Sind Frontier, Beloochistan, and Southern Afghanistan; Africa, Madagascar, S. and W. Europe. Breeds nearly throughout Afghanistan and Beloochistan during March. Eggs, in size, shape and colour the counterpart of *M. govinda.*

Gen. **Elanus.**—*Savigny.*

Bill small, ridge (without cere) greater than half of middle toe without claw; tip much hooked and lengthened; edge of upper mandible slightly sinuate. Cere small; nostrils oval. Loreal space feathered. Wings reaching to end of tail, pointed; 2nd quill longest; the 1st emarginate near the tip. Tail short. Tarsi short, plumed above, covered with small round scales. Middle claw keeled.

55. Elanus cæruleus, *Desf. Mem. Acad. R. des Science,* p. 503, pl. 15. Falco melanopterus, *Daud. Traite,* ii. i. p. 152; *Bree, Birds Eur.* i. p. 108. Elanus melanopterus, *Leach, Zool. Misc.* p. 5; *Jerd. Birds of Ind.* i. p. 112,

No. 59; *Sharpe, P. Z. S.* 1869, p. 570; *Hume, Rough Notes*, ii. p21; *Str. F.* i. pp. 21, 163; *Murray, Zool., &c., Sind*, p. 117; *id. Vert. Zool. Sind*, p. 92.—The BLACK-WINGED KITE.

Adult.—Entire upper parts ashy grey, lighter on the head; forehead, eyebrow, lores and sides of face white; ear-coverts ashy grey; supercilium dark brown or black; lesser and median wing coverts and winglet glossy black; greater coverts concolourous with the back. Axillaries and under wing coverts white; inner lining of wing dark grey; primary coverts and quills ashy grey, the latter white at the base and black-shafted. Tail ashy, the two centre feathers greyish; entire under parts white. Cere, orbits, and feet yellow; bill black; irides crimson.

Length.—13 inches; wing 10·6 to 11; tail 5·6; tarsus 1·4.

Hab.—South-Eastern Europe, Africa, India and Ceylon. Very widely distributed. Recorded from Egypt, Gambia, Transvaal, South Africa, and the Mediterranean; also from Kutch, Kattiawar, Jodhpore, Sambhur, North Guzerat, the Concan and Deccan, Pegu, Burmah and Nepaul. Breeds almost throughout Upper India. Nest circular, composed of small twigs and sticks, and lined with fine grass roots and fibres. Eggs, bluish white or creamy, streaked and blotched with pale yellowish brown or brownish red.

As to the habits of this species there is not much recorded; it usually flies low, skimming above the surface of the ground, or hovers in the air much like a kestrel, but dropping suddenly to the ground. It is not uncommon to see it perch on telegraph wires, on the bare end of a bough, or on some dry tree in the vicinity of water. It feeds chiefly on rats, mice, beetles, grasshoppers, and other insects.

It is a resident in Sind, and affects chiefly the acacia forests lining the banks of the Indus. Breeds in the Narra districts from June to August.

Gen. **Machæramphus.**—*Westermann.*

Bill small, feeble, and keeled; culmen, with a sharp cutting edge, which has two faint sinuations on the upper mandible; cere small; nostrils long, oblique, pierced near the margin of the cere; loreal plumes produced above half the nostril; tail of 12 feathers; tarsi feathered in front for three-fourths of an inch, reticulate; outer and inner toes, with claws of the same length.

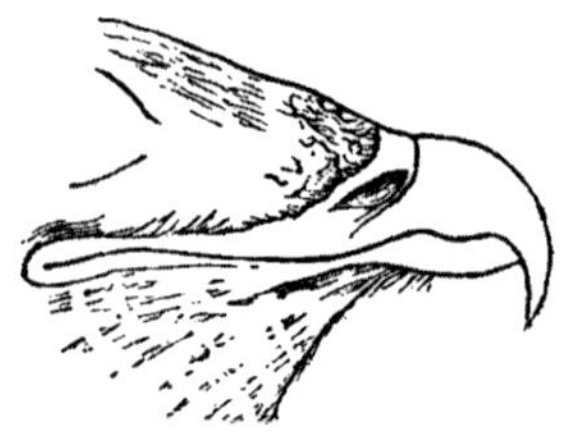

56. Machæramphus alcinus, *Westerman, Bijd. tot. d. Dierk.*, i. p. 29, pl. 12; *Sharpe, P. Z. S.* 1871, p. 502; *id. Cat. Acc. B. M.* p. 341; *Hume, Stray F.*, iii. p. 269; *id.* Vol. vi. p. 24.

Adult Male.—Black throughout, shaded with brown; throat and front of the neck white; chin with a diamond-shaped patch of black, continued as a line down the centre of the throat; breast white; a band of white above and below the eye; head with an occipital crest of pointed lanceolate feathers; irides bright yellow; bill and claws black; legs and feet pale plumbeous; cere black.

Length.—18·0 to 18·5 inches; expanse 46·0; tail 7·37; wing 14·62; tarsus 2·5; bill, from gape, 1·8; from edge of cere to point (straight) 0·75; greatest height of upper mandible 0·4.

Hab.—Southern extremity of the Tennaserim provinces at Malewoon, and Malacca.

The above particulars as to the colors of the soft parts and measurements have been extracted from Mr. Hume's notice of the species in *Str. F.*, vol. iii. Mr. Sharpe does not seem to have had a specimen to describe them. Of the habits of this remarkable species I have no information. The wood-cut of the head and bill is that of an allied species, *M. Anderssoni*, copied from Mr. Sharpe's work, to show their peculiar structure.

Gen. **Pernis.**—*Cuv.*

Bill curved from the base; the margin straight; lores clothed with scale-like feathers; tarsi short, reticulate, half plumed in front; scales on toes transverse; wings and tail long.

57. Pernis ptilonorhynchus, *Steph. Gen. Zool.* xiii. pl. 35; *Holdsw. P. Z. S.* 1872, p. 414; *Sharpe, Cat. Acc. B. M.*, p. 347. Pernis cristata, *Cuv. Regne An.*, i. p. 335; *Jerd. B. Ind.*, i. p. 108, No. 57; *Hume, Rough Notes*, ii. p. 330. *Stray F.*, vol. iii. p. 448, vol. ix. p. 375.—The HONEY BUZZARD.

Adult.—General color above and below rich chocolate brown, with indistinct black shaft stripes; the crown and sides of head, as well as the throat, ashy grey; the lower throat blackish; quills and tail brownish ashy, the latter with 3 dark bands, the uppermost hidden by the upper tail coverts, the terminal one tipped with greyish white; crest undeveloped; cere black, greenish towards commissure and nostrils; gape and lower mandible pale blue; feet bees'-wax-yellow; irides yellow.

Length.—24 to 25·5 inches; wing 15·5 to 16·5; tail 11·5 to 12·75; tarsus 2·1 to 2·2. The female is larger. The intermediate and young stages of the Honey Buzzard are so very variable, that it is scarcely necessary to describe them. Mr. Sharpe says: "Great variations exist in the tone of the intervening stages, the color varying from tawny to fulvous brown, while the extent of black stripes on the throat is also a very variable character." Again, he adds, under "Obs." that, the young of *P. ptilonorhynchus*, if they happen to be crestless, are undistinguishable in plumage from the immature of *P. apivorus*;

and I have seen young birds from India which I could not separate from European examples. A natural inference is that these may not be *P. ptilonorhynchus* but *P. apivorus*, the young of which may migrate to India in the winter." Mr. A. O. Hume's remarks are also to nearly the same effect.

Hab.—The whole of India, except Sind; the Himalayas, Burmah, the Malayan Peninsula, Sumatra and Java, also Nepaul and Ceylon.

Breeds in May and June, on trees, making a moderate-sized nest of sticks and twigs lined with leaves or grass; eggs normally 2 in number, spherical nearly, or a very broad oval, white or buffy with red, reddish brown, or blood red markings and varying in size, from 1·82 to 2·2 in length and from 1·5 to 1·9 in breadth. The food of the Honey Buzzard is young birds, frogs, mice, bees, and reptiles generally. It has a rapid flight, soars very high and gracefully, and glides through the air without apparent effort. It is easily tamed, bears confinement well and does not show the fierceness of other birds of prey. Another species, *Pernis brachypterus*, Blyth, has been mentioned in *Stray Feathers*, Vol. III. p. 36, as having been found in Upper Pegu. The description is certainly very curt, and I have seen birds answering it from the Punjab and the Deccan. The extremely variable character of the plumage of the intermediate and crested stages of the species, leaves room to doubt its validity.

Sub-family—FALCONINÆ, Falcons.

Bill short, suddenly curved from the base; upper mandible distinctly toothed; nostrils, either round, oblique, or linear oval; cere short; tarsi, slender, naked; hinder aspect reticulate. Outer toe only connected to mid-toe by interdigital membrane; tibia longer than tarsus.

Gen. Baza.—*Hodgs.*

Bill small, much hooked, grooved on its side; upper mandible with two sharp teeth on each side, lower with 3-4; lores covered with feathers; nostrils transverse, narrow; head crested; wings moderate; the 3rd quill longest, the 1st three slightly emarginate towards the tip; tarsi covered with small smooth hexagonal scales; claws small, subequal.

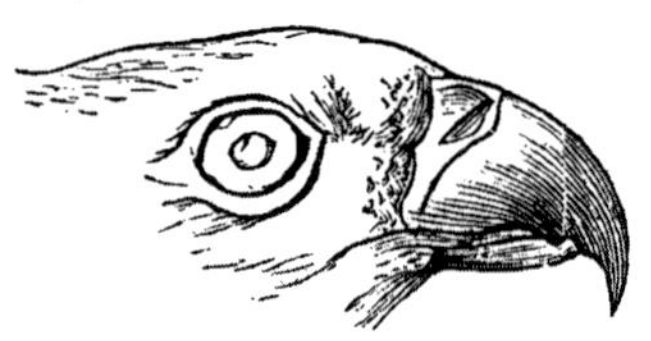

58. Baza lophotes, *Tem. Pl. Col.* i. pl. 10; *Gray List, Gen. B.*, p. 4, *Blyth. Cat. B. Mus. Soc. Beng.*, p. 17; *Jerd. B. Ind.*, i. p. 111, No. 58; *Bly. Ibis*, 1863, p. 11; *Wall. Ibis* 1868, p. 19; *Hume, Rough Notes*, p. 337; *Hold., P. Z. S.* 1872, *Sharpe, Cat. Acc. B. M.*, p. 352; *Hume, Str. F.*, vi. p. 24; viii. p. 191.—The Black Crested Kite.

Above glossy greenish black with a very long occipital crest; thigh coverts under-tail and under-wing coverts also glossy greenish black; quills black, greyish underneath; outer webs of the secondaries deep chestnut at base and towards the tip which is greenish black, rest of the feathers white; scapulars and some of the coverts next them white internally and tipped chestnut, forming a conspicuous interrupted white wing band; tail greenish black above, ashy grey beneath; entire sides of the face and neck as well as the throat black, tinged with brown; foreneck and chest white, forming a very broad band, followed by an indistinct line of blackish feathers, and another broad band of chestnut covering the upper breast; lower breast creamy white and banded with chestnut, narrow on the lower part and flanks; thighs, lower abdomen, under tail-coverts and underwing-coverts greenish black, the lower ones of the latter ashy grey; bill and legs plumbeous; irides dark brown.

Length.—13 to 14 inches; wing 9 to 9·85; tail 5· to 5·7; tarsus 1·3 to 1·5.

Hab.—Southern India, Ceylon, the Malayan Peninsula, Lower Bengal, Assam, Tipperah and the Tennaserim provinces of British Burma.

Of the nidification of this species nothing is known.

59. Baza sumatrensis, *Lafr. Rev. Zool*, 1848, p. 216; *Gray Gen.* B. III. App. p. 2, 1849; *Wall Ibis*, 1868, p. 18; *Sharpe Cat. Acc.*, p. 357; *Stray F.* ii. p. 378; iii. p. 313; iv. p. 248; vi. p. 25; viii. p. 444.—THE SUMATRAN CRESTED KITE.

Male.—Hume's specimen from Tennaserim—*Baza incognita*, nobis. Forehead, and a broad but inconspicuous band from the latter over the eyes to the nape pale whitey brown (not noticeable in Sharpe's figure); the shafts darker brown; crown of the head, occiput, nape and sides of the neck rufescent buff; the feathers broadly centred with dark brown; crest black, narrowly and obsoletely barred the feathers with white tips; lores and an inconspicuous band under the eye and the base of the ear-coverts grey, the feathers darker shafted; rest of ear-coverts and lateral portions of the throat fulvous, the feathers dark shafted; chin and throat pure white, slightly tinged with yellowish, *and with a narrow and conspicuous black central stripe*; upper breast mingled white and a pale brownish rufous; lower breast, sides, flanks, axillaries and abdomen white with broad regular transverse brownish rufous bands; vent and lower tail coverts white or buffy with traces of rufous barring; wing lining yellowish white with rufous bars and mottlings; quills brown on the outer webs, banded obscurely with darker brown, their inner webs with a dark drab brown at the tips and white basally, with several broad, blackish brown transverse bands and tipped white; also the secondaries and some of the median coverts; lower surface of quills French grey at the tips; tail pale drab with a subterminal band, which is black, and 3 others; under surface of tail greyish white, the dark bands showing through on the outer webs.

Length.—18·5; wing 13·12; tail 9·62; tarsus 1·6; bill from gape 1·35; legs and feet white tinged with blue. Irides bright yellow; cere and upper mandible blackish; base of lower mandible paler.

The female is very similar to the male except that the head, nape and sides of the neck are more rufescent and have less conspicuous dark brown central stripes, the mantle is a much less dark brown, there is less of the purple gloss and the marginal fringes of the feathers are broader and more rufous; there is no grey about the cheeks, which are pale fulvous fawn; the chin and throat too are fulvous white and the throat stripe is brown, instead of black, as in the male; the coverts are also paler and more rufescent.

Length.—22·0 inches; wing 13·75; tail 10·25; tarsus 1·7; bill from gape 1·3.

Mr. Sharpe *Cat. Acc.*, describes a young female from Sumatra, but Messrs. Hume and Gurney, two profound Ornithologists, suggest that it was not correctly sexed, and that the specimen is a young male, and not female. The following is Mr. Sharpe's description.

Young female.—Head and hind-neck creamy buff, washed with tawny rufous, the feathers on hinder part of crown dark brown in the centre; occipital crest very long, black, with cream-coloured tip; back brown with fulvous edgings, the scapulars and secondaries further margined with white; quills ashy brown, barred with darker brown, the tail similarly coloured, narrowly tipped with white; the feathers washed externally with rufous near the base; the bars on the tail four in number, one being concealed; the under-surface of both wings and tail paler and more ashy white; entire sides of face, throat and under-parts creamy buff washed with pale tawny rufous; the breast and sides of the body broadly barred with the latter colour; under-wing coverts creamy buff; bill black; pale at base beneath; feet yellowish white; iris yellow.

Length.—20·5 inches; culmen 1·4; wing 12·75; tail 9·6; tarsus 1·6.

Hab.—Sumatra, Tennaserim, B. Burmah.

60. Baza ceylonensis, *Legge, Birds of Ceylon*; *Stray F.*, iv. p. 247; viii. p. 444 :—THE CEYLON CRESTED KITE.

Lores blackish; head brownish tawny; centre of forehead and crown, black, edged with rufous; occipital crest 1¾ inches in length, black, conspicuously tipped with white; the feathers of the hindneck deeply edged with rufous tawny, the centre parts being black; back, scapulars, rump, upper tail coverts primary and lesser wing coverts blackish brown, the latter the deepest and with a cinerous tinge; upper tail coverts paler than the back; median and greater wing coverts pale or fulvous brown; quills black, the outer webs with smoky grey bars, the corresponding band on the inner web being brown; tertials and secondaries tipped with white; tail dark smoky grey, tipped greyish white and with four blackish bars, the terminal one about 1½ inches in depth; cheeks and ear-coverts slaty grey with dark shafts, the dark feathers of the occiput passing round to meet the latter region; chin and throat buff with a broad mesial black streak; sides and lower part of foreneck with the upper edge of the pectoral region tawny cinerous, the feathers with brownish shafts; below this, the under-surface, under-tail and under-wing coverts are white, with broad rufescent brown edges; iris yellow, also the tarsi and feet; bill blackish leaden; lower mandible pale at base; cere dusky plumbeous.

Length.—To front of cere 16·5; culmen 0·10; total length 17·5; wing 11·7; tail 7·5; tarsus 1·5; bill to gape 1·2.

Hab.—Southern India (The Wynaad) and Ceylon (Kandy district). Nothing is known of its habits, &c.

Gen. **Microhierax.**—*Sharpe.*

Bill short; upper mandible with a tooth and a notch on each side; wings short; 2nd and 3rd quills equal; tarsus short, with large transverse scutæ in front.

61. Microhierax cærulescens, *Linn. S. N.* i. p. 126; *Sharpe, Cat. Acc. B. M.*, p. 366. Harpagus cærulescens, *Sws. Classif. B.*, ii. p. 213. Hierax bengalensis, *Bly. J. A. S. B.* xi. pt. ii. p. 789. Hierax Eutolmus, *Gray. Gen. B.*, i. p. 21; *Jerd. B. Ind.*, i. p. 42, No. 20; *Hume, Rough Notes*, i. p. 3.—The WHITE-NAPED PIGMY FALCON.

Adult.—Forehead, supercilium continued to down the sides of the neck, and connecting the broad collar on the nape, white; round the eye and a broad streak to the ear coverts black; throat, lower abdomen, under tail coverts, and thighs chestnut; occiput to the white collar black, also the mantle, wings, and tail; quills black, barred with white on their inner web; tail spotted with white on the inner webs; lower throat, breast, and abdomen silky white.

Length.—5·5 to 6·5 inches; wing 4 to 4·5; tail 2·1 to 2·5; tarsus 0·75 to 0·85.

Hab.—Southern and Upper India, Nepal, and Assam, Sikkim, Arrakan, British Burma, the Tennaserim Provinces, Darjeeling.

Affects open jungle, and are often seen perched on dead trees in parties of 5 or 6. Mr. Davison found that they affected the top of some large tree rising higher than its neighbours, and from this commanding perch they took longer or shorter flights, after insects apparently. Their flight is rapid and as far as my observations go, they feed both on insects and small birds. They are quick and lively in their motions. Of the nidification of this, the red-legged Falconet, nothing is known.

62. Microhierax fringillarius, *Drap. Dict. Class d'Hist. Nat.* vi. p. 412, pl. v. Hierax cærulescens, *Vig. Zool. Journ.* i. p. 339; *Bly. J. A. S. B.*, xii. p. 180; *Wall. Ibis.*, 1868 p. 6. Hierax Malayensis, *Strickl. Ann. N. H.*, xiii. p. 33.—THE BLACK-LEGGED FALCONET.

Adult.—Above deep blue black, quills and tail also black, but barred with white on their inner web; forehead and a stripe from behind the eye down the sides of the neck white, lores, round the eye, ear coverts and hinder part of cheek black; under parts silky white; the throat slightly, the abdomen and under tail coverts more richly washed with ochre; sides of body, flanks, and outer face of thighs glossy black.

Length.—5·75 to 6·45 inches; wing 3·62 to 3·82; tail 2 to 2·75; bill from gape 0·45 to 0·55; tarsus 0·65 to 0·75; bill legs, and feet black; irides dark brown; orbital skin plumbeous.

The female is larger.

Length.—6·4 to 6·7; wing 3·82 to 4·15; tail 2·25 to 2·62.

In the young bird the bill is yellow; frontal band and streak behind the eye tinged with pale ferruginous; upper tail coverts and tail feathers margined with buff.

Hab.—The Malayan Peninsula, Java, Sumatra, Borneo, Tennaserim, Malacca and Singapore.

The black-legged falconet is common in the southern portions of the Province of Tennaserim, as high up as 3,500 feet elevation. It is not known from any other part of British India. It feeds generally on small birds and insects, and its habits are quite those of *M. cærulescens.*

Gen. Poliohierax.—*Kaup.*

Nostrils perpendicular, oval, with no overhanging membrane or central tubercle; bare part of tarsus greater than outer toe and claw.

63. Poliohierax insignis, *Wald. P. Z. S.* 1871, p. 627, *et Ibis.* 1872, pp. 200-471; *Sharpe, Cat. Acc. B. M.* p. 370; *Stray. F.*, vi. p. 2. Lithofalco fieldeni, *Hume, J. A. S. B.* 1872, p. 70.—FIELDEN'S FALCONET.

Adult Male.—Forehead, lores and feathers round the eye greyish white with dark shafts; rest of the top, back, sides of the head and upper back slaty blue, each feather with a linear dark shaft stripe; lower back, rump and upper tail coverts white; tail feathers black, tipped with white and with a few white spots, the remains of narrow transverse bars, not very apparent on the central tail feathers; quills blackish brown or black (the later secondaries and tertiaries more or less tinged slaty) with a few small white spots, most conspicuous on the outer webs of all but the first primary and numerous broad white bars on the inner webs; chin, throat, and whole lower surface, including wing lining, white; some of the feathers of the throat with narrow, central brown shaft stripes and those of the sides and upper abdomen with broad grey brown dashes; cere, orbits and feet yellow; bill leaden black, yellow at base.

Male.—Length 10·5 inches; wing 5·5; tail 5·8; tarsus 1·55; culmen 0·85.

The female is like the male, but distinguished by its bright ferruginous head and markings; forehead, eyebrow, and sides of face ashy white with narrow linear black shaft stripes.

Length.—10·7 to 10·9 inches; wing 5·9 to 6; tail 5·8; tarsus 1·5 to 1·6.

Hab.—Pegu, Toonghoo, and Tennaserim. Capt. Fielden says it is common about Thayetmyo. Mr. Oates, (*S. F.* iii.), says, from the Irrawady to the summit of the Pegu hills, also Arracan.

According to Capt. Fielden's observations its food consists of insects, with an occasional mouse, snake, or lizard. He adds that "the ordinary note of this bird is like that of the white-eyed buzzard, but of course not so loud. During the pairing season, its call-note is a kind of whistling hoot, which appeared to me to resemble 'tooovey,' the 'too,' very much prolonged. I once saw a pair meet, when they uttered a succession of loud harsh screams which resembled the cries of a flock of red-wattled plovers when disturbed, but before they rise. They pair about the last week in January. I found an unshelled egg in March (on dissection). I think I found an old nest in the fork of a tree as I shot a young bird a short distance off, but I only mention this as a help to others in looking for the nest. It resembled a small hawk eagle's nest both in make and position.

"The habits of these birds are very peculiar, in something resembling those of the magpie. They perch exactly like a falcon; but if they wish to move along a branch, they hop sideways, or if the branch is pretty upright, walk up it foot over foot, if I may use the expression, in the same manner as a Magpie. When at all alarmed they jerk their tail, and when much excited by the approach of any one, lower their heads exactly in the same way as some of the owlets. Altogether, when moving about the branches of a tree, they might at a short distance be mistaken for a magpie, except for the shape of the head. The flight is also peculiar, a few tolerably rapid strokes ending, if I remember rightly, in a slightly upward jerk, then a short sail through the air, and then a few more strokes, and so on.

"I have invariably found them on cleared ground in the middle of jungles, seated on trees, and once on a fallen hut. The exception to this being when I found them at a spot where several jungle roads meet and form an open space, or on low gravelly hills thinly covered with bushes, and an occasional tree. Their most favourite seat seems to be a dead tree, barked by the Burmese, in the middle of one of their half-cleared cotton fields. I once saw a pair on a tree in a dry rice field, but on every other occasion the ground was covered partially with bushes, cotton plants, &c. I have found them from the level of the Irrawady to the highest cultivated patches in the hills about Thayetmyo. I have never seen one in a large open space or in thick jungle."

Gen. **Falco**.—*Linn.*

Nostrils round with a central tubercle. First one or two quills notched internally, second quill longest; tarsus feathered at the knee; toes long, scutellated.

64. Falco communis, *Gm., S. N. p.* 270; *Less. Traité*, p. 88, pl. 16; *Sharpe, Ann. N. H.* xi. p. 222; *id. Cat. Acc. B. M.* p. 376. Falco peregrinus, *Gmel. S. N.*, vol. i. p. 272; *Jerdon, Birds of India*, vol. i. p. 21; *Ibis*, 1871; *Gray, Cat. Br. Mus.*, p. 11; *Hume, Rough Notes*, vol. i. p. 49; *Sharpe, Cat. Acc. Br. M.*, p. 376; *Murray, Hdbk., Zool., &c., Sind*, p. 106. *Bhyri* (the female), *Bhyri Bacha* (the male). Hind. Falco atriceps, *Hume, Ibis*, 1869, p. 356; *id. Rough Notes*, 1 p. 58; *id. Ibis*, 1871, p. 24; *Jerd. Ibis*, 1872, p. 2. Falco Brookii, *Sharpe, Ann. N. H.* (4) ii. pp. 20, 222, 1873.—THE PEREGRINE FALCON.

Adult Male.—Above bluish grey, paler on the rump and upper tail coverts, and barred with blackish. Head, neck, upper part of mantle and wing-coverts blackish, with grey barring, more or less indistinct on the latter. Cheeks, ear-coverts, and a short moustachial band blackish. Forehead, sides of neck, chin, throat, under surface of body and breast white, the latter with a tinge of pale fawn, as also the lower abdomen; the chest with a few narrow black shaft-stripes almost disappearing in old individuals; abdomen with some small heart-shaped spots, some similar marks on the under-tail coverts also. Thighs transversely barred with narrow black lines. Quills brownish black, primaries slightly shaded with greyish, the secondaries clearer grey, crossed by dull blackish bars, the smaller median quills tipped white. Tail feathers greyish, broadly barred with black and tipped with white. Bill bluish, black at the tip; cere, legs and feet yellow; claws black; iris hazel-brown.

Length.—15 to 16; inches culmen 1·2; wing 12·2 to 12·7; tail 6·5. (*Adult female* similar to the adult male, but larger. *Length*, 17 to 19; inches, culmen 1·35; wing 14·5; tail 7·5; tarsus 2·3.)

The young bird is brown, all the feathers edged with pale buff shading into whitish; under surface of the body whitish, the throat unspotted, all the rest of the feathers dark brown in the centre, lower flanks barred; head more edged with whitish; cheek stripe brown. Wings darker than the back; the inner webs spotted or barred with rufous. Tail feathers brown, broadly tipped with white; the outer web spotted and the inner one barred with pale rufous more or less distinct.

Very widely distributed species. A winter visitant to India—Occurs in Sind, Punjab, N.-W. Provinces, Oudh, Bengal, Rajpootana, Kutch, Central and South India, Guzerat, Concans and Deccan, also Beloochistan, Persia, and S. Afghanistan. Rare in Pegu and Tennaserim. Has been found in Nepaul, and also in Ceylon.

The peregrine is believed to breed below Ferozepoor along the banks of the Indus, but nothing certain is known. Mr. Hume, in his "Rough Notes" mentions having a nestling shot by a shikaree in the interior of the Himalayas, not far from Kotegarh. In Europe it builds on rocks and cliffs. Eggs 2,3 or 4, of a light russet red colour marbled over with darker shades, patches, and streaks of the same. Nest composed of sticks, seaweed, hair, and other such materials. The flight of the peregrine is extremely rapid and by repeated beatings of its wings. 150 miles an hour has been calculated as its rate of flight. It is much prized for its value in falconry on account of its courageous spirit and fearlessness. The food of the species consists principally of birds, such as seagulls, partridges, plovers, grouse and ducks; but it also feeds on hares, rats, &c. It has frequently been known to stoop upon and carry off game from before the sportsman.

65. Falco peregrinator, *Sundev. Phys. Tidskr. Lund.* 1837, p. 177, pl. 4; *Gray, Gen. B.* i. p. 19; *id. Cat. Mam. and B. Nepal Hodgs.* p. 44; *Blyth, J. A. S. B.* xix. p. 321; *Jerd. B. Ind.* i. p. 25; *Hume, Rough Notes,* i. p. 557; *Jerd. Ibis,* 1878, p. 237; *Sharpe, Ann. and Mag. Nat. Hist.* xi. p. 223, 1873; *id. Cat. Acc. B. M.* p. 382; *Str. F.* V. 500; *id.* vii. 423. Falco Shaheen, *Jerd. Madr, Journ.* x. p. 81; *id. Ill. Ind. Orn.* pls. xii. and xxvii.—The SHAHEEN FALCON.

Adult.—Head, nape, neck, interscapulary region, cheek stripe and wing coverts deep black, the latter shaded with bluish grey; lower back, rump and upper tail coverts slaty or bright bluish grey, the latter with remains of or without obsolete blackish cross markings. Quills black, externally washed with greyish, the inner web with a few nearly obsolete rufous bars; secondaries tipped with fulvous. Tail bluish grey, the tips tawny, the blackish bars nowhere distinct; chin, throat and upper breast white; rest of under surface rufous, or tawny ferruginous; flanks, thighs and under tail coverts with a few spots or bars. Under wing coverts rufous with black bars. Cere yellow; bill slaty, blue black at tip; feet yellow; iris deep brown.

Length.—16 to 16·5 inches; wing 12·25 to 12·77; tail 6·5 to 6·8; tarsus 2·2 to 2·25.

Hab.—The whole of India, the Himalayas, Nepaul, Ceylon, B. Burmah, Afghanistan, and extending into Western Asia.

The Shaheen Falcon, like the Peregrine, is much prized in falconry. All the peculiarities which are sought for in the Peregrine are also exhibited in this species which is considered a better bird. Its native habits have not been studied much. It however affects both rocky hills and forest land, and destroys much game. It has been found breeding in Central and Southern India during March and April, building on inaccessible cliffs.

66. Falco barbarus, *Linn. Syst. Nat.* i. p. 125; *Salvin, Ibis*, 1859; *Heugl. Orn. Afrik.* i. p. 21; *Hume, Str. F.*, i. p. 19; *Saunders, P. Zool. Soc.*, 1872, p. 356; *Sharpe, Cat. Acc. Br. Mus.*, p. 386; *Murray, Zool., &c., Sind*, p. 107; *id. Vert. Zool. Sind*, p. 68. Falco pelegrinoides, *Tem. pl. col.* 479; *Gray, Gen. B.*, i. page. 19.—THE BARBARY FALCON.

The forehead presents a mixture of rufous and dull white. This part of the head is encircled by a black (or dark slaty) horse-shoe shaped band, of which the lateral branches pass over the eyes, their extreme points joining in front of the eyes, the moustachial stripes, which extend along the sides of the neck. The occiput and nape are covered by a rufous half collar marked with three black spots, of which the centre one forms a band on the nape. The back and wings are a light bluish grey, with large spots and irregular bars of bluish black.

The tail, which is a lighter grey than the back, is barred transversely with black bands, very narrow towards the bases of the feathers, but widening gradually towards their ends, the tips of which are white. The chest is pure isabelline. The flanks, vent and abdomen of the same colour, but the feathers bear very narrow longitudinal striæ and little triangular black spots. The base of the beak is yellow, but the point blue. The cere and feet beautiful yellow, and the orbital skin orange. (*Tem. Ex. S. F.* 1.19.)

Length.—Female 15·5 inches; expanse 36·4; wing 11·4; tail 6·4; tarsus 1·8. Male *Length.*—14 inches; wing 10·8; tail 5; tarsus 1·6.

Hab.—Sind (winter visitant), Persia, Kutch, and the Central Provinces. Sharpe, (*Cat. Acc.*) gives its range as N. and N.-E. Africa as well as Senegambia on the West Coast, ranging into N.-W. India and the Himalayas.

67. Falco babylonicus, *Gurney, Ibis*, 1861, p. 218, pl. vii.; *Jerd. B. of Ind.*, vol. i. p. 32; *Ibis*, 1866, p. 221; *Hume, Rough Notes*, i. p. 79; *Sharpe, Ibis*, 1870; *Cat. Acc. Br. Mus.*, p. 388; *Str. F.*, vii. p. 329; *Murray, Hdbk., Zool., &c., Sind; id. Vert. Zool. Sind*, p. 67.—THE RED-HEADED LANNER.

Young Male.—Dark earthy brown, some of the feathers of the crown obscurely margined, the nape and hind neck mottled, the lower back and rump edged, and the upper tail-coverts barred with rufous. Tail dark brown, spotted on the outer web and banded on the inner one with rufous, the two centre feathers nearly obsoletely barred. Quills dark brown, barred with pale buff on the inner web; the secondaries paler brown, edged and spotted on the outer web with rufous. Feathers under the eye and cheek stripe blackish brown. Sides of the face and ear-coverts strongly tinged with rufous; throat whitish; rest of under surface earthy buff, with central dark brown streaks to the feathers inclining to bars on the vent and under tail coverts. Under wing coverts brown, spotted and barred with clear buff. Cere pale sea-green; bill pale bluish-green, blackish on the culmen and tip; feet bright yellow; iris dark brown.

Length.—15·5 to 16 inches; wing 11·87 to 12tail; 6 to 6·6; tarsus 1·9.

Adult Male.—Above bluish grey, the feathers with pale fulvescent margins, and having indistinct bars of darker grey; the lower back, rump and upper tail coverts paler and clearer blue grey, transversely barred with dark grey, the bars somewhat irregular and arrow-shaped on the upper tail coverts. Wing coverts con-colorous with the back, the greater series rather lighter grey. Quills brown, externally shaded with grey; the secondaries margined and broadly tipped with buffy white, and barred across with darker grey, the bars very distinct on the lower surface of the wing and especially numerous on the primaries. Tail grey, tipped with fulvous and crossed with nine or ten bars of darker grey, the light grey interspaces sometimes tinged with rufous, the lower surface of the tail whitish, the bars very distinct. Head and hind neck clear rufous, the crown more or less inclined to greyish black, of which colour many of the feathers are composed, having only a slight margin of rufous. A rufous half collar round the back of the neck, mottled somewhat with slaty. Sides of the face buffy white, tinged with rufous; the ear coverts streaked with brown, collecting on the cheeks and forming a distinct moustache. Throat pure white; chest also white, with a few narrow central streaks of brown; remainder of under surface whitish, slightly tinged with buff and numerously marked with arrow-head spots of brown in the centre of the body, and barred on the sides of the breast, flanks, and under wing coverts with the same colour. The bars on the thighs and under tail coverts narrower than on the greater series of the under wing coverts. Cere, gape, orbits and feet bright yellow; bill bluish, blackish at the tip; iris deep brown.

Length.—17·25 inches; wing 13; tail 7·25; tarsus 1·75.

Hab.—The Punjab, Beloochistan and Persia, N.-W. Provinces, Nepaul, N.-E. Africa, Mesopotamia, Central Asia. It is said to breed in Cashmere. A winter visitant. Not uncommon from November to February in Sind and Northern India.

68. Falco juggur, *J. E. Gray, Ill. Ind. Orn.* ii. pl. xx.; *id. Cat. Mammals, and Birds Nepaul*; *Hume, Rough Notes*, vol. i. p. 70; *Str. F.* vol. i. p. 152; *Sharpe, Cat. Acc. Br. Mus.*, p. 393; *Murray, Hdbk., Zool., &c., Sind; id. Vert. Zool., Sind*, p. 67. Falco luggur, *Jerd. Madras Journ.* x. p. 80; *id. Ill. Ind. Orn.* pl. xliv. 1847. *Lugger* (female), *Juggur* (male), Hind.—THE LUGGUR FALCON.

Adult Male.—Above dusky ashy or slate colour; crown of head dull rufous with central ashy black striations. Lores, forehead, chin, throat and eyebrow white; moustachial stripe black; wing coverts con-colorous with the back, the carpal margin white. The breast white, with a few brown spots. Lower abdomen, flanks, and thighs ashy brown. Tail clear ashy grey with pale rufous bars on the inner webs and a white tip.

Length.—15·5 to 17 inches; wing 11·8; tail 7; tarsus 1·95; culmen 1. *Female.*—17 to 19 inches; wing 13·6 to 15·5; tail 8 to 8·5; tarsus 1·95 to 2.

Young, of a chocolate brown above and below; wing coverts with rufous margins. Head yellowish-fawn or pale rufous. Forehead and eyebrow whitish. Chin and throat white. Under tail coverts dirty white with faint brown markings.

The Luggur Falcon is the most common of the Lanners, and very generally distributed. It has been recorded from the whole of India; also from Beloochistan and Afghanistan. In the more moist climate, and wooded districts of Malabar, it is found, but not in any numbers. Jerdon remarks, that while the Byri prefers the sea-coast and the neighbourhood of lakes, rivers, and wet cultivation, and the Shaheen delights in hilly and wooded regions, the Luggur, on the contrary, frequents open, dry plains and the vicinity of cultivation. It breeds during January, February and March, particularly in Sind, Punjab, and N.-W. Provinces; also in the Deccan; but is partial, for this purpose, to a dry climate. The nest is placed either on a high tree or on a rocky ledge, but in Sind almost always on ledges of high buildings and mosques or church steeples. The normal number of eggs is 4; five have, however, been occasionally found; in colour reddish, brownish, or yellowish brown, thickly spotted and speckled all over with brick red or reddish brown. In size they vary from 1·85 to 2·15 in length and 1·48 to 1·65 in breadth; generally broad ovals, slightly pointed at one end, glossless, of a slightly chalky but compact texture.

The Luggur Falcon preys chiefly on small birds, also field rats, for which it may be often seen hawking over plains infested by them. It is trained by natives to bring down water-birds of kinds, as, the herons generally, also partridges, floriken, quail and snipe, but at this latter it is not dexterous. Jerdon has a footnote stating that it is also used to strike the Houbara, *Otis macqueeni* and hares.

69. Falco subbuteo, *Linn. Syst. Nat.* i. p. 127; *Gould, B. Eur.* i. pl. 22; *Blyth, Ibis,* 1863, p. 9. Hypotriorchis subbuteo, *Boie, Isis,* 1826, p. 976; *Gray, Gen. B.* i. p. 20; *Jerd. B. Ind.* i. p. 33, No. 13; *Hume, Rough Notes,* i. p. 85; *id. Stray F.* ix. 282.—The HOBBY.

Adult Male.—Top of head, back, scapulars and wing-coverts bluish black, the latter sometimes tinged with rusty; lower back and rump clear slaty grey. Forehead and eyebrow, whitish; nape tinged with rufous, forming two indistinct rufous spots. Lores, cheek stripe, feathers below the eye and ear-coverts black. Throat and sides of the neck, creamy white, tinged with rufous, the breast and abdomen the same, streaked mesially with dark brown, narrow on the centre of the abdomen, and wider on the flanks; vent, under tail coverts and thigh coverts rich ferruginous. Under wing coverts buffy white with some transverse dark bars. Quills blackish, barred internally with rufous. Tail dark slaty or slaty grey, barred on their inner webs with rufous, and tipped with whitish.

Length.—11 to 11·5 inches; wing 9·5 to 9·6; tail 5·5; tarsus 1·25. Females are larger. *Length*—13·5; wing 10·6; tail 6·5; tarsus 1·4.

The young bird is dark or grey brown above, the feathers edged with fulvous. Cheek stripe darker. Forehead and superciliary fulvous white; sides of the neck, nape, throat, and under surface creamy buff; lower abdomen and thigh coverts with a rufous tinge, and streaked mesially with brown. These streaks are rather broad and distinct on the breast, and long and narrow on the under tail coverts. Wings and tail as in the adult—black, and banded with rufous.

Hab.—The whole of Europe and Northern Asia, extending to India and North China, and migrating in winter to South Africa (*Sharpe*). It has also been found in Nepaul and Darjeeling, also in Kumaon, Oudh, Dhurmsala, between Mussoorie and Gangootri, Northern Guzerat, Kutch, and Jerdon killed one at Jaulnah. In Sind it was obtained by Mr. S. Doig at Hydrabad in the month of June.

The Hobby is a winter visitant. Nothing is known of its breeding habits in India. Mr. Hume says, although common enough in some parts of the Himalayas, it is a rare visitant and if it breeds anywhere within our limits, it would probably be in the higher ranges of the hills. From Kumaon, Mr. R. Thompson, writing to Mr. Hume in September, says he saw flocks of the Hobby hunting about for insects which appear to be its food. Snipe, plovers, swallows and sandpipers, it is also very partial to. The nest of the Hobby which is built of sticks and lined with moss or hair is usually placed in the topmost branches of trees in forests. Eggs 2 to 4 in number, short and oval, of a dingy white or bluish white ground colour, much speckled all over with reddish or yellowish brown.

70. Falco severus, *Horsf. Tr. Lin. Socy.* xiii. p. 135; *Blyth, Ibis.* 1863, p. 8. Hypotriorchis severus, *Gray, Gen. B.*, i. p. 20; *Jerd. B. Ind.* i. p. 34; No. 14; *Hume, Rough Notes*, i. p. 87; *Sharpe, Cat. Acc. B. M.* p. 397; *Stray F.* iv. p. 354; and pp. 533-5.—The INDIAN HOBBY.

Adult.—Dark slaty blue above, black on the cheeks and ears; beneath deep rusty red, unspotted. Cere, orbital skin, and legs reddish yellow; bill plumbeous.

Length.—Male, 10·5 inches; wing 9; tail 4·5.

Mr. Sharpe (*Cat. Acc.*) describes an adult female. Above black, with a slight slaty grey shade, more distinct on the lower back, rump and tail, the bars on the latter obsolete; head, cheek and ear coverts black. Under surface of body, bright chestnut; throat and sides of neck creamy white, the latter with a slight wash of chestnut. Under wing coverts bright chestnut, some of the lower ones barred with black. Primaries black with a few rufous bars near the base. Cere, orbits and feet yellow; bill bluish black, yellow at base; iris dark brown.

Length.—13·5 inches; wing 8·5 to 8·75; tail 4·5 to 4.62; tarsus 1.15.

Hab.—Northern and Southern India; Nilgherries, Travancore Hills, Barrackpore; the lower ranges of Kumaon and Gurhwal and the Himalayas generally. Out of India proper, Mr. Sharpe gives the Indo-Malayan sub-region and Nepaul. Supposed to breed in the dense forests of Gurhwal.

71. Falco chiquera, *Daud Traite*, ii. p. 121; *Blyth, Cat. Mus. As. Socy. Beng.* p. 14; *Sharpe, Cat. Acc. Br. Mus.* p. 403. Hypotriorchis chiquera, *Gray, Gen. B.* i. p 20; *Jerdon, B. Ind.* i. p. 36, No. 16; *Murray, Hdbk. Zool., &c., Sind*, p. 108. Chiquera typus, *Bp. Rev. Mag. de. Zool.* p. 536, 1854; *Hume, Str. F.*, i. p. 157. Lithofalco chiquera, *Hume, Rough Notes*, i. p. 91; *Anderson, P. Z. S.* 1871, p. 681. The *Turrumti*, Hind.—The RED-HEADED MERLIN.

Adult Male.—Crown, nape, back, and sides of the neck chestnut; forehead white; sides of the face, chin, throat and neck white, except a faint, short, moustachial stripe. Eyebrow and a narrow streak below the eye, black; back, scapulars, tertiaries, wing and primary coverts and secondaries slaty blue, the feathers with dark shafts and barred with dark brown. Primaries dark or blackish brown, their inner webs barred with white. Under wing coverts white, barred with blackish brown; breast white, some of the feathers with dark shaft-streaks; rest of under surface white, barred transversely with black. Tail like the back, the feathers barred with black, tipped white and with a broad subterminal black band. Cere, orbits and feet yellow. Claws black; bill greenish yellow at base, black at the tip; irides light brown.

Length.—11·5 to 12 inches; wing 8·25; tail 4·75 to 6; tarsus 1·5; culmen 0·85.

The adult female is similar to the male, but larger. *Length.*—13 inches; wing 9; tail 6·5; tarsus 1·5 to 1·55.

Hab.—Sind, Punjab, N. W. Provinces, Bengal, Nepaul, Kutch, Kattiawar, Jodhpore, N. Guzerat, and throughout the Indian Peninsula; also Beloochistan, Persia and Afghanistan.

Affects open country in the vicinity of cultivation. It is said to be easily reclaimed and flown at partridges and quails, which it pursues very perseveringly. Like the European sparrow-hawk, it is a very courageous bird, and the propensity of attacking larger birds of prey than itself seems to be more developed. Jerdon says it even drives away the *Wokhab* (*Aquila fulvescens*) from the vicinity of its nest or perch. Breeds in February, March, April and May, nearly everywhere on trees; nest fixed in a fork near the top. Eggs 3—4 in number, variable in shape; in color, they are pale yellowish brown, with from, a few reddish brown specks to a nearly uniform dark brownish red obscurely mottled and blotched with a somewhat purer and darker. Size 1·6 to 1·75 in length, and 1·25 to 1·32 in breadth.

72. Falco regulus, *Pall Reis. Russ. Reichs* II. *Anhang*, p. 707: *Gmel. Syst. Nat* i. p. 285; *Sharpe, Cat. Acc. Br. Mus.*, p. 406. Falco æsalon, *Gmel. Syst. Nat.* i. p. 284; *Heugl. Orn. N. O. Africa.* Hypotriorchis æsalon, *Gray, Gen. B.* i. p 20, *Jerd. B. of Ind.* vol. i. p. 35, No. 15. Lithofalco æsalon, *Hume, Rough Notes*, i. p. 89; *Jerd. Ibis.* 1871, p. 242; *Murray, Hdbk., Zool., &c., Sind*, p. 108.—The MERLIN.

Adult.—Above clear slaty blue, paler on the rump and upper tail coverts, the black shafts on all the feathers distinctly indicated. Head dark slaty, with broad shaft-stripes; forehead, lores and sides of the face whitish, the feathers with dark mesial streaks. Eyebrow and nape strongly mixed with rufous. Ear coverts tinged with grey on the hinder part; chin and throat pure white. Sides of the neck and entire under parts white, washed with rufous, the feathers dark shafted; under wing coverts white, spotted and barred with black. Quills black, the inner web barred with greyish white and the outer washed with bluish grey near the base. Inner secondaries concolorous with the back, dark shafted. Tail slaty blue, tipped with white, with a broad subterminal black band. Cere yellow; bill bluish horn colour, darker at the tips; feet yellow; iris dark brown.

Length.—Male, 10 to 11·25 inches; wings 7·75 to 8; tail 4·5 to 5; tarsus 1·45. Female browner in color, under surface less rufous. *Length.*—12 to 13 inches.

The young bird is like the adult female in colour, but tinged grey, with dark shafts and rufous edges to the feathers; the head rufous, with dark streaks, the tail ashy brown, barred with rufous and with a white tip.

Hab.—Sind, Kutch, Punjab, Beloochistan, and Afghanistan. The whole of Europe and Northern Asia, extending into India and China.

The Merlin is a winter visitant and is chiefly found in Sind, Punjab and the N.-W. Provinces, also in Beloochistan and Southern Afghanistan. Outside of these limits, it is recorded from all over Europe, Malta, Egypt, Lower Palestine and according to Swinhoe in Pekin, Amoy and Foochow.

Mr. Hume says it is commonly captured about Umritsur and sold by native huntsmen. It comes down in some numbers into the Peshawar Valley, and is always to be met with early in the year in the salt range. He adds that it is therefore probable that it breeds in Cashmere and the neighbouring regions of the Himalayas, but of this there is nothing known for certain. The nest in England is generally built on the ground, and the eggs are laid in them. On the Continent the Merlin is said to breed on trees. The eggs are 3 or 4, in number; Bewick says sometimes 5 or 6 (?), bluish white blotched at the larger end with reddish brown or greenish brown, and sometimes of a deep dingy red; in shape a broad oval, slightly compressed towards one end about 1·6 × 1·25 inches in breadth.

The Merlin flies low, and does not often mount above its prey, which is generally birds, as partridges, pigeons, plovers, &c. Snipe and Sandpipers are chased to the edge of the water and are seldom missed.

Gen. **Hierofalco.**—*Cuv.*

Outer and inner toes, (measured without claws) about equal in length. Distance between tips of primaries and tips of secondaries about equal to or less than half the length of tail; tarsus finely reticulate in front and not twice the length of mid-toe; nostrils round with distinct central tubercle.

73. Hierofalco saker, *Briss. Orn.* i. p. 337: *Sharpe, Cat Acc. B. M.* p. 417. Falco sacer, *Gm. Syst. Nat.* i. p. 273; *Bree, B. Eur.* i. p. 31. *Jerd. B. Ind.* i. p. 29, No. 10; *Hume, Str. F.* i. p. 152; *Hume, Rough Notes,* i. p. 62; *Murray, Handbook, Zool. &c., Sind*; *id. Vert. Zool. Sind* p. 66. Falco lanarius, *Pall. Zoog, Rosso, As.*-i. p. 330; *Gould, B. Eur.* i. pl. 20. Falco Hendersoni, *Hume, Ibis.* 1871, p. 407; *id.* and *Henderson, Lahore to Yarkand,* p. 171.—The Cherrug Falcon.

Adult Male.—Above pale earthy or slaty brown, all the feathers margined with rufous. Head pale rufous, reddish ash or bleached nearly white; the feathers with narrow mesial streaks. Chin, throat, abdomen, and under tail coverts white; cheek stripe indistinct; breast and lower parts white, with oblong slaty spots, more thickly on the breast and flanks; quills brown, deeply indented with white or rufous-white notches or bars, less in number on the secondaries; tail pale brown, barred with whitish on the inner web, and ovally spotted on the outer. Thighs streaked with brown. Under wing coverts and axillaries white, streaked with brown; cere greenish white; orbits and feet yellow.

Length.—18 to 18·5 inches; wing 12·5 to 13·2; tail 7·3 to 7·5; culmen 1·2; tarsus 2. *Female,* 20 to 24 inches; wing 14 to 15·8; culmen 1·3; tail 9·8; tarsus 2·1.

Hab.—The whole continent of India from Cape Comorin to the Himalayas (Bengal, Sind, Punjab, N. W. Provinces and Kutch), affecting open plains. Outside of India it is found in Asia Minor, Egypt, Nepaul and Yarkand.

It is not common in Sind, and occurs during winter only, arriving at the same time as *F. peregrinus,* but of its departure nothing is on record. All specimens obtained in Sind are in the young or immature phase, with the upper parts brown, the head a yellowish white colour, and the body beneath brown. Nothing is known of the breeding of the Cherrug within Indian limits. In "Rough Notes" Mr. Hume says the Ameer of Kabool mentioned that the birds he had, bred in Afghanistan. Eggs are said to be 4 in number, of a slightly elongated oval form, and varying in color and markings from a light red to dirty reddish white with spots and blotches of brighter red. The Cherrug is trained to strike at Cranes, Bustards and other large game.

Hab.—The whole of Europe and North Asia; the Indian Peninsula as a winter visitant; N. E. and South Africa, Sind, Punjab, N. W. Provinces, Oudh, Bengal, Kutch, Kattiawar, and along the Western Coast; Central and Southern India to Nepaul; also Beloochistan, Persia, Afghanistan, and Eastern Turkestan.

A very useful bird to cultivators, preying only, as it does, chiefly on field-mice, which are its favourite diet.

74. Cerchneis tinnuncula, *Boie, Isis,* 1828, p. 314; *Sharpe, Cat. Acc. B. M.* p. 425. Tinnunculus alaudarius, *Gray, Gen. Bird,* i. p. 21; *Jerd. B. Ind.* i. p. 38, No. 17; *Blyth, Ibis,* 1863; *Hume, Rough Notes,* p. 96; *Murray, Hdbk., Zool., &c., Sind,* p. 108. (*Narzi,* the female; *Narzanak,* the male, Hind.)—The KESTREL.

Adult Male.—Forehead buffy white; crown of the head, nape, neck behind and on the sides, blue grey, the feathers with narrow dark shaft-stripes. Eyebrow buffy white; sides of the face, except a dark moustachial stripe, silvery white; chin and throat, also the under tail coverts, unspotted buff. Upper back, scapulars, tertiaries and wing coverts, brick-red or vinaceous, the feathers with a subterminal heart-shaped black spot, larger on the tertiaries. Primaries and their coverts, and secondaries dark brown, the primary coverts margined with rufous; outer secondaries narrowly edged and tipped with fulvous or buffy white, and the primaries barred on their inner webs with white; the inner primaries with bars of a rufescent hue. Lower back, rump, upper tail coverts and tail blue grey, the tail with a broad subterminal black band and tipped with white; breast, abdomen and flanks, rufous fawn, the feathers on the breast, and flanks with mesial dark streaks, which take an oval shape lower down. Thigh coverts unspotted rufous fawn. Under wing coverts white, with a buffy tinge, and spotted black. Bill bluish-horn, black at the tip and yellowish at the base. Cere, orbits and legs yellow. Irides brown.

Length.—12·5 to 13 inches; wing 9·5 to 10; tail 6·5 to 6·7; culmen 1·75; tarsus 1·6.

The adult female is less rufous in colour above, and with the subterminal spots wider and forming bands. Head rufous with longitudinal streaks. Tail rufous, banded with dark brown, tipped with white and with a subterminal black band as in the male.

75. Cerchneis naumanni, *Fleisch in Fischer, Jahrg.* 1818 (*teste Naumann*; *Sharpe, Cat. Acc. B. M.* p. 435; *Str. F.* vii. 331; *id.* ix. p. 236, 371. Falco tinnunculoides, *Tem. Man. d'Orn.* i. p. 30; *Gould, B. Eur.* i. pl. 27; *Bree, B. Eur.* i. p. 48. Falco cenchris, *Cuv. Regn. An.* i. p 322; *Sharpe and Dresser B. Eur.* pt. 3. (1871). Tinnunculus cenchris, *Bp. Cat. Met. Ucc. Eur.* pt. 21; *Tristram, Ibis.* 1865, p. 259.—NAUMANN'S KESTREL.

Adult Male.—Head, hind neck, lower back, rump, upper tail coverts and tail blue grey, the latter tipped with white, and with a black subterminal band; lores and a few streaks on the cheeks whitish. Upper surface of body rich cinnamon rufous, also the lesser and median wing coverts, a few of the outer ones of the latter series washed with blue grey; greater coverts and inner secondaries blue grey washed with rufous externally; primaries dark brown; throat deep fulvous white; breast pale cinnamon or vinous with a few blackish spots, which become larger on the sides of the body; thighs unspotted pale rufous; abdomen and under tail coverts yellowish white; under wing coverts white, with a few tiny oval spots, larger on the axillaries; bill lightish blue, yellow at base and blackish at tip. Cere, orbits and feet beautiful yellow, the claws generally white; iris dark brown.

Length.—12·5 inches; culmen 0·75; wing 9·1; tail 6, tarsus 1·2.

The Adult Female is dissimilar to the Male. Tawny rufous above with transverse bars of blackish brown, narrower and more obscure on the lower back, rump, and upper tail coverts, the latter of which are strongly inclined to grey; tail rufous, barred with black, with a broad black subterminal band and tipped with whitish. Head and neck rather pale rufous, the former broadly, and the latter narrowly streaked with blackish shaft stripes; forehead and a distinct eyebrow whitish; cheeks and ear coverts silvery white with narrow black shaft streaks. Primaries dark brown, barred on the inner web with rufous; secondaries like the back, outer ones narrowly margined with white at the tip; throat, vent and under tail coverts unspotted fulvous white; breast inclining to rufous fawn, all the feathers mesially streaked with blackish, broader on the flanks and tiny on the thighs, which are also rufous.

Length.—12·5 inches; culmen 0·7; wing 9·3 tail 5·9; tarsus 1·2. (Sharpe).

Hab.—South and South-Eastern Europe, migrating to S. Africa and India, during winter. Recorded from the Concan, Deccan, South India and Nepaul.

76. Cerchneis pekinensis, *Swinh. P. Z. S.* 1870, pp. 44?, 448; *Sharpe, Cat. Acc. B. M.* p. 437. Erythropus cenchris, *Jerd B. Ind.* i. p. 40, No. 18; *Hume, Rough Notes,* i. p. 103.—The LESSER KESTREL.

Adult Male.—Similar to *C. Naumanni*, but darker and more vinous red above; below darker colored and unspotted. Wing coverts entirely blue grey, the innermost washed with rufous. (Sharpe).

Length.—Male 12 inches; wing 9·6; tail 5·8; tarsus 1·45; bill 0·8. The female is larger and Mr. Hume's measurements of one from Coimbatoor, are as follows: Length, 13 inches; wing 9·75; tail 6·75; tarsus 1·81. Bill from gape 0·88. Bill plumbeous, dark at the tips.

Hab.—South and South-East Europe; North Africa, Abyssinia, the Himalayas; (Nepaul;) Umballa, and Delhi (Punjab and N.-W. Provinces) Oudh, Bengal, the Concan, Deccan and South India; also N.-E. Cachar.

Nothing is known of the breeding of this species in India, beyond what Dr. Jerdon mentions of his having found it breeding on the cliffs of the Neilgherries in May and June. In the Ibis for 1865, Mr. Tristram gives a full account of its nidification in Palestine. According to him, it breeds in communities, usually in narrow fissures of rocks or crevices of ruins; the Common Kestrel too breeding in the same place. Although closely allied, the eggs of both species are not difficult to discriminate. There is no regular nest and the eggs, 4 in number, are placed in a depression in the bare wall, amongst bits of lime with the hard parts of Coleopterous and other insects, which form the food of this species. The eggs, by Degland's account, quoted by Bree, are very short, smaller than those of the Common Kestrel, of a mingled reddish white color, with a great number of minute spots of a brick red, together and mixed with small brown spots. The figure by Bree measures according to the drawing 1·42 by 1·17 inches.

77. Cerchneis amurensis, *Homey, J. F. O.* 1868, p. 251; *Sharpe, Cat. Acc. B. M.* p. 445. Erythropus amurensis, *Gurney, Ibis.* 1868, p. 251. Erythropus Vespertinus, *Swinh. Ibis.* 1861, pp. 253, 327; *Jerd. B. Ind.* i. p. 40. No. 19; *Hume, Rough Notes,* i. p. 106; *Jerd. Ibis.* 1871, p. 243. Hypotriorchis concolor, *Gurney, Ibis.* 1866, p. 127.—The Red LEGGED HOBBY.

Adult Male.—Above leaden black, paler on the lower back and secondaries; greater wing-coverts and primaries washed externally with silvery grey; tail greyish black above, paler below; under surface of body pale grey; lower abdomen, thighs, vent and under tail coverts bright chestnut; under wing coverts and axillaries pure white. Cere, orbits and feet dark orange; claws whitish; bill yellowish horn color, blackish at tip; iris hazel.

Length.—9·5 inches; culmen 0·75; wing 9; tail 5·3; tarsus 1·15.

Adult female, is dull leaden grey above, darker on the interscapulary region, clearer on the scapulars, lower back and rump, all the feathers crossed by indistinct bars of black; tail bluish grey crossed by a broad subterminal and other narrow bars of black. Quills brownish black, externally washed with grey and barred with white about half way up the inner web; crown of the head, lores, feathers round the eye, and a slight moustachial streak dull blackish; sides of the face, neck and throat unspotted creamy white, also the breast; the latter with mesial streaks of black on each feather; flanks barred; thighs, vent and under tail-coverts pale rufous. Under wing-coverts white with black spots.

Length.—10·5 inches; culmen 0·75; wing 9·5, tail 5·3; tarsus 1·1.

Hab.—Mr. Sharpe gives, Amoor Land, N. China, Nepaul, E. Coast of Africa and Natal. It migrates during winter to India, and has been found in the Punjab, N.-W. Provinces, Central India, the Concan, Deccan, and also in N.-E. Cachar and British Burmah.

Its habits are quite like those of the Lesser Kestrel, building in communities and hunting in company for grass-hoppers and other insects.

SUB-ORDER,—PANDIONES.

Outer toe reversible; toes devoid of feathers; eyes lateral; no facial disk; plumage close and compact. Nostrils not concealed by bristles.

Gen. **Pandion.**—*Savigny.*

Bill short rounded above and curved from the cere. Upper mandible with a slight festoon. Nostrils small, obliquely transverse; wing lengthened; second quill longest; distance between tips of primaries and secondaries greater than length of tarsus; legs naked; tarsi with reticulate scales.

78. Pandion haliætus, *Lin. Syst. Nat.* i. p. 129; *Sharpe, Cat. Acc. B. M.* i. p. 450; *Less. Man. d'Ornithology*, i. p. 86; *Sw. and Rich. Faun. Bor. Am. Birds*, p. 20; *Gould. Birds of Eur.* pl. 12; *Bp. Consp.* i. 16; *Jerd. B. Ind.* i. p. 80, No. 40; *Hume, Rough Notes*, i. p. 234; *id. Stray Feathers*, i. p. 159; *Blanford, Eastn. Persia*, p. 114; *Murray, Hdbk., Zool., &c., Sind*, p. 110; *id. Vert. Zool. Sind*, p. 81; *Shelley, B. Egypt*, p. 203. Pandion indicus, *Hodgs. in Gray's Zool. Misc.* p. 81. *Muchee-Mar*, Sind; *Much Murrung*, Hind.—The Osprey.

Head and nape white, the feathers of the forehead and crown with dark brown stripes; a dark brown streak from the eyes over the ears; upper plumage rich hair brown; quills blackish; tail pale brown with dark bars, whitish on the inner web; beneath pure white with some brown spots on the breast, longitudinal in youth, broader in advancing age, and tending to coalesce in the fully adult; irides bright yellow; legs and feet plumbeous yellow.

Length.—Of a female 26 inches; wing 20; tail 9; tarsus 2·4; bill black.

Hab.—Sind, Beloochistan, and Persia; also the Punjab, N.-W. Provinces, Bengal, British Burmah, Nepaul, Kutch, Kattiawar, Concan and Deccan, and nearly throughout the Indian Peninsula in suitable localities. Occurs also all over Europe and Africa, N. and S. America, China and Japan. Very widely distributed. Most abundant along the coasts, large rivers and lakes. In Sind it is a winter visitant.

Mr. Sharpe (*Cat. Acc.* p. 450) remarks that "Ospreys seem to get whiter on the head with age; the mottling on the breast is strongly marked in all old birds, and that the tail becomes more uniform brown with age, so that a strongly barred tail is a sure sign of immaturity."

It is believed the Osprey breeds in the Valley of Kumaon, where Mr. Hume saw the nest of one, and Mr. Thompson believes it breeds on the Ganges above Hurdwar. Nothing certain is however known. In the British Isles it is said to make a large nest either on trees, on rocks, or about old ruins near large pieces of water, and to lay 2 or 3 eggs, oval in form, and typically have a white ground, here and there clouded with pale purple and very richly blotched and streaked, most densely towards the large end with deep red, becoming in its intensity almost black.—Size 2·52 × 1·89 to 1·93.

Gen. **Polioaetus.**—*Kaup.*

Tarsus feathered in front for one-third its length, scutellate in front. Distance between tips of primaries and secondaries less than length of tarsus.

79. Polioaetus ichthyaetus, *Horsf. Tr. Linn. Socy* xiii. p. 136; *Sharpe, Cat. Acc.*, p. 453; *Kaup. Contr. Orn.* 1850, p. 73; *Jerd. B. Ind.* i. p. 81; *Hume, Rough Notes*, ii. p. 1. Haliaetus plumbeus, *Hodgs. J. A. S. B.*, vi. p. 367.—The EASTERN WHITE-TAILED EAGLE.

Adult Male.—Head and neck all round ashy grey; breast a little lighter brown than the back; wings darker; primaries blackish. Under surface of wing leaden brown with a whitish spot at the base of the primaries; tail white with a terminal bar of brown. Abdomen, vent, thighs, lower flanks and under tail coverts white, under wing coverts ashy brown. Cere and bill blackish; feet dirty yellowish white; iris brown.

Length.—26 inches; wing 18; tail 10; tarsus 3·75 culmen 2·3.

Adult female.—Similar, but larger. *Length.*—29 inches, with a wing of 20·4, and tarsus 3·9.

The young bird is lighter brown above. All the feathers edged and tipped with whitish; feathers beneath pale reddish brown, with mesial pale streaks; thighs white, mottled with reddish brown; quills as in the male with a larger white basal patch below; tail fulvous brown, mottled with dark brown, tip uniform dark brown, forming a distinct band.

Hab.—Punjab, N.-W. Provinces, Oudh, Bengal, Rajpootana, Central India, the Southern Mahratta country (Dharwar), Central Provinces, Kutch, the Concans and British Burmah, extending to Nepaul and Assam. Breeds in January to as late as April, chiefly in the N.-W. Provinces and Bengal (although it may be found breeding in other parts of India), building a nest of stout sticks on high trees on the bank of some river or in the proximity of some considerable piece of water. The nest is usually lined with some soft material as grass, weeds and green leaves; this latter is generally the uppermost layer on which the eggs are laid. Eggs normally three in number, a broad and perfect oval in shape; texture rough and pitted, and with a slight gloss, and unspotted white.—2·72 to 2·8 inches in length, and from 2·1 to 2·15 in breadth.

80. Polioaetus humilis, *Mull and Schleg. Verz. Nat. Gesch. Zool. Aves.* p. 47 pl. 6; *Kaup. Contr. Orn.* 1850, p. 73; *Wall. Ibis.* 1868, p. 14; *Walden. Tr. Z. S.* viii. p. 35; *Sharpe, Cat. Accr.* p. 454. Ichthyaetus nanus, *Bly. J. A. S. B.* xi. p. 202. Pandion humilis, *Gray, Gen. B.* i. p. 17; *Blyth, Ibis.* 1866, p. 244; *Str. F.* v. p. 130; *id.* ix. 244.—The LESSER SEA EAGLE.

Adult female.—Above ashy brown; the back and wings darker and more chocolate brown; the feathers of the crown and hind neck slightly fulvescent towards their tips; lores and an indistinct eyebrow whitish; cheeks, throat, breast and under wing coverts entirely ashy brown; a few whitish streaks on the throat and forepart of cheeks; lower abdomen, thighs, vent, and under tail coverts white; primaries black, whitish at base of inner web; secondaries brown like the back; tail pale brown at base, gradually becoming darker brown towards the tip which is white; bill and cere dusky lead colour; feet pale bluish white; iris light yellow.

Length.—23 inches; wing 6·2; tail 8·8; tarsus 2.85; culmen 2·05.

The young is brown with large fulvous tippings to the feathers. *Length.*—18·5.

Hab.—From Assam, down the Malayan Peninsula, to Sumatra and Celebes.

Found in N.-E. Cachar; also Bengal.

SUB-ORDER.—STRIGES

or

NOCTURNAL BIRDS OF PREY.

Head large, eyes surrounded with a circle of radiating feathers forming a facial disk and directed forwards; ears large. Nostrils generally hidden by stiff bristles; feet generally feathered to the toes; outer toe reversible; tibia more than double the length of tarsus; plumage soft and fluffy.

Family.—BUBONIDÆ.

Hinder margin of sternum with two or more distinct fissures or clefts; furcula free, not attached to keel of sternum; inner margin of claw of middle toe not serrated; mid toe longer than the inner one.

Sub—Fam., BUBONINÆ,—Eagle and Scops Owls.

Ear conch not larger than the eye, and without an operculum.

Gen. Ketupa.—*Lesson.*

Bill long, strong, straight at base, moderately compressed and hooked. Wings do not reach the end of the tail; tarsi naked, reticulate; soles of feet with tiny prickles; ear-tufts large.

81. Ketupa ceylonensis, *Gmel. Sys. Nat.* i. p. 287; *Gray, Gen. Birds*, i. p. 38; *Jerd. Birds of Ind.* i. p. 133, No. 72; *Hume, Rough Notes*, ii. p. 379; *Str. F.* i. p. 341, ii. p. 469; *Sharpe, Cat. Striges*, p. 4; *Murray Hdbk., Zool., &c., Sind*, p. 119; *id. Vert. Zool. Sind*, p. 92.—The Brown Fish-Owl.

Adult.—Above fawn-brown, the feathers broadly centred black and mottled brown and fulvous on both webs. Feathers of the hind neck thinly barred with brown; the ear tufts with dark central longitudinal streaks. Quills dark brown, the primaries tipped and spotted on the outer web with creamy buff, the same spots on the inner webs, being dull fawn-brown; secondaries dark brown, with less distinct spots and bars, and more mottled with brown. Tail brown with a fulvous tip, and 3 or 4 pale fulvous bands. Chin and throat white streaked with dark brown. Loreal plumes whitish; under surface of body fulvous-fawn or vinaceous-rusty, all the feathers mesially streaked with broad black centres and with wavy bars. Disk rusty with dark brown stripes; cere greenish grey. Bill pale horny yellow. Legs and feet dusky yellow. Irides bright yellow.

Length.—21 to 24 inches; wing 16·25; tail 8; tarsus 2·65.

Hab.—India, Ceylon, Assam and Tenasserim. I have had it at Khandalla and Poona in the Deccan. At Madras it is not uncommon, as also in Nepaul and Behar, Sind, Beloochistan, Afghanistan, N.-W. Provinces, Oudh, Bengal, Punjab; also Rajpootana (scarce) Central India, the Central Provinces, Concan, Deccan, South India, British Burmah and Nepaul. There is no record of its occurrence in Kutch and Guzerat.

Breeds throughout India from December to March or April, making its nest on a shelf of rock, clay cliffs, or high banks near water. Normally this species lays two eggs, very perfect broad ovals, white, with in most specimens the faintest possible creamy tinge. The shell is close-grained, and compact, freely pitted over its surface, but more or less glossy. In size they vary from 2·29 to 2·44 in length, and from 1·84 to 1·94 in breadth. In Sind it affects the forests and breeds in holes of decayed trees. Of its food it is not particular. Fish, young birds, quails and partridges, it is quite partial

82. Ketupa Javanensis, *Less. Traite*, p. 114; *Gray, Gen. B.* i. p. 38; *Blyth, Cat. B. Mus. A. S. B.* p. 37; *Wall. Ibis.* 1868, p. 65. *Hume, Rough Notes*, ii. p. 384; *Sharpe, Striges*, p. 8. Bubo Ketupa, *Kaup. Tr. Z. S.* iv. p. 242.—The MALAYAN FISH OWL.

General colour a somewhat orange, light rufous, or bright rufous buff, the lower parts with long blackish brown central stripes; throat pure white; the head, aigrets and back of neck similarly marked to the breast, but the stripes broader and closer set; the back, scapulars and wing coverts with broad very closely set, imperfect transverse black or blackish brown bars. The quills and tail feathers blackish brown, intersected at wide intervals by somewhat narrow rufous yellow bars, and all tipped whitish. Face reddish buff, the feathers dark shafted, and at the sides of the disk tipped with blackish brown.

Length.—16 to 20 inches; wing 13 to 13·2; tail 6·5; tarsus 2·45; culmen 2·1. Auricular tufts 2·0, auriculars pale tawny, streaked with black.

Hab.—Burmah, Siam, and the Malay Peninsula to Sumatra, Java, and Borneo. Common in the Irrawady Delta; also in Tennaserim, Malewoon and the Thoungyeen Valley.

In all its habits like *K. Ceylonensis.* Nothing is known of its nidification. This species issues from its roost just after sunset with a powerful and heavy flight generally over the course of creeks, hunting for its prey. Feeds chiefly on insects and probably fish and crabs.

Gen. **Bubo**.—*Auct.*

Nostrils oval, situated in the anterior margin of the cere; cere not inflated. Ear tufts distinct, tarsi never naked.

83. Bubo bengalensis, *Frankl, P. Z. S.* 1831, p. 115; *Gray, Gen. Birds*, i. p. 37; *Hume, Str. F.* i. p. 163; *Sharpe, Cat. Striges*, p. 25. Urrua bengalensis, *Jerd. B. of Ind.* i. p. 128, No. 69; *Murray, Hdbk., Zool., &c., Sind*, p. 118. Ascalaphia bengalensis, *Blyth, Ibis.* 1866, p. 252; *Hume, Rough Notes*, ii. p. 366.—The ROCK-HORNED OWL.

Adult.—Forehead and crown dark brown, nearly black, the feathers narrowly margined with light fulvous; back of neck, light yellowish buff, the feathers mesially streaked with dark brown. Ear tufts black, narrowly edged with fulvous; back and scapulars deep brown, mottled and barred with light yellowish buff; the outer scapulars whitish on their external web, forming a conspicuous shoulder-patch. Primaries rich tawny buff, barred across and tipped with brown; their coverts dark brown at tip, and with slightly vermiculated fulvous bars; secondaries dull tawny buff, also barred across and tipped with dark brown, the tawny interspaces on the external web vermiculated with brown, the internal ones clear rufous and margined with white; tertiaries mottled with fulvous and brown. Lower back, rump and upper tail coverts clear fulvous or tawny buff, vermiculated at the tips, and with irregular narrow bars of brown. Tail tawny with seven brown bars, the central feathers brown with much mottled fulvous bars. Loreal plumes white, with black shafts at the tip. A small black patch above the eye. Cheeks whitish; ear coverts dirty fulvous, the feathers tipped black and with dark shafts. Ruff blackish, the feathers edged with fulvous. Chin white. Throat with a band of stiff fulvous feathers, mesially streaked with brown; below this a patch of white, some of the feathers of which with mesial brown streaks. Breast and sides of the neck light yellowish buff, the feathers mesially streaked and finely spotted with dark brown; abdomen, flanks and thigh coverts buffy white, with narrow transverse wavy bars of brown, the feathers of the lower breast with distinct mesial streaks; under tail coverts fulvous, with narrow wavy brown bars. Tarsal plume buffy white, fulvous on the sides and behind, and with a few indistinct brown markings. Under wing coverts tawny buff, with narrow brown markings. Bill horny black; irides yellow.

Length.—20 to 22 inches; wing 16; tail 8·8 to 9; tarsus 2·95 to 3.

Hab.—The Peninsula of India and Ceylon; also Beloochistan, Afghanistan, and Nepaul. In India it has been recorded from Behar, Kutch, Kattiawar, Jodhpore, North Guzerat, the Neilgherries, Mhow, Malabar Coast, the Concan and Deccan, Punjab, N.-W. P., Oudh, Bengal; also British Burmah. It is a permanent resident in India, breeding in March and April, laying from 2 to 4 eggs of a creamy white colour.

The precipitous banks of canals and rivers are the breeding places of this species.

84. Bubo coromandus, *Lath. Ind. Orn.* i. p. 53; *Sharpe, Cat. Striges. B. M.* p. 35. Bubo coromanda, *Gray, Gen. B.* i. p. 37; *Hume, Str. F.* p. 164. Urrua coromanda, *Hodgs. J. A. S. B.* vi. p. 373; *Jerd. B. of Ind.* i. p. 130, No 70; *Hume, Nest and Eggs, Ind. B.* p. 63; *Murray, Hdbk., Zool, &c., Sind.*, p. 118. Ascalaphia coromanda, *Blyth, Ibis.* 1866, p. 253; *Hume, Rough Notes,* ii. p. 371.—The Dusky-horned Owl.

Adult.—Head, neck, ear-tufts, back, rump, scapulars and upper tail coverts greyish brown, the feathers thickly vermiculated and crossed with numerous narrow fulvous bars, and with dark mesial streaks. Loreal plumes greyish white, with dark shafts to the tips. Ear coverts dark grey with black shafts, a black patch on the hinder edge of the ear coverts. Chin whitish, quills ashy brown, the primaries tinged with fulvous and crossed with broad bands of dark brown. Outer scapulars with yellowish white spots forming a shoulder patch. Tail dark brown, with 4 broad fulvous bands and a buffy white tip. Entire under surface pale earthy brown with a fulvous tinge, the feathers mesially streaked with dark brown and faintly barred with zigzag lines. Thigh coverts and tarsal plumes fulvescent, with narrow bars of zigzag lines. Feet sparsely feathered. Claws horny brown. Bill greyish at the base, horny yellow at tip.

Length.—21 to 23 inches; wing 16; tail 9; tarsus 2 to 2·65.

Hab.—Sind, N.-W. Provinces (Futtehgur, Delhi), Oudh, Nepaul, Lower Bengal, Arrakan, Lower Himalayas, the Carnatic, Malabar Coast, Rajputana and North Guzerat. Like the last it is a resident in India. Breeds in December, constructing nests of sticks in the fork of trees, lined with some soft material as grass or green leaves. Eggs, 2, 3, varying in size and shape. Typically they are broad ovals. In colour slightly glossed creamy white and varying in size from 2·2 to 2·55 in length, and from 1·75 to 2·0 in breadth.

85. Bubo nipalensis, *Hodgs. As. Res.* xix. p. 172; *Sharpe, Cat. Striges,* p. 37. Huhua nipalensis, Hodgs. *J. A. S. B.* vi. p. 362; *Jerd. B. Ind.* i. p. 131. No. 71; *Blyth, Ibis.* 1866, p. 254; *Hume, Rough Notes,* p. 378; *id. Str. F.* i. p. 431. Bubo orientalis, *Blyth, Cat. B. Mus. As. S. B.* p. 34. Huhua pectoralis, *Holds. P. Z. S.* 1872, p. 416.—The FOREST EAGLE OWL.

Adult.—Above brown narrowly tipped and banded across with tawny buff over the whole of the upper surface, these bars less distinct on the crown, but broader and deeper colored on the hind neck. Outermost scapulars tipped and spotted with yellowish buff on the outer web, forming a distinct shoulder patch. Primary coverts nearly uniform dark brown, with faint indications of lighter brown bars. Quills dark brown, barred darker; tail dark brown, broadly tipped with whitish and crossed with six other bands of fulvous; face dusky brown with whitish shaft streaks; feathers above the eye blackish. Ear tufts 3·1 inches long, dark brown, notched and barred with fulvous or white on the inner web. Cheeks with white stiff feathers mesially streaked with brown; chin whitish—rest of under surface of body white, washed here and there with fulvous and barred across with dark brown; under tail coverts the same, also the under wing coverts.

Length.—23 to 25 inches; wing 16·5 to 18·1; tail 11; tarsus 3·2; bill at gape 2·5, bill horny yellow; irides brown.

Hab.—Southern India and the Himalayas, ranging Eastward into Tennaserim; also Ceylon and Malabar.

I have nothing to record in regard to its nidification. It preys on rats, snakes, hares and pheasants. Mr. Gurney in *P. Z. S.* 1884, p. 558, plate 52, gives an excellent figure of this large owl, from a living specimen in the Zoological Society's Garden, captured as a nestling on a precipitous ledge of a lofty mountain in the Karenne Country to the N. E. of Pegu. It has lived in the Gardens since 1878, at which time a note was made of the circumstances of its capture. (*P. Z. S.* 1878, p. 790), under the name of *Bubo* (*Huhua*) *Orientalis.* Mr. Gurney, now has no doubt that it is really an example (now fully adult) of *H. Nipalensis.* Mr. Gurney says "the present is probably the most eastern example of *Huhua Nipalensis,* of which the locality has as yet been ascertained, as there appears to be considerable doubt whether a young owl obtained by Col. Tickell on the Mooleyit Mountain in Tennaserim, belonged to this species or to its congener, *H. Orientalis.* Mr. Blyth held the former opinion (*Ibis.* 1872, p. 89,) and Mr. Hume advocated the latter in *Stray F.* vol. vi. p. 31. Capt. R. G. Wardlaw Ramsay possesses a specimen of *H. Nipalensis* in immature dress, which was shot at Tonghoo, a locality nearly as far eastward as that from which the bird now in Regent's Park was obtained. Col. Godwin-Austen has recorded a much more northern specimen of this species obtained in the Darrang Dist. of Assam, *J. A. S. B.*, vol. xiv., pt. 2, p. 68; while Mr. W. T. Blanford records its occurrence (*J. A. S. B.* vol. xli., pt. 2, p. 154) in the Tista Valley in Sikkim, and Hodgson in *Asiatic Researches*, vol. xix., p. 173, says it is found in all parts of the kingdom of Nepaul. Major Fitzgerald obtained the young of this species in the Darjeeling District, and says (*Ibis.* 1878, p19), that though not a common bird, it is met with in most parts of the Himalayas in the more temperate valleys. The presumption in favour of the Malabar bird being identical with *H. Nipalensis* is strengthened by the fact of this species being an inhabitant of Ceylon."

86. Bubo orientalis, *Horsf, Tr. Lin. Soc.* xiii. p. 140; *Sharpe, Cat. Striges, B. M.* vol. v. p. 39; *Hume and Davison, B. G. Tennaserim, Str. F.* vol. vi. p. 31. Bubo strepitans, *Less. Traite*, p. 114. Strix Sumatrana, *Raffl., Tr. Lin Soc.* xiii. p. 279.—HORSFIELD'S HORNED OWL.

Male.—Upper set of loral bristles, feathers immediately over and round the upper portion of the eye black, the bristles white at base and the terminal halves of the longer ones blackish brown; point of forehead and an obscure band on each side of the anterior half of the crown greyish white; middle of forehead barred greyish white and brown; crown, occiput, nape, upper portion of sides of the neck and entire mantle deep brown, with narrow, wavy pale rufescent transverse bars, narrowest on the crown; aigrettes of numerous feathers from 2·0 to 2·5 inches long; upper feathers barred like the forehead, the lower ones blackish brown, unbarred or only slightly barred towards their margins or tips. Some of the under scapulars white with black bars; coverts about the shoulder of the wing, winglet and primary greater coverts plain, very dark brown; rest of the coverts and scapulars much like the upper back, but the rufescent bars wider and with mottled brown centres and a few of the coverts white-tipped; upper tail coverts hair brown, with narrow transverse rufescent bars like the upper back; tail deep brown conspicuously white-tipped, and with fine rather narrow transverse rufescent white bars mottled and spotted with brown. Primaries beyond their emarginations dark brown with traces of paler bars; inner webs of quills broadly banded with paler; cheeks and ear coverts mottled grey brown and dingy white; chin, bristles of the gape and base of lower mandible white; entire throat and breast white, the tips banded with close bars of blackish brown. Abdomen, sides, flanks, vent, and lower tail coverts white, with broad, widely separated blackish brown bands; tibial and tarsal plumes, similar, but more narrowly banded; lower portion of feet and inner portion of tarsi unbarred; axillaries barred; wing lining irregularly barred or spotted with blackish brown; feet clear or chrome yellow; claws black; bill, cere and eyelids, yellow; irides dark brown.

Length.—18 to 18·25 inches; tail 6·75; wing 13·75; tarsus 2; bill from nostril to point 0·96; from gape 1·7 to 1·9 (Hume and Davison). The adult female is described in the *B. M.* vol. *of Striges*, by Mr. Sharpe on p. 40. It is not unlike the male, except that the wavy cross bands are a tawny rufous; and altogether much lighter in the general tone of colour throughout; some of the scapulars have the outer webs white forming a shoulder stripe. *Tail crossed with six dull tawny bands*, instead of five, and tipped as in the male with white.

Length.—20·5 inches; culmen 2·3; wing 13·5; tail 7·2; tarsus 2·3; ear-tufts 2·6.

Hab.—Malacca, Java, Sumatra, Borneo, Bangka and the Tennaserim Province of British Burmah; according to Mr. Hume rare in the latter. Mr. Davison notes that he met with it in dense forest on the road between Malewoon and Mergui. It was a pouring wet day and the bird being quite drenched, he had no difficulty in *catching* it alive after a short chase.

Gen. **Scops**.—*Sav.*

Ear tufts large, Ear orifice moderate. Lateral margin of bill somewhat curved. Cere not inflated; nostrils oval, situated in the anterior margin of the cere. Wings long, reaching nearly or quite to the tip of the tail; 3rd and 4th quills longest; tail short; toes generally feathered; tarsi never naked.

I quite agree with Messrs. Sharpe and Hume, that it is most difficult to understand the owls, especially the species of the *Genus Scops* which are in every way the most difficult to identify.

Mr. Sharpe has, however, done something towards characterizing the various species and had necessarily from want of a large series of skins to make "races" or "subspecies." He says, "these races *do* exist in nature, and they may be called by whatever name Naturalists please. "Varieties" "races" "subspecies" "climatic forms" &c., but it has seemed to me better to keep these forms distinct from one another, than to merge them all in one species and thus to obliterate all records of natural facts which are plain enough to the practised eye of the Ornithologist though difficult to describe in words."

87. Scops pennatus, *Hodgs. J. A. S. B.* vi. p. 369; (pt.); *Blyth, J. A. S. B.* xiv. p. 183; *Str. Feathers,* iii. 38; vi. 34; vii. 180; *Murray, Vert. Zool. Sind,* p. 95. Ephialtes pennatus, *Jerd. B. Ind.* i. p. 136, No. 74; *Murray, Hdbk, Zool., &c., Sind,* p. 119; *Sharpe, Cat. Striges,* p. 53 (Sub-Sp. B.)—The Indian Scops Owl.

This little owl is very similar to *S. giu,* but of a greyer colour ordinarily. Specimens from Sind are usually of the rufous phase. Jerdon describes both phases, which I extract.

Adult.—Above ashy grey, more or less tinged with rufous or rufous-grey, the feathers dark-shafted, finely mottled with brown and with a white subterminal spot; wings more rufescent and without the white spots, except on the outer scapulars as usual, and some of the greater coverts; quills rufescent, with darkish double bars, the interval between the bars dusky or mottled, and the light spaces or ground colour, on some of the outer primaries, rusty white in some specimens, or it may be said that the quills are dusky rufescent, mottled with pale bands; the tail rufescent with double bars, in some mottled almost throughout; beneath, the feathers are streaked dark brown, banded with white, and mottled rufous-grey and brown, mostly grey on the upper part and white on the lower part of the abdomen; tarsal feathers barred and mottled; disk ashy white, with a few darker specks, and the shafts of the frontal bristles white; ruff marked with dark brown and rufous.

In the rufous phase, the upper parts are uniform bright golden chestnut red, with black shafts, inconspicuous on the back, more distinct on the forehead, ear plumes and shoulders of the wings; outer edge of scapulars whitish; disk rufous with some of the feathers white-shafted; ruff deep brown with the outer feathers black tipped or black; beneath deeply tinged with the hue of the back, but with more or less white on the belly and under tail coverts; the breast and sides of the belly with brownish central black streaks, the latter with transverse pencillings; four faint bars on the inner webs of the tail feathers, and the primaries also distinctly barred with dusky or mottled. The young bird has all the feathers duller red, more black-shafted, and there is much white on the lower surface; the disk too has a good deal of white, scapulars white externally, with black tips, and the bars on the quills and tail feathers are more distinct, brown and mottled. Bill dusky greenish; iris pale golden yellow; feet fleshy grey.

Length.—$7\frac{1}{2}$ to 8 inches; wing 5 to 6; tail $2\frac{1}{2}$ to 3.

Hab.—Sind, Kutch, Rajputana, Concan, Deccan, South and Central India, Bengal, Punjab, N.-W Provinces and Oudh; Central Provinces, Guzerat, Nepaul, Beloochistan and Afghanistan. Recorded also from Upper Pegu, Malacca and Tennaserim.

In Sind it appears to be a winter visitant.

Except Mr. Thompson's note that this species breeds from March till August in holes of trees, at no height from the ground, nothing is known of its nidification or eggs. It is a common bird in the Gurhwal forests. Mr. Hume says, in Lower Bengal he has occasionally obtained specimens by capturing them in the "Jalmil" or Jalousie of his house where they resort to by day.

88. Scops rufipennis, *Sharpe, Sub. Sp.* f. of the *giu* group, *Cat. Striges, B. M.* p. 60. Scops pennatus, *Jerd. Madr. Journ.*, xiii. pl. 2, p. 119.—The Rufous-winged Scops Owl.

There is a single specimen only of this species in the British Museum from the Eastern Ghauts, collected by the late Dr. Jerdon and named by him *Scops pennatus*; but Mr. Sharpe has separated it from among his large series of *Scops*. He says, it is of the *Scops giu* group and closely allied to *S. Malayanus* resembling it in the dusky grey ear coverts, but distinguished by the absence of the white ocellations on the hind neck and of the bars on the centre tail feathers, and more especially by its rufous quills. The following is his description of the *type* in the British Museum.

Adult.—General aspect of upper surface more uniform than is usual in species of this genus, being of a dusky greyish brown, the feathers being blackish in the centre, but scarcely to be called streaked, excepting on the fore part of the crown, where the black shafts are very broad and distinct, all the feathers of the upper surface so finely pencilled with dark brown as to appear almost uniform, with here and there a few sandy-coloured mottlings, more distinct on the head, to which they impart a slightly spotted appearance; the collar on the hind neck very distinct, some of the feathers being barred with fulvous and crossed with narrow bars of blackish; on the scapulars the blackish cross lines are a little more coarsely defined than on the back, washed with orange buff, and having the outer web pure white, tipped with black, forming a conspicuous shoulder patch; wing coverts greyish like the back, the vermiculations very faint and often obsolete on the greater series, which have rather large white spots on the outer web; the median coverts coarsely vermiculated with sandy buff; the feathers with blackish shaftstreaks; the least series rufous with obscure blackish cross vermiculations; the outermost of the greater series, and the primary coverts strongly rufescent, almost chestnut in tone, the latter finely vermiculated with blackish; innermost secondary quills colored like the back, and finely vermiculated in the same manner, their centres streaked with dusky blackish along the shaft; the rest of the quills rufous, barred with dusky brown; these bars are more or less vermiculated; the inner webs almost entirely dusky brown barred with pale rufous inclining to yellowish on the inner web; the rufous bars on the outer web of the primaries inclining to white, and producing somewhat a chequered appearance; upper tail coverts exactly like the back; the centre tail feathers likewise strongly resembling the upper surface inasmuch as they are without any distinct trace of cross bars; the outer feathers dark brown, vermiculated with sandy rufous, and crossed with seven bars of rufous; the subterminal one very indistinct and lost in the vermiculations at the tips, the light bars inclining to white on the outer edge of the external web; loral plumes whitish; the shafts black, and produced into long hair-like bristles; feathers over the eye buffy white, tipped with blackish; sides of face dusky grey, indistinctly varied with fine cross lines of dull brown; behind the ear coverts a tolerably distinct ruff of orange-buff, and the feathers broadly tipped with black, this ruff extending across the throat, but the feathers here finely barred with blackish; chin feathers dull white; chest dull orange buff; the feathers broadly centred with black and crossed with a few narrow zigzag lines of brown and vermiculated with the same at the tips, many of the feathers inclining to white; on the breast and the rest of the lower parts the white predominates, many of the feathers only having a few zigzag markings of brown, on many of them a strong tinge of rufous with broad black central streaks; some of the flank feathers slightly washed with grey; under tail coverts almost entirely white, except an arrow-shaped mark of rufous or brown near the tip; leg feathers buffy white, the tarsus slightly streaked with brown; under wing coverts fulvous, those near the edge of the wing mottled with brown; the lower series ashy brown with yellowish white base, the quills being also ashy brown below, but inclining to rufous near the tips, the bands being entirely of this colour, and fulvous only near the base of the inner webs.

Length,—8 inches; wing 5·1; tail 2·7; tarsus 0·85. (Sharpe).

Unique. A single specimen from the Eastern Ghauts, Madras. Nothing is known of its habits or nidification. I am, however, strongly inclined to group this as a variety of *S. spiolcephalus*.

89. Scops brucii, *Hume, Stray Feathers*, vol. i. p. 8; *Murray, Handbook, Zool. &c., Sind*, p. 119; *Sharpe, Cat. Striges*, vol. ii. p. 63; *Murray, Vert. Zool. Sind*, p. 495; *Str. F.* vol. ii. p. 491; iv. 254; vii. 352; *Descr.* ix. 36, 312 376-452.—The STRIATED SCOPS OWL.

Cheeks and feathers under the eye greyish white, excessively fine and indistinctly barred with brown; the lores and stripe running up from them to the top of the eye creamy white. The longer feathers that meet over the base of the upper mandible tinged brownish, a few tiny dark brown feathers on the eyelids. Chin and throat creamy white, with very narrow central shaft-stripes towards the tips and excessively finely vermiculated with brown. Feathers of the ruff, which is inconspicuous, very pale buff, narrowly edged with dark brown. The whole of the forehead, crown, back of head, back and sides of neck, back, scapulars, wing coverts, rump, and upper tail coverts, very pale buff or creamy white, so minutely and closely powdered with pale brown, that looked at from a little distance, the feathers appear to be a uniform pale earthy brown. Every feather has a narrow central dark-brown stripe, some of the outer scapulars have inconspicuous patches of buff on their outer webs, and the ground colour of the feathers on each side of the crown immediately above the eye is slightly paler; but beyond this the whole of the upper plumage above described is singularly uniform in tint and appearance, and is absolutely devoid of those white spots and blackish brown or buff dashes and streaks so characteristic of the other Indian species. The primaries are pale dingy buff, with broad transverse brown bars, which towards the tips are with the ground colour mottled and freckled over, the ground colour with brown, and the bars with dingy fulvous. Nearer the base of the feathers, the light bars are on the exterior webs pure pale buff, while the dark bars continue freckled as already described. On the inner webs, the dark bars are nearly uniform and unmottled, while the light bars are pure and unmottled towards the edge of the webs, and suffused with brown towards the shafts. The tertiaries and the tips of the secondaries approximate closely to the plumage of the back and coverts. Of the breast and abdomen, the ground colour is similar to that of the upper parts, but the brown powdering is coarser, so that more of the ground colour is seen, and the dark brown central shaft stripes are somewhat broader; towards the vent, on the flanks and lower tail coverts, the ground colour becomes almost pure white, and the brown powdering very sparse, while the shaft stripes are reduced as on the back and wing coverts to well-marked dark lines. The short dense tibial and tarsal plumes are brownish white, each little feather with its dark central shaft stripe. The axillaries and wing lining are cream-coloured or yellowish white, entirely unstreaked and unmottled.

The legs and feet, including the base of the toes, densely feathered; terminal portions of toes with small transverse scutæ, slate-coloured; claws black, well curved, slender, and very sharp; toes very slender, but pads largely developed, so as to make a broad sole; exterior toe more or less versatile; irides bright yellow; bill dusky.

Male, Length.—9 inches; expanse 22 inches; wing 6·4 inches; tail 3·25 inches; tarsus 1·45 inches; foot greatest length 1·87 inches; greatest width 1·75 inches; mid-toe to root of claw 0·8 inch; its claw straight, 0·39 inch; hind toe 0·35 inch; its claw straight, 0·28 inch; inner toe 0·67 inch; its claw straight, 0·4 inch. Bill straight from forehead to point including cere, which is ill-defined, 0·7 inch, from gape 0·73 inch; height at front at margin of cere 0·29 inch, wings when closed are even with the end of tail. Lower tail coverts reach to within 0·9 inch of end of tail. The third and fourth primaries are the longest; the first is 0·75 inch, and the second is 0·08 shorter. The exterior tail feathers are 0·3 inch shorter than the central ones. Weight 4 oz. (*Hume, Stray Feathers*, vol. i., p. 8.)

Mr. Vidal obtained this species at Khed in the Southern Concan, and the Rev. Mr. Fairbank near Nuggur. Major Biddulph records it from Gilgit, and I have myself taken specimens in Southern Afghanistan, where it is not uncommon and breeds in April; eggs 3 in number, pure white, round, 1·77 × 1·0 inches. It nests in holes of old *Pistacia Kinjuk* trees, on the Khojak, and below. Every orchard after dusk is alive with them, and they make night hideous with their melancholy cry.

90. Scops spilocephalus, *Blyth, J. A. S. B.* xv., p. 8; *Hume, Nest and Eggs, Ind. B.* i. p. 66; *Sharpe, Cat. Acc. Br. Mus.* p. 63. Scops pennata, *Hodgs. J. A. S. B.* vi. p. 369, *partim.* Phodilus nipalensis, *Gray, Handl. B.* i. p. 53. Ephialtes gymnopodus, *Hume, Rough Notes*, ii. p. 390; *Jerd. Ibis.* 1871, p. 347.—The BARE-FOOT SCOPS OWL.

Forehead and a broad stripe over the eye pale rufous white or fawn colour. Some of the feathers with a few minute brown spots towards the tip ; loral bristles pale fawn color, more rufous towards the tips, which are black. Feathers under the eye and ear coverts pale fawn color, more or less tinged rufous, and freckled, mottled or imperfectly barred with brown. Top of head, back of neck, back, scapulars, rump and upper tail coverts, also lesser wing coverts with a more or less dark rufous fawn ground, very finely freckled with dark, in some almost blackish brown. An irregular ill-defined, broad, white, or yellowish white half collar at the base of the neck ; most of the exterior scapulars with the outer webs white or yellowish white, and tipped dark brown. Tail rufous fawn with from 7 (Hume) 9 (Sharpe) somewhat freckled transverse brown bars, 8 of which are distinctly traceable on the centre feathers. (In the specimen from the Kumaons—a single one—8 only are traceable on all the feathers.) Quills rufous fawn, broadly barred and clouded with dusky brown, which suffuses the. greater portion of the inner webs near the tips. Carpal joint of wing whitish. Chin and throat rufous white or pale fawn. Some of the feathers of the throat with narrow, somewhat irregular transverse brown bars; the feathers of the ruff tipped with the same. Breast, abdomen and flanks pale rufous white or fawn color, thickly freckled and vermiculated with dark brown, thickly on the breast and sparingly on the abdomen and flanks. Tarsal and tibial plumes ferruginous or rufous white, spotted, or obscurely barred with dusky. Wing lining and axillaries silky yellowish white.

Length.—7 to 7·75 inches; wing 5·4 to 5·6; tail 2·75 to 3·1; tarsus 1·2 to 1·25. (Hume).

Hab.—The Himalayas, in the neighbourhood of Mussoorie, Kumaon, Gurhwal, below Simla and Nepal.

Captain Hutton says this species occurs in the Himalayas near Mussoorie at an elevation of five thousand feet, and nidificates in hollow trees, laying 3 pure white eggs of a rounded form, on the rotten wood, without any preparation of a nest. Diameter of egg 1·19 × 1·0 inch. The nest was found on the 19th March. *Scops gymnopodus* follows in order, but it is not possible to admit the species as Indian without further proofs. Mr. Sharpe himself doubts its Indian habitat, as Mr. Reeves' specimens on which the species is founded came from Malacca and China.

91. Scops sunia, *Hodgs. As. Res.*, xix., p. 175; *id. in Gray's Zool. Journ.* p. 82 ; *Blyth, J. A. S. B.* xiv., p. 182 ; *Jerd Ill. Ind. Zool.* pl. xli ; *Sharpe, Cat. Striges*, vol. ii. p. 67. Ephialtes sunia, *Gray, Cat. Mamm., &c., Nepaul; Coll. Hodgs.*, p. 51 ; *Holdsw. P. Z. S.* 1872, p. 418. Ephialtes Bakkamæna, *Blyth, Ibis.* 1866, p. 255. Scops pennatus, *Hume, Nest and Eggs, Ind. B.* i. p. 65. Ephialtes pennatus, *Hume, Rough Notes*, ii. p. 386.—HODGSON'S SCOPS OWL.

Adult.—Above clear cinnamon rufous, nearly uniform, most of the feathers with a narrow central shaft line of black, a little broader than on the crown; scapulars externally yellowish buff or pure white, with a black subterminal bar; wing coverts rufous like the back with the same dusky black shaft lines, broader on the greater series, which are white at the tips of their external webs; the spurious quills externally whitish, broadly barred with dark brown; primary coverts, cinnamon, with a spot of yellowish white near the tip of the outer web, the inner web blackish brown; quills dull cinnamon rufous with faint cross-bars of brown, almost obsolete on the innermost secondaries, less distinct on the outer ones, but plainer on the primaries, many of the light interspaces on the outer webs of the latter inclining to whitish; tail cinnamon, the centre feathers nearly uniform, with only faint indications of narrow blackish cross-bars, these are broader and more distinct on the outer feathers, the exterior ones having slight indications of whitish spots on the light interspaces; lores white, the elongated bristly shafts blackish at tip; over the eye a patch of white feathers narrowly margined with black at their tips; sides of face cinnamon with silvery white shaft lines to the feathers; behind the ear coverts a distinct ruff of deep cinnamon feathers broadly terminated with black; plumes on the chin whitish; chest cinnamon, some of the feathers buffy white at the tips, with broad mesial streaks of black; rest of under surface of body for the most part white, broadly streaked down the centre with black, barred with cinnamon and freckled and grizzled with zigzag lines of blackish. Under tail coverts white, slightly washed with cinnamon at the tips, and with few indications of a central dark brown streak. Under wing coverts yellowish, those near the edge of the wing rufous mottled with brown. Edge of wing white. Bill dusky horn; feet fleshy brown. Iris bright yellow.

Length.—6·7 inches to 7·5; wing 5·3 to 5·7; tail 2·5; tarsus 0·9 to 1·0 (Sharpe.)

The above is a description by Mr. Sharpe, taken from a Nepaul skin collected by Mr. Hodgson.

Mr. Sharpe observes that some specimens show considerable differences, principally on the breast and abdomen, both the Penang and Madras specimens having the central black streaks very indistinct on the under-parts, while they vary *inter se* in the mottling of the abdomen. Mr. Sharpe's description answers exactly to a specimen of Scops very near *pennatus*, now in the Kurrachee Museum, collected at Kurrachee, except that the tibial and tarsal plumes are unspotted white, also the under tail coverts; another specimen has the tibial and tarsal plumes rufous fawn, with faint indications of small brown spots; the primaries too have the outer webs broadly barred with yellowish white and dark brown.

Hab.—India generally, ranging down the Malayan Peninsula as far as Penang. Recorded from Madras, Penang, and Nepaul; also Sind, the Punjab, and the lower ranges of the Himalayas to Darjeeling, and everywhere where *pennatus* occurs. I cannot from the series I possess of these Scops sufficiently separate them.

In my opinion it bears the same relation to *pennatus* as *plumipes* of the Himalayas does to *S. lettia.*

92. Scops plumipes. *Hume, Rough Notes,* ii. p. 397; *Sharpe, Cat. Striges, B. M.* p. 85,—The Plume-Foot Scops Owl.

This species, if it is to be distinguished at all, or specifically separated from the next (*E. lettia*) may be distinguished by the toes being feathered to the base of the toes, the general tone of colouring as shown by Mr. Hume darker, and as a rule less rufous or buffy, and the dark blotches on the head, back, ruff, breast and abdomen more conspicuous.

Length.—9·5 to 10-inches; wing 6·7 to 7.3; tail 3; tarsus 1·6 to 1·7; horn from gape 0·92. (Rough Notes.)

Hab.—Punjab, N.-W. Provinces, and the Himalayas (Murree, Kotegurh and Gurhwal).

According to Mr. Hume, *S. plumipes* has been found breeding at Kotegurh. A female and 4 eggs were taken from a hole in a tree on the 13th May. The eggs are intermediate in size between those of *Athene brama* and *A. cuculoides* but more spherical. They are pure white and slightly glossy, and vary in size from 1·25 inches to 1·28 in length, and from 1·1 to 1·5 inches in breadth, and not quite as large as some of those he possesses of *E. griseus, Jerd.*

93. Scops lettia, *Hodgs. As. Research,* xix. p. 176; *Sharpe Cat. Striges. p.* 85; *Hume, Nest and Eggs, Ind. B.* i. p. 67. Ephialtes lempiji, *Gray. Cat. Mamm. &c., Nepaul Coll. Hodgs.* p. 51; *Jerd. B. Ind.* i. p. 138; *id. Ibis.* 1871, p. 256. Ephialtes lettia, *Hume, Rough Notes,* ii. p. 393; *Oates, B. Br. Burmah,* ii. p. 155.—The Nepaul Scops Owl.

Forehead, a broad streak over the eye running down the interior web of the aigrettes, feathers under the eye, most of the ear coverts, loral bristles and chin white, with a greyish or yellowish tinge, most of the feathers tipped or imperfectly barred with dark brown. Top of the head, back of the neck, exterior webs of the aigrettes, back, scapulars and tertiaries, also the lesser wing coverts, rump and upper tail coverts with a rufous fawn, or in some buffy yellow ground color, everywhere except on the outer webs of the scapulars, and in a broad half collar at base of neck, very closely and finely freckled or irregularly barred with minute zigzag lines of dark brown. Many of the feathers, especially of the head and aigrettes, with large deep brown blotches towards the tips, confined in the aigrettes to the outer webs. Outer webs of quills rufous fawn or buffy yellow, palest on the first few primaries, and with 5—6 broad irregular mottled and imperfect transvese brown bars which extend to the inner webs. Outer webs of secondaries also buffy and much freckled and mottled with brown. Tail brown, with 5—6 imperfect and irregular transverse rufous fawn bars, the interspaces much freckled. Throat and ruff white, suffused with rufous fawn towards the tips; those of the throat with 2—3 very narrow transverse brown bars towards the end, and those of the ruff broadly blotched at the tips with deep brown. Breast and abdomen white, pale yellowish or rufous white, closely and irregularly barred with delicate wavy brown lines, many of the feathers with dark brown shaft stripes or lengthened blotches. Vent and the lower tail coverts white with or without an imperfect bar or two towards the tip; tibial and tarsal plumes white or slightly rufescent, with a few indications of narrow brown cross markings. Under wing coverts yellowish white, mottled with cross lines of dark brown near the edge of the wing, which is white. Feet yellowish fleshy; bill yellowish horny, brown at the tip and on the side of upper mandible and the edge of the lower.

Length.—8·5 to 10·5 inches; wing 6·3 to 7·2; tail 3·2 to 3·3; tarsus 1·4 to 1·5; bill from edge of cere 0·6 to 0·7.

Hab.—Punjab, N.-W. Provinces, Bengal, Concan, South India, Malabar, British Burmah, Nepaul and Sikkim. Recorded as most plentiful at Kumaon, Darjeeling, Dhurrumsalla, Kotegurh, Simla and Gurhwal. It is recorded from Arrakan, and according to Oates is common over the greater part of Pegu. Captain Ramsay procured it at Rangoon and on the Karenne Hills.

Of the habits of this species very little is known. Like most Scops Owls it issues from its retreat at sunset. It is known to breed in the valley of Surjoo between Petoraguth and Almorah in Kumaon, and Oates says, he found a nest in March. The nest according to Hume, *Rough Notes*, was a few small sticks or twigs, amongst which a few feathers were interspersed, and was placed in a narrow cleft on an overhanging precipice. Eggs 3 in number, very spherical in shape, pure white and very glossy, varying in size from 1·33 to 1·38 in length, and from 1·18 to 1·2 in breadth.

94. Scops lempiji, *Horsf. Tr. Lin. Soc.* xiii., p. 140; *Sharpe, Cat. Striges*, p. 91; *Blyth, J. A. S. B.* xv. pt. i. p. 182. Ephialtes lempiji, *Gray, Gen. B.* i. p. 38; *Wall. Ibis.* 1868, p. 24; *Hume, Str. F.* ii. p. 469; *id.* 1st *list. B. Pegu*, vol. iii. pp. 14, 28; *Hume and Davison, B. Tennaserim*, vol. vi. p. 35; *Ball, Ganges to the Godavery*, vol. vii. p. 201; vol. viii. *B. West half Malay Pen.*; *Bingham, B. Tennaserim*, vol. ix. p 147; *Oates, B. Br. Burmah*, ii. p. 156.—HORSFIELD'S SCOPS OWL.

Above clear sandy brown, coarsely vermiculated with wavy cross lines of. black, many of the feathers with broad but irregularly formed streaks of black; scapulars more or less sandy buff on the outer web, the cross lines apparent on the tips of the lower ones, but nearly absent on the upper scapulars, some of which are entirely sandy buff on both webs; round the hindneck a tolerably distinct collaret of sandy buff feathers, only varied with blackish markings towards the tips of the feathers; crown of head blackish in the centre, the plumes laterally rufous buff with very narrow black cross lines. Forehead and a broad streak on each side of the crown sandy buff, the feathers narrowly streaked with black along the shaft and varied towards the tip with a few blackish cross lines; the ear tufts (1 inch long) which form part of the light lateral band on the sides of the crown being pale sandy buff, slightly varied with zigzag lines of black towards the tips, which are very broadly black; over the eye a patch of buffy white feathers each terminally margined with a narrow line of black; lores sandy buff with whitish bases; sides of face sandy buff, indistinctly barred across with narrow lines of dusky black, the hindermost ear coverts rather broadly tipped with the same; behind the ear coverts an indistinct ruff of sandy buff feathers extending across the centre of the throat, many of the plumes narrowly barred across with blackish lines and all rather broadly tipped with black; rest of under surface of body entirely sandy buff, varied with narrow cross lines of dark brown, the chest with broad central spots or streaks of blackish brown, much narrower and more linear on the abdomen and flank feathers; under tail coverts nearly uniform sandy buff with a few wavy lines of blackish near the tips of the feathers; leg feathers sandy buff, the tarsal plumes crossed with distinct wavy blackish cross lines, under wing coverts sandy buff, the inner ones nearly uniform, the outermost mottled or barred with dark brown near the edge of the wing, which is whitish, the lower series entirely ashy brown; the inner lining of the quills nearly uniform ashy brown, barred with yellowish white near the base of the inner web, and with sandy buff near the tips of the feathers. Upper wing coverts darker than the back, being blackish brown, the spurious quills externally notched with sandy buff, the innermost of the least series sandy buff, mottled with zigzag blackish lines, the greater series dark brown widely notched with sandy buff towards the tip of the outer web; primary coverts blackish brown with indications of sandy buff bars, thickly obscured with blackish vermiculations; quills dark brown, barred with lighter or ashy brown on the inner webs, these light bars being represented by corresponding ones of sandy buff on the outer webs of the primaries, giving a chequered appearance to the external aspect of the wing; the secondaries outwardly sandy buff, vermiculated with lines of dark brown, the innermost sandy brown mottled and vermiculated exactly like the scapulars; rump and upper tail coverts darker sandy brown than the back, thickly obscured with blackish vermiculations; tail dark brown mottled with sandy buff, nowhere forming very distinct bars and particularly broken up towards the tips of the feathers; on the outer ones the bars are a little more distinct, about eight being distinguishable, all the light markings everywhere somewhat obscured by brown vermiculations. (Sharpe).

Length.—Adult Females: 8·75; wing 6·6. Males: *Length*—8·5; wing 5·8 to 6·4; tail 3·25; tarsus (not plumed the whole way, the junction of the toes always bare) 1·25; bill yellowish at tip, plumbeous at base; iris brown, tinted with olive; feet and eyelids purplish brown.

Hab.—Borneo, Bangka, Java, Sumatra, Malayan Peninsula, ranging northwards in the Tennaserim Provinces of British Burma and Nepaul, and occurring in the N.-W. Provinces, Oudh, Bengal, Kutch, and the Concan.

In vol. iii. of *Stray Feathers* Capt. Fielden says that this little owl appears able to lower its ear-tufts, and that he has always seen them erected, standing out much like a cat's ears; also, that they appear to live in holes of trees during the hot weather, and during the rains are to be seen on the shady side of bamboo clumps or on fallen bamboos partly buried in long grass. According to Capt. Fielden, this species is very tame and does not fly out of range of shot when disturbed, and is chiefly found near watercourses in Thayetmyo. Hume and Davison in vol. vi. of *Stray Feathers* give as localities in Tennaserim, the Karen Hills (Rams), Pahpoon, Tavoy, Pabyin, Mergui, Tennaserim Town, and Bankasoon, generally distributed throughout the better wooded portions of the Province. Mr. Sharpe like Mr. Hume unites the Malaccan and Sumatran forms. The Tennaserim forms Mr. Hume says, are not separable, and are clearly *lempiji* of Mr. Sharpe's Catalogue, characterized by the completely unfeathered toes. Capt. Bingham in vol. xi. of *Stray Feathers* mentions having taken three eggs of this species from a hole in a tree from 15 to 20 feet from the ground. The eggs were white, round and nearly glossless, and were laid on the bare wood in a natural hollow in the branch.

95. Scops malabaricus, *Jerd. Madr. Journ.* x. p. 89; *Sharpe, Cat. Striges*, p. 94, Sub-Sp. B.; *Str. F.* vol. v. p. 135; *Bourdillon, B. S. Travancore, S. F.* vol. vii. p. 34; *Hume, Str. F.* vol. vii. p. 361. Descr. Scops griseus, *Jerd. Madr. Journ.* xiii. pt. 2, p. 119. Scops lettoides, *Blyth, J. A. S. B.* xiv. pl. i. p. 182. (*ex. Jerd. Ms.*) Ephialtes malabaricus, *Hume, Rough Notes* ii. p. 402; *Jerd. Ibis.* 1871, p. 348. Scops indicus, *Gmel. Stray Feathers*, v. 135, vii. pp. 359, 506. Scops bakkamæna, *Forst.*; *Hume, Nest and Eggs, Ind. B.* p. 69. Ephialtes griseus, *Hume, Rough Notes*, p. 398; *Murray, Hdbk., Zool., &c., Sind*, p. 121.—The Malabar Scops Owl.

A prominent tuft of disunited-webbed, bristly white feathers (with dark naked tips to the shafts, and traces on those nearest the eye of dark cross bars,) on each side of the upper mandible at its base; a faint tinge of buffy at the anterior angle of the eye; rest of the lores, feathers below and behind the eyes, including ear coverts, loose-webbed, silky and greyish white with traces of faint minute transverse brown bars; chin white; the feathers of the extreme tip somewhat bristly and curving upwards round the lower mandible; across the throat and upwards, immediately behind the ear orifice, as far as the base of the aigrettes, a band of creamy or pale buff feathers, with numerous minute, transverse, wavy brown pencillings and bars; those from the aigrettes to the sides of the throat with conspicuous dark brown tippings, which from the defining line of the disc, and a few of those in the centre of the throat with similarly coloured spots at the tips; forehead and a broad supercilium running up the inside webs of the aigrette feathers, and a curved band at the back of the head, extending from the point of one aigrette to the point of the other, a silvery grey or greyish white, the feathers with dark brown shafts and numerous minute transverse pencillings of that colour, and some of them with terminal spots; centre of forehead, top of head, a triangular space surrounded by this grey band, a rich dark brown, purest on the centre of the forehead, with small twin spots or imperfect transverse bars and mottlings, to a greater or less extent, of pale buff; the outside webs of the aigrettes are similar, as are the feathers of the band outside and contiguous to the curved grey band, which latter seems continuous with the dark line of the outer webs of the aigrette, while the former seems to start immediately above the centre of the eye; below the dark band at the base of the neck, is another band of very similarly marked feathers, but whereas the dark brown predominates in the former, the buff much predominates in the latter. The back, rump, upper tail coverts, scapulars, wing coverts, except the greater ones of the primaries, a mixture of pale brownish grey and pale buffy, with dark brown central streaks, and numerous transverse wavy brown pencillings and mottlings. In the outside line of the scapulars the buff is very pure, and in some positions conspicuous, and while the rump, upper tail and lesser wing coverts are dingier and greyer, the centre of the upper back and the median and secondary wing coverts show more of a pale buff; the primary greater coverts are very dark brown with broad transverse buffy mottled bars; the quills are darkish brown, with numerous broad transverse greyish more or less dingy white bars, much more conspicuous on the outer webs; with the exception of a few bars on the upper portion of the outer web of the earlier primaries, which are unmottled and slightly tinged with creamy, all the rest of these bars are closely mottled and pencilled with brown; the second, third and fourth primaries are just perceptibly emarginate on the outer webs, and the first to the fourth are conspicuously notched on the inner webs; the sides of the neck behind the dark line, the breast, sides, abdomen and thigh coverts, a sort of creamy grey, very soft and silky, the feathers with narrow rich brown central streaks and numerous minute irregular, wavy, transverse pencillings; greater portion of wing lining, vent feathers and lower tailcoverts, silky greyish white, the latter, some of them, with dark central streaks towards the tips; tarsal feathers silky greyish white, with a faint buffy tinge towards the joint, and with several narrow, somewhat irregular transverse brown bars; tail feathers greyish brown with imperfect transverse mottled bars of very pale dingy buff, and with the interspaces, too, more or less mottled with the same colour. Toes and claws pale greyish brown. Soles creamy white; pads and papillæ much developed and soft; irides brownish yellow or dark brown; bill dark brown; cere dusky grey.

Length—7·88 to 9 inches; wing 5·6 to 6·75; tail 2·5 to 3·37; tarsus 1·06 to 1·19.

The above is Mr. Hume's description of *Scops indicus, Gm.*, which, he says (on page 506, vol. vii. *Str. F.*) is identical with *Scops griseus* (*malabaricus* of *Sharpe, Cat. Striges, B. M.*) and *Scops bakkamœna* of *Forster*. Sharpe, however, does not in his references to the literature of this species allude to the names given by Gmelin and Forster.

Hab.—Sind, Punjab, N.-W. Provinces, Oudh, Bengal, Central India, Madras, Malabar Coast, Travancore, Ceylon, Eastern and Western Ghauts, North Guzerat, and Ratnagiri (S. Concan). Like the preceding species, it occurs in Sind, but is uncommon, and affects wooded districts only.

Breeds in holes of trees; nest commonly lined with leaves; eggs white, glossy and spherical. Nests have been taken during March and April in Sind, Central Provinces (Etawah) and near Hansi.

96. Scops sagitatus, *Sharpe, Cat. B. Br. Mus.* ii. p. 98; *Oates, B. Br. Burmah*, vol. ii. p. 156; *Hume and Davison, S. F.* vi. p. 35; *Hume, S. F.* viii. p. 83. Ephialtes sagitatus, *Cass. Journ. Acad. Philad.* ii. p. 90, pl. 12.—THE LARGE MALACCAN SCOPS OWL.

The whole upper plumage a rather rich chestnut; the wings barred on the inner webs with brown and the tail irregularly banded with the same; each feather of the upper plumage with small arrow-head fulvous marks in the centre, and some narrow wavy black lines across; the forehead for a depth of nearly an inch, a broad supercilium and the inner webs of most of the feathers of the eartufts white; the shafts of the feathers of the forehead nearly black; the tips of the tufts and the top of the head a darker chestnut than the back, and without any marks. The long feathers on the sides of the neck, indicating a ruff, whitish, broadly tipped with blackish; lower webs vermiculated with brown; the breast with small dark brown shaft spots and a narrow vermiculation; abdomen and vent with some rather large distinct black shaft spots on the feathers.

Bill, feet and claws, bluish white; cere pale bluish green; irides deep brown. (*Davison*). *Ex. Oates.*

Length.—10 to 11·5 inches; wing 7·15 to 7·2; tail 4·5 to 5; tarsus 1·2 to 1·25.

Hab.—Malewoon in South Tennaserim; the Southern slopes of the Mooleyit Mountain. (*Davison*)—and Malacca. Of its habits and nidification nothing is known.

97. Scops balli, *Hume, Str. F.* i. p. 53; *Sharpe, Cat. Striges*, vol. ii. p. 100. Ephialtes spilocephalus, *Ball. Str. F.* i. p. 53.—BALL'S SCOPS OWL.

Adult (type of species).—General color above rufous chocolate, with a few fine nearly obsolete vermiculations of black, the whole upper surface with more or less concealed spots of rufous buff, very minute on the crown, but much more distinct on the back, where they form almost bars, all the light spots having a blackish margin; scapular feathers externally barred with white, the interspaces very pale, and inclining to ochraceous; wing coverts colored like the back, the bases dark brown, the tips chocolate rufous, with rather more distinct vermiculations of black, the spots very plain, and forming notches on the outer web of some of the greater series; primary coverts exactly like the other, brown at base, rufescent at tips, but without the light spots; quills dark brown, nearly uniform on the inner web, and chocolate rufous at the tips of the primaries, and on the outer webs of the secondaries, which are minutely notched with fulvous; the primaries very distinctly chequered with white on the outer webs, the innermost secondaries spotted with rufous buff, resembling the scapulars; tail dark brown near the base, crossed with about six bars of dull rufous, these becoming obsolete towards the tips of the feathers, which are rufous chocolate, very finely vermiculated with black; the outer feather externally notched with fulvous, and all the feathers of the wings and tail barred with fulvous on the inner web, especially towards the base; forehead and feathers over the fore part of the eye creamy white, narrowly tipped with brown; loral plumes rufous, the shafts ending in black hair-like bristles, barred obscurely with black; ear coverts rufous chocolate, barred and tipped with black; cheeks fulvous, all the feathers tipped, and some of them barred across with dull black; general colour of under surface rufous sandy obscured with grey, and finely vermiculated with blackish cross lines, the bases of the feathers, especially those of the flanks, strongly rufescent, broadly barred with fulvous, inclining to white near the tips of most of the feathers; and before this whitish tip, appears generally a slight indication of a diamond-shaped spot of black, evidently the remains of a streak; all the above markings, though distinct on the abdomen and flanks, are less plainly characterized on the chest, which is consequently more dusky; leg-feathers orange tawny, narrowly barred with dark brown; under wing coverts fulvous, slightly marked with brown and spotted with sandy buff near the edge of the wing, which is whitish; the lower series dark brown, fulvescent at base, resembling the inner lining of the quills, which are dark brown, notched on the outer web and barred on the inner with fulvous. Total length 7·5 inches; wing 5·45; tail 3·2; tarsus 1·15. (*Mus. Ind. Calc.*)

Obs.—Another specimen, very kindly lent me by Mr. Hume, differs considerably from the one described. It is not such a deep rufous in color, and is much more thickly spotted both above and below, recalling *Scops spilocephalus;* the under surface is much paler and greyer, the white bars very large and distinct and extending even on to the chest. Total length 7·5 inches; wing 5·6; tail 3·2; tarsus 1·15.

Hab.—Andaman Islands, Nepaul. Mr. Sharpe again observes that, "it has been suggested by Mr. Hume, that the bird from the Andamans, named *Scops modestus* by Lord Walden, must be the young bird of *S. Balli*, and I confess that until I examined and compared the types, I entertained a similar impression. Lord Walden, however, having kindly lent me the original specimen of *S. modestus* for examination, I have come to the conclusion that the two species are quite distinct. Lord Walden has two specimens precisely similar; and they seem to me to represent the young of some species of the *S. malayanus* type. Immature they certainly are; but they present too many differences for me to refer them to *S. Balli.* The type of the latter has been lent to me by Mr. Hume, and as the wings and tail in *S. modestus* are doubtless those of the adult bird, I draw attention to the following characters which as it seems to me must separate the two; for in no other species of *Scops* is such a difference known between the young and the adult stages":—

Scops Balli.	*Scops modestus,* Juv.*
Adult.—Greater wing coverts and secondary quills dull brown, externally rufous chocolate, with minute vermiculations of black, and a few small notches of fulvous.	Greater wing coverts and secondary quills alternately barred with sandy rufous and dark brown, the latter bars rather broken up into vermiculations, especially on outer margin; the greater coverts with white spots near the tip of outer web, not present in the secondaries.
Primary coverts nearly uniform blackish brown, vermiculated with rufous chocolate at the tips. Primaries dull brown, rufescent at the tips, notched with white on the outer web, the interspaces inclining to rufous chocolate.	Primary coverts and primaries dull brown on inner web, but regularly banded with sandy rufous and dark brown on outer web; some of the primaries with whitish notches.
Tail for the most part rufous chocolate, like back, with indications of lighter bars, the outer feather externally notched with whitish.	Tail regularly banded with dark brown and sandy rufous, the dark bars somewhat broken up into vermiculations on the centre feather.

Again, the feathering of the tarsus is very different, not extending nearly so far down the leg in *S. Balli* as it does in *S. modestus.*

The above is Mr. Sharpe's description in its entirety of this rare species.

98. Scops modestus; *Wald. Ann. and Mag. N. History*, vol. xiii. p. 123, 1874; *Ibis.* 1874, p. 129; *Sharpe, Cat. Striges, B. M.*, pp. 101-102.

The following is Lord Walden's description, taken from the *Annals and Mag. Nat. History*, p. 12 (1874):—

*Scops Modestus.—*Wald. Ann. & Mag. N. H.* xiii., p. 12. *id. et Ibis.* 1874, p. 129.

Stiff loral bristles pure white at base, some tipped with fulvous, some with dark brown or black; those of the chin pale fulvous, nearly white; over each eye a distinct broad whitish band formed by pure white feathers narrowly tipped with yellowish brown, which again in some is narrowly fringed with black; some nearest the eyes also edged throughout their length with yellowish brown. Feathers of the head and nape, pale yellowish rusty, each traversed by three or four narrow irregular light brown lines. Interscapulars and feathers of the back and rump, colored and marked like the plumage of the head and nape, but the brown transverse bands are broader and fewer; scapulars the same, but a few more or less pure white, mottled towards the tip with the prevailing tints; ear coverts and cheeks principally white with brown and very fulvous markings; throat feathers albescent with one or more narrow brown cross bands; a half collar below the throat, of feathers marked and colored like those of the nape; breast feathers tipped with brown, a sub-terminal band of pale fulvous, then a brown band followed by a much broader pure white band; abdominal feathers white, tipped with an irregular ocellated mark, centred with pale rusty fulvous and encircled with brown, then a broad white band, with a basal and narrower brown band in many of the abdominal feathers, the ocellated markings are replaced by an irregular cross band of mixed fulvous and brown; under tail coverts white, with faint subterminal fulvous brown bands; tarsus clothed with white feathers faintly barred with pale brown; ground color of the primaries and secondaries brown, each quill traversed by three or more pale rufo-fulvous narrow bands more or less complete, the brown intervals towards the apices of the primaries and on their outer webs much freckled with rufo-fulvous; on the outer web of the second, third and fourth primaries, the pale rufo-fulvous bands change to fulvous white or pure white; under wing coverts greyish white; median rectrices marked and colored like the apices of the primaries; lateral with clear rufo-fulvous bands running through, all tipped like the median shoulder edge, with white; tarsi feathered to within an eighth of an inch of the base of the toes; fourth and fifth quills equal; third slightly longer than sixth.

Wing 4·75 inches; tail 2·37; tarsus 1·0; middle toe with nail 1·12; bill from nostril (in a straight line) 0·65.

Hab.—Port Blair, S. Andamans. Occurs also in Nepaul.

Nothing is known of the habits or nidification of this species.

Gen. **Carine**.—*Kaup.*

Cere swollen; 1st primary much lengthened; 5th escolloped on the outer web like the fourth; hind tarsus plumed; nostril pierced near the anterior margin of the cere; bill short, curved from the base, hooked; lower mandible notched.

99. Carine brama, *Tem. Pl. Col.* ii. pl. 68; *Sharpe, Ibis.* 1875, p. 258; *Cat. Striges*, p. 139. Noctua indica, *Frankl. P. Z. S.* 1831, p. 115. Athene brama, *Blyth, Ann. N. H.* xii. p. 93; *Grey, Gen. B.* i. p. 34; *Jerd. B. Ind.* i. p. 141, No. 76; *Murray, Hdbk., Zool., &c., Sind*; *Hume, Rough Notes*, ii. p. 404; *Murray, Vert. Zool., Sind*, p. 99; *Reid, Cat. Lucknow Prov. Mus.*—THE SPOTTED OWLET.

Adult.—Above greyish brown, each feather with two white spots; scapulars barred with white, more broadly on the outer webs; wing coverts concolorous with the back, and spotted with white; primaries and their coverts brown, externally notched with white, and barred on the inner web; upper tail coverts and tail brown, also barred with white; head and hind neck closely spotted with white; lores, eyebrow, chin, a demi-collar and patch on the breast pure white; ear coverts brown, the feathers tipped with greyish; fore neck white, the tips of the feathers brown, forming a brown band between the white patch of the breast and foreneck; rest of under surface white, barred transversely with brown; under tail coverts, tarsal plumes, and under wing coverts pure white, the latter streaked with brown; cere dusky; bill greenish horny; toes sparsely covered with stiff bristles; irides bright yellow.

Length.—9 inches; wing 6; tail 3 to 3·5; tarsus 1·4.

Hab.—India generally to the foot of the Himalayas and Nepaul. Extends into Beloochistan, Persia, Afghanistan, Burmah and Ceylon. Extremely common in Sind, the Punjab, N.-W. Provinces, Oudh, Bengal, Rajputana, Jodhpoor, Kattiawar, Central India, the Central Provinces, Kutch, Guzerat, Concan, Deccan, and South India.

Breeds during February, March, and April wherever found in holes of old trees, or in old buildings and clefts of rocks; nest scantily lined with leaves and feathers. Eggs 4-5 in number, pinkish when fresh, white when blown, of a satiny texture. In shape oval and varying in size from 1·15 to 1·45 in length, and from 0·93 to 1·1 in breadth.

The species always issues from its hiding place at about dusk, when it may be seen perched either on the branch of a withered tree, or on the telegraph wire. Barnes, in his *Birds of the Bombay Presidency*, says if they can affect an entrance beneath the eaves of a bungalow they do so, and there rear their families; in such cases they become an intolerable nuisance, being noisy disagreeable birds, and not easily driven away. Lt. Barnes has even taken the eggs of this species from holes in haystacks.

In the Mahratta Country it is known as Pinglee. Mr. W. F. Sinclair, the Collector of Alibag, says it has a habit of hovering over one spot and dropping on its prey like a kestrel or kingfisher. He has noticed this in the dry bed of the Sabarmati near Ahmedabad, and thinking them (there were 5 or 6) kingfishers, went out to see what they were catching on the sand.

Carine glaux occurs in Kandahar, and probably in Beloochistan, but there is no information as to its occurrence anywhere in India.

100. Carine pulchra, *Hume, Str. F.* i. p. 469; *id. op. cit.* iii. p. 39; *Sharpe, Cat. Striges*, p. 140; *Subsp. a. id. Ibis.* 1875. p. 258; *Hume, Str. F. Birds of Pegu*, iii. pp. 14, 39; iv., p. 47.—THE LESSER SPOTTED OWLET.

Mr. A. O. Hume characterizes this species as closely allied to *Carine brama*, but much smaller, the color of the upper surface usually a darker and purer brown, and the white markings smaller. Sharpe, however, gives a detailed description of an adult male from Lieut. Wardlaw Ramsay's collection, which I transcribe.

Adult Male.—General color above slaty brown with more or less concealed spots of white, very small on the head, where they are plainly defined; hind neck barred with white, forming an indistinct kind of collar; scapulars barred across with white, broader on the outer web; wing coverts dark slaty color, externally notched with white, the median and greater series with large rounded spots of white on the outer web; the primary coverts and quills dark slate color, notched on the outer web and barred on the inner ones with white; tail slaty brown crossed with 6 narrow bars of white, rather broader on the outer feather; forehead and eyebrow white; the lores developing into hair-like bristles; fore part of cheeks whitish; ear coverts dark slaty, barred across with white; entire throat white, extending backwards in a triangular patch below the ear coverts; a black mark running down the sides of the neck, rest of under surface white, barred with ashy brown, the bars fainter on the lower flanks; leg feathers and under tail coverts pure white, also the under wing coverts, the lower series of the latter ashy brown at tip; inner lining of quills ashy brown below and barred with white; bill brownish; the tip and culmen greenish yellow.

Length.—7 to 8 inches; wing 5·4 to 5·5; tail 3·1 to 3·5; tarsus 1·05 to 1·1.

Hab.—Burmah and Pegu; very common at Thyetmyo and Prome, and Dr. Anderson obtained specimens of it in independent Burmah.

Mr. Oates in *S. F.* iii., p. 39, (Hume) remarks that this is possibly the noisiest of all the small screech owls. They are continually quarrelling with each other at night, and even in the day time, a pair will commonly come out of some hole in a tree and screech away for a quarter of an hour.

Gen. **Heteroglaux**.—*Hume.*

Size medium; head small; disc imperfect; nostrils situated in the centre of the cere. Ear orifice smaller than the eye, circular, without operculum, wings short; first four primaries conspicuously notched on the inner webs; 4th primary longest; tarsi short, stout, densely covered with feathers; upper surface of toes thickly covered with stiff bristly shafted feathers.

101. Heteroglaux Blewitti, *Hume, Str. F.* i., 467; *Ball op. cit.* ii, p. 382;. *Sharpe, Cat. Striges, B. M.* p. 141.—BLEWITT'S HETEROGLAUX.

Forehead, top and back of head, back and sides of the neck, scapulars and interscapulary region an uniform rather dark earth brown; feathers of the back of the neck and scapulars with a white bar about midway, but not visible when the feathers are in repose; lores, a line over the eye, another broad one under the eye, and a triangular patch immediately behind the eye white; bristles of the lores with the terminal halves black, longest bristles reach the tip of the bill. From the gape runs a stripe backwards, enveloping the whole of the ear coverts, in color a rather dark earth brown obsoletely barred with albescent; chin and throat and the sides of the lower mandible below the stripe pure white; a dark brown band across this, from the base of the lower mandible on one side to the base on the other; wings hair brown, darkest on the primaries, secondaries and their greater coverts, and more nearly concolorous with the scapulars, the lesser and median coverts and tertiaries. Quills with 4—5 conspicuous white spots on the outer webs, and corresponding imperfect bars on the inner webs, which are pale brown towards the tips, and pure white higher up; winglet almost blackish brown and similarly marked. Primary greater coverts similar, the rest of the greater and some of the median coverts with very large conspicuous white spots near the tips on the outer webs; lesser and most of the median coverts unspotted. Rump and upper tail coverts uniform brown. Tail hair brown, tipped white, and with three conspicuous transverse white bars, a fourth, less perfect one concealed by the upper tail coverts. Breast white, broadly tipped with hair brown. Abdomen, the tibial and tarsal plumes, toe feathers and lower tail coverts pure white; sides of abdomen, sides, and flanks broadly banded with hair brown.

Length.—9·5 inches; expanse 22·5; wing 5·8; tarsus 0·91. Bill straight from nostril to point 0·55; tail from vent 2·9.

Hab.—The Central Provinces. Frequents the densest forests of the Western portion of the Tributary Mehals.

Gen. **Ninox**.—*Hodgs.*

Head small; disc obsolete; bill short, cere large; wings long and pointed, the distance between it and the tip of the tail equal to, or less than the tarsus; distance between tip of first primary and that of the third equal to, or greater than the length of tarsus. Tarsus not twice the length of the middle toe, feathered toes clad with bristles.

102. Ninox lugubris, *Tickell, J. A. S. B.* ii. p. 573; *Sharpe, Cat. Striges*, p. 154; *Stray F.* vol. iv. p. 378; *Ball Avifauna Chota Nagpur S. F.* ii p. 383; *id.* iv. p. 285, 286, 374; *id.* v. 13. 413; *id.* ix. p. 42, 377; *Reid, B. Lucknow S. F.* x. p. 17; *id. Cat. B. Prov. Mus. Lucknow, Barnes, B. Bom. Pres.* p. 77. Ninox Nepalensis, *Hodgs. Madr. Journ.* v. p. 24, pl. 14. Otus lugubris, *Jerd. Madras Journ.* x. p. 87. Ninox scutellatus, *Blyth, J. A. S. B.* xvi. p. 5 iii; *Jerd. B. Ind.* i. p. 147; *Hume, Rough Notes*, p. 420.—The Brown Hawk Owl.

ASIO ACCIPITRINUS.

Ignatius Siqueira, Lith. *B. E. S. Press.*

NINOX AFFINIS, *Beavan.*

Mintern Bros. lith.

Adult female.—Above ashy brown, the head very much greyer, the sides of the face and neck being decidedly light grey; forehead, lores, forepart of cheeks and chin very conspicuously white, the loreal plumes with hair-like black shaft lines; feathers round the eyes greyish; scapulars marked externally with large bars of white, not very distinct and often half concealed; upper-wing coverts ashy brown like the back; the outer median coverts and the primary coverts deeper and more inclining to sepia brown; quills dark brown, a little deeper than the back, barred across with light ashy or greyish brown, inclining to whitish on the outer web of some of the primaries and inner secondaries, most of which are narrowly tipped with white; under surface of body white, the throat yellowish buff, streaked longitudinally with greyish brown; the chest broadly streaked with rufescent brown, the abdomen spotted, and each feather subterminally barred with the same; under-tail coverts pure white, basal ones with a few brownish bands; tail very pale greyish brown, inclining to white at the base and also tipped with white, and crossed with six blackish brown bands; leg feathers rufous brown, very slightly mottled with whitish cross markings; under-wing coverts white, barred across with dark brown, the outermost almost entirely brown, the edge of the wing white; the greater series dusky greyish brown barred with buffy white, thus resembling the inner lining of the wing, which is greyish brown barred with buffy on the inner web, these bars inclining to fulvous near the base; cere and bill green, the tip of the latter dusky; feet greyish or reddish yellow; iris bright golden yellow.

Length.—13·5 inches; wing 9·15; tail 5·7; tarsus 1·35.

The adult male is smaller than the female, and has only five blackish bands on the tail.

Length.—11·5 to 12·5 inches; wing 8·5; tail 5·3 to 5·6; tarsus 1·1 to 1·15; bill 1·0.

Hab.—The Indian Peninsula and the Himalayas, Punjab, N.-W. and Central Provinces, Oudh, Bengal, Concan, Deccan, and Nepaul.

103. Ninox affinis, *Beavan, Ibis,* 1867. pp. 316, 334; *Hume, Rough Notes,* p. 421; *Walden, Ibis,* 1874, p. 129, pl. v.; *Hume, Stray F.* 1874, p. 152; *Sharpe, Ibis,* 1875, p. 159; *Sharpe, Cat. B. Br. Mus.* ii., p. 155.—The ANDAMAN HAWK-OWL.

PLATE.

All the upper surface rufous brown; bases of the lax feathers slaty and showing through in many places; chin albescent; throat, breast, and abdomen rufous; breast and flanks albescent near the margins of the feathers, rufous at the tips and darker near the shaft; vent and under-tail coverts white; thighs, tarsi, and under-wing coverts rufous; toes covered with bristle-like feathers, albescent brown in colour. Quills brown, barred with darker brown and washed with rufous on the outer web; primary coverts sepia brown. Upper-tail coverts dark brown, barred with fulvous; tail dark brown with 5—6 bars of darker brown. Head and ear coverts greyish chocolate, nostrils and base of upper mandible covered with stiff, white, black-shafted, lax feathers; face and a part of the forehead albescent. Bill yellowish or yellowish horny, slaty towards the base; feet and irides pale yellow. Axillaries pale buff or orange chestnut, barred or not with brown.

Length.—10 inches; wing 6·6 to 6·9; tail 4·3 to 4·5; tarsus 1·0; bill from gape 0·8.

Hab.—Port Blair, the Andamans, British Burmah and the Nicobars.

Mr. Hume describes this species from specimens received from Col. Tytler and Mr. Sharpe from specimens in Lord Walden's collection. It is no doubt very closely allied to *N. scutulata,* but differs from it in some very material particulars, especially in the markings on the abdomen and flanks, which have a streaked appearance, also in the general tone of colouring of the upper parts and in size, being much smaller (10 inches against 12·5). It is said to affect heavy forests and jungles. Mr. Davison says (*S. F.* ii. 153), he saw a bird fly off a stump, hover in front of a frond of a cocoanut palm for about four or five seconds and return to its original perch, from which it would take short circular flights, dart straight up, and again swoop almost to the ground, hawking like a *Caprimulgus,* and capturing small moths.

104. Ninox scutulata, *Raffl. Tr. Linn. Soc.* xiii. p. 280; *Jerd. B. Ind.* i. p. 147; *Armstrong, Str. F.* iv. p. 373; *Hume, Rough Notes,* p. 420; *Sharpe, Cat. B. Br. Mus.,* ii. p. 156; *Bl. and Walden B. Burmah,* p. 67; *Hume, Str. F.* viii. p. 84; *Kelham Ibis,* 1881, p. 37. Athene scutulata, *Gray, Gen. B.* i. p. 35; *Wall. Ibis,* 1868, p. 22. Ninox hirsutus, (*Tem.*), *Hume S. F.* iii. p. 40; *id.,* 1874, pp. 141. 469, *et* 1875, p. 441. Ninox Burmanica, *Hume, S. F.* iv. p. 285; *Hume* and *Davison S. F.* vi. p. 40; viii. p. 84; ix. p. 245. Ninox innominata, *Hume, Str. F.* iv. p. 286; v. p. 16.—The Brown Hawk-Owl.

Head, sides of the face and also of the neck chocolate brown; forehead, lores and chin whitish with mesial dark streaks. The whole upper surface, wing coverts and tertiaries dark chocolate brown, the scapulars with large concealed white spots; primaries and secondaries dark brown, barred with white on the inner webs; a few of the primaries edged with rufous; throat rufous streaked with brown; breast rufous chocolate, each feather edged with white; rest of under surface rufous chocolate, barred with white. Tail ashy brown, paler at tip and with 5—6 dark bars, the basal one concealed. Under-tail coverts pure white; under-wing coverts and axillaries rufous, barred with white; edge of the wing whitish.

Irides bright yellow; cere dull green; bill bluish black; culmen and tip of lower mandible yellowish green; feet pale yellow.

NINOX OBSCURA.

Mintern Bros lith.

Length.—11 to 12·5 inches; wing 8 to 8·75; tail 4 to 5·5; tarsus 1·1 to 1·15.

Hab.—Rare in the Punjab, and N.-W. Provinces, also in Rajpootana and the Deccan. Common in all the more wooded countries, as the Carnatic, the Malabar and Rutnagherry coasts and Ceylon; also in Central India, Lower Bengal and the Himalayas, extending through Assam, Burmah, Malaya to Nepaul, and to China and Japan. The Brown Hawk-Owl frequents the skirts of dense forests. It is nocturnal in its habits, issuing forth at dusk. It seats itself generally on stumps of dead trees whence it swoops, or rather skims along the surface of the ground or water in search of insects, which are its chief food; Jerdon says, and occasionally mice or reptiles. It has a peculiar call which it frequently utters at night, resembling, as Tickell says, the cries of a strangling cat; Buchanan likens it to the cry of a hare when caught by hounds, and Elliott, "the cries of a child." Oates says its note resembles the word *Whoo-wuk*, repeated several times.

Nothing is known of its nidification.

105. Ninox obscura, *Hume, Str. F.* i. pp. 11, 421; *Ball, Str. F.* i. p. 55; *id. J. A. S. B.* xxxix. 1870, p. 240; *Walden, Ibis,* 1874, p. 129, pl. iv; *Hume, Str. F.* ii. p. 153; *Sharpe, Ibis,* 1875, p. 258; *id. Cat. Striges, B. M.* p. 177; *Gurney, Ibis,* 1854, p. 171.

PLATE.

Lores and forehead, yellowish white; tips of bristles in front of and below the eye black; cheeks, ear coverts and sides of neck deep chocolate brown; chin whitish. Whole upper surface a rich, uniform chocolate brown, darker on the head and nape; throat yellowish white with a rufous brown patch; rest of under surface of body reddish or rufous chocolate, darker on the fore-neck and breast, paler on the flanks and abdomen, the former with some imperfect, and concealed fulvous bars or spots. Under-tail coverts buffy white, barred with dark brown; under-wing coverts like the back, with a rufescent tinge in some specimens. Primaries like the back, but margined on the outer web with buffy white or whity brown, their coverts blackish; tail dark brown narrowly tipped with whitish, and with 3—4 narrow bars of yellowish brown. Bristles on the sides of the toes dark brown. Cere and culmen greenish slate; iris bright yellow; feet pale yellow; claws black.

Length.—11 to 12 inches; wing 7·55 to 8·5; tail 4·75 to 5; tarsus 1 to 1·1; bill at front ·75.

Hab.—The Islands of the Bay of Bengal, Nicobars, Port Blair, and the Andamans.

Mr. Gurney notices this species in his article on "Eastern Owls," and says it bears a curious similarity in the nearly uniform fuscous colouration of its under parts to the more southern *N. Theomacha,* from which it is readily distinguishable by its larger size and darker abdomen, as well as by the tail having 4—5 dark (3—4 yellowish white) bars and also bearing a white tip.

Lord Walden in the *Ibis* for 1874, p. 129, notes, that the fourth primary of a ♂ from South Andamans, slightly exceeds the 3rd and is the longest; the third exceeds the 5th; and Mr. Gurney, from examination of three specimens (1 ♂ and 2 ♀ ♀) also from the same locality, remarks that the male bird exhibits the curious peculiarity of being longer in the wing than the two females (8·80 inches against 8·20 and 8·40 inches of the two females).

Mr. Davison, the Curator of Mr. Hume's Museum, and one of the most energetic and experienced collectors in India, secured two specimens of this bird at Port Monat, S. Andamans. He says, he knows next to nothing about the habits of the species, and adds that the first specimen he saw flitted by him and settled on a small tree close to the water's edge. On the following evening (15th April), he secured a second specimen which was seated on the stump of a tree. It rose as he approached, took a long sailing circular flight and returned to its perch. The hoot, he says, is a peculiar one, quite unlike that attributed to the Common Hawk-Owl. It is a low, subdued, but clear double note.

Gen.—**Glaucidium**.—*Boie.*

Nostrils tubular in the middle of a swollen cere; wing short and rounded, the distance between it and the tip of tail much greater than the length of the tarsus, which is feathered and is as long as the mid toe; 1st quill shorter than the next four, emarginate; 4th and 5th about equal. Tail rounded.

106. Glaucidium brodiei, *Burton, P. Z. S.*, 1835, p. 152; *Schl. Mus. P. B. Striges*, p. 38; *Jerd. B. Ind.* i. p. 146, No. 80; *Hume, Rough Notes*, ii. p. 417; *Sharpe, Ibis*, 1875, p. 259; *Str. F.* vi. 39; ix 148. Athene brodiei, *Blyth, J. A. S. B.* xi. p. 163; *Gould, B. Asia* pl. xxii; *Oates, B British Burmah*, ii. p. 159.—The Collared Pigmy Owlet.

Head, back, wings and tail dusky brown, banded rather broadly on the head and narrowly on the back with white or fulvous white; forehead with small spots of the same. Hind neck with a fulvous collar and a patch of black on each side. A white shoulder patch formed by the white markings on the outer web of the scapulars. Primaries dark brown with notches of white on the outer web; secondaries the same, the bars on the inner ones larger. Upper-tail coverts dark brown, barred and spotted with white or fulvous white. Tail tipped with whitish and with 7—8 bars across. Lores and supercilium white, the lores intermixed with black bristly feathers. Chin and fore neck white, separated by a dark band; rest of under surface brown with pale fulvous or white bars; under-wing coverts white, in some tinged yellowish with some few brown markings near the edge of the wing. Bill pale greenish yellow; toes a deeper yellow; irides bright pale yellow.

Length.—6·5 to 7 inches; wing 3·45 to 3·75; tail 2·75 to 2·8; tarsus 0·8.

Hab.—Northern India, the Punjab, N.-W. Provinces, Bengal, Assam, the Himalayas, and Nepaul. Besides the latter it is noted from Mussoorie and Darjeeling, also from Amherst, Mergui and Tennaserim, from Tavoy northwards.

Mr. Hume says this pretty little owlet though nocturnal in its habits is very watchful by day; when seated motionless it appears as a knot or excrescence on the branch, but "point in its direction," or the moment your eyes are on it, it is aware that it has been recognized and darts away. It is said to be as daring as the Falconets. Breeds during May and June, making little or no nest in the hollow of trees. Nest usually lined with feathers. Eggs 3—4, nearly round, and pure white. Feeds on young birds, mice, and insects. The flight of this bird, Mr. Thompson says, is rapid and vigorous. *Glaucidium castaneonotum, Bly.*, occurs in Ceylon, and may be found in Travancore or some part of Southern India. *G. castonopterum*, a Javan species, is said to occur in Tennaserim, but of this there is no reliable information, and Mr. Hume surmises that if such a bird should be found in British Burmah, it will prove a distinct species. The coloration of the Javan bird is a deep chestnut with the usual barrings and a chestnut streaked abdomen. Wing 5·7 inches.

107. Glaucidium radiatum, *Tick. J. A. S. B.* ii. p. 572; *Sharpe, Ibis*, 1876, p. 259; *Walden, Ibis*, vol. vi. 1876, p. 343; *Sharpe, Cat. Striges B. M.* p. 217. Athene radiata, *Bly. J. A. S. B.* xv. p. 281; *Jerd. B. Ind.* i. 143, No. 77; *Ball Str.* ii. p. 383; *Str. F.* iv. 373; vi. 36; *Hume, Rough Notes*, ii. p. 409; *id. Nests and Eggs Ind. B.* i. p. 70; *Vidal, B. South Concan, Str. F.* p. 39.—The JUNGLE OWLET.

Above dusky brown, barred with rufous buff or rufescent whitish, rather broader on the hind neck; outer web of scapulars whitish with a few dusky spots or bars. Wing coverts rufescent, the bars broader than on the back. Edge of the wing white. Some of the outer webs of the greater coverts with large white spots; primaries and their coverts and secondaries dark brown, banded with rufous, the bands on the secondaries narrower than those on the primaries; tail dark brown *narrowly tipped with whitish and with eight narrow white bands;* chin, throat, and cheeks whitish; rest of under surface barred, except the centre of the body, which is barred transversely with dusky and whitish, the bars on the sides of the breast rather fulvous. Under-tail coverts white, with brown spots. Bill and feet greenish horny; iris golden yellow; claws dusky.

Length.—8 to 8·5 inches; wing 4·9 to 5; tail 2·85 to 3; tarsus 1·0.

Hab.—India generally, from the Himalayas southwards through the Peninsula, but not extending far below the Neilgherries. Recorded from the N.-W. Provinces, Bengal, the Central Provinces, the Concan, Malabar and Travancore, also Rutnagherry, South India on the Neilgherries, British Burmah (?) and Nepaul. Whether this species is distinct from *Malabaricum* or not, has not been quite settled. Much has been written on the various phases of plumage of both these species, and it is argued that this is due to climatic influence. Sharpe, however, keeps the northern and southern forms distinct, calling *Malabaricum* a sub-species of *radiata*. I have not had a sufficient number of specimens of the two forms, and hence cannot give an opinion. I follow Sharpe in keeping both separate till some one with enough materials will decide the points raised.

The Jungle Owlet breeds in the early part of the summer in holes of trees, during April, May, and June.

The eggs are pure white, round, and measure 1·2 by 1·0. The young are generally fully fledged by the end of June. It is easily tamed, and in confinement will eat readily of raw or cooked meat, insects, frogs, &c. Both adults and young are excessively noisy, and when teased make a peculiar hissing chattering tremulous noise. The cry, according to Mr. R. Thompson, is a too-roo-roo-roo, &c., drawn out to a considerable length, and resembles that of the Common Goanna or Monitor Lizard.

108. Glaucidium malabaricum, *Bly. J. A. S. B.* xv. p. 280, *et.* xix. p. 500; *Jerd. B. India,* I. p. 144, No. 78; *Hume, Rough Notes,* ii. p. 413; *Sharpe, Ibis,* 1875, pp. 6, 259; *id, Cat. Striges. B. M.* p. 218. Athene castanoptera, *Bly. J. A. S. B.* xiv. p. 184. *Str. F.* iv. 372; v. 201.—The MALABAR OWLET.

Head, neck, and interscapulars uniform lightish rufous with narrow close dusky bars; wings the same, but the colour deeper and the bands broader; primaries dark rufous, the first three barred throughout with dusky, the rest mostly unspotted or obscurely banded at the base and distinctly at the tip; secondaries barred throughout with rufous and dusky; outermost scapulars with large white spots forming a shoulder patch. Under surface of body barred throughout with rufous and dusky on the breast and dusky and white on the belly and flanks. Vent and under-tail coverts pure or buffy white; upper-tail coverts dusky barred with white; tail dusky tipped with white and crossed with nine other bars of white. Under-wing coverts white with a few brown markings near the edge of the wing; the greater series with dusky tips, tibial and tarsal feathers white, with a few remains of dark bars. Bill and claws black; irides yellow.

Length.—7·8 to 8 inches; wing 4·5 to 4·8; tail 2·5 to 2·9; tarsus 0·9.

Hab.—Southern India. Recorded from the Malabar Coast, Cochin, Wynaad, Southern Mysore, Travancore, Madras and the Concan.

Habits like the last.

Mr. Frank Bourdillon, writing to Mr. Hume, says, this is a resident in Travancore, preferring the low jungles, though he has often heard one as high as 2,500 feet in heavy jungle. Feeds during the hour after sunrise and before sunset. Mr. Hume observes that all the specimens got from Travancore are typical *Malabaricum* with the upper parts strongly ferruginous.

109. Glaucidium cuculoides, *Gould, Cent. Him. B.* pl. 4; *Sharpe, Ibis,* 1875, p. 259; *id. Cat. B. Br. Mus.* ii. p. 219; *Hume, and Dav. S. F.* vi. p. 37; *Hume, Str. F.* viii. p. 84; *Bingham, Str. F.* ix. p. 148; *Oates, Str. F.* x. p. 183; *id. B. Br. Burmah,* ii, p. 162. Noctua cuculoides, *Vig, P. Z. S.,* 1831, p. 8. Athene cuculoides, *Jerd. B. Ind.,* i. p. 145, No. 79; *Hume Rough Notes,* ii. p. 414; *id. Nests and Eggs,* p. 71; *id. Str. F.* iii. p. 39; *Wardlaw-Ramsay, Ibis,* 1887, p. 454; *Marshall, B. Chumba, N.-W. Himalaya,* p. 408.—The LARGE-BARRED OWLET.

Whole upper plumage and wings brown, closely barred all over with ochraceous; ear coverts, sides of the neck, a band across the throat and the whole breast similarly banded. A broad moustachial band reaching to the ear coverts, and a large patch on the foreneck white; outer webs of some of the scapulars and outermost wing coverts with large patches of white; centre of abdomen, vent and under-tail coverts white, the sides of the former and flanks streaked with rufous; axillaries and under-wing coverts pale buff. The latter with a few brown streaks; tail blackish, tipped with white *and with six bars of the same colour*; thighs in front rufous; iris bright yellow; eyelids greenish plumbeous; cere brown; bill pale green, the tip of the upper mandible yellow. Legs greenish yellow; claws brown.

Length.—8·7 to 8·9 inches; wing 5·7 to 5·8; tail 3·2 to 3·8; tarsus 1 to 1·02; bill from gape 0·9. Females larger.

Hab.—The Himalayas to Nepaul, extending to Burmah and Siam. Found in Assam, Arracan, and Tenasserim, and also in China. Recorded from the Punjab, N.-W. Provinces, Bengal, the Central Provinces, British Burmah, and Nepaul. Spread all over British Burmah and along the lower ranges of the Himalayas, and generally throughout Northern India. Breeds in the Himalayas from March to May, laying 3—4 eggs, which are pure white and glossy. In shape almost spherical to broad ovals, and measure from 1·38 to 1·48 × 1·17 to 1·24 inches. The nests are made in holes of trees, without any lining. The species inhabits forests, gardens, and bamboo groves or large orchards. *G. Whitelyi* is another species found as yet only in Japan and China, and is believed to occur in Burmah.

Sub-Family II.—SYRNIINÆ.—HOOTING OWLS.

Wings moderate, somewhat rounded; tarsus feathered. Head larger than in the last; ear conch larger than the eye, with large operculum shutting in the ear; facial disk distinct; wings long; 2nd and 3rd quills longest.

Gen. Asio.—*Briss.*

Characters, same as those of the Sub-Family.

110. Asio otus, *Lin. S. N.* i. p. 132; *Sharpe, Cat. Striges*, p. 227. Otus vulgaris, *Fleming, Brit. An.* p. 56; *Gray, Gen. B.* i. p. 40; *Gould. B. Eur.* pl. 39; *Jerd. Birds Ind.* i. p. 125, No. 67; *Loche Exp. Sci. Alger. Ois.* p. 96; *Hume, Rough Notes*, ii. p. 363; *Murray, Hdbk., Zool., &c., Sind*, p. 121. *Murray Vert. Zool. Sind*, p. 99.—Otus communis, *Less. Traité.* p. 110.—The Long-eared Owl.

Head, neck, and breast yellowish brown, or tawny yellow, with mesial dark brown longitudinal streaks to the feathers, many of which are margined whitish and pencilled with dusky brown; ear-tufts 1—1½ inch, brownish black in the middle, edged tawny, the upper edge of the inner web whitish; forehead finely mottled, whitish, dusky and ferruginous; face dusky white with hair-like lines of black; feathers round the eye blackish; ear coverts yellowish, tipped with dusky brown; facial ruff white, the feathers tipped with black; chin white; throat with stiff feathers in continuation of the ruff, spotted and centred with dark brown; rest of under surface orange-buff, sometimes whitish, with a broad mesial streak of dark brown, the feathers of the abdomen having also dusky frecklings. Under-wing coverts buffy or light tawny, a few of the feathers narrowly lined with brown. Back dusky brown, much mottled with orange-buff and whitish; wing coverts and scapulars with a large oval spot on the outer web. Edge of wing white; wing underneath yellowish white, the dark bars on the inner webs distinct. Primaries dusky brown, with bars of tawny or reddish yellow, the tawny interspaces towards the tips of the feathers narrow, and vermiculated with brown; the tips entirely brown. Secondaries greyish white, barred with dusky; the margins of the inner webs buffy; upper-tail coverts yellowish brown, edged and vermiculated with dusky brown. Upper-tail coverts white, the shafts towards the tips of some of the feathers with a broad dusky spot. Tail tawny buff or yellowish brown, crossed by seven bands of dark brown and vermiculated near the tip, the outer feathers with ten narrow dark brown bands. Tarsal plumes tawny or yellowish buff and unspotted. Bill of a dusky horn colour. Irides orange yellow.

Length.—13·5 to 14 inches; wing 11·75; tail 6; tarsus 1·6.

Hab.—Throughout Europe, across Siberia to Japan and China (Sharpe); the Himalayas from Nepaul to Cashmere, N.-W. Provinces, the Punjab and Afghanistan. It it also recorded from Eastern Turkistan, N. Africa and Egypt. In Sind it is a winter visitant. Nothing is known of the breeding of this species in India. Mr. Hume, however, in *Rough Notes*, says he has reason to believe it is a permanent resident of the forests of the interior of the Himalayas. Yarrell and others assert that it does not make a nest for itself, but occupies the deserted habitation of some other bird, as the crow, ringdove,

&c. The eggs are four in number, white, oval and smooth, 1·7 by 1·29. The young are hatched by the end of April.

111. Asio accipitrinus, *Pall. Reis. Russ. Reichs.* i. p. 455; *Sharpe, Cat. Striges,* p. 225. Strix brachyotus, *Forst. Phil. Trans.* lxii. p. 384; *Gm. S. N.* i. p. 289. Otus brachyotus, *Steph. Gen. Zool.* xiii. pl. 2, p. 57; *Jerd. B. Ind.* i. p. 127, No. 68; *Gurney, Ibis,* 1868, p. 150; *Hume, Rough Notes,* ii. p. 364; *Murray, Zool., &c., Sind,* p. 118. Asio brachyotus, *McGill. Br. B.* iii. p. 461. Asio accipitrinus, *Newt. Ed. Yarr. Brit. B. Shelley, B. Egypt.*—THE SHORT-EARED OWL.

PLATE.

Adult.—Head, neck and back dark brown, the feathers broadly margined with ochraceous buff; the scapulars much paler on their outer margins, and with brown irregular markings, which form ovate spots of whitish buff. Secondaries brown, mottled with ochraceous buff and tipped and margined on the inner web with whitish buff; primary coverts dark brown with a few ochraceous spots. Quills ochraceous buff, tipped whitish and with dark brown bands, which are distinct on both webs. Upper-tail coverts ochraceous, faintly edged with a darker shade; under-tail coverts pale fulvous, with a mesial dark streak on some of the feathers; tarsal plumes unspotted ochraceous. Ear-tufts 0·5 inch long; chin whitish, in some specimens buffy. Ruff whitish, or whitish buff, and speckled with spots of brown; plumes above the eye whitish buff, with mesial dark brown streaks; facial aspect dull white, the lores brownish; feathers round the eye black; ear coverts ochraceous, with narrow black shaft-lines. Breast and entire under parts ochraceous buff streaked with dark brown mesially, these streaks narrowing into linear shaft lines on the lower breast and abdomen. Under-wing coverts buffy white, with a few dark streaks. Tail dark brown, whitish at tip, and with 6 bars of ochraceous buff mottled with brown. Cere and bill brownish black.

Length.—14 to 15 inches; wing 13; tail 5 to 6; tarsus 1·75. *Female, length*—15·5 inches; wing 12·5; tail 6·7; tarsus 1·85.

Hab.—Throughout Europe, and nearly all India; it occurs in Beloochistan, Persia, Egypt, East Turkistan, Gilgit (Cashmere) and Nepaul; also in the Punjab, N.-W. Provinces, Oudh, Bengal, Central and Southern India, Kutch, Guzerat, Rajputana, the Concan and Deccan. In Sind it is a winter visitant, and is not uncommon, especially in the Northern and Central parts, keeping to low jungle and long grass.

This is another species of whose breeding in India nothing is known. In England it is known to lay its eggs on the ground in long grass. Eggs 3—4 in number, smooth and white, 1·67 + 1·29 inches. Breeds in April and May. In India it is found in long grass. It is a migrant coming in about the beginning of winter.

Gen. **Syrnium**.—*Savigny*.

Head not so large as in the *Striges*. No ear-tufts; toes thickly feathered, with hair-like bristles or entirely bare; feet stout. Ears moderately large and operculate.

112. Syrnium Butleri, *Asio Butleri, Hume, Str. F.* vii. 1878, p. 316; *Tristram, Ibis,* 1880, p. 245.—THE MEKRAN WOOD-OWL.

Chin, cheeks, entire space inside the ruff white, tinged fawny below and behind the eye; some few of the loral bristles dark-shafted towards their tips, but inconspicuously so; feathers of the ruff across the throat and as far as opposite the gape, are grey brown, margined throughout their length pretty broadly, and tipped with cream colour, more rufescent and fawny towards the tips; the rest of the feathers of the ruff from gape round and behind the eye are very peculiar; when examined closely they are rather pale, French grey on one surface, warm brown on the other, and obscurely tipped with rufescent fawn; forehead, crown, occiput and nape pale rufescent fawn obscurely mottled with dusky brown; when the feathers are closely examined, the basal portions are bluish dusky, the rest pale rufescent fawn or buff with an obscure ill-defined dusky brown bar, some little distance from the tip, and another imperfect bar or spot of the same colour near the tip; lesser-wing coverts from the carpal joint uniform smoky brown, somewhat intermediate between a hair brown and an earth brown; scapulars, back, median and greater-wing coverts dull pale rufescent fawn, clouded and streaked with brown, most of the secondary, median and greater coverts having more or less pure white spots or blotches on the outer webs near the tips. First primary almost uniform brown, edged creamy white on the outer web, and a mottling of the same towards the middle of the inner web near the base; rest of the quills lighter brown, regularly barred with pale fawn colour, duller and shaded with grey brown on the inner webs towards the tips becoming white away from the shaft towards the bases; tail tipped with nearly pure white, and exactly of the same character as the quills, but the bars on the two central feathers are reduced to mere blotches on either side of the shaft; breast and abdomen creamy, the sides of the breast with a few indistinct transverse dusky bands, and those of the latter with narrow brown shaft stripes. Entire wing-lining, basal portions of the quills, vent, lower-tail coverts, legs and feet pure white; lower surface of the tail grey brown barred with white.

Bill and cere blackish horny; culmen and tips of both mandibles pale yellowish horny; feet greenish olive.

Length.—14 inches; wing 9·95; tail 6; tarsus 2·05; bill from gape 2·0; from margin of cere to point 0·6.

Hab.—Oormara on the Mekran Coast.

This bird has been included in the Indian Avifauna owing to the country in which it was first discovered, being under British Administration. Oormara is only about 60 miles from Kurrachee, the seaport of Scinde, and it is not unlikely it may be found to occur there. Of its habits and nidification nothing is known.

113. Syrnium nivicolum, *Hodgs. in Gray's Zool. Misc.* p. 82; *Blyth, J. A. S. B.* xix. pp. 185, 550; *Jerd. B., Ind.* i. p. 124, No. 66; *Hume, Rough Notes,* ii. p. 359; *Sharpe, Cat. Striges,* iii. p. 250.—THE HIMALAYAN WOOD-OWL.

Above mottled dark brown and fulvous, the outer webs of the scapulars white or with a fulvous tinge, and forming a conspicuous shoulder patch. Quills brown with whitish interrupted bands; tail brown with 8—9 bars of light brown marbled towards the tips; sides of the neck and eyebrows also with a good deal of white; chin whitish; disc greyish mottled with brown, slightly darker round the eyes; ruff with a few brown markings; lower parts mottled with brown, white and fulvous bars and lines; tarsal feathers narrowly barred brown, and the toes feathered to nearly the tips, where there are 2—3 moderate transverse scales. Irides dark brown; bill pale fleshy yellow; cere faintly brown.

Length.—16 to 18 inches; wing 11 to 12·7; tail 7 to 7·7; tarsus 2 to 2·15.

Hab.—The Punjab, N.-W. Provinces, and from Murree (the Himalayas), extending into Western China. Mr. Hume has had it from Darjeeling and Kotegurh, and Capt. Marshall got one at Kussowlie, at a height of only 5,000 feet above the sea.

The species is allied to the European *S. Aluco*; the difference is in the smaller size of *Aluco*, and the proportionally larger and stronger bill and claws of the Indian species.

Nothing appears to be known of its nidification.

114. Syrnium sinense, *Lath. Ind. Orn. Supp.* p. xvi. Strix seloputo, *Horsf. Trans. Lin. Socy.* xiii. p. 140. Strix pagodarum, *Tem.* pl. col. 230. Bulaca sinense, *Hume, Rough Notes,* ii. p. 357. Syrnium sinense, *Sharpe, Cat. Striges, B. Mus.* ii. p. 261; *Hume, S. F.* iii. p. 37; *id. and Davison S. F.* vi. p. 28; *Oates, S. F.* vii. p. 45; *Hume, S. F.* viii. p. 83; *Bingham, S. F.* ix. p. 146; *Oates, S. F.* x. p. 182; *id. B. British Burmah,* ii. p. 164.—THE MALAYAN WOOD-OWL.

Forehead, chin, and facial disc rather bright ferruginous without marks; lower edge of disc whitish; a large patch on the throat pure white; a space between this patch and the chin ferruginous; ear coverts black, barred slightly at the lower end with ferruginous; top of head and neck very dark chocolate brown, each feather with two white spots on either web, the spots becoming larger as they recede from the front of the head; sides of the neck darker, the spots turning into bars; the back, scapulars, rump and upper-wing coverts chocolate brown, paler than on the head; the back with large white bars; the lesser-wing coverts with a few white spots; the greater-wing coverts with large white spots on both webs; the rump barred with white; the scapulars with large bar-like drops of white; the exterior feathers, which are usually concealed, being almost entirely white, with ferruginous brown bars; primary coverts, plain rufous brown, the general colour of the wings much the same as that of the upper plumage, but duller; the primaries and secondaries barred with fulvous on both webs, except on the first four primaries, where the outer webs are barred with whitish; the tertiaries broadly barred with white, turning to rufous bars at the bases of the feathers; tail much the same tint as the back, the central rectrices very sparsely barred with whitish (probably disappearing with age), the others barred narrowly on the outer and broadly on the inner web with fulvescent white; all the rectrices tipped with dull white; the lower plumage with the under-wing coverts white with numerous bars of dark brown; bases of the feathers which are very much decomposed and bright fulvous in colour, show through the plumage in patches; the bars on the thighs narrower and more numerous.

In the young the whole upper plumage is white, barred with chocolate brown, the tips to the tail feathers very white and broad; the whole lower plumage white, closely barred with brown; thighs plain fulvous white; facial disc as in the adult.

Bill and cere dark horny brown; the mouth flesh colour; iris dark brown; edges of the eyelids pink; toes brown; claws dark horn.

Length.—18 to 20·5 inches; tail 7·6 to 9; wing 14·4 to 15·6; tarsus 2·15 to 2·3; bill from gape 1·5 inches.

Hab.—British Burmah, Java, Siam, Cochin-China, Borneo, and Penang; distributed over Pegu and Tennaserim. Common near Kyrikpadien and the towns of Pegu and Rangoon. Capt. Fielden procured some at Thayetmyo, and Mr. Davison and others in the extreme south of Tennasserim, while Capt. Bingham heard its note in the Thoongyeen Valley. According to Oates the species frequents ever green forests and groves of trees near pagodas and ruined temples or monasteries. It is strictly nocturnal in its habits, and feeds principally on insects. During the day it roosts on a high branch well protected by leaves. Of its eggs I have no record, but Oates says he took the young birds in March, and that the eggs appear to be deposited in a roomy fork of some large tree, at no great height from the ground.

115. Syrnium ocellatum, *Less. Rev. Zool.* 1839, p. 289; *Gould, B. Asia* pt. xxii.; *Sharpe, Cat. Striges*, ii. p. 263. Bulaca ocellata, *Hume, Rough Notes*, ii, p. 383; *id. Nests and Eggs, Ind. B.* p. 61. Syrnium sinense, *Blyth, J. A. S. B.* xi. p. 162; *Jerd. B. Ind.* i. p. 123. Bulaca sinensis, *Gray, Cat. Acc.* 1844, p. 43; *Blyth, Ibis*, 1865, p. 29.—The Mottled Wood-Owl.

General colour above rufous-orange, the feathers of the crown and hind-neck mottled with black and white, each feather having a double white spot at the tip, preceded by a distinct black bar; back greyer, each feather being orange at the base, but for the terminal half crossed with distinct zigzag bars of dark brown, the interspaces being white, thickly mottled with brown vermiculations; the scapulars externally white, crossed with narrow brown bars, forming a conspicuous shoulder patch; wing coverts coloured like the back and mottled with grey in the same manner, the greater series rather whiter than the rest; primary coverts dark brown with a few zigzag markings of ashy grey on the outer web. Primaries dark brown, barred across with lighter brown, these bars nearly obsolete on the inner web and represented by an ashy spot on the outer one, the spots clouded and obscured by brown vermiculations, the inner webs orange for the basal half with brown cross bars; secondaries for the most part ashy white like the back, vermiculated with brown; the tips of the feathers brown, crossed in the same way with ashy whitish bars, there being altogether 8—9 in number on the tail; sides of the face greyish-white, mottled all over with minute black bars, the ear coverts orange in the centre; facial ruff dark chocolate brown, many of the feathers spotted with white, those on the lower parts inclining to orange and the plumes under the chin being white with narrow black bars, in both instances assimilating to the adjacent parts of the body; chin and the patch on the fore-neck white, the plumes on the latter with a few narrow terminal bars of dark brown; rest of under surface white, narrowly barred with dark brown, the whole of the feathers orange at base, this colour showing conspicuously on the chest; leg feathers as well as under-wing and tail coverts white, barred with dark brown; the greater series of under-wing coverts blackish with light. orange-buff bases, thus resembling the inner lining of the wing which is orange-buff for the greater part of the inner webs of the feathers, the ends being brown barred across with lighter brown; bill horny black, pale and greyish on lower mandible; cere dingy, a dirty pinkish, brownish or yellowish horny. Varies a good deal. Bare part of toes pale greenish brown; soles yellowish white; iris brown, light in some species, and deep or dark in others. (Hume.)

Length.—17·9 to 21 inches; wing 13·0 to 13·9; tail 7·4 to 8·5; tarsus 2·05 to 2·4.

Hab.—Throughout the greater part of India, east of the Sutlej, and of the Indus below its junction with the former, and west of the Ganges. It is recorded from the Punjab, N.-W. Provinces, Central and Southern India, the sub-Himalayan Valleys, the Central Provinces, Kutch, Kattiawar, Guzerat, Mount Aboo, the Concans and Deccan. According to Jerdon in the Carnatic, in parts of Mysore and the forests of Malabar, but not in Ceylon nor in Lower Bengal.

This beautifully plumaged species is only found in well-wooded districts at no great elevation. Its hoot is loud, harsh and resonant. Of its nidification little is known. The normal number of eggs is two, deposited, like as in the previous species, in large depressions or in the fork of trees, generally peepul or mango at about from 10 to 20 feet from the ground. There is no nest, so to speak, but a little dry touchwood, and a few dead leaves. The eggs are round, oval, white, and in some instances with a delicate creamy tinge. In length they vary from 1·94 to 2·1 inches and in breadth from 1·63 to 1·75. The months in which the young are hatched are generally April and May, sometimes at the end of March. Lieut. Barnes, however, says he took full fledged nestlings from a large hole in a tree at Saugor, Central Provinces, as early as the 22nd February.

116. Syrnium newarense, *Hodgs. Asiat. Res.* xix. p. 168; *Hume, Rough Notes,* ii. p. 348; *id. Nests and Eggs, Ind. B.* p. 60; *Jerd. B. Ind.* i. p. 122, No. 64.—THE NEPAUL BROWN WOOD-OWL.

Upper parts rich brown, quill and tail feathers barred whity brown, under surface pale rusty, with numerous narrow brown bands; inner scapulars the same; throat white; rump and upper-tail coverts also faintly barred; forehead, crown and occiput deep blackish brown; the stiff bristle-like feathers in front and above the angle of the eyes dark-shafted; legs and feet densely feathered to the last joint of the toes; bill greenish horny, bluish towards base; cere (?) plumbeous.

Length.—21·5 to 24 inches (28 ? *Sharpe*); wing 15·2 to 15·5; tail 9·75 to 10·75; tarsus 2·75 to 3.

Hab.—N.-W. Provinces, the Himalayas, and Nepaul. Recorded from Simla, Koteghur, B. Burmah (?), Bussahir, Kumaon, and the Neilgherries (?)

This species, Mr. Hume says, so far as he knows, lays in May. He says, "contrary to what might have been expected, the nest was placed on a shelf projecting from the face of a low precipice; immediately above it projected a large point of rock from which depended a perfect curtain of bushes which reached the tops of the trees growing at the foot of the precipice. The nest, according to the Paharees, with Mr. Hume, was composed of sticks with a few feathers intermingled. The nest contained (6th June), three very young birds. Mr. Hume like other Ornithologists, who have of late years worked at the subject, doubts the distinctness of this species from *S. indranee.* The following remarks are his, and the quotations too from his invaluable Scrap-book, which gives some very material information in regard to measurements of such of the specimens of this species in his possession, from which it will be seen that the dimensions very little exceed those given by Dr. Jerdon for *Indranee,* and fall short of those which he gives for *Newarensis.* A Burmese *skin* differed in none of its dimensions by more than a mere fraction from the skin of an old and a young male; he adds that notwithstanding Mr. Blyth's opinion." I nevertheless still hold, that the distinction of size is, *to say the least*, neither so constant nor so material as has been asserted, and has by no means been so established as to render (if Dr. Jerdon's measurements of the Southern race are reliable), a specific separation of the Northern and Southern birds, *certainly* requisite. Dr. Jerdon gives the wing of Southern species at from 13 to 14 inches.

The Burmese bird has them...	14·8	,,
The two Simla specimens (Young)........ ...	15·2	,,
The adult	15·5	,,
A Bussahir specimen	16·2	,,
A large Kumaon one............................	16·7	,,

While Dr. Stohckza wrote to say, that a specimen 21 inches in length had wings a little over 18 inches, and a Himalayan specimen from Baron Hugel was decidedly smaller, the wing measuring 15 inches. The species affects well-wooded localities, but so far as Mr. Hume's experience goes, affects small precipices on the sides of wooded hills. It is like *sinense*, strictly nocturnal in its habits, and feeds on large insects.

I have not sufficient material to give an opinion either way; Mr. Sharpe too has not given his opinion, and has placed *S. indranee* as an inhabitant of the Peniusula of India, Ceylon and the Malayan Peninsula.

With Mr. A. O. Hume's large Museum at his elbows, it is hoped, the question will soon be worked out. In the meantime it would be well to keep Sykes' *Indranee* as a distinct species.

117. Syrnium indranee, *Sykes, P. Z. S.* 1832, p. 82; *Horsf. and Moore, Cat. B. M. E. I. Co.* i. p. 83; *Jerd. B. Ind.* i. p. 121, No. 63; *Holdsw, P. Z. S.* 1872, p. 415; *Hume, Str. F.* 1873, p. 429; *Legge, Str. F.* 1874, p. 349; *Sharpe, Cat. B. Br. M.* p. 282. Bulaca indranee, (*Kaup,*) *Hume, Rough Notes*, ii. p. 347.—THE SOUTHERN WOOD-OWL.

Above hair brown darkest on the head and neck; the greater coverts, scapulars, and tertiaries banded with white, the outer scapulars being almost white with brown bars; rump and upper-tail coverts also faintly barred with fulvous; quills brown, barred with pale fulvous on both webs, and, with narrow whitish bars and a white tip; disc black round the eye, with a pale whitish upper edge or supercilium, rufous externally; ruff brown with some white markings; beneath pale fulvous white, narrowly and closely barred with brown; quills and tail beneath dusky brown, with white bars; bill pale greenish; irides deep brown; claws horny reddish.

Length.—19 to 21 inches; wing 13 to 14; tail 8 to 9; tarsus 2·5; mid toe and claw 2·5; toes feathered three quarters of their length, with strong scuta beyond; wings reach nearly to the end of tail. The above is Dr. Jerdon's description. He gives the habitat as "throughout Southern India, in Ceylon and the Malayan Peninsula, not yet in Burmah. Refer to notes for distribution under *S. newarense*.

Family—STRIGIDÆ.

Hinder margin of sternum entire, with no distinct cleft; inner margin of middle claw serrated. Head large, densely feathered. Eyes surrounded with a circle of radiating feathers; between the anterior portion of the facial area a frontal patch of small stiff feathers always present. Bill short, covered by stiff bristles. Feet feathered to the toes.

Gen. Strix.—*Linn.* (*in pt.*)

Nasal fossæ large; nostrils lunate. Wings reaching far beyond the tail; tail short, slightly rounded; 2nd quill longest; tarsi scantily feathered.

118. Strix flammea, *Lin. S. N.* i. p. 133; *Tem. Man. d'Orn.* i. 91; *Gould, B. Eur.* i. pl. 36; *Murray, Vert., Zool., Sind,* p. 101. Strix Javanica, *Gm. S. N.* i. p. 295; *Jerd. Mad. Journ.* x. p. 85; *id. Birds of Ind.* i. p. 117, No. 60; *Hume, Nests and Eggs, Indian Birds*; *Murray Hdbk., Zool., &c., Sind.*, p. 119. Strix indica, *Blyth, Ibis,* 1860, p. 25; *Hume, Rough Notes,* ii. p. 342; *id. Str. F.* 1873, p. 163 *et* 1875, p. 37.—THE INDIAN SCREECH OWL.

Head pale buff, mottled with light grey, each feather tipped with a white spot and edged darker. Neck silky white, sometimes tinged yellowish and with small brown spots; the ruff the same, with darker tips; chin, throat, and breast, and under parts white, the feathers of the breast and abdomen with small black specks. Scapulars and back pale buff, mottled with grey, each feather with a terminal dark-edged white spot. Primaries buff on the outer web and paler on the inner, edged with white and barred with brown, the outer web finely speckled. Tail pale buff with 4—5 dark bars, tip whitish, and the inner web of the lateral feathers pure white. Under tail coverts and tarsal plumes white; under wing and thigh coverts white with small dark spots; facial disc pure white with a rufous spot in the corner of each eye. Bill yellowish white, irides black; cere flesh coloured.

Length.—13 to 14 inches; wing 11; tail 2·5; tarsus 2·5 to 2·75.

Hab.—Throughout Europe, India, Beloochistan, Afghanistan and Ceylon, extending through Burmah. Oates says it is abundant in Pegu and Arrakan, and Capt. Bingham records it from near Moulmein. In Burmah it is found chiefly in woods. It breeds in holes of trees or in the ground. Eggs 5 in number.

119. Strix candida, *Tick. J. A. S. B.* ii. p. 572; *Jerd. Ill. Ind. Orn. pl.* 30; *Jerd. B. Ind.* i. p. 118, No. 61; *Gould B. Asia*, pt. xxiv.; *Sharpe, Cat. B. M.* ii. p. 308; Glaux candida, *Blyth, J. A. S. B.* xix. p. 513; *Ball, Str. F.* 1874, p. 381; *Hume, Rough Notes*, ii. p. 345; *id. Nests and Eggs, Ind. B.* p. 60. Strix candida, *Hume, Str. F.* viii. p. 83; *Oates, Str. F.* x. p. 181.—The Grass-Owl.

The whole of the plumage, with median and greater wing coverts, dark glossy brown, the feathers yellow at the base, this colour being more or less mixed with the brown, according to the disarrangement of the plumage; each feather with a small spot of white near the tip; lesser wing coverts pale orange-buff spotted with brown; tail buffy white; the central feathers completely barred across with dark brown, the others successively less barred, the outermost feathers being nearly pure white; the quills in general orange-buff, barred with brown, and the tips also brown; the whole of the face and sides of the neck white; a patch of black in front of the eye; whole lower plumage pure white; the abdomen, under wing coverts, sides of the breast and body spotted with brown; irides very dark brown; bill horny; legs livid. (Jerd.)

Length.—14 to 14·5 inches; tail 5·2 to 5·5; wing 13·3; tarsus 3·1 to 3·2.

Hab.—India, Burmah, Upper Assam, and the Indo-Chinese sub-region; also the Phillipine Islands and N. Australia. Jerdon says he procured it on the Neilgherries at about 6,000 ft. elevation, also in the Carnatic and in Central India. According to Tickell (Jerd.), it is found throughout Bengal and the Upper Provinces. In Burmah Colonel Lloyd got it at Toonghoo. In Eastern Bengal it is common, and lays its eggs on the ground during November and December. In Dehra Dhoon a young bird was shot by Mr. R. Thompson during March and April. As its English name implies, it lives in long grass.

Gen. **Phodilus.**—*Isid. Geof. St. Hilaire.*

Facial disc irregular, the area above the eye being not equal to that below it. Wings rounded, reaching to nearly the tip of the tail; 1st quill equal to the 10th; tarsus feathered, inner toe longer than midtoe; outer toe reversible.

120. Phodilus badius, *Horsf. Tr. Lin. Soc.* xiii. p. 139; *id. Zool. Research., Java,* pl. 37; *Isid. G. St. Hilaire, An. Sc.* xxi. p. 201; *Jerd. B. Ind.* i. p. 119, No. 62; *Wall. Ibis.* 1868, p. 26; *Gray, Hand. l. B.* i. p. 52; *Gould B. Asia,* pl. xxii.; *Walden, Ibis,* 1872, p. 365; *Hume, Rough Notes,* ii. p. 346; *id. Str. F.* 1873, p. 429; *Hume and Dav. S. F.* vi. p. 27; *Hume, S. F.* viii. p. 83; *Oates, S. F.* x. p. 181; *id. B. Burmah,* ii. p. 166; *Sharpe, Cat. B. B. M.* ii. p. 309.—The BAY SCREECH OWL.

Forehead and anterior half of the crown, delicate pinkish white; remainder of the crown and nape very deep chestnut; the whole upper plumage, wings, and tail lighter chestnut; quills banded black on the inner web; the first two or three on the outer web also; the first primary and first primary-covert as well as the winglet with their outer webs white and with broad transverse dark bars as on the quills; tail with more or less perfect bars on both webs; the feathers of the other parts each with a small black mark, and those of the greater wing coverts, scapulars and tertiaries with some white shaft spots; feathers round the eye deep chestnut; disc whitish, marked with chestnut; under surface fulvous pink, sparingly spotted with brown, except on the tarsi and under-tail coverts; bill fleshy white; toes pale livid; irides brown.

Length.—11 to 12 inches; wing 7·3 to 7·5; tail 3·3 to 3·5; tarsus 1·7 to 1·9. Females slightly larger.

Hab.—Nearly all India to the North, ranging through Burmah, Pegu, Java and Borneo, the Eastern Himalayas and Ceylon. Mr. Thompson records it from Dehra Dhoon, and Jerdon obtained specimens at Darjeeling and Khasia Hills. In Burmah Captain Fielden obtained it at Thayetmyo, and Captain Wardlaw-Ramsay at Toonghoo and on the Kharen Hills, east of Toonghoo.

Nothing is known of the habits of the Bay Screech-Owl, nor anything of its nidification. The natives assert that it approaches the tiger, with the same familiarity as *Pastor Jalla, Horsf.*, does the buffalo, and does not fear to alight on the tiger's back.

Asio otus.

In beginning the second Order, *viz.*, the *Passeriformes*, or Perching Birds, I follow Mr. Bowdler Sharpe in the arrangement of the orders and sub-orders, as well as the various divisions and sections which this most extensive group cannot but contain. Mr. Sharpe explains that the system of classification for the higher groups of Passerine birds followed in his work is that of Professor A. H. Garrod, who, after an exhaustive consideration of many points in their anatomy, has established his classification on several characters after devoting his attention to the characters given by Professor Sundevall and Dr. Elliott Coues. For the lower groups he follows as far as possible the divisions of Professor Sundevall's "Tentamen" without adopting their exact order. All the great ornithologists have been consulted, and such authorities as Professor Garrod, Mr. Wallace, Professors Baird and Ridgeway have helped him in his great work, which cannot but be of the greatest assistance to students and working ornithologists. In regard to Genera, though following Sharpe, it will be necessary in this work to modify their characters to a certain extent.

ORDER II.—PASSERIFORMES.

Perching birds, with a nude oil gland and colic cæca. *Cf. Garrod, P. Z. S.*, 1874, p. 119; (*Sharpe, Cat. Pass. B. B. Mus.*)

SUB-ORDER I.—PASSERES.

Anomalogonatous birds with the second, third, and fourth toes directed forwards and the hallux backwards; the *flexor longus hallucis* muscle independent of the *flexor perforans digitorum*, the cæca coli short but at the same time of characteristic shape; oil gland nude; palate ægithognathous; *tensor patagii brevis*, specialized and quite peculiar. (*Garr.*)

DIVISION I.—ACROMYODI.

Sub-Division I. Passeres Normales.

Section A.—*Turdiformes*. Typical or Thrush-like Passeres, with 10 primaries, the first more or less markedly reduced in size. (*Cf. Wallace.*)

GROUP I.—COLIOMORPHÆ.

Bill stout, generally of large size, not deflected at all or very little so. Chin angle produced before the line of the nostrils; cutting edge of lower mandible simple; tongue thick and fleshy, the tip horny, slight, divided or split in various ways; feet in most, strong and large, with the claw of the midtoe oblique. (*Cf. Sund. Av. Tent.*); *Sharpe, Cat, Pass. B. B. Mus.*

Family.—CORVIDÆ.

Bill without a distinct sub-terminal notch in the upper mandible; hallux strong; its claw not as long as the midtoe and claw. Toes normal.

Many of the birds which constitute this family are nearly alike in their plumage and habits. It includes the Rook, the Raven, the Magpie, the Crows, the Jackdaw, the Chough, and others. Members of this family are found in almost every part of the known world. While some feed on earthworms, insects as well as reptiles, others act the part of scavengers by feeding on putrid flesh and removing noxious matter. Though restless and noisy—the crows especially—they are active and sagacious, and have strong propensities for thieving. In general the family constitutes many which are readily tamed and taught to talk or articulate words. As for the Corvus genus, every one could testify to their voracious habits. They have been known to commit such havoc in some countries, that it became necessary to set a price on their heads. They are monogamous, and live in a kind of society. They moult only once a year.

Gen. **Trypanocorax**. *Bp.*

Wing never falling short of the tip, more than the tenth of tarsus; face and nostrils bare.

121. Trypanocorax frugilegus, *Linn. S. N.* i. p. 150; *Gould, Birds Eur.* iii. pl. 24; *McGillivray, Brit. B.* i. p. 535; *Yarrel, Brit. B.* ii. p. 91; *Jerd. B. Ind.* ii. p. 302; *Hume, Ibis*, 1871, p. 404; *Shelley, B. Egypt*, p. 159; *Blanford, East. Persia*, p. 263; *Sund. Meth. Av. Tent.*—The Rook.

PLATE.

Whole plumage above black glossed with purple; richer on the head and neck, and with a greenish shade on the eyes and ear coverts; forehead, lores, base of the bill, nostrils and forepart of the cheeks, also the throat, bare, being covered with a scabrous skin. Under surface dull purplish black. First quill shorter than the second, which again is shorter than the fourth.

Females similar to the male. Bill and feet black; irides blackish brown.

Length.—16 to 18 inches; culmen 2·2; wing 12 to 12·2; tail 7·4 to 7·5; tarsus 2·1.

Hab.—The whole of Europe ranging into Persia, the Punjab, N.-W. Provinces, Afghanistan, and Cashmere.

The rook is so well known that its habits scarcely need description. It is well known to be gregarious. Cultivated districts are its chief haunts. Grain and insects especially form its chief food; and no doubt the farmers are fully repaid for so much of the seed that they lose, by its clearing their farms of wire-worms and cock-chafers (*Melolontha vulgaris*).

Rooks live together in large societies, and build on trees close to each other, and frequently in the midst of populous towns. They occupy the same nests from year to year. The nests are built of sticks and twigs, cemented

TRYPANOCORAX FRUGILEGUS.

with clay mixed with tufts of grass. The eggs, 4—5 in number, are a pale green, blotched and spotted with darker and lighter patches of yellowish and greenish brown. As among the ravens and crows, pied varieties are not uncommon.

Gen. **Corvus**.—*Lin.*

Bill straight, large, compressed, a little swollen laterally, convex and curved towards the point, its edges cutting. Nostrils in a more or less distinct groove covered by bristly plumes, the space between the tips of which and the eye is less than the uncovered portion of the bill.

122. Corvus corax, *Linn. S. N.* i. p. 155; *Tem. Man. de Orn.* i. 107; *Yarrell, Br. B.* i. p. 498; *Jerd., B. Ind.* ii. p. 293; *Str. F.* vi p. 63.—The Raven or Great Corbie Crow.

PLATE.

Above glossy steel black, the feathers greyish at base; wings duller and with bronze reflections, their coverts and the secondary quills purplish at base, the secondaries purplish externally. Primaries steel black; tail purplish, the two outer tail feathers nearly steel black; head like the upper surface of body; face, and the long lanceolate hackles silky black, glossed with a purplish brown. Entire under surface of body glossy blue-black, shaded with purple; bill and legs black; irides brown.

Length.—22 to 25 inches; culmen 2·9 to 3·4; wings 16·5 to 16·6; tail 10 to 11·2; tarsus 2·5 to 2·8.

Hab.—The whole of Europe, Northern and Central Asia, North America, and Mexico, ranging into Cashmere, N.-W. Himalayas, Upper Sind, Punjab, and Afghanistan, as a migrant. Morris says its geographical distribution is soon told. He is a citizen of the world (*barring the greater part of India*). His sable plumage reflects the burning sun of the Equator and his shadow falls upon the regions of perpetual snow; he alights on the jutting peak of the most lofty mountain and haunts the centre of the most untrodden plain, * * * "No ultima thule," is a *terra incognita* to him. He is known since the day of Noah as a deserter, and there is scarcely a worse-abused scavenger in the present day. Although fulfilling its place in the economy of Nature, it is quite partial to poultry, lambs, rabbits, and the like.

Of its nidification, Morris says it commences about January. Incubation 20 days. Nest composed of the same materials as those used by the preceding species, and all crows. Eggs, 4—7 in number, of a bluish green colour, blotched with stains of darker or brown.

123. Corvus umbrinus, (*Hedenb.*) *Sundev. Œfv. K. vet. Akad. Forh. Stockh.* 1838, p. 199; (*ex Hedenb. Ms.*); *Heugl. Orn. N. O. Afr.* pp. 505, 125; *Shelley, B. Egypt*, p. 158; *Dresser, B. Eur*, pl. xxxiv., xxxviii.; *Blf.*

East, Pers.; *Murray, Str. F.* vol. vii. p. 113; *Hume, Str. F.* vii. p. 120; *Murray, Hdbk., Zool., &c., Sind*, p. 173. Corvus infumatus, *Wagn. Munch. gel. Anz.* 1839. Corvus corax, *Horsf. and Moore, Cat. B. Mus. E. I. Co.* ii p. 552; *Murray, Vert. Zool., Sind*, p. 175.—The Afghan Brown-necked Raven.

Head and neck glossy umber brown, also the ear coverts, sides of the face and sides of the neck, the latter scarcely glossed; lores, incumbent nasal bristles, feathers round the eye, at base of bill and at the gape, black; back, scapulars, wings, wing-coverts, upper tail-coverts and tail glossy black with a violet blue gloss; chin, throat and breast dark glossy umber brown; rest of under surface brown, glossed with purple on the breast, flanks, abdomen and vent; under tail coverts glossy purplish black; axillaries and under wing coverts purplish black; bill and legs black; irides dark brown.

Length.—21·5 to 23 inches; wing 15 to 16·4; tail 8·6 to 9; tarsus 2·9; bill at front 2·9 to 3.

Hab.—This fine Raven occurs during winter in the northern parts of Sind, where it is not uncommon at Larkhana and Jacobabad from December to March. It has hitherto been known from N. E. Africa, Palestine, and Beloochistan, about as far as 62° East long. Its occurrence at Jacobabad extends its range to nearly 69° East long. Occurs also in Beloochistan, S. Afghanistan, Punjab (Ferozepore), Egypt, Mesopotamia, and Cashmere (Gilgit).

124. Corvus lawrencei, *Hume, Lahore to Yarkand*, p. 235; *id. Str. F.* vol. i. p. 205; *Adam*, t. c. p. 385; *Hume, Nests and Eggs, Ind. B.* p. 408; *Stol. S. F.* 1864, p. 474; *Ball. S. F.* 1875, p. 207; *Murray, Hdbk. Zool., &c., Sind*, p. 172; *Sharpe, Cat. B. Br. Mus.* vol. iii. p. 15.—The Indian Raven.

Uniform blue-black throughout, with a purplish tinge on the throat and upper breast; feathers of the chin and throat lanceolate; bill black; incumbent bristles in front extend to beyond more than half of the length of the bill, which is much arched; irides dark brown or grey brown; legs black.

Length.—23·75 to 24·75 inches; wings 16·3 to 17·4, when closed reach to about from 0·3 to 0·5 of the end of the tail; bill at front 2·8.

Hab.—Sind, Punjab, N.-W. Provinces, Kutch, Kattiawar, Rajputana, Beloochistan and Afghanistan; found in some numbers in Upper Sind and usually in flocks of from 30 to 50 at the beginning of winter, when a great number are to be seen dead under the trees about Jacobabad and Shikarpoor.

Gen. **Colœus**.—Lin.

Tarsus longer than culmen, which is more or less shorter than the head; face feathered; nostrils covered by bristles.

COLÆUS MONEDULA

CORONE CORNIX.

125. Colœus monedula, *Linn, S. N.* i. p. 156; *Jerd. B. Ind.* ii. p. 302; *Hume, Nests and Eggs, Ind. B.* p. 414; *Scully, Str. F.* 1876, p. 258; *Blanf. East Pers.* p. 263.—The JACKDAW.

PLATE.

Crown of the head, blue-black, forming a cap; back of neck and nape fine hoary bluish grey; rest of the plumage black; the primaries and innermost secondaries glossed green, also the tail on the edges of the feathers; under-wing and tail-coverts greenish black; first quill shorter than the second, which again is shorter than the third, the third and fourth sub-equal; bill, legs and feet black.

Length.—13 inches; bill 1·35; wing 9·5; tail 6·1; tarsus 1·7.

Hab.—Europe and Africa, ranging into Persia, Afghanistan and the Punjab. The Jackdaw is an active and sprightly bird, and like most of the family to which it belongs noted for thievery. It is readily tamed, and soon learns mimicry. Jackdaws are social birds, and live, like the Rook, in large communities. They feed on insects, shellfish, putrid matter, and almost any garbage. They are not particular as to the site they build on,—cliffs, roofs of buildings, hollow trees, and even chimneys quite suit them. The nest though built of sticks is lined with wool, hair, or other soft material. They lay 4—5 eggs of a pale bluish white colour, spotted with grey and brown. The young are hatched by the end of May. Nothing is known of the nidification of the Jackdaw in India.

Gen. **Corone.**—*Kaup.*

Differs from *Corvus* by the first primary being longer than the foremost secondaries, but not longer than the inner. Nasal bristles directed horizontally over the nostrils; tarsi stout, scutate.

126. Corone cornix, *Linn. S. N.* i. p. 156; *MacGill. Brit. B.* i. p. 529; *Jerd., B. Ind.* ii. p. 298; *Scully, Str. F.* 1876, p. 156; *Blanf., E. Persia*, p. 262; *Str. F.* vii. p. 406, 517; *Sharpe, Cat. B. Br. Mus.*, vol. iii. p. 31. Corone cornix, *Kaup. Nat. Syst.* p. 99. Corone capellana, *Sclater, P. Z. S.* 1876; *Sharpe, Cat. B. Br. Mus.* vol. iii. p. 32. THE HOODED CROW.

Adult.—Head, foreneck, and breast glossy blue-black; wings and tail the same, but with purplish and steel green reflections; wing coverts blue-black; axillaries greyish; upper tail coverts purplish brown, the edges grey; thighs dusky black; rest of the plumage drab-grey; bill and legs black; irides dark brown.

Length.—17 to 18 inches; wing 12·2 to 12·5; tail 7·5 to 7·8; culmen 2·35 to 2·4; tarsus 2·2 to 2·25.

Hab.—Great Britain, Central and Southern Europe, Beloochistan, Afghanistan, Persia, and the Punjab.

In Mesopotamia (Fao), this species appears to be the lighter drab, or nearly white form, which, according to Sharpe, is *Corone capellana*, Sclater, but, examining a series the lighter or whitish colour is not so apparent as to separate it as a distinct species. According to Sharpe, it has also been found in the Deccan; this must surely be an error, or the bird is very rare.

Wherever the Hooded Crow occurs, it always keeps about towns and villages. Its habits are those of *C. splendens*. In India (*e.g.*), Punjab, it is a migrant, while in Persia it remains throughout the year. In Beloochistan it is fairly common above the Bolan Pass, but during the autumn only.

127. Corone splendens, *Vieill. N. Dict. d'Hist. Nat.* viii. p. 44; *Tem. Pl. Col.* ii. pl. 425; *Gray, Gen. B.* ii. p. 315; *Jerd. B. Ind.* ii p. 298; *Hume, Str. F.* vol. viii.; *Murray, Hdbk. Zool., &c., Sind*, p. 173. Corvus impudicus, *Gray, Handlist B.* ii. p. 14; *Hume, Str. F.* i. p. 206; *Str. F.* ii. pp. 418, 493; *Murray, Vert. Zool. Sind*, p. 176; *Oates B. Burma*, p. 398. Corone insolens, *Hume, Str. F.* 1875, p. 144; *Sharpe, Cat. B. Br. Mus.* vol. iii. p. 34; *Oates B. Burma.* vol. i. p. 399.—The Common Indian Crow.

Nasal bristles, crown of head, lores, sides of face, chin, throat, back, wings and tail glossy black with purplish, or steel blue reflections; lower abdomen flanks, vent, under tail and thigh coverts dull black; nape, hind neck, sides, of the neck, and part of the upper back a greyish drab; breast and upper part of the abdomen dark ashy; under wing coverts and axillaries dull black; bill and legs black; irides deep brown.

Length.—16 to 17 inches; wing 11 to 11·25; tail 7; bill at front 1·12.

Hab.—Throughout India to the foot of the Himalayas and Ceylon, Assam, B. Burmah, Tennaserim and Malacca.

The Indian House Crow like its congeners, is extremely social, and lives about towns feeding on almost anything and everything; dead mice, rats, putrid flesh, fruit, &c., in fact, is a general scavenger. Breeds from the middle of March to the beginning of June, laying generally four eggs of a greenish, colour, marked with various shades of brown. The nest is made of twigs, lined with grass, hair, rags, or any other soft material.

I do not separate *splendens* and *insolens.* From an examination of a large series of *insolens* sent to me by Mr. Calthrop from Tonghoo, Karenne, and other parts of Burmah and Tennaserim, I have come to the conclusion that it cannot be specifically separated from *splendens.* If shades of colour, especially of grey and brown are to constitute species, Ornithology will soon reach a state of confusion, from which it will never be extricated. Races and sub-species, sound well, but both help to make what never should be.

128. Corone corone, *Linn. S. N.* i. p. 155; *MacGill, Br. B.* i. p. 516; *Jerd., B. Ind.* ii. p. 295; *Hume, Nests and Eggs Ind. B.* p. 410; *Scully, Str. F.* 1876, p. 156; *Sharpe, Cat. B. Br. Mus.* iii. p. 36.—The Carrion Crow.

CORONE CORONE

Whole plumage above and below glossy blue or steel black, glossed with green; the throat with purplish; tail purplish black.

Length.—19 to 19·5 inches; wings 12·16 to 13·3; tail 7·8 to 8; culmen 2·15 to 2·25; tarsus 2·5.

Hab.—Throughout Europe; ranging into the Punjab and the N.-W. Provinces. It has as yet only been found in the Punjab, and on the borders of the N.-W. Provinces.

The Carrion Crow, as its name implies, feeds on all sorts of animal food, alive and dead. Young pigeons, chickens, sparrows, crustacea, shellfish, fruit, vegetables, frogs, mice, and insects, it is very partial to, as well as garbage. House refuse of every kind does not come amiss to it. It is a predaceous bird, and a relentless destroyer of everything it can devour. Its sense of perception, too, is very acute. Nidificates on rocks or on trees, during March. Nest of twigs, cemented with clay, and unsparingly lined with rags, grass, hair, wool, or any other soft material within its reach. Eggs 4—6 in number, greenish spotted, and streaked with various shades of brown.

129. Corone macrorhynchus, *Wagl. Syst. Av. Corvus, sp.* 3; *Hume, S. F.* v. p. 461; *Legge, Birds, Ceylon*, p. 346; *Hume, S. F.* viii. p. 105. Corvus Levaillantii, *Les traite*, p. 328; *Hume, Nests and Eggs*, p. 411; *id. S. F.* ii. p. 295; *Anderson, Yunnan Exped.* p. 589. Corvus culminatus (*Sykes*), *Jerd. B. Ind.* ii. p. 295. Corvus Vaillantii (*Less*), *Bl. B. Burm.* p. 86; *Oates, S. F.* v. p. 159. Corone macrorhynchus, *Sharpe, Cat. B. Br. Mus.* iii. p. 38; *id. Cat. B. Br. Mus.* iii. p. 39; *Oates B. Br. Burmah*, i. p. 397.—The INDIAN JUNGLE CROW.

Whole upper plumage deep black glossed with purple, blue and green; bill, legs, and feet black; irides dark brown.

Length.—19 to 21 inches; tail 7·6 to 9·2; wing 12·2 to 14; tarsus 2·3; bill from gape 2·3.

Hab.—The whole Continent of India, Ceylon, Andaman Islands, the Indo-Burmese countries and China, extending to Eastern Siberia. Southerly it extends down the Malayan Peninsula to Sumatra, Java, Borneo and Timor. In India it is found in Sind, Punjab, N.-W. Provinces, Oudh, Rajputana, Central India, the Central Provinces, Concan, Deccan and South India, also in British Burmah and Nepaul.

It will be seen that *Levaillanti* has been made a synonym of *macrohynchus*. Sharpe makes the former a Sub.-Sp., but it must not stand thus. Hume has worked out the Crows to some purpose, and like him, I am of opinion, that these two cannot be specifically separated. Except from Kutch and Guzerat, I have had specimens of this species from all parts of India for examination, and not less than 13 from various parts of Burmah and Tennaserim, and though in a few the pale bases to the feathers are apparent, in others it is either absent, (though from one locality) or distributed here and there over different parts of the body. This may be a sign of nonage.

The Jungle Crow does not affect forests only, but it also frequents towns and villages, associated with the House Crow. Nesting and breeding season the same; also the eggs, though slightly larger.

Gen. **Nucifraga.**—*Briss.*

Outer secondaries longer than the inner; bill conical, nearly straight; tip blunt; base of bill with short incumbent feathers, under which the nostrils are hidden.

130. Nucifraga hemispila, *Vigors, P. Z. S.* 1830, p. 8; *Gould. Cent. Him. B.* pl. 36; *Hodgs. in Gray's Zool. Misc.* p. 84; *Gray, Cat. B. Nepal*; *Jerd. B. Ind.* ii. p. 304; *Hume, Nests and Eggs, Ind. B.* ii. p. 415; *Sharpe, Cat. B. Br. Mus.* iii. p. 54.—The NUTCRACKER.

Crown of the head black; bristles over the nostrils blackish, streaked with white; lores white; sides of face and neck blackish brown, streaked with white; throat and under surface of body chocolate brown; the chin streaked with white; the breast tipped with triangular spots of white, the abdomen uniform brown. Under tail coverts white. Back and scapulars brown, streaked on the mantle with white; lower back, rump and upper tail coverts brown, the latter glossed with greenish; wings glossy greenish black; under wing coverts dark brown, the outermost tipped with white; tail greenish black, all the feathers except the two central ones with a broad white tip increasing in width till the outermost is white for the terminal half. Bill and feet horny black; irides reddish brown.

Length.—16 inches; wing 8·4; tail 6·6; tarsus 1·75; culmen 1·8 (*Sharpe*).

Hab.—The Himalaya Mountains. Recorded from Bengal (Darjeeling), Sikkim, N.-W. Himalayas and Nepal.

The Himalayan Nutcracker like its congeners lives on fruit, seeds, berries and insects generally. Nuts and other hard seeds it fixes in the crevice of a tree, and pecks at it till the shell is broken. It nests in holes of trees, and lays from 5 to 6 eggs, of a yellowish grey colour, spotted with lighter or darker shades of brown.

Gen. **Pica.**—*Briss.*

Wings short; tail long, graduated, the centre feathers longest. Head not crested. Eye without a nude space. 1st primary sinuated and ending in a long point. Bill as in Corvus, but more slender.

131. Pica rustica, *Scop. Ann.* i. p. 38; *Dresser Birds Eur.* part xxii.; *id. Ibis*, 1875, p. 238; *Blanf. Zool. E. Persia*, p. 264. Corvus pica, *Lin. S. N.* i. p. 157; *Wilson Am. Orn.* iv. p. 75, pl. xxxv. fig. 2. Pica caudata, *Keys. u. Blas. Wirb. Eur.* p. 45; *Gould, Birds Eur.* iii. pl. 216. Pica bottanensis, *Deless, Rev. Zool.* ii. p. 100; *Jerd. B. Ind.* ii. p. 305, No. 668. Pica pica, *Sharpe, Cat. B. Brit. Mus.* vol. iii. p. 62.—The MAGPIE.

PICA RUSTICA.

PLATE.

Head, crown, neck and nape glossy purplish black, with a shade of shining deep green on the crown; chin and throat black, the shafts of some of the feathers greyish white; breast above black; below white; back black with shining deep green reflections; wings blue, the outer edge, primary coverts and external web of primaries green; shoulders white; primaries black with an elongated patch of white on the inner web of each of the first ten feathers; secondaries and tertiaries fine blue. Tail of bright iridescent blue and purple shades terminally, green at the base and tipped dusky; the inner webs of all except the centre pair purplish black; rump and upper tail coverts purplish black. Under surface of body pure white; lower abdomen and under tail coverts purplish black, also the thighs and under wing coverts.

Bill and legs black; irides brown.

Length.—16 to 16·5 inches; wing 7·6 to 8·2; tail 9·7 to 10·5; tarsus 1·9 to 2; culmen 1·4 to 1·5.

Hab.—Europe, Asia, Africa, and America. Found in Spain, France, Italy, Belguim, Sweden, Asia Minor and Siberia; also in India, China, Japan and the United States. It is common also in Upper Beloochistan, along the Bolan Pass; on the Khojuk, or Amran range of mountains; throughout Afghanistan, and the highlands of Persia, in British Burma, at Bhamo and on the Khakyeen Hills and in Nepaul.

Of the Magpie much need not be said. Even the schoolboy has it for his lesson. It is a sly and wary bird, as well as crafty; while being always on the alert, its chatter and noise at the sight of almost any creature warn other birds. The wing being short and rounded it has to fly with quick flappings of its wings. Its food is chiefly insects, fruit and seeds. Nidification begins in spring. The nest not unlike that of the crow is made of strong sticks and twigs, cemented with mud and lined with grass, fibres, &c., and domed on top, leaving an aperture on one side for entrance and exit. Eggs 6—8, pale bluish white, spotted all over with grey and greenish brown.

Gen. **Urocissa**.—*Cab.*

Wings short and rounded; tail with the two centre feathers longer than the others, but not spathulate at tip. Head not crested. Eye without a nude space, Bill stout, much curved. Nostrils not densely feathered.

132. Urocissa occipitalis, *Blyth, J. A. S. B.* xv. p. 26; *Jerd. B. Ind.* ii. p. 309; *Hume, Nest and Eggs*, p. 419; *Sharpe, Cat. B. Br. Mus.* iii. p. 70; *Hume, Str. F.* viii. p. 105; *Scully, Str. F.* viii. p. 327; *Bingham, Str. F.* ix. p. 191; *Oates B. Br. Burmah* i. p. 400. Psilorhinus magnirostris *Bl. J. A. S.* B. xv. p. 27: Urocissa magnirostris, *Bl. B. Burma*, p. 88;

Hume, Str. F. iii. p. 144; *Sharpe, Cat. B. Br. Mus.* iii. p. 71; *Wardlaw-Ramsay, Ibis,* 1877, p. 460; *Hume, and Davison, Str. F.* vi. p. 385; *Anders. Yunan Exped.* p. 592; *Hume, Str. F.* viii. p. 105. Urocissa sinensis (*Lin.*), *Jerd. B. Ind.* ii. p. 30.—The BLUE MAGPIE.

Above pale purplish brown. Head, throat and foreneck, also the breast black; a large patch of white on the nape continued down the back of the neck; some of the feathers of the crown tipped with white; rest of under surface of the body, also the under wing and tail coverts silky white, in some with a purplish tinge; wings brown, the first two primaries edged with blue, the next five edged with blue above the emargination and with bluish white below and tipped with white, the other primaries and secondaries almost entirely blue on the outer web, the tertiaries blue on both webs; back, scapulars and rump azure blue; the wing coverts brighter. Upper tail coverts azure blue, tipped with black and with a subterminal band of bluish white; flanks and thighs light bluish grey.

Bill coral red; legs reddish crimson or orange; irides brown.

Eyelids greyish white; claws horn colour.

Length.—20 to 24 inches; wing 7·5 to 8; tarsus 1·9 to 1·95; tail 17 to 18; culmen 1·6.

Hab.—The Himalayas, extending to Nepaul, Burmah and Siam. Oates obtained it in Thayetmyo, Captain Ramsay at Tonghoo, Davison at Pahpoon, Capt. Bingham in the Thoungyeen valley. It has also been found in Arrakan, Sikkim, Nepaul, Kumaon and in the Valley of the Sutlej.

The Blue Magpie is said to be easily tamed, and to bear confinement well as a cage-bird. Although a forest bird it affects camps and villages. It feeds chiefly on the ground. It breeds during March and April, making a nest constructed of twigs and branches and lined with grass and slender twigs on the topmost branches of trees. Eggs 3—4, white, with streaks and spots of a claret colour. (Oates.)

U. magnirostris has been made a synonym of *Occipitalis*, as there does not appear to be any marked difference, either in size, or colour. Taking the bill alone, of the several examples of both species sent to me by Mr. A. O. Hume the difference is scarcely a tenth, while most have it of the same length as *occipitalis*. The colour of the irides, too, as given by several ornithologists, also of the legs, cannot be accepted as distinctive characters, being variable in most birds at certain seasons.

133. Urocissa flavirostris, *Blyth. J. A. S. B.* v. p. 28; *Cat. Mus. Hein. Th.* 1. p. 87; *Jerd. B. Ind.* ii. p. 310; *Hume, Nests and Eggs, Ind. B.* p. 419; *Henderson and Hume, Lahore to Yarkand*, p. 242. Cissa cucullata, *Gould. B. Asia*, part xiii.—The YELLOW-BILLED BLUE-MAGPIE.

Head, neck, and mantle deep black; a nuchal patch of white glossed with light blue; under surface ashy grey, paler on the abdomen and under tail

AVIFAUNA OF BRITISH INDIA.

DENDROCITTA OCCIPITALIS.

? Urocissa

Mintern Bros. lith.

coverts; under wing coverts yellowish. Edge of the wing and upper wing coverts washed with lavender. Upper surface lavender, tinged with azure blue; wings the same; primaries externally greyish for their apical two-thirds, the secondaries tipped with white; upper tail coverts azure blue with a narrow subterminal bar of bluish white and tipped with black; tail azure blue, broadly tipped with white; all but the two centre feathers subterminally barred with black. Legs orange yellow; bill yellow; irides brownish red.

Length.—20 inches; wing 7·3; tail 16; tarsus 1·9; culmen 1·45.

Hab.—The Himalaya Mountains, Nepal, Sikkim, Darjeeling, Kumaon, Kooloo, Ladakh, and Cashmere. (Sharpe.)

Gen. **Dendrocitta.**—*Gould.*

Base of the culmen unfeathered; middle tail feathers broad at the ends; nostrils concealed by incumbent feathers; 5th and 6th quills longest; secondaries nearly as long as the primaries.

134. Dendrocitta rufa, *Scop. Del. Fauna et Flor. Insubr.* ii. p. 86; *Hartl. Syst. Verz.* p. 63; *Jerd. B. Ind.* ii. 314, No. 674; *Murray, Vert. Zool. Sind,* p. 177; *Sharpe, Cat. B. Br. Mus.* iii. p. 76; *Gray, Handlist B. Br. Mus.* ii. p. 8; *Hume, Str. F.* i. pp. 206, 386; *Murray, Hdbk. Zool., &c., Sind,* p. 174. Crypsirrhina pallida, *Blyth, J. A. S. B.* xv. p. 30. Dendrocitta pallida, *Blyth, Cat. Mus. A. S. B.* p. 336; *Jerd. B. Ind.* ii. p. 315, No. 675.—The Common Indian Magpie.

Adult.—Head, neck all round, part of upper back, chin, throat, breast and ear coverts dark sooty brown, paler on the upper back; lores blackish brown; back and scapulars orange brown; rump and upper tail coverts bright orange or yellowish buff; abdomen and under tail and thigh coverts, like the rump, orange, yellowish buff or dark ferruginous; primaries and secondaries black; tertiaries black, greyish white on their outer webs; wing coverts white; edge of the wing and under wing coverts greyish white; tail greyish white, or grey, the centre feathers elongated much beyond the rest, and all broadly tipped with black; bill black; legs slaty; irides blood-red.

Length.—16—17 inches; wing 5·9; tail 10; tarsus 1·45; bill at front 1 to 1·25. The young is much paler throughout, and has the tail feathers tipped whitish buff.

Hab.—The whole of India, through Assam and Burmah to Tennaserim and Cashmere; Sind, Punjab, N.-W. Provinces, Bengal, Southern India, Travancore, Central India, Kutch, Kattiawar, Rajputana, Concan, and Deccan.

The common Indian Magpie is an inhabitant of forests as well as of open country, and is usually found in small flocks of 5 or 6. It nests on trees, select ing the highest, and generally in the vicinity of water, for what reason it is difficult to say. The nest is constructed of twigs, usually of thorny trees, and lined with grass, fibres, or other such soft materials. It breeds from April to June. The eggs, generally four and sometimes five in number, vary much in colour, size, and markings; typical eggs may be said to be of a dirty greenish white colour, richly blotched with reddish brown, purplish, or umber brown. In size they also vary from 1·15 to 1·18 × 0·85 to 0·87.

135. Dendrocitta frontalis, *McClell., P. Z. S.* 1839, p. 163; *Jerd. B. Ind.* ii. p. 317, No. 677; *Sharpe, Cat. B. Br. Mus.* iii. p. 780. Crypsirrhina frontalis, *Blyth, J. A. S. B.* xii. p. 933; xv. p. 30. Crypsirrhina altirostris, *Blyth, J. A. S. B.* xii. p. 932.—The BLACK-BROWED MAGPIE.

Hinder part of head, entire hind neck, mantle, sides of the neck, foreneck, and breast whitish grey; rest of head, sides of the face, entire throat, bastard wing, primary coverts, quills, tail, bill and feet black; upper surface orange chestnut; lower surface of body bright orange chestnut, deeper on the lower tail coverts; thighs and under wing coverts grey, washed with orange; upper wing coverts blue grey; iris brownish red.

Length.— 14 inches; wing 5·15; tail 9·3; tarsus 1·2; culmen 1·05.

Hab.—The Himalayas. Recorded from Nepaul and Darjeeling; also Sikkim and Assam.

Nothing is known of its habits and nidification.

136. Dendrocitta leucogastra, *Gould. P. Z. S.* 1833, p. 57, et. *Tr. Zool. Soc.* 1. p. 89, pl. 12; *Jerd. B. Ind.* ii. p. 317, No. 678; *Hume, Nests and Eggs, Ind. B.* p. 424, No. 678; *Sharpe, Cat. B. Br. Mus.* iii. p. 79; *Str. F.* iv. p. 402.—The WHITE BELLIED MAGPIE.

Crown of the head, sides of face, cheeks, throat, foreneck, tail, terminal third of the two long central feathers, wings (except a white star patch at base of primaries), thighs, under wing coverts and bill black; back and scapulars orange brown; hind crown, hind neck, rump, upper tail coverts, under surface of the body (except the under tail coverts, which are rufous), a band across the inner lining of the quills white; basal two-thirds of the long central tail feathers grey; bill black; legs and feet dark plumbeous; irides blood-red.

Length.—17 to 18 inches; wing 5·5 to 5·8; tail 11 to 11·5; tarsus 1·25; culmen 1·3.

Hab.—Southern India, Malabar Coast and the Neilgherries; also Peria Forests, Wynaad, where it is said to be abundant. Jerdon gives Coorg and Travancore, also, as countries where it is found.

137. Dendrocitta himalayensis, *Blyth. Ibis,* 1865, p. 45; *Hume Str. F.* 1874, p. 480; *id. Nests and Eggs, Ind. B.* p. 423; *Blyth B. Bur.* p. 88; *Sharpe, Cat. B. Br. Mus.* iii. p. 79; *Wardlaw-Ramsay, Ibis,* 1877, p. 459; *Hume and Davison, Str. F.* vi. p. 386; *Hume, Str. F.* vii. p. 106;

DENDROCITTA BAYLEYII, *Tytler.*

Mintern Bros. lith.

Scully, Str. F. viii. p. 329. Dendrocitta sinensis, (*Lath.*) *Jerd. B. Ind.* ii. p. 316. Dendrocitta assimilis, *Hume, Str. F.* v. p. 117; *Hume and Davison, Str. F.* vi. p. 386; *Hume, Str. F.* vii. p. 519; viii. p. 106; *Reid, Cat. Birds Provincial Mus.* i. p. 123.—The HIMALAYAN TREE MAGPIE.

Forehead, lores and feathers above the eye black, also the wings and their coverts; also all the primaries except the first two, with a white spot at the base; the terminal third of the two central and other tail feathers black, the basal two-thirds of the former and bases of the latter ashy, or greyish white. Sides of the head, chin, and throat dark sooty brown, paling on the sides of the neck and breast; nape and upper back, rump and upper tail coverts ashy; rest of back and the scapulars brownish buff, abdomen and flanks cinereous; thighs blackish; vent and under tail coverts chestnut or orange; under wing coverts glossy black; bill horny grey, blackish in some; irides reddish brown; legs dusky black.

Length.—11 to 13 inches; wing 5·4 to 5·5; tail 8·7 to 8·9; tarsus 1·1 to 1·15; culmen 1·3.

Hab.—The Himalayas. Has been found in Nepaul, Purneah, Darjeeling, Kumaon, and the mountains of Arrakan. According to Capt. Ramsay it occurs on the Tounghoo Hills and in Karenne. Davison procured it on the Mooleyit mountains in Tennaserim. It occurs also in Assam, Cachar, in the hills of Eastern Bengal, N.-W. P., Oudh, and the hills of Southern India. Jerdon says, "Horsfield got a specimen from Madras; that on the Himalayas it is very abundant from 4,000 to 7,000 feet, and that it is found in the more open forests and near cultivation and villages." Like its congeners it is a noisy bird, and has a variety of notes similar in character to those of *D. rufa.* Feeds on insects and fruit. It breeds from March to June, making a nest of sticks and roots, partially cemented with clay and lined with fibrous grass. Capt. Wardlaw-Ramsay found a nest on the Karin Hills which contained two eggs: Jerdon says he had nests of the Himalayan Magpie brought to him at Darjeeling, and that the number of eggs are three or four, of a pale greyish fawn colour with a few pale reddish brown spots and blotches, sometimes very indistinct. Hutton also took the eggs at Mussoorie. He describes them as "dull greenish ash with brown blotches and spots somewhat thickly clustered at the larger end." The eggs no doubt, like those of the Corvinæ family, vary much both in colour and markings, as well as in size and shape.

138. Dendrocitta Bayleyi, *Tytler, J. A. S. B.* 1863, p. 88; *Beavan, Ibis,* 1867, p. 329; *Ball, Str. F.* 1873, p. 75; *Hume, Str. F.* 1874, p. 245; *Walden, Ibis,* 1874, p. 145, pl. vi.; *Sharpe, Cat. B. Br. Mus.* iii. p. 82.—BAYLEY'S BLUE TREE MAGPIE.

PLATE.

Adult Male.—Back and scapulars dull tawny brown, becoming slightly more orange on the rump; head black shading off into leaden grey on the hind neck and on the upper breast, the rest of the under surface bright orange chestnut ; thighs blackish ; under wing coverts blackish, the inner ones shaded with grey ; wings above black, the lesser and median coverts slightly shaded with leaden grey ; a very distinct alar speculum, caused by the outer webs of all the secondaries, except the innermost, being white at the base ; upper tail coverts leaden black ; tail entirely black, with a slight leaden grey shade near the base. (Sharpe.)

Bill, legs, and feet black ; iris bright yellow, sometimes golden yellow. (Hume.)

Length.—12·5 inches ; wing 4·55 ; tail 7·7 ; tarsus 1 ; culmen 1.

The adult female differs from the male in being slightly duller coloured. The young are coloured like the adults, but not so bright ; the head and throat browner, the chest reddish brown instead of grey.

Hab.—Andaman Islands (Port Blair South Andamans), British Burmah, and Nepaul.

Of its habits and nidification nothing is known.

Gen. **Crypsirhina**—*Vieill.*

Tail long, the two central feathers exceeding the rest ; head not ornamented with a distinct crest ; eye without a nude ring ; nostrils densely feathered, forming a crest of velvetty feathers covering the base of the culmen.

139. Crypsirhina varians, *Lath. Ind. Orn. Suppl.* p. xxvi. ; *Walden, P. Z. S.*, 1866, p. 552 ; *Bly. B. Bur.* p. 88 ; *Hume, Str. F.* iii. p. 146 ; *Sharpe, Cat. B. Br. Mus.* iii. p. 83 ; *Wardlaw-Ramsay, Ibis*, 1877, p. 459 ; *Oates, Str. F.* v. p. 159 ; *Hume and Dav. Str. F.* vi. p. 386 ; *Hume, Str. F.* viii. p. 106.—The Black Racket-tailed Magpie.

The whole plumage metallic bronze green, tinged with bluish on the head ; the forehead, lores, a circlet of feathers round the eye and a spot at the base of the lower mandible velvetty black. Wings brown, the outer webs of the primaries greenish, the other quills more or less entirely suffused with green ; tail black, overspread with a metallic green lustre. Bill and feet black ; irides bright blue.

Length.—13 inches ; wing 4·6 to 4·7 ; tail 7·8 to 8 ; tarsus 1·1 ; culmen 1.

Hab.—Java, Burmese countries from Tennaserim northwards and eastwards also to Cochin. Found in Lower Pegu, whence it extends to Bassein. Davison procured it in Mergui. Malacca and the Province of Wellesley are other countries where it has been met with. According to Blyth it occurs in Lower Siam, and also in Cochin-China.

The Racket-tailed Magpie affects secondary jungles. It is said to be common in gardens, and wherever found has always been noticed in pairs. Breeds from May to July. Nest cup-shaped, generally made on a bamboo branch. Eggs 2—3, whitish, marked with brownish.

140. Crypsirhina cucullata, *Jerd. Ibis*, 1862, p. 20; *Hume, Str. F.* iii. p. 147; *Bly. B. Burma*, p. 88; *Sharpe, Cat. B. Br. Mus.* iii. p. 84; *Wardlaw-Ramsay, Ibis*, 1887, p. 459; *Hume, Str. F.* viii. p. 106.—The HOODED RACKET-TAILED MAGPIE.

Head, chin, throat, primaries and their coverts black; neck with a collar of ashy white. Upper plumage, wing coverts and tertiaries vinaceous grey; under surface the same, but more rufous; central tail feathers black, the others like the back paling to whitish at the tips; secondaries black, edged with ashy white; under wing coverts and inner bases of the quills whitish; irides blue; eyelids plumbeous; bill black; legs dark brown.

Length.—10·5 to 12·5 inches; wing 4 to 4·1; tail 6·8 to 7·8; tarsus 0·95.

The young differs from the adult in having the hood dusky ashy instead of black; lores, ear coverts and chin blackish brown and the top of the head darker brown; no white ring round the neck, the grey of the plumage duller and dingier, and the quills and central tail feathers altogether duller coloured (Hume), basal portion of bill, edges of the eyelids and inside of the mouth orange. (Oates).

Hab.—Burmah and Upper Pegu. Has been noted from Thayetmyo, Palow and Tounghoo. Affects bamboo brakes chiefly. Nothing is known of its nidification.

Gen. **Cissa**.—*Boie.*

Eye surrounded by a fleshy ring. Head crested.

141. Cissa chinensis, *Bodd, Tab. Pl. Enl.* p. 38; *Sharpe, Cat. B. Br. Mus.* iii. p. 85; *Hume, Str. F.*, viii. p. 106. Corvus speciosus, *Shaw, Gen. Zool.* vii. p. 364. Cissa sinensis (Briss), *Jerd. B. Ind.* ii. p. 312; *Bly. B. Burma*, p. 89; Cissa speciosa, *Hume, Nests and Eggs*, p. 421; *id. Str. F.* iii. p. 145; iv. p. 509; *Bingham, Str. F.* v. p. 85.—The GREEN JAY.

General colour green (in life), pale blue (in skin). Head crested; lores feathers round the eye, extending in a band round the nape and forming a nuchal collar black; cheeks, sides of neck and under surface of the body light green or blue; wings reddish brown; the least wing coverts green like the scapulars; all the quills dull brown on the inner web, the innermost secondaries broadly tipped with bluish white, before which is a subterminal bar of black; tail pale blue or green, the two middle feathers white at tip, the rest broadly tipped with white and with a broad subterminal band of black; bill and legs bright coral red; bare skin round the eye vermilion (Jerd.); edge of eyelid coral red; rest of it yellowish brown (Oates). Iris dark reddish brown, (Jerd.), blood-red (Oates & Sharpe).

Length.—15 to 15·5 inches; wing 5·8 to 5·9; tail 7·8 to 8·5; tarsus 1·7 to 1·9; culmen 1·45 to 1·6.

19

Hab.—The Himalayas, Assam, Sylhet, Arracan, Sikkim, Tennaserim, Nepaul and the whole of British Burmah. Oates says from Arrakan down to Mergui in Tennaserim. It is abundant on the Pegu Hills. Davison met with it as far south as Meetamyo in Tennaserim; Bingham also noticed it in the Thoungyeen Valley, and Captain Wardlaw-Ramsay on the Karin Hills.

The Green Jay is essentially a forest bird, and is found either singly or in pairs; and according to Oates feeds principally on insects. They are frequently tamed and caged, and Blyth says are very amusing and imitative. Oates found the nest in April on the Pegu Hills; a large cup-shaped structure made of leaves and coarse roots and lined inside with fibres and fine roots. It was placed in a small tree about 20 feet from the ground and contained three eggs, which were greenish white, marked with yellowish brown.

The change which the plumage of this bird undergoes, both in life and in death, though remarkable, has not yet excited the interest of physiologists as the chameleon did. During life when newly moulted it is said to be of "a lovely green colour, the wings bright sanguine red, and the bill and legs deep coral;" the green however changes both in life and after death to verdigris or dull blue. *Cissa ornata* is a Ceylonese form. Though Ceylon is a British possession, it is not comprised in India, and hence the avifauna of that country, so well written of by Capt. Legge, is omitted. It differs from *Chinensis* in having a chestnut head and no black nuchal collar.

Gen. **Platysmurus**,—*Reich.*

Tail moderately long and graduated, the two centre feathers not much longer than the others; nostrils covered by a dense tuft of bristles; bill deep and compressed.

142. Platysmurus leucopterus, *Tem. Pl. Col.* 265; *Less. Traité* p. 341; *Sharpe, Cat. B. Br. Mus.* iii. p. 90; *Tweed. Ibis*, 1877, p. 318; *Hume and Dav. Str. F.* vi. p. 387; *Hume, Str. F.* viii. p. 106.—The WHITE-WINGED JAY.

Whole plumage black, except a bar formed by the tips of the greater coverts and the basal two-thirds of the central secondaries which are white; forehead crested, the feathers recurved; eye surrounded by scale-like black feathers; bill, legs, and feet black; irides lake-red to crimson.

Length.—16 inches; wing 7·6 to 7·8; tail 7·8 to 8; tarsus 1·55; culmen 1·25.

Hab.—Throughout the Malay Peninsula and Sumatra, ranging into Tennaserim. Mr. Davison observed it in Tennaserim from Meetamyo down to the extreme southern point at Malewoon. According to him, it "keeps entirely to the forests, going about usually in parties of from four to six. They have a deep rolling metallic note which they continually utter as they move from tree to tree. They are excessively restless, and always on the move flying at a considerable height. They restrict themselves to the evergreen forests."

Gen. **Garrulus**.—*Briss.*

Bill moderately compressed, short, thick, as high nearly as broad; nostrils covered with incumbent bristles; wings and tail about equal in length; secondaries moderately long; second primary about as long as the secondaries; culmen decurved.

143. Garrulus atricapillus, *Geoffr. St. Hilaire, Etud. Zool.* fasc. i.; *Dresser, B. Eur.* part xx. Garrulus melanocephalus, *Gene. Mem. Acad. Torino*, xxxvii. p. 298; *Bree. B. Europe*; *Blf. Eastern Persia*, vol. ii. p. 265; *Hume, Str. F.* i. p. 206; *Murray, Zool. &c., Sind*, p. 173; *Sharpe, Cat. B. Br. Mus.* iii. p. 97.—The BLACK-HEADED JAY.

Adult Female.—General colour above clear vinaceous, washed with grey; the rump and upper tail coverts white (wings and tail much as in *G. cervicalis*); wing coverts grey, the least coverts barred with chestnut, the median series broadly chestnut at tip; the greater series velvety black, the outermost barred with blue and black; the bastard wing and primary coverts cobalt blue, narrowly barred with black; quills brownish black, externally greyish white; the secondaries white for two-thirds of the outer web, with slight indications of blue bars, the innermost black, inclining to chestnut on all but the tip of the last secondary; tail brownish black, bluish grey at base, and barred with the same colour for more than half the length of the centre feathers; nasal bristles white, washed with vinaceous at the tip; forehead, feathers round the eye, a broad eyebrow and the sides of the face and neck, as well as the throat, white; a broad malar bar of black; rest of under surface pale vinaceous, deeper on the sides of the body and under wing coverts, and inclining to buffy white on the centre of the abdomen, thighs and under tail coverts.

Length.—12·7 inches; culmen 1·2; wing 6·7; tail 6.

Adult Male.—Similar to the female but showing less grey on the back and rather more on the chest; the face and throat sometimes washed with a vinous tinge.

Length.—14·5 inches; wing 7·6; tail 7; culmen 1·4.—(*Sharpe, Cat. B. Br. Mus.* vol. iii. pp. 97, 98.)

Hab.—Sind, on the hills dividing Sind from Khelat (Hume). Syria and Palestine eastwards into Persia (Sharpe). Mr. Hume, in vol. i. p. 206 of *Stray Feathers*, states that he satisfied himself from the description given him of this bird, that it occurs on the hills dividing Sind from Khelat. I have no specimen from Sind, nor has Mr. Hume; but I give the above description of the bird to help its identification if met with.

144. Garrulus leucotis, *Hume, Proc. A. S. B.* 1874, p. 106; *id. Str. F.* ii. p. 443; *Wald. in Bly. B. Burm.* p. 89; *Sharpe, Cat. B. Br. Mus.* iii. p. 99; *Wardlaw-Ramsay, Ibis*, 1877, p. 460; *Hume and Davison, Str. F.* vi. p. 384; *Hume, Str. F.* vii. p. 105.—The BURMESE OR WHITE-EARED JAY.

PLATE.

Forehead and front of head white, with brown shaft streaks; lores, sides of the face, feathers above the eye, ear coverts, entire throat, rump and upper tail coverts white; crown and nape black, also the tail and a broad moustachial stripe; back ashy fawn colour, purer on the scapulars and lower back; abdomen and flanks ashy fawn colour; vent and under tail coverts white; under wing coverts chestnut, the lower series ashy; winglet, primary coverts and the outer greater series barred with black and cobalt blue; secondaries black, the basal two-thirds barred with black and cobalt blue; upper wing coverts chestnut; primaries black, margined with whity brown on the outer webs towards the tip; innermost secondaries deep chestnut at base; tertiaries black, the inner ones partly chestnut; bill blackish horny, whitish at tip; legs and feet flesh colour; irides wood brown (Davison).

Length.—12·5 to 12·8 inches; wing 6·7 to 6·8; tail 5·7; tarsus 1·6 to 1·7; culmen 1·25 to 1·5.

Hab.—The Burmese countries, extending to Cochin-China.

The Burmese or White-eared Jay occurs in Burmah and Tennaserim. Davison procured it at Kyouknyat and also on the Mooleyit mountains. Capt. Bingham at Kaukarit and Capt. Ramsay near Tounghoo, where, he says, it is generally distributed on the hills and plains. Davison says he found it usually in small parties, occasionally in pairs or singly, going about the tops of trees, one occasionally perching itself upon the very top of some tree in the self-sufficient way in which only a Jay can. The habits are quite those of other Jays. Food, insects.

145. Garrulus bispecularis, *Vigors, P. Z. S.*, 1830, p. 7; *Gould, Cent. Him. B.* pl. 38; *Henderson and Hume, Lahore to Yarkand*, p. 242; *Jerd. B. Ind.* ii. p. 307, No. 669; *Hume, Nests and Eggs, Ind. B.* p. 416; *Sharpe, Cat. B. Br. Mus.* iii. p. 100; *Reid, Cat. B. Prov. Mus. Oudh*, p. 118. Garrulus ornatus, *J. E. Gray, in Hard. Ill. Ind. Zool.* i. pl. 23.—The HIMALAYAN JAY.

Above vinaceous fawn colour, paler on the forehead, which is almost isabelline; moustachial streak black; under surface of body pale vinaceous fawn colour, the throat and abdomen paler; upper and under tail coverts and thighs white; least wing coverts vinaceous chestnut, deeper on the median series which are ashy black at base, the outermost having some transverse rays of grey; winglet and outer webs of the primary coverts barred with black and

GARRULUS LEUCOTIS, *Hume.*

Mintern Bros. lith.

cobalt blue; other coverts black; the innermost chestnut with a black tip; primaries black, edged with white on the outer web; secondaries barred externally with black and cobalt blue for two-thirds their basal length; tail black with indications of grey bars near the base; "bill dusky horny; legs dull yellowish; iris red brown." (Jerdon).

Length.—12 inches; wing 6·35; tail 6; tarsus 1·55; culmen 1·15.

Hab.—The Himalayas, fairly common in the N.-W. Provinces, and Bengal; also Sikkim, Ladakh, and Nepaul. It is recorded as being abundant about Darjeeling.

146. Garrulus lanceolatus, *Vig. P. Z. S.* 1830, p. 7; *Gould, Cent. Him. B.* pls. 39, 40; *Hutton, J. A. S. B.* xvii. pl. ii. p. 5; *Jerd. B. Ind.* ii. p. 308, No. 670; *Hume, Nests and Eggs, Ind. B.* p. 417; *Brooks, Str. F.* 1875, p. 253; *Sharpe, Cat. B. Br. Mus.* iii. p. 252. Garrulus vigorsii, *J. E. Gray in Hard. Ill. Ind. Orn.* pl. 9.—The BLACK-THROATED JAY.

Whole head, crest, face and nape black; neck behind, and back pale vinaceous grey; throat blackish with broad lanceolate streaks of white, the foreneck shading off into blue grey, with a few nearly obsolete whitish streaks; rest of under surface vinaceous red; scapulars like the back; quills and bastard wing black, tipped with white, the primaries edged with grey, and all barred with deep cobalt blue and black on the outer web, the blue increasing on the outer secondaries and extending to nearly the tips of these feathers; primary coverts white, black basally and banded blue on the outer web of the first two; upper tail coverts grey; tail blue, narrowly barred with black and with a terminal white band; under wing coverts greyish black; bill horny; legs yellowish; irides reddish brown. In the young, the white shafts of the feathers on the throat are not developed.

Length.—12 to 13 inches; wing 5·7 to 6; tail 5·7 to 6; tarsus 1·25 to 1·5; culmen 1.

Hab.—The Himalayas, extending to Ladakh, Nepaul and Cashmere. Common about Mussoorie, Darjeeling, and Simla in small parties of 4 to 6. Breeds in May. The nest is a loose structure of twigs, roots, and fibres Eggs 3—4 in number, stone grey with a greenish tinge, spotted and streaked with dark and dusky.

Sub-family II.—FREGILINÆ.

Bill more or less lengthened, slender, arched and bright coloured; nostrils covered with plumes; wings long and pointed.

Gen. Graculus.—*Koch.*

Wings long, but not reaching the tip of the tail; bill long, curved, slender, compressed; the base of lower mandible feathered; the nostrils covered with setaceous plumes; 4th and 5th quills longest; tarsus robust, strong.

147. Graculus eremita, *Koch, Syst. baier, Zool.* p. 91; *Reid, Cat. B. Prov. Mus., Oudh,* p. 122. Corvus graculus, *Linn. Syst. N.* i. p. 158. Gracula pyrrhocorax, *Scop. Ann.* i. p. 42 (*nec. L.*). Fregilus graculus, *Cuv. Regne Anim.*, 1817, p. 406; *Gould, Birds Eur.* pl. 210. Pyrrhocorax graculus, *Tem. Man.* i. p. 122; *Dresser, B. Eur.* pl. xxxvii. Fregilus himalayanus, *Gould, P. Z. S.*, 1862, p. 125; *Jerd. B. Ind.* ii. p. 318, No. 679. Graculus graculus, *Sharpe, Cat. B. Br. Mus.* ii. p. 146.—The HIMALAYAN CHOUGH.

Above and below black, glossed with purple and green; wings black, externally dull green; tail dull greenish black; bill deep vermilion or coral red; legs the same; iris brown.

Length.—15 to 16 inches; wing 11 to 12·75; tail 5·8 to 6·75; culmen 1·95 to 2·2.

Hab.—Europe, Central Asia, N. and N.-E. Africa, the Himalayas, Beloochistan, in the Bolan Pass, Afghanistan, Persia, the N.-W. Provinces of India, Cashmere and Nepaul. In the Punjab and N.-W. Provinces it has been recorded from Kumaon and Darjeeling. Jerdon says it is found on the Himalayas in flocks, some of them emigrating with the Jackdaw to the plains of the Punjab. Blanford met with it between Bampur and Narmashir in April, at not more than 4,000 feet above the sea, and again in the higher parts of the Elburz Mountains. The Chough is as full of curiosity and as noted for petty thefts as its cousin, the Crow. It is easily tamed, but restless in captivity. It is extremely shy in the wild state, and does great service in killing the grubs which affect cultivation. Insects as grasshoppers, grubs of every kind, beetles and grain are its chief food. Of its nidification in India nothing is known. In England the nests are placed in clefts and cavities of inaccessible cliffs. The eggs are 4—5 in number, dull white, spotted with grey and brown, rather thickly at the larger end.

Gen. **Pyrrhocorax.**—*Vieill.*

Bill shorter and stronger than in *Fregilus*, also less curved, the tip of upper mandible toothed, and the base of lower mandible bare of feathers; feet robust; wings reaching to nearly the tip of the tail.

148. Pyrrhocorax alpinus, *Vieill. N. Dict. d'Hist.* vi. p. 568; *Gould. B. Eur.* iii. pl. 218; *Bly. Cat. B. Mus. A. S. B.* 90; *Jerd. B. Ind.* ii. p. 319, No. 680; *Henderson and Hume, Lahore to Yarkand,* p. 249; *Dresser, B. Eur.* pl. xxxviii; *Ibis,* 1875, p. 237; *Scully, Str. F.*, 1876, p. 162; *Blf. East Pers.* p. 263; *Sharpe, Cat. B. Br. Mus.* iii. p. 149.—The ALPINE CHOUGH.

PLATE.

Glossy black all over, with iridescent tints; bill yellow; legs bright red or dark vermilion red; iris brown.

FREGILUS GRACULUS.

Length.—16·5 inches; wings 10·75 to 11·25; tail 6·8 to 7; tarsus 1·9 to 2; culmen 1·4.

Hab.—Europe, ranging to the Himalayas, the N.-W. Provinces, the Punjab, and Nepaul.

The Alpine Chough is plentiful between Simla and Mussoorie. It has also been met with in Darjeeling and the higher parts of the N.-W. Provinces, but rarely in the plains of the Punjab. It is found in large flocks in the Himalayas, where it feeds chiefly on various fruits as the mulberry; and breeds in holes in rocks. Of the sub-family, *Fregilinæ*, are three species of Podoces, viz., *Hendersoni*, Hume, *Ibis*, 1871, p. 408; *Hab.* Yarkand; *Biddulphi* Hume, *Str. F.* ii. pp. 503, 529, collected by Dr. Stolickza in Eastern Turkestan, and *humilis*, Hume, *Ibis*, 1871, p. 408, obtained by Dr. G. Henderson in the Sanju Pass, Yarkand. This last will probably be found to range to the Himalayas.

Fam.—ORIOLIDÆ.

Bill long, strong, moderately broad at the base, hooked, and distinctly notched at the tip; nostrils in front of the base of the bill and quite bare; tail rather short; tarsi short; feet small; claws curved.

Gen. **Oriolus.**—*Lin.*

Characters those of the family; the culmen keeled; wings with the 1st quill very short, 2nd shorter than the third, which is the longest; upper tail coverts long. Lores feathered, but generally with a small bare space behind the eye. Outer toe syndactyle. Nostrils lateral.

149. Oriolus galbula, *Linn. S. N.* i. p. 160; *Naum. vogl. Deutsch* ii. tab. 61; *McGill. Br. B.* ii. p. 69; *Gould. B. Eur.* ii. pl. 71; *Gray, Gen. B.* i. p. 232; *Layard, B. South Afr.* p. 135; *Shelley, B. Egypt*, p. 156; *Sharpe, Ibis*, 1870, p. 215; *id. Cat. Afr. B.* p. 53; *Hume, Str. F.*, 1873, p. 182; *Murray, Hdbk. Zool., &c., Sind*, p. 143; *Murray, Vert. Zool. Sind*, p. 136.— The Golden Oriole.

Adult Male.—Golden yellow, a blackish brown spot between the eye and the bill; wings and tail black; a yellow spot on the quills not far from the middle of the wing when closed; tail feathers terminated with yellow; bill reddish maroon; iris red; feet bluish grey.

Length.—10 to 10·5 inches; bill at front 1; wing 5·9; tail 3·1; tarsus 0.8.

Adult Female.—Greenish olive above, greyish white with a yellowish tinge below, where the plumage is marked by some white distant greyish brown stripes or dashes disposed longitudinally; wings brown, bordered with olivaceous grey; tail olivaceous, tinged with black; beneath yellowish with a brownish black mark somewhat in the form of an irregular Y; no dark streak behind the bill and the eye.

The young of the year resembles the female, but the longitudinal stripes of the lower parts are more numerous and deeper in colour; bill blackish grey; iris brown.

It is said to breed in parts of Europe, laying generally four or five eggs, white or purplish white, speckled with lake red and dusky.

Hab.—The whole of Europe, S.-W. Asia, South Asia, South Africa and Persia. A visitant in Sind during October and November.

150. Oriolus kundoo, *Sykes, P. Z. S.*, 1832, p. 87; *Gray, Gen. B.* i. p. 232; *Blyth, J. A. S. B.* xv. p. 49; *Jerd. B. Ind.* ii. p. 107, No. 470; *Hume, Lahore to Yarkand*, p. 167; *Murray, Hdb. Zool. &c., Sind*, p. 143; *Murray, Vert. Zool. Sind*, p. 137; *Reid. Cat. B. Prov. Mus. N.-W.-P. and Oudh*, p. 92.—The INDIAN ORIOLE.

Adult Male.—Bright golden yellow above and below; lores, feathers round the eye and a streak through the eye black; scapulars externally black; the edge of the wing and a bar formed by the primary coverts yellow; the bases of the primary coverts black; quills black; the primaries edged with yellow; secondaries with yellow tips; tail with the central feathers black and narrowly yellow tipped, the next pair black, with a broad yellow tip, the others black at the base and yellow for the greater part of their terminal length; under wing and tail-coverts golden yellow; bill deep lake red; legs plumbeous; irides blood-red.

Length.—9 to 9·5 inches; wing 5·5; tail 3·5; tarsus 0·95. The female is like the male, but with a slightly greenish tint.

Hab.—Throughout India to Nepaul, Cashmere and Eastern Turkistan. Probably a resident in Sind, but nothing is known of its nidification in the Province. Specimens have been obtained in April, June, September and December. The September birds were the young of the year.

151. Oriolus diffusus, *Sharpe, Cat. B. Br. Mus.* iii. p. 197; *Legge, B. Ceylon,* p. 355. Oriolus indicus, *Jerd. Ill. Ind. Orn.* pl. 15; *id. B. Ind.* ii. p. 109, No. 471; *Salvad Ucc. Born.*, p. 275; *Hume, Str. F.* vii. p. 132; *Bl. and Walden, B. Burm.* p. 139; *Hume and Dav. Str. F.* vi. p. 329; *Hume, Str. F.* viii. p. 99; *Oates, B. Br. Burm.* i. p. 211. Oriolus cochinchinensis, *Apud David et Oust. Ois. Chine,* p. 132.—The BLACK-NAPED ORIOLE.

Above and below bright yellow; lores, and a band through and above the eye continued to the nape, on each side black. Primaries and secondaries black, tipped and edged narrowly with yellowish white, the latter more broadly; outer webs of tertiaries and a portion of the inner webs next the shaft yellow; primary coverts black, tipped broadly with yellow; inner webs of greater coverts black, also the winglet; tail black, tipped with yellow; the central pair narrowly and the others progressively broader towards the outer feathers.

The young have the feathers of a greenish tinge, and dark-shafted on the breast and abdomen, the band on the nape indistinct; tail greenish with yellowish tips; irides and eyelids pinkish; legs and feet plumbeous; bill pinkish red.

Length.—9·6 to 10 inches; wing 5·85 to 6; tail 3·85 to 4; tarsus 1 to 1·05; culmen 1·25 to 1·4.

Hab.—The Indian Peninsula to Tennaserim, China, and Mongolia. Oates says it appears to be a winter visitant to British Burmah. Blyth records it from Arrakan. It is said to be common about Pegu, Rangoon, and in the Irrawady delta. Davison met with it in Tennaserim from Thatone to Malewoon during winter. Jerdon procured it from the Malabar jungles, and mentions it as having been procured at Dharwar, and to be found near Calcutta.

The black-naped Oriole affects forests, large groves and gardens. It feeds on fruit and insects, and is strictly arboreal in its habits.

152. Oriolus tenuirostris, *Bly. J. A. S. B.* xv. p. 48; *Hume, Str. F.* iii. p. 131; *Bl. B. Burm.* p. 140; *Sharpe, Cat. B. Br. Mus.* iii. p. 198; *Hume and Dav. Str. F.* vi. p. 329; *Hume, Str. F.* viii. p. 99; *Scully, Str. F.* vii. p. 298; *Oates, B. Br. Burm.* i. p. 212.—The BURMESE BLACK-NAPED ORIOLE.

Similar to *O. diffusus*, but differs in having a more slender and slightly smaller bill, the alar speculum larger, the tail feathers more broadly yellow terminally, and the nape band narrower in width, ·4 against ·7 in *O. diffusus.* Bill pale pink, black in the young; inside of mouth fleshy; legs plumbeous; irides crimson.

Length.—9·5 to 10 inches; wing 5·35 to 5·9; tail 3·5 to 3·7; tarsus 1; culmen 1·3 to 1·35.

Hab.—This species has a very wide range, especially in the Indo-Burmese countries. It is spread over the whole Pegu division. Abundant in the Thayetmyo districts. Wardlaw-Ramsay obtained it in Karenne, and Col. Lloyd at Tounghoo. In Tennaserim it is rare. It is recorded from Arrakan, also from Cachar, Munipoor, and Nepaul. (Oates.) Habits those of the last.

153. Oriolus andamanensis, *Tytler and Beavan, Ibis,* 1867, p. 326; *Ball, Str. F.,* 1873, p. 72; *Hume, Str. F.* 1874, p. 227; *Sharpe, Cat. B. Br. Mus.* iii. p 200. Oriolus Horsfieldi, *Blyth, in Mouatt's Andaman Isl.* p. 352 (nec Sws). Broderipus andamanensis, *Walden, Ibis,* 1873, p. 305.—The ANDAMAN ORIOLE.

Adult Male.—General colour above and below brilliant yellow; crown of head yellow like the back, from which it is separated by a horse-shoe band of black, drawn from the lores, enclosing the eye and passing round the nape; wing coverts yellow; the greater series black on the inner web; primary coverts black, tipped with yellow; but not very broadly; *rest of the wings black with only a faint terminal edging of yellow to the quills, forming a little larger spot on the inner secondaries*; central tail feathers black, tipped with yellow and slightly washed with olivaceous near the base; all the other feathers black at base, which decreases in extent towards the outer tail feathers. (Sharpe.) "Bill carneous or delicate pink; legs and feet plumbeous, sometimes tinged with green, the soles dirty grey; iris carmine; the eyelids brownish red." (Hume.)

The adult female is duller in colour, and the yellow of the feathers decidedly tinged with olivaceous. Bill in the young black.

Length.—9·5 inches; wing 5·3; tail 4·1; tarsus 0·95; culmen 1·2.

Hab.—The Andaman Islands; Port Blair.

Nothing is known of the nidification of this species nor of *Oriolus macrurus,* Blyth, a species found in the Nicobars. It is possible this latter will be found in Burmah. A description is, however, given of the species.

Above and below bright yellow; forehead yellow; the lores, feathers round the eye and remainder of head and nape black; wings black; wing coverts yellow, the greater series black on the inner web; primaries externally edged with grey; secondaries narrowly edged with yellowish near the tip, almost imperceptible; primary coverts tipped with yellow forming an alar speculum; two centre tail feathers black with a narrow yellow tip, rest of the feathers yellow with black bases, the extent of the black greater on the inner web; *outer tail feathers* almost entirely yellow with a very little black near the base. (Sharpe.) Bill carneous; legs and feet plumbeous; claws horny; iris carmine. (Hume.)

Length.—11 inches; culmen 1·4; wing 5·2; tail 4·7; tarsus 1·1.

The young bird has the bill of a dull fleshy colour; iris dull red-brown. (Hume.)

154. Oriolus xanthonotus, *Horsf. Tr. Lin. Soc.* iii. p. 153; *Tem. pl. col.* 214; *Horsf. Zool. Res. Java*; *Stolickza, J. A. S. B.* xxxix. pt. ii. p. 317; *Salvad. Ucc. Born.* p. 277; *Sharpe, Cat. B. Br. Mus.* iii. p. 213; *Tweed. P. Z. S.*, 1878, p. 616; *Hume and Davison, Str. F.* vi. p. 330; *Hume, Str. F.* viii. p. 99. Oriolus castanopterus, *Blyth, J. A. S. B.* xi. p. 796; *Oates B. Br. Burmah*, i. p. 215.—The SMALL BLACK-HEADED ORIOLE.

Head, neck, chin and throat black; breast, abdomen and flanks white, streaked with black; under tail coverts yellow; sides of the breast tinged with yellow; axillaries grey; under wing coverts black, margined with yellow; back, scapulars, lesser wing coverts, rump and upper tail coverts yellow; median wing coverts black, broadly tipped with yellow; rest of the coverts and all the quills black, most of them very narrowly edged with yellow; tail black, tipped with yellow, very narrowly on the central pair of feathers and progressively increasing in extent on the outer feathers.

Length.—7·5 inches; wing 4·35; tail 3·1; tarsus 0·75; culmen 0·9.

Immature specimens have black edgings to the feathers of the back and mesial dark streaks on the upper tail coverts.

The adult female has the whole upper plumage with the lesser wing coverts and tertiaries olive yellow, and the feathers of the head with dusky striations; lores grey; feathers round the edges of the eyelids yellow; ear coverts olive yellow with paler shafts; chin and throat whitish; breast, abdomen, and flanks white, streaked with black; under tail coverts yellow; rest of the plumage as in the male, but everywhere more dull. Legs and feet plumbeous; bill dark fleshy; irides crimson.

Length.—8 inches; wing 4·4; tail 2·8; tarsus ·8; culmen 1·1.

Hab.—Malacca, Java, Sumatra, Borneo, Labuan, the Indian Archipelago, Malay Peninsula, and the extreme south of Tennaserim, where it was procured by Davison.

Habits those of its congeners.

155. Oriolus melanocephalus, *Lin. S. N.* i. p. 160; *Jerd. B. Ind.* ii. p 110, No. 472; *Hume, Nests and Eggs, Ind. B.* p. 301; *Bly. B. Burm.* p. 139; *Sharpe, Cat. B. Br. Mus.* iii. p. 215; *Oates, S. F.* vii. p. 48; *Cripps, Str. F.* vii. p. 99; *Anderson, Yunnan Exped.* p. 660; *Hume, Str. F.* vii. p. 99; *Legge, B. Ceylon*, p. 57; *Oates, B. Br. Burm.* i. p. 214. Oriolus Ceylonensis, *Bonap. Consp.* i. p. 347; *Jerd B. Ind.* ii. p. 311; *Hume, Str. F.* i. p. 439. Oriolus Himalayanus, *Legge, B. Ceylon*, p. 358.—The BLACK-HEADED ORIOLE.

Above and below bright golden yellow; head, chin, throat and upper breast black; scapulars and wing coverts bright yellow; winglet and primary coverts black, the latter yellow for their terminal half, forming a large alar speculum; upper wing coverts yellow; first primary black; the others black, tipped with yellow, which increases in extent towards the secondaries, the innermost of which have the entire outer web yellow; base of primaries yellow; tail yellow, the two central feathers with a broad subterminal bar of black; the next on either side with a patch of black.

The female is not unlike the male, but the yellow is less bright and has an olivaceous or a greenish tinge. The young is duller in colour everywhere, the forehead is streaked with black, the feathers of the crown and nape edged with yellowish; throat white, streaked with black. Bill lake red; irides rich red; legs plumbeous.

Length of adult male and female—9·5 to 10 inches; wing 5·4 to 5·55; tail 3·4 to 4; tarsus 1· to 1·05; culmen 1·15 to 1·3.

Hab.—Throughout the Peninsula of India, extending down the Malay Peninsula. Occurs throughout Burmah and Ceylon; also in Cochin-China and Siam. It is found in the Punjàb, N.-W. Provinces, Bengal, Rajpootana, Central India, the Concan, Deccan, South India, the Malabar Coast, the Carnatic, Pegu, Tennaserim, British Burmah, the Andamans and Nepaul. I do not follow Sharpe in separating *O. ceylonensis*, either as a distinct species of or sub-species, nor Captain Legge in calling the larger form *O. himalayanus*. Mr. Sharpe (*Cat. B. Br. Mus.*) observes, that *O. ceylonensis* "although rather smaller than Himalayan examples, the alar speculum is larger than in the Cingalese form, and he looks upon it as intermediate between the continental and insular birds. *O. ceylonensis* is not at all a good species, and perhaps in a large series would be found to be inseparable,—*which it certainly is* from *O. melanocephalus*."

The black-headed Oriole affects both the densest forests and open jungles, also orchards and gardens. Oates says, its exquisite call of five whistling notes is one of the most charming sounds heard in the jungle, and it seems to be uttered at all hours of the day and almost all the year round. It nests from March to June, generally at a considerable height from the ground. The nest is suspended between two twigs, and in shape is like a cup. The materials used are leaves, fine twigs and vegetable fibres. Eggs 2—3, pinkish white, spotted with black. It feeds chiefly on fruit. Jerdon says, the figs of the Banian, peepul and other *Fici*, also mulberry, blossoms, and buds.

156. Oriolus trailli, *Vig. P. Z. S.*, 1831, p. 175; *Jerd. B. Ind.* ii. p. 112, No. 474; *Sharpe, Cat. B. Br. Mus.* iii. p. 222; *Hume, Str. F.* viii. p. 99; *Scully, Str. F.* v. p. 299. Psaropholus trailli, *Jerd. and Selby, Ill. Orn.* iv. pl. 20; *Bly. and Walden, B. Burm.* p. 139.—The MAROON ORIOLE.

Whole head, neck, chin, throat and wings glossy black; rest of the plumage maroon-red.

The young have the crown and nape dark brown; the back, rump, scapulars and wing coverts also dark brown, each feather edged with rufous. Upper tail coverts maroon-red, with black shafts; the tail maroon-red, the greater part of the central feathers and the edges of the outer webs of the other feathers brown; under surface white, streaked with brown. Bill pale bluish-grey; irides pale buffy-yellow; feet plumbeous; claws blue at base, pale horny at tip. (Scully.)

Length.—11 inches; tail 4·5; wing 6; tarsus 1; bill from gape 1·45.

Hab.—The Himalayas, extending to Nepaul, Sikkim, Assam, Arrakan, Burmah and Tennaserim. Occurs in Darjeeling, Nynee Tal, Bhootan, and Kumaon. Rare in Burmah. Obtained by Capt. Wardlaw-Ramsay, at Tounghoo, Karenne and on the Karin Hills.

The Maroon Oriole is said to be found in small flocks, keeping to high trees. It has a fine loud mellow call. Feeds on insects, as caterpillars.

Family—DICRURIDÆ—DRONGO SHRIKES.

Bill rather large, wide at base, thick, culmen curved and keeled, tip notched; rictal bristles moderately developed; nostrils basal, concealed by short plumes; tail usually long and furcate; outer feathers generally much lengthened. Plumage generally black or steel blue.

Gen. **Dicrurus.**—*Vieill.*

Characters same as that of the family. Tail nearly square, more or less forked, the outer feathers not ending in a racket, nor curved upwards.

157. Dicrurus annectens, *Hodgs. Ind. Rev.* i. p. 326; *Sharpe, Cat. B. Br. Mus.* iii. p. 231. Edolius annectens, *Blyth, J. A. S. B.* xi. p. 173. Dicrurus balicassius (*nec Lin.*), *Blyth, J. A. S. B.* xi. p. 175; *id.* xv. p. 298; *Jerd. B. Ind.* i. p. 430, No. 279; *Hume, Str. F.* 1874, pp. 209, 474; *Bly. and Walden, B. Burm.* p. 131; *Tweedd. Ibis.*, 1878, p. 72. Dicrurus annectens, *Hume and Davison, Str. F.* vi. pp. 213, 509; *Hume, Str. F.* viii. p. 91; *Oates, Str. F.* x. p. 201; *id. B. Br. Burm.* i. p. 217.—The CROW-BILLED DRONGO.

Black, glossed with steel blue, except the lores, ear coverts, inner webs of quills, axillaries and under wing coverts. Young and adolescent birds have the under wing coverts and under surface tipped with greyish white. Bill and legs black; iris red.

Length.—10 to 11 inches; wing 5·45 to 6; tail 4·1; to tip of outer feather 5·15 to 6; culmen 1·1; tarsus 0·75 to 0·82.

Hab.—The Malay Peninsula, Sumatra, Cochin-China. Found also in Nepaul, where Jerdon says it is rare. Extends thence eastward through Lower Bengal and Dacca to Assam, Burmah and Malacca. Found also in the Oudh

Terai. Oates says, it sweeps through Pegu every year in October; but whether it comes from the North or from the South he is unable to say; it is not seen at other times. Capt. Wardlaw-Ramsay procured it in Rangoon. Mr. Davison says it is not uncommon in the southern third of Tennaserim. Oates had examples from Malewoon, procured from December to February. Its habits are said to be those of the Common Drongo Shrike.

Gen. Chibia.—*Hodgs.*

Bill lengthened, compressed, curved and keeled on the culmen, tip hooked and obsoletely notched; rictal bristles short; forehead crested with hairs which fall over the neck; tail forked, outer feathers slightly lengthened, turned up; feathers of head and neck lanceolate.

158. Chibia hottentottus, *Lin.*, *Syst. Nat.* i. p. 155. Chibia hottentotta, *Jerd. B. Ind.* i. p. 439, No. 286; *Bly. B. Burm.* p. 128; *Anders. Yunnan Exped.* p. 651; *Hume, Nests and Eggs*, p. 194; *Hume, Str. F.* iii. p. 101; *Sharpe, Cat. B. Br. Mus.* iii. p. 235; *Tweedd. Ibis*, 1878, p. 73; *Hume and Davison, Str. F.* vi. p. 222; *Hume, Str. F.* viii. p. 92; *Oates, Str. F.* viii. p. 167; *Scully, Str. F.* viii. p. 272; *Bingham, Str. F.* ix. p. 174; *Oates, B. Br. Burm.* i. p. 227.—The Hair-crested Drongo.

Whole plumage black, with metallic blue reflections on the back and lower parts; lores and frontal plumes black, with a crest of long hairs springing from the base of the forehead and falling over the nape; sides of face purplish black; feathers of the head and sides of neck metallic steel green, those on the neck, long and lanceolate; feathers of the throat and neck tipped with metallic steel green. Upper surface of wing metallic bronze green; rest of the plumage black with metallic steel blue or green reflections; outer feathers of the tail recurved inwards at the tips. Bill and legs black; iris dark brown.

Length.—12·5 to 13 inches; wing 6·5 to 6·95; tail 5·6 to 6·5; culmen 1·55 to 1·6; tarsus 0·9 to 1.

Hab.—India, ranging through Assam and Burmah to China. Jerdon records it from Southern India, the Eastern Ghauts, Malabar, Wynaad, and Chota Nagpur, and says that it is found also about Calcutta, in the Sunderbuns and in the Himalayas. Blyth observed it in parts of the forests of Upper Martaban, and Jerdon himself procured specimens in the warmer valleys near Darjeeling. According to Oates, it is found over the whole of Burmah, except, perhaps, in the southernmost portion of Tennaserim. It is said to occur in Arrakan and in many parts of Pegu. Fairly common at Prome. Davison got it in Tennaserim and Captain Bingham in the Thoungyeen Valley. It has also been procured at Tounghoo and on the Karin Hills.

The Hair Crested Drongo is an inhabitant of thick forests or groves. It is said to feed on insects as wasps, bees, beetles, &c. Breeds in May and June. Nest constructed of fine twigs, placed generally in a fork at the top of very high trees. Eggs three in number, white, spotted and streaked with reddish brown, or purplish and claret.

Gen. **Chaptia**.—*Hodgs.*

Tail strongly forked; outer tail feathers not much recurved at tip; plumage spangled with metallic bronze tips; frontal plumes dense. Bill depressed and more feeble than in *Dicrurus*. 1st quill short, 4th longest, 3rd and 6th equal.

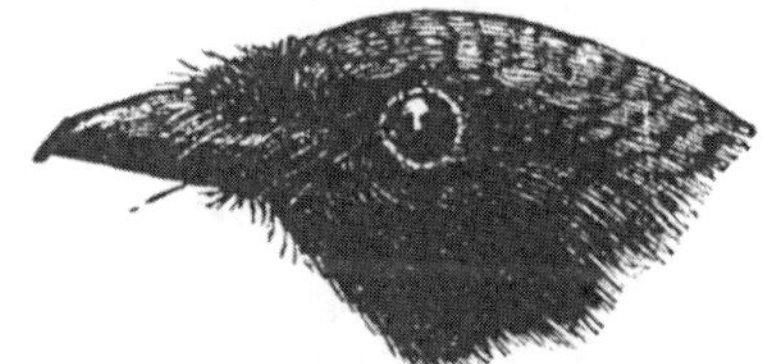

159. Chaptia ænea, *Vieill, N. Dict. d' Hist.* ix. p. 586; *Jerd. B. Ind.* i. p. 433; *Hume, Nests and Eggs*, p. 192; *Bly. and Wald. B. Burm.* p. 128; *Hume, Str. F.* iii. p. 100; *Armstrong, Str. F.* iv. p. 320; *Sharpe, Cat. B. Br. Mus.* iii. p. 243; *Anders. Yunnan Exped.* p. 652; *Hume and Davison, Str. F.* vi. p. 217; *Hume, Str. F.* viii. p. 92; *Oates, Str. F.* viii. p. 166; *Scully, Str. F.* viii. p. 272; *Bingham, Str. F.* ix. p. 173; *Oates, B. Br. Burm.* i. p. 223. Edolius picinus (*S. Mull*) *Bonap. Consp. Av.* 1. p. 352.—The Bronzed Drongo.

Whole plumage black, glossed with metallic bronze on the upper and under surface, except the rump, vent, under tail coverts, and lower abdomen, which are dull greyish brown; throat and breast spangled with metallic bronze tips to the feathers; under wing coverts black, only slightly glossed with bronze; lores and sides of face unglossed dull or brownish black. Bill and feet black; iris blackish brown (pinkish hazel, *Oates*). Eyelids purplish grey.

Length.—9 to 9·5 inches; wing 4·75 to 5; tail 4·75 to 5; tarsus 0·65; culmen 1·0.

Hab.—The moist climates of India generally, extending to Assam and Burmah. Occurs along the Malabar Coast, in Travancore, Southern India generally, Lower Bengal, Central India and on the slopes of the Himalayas to Nepaul. Oates says it is found in every part of Burmah, and that Mr. Blyth gives it from Arrakan. He procured it in Pegu, and both Davison and Captain Bingham found it abundant in all parts of Tennaserim, while Captain Wardlaw-Ramsay obtained it at Tounghoo, in the Karen Hills and in Karenne.

The Bronzed Drongo is an inhabitant of dense and lofty forests, and is usually found in small parties, near the top of some lofty tree, whence it sallies forth, darts on passing insects, and returns generally to the same perch. Oates found a nest in April. It was cup-shaped, placed at the top of the higher branches of a Jack tree, *Artocarpus integrifolia,* and made of fine grass, strips of plantain bark and vegetable fibres over-laid at the edges with cobweb. Eggs two in number, of a salmon colour and marked with darker shades of the same.

160. Chaptia malayensis, *Blyth. J. A. S. B.* xv. p. 294 (*ex. A. Hay MS.*) ; *Jerd. B. Ind.* i. p. 434 ; *Sharpe, Cat. B. Br. Mus.* iii. p. 244. Chaptia malayana, *Sharpe, Ibis,* 1876, p. 45.—The MALAY DRONGO.

Differs from *C. ænea* in having the whole plumage, including the vent, rump and upper and under tail coverts of a glossy metallic greenish black colour, the abdomen and flanks greyish black. It is also much smaller, adults measuring 8·3 against 9·5 inches in length ; wing 4·5 ; tail 4 ; tarsus 0·6 ; culmen 0·85.

Hab.—The Malay Peninsula, Sumatra, Borneo and, according to Dr. Tiraud, Cochin-China. Habits, those of the last.

Gen. **Buchanga.**—*Hodgs.*

Bill moderate, depressed at base and slightly hooked ; culmen keeled and notched at tip ; rictal bristles strong ; frontal plumes dense, but not elongated to form a crest. Plumage black ; tail forked.

161. Buchanga atra, *Herm. Obs. Zool.* p. 208 ; *Murray, Vert. Zool. Sind,* p. 126 ; *Sharpe, Cat. Passerif. B. Br. Mus.* p. 246. Dicrurus macrocercus, *Viell. N. Dict.* ix. p. 588 ; *Jerd. Mad. Journ.* xiii. pt. ii. p. 121 ; *id. B. of Ind.* i. p. 427, No. 278 ; *Gray, Gen. B.* i. p. 286 ; *Str. F.* iv. 278 ; vi. 213 ; vii. 272 ; *Murray, Hdbk., Zool., &c., Sind,* p. 137. Buchanga albirictus, *Hodgs. Ind. Rev.* p. 326 ; *Hume, Str. F.*, 1873, p. 178 ; *Ball. Str. F.*, 1874, p. 402. Dicrurus balicassius, *Sykes, P. Z. S.* 1832, p. 86 (*nec. l.*).—The COMMON DRONGO SHRIKE or KING CROW.

Head, hind neck, back, upper tail coverts, lesser and median wing coverts glossy blue-black ; a white spot at the gape ; chin, throat, lores, sides of the face, and under surface of the body black, less glossy than the upper surface, and with a greenish cast ; greater and primary coverts black, glossed greenish, also the secondaries and tertiaries ; primaries and tail duller black ; the inner webs of the primaries and under surface of the tail dusky. Young with whitish lunules on the under surface of the body. Bill and legs black ; irides red.

Length.—12 inches; wing 5·75; tail 6·25 to tip of outer feather; tarsus 0·9.

Hab.—The whole of India and Ceylon, extending to Assam, the Indo-Chinese region, China, Formosa and Burmah. Occurs also in Java, Siam, Cochin-China, the N.-W. Himalayas, Nepaul, Beloochistan and Afghanistan. If is found throughout the Punjab, N.-W. Provinces, Oudh, Bengal, Rajpootana, Central India, Kutch, Guzerat, Konkan, Deccan, Travancore and South India generally. According to Oates it is a common bird in Burmah and Pegu. In the latter it is common from October to January. Dr. Armstrong found it common in the Irrawaddy delta; Davison found it common in Tennaserim from Moulmein to Malewoon, and Captain Bingham met with it at Tounghoo.

The King Crow is chiefly found in open jungle, and seldom or never in forests. It is a conspicuous bird everywhere about a station. Its presence is readily known simply by its cheerful and pretty notes. Perched on a telegraph wire, wall, or on a bare branch, its sweet notes are uttered, not forgetting now and again its rather harsh cry. A couple of pairs within one's grounds often make their chattering, as if one to another for half an hour at a time, sound disagreeable. Its loquacity is unsurpassed, especially in the early morn. It is often seen on the backs of cattle, sheep and goats when out grazing in company with *Acridotheres tristis* or *ginginianus*, the common crow, and not unfrequently *Neophrons*.

The food of the King Crow is chiefly insects of sorts, as grasshoppers, mantises, bees, wasps, ants, dragon flies, moths and butterflies. I don't know that it has a predilection for anything higher than members of the Invertebrates. During the breeding season, which lasts from May to July, March to April, and August and September, according to locality, the King Crow is very pugnacious. It pursues and drives away every bird it suspects, even hawks, kites, and crows, especially when the female is sitting for incubation. It places its nest generally in the fork of the outer branches of a tree, selecting generally an *Acacia*. It is cup-shaped and shallow, and made of fine twigs and grass. In some instances lined outside with cobwebs and inside with a little hair or feathers. Eggs generally 4 in number, reddish or pinkish white, prettily streaked, spotted and blotched with brick red or brown.

162. Buchanga longicaudata, *A. Hay, Jerd. Mad. Journ.* xiii. p. 121; *Jerd. B. Ind.* i. p. 430, No. 280; *Wald. P. Z. S.* 1866, p. 549; *Hume, Nests and Eggs*, p. 189; *Hume, Str. F.* iii. p. 97; *Wald. in Bl. B. Burm.* p. 130; *Sharpe, Cat. B. Br. Mus.* iii. p. 249; *Hume and Davison, Str. F.* vi. p. 213; *Legge, B. Ceylon*, p. 390; *Tweedd. Ibis*, 1878, p. 74; *Hume, Str. F.* viii. p. 91; *Scully, Str. F.* viii. p. 270; *Oates, Str. F.* x. p. 202. Dicrurus himalayanus, *Tytler, Ibis*, 1868, p. 200. Buchanga Waldeni, *Beavan, Ibis*, 1868, p. 497; *Oates, B. Burm.* i. p. 220.—The DARK-ASHY OR LONG-TAILED DRONGO.

Whole upper plumage including the wings and tail blackish ashy, with a greenish gloss; sides of the face, frontal plumes and under surface of the body

21

dark ashy, paler towards the vent; under tail coverts dull greyish white, paler and nearly white at the tips; under wing coverts similarly tipped; in old or fully adult birds, these whitish tippings are absent. Bill and legs black; iris red.

Length.—11 to 11·5 inches; wing 5·5 to 5·6; tail, including outer feathers, 6·5 to 6·7; tarsus 0·8; culmen 1.

Hab.—India generally, the Indo-Burmese countries, Ceylon, N.-W. Himalayas to Nepaul and Ladakh. Found in Travancore, and Southern India generally; also on the Malabar Coast, Wynaad, Coorg, the Neilgherries, Bengal, Punjab, N.-W. and Central Provinces. In Southern and parts of Western India, it is a permanent resident, also in S. Pegu. Davison found it in Tennaserim from Moulmein to Mergui. In Upper Pegu it is said to be replaced by *B. leucoophæa.*

Its habits are quite those of *B. atra,* but unlike it, it inhabits or rather affects forests, and has a pleasant song. Breeds during April and May. Nest similar to that of *B. atra.* Eggs, 3—4 in number typically white with brick red spots.

163. Buchanga cineracea, *Sharpe, Cat., B. Br. Mus..* iii. p. 250. Edolius cineraceus, *Horsf. Tr. Linn. Soc.* xiii. p. 145. Dicrurus leucophæus, *Gray. Gen. B.* i. p. 287. Dicrurus intermedius, *Bly. J. A. S. B.* xv. p. 298. Dicrurus leucophæus, *Vieill. N. Dict. d'Hist. Nat.* ix. p. 587; *Hume, Str. F.* iii. p. 99. Buchanga pyrrhops, (*Hodg.*) *Wald. in Bl. B. Burmah,* p. 130; *Armstrong, Str. F.* iv. p. 320; *Sharpe, Cat. B. Br. Mus.* iii. p. 251; *Hume and Dav. Str. F.* vi. p. 216; *Hume, Str. F.* viii. p. 92; *Oates, Str. F.* x. p. 202. Buchanga leucophæa, *Hume and Dav. Str. F.* vi. p. 317; viii, p. 92.—The PALE-ASHY DRONGO.

Whole plumage bluish ashy, glossy above, paler underneath and unglossed on the breast; frontal plumes and lores black, upper wing coverts like the upper surface but centred darker; quills tinged with ashy on the outer webs. Tail bluish ashy; the shafts black and the tips brownish. Bill and legs black; iris crimson.

Length.—10 to 11 inches; wing 5·2 to 5·75; tarsus 0·8; culmen 2.

Hab.—Dacca (Bengal) to the N.-W. Himalayas, and Nepaul, ranging to Pegu, Burmah and Java. Occurs also in Siam, Cochin-China, and Eastern China.

The habits of this Drongo are quite those of its congeners. The structure of the nest and the size and colour of its eggs like those of *B. longicaudata.* It is found in all the well-wooded districts of Burmah and Bengal.

164. Buchanga leucogenys, *Wald. Ann. and Mag. Nat. Hist.* v. p. 219; *id. in Bl. B. Burm. p.* 131; *Sharpe, Cat. B. Br. Mus.* iii. p. 251; *David et Oust. Ois, Chine,* p. 108, pl. 77; *Tweedd. Ibis,* 1878, p. 69; *Hume*

Family, ARTAMIDÆ.—Swallow Shrikes.

Bill moderate, wide at base, deep and slightly curved; commissure slightly curved; nostrils basal, with a minute tuft of bristles at their base; tarsus short and strong; claws well curved, acute; wings long; 1st quill minute, 2nd longest; tail short. (*Jerd.*) Plumage grey. They are called Swallow Shrikes, owing to their feeding like the swallows in the air.

Gen. **Artamus**—*Vieill.*

Characters those of the Family.

165a. Artamus fuscus, *Vieill., Nouv. Dict. d'Hist. Nat.* xvii. p. 297; *Jerd., B. Ind.* i. p. 441, No. 287; *Hume, Nests and Eggs, Ind. B.* p. 194; *Blyth, B. Burm.* p. 127; *Hume, Str. F.* iii. p. 102; *Armstrong, Str. F.* iv. p. 321; *Dav. et Oust. Ois. Chine,* p. 101; *Cripps, Str. F.* vii. p. 273; *Sharpe in Rowley's Orn. Misc.* iii. p. 191; *Legge, B. Ceylon,* p. 666; *Hume, Str. F.* viii. p. 92; *Oates, Str. F.* x. p. 203; *id., B. Br. Burm.* i. p. 396.—The Ashy Swallow Shrike.

Lores black; head and neck ashy grey, also the back, scapulars, rump and shorter upper tail coverts, but these with a rufescent or vinous tinge; longer upper tail coverts white; tail dark grey, tipped with whitish; wings and their coverts deep grey; quills narrowly margined with white near the tips and on portions of the inner webs; breast, abdomen, under wing and under tail coverts pale purplish brown, the latter finely barred with ashy. Bill pale blue, darker at the tip; legs slaty; irides dark brown.

Length.—7 to 7·3 inches; wing 5·2; tail 2·5; tarsus 0·65; bill from gape 0·95.

The young are barred above, the quills are broadly margined with whitish, and the under wing coverts tipped with rufous.

Hab.—Throughout nearly the whole of the moist regions in India and Ceylon. Jerdon says it is more abundant in the wooded districts, especially where palm trees abound, more particularly the Palmyra palm. He found them most abundant in the Carnatic, the Malabar Coast, the Northern Circars and Bengal; rare in the Deccan and Central India. Occurs also at Darjeeling, spread throughout Assam, British Burmah and Ceylon. It has been found at Arracan, Tenasserim and Pegu in large flocks. The nests are built on palm trees, and are made of grass, twigs and fibres. Eggs, 4 in number, whitish, marked at the larger end with yellowish brown and lilac.

Artamus leucorhynchus, a species with the rump and lower surface of the body white and the back and wings chocolate brown, is found in the Andamans.

Vol. I., p. 157.

and Dav. Str. F. vi. p. 216; *Hume, Str. F.* viii. p. 92; *Oates, B. Br. Burmah* i. p. 222. Dicrurus leucophæus (*Vieill.*) *apud. Hume, Str. F.* ii. p. 210.—The WHITE-CHEEKED DRONGO.

Whole upper plumage clear pale ashy grey; shafts of the quills and tail and tips of the first 6—7 primaries black; upper tail coverts and tail lighter grey, inclining to blackish brown at the tips. Nasal bristles black; lores, feathers round the eye and ear coverts pure white. Cheeks and under surface of body pale ashy grey, lighter and nearly white on the abdomen and under tail coverts; under wing coverts light grey edged with white. Bill and legs black; iris red.

Length.—10·2 to 10·5 inches; wing 5·5; tail 4·5; to tip of outer feathers 5·7; tarsus 0·7; culmen 0·95.

Hab.—Malacca, ranging through the Indo-Chinese region to China and Japan. (Sharpe.)

Extends down the Malay Peninsula, and is found in Siam and Cochin-China. Davison procured it in South Tennaserim, where he says it was abundant as far north as Mergui. He adds that "it is much more of a forest species than any of the other King Crows. It also occurs in clearings and occasionally in gardens. Its notes and habits are much the same as those of the other species, and like them it is fond of perching on the top of some dead tree, or other commanding station from which it constantly makes short sallies after passing insects. It is always seen singly."

165. Buchanga cærulescens, *Linn, Syst. Nat.* i. p. 134; *Sharpe, Cat. B. Br. Mus.* iii. p. 252. Dicrurus cærulescens, *Vieill. N. Dict. d'Hist. Nat.* ix. p. 587; *Jerd. Madras Journ.* x. p. 239; *Bly. Ann. and Mag. Nat. Hist.* xiv. p. 47; *Jerd. B. Ind.* i. p. 432, No. 281.—The WHITE-BELLIED DRONGO.

Whole upper plumage, including wings and tail, slaty grey, with a metallic steel blue gloss; chin, throat and breast ashy brown, glossed with steel blue on the sides of the neck and sides of the upper breast; abdomen and lower tail coverts white; under wing coverts ashy brown and slightly glossed; thighs glossy black; bill and feet black; iris lake-red.

Length.—9·5 to 9·6 inches; wing 4·75 to 5·05; tail 3·65; to tip of outer feathers 5; tarsus 0·8; culmen 0·95.

Hab.—India generally. Recorded from Malabar, the slopes of the Neilgherries, Madras, Nellore, Central India, Calcutta, Central Provinces, Behar, Kattyawar, N.-W. Himalayas to Nepaul.

The White-bellied Drongo affects well-wooded districts generally. It is seldom seen in clearings, groves, or near habitations. Like other species of *Buchanga*, it seizes its prey on the wing, and has the usual sweet song and harsh cry of the family.

Gen. **Dissemuroides**.—*Hume*.

Outer tail feathers produced and recurved at tip; forehead with a few bristles.

166. Dissemuroides andamanensis, *Hume, Str. F.*, 1874, p. 211; *Sharpe, Cat. B. Br. Mus.* iii. p. 255. Dicrurus andamanensis, *Tytler and Beaven, Ibis*, 1867, p. 322; *Gray, Hand-l. B.* i. p. 285; *Ball, J. A. S. B.* xii. p. 282. Buchanga (Dicrurus) andamanensis, *Ball, S. F.*, 1873, p. 66. Dissemuroides dicruriformis, *Hume, Str. F.*, 1873, p. 408; *id.*, 1874, p. 211; *Sharpe, Cat. B. Br. Mus.* p. 255.—The ANDAMAN DRONGO.

Adult Male.—General colour black, with a slight purplish gloss on the back; wings glossed with metallic steel-green, as also the secondaries; quills brown, with reddish brown shafts, and slightly glossed with greenish at the base of the outer web; tail black, with a steel green gloss on the outer web; lores, sides of face, and under surface deep black with a slight purplish gloss on the breast; under wing coverts like the breast, but tipped with white; bill and legs black; iris hair-brown, sometimes very deep and almost blackish.

Length.—11·25 to 12·0 inches; wing 5·0 to 5·25; tail 7·0 to 8·25; bill from gape 1·2 to 1·35; tarsus 0·8 to 0·9.

Adult Female.—Rather smaller than the male.

Hab.—Andaman and Great Cocos Islands.

I have united Hume's *D. dicruriformis* with this species, as I cannot find any good character which would serve to give it specific rank. It is certainly a larger bird, but I think with Mr. Sharpe that it can only be looked upon as a race. The comparative measurements of *Andamanensis* and *dicruriformis* are as under:—

	Length.	Wing.	Tail.	Tarsus.
dicruriformis	13·25 to 14·6	5·6 to 5·9	8·75	0·9 to 1·0
Andamanensis	11·25 to 12	5 to 5·25	7 to 8·25	0·8 to 0·9

Gen. **Bhringa**.—*Hodgs*.

Bill moderately depressed at base; culmen curved, hooked and notched at the tip; rictal bristles feeble; base of bill covered with recurved feathers. Nostrils covered with bristles; 4th quill longest. Tail nearly even, forked, the outer feather ending in a racket.

167. Bhringa remifer, *Tem. Pl. Col.* 178; *Jerd. B. Ind.* i. p. 434; *Sharpe, Cat. B. Br. Mus.* iii. p. 257; *Hume and Davison, Str. F.* vi. p. 218; *Tweedd., Ibis,* 1878, p. 80; *Hume, Str. F.* viii. p. 92; *Oates, B. Br. Burm.* i. p. 224. Bhringa tectirostris, (*Hodgs*), *Hume, Nests and Eggs,* p. 193; *id. Str. F.* iii. p. 101.—The LESSER RACKET-TAILED DRONGO.

Whole plumage black, with a brilliant metallic gloss, the feathers of the crown spangled with metallic-violet; also those of the throat and breast; under tail coverts washed with steel green; abdomen blackish grey with a steel gloss; outermost tail feathers produced into a long shaft with an elongated black spatule at end. Bill and legs black; iris red.

Length.—9·6 to 10·5 inches; wing 5·25; tail to tip of outer feathers 12 to 14.

Hab.—Nepaul, N.-W. Himalayas, Burmese Provinces, Tennaserim and Java. Sparingly distributed over Pegu, and confined to deep forests. According to Jerdon, it is also found in Assam. At Darjeeling it is found in the warmer valleys. Breeds from April to June and July; nest a loose cup-shaped structure. Eggs, 3—4, reddish white with reddish brown spots and blotches. Habits the same as other Drongos.

Gen. **Dissemurus**.—*Gloger.*

Characters the same as in *Bhringa*. Crest more full and developed, and falling back on the forehead; tail forked, the outermost pair with the outer web gradually thinning off; shaft bare for some distance, and terminating in a racket.

168. Dissemurus paradiseus, *Linn, Syst. Nat.* i. p. 172; *Bl. Wald. B. Burm.* p. 128; *Armstrong. Str. F.* iv. p. 321; *Sharpe, Cat. B. Br. Mus.* iii. p. 258; *Tweedd. Ibis,* 1878, p. 80; *Hume and Davison, Str. F.* vi. p. 219; *Legge, B. Ceylon,* p. 399; *Hume, Str. F.* viii. p. 192; *Bingham,*

Str. F. ix. p. 174; *Oates, Str. F.* x. p. 203; *id. B. Br. Burm.* i. p. 225. Dicrurus platurus, *Vieill. N. Dict. d'Hist. Nat.* i. p. 588. Edolius Rangoonensis, *Gould. P. Z. S.*, 1836, p. 50. Edolius grandis, *Gould. P. Z. S.*, 1836, p. 5. Chibia malabaroides, *Hodgs. Ind. Rev.* i. p. 325. Dicrurus retifer, *Jerd. Mad. Journ.* x. p. 241. Edolius cristatellus, *Bly. J. A. S. B.* xi. p. 171. Edolius brachyphorus, (*Temm.*) *Bonap. Consp. Av.* i. p. 351. Edolius paradiseus (*Linn.*) *Jerd. B. Ind.* i., p. 435. Edolius malabaricus, (*Scop.*) *Jerd. B. Ind.* i. p. 437. Dissemurus malabaroides (*Hodgs.*), *Hume, Nests and Eggs, Ind. B.* p. 123; *id., Str. F.* iii. p. 101. Dissemurus grandis, (*Gould.*), *Hume, Str. F.* viii. p. 92; *Oates, Str. F.* viii. p. 166; *id., Oates, B. Br. Burm.* i. p. 225.—The GREAT RACKET-TAILED DRONGO.

Whole plumage black, glossed with steel blue, except on the inner webs of the quills, the throat, lower abdomen and vent. The outer pair of feathers in both sexes lengthened and furnished with a racket; in the young the gloss is less developed, and the under wing coverts are tipped with white; bill, legs and feet black; irides red (brown in the young).

Length.—14 inches; wing 6·6; tail 7; outer feathers 13 to 15; tarsus 1·15; culmen 1·3.

Hab.—The Indian Peninsula, Ceylon, Andaman Islands, Indo-Chinese and Indo-Burmese Countries, the Malayan Peninsula, Java and Borneo; also Sumatra, Cochin-China and Nepal. It is recorded as occurring from the Himalayas to the Eastern Ghats as far South as N. L. 15°; also at Nellore, Goomsoor, Central and S. India, N.-W. Provinces, Lower Bengal, the Sunderbuns, Assam, Sylhet, Burmah and Tennaserim. Mr. Sharpe has very carefully gone into the question, whether all the species hitherto described as distinct, were so or not. *Brachyphorus* from Borneo, appeared to be a distinct form, but there was not sufficient ground upon which it could be specifically separated. The specific characters held to constitute a species were the length of tails, the size of the rackets on the outer feathers, and the development of the crest. These Mr. Sharpe has carefully studied, and the outcome is that he has united all under one species (*Dissemurus paradiseus*). He says that after a careful study of what has been written on the subject of these racket-tailed Drongos, and after comparison of the series in the British Museum collection, he has arrived at the conclusion that between *D. malabaroides* (a very full-crested form) of the Eastern Himalayas and *D. brachyphorus* of Borneo, an unbroken chain of races exists. Blyth came to the same conclusion in 1849, Mr. Sharpe adds, that he does not see that the labors of ornithologists have tended to upset this conclusion. His review of these species ends with the following remarks;—"Finding it, however, quite impossible to define exact specific characters for these supposed species, I have united them under one name, and merely keep the specimens arranged under different headings; for I fully believe that a larger series will only show more connecting links, and that it will be found more and more impossible to give specific characters for those differentiated under the various titles mentioned."

The large racket-tailed Drongo affects forests, and well-wooded districts. Like the Drongos in general it selects the extreme end of a bough or branch for its perch, which it now and again leaves for the purpose of capturing a passing insect. It always returns to the same perch. Its song is said to be rich and mellow, especially during the breeding season. The nest is built in a fork on the very tip of a bough on the highest tree in the place, and almost inaccessible. In structure it does not differ from that of its congeners. The eggs, usually three in number, are white or pinkish, marked with reddish brown.

Gen. **Irena.**—*Horsf.*

Bill stout, of moderate length; culmen rather elevated and slightly arching from the base, tip notched; nostrils covered with short plumes. Wings with the 4th quill longest; tarsus short.

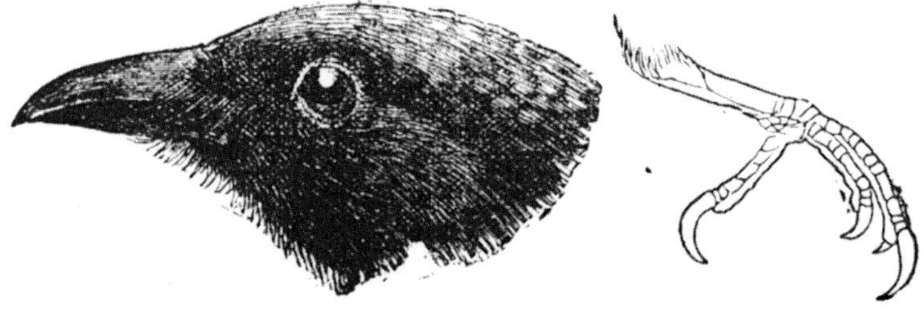

169. Irena puella, *Lath. Ind. Orn.* i. p. 171; *Jerd. B. Ind.* ii. p. 105; *Stol. J. A. S. B.* xxxix. p. ii. p. 318; *Wald. Ibis,* 1871, p. 170; *Hume, Nests and Eggs,* p. 298; *Hume, Str. F.* ii. p. 226; iii. p. 130; *Bl. and Wald. B. Burm.* p. 138; *Armstrong, Str. F.* iv. p. 326; *Bourdillon, Str. F.* iv. p. 400; *Wardlaw-Ramsay, Ibis,* 1877, p. 467; *Hume and Dav. Str. F.* vi. p. 328; *Hume Str. F.* viii. p. 99; *Legge, Birds, Ceylon,* p. 466; *Sharpe, Cat. Birds, B. Mus.* vi. p. 177; *Bingham, Str. F.* ix. p. 184; *Oates, Str. F.* x. p. 211; *Oates, B. Br. Burm.* p. 209.—The Fairy Blue Bird.

Whole upper plumage, including the lesser wing coverts, brilliant glistening cobalt blue. Sides of the head, quills and tail deep black; the secondaries and central tail feathers with a shade of blue; lores, feathers over the eye, sides of neck and entire under surface, also the thighs and under wing coverts, black; under tail coverts purplish black.

The female has the whole of the upper plumage dull prussian blue, brighter on the rump and upper and under tail coverts; primaries and secondaries dark brown, also the greater wing coverts, primary coverts and tertiaries, but these with a bluish tinge on their outer webs.

Bill and legs black; iris crimson.

Length.—10 to 10·3 inches; wing 5; tail 4·2 to 4·4; tarsus 0·85; culmen 0·95 to 1.

Hab.—The Malabar Coast, Southern India generally, and Travancore; also Assam, Arrakan, and British Burmah. It also occurs in Siam and Cochin-China, in the Khasia Hills, Cachar, Ceylon and the Andamans.

The Fairy blue bird affects evergreen, dense, woody forests, and is more abundant in the hilly tracts than in the plains. It is found in the Pegu Hills down to Rangoon; in the Irrawaddy delta, and according to Davison, in all the evergreen forests of Tennaserim. It is generally found in pairs, but parties of 6 or 7 are not uncommon. Capt. Bingham found the nest in Tennaserim. It was cupshaped in form, and in structure like that of a Drongo. Eggs, two, greenish white, marked with brown.

Family.—PRIONOPIDÆ.

Bill with a notch in the upper mandible. Nostrils more or less covered with plumes. Tail moderate, rounded or square, and of 12 feathers.

Sub-family.—PRIONOPINÆ.

Bill higher than broad, wings short, not reaching the tip of the tail.

Gen. Tephrodornis.—*Swainson.*

Bill moderately hooked and notched at tip; a few rictal bristles, nostrils covered with procumbent plumes; wings moderate; tarsus and toes short. Outer toe longest and slightly syndactyle.

170. Tephrodornis pondiceriana, *Gmel. S. N.* i. p. 939; *Bly. J. A. S. B.*, 1846, p. 305; *Jerd. B. Ind.* p. 410, No. 265; *Murray, Vert. Zool., Sind*, p. 123; *Hume, Str. F.* i. 435; *Murray, Hdbk., Zool., &c., Sind*, p. 134. Tephrodornis indica, *Cat. Hodgs. Coll. B. M.* p. 90. Tentheca leucura, *Hodgs. Ind. Rev.* i. p. 447.—The Common Wood-Shrike.

Head, hind neck, scapulars, back and rump ashy brown; the feathers of the rump edged white; superciliary streak fulvous white; a dark brown streak from the nostrils to the ear coverts; upper tail coverts dark brown; wings dusky brown; tail dark brown, with the two outer feathers white, and margined dusky on the outer web at the tip, basally dark brown; chin and throat white; breast and upper abdomen greyish brown; lower abdomen, vent and under tail coverts white; bill dusky horny; legs plumbeous; irides greenish yellow.

Length.—6·5 to 7 inches; wing 3·5; tail 2·75; bill at front 0·62.

Hab.—India generally, Burmah, Assam, Bengal, extending to the foot of the Himalayas. Occurs in the Deccan, North Guzerat, Kutch and Kattiawar. In Sind it is a seasonal visitant, arriving in April, breeding and leaving the Province early in September. I obtained nestlings in May and June, and during July and August. Of the eight specimens collected, five were young birds. None were seen in September. Its presence is easily known by a very pretty, unmistakable little song, quite unlike that of any of the *Laniinæ*.

171. Tephrodornis pelvicus, *Sharpe, Cat. B. Br. Mus.* iii. p. 276. Tentheca pelvica, *Hodgs. Ind. Rev.* i. p. 447; Tephrodornis pelvica, *Jerd. B. Ind.* i. p. 409, No. 263; *Hume, Str. F.* iii. p. 92; *Bl. B. Burm.* p. 122; *Hume and Dav. Str. F.* vi. p. 205; *Hume, Str. F.* viii. p. 91.—The NEPAUL WOOD-SHRIKE.

Above pale ashy brown; forehead whitish; head, nape and hind neck cinereous grey; rump greyish white, barred with brown near the tip; upper tail coverts white, the longer ones brown. Tail brown, with a rufous tinge, the shafts reddish and the tips whitish; quills ashy brown, rufous shafted, all edged and tipped brighter; lores, ear coverts and feathers under the eye black; sides of face, sides of neck, and under surface white, tinged with pinkish on the breast.

Length.—8·5 inches; wing 4·5; tail 3·5; tarsus 0·85; culmen 0·95 to 1.

Hab.—N.-W. Provinces of India, Oudh, N.-W. Himalayas, Sikkim, Arrakan, Assam, the Indo-Burmese countries, Tipperah, Cachar, and from Bhootan to Nepaul. Davison found it generally distributed over Tennaserim, and Oates says over the whole of Pegu.

The Nepaul or Hodgson's Wood-Shrike frequents thick evergreen forests in preference to other localities. It feeds on insects as grylli, mantises, crickets, grubs and caterpillars, which it picks off the leaves.

172. Tephrodornis sylvicola, *Jerd. Madr. Journ.* x. p. 236; *Bly, J. A. S. B.* xv. p. 304; *Bp. Consp.* i. 357; *Jerd. B. Ind.* i. p. 408.—The MALABAR WOOD-SHRIKE.

Above slaty cinereous; rump, white; wings, tail and some of the upper coverts dusky brown; upper tail coverts white; the longer ones dusky brown; nasal plumes, lores, feathers under and above the eye, and ear coverts black, more defined than in *pondiceriana*; cheeks and entire under surface of body white. Eyebrow faintly indicated. Bill blackish; legs plumbeous; iris was yellow.

Length.—8·5 inches; wing 4; tail 4·4; tarsus 0·8; culmen 0·8.

Hab.—Southern parts of the Indian Peninsula. Jerdon says it is only found in the forests of the Malabar Coast, and ascends the Neilgherry and other ranges. It climbs and hops about the larger boughs of trees, picking insects of various kinds off the leaves. Found in small flocks.

173. Tephrodornis grisola, *Blyth, J. A. S. B.* xii. p. 180; *Jerd. B. Ind.* i. p. 411, No. 266; *Bly. Ibis*, 1865, p. 43. Hyloterpe grisola, *Wald. Ibis*, 1874, p. 141. Muscitrea cinerea, *Bl. J. A. S. B.* xvi. p. 121; *Hume, Str. F.* v. p. 101. Hyloterpe philomela, (*Mull.*) *Cat. Arch. f. Wat.* 1847, p. 322. Muscitrea grisola, *Hume and Dav. Str. F.* vi. p. 206; *Hume, Str. F.* viii. p. 91; *Oates, B. Br. Burmah*, i. p. 257.—The GREY WOOD-SHRIKE.

Lores, head from the forehead to the nape dull earthy brown; back, rump, scapulars, upper tail and upper wing coverts rufous brown; wings and tail hair brown, the quills of the former margined exteriorly with rufous brown. Chin, throat, breast and flanks pale brown; abdomen, vent, under tail and under wing coverts pure white. No white supercilium as in *pondiceriana*. Bill dark brown; iris reddish brown; legs plumbeous; claws pale horn colour.

Length.—6·5 to 6·6 inches; wing 3·25; tail 2·5 to 2·6; tarsus 0·84; culmen 0·8.

Hab.—Eastern side of the Bay of Bengal, from Arrakan down to Malayana, also the Andaman Islands and Java. It is recorded from Bengal, also from Pegu. It has also been found in Sumatra and Borneo. According to Davison it is rare in Tennaserim.

Gen. Hemipus.—*Hodgs.*

Characters as in *Tephrodornis*; bill more depressed, and wider at base; 3rd quill nearly equal to 4th.

174. Hemipus picatus, *Sykes, P. Z. S.* 1832, p. 25; *Sharpe, Cat. B. Br. Mus.* iii. p. 307; *Jerd., B. Ind.* i. p. 412; *Hume, Nests and Eggs*, p. 178; *id. Str. F.* i. p. 435; iii. p. 93; *Hume and Davison*, vi. p. 207; *Hume, Str. F.* viii. p. 91.—SYKES'S PIED SHRIKE.

Whole upper plumage, with the lores and ear coverts glossy black; rump feathers broadly tipped with white; chin, vent, and upper tail coverts pure white; the remainder of the lower plumage pale vinaceous; the cheeks and the sides of the neck white, produced so as to form an indistinct white collar round the neck; lesser wing coverts black; median coverts black, broadly tipped with white, the outer greater coverts black; primary coverts and quills black, the later secondaries broadly edged with white; tail black, all but the central feathers tipped with white, which extends over the whole outer web of the outermost feathers; bill black; iris hazel; eyelids plumbeous; legs plumbeous brown.

Length.—5·4 inches; wing 2·5; tail 2·4; tarsus 4·5; culmen 7.

Hab.—N.-W. Provinces, Oudh, Central India, Concan, Deccan, South India, Travancore, Ceylon, British Burmah and Tennaserim.

The little Pied Shrike is generally seen in small parties of five or six, wandering about from tree to tree, every now and then darting on insects in the air. It has a pleasant song, which, however, is not often heard. It frequents thick forests, and like the Drongo, perches on the outer branches of a tree. According to Davison it also searches the leaves like a Wood Shrike. A nest taken by Mr. Davison at Ootacamund, was a small shallow cup made of grass and roots, covered with cobwebs and lichens and sparingly lined. It was placed on a branch of a tall tree and contained three eggs, which were pale greenish marked with umber-brown. Jerdon says the markings of the eggs he obtained at Darjeeling were a few rusty red spots.

175. Hemipus obscurus, *Horsf. Tr. Linn. Soc.* xiii. p. 146; *Bly. J. A. S. B.* xv. p. 305; *id. and Wald. B. Burm.* p. 122; *Jerd. B. Ind.* i. p. 413; *Sharpe, Ibis,* 1877, p. 20. Tephrodornis obscura, *Gray, Gen. B. App.* p. 13.—HORSFIELD'S OBSCURE OR PIED SHRIKE.

Wings, tail and the whole upper plumage glossy greenish black, except the shorter upper tail coverts and the tips of the feathers of the rump, which are white; outer tail feathers edged on either side with white. Cheeks, sides of neck and entire throat pure white; breast pinkish ashy, rest of under surface pure white, the flanks washed with greyish; thighs whitish.

The female is similar to the male, but the black is replaced everywhere by brown.

Iris brown; bill and legs black.

Length.—5·5 to 5·7 inches; wing 2·6; tail 2·25; tarsus 0·5; culmen 0·6.

Hab.—Java, Sumatra, Borneo, Malacca, ranging into Burmah and Tennaserim.

176. Hemipus capitalis, *McClell. P. Z. S.*, 1839, p. 157; *Blyth, Cat. B. Mus. A. S. B.* p. 154; *Godwin Austen, J. A. S B.*, 1870, p. 99; *Jerd. Ibis,* 1872, p. 116. Hemipus picatus (*nec Sykes*) *Gray, Cat. Mam., &c., Nepaul*; *Bly. and Wald B. Burm.* p. 122.—The BROWN-BACKED PIED SHRIKE.

General colour above brown, the lower back with a distinct white bar across it, caused by the feathers being white with brown subterminal bars; rump pure white; upper tail coverts glossy black; some of the outer ones with tiny white tips; head and nape glossy greenish black; chin and cheeks white; throat, breast and sides of body drab-brown; abdomen under tail and under wing coverts white; thighs brown; wing coverts glossy greenish black, the least series washed with the same brown as the back, the median and greater series broadly edged with white, forming a wing bar; quills black, the secondaries externally margined with white, in continuation of the bar formed by the coverts; tail glossy black, all but the two central feathers tipped with white, increasing very much in extent towards the outermost, which are edged with white along the outer web for all but the basal third; bill and legs black; iris sienna yellow.

Length.—5·3 inches; wing 2·5; tail 2·55; tarsus 0·55; culmen 0·6. (Sharpe.)

The adult female differs from the male in having the head brown, only a little darker than the back; wings brown; tail blackish brown, the markings on both these exactly as in the male. (Sharpe.)

Hab.—The N.-W. Provinces, Himalaya Mountains, ranging into Burmah. Sharpe records it from the Himalayas, Nepaul, Darjeeling, and Kakhyen Hills.

Gen. **Hypocolius**.—*Bp.*

Bill hooked at tip, and notched; 3rd quill longest; feet scutellated; tail long, subcuneate.

177. Hypocolius ampelinus, *Bonap. Consp.* i. p. 336 (1850); *Hume, Str. F.* iii. 358; v. 349; *Murray, Hdbk. Zool. &c., Sind,* p. 135. Ceblypyris isabellina, *Heugl. Syst. Uebers. Vog. N. O. Africa; Sitzungsber. K. Akad. Wien.* xix. p. 284, No. 308; *Ibis*, 1868, pp. 181, 182, pl. v.

Upper parts generally ashy grey, with a slight rufous tinge on the head, which is more marked on the frontal portion, where the feathers are rather lighter and more isabelline in tint; feathers above the nostrils, lower parts of the lores, all round the eye, and a band round the nape black, so that there is a black ring all round the head, except in the centre of the forehead; ear coverts dark silver grey, looking black in some lights in the preserved skin; primary quills black, with rather long white tips, the tip on the first long primary being wholly, and on the second partially, dusky; outer secondaries black with grey edges, the black diminishing in amount, until it disappears completely on the feathers near the body; tail feathers the same colour as the back with black tips about three-quarters of an inch long; chin and throat isabelline; breast grey, like the back; abdomen and lower tail coverts pinkish isabelline; under wing coverts light grey; legs flesh-coloured; bill horn coloured, dusky towards the tip.

Length.—Before skinning 10·25 inches; wing 4·2; tail (from insertion of central feather) 4·75; tarsus 1; midtoe and claw 0·95; wing short of end of tail 3·6; culmen (point of bill from rise of skull) 0·85; bill from front 0·5; from gape 0·9.

The female is described by Heuglin as slightly smaller, isabelline grey in colour, with an olivaceous tinge, darker above than below, wanting altogether the black marking on the head, and having much less distinct black tips to the tail feathers. The ends of the primary quill feathers, the two first excepted, blackish with white margins.—*Blf. Str. F.* iii. p. 358.

Hab.—Abyssinia, Bushire (Persian Gulf) and Nal in Khelat. Rare in Sind. A single specimen was obtained by Mr. Blanford on the lower hills, on the eastern flank of the great Kirthur Range, which forms the boundary between Sind and Khelat.

Gen. **Platylophus**.—*Swainson.*

Occipital crest long.

178. Platylophus ardesiacus, *Cat. Mus. Hein. Th.* i. p. 219; *Bp. Consp. Av.* i. p. 374; *Sharpe, Cat. B. Br. Mus.* iii. 317; *Hume and Dav. Str. F.* vi. p. 380; *Hume, Str. F.* viii. p. 105; *Oates, B. Br. Burmah*, i. p. 410.—The CRESTED JAY.

Whole head, crest, chin, throat and entire lower plumage black; back, scapulars, wings and wing coverts, rump and upper tail coverts rich olive brown; tail dark brown; a large patch of white on either side of the neck, two white patches of the same at the back of the eye. The young is paler brown, the forehead greyish, lores whitish, the white patch behind the eye and on the neck, margined with blackish; wings reddish brown; under surface of body slaty; bill and legs black; irides reddish brown.

Length.—11 inches; wing 5·5; tail 5; tarsus 1·3; culmen 1·35.

Hab.—The Malay Peninsula, and Tennaserim.

The Crested Jay has been met with in Tennaserim by Mr. Davison, and Oates procured several specimens at Malewoon. Davison says it occurs only in the evergreen forests of the extreme south of Tennaserim. It is a restless bird flying from tree to tree and branch to branch incessantly, sometimes close to the ground; and sometimes high up. Even when seated it appears to be unable to keep the body quiet, but keeps bobbing and bowing. It always keeps its crest fully erect, and as Dr. Stolickza remarked, it looks like a gigantic *Lophophanes*, Its note is very peculiar, and once heard not easily forgotten. It is a sharp, clicking metallic rattle. The food is believed to consist entirely of insects, such as beetles. It is almost always seen in pairs.

Platylophus coronatus is recorded from Southern Borneo.

Gen. **Cochoa**.—*Hodgs.*

Bill short, wide at base, depressed, straight, the tip slightly bent and notched. Nostrils covered with a few incumbent bristles; wings long, and pointed; 1st quill minute, 2nd and 3rd graduating; 4th quill longest; tail moderate; tarsi short; head subcrested.

179. Cochoa viridis, *Hodgson, J. A. S. B.* v. 359; *Blyth, Cat. B. A. S. B.* 1174; *Gould. B. Asia.* pt. i. pl. 12; *Jerd. B. Ind.* ii. p. 243, No. 608; *Sharpe, Cat. B. Br. Mus.* vol. iv. p. 1.—The GREEN THRUSH-TIT.

Head, nape and back of neck fine cobalt blue; supercilium and ear coverts black, tinged with blue; a small nude space behind the eye; body above dull blue green; lesser wing coverts green, with black lunules; the greater coverts pale blue externally, green on the inner web, and tipped with black; the primary coverts blue basally and tipped with black; primaries and secondaries black, basally blue banded; tail dull cobalt-blue, tipped with black; under surface of body green, the throat and lower abdomen tinged with blue. Bill black; legs fleshy brown; irides brown.

Length.—10·75 to 11 inches; wing 5·6 to 5·7; tail 4·75; culmen ·75; tarsus 1·0.

The female is paler in color throughout, and the young have the feathers of the upper surface lunated with black; the wings paler in colour.

Hab.—The N.-W. Provinces, Nepaul and Sikkim.

The Green Thrush-Tit, although found occasionally about Darjeeling, is very rare, but not so at higher altitudes. It is fairly numerous about Nepaul and Sikkim, and according to Jerdon, Major Tickell obtained specimens near Kurseong during winter.

180. Cochoa purpurea, *Hodgs. J. A. S. B.* v. p. 359; *Jerd. B. Ind.* ii. p. 243, No. 607; *Hume, Nests and Eggs*, p. 388; *Hume and Davison, Str. F.* vi. p. 367; *Hume, Str. F.* viii. p. 104; *Sharpe, Cat. B. Br. Mus.* iv. p. 3; *Oates, B. Br. Burm.* i. p. 136.—The PURPLE THRUSH-TIT.

Head and nape lavender-blue; lores and sides of the head, including the ear coverts black; back, rump, upper tail coverts and the lesser wing coverts dull or ashy purple; median and greater wing coverts bluish purple; primaries black, all except the first two, and the primary coverts with the basal third of the outer webs lavender-blue; the basal two-thirds of the outer webs of the secondaries and all the tertiaries bluish purple; the terminal third of the outer webs of the secondaries; and their entire inner webs black; tail bluish purple, tipped with black. Entire under surface brownish purple.

The female is similar to the male except that where the male is purple she is reddish brown, and the wing spot is duller. The young is not unlike the female, but have the feathers edged with whitish and the under surface reddish brown, barred with dusky. Bill black; legs and feet dark or plumbeous brown; irides dark brown.

Length.—10·5 to 10·9 inches; wing 5·5; tail 4·2 to 4·5; culmen 1· to 1·2; tarsus 1· to 1·1.

Hab.—The Himalayas to Nepal, Kumaon and Sikkim; also British Burmah. The Purple Thrush-Tit is rare about Darjeeling. Davison procured it on the higher slopes of the Mooleyit Mountains in Tennaserim, and Capt. Bingham got it in the Thoungyeen Valley. According to Hodgson it is common to all the three regions of Nepaul. He remarks "They are shy in their manners, adhere exclusively to the woods, live solitarily or in pairs, breed and moult but once a year, nidificate on trees and feed almost equally on the ground and on trees. He adds that he has taken from their stomachs several sorts of stony berries, small univalve mollusca, and sundry kinds of aquatic insects. The nest is strongly built of moss and lined with lichens. Eggs of a greenish colour, spotted and blotched with brown.

Gen. **Artamides.**

Bill of moderate length, hooked and slightly notched; the culmen curved; the base as wide nearly as in the Genus *Graucalus*; rictal bristles well developed; 4th quill longest, 3rd and 5th equal.

181. Artamides Dobsoni, (*Ball.*) *Sharpe, Cat. B. Br. Mus.* iv. p. 9. Graucalus Dobsoni, *Ball. Str. F.* i. p. 66; p. ii. 206.—DOBSON'S THRUSH-TIT.

Point of the forehead, lores, a stripe under the eyes and the ear coverts black; whole of the front, top, and back of the head, back and sides of the neck, scapulars and lesser wing coverts, rump and upper tail coverts an uniform dark iron grey, slightly paler on the rump; quills, greater and median coverts dark hair brown, paler on the inner webs, every feather with a *very* narrow pale edging, grey on the coverts, pale brown on the tips of the primaries and only at all conspicuous on some of the primaries above the emarginations, and some of the later secondaries towards their tips. Tail black, browner towards the base, outer tail feathers pale brown on the outer webs and at the tip, which again is narrowly tipped with white; the next pair on either side tipped with brownish white, and the 3rd pair with only a trace of this white tip. Chin, throat, and upper breast pale iron grey; lower breast, entire wing lining, axillaries and entire lower parts white, narrowly, closely and strongly barred with blackish brown.

The female is like the male, but the point of the forehead is iron grey, not black; and the chin, throat and upper breast are barred like the under surface.

The young have the whole chin, throat, and breast strongly tinged with ferruginous; the tertiaries, secondaries and later primaries comparatively broadly margined, and tipped with pale rufous or rufescent white; the tertiaries and later secondaries with also a rufous spot near the tips; a faint rufous supercilium from the nostrils over the eyes; lores dusky with tiny white spots; cheeks dusky; the feathers white shafted. Bill, legs and feet black; irides crimson lake, tinged with brownish in the young.

Length.—11·5 to 12·25 inches; wing 6·1 to 6·42; tail 5 to 6; bill at front 0·95 to 1·06. (Hume.)

Hab.—The Andaman Islands; probably also in Burmah.

Mr. Davison says, "this species unlike *G. macei* is exclusively a forest bird, never venturing out in the open fields; it usually is seen in pairs keeping moderately high up in trees; its flight is weaker than that of *G. macei* and undulating, seldom extended, except from branch to branch or from one tree to another. It is not uncommon at Mount Harriet and other well-wooded portions of the settlement."

Gen. **Graucalus**.—*Cuv.*

Bill of moderate length, strong and wide at base, the culmen curved, hooked and slightly notched; rictal bristles not much developed; wings long and pointed; tail moderate, slightly rounded.

182. Graucalus Macii, *Less. Traite* p. 349; *Jerd. B. Ind.* i. p. 417, No. 270; *Wald. Ibis*, 1872, p. 311; *Blanf. J. A. S B.* xli. pt. ii. p. 156; *Hume, Nests and Eggs*, p. 181; *id. Str. F.* ii p. 204; *Ball, Str. F.* ii. p. 400; *Bl. B. Burm.* p. 123; *Anderson, Yunnan Exped.* p. 647; *Legge, B. Ceylon*, p. 360; *Sharpe, Cat. B. Br. Mus.* iv. p. 34; *Hume, Str. F.* viii. p. 91; *Scully, Str. F.* viii. p. 267. Graucalus layardi, *Bl. Ibis*, 1866, p. 35; *Jerd. Ibis*, 1872, p 117; *Legge, Ibis*, 1875, p. 287; *Murray, Vert. Zool, Sind*, p. 124.—The INDIAN CUCKOO-SHRIKE.

Head, neck, back, rump, upper tail coverts and scapulars french-grey; primaries and their coverts black, externally edged with whitish; secondaries french-grey on the outer webs, and margined and tipped whitish; the inner webs dusky; tail with the two centre feathers grey, tipped with white; the rest black, broadly tipped with white. A narrow frontal line, lores, below the eye, and at the gape black. Sides of face, and ear coverts darkish grey beneath; the neck and breast french-grey; upper abdomen lighter, with numerous dull white transverse lines; lower abdomen, vent and under tail coverts white; under wing coverts and axillaries white, with a few cross lines of grey at the edge of the wings; bill blackish; irides rich lake; legs plumbeous.

The female is paler in colour throughout and has not the black on the face; generally there are present nearly obsolete barrings on the under surface. The young have the upper plumage tipped and margined with pale ferruginous, and the under surface nearly pure white.

Length.—11·8 to 12 inches; wings 6·5 to 7; tail 5 to 6; tarsus 1 to 1·05; bill at front 1.

Hab.—The Indian Cuckoo-Shrike is found over all India, from the Himalayas to the extreme South. It is abundant in Southern India and Ceylon, spread over the whole of British Burmah, recorded from Nepaul, Pegu, Assam, and Port Blair; also the N.-W. Provinces, Punjab, Oudh, Bengal Rajpootana, Kutch, Kathiawar, Jodhpoor, North Guzerat and Travancore. Blyth records it from Arrakan, Mr. Davison from Tennaserim, and according to Dr. Tiraud it is found in Cochin-China. It affects thin forest, jungles, gardens, orchards, avenues and thick growths of high bushes. Feeds chiefly on insects as caterpillars, mantides, locusts, and grasshoppers, and probably also small fruit. Jerdon says it is rather a shy bird, flying before you from tree to tree uttering as it alights two or three rather sweet and mellow notes, but it has also a very harsh rattling scream. It flies in an easy undulating manner, with but few flappings of its wings. Its flesh is said to be eaten by the natives. Breeds almost everywhere about the beginning of the rains. Nest usually placed in the fork of a lofty branch of a tree, constructed of fine twigs and grass, cup-shaped in form. Eggs three, of a greenish colour, marked with spots and blotches of brown and pale purple.

Gen. **Campophaga.**—*Vieill.*

Bill shorter than in *Graucalus*, broad at base, compressed at tip and notched; rictal bristles absent or a very few; nostrils partly concealed; wings long; the 3rd and 4th quills equal and longest.

183 Campophaga lugubris, *Sund, Ind. Rev.* i. p. 328; *Sharpe, Cat. B. Br. Mus.* iv. p. 65. Volvocivora melaschistos, (*Hodgs.*) *Jerd. B. Ind.* i. p. 415, No. 269; *Str. F.* v. p. 205.—The Dark Grey Cuckoo-Shrike.

Iron grey throughout, except on the quills and tail, which are dark brown, the latter tipped with white on all but the central tail feathers.

The young have the whole of the lower plumage dark brown, almost unicolorous from the chin to the vent. Nestlings only just fully fledged have the upper plumage barred with white. Bill and legs black; irides hazel-brown.

Length.—9·5 to 10 inches; wing 4·6; tail 5·25 to 5·5; culmen nearly 1·0.

Hab.—N.-W. Provinces, Oudh, Bengal to Nepaul. Rare in South India. Habits and food those of the last. Hutton says it has a plaintive note which it utters repeatedly when searching for insects. Affects the more wooded districts, and is found in small parties on the higher branches generally, though it freely descends to the ground also to feed. According to him it is a summer visitor to Darjeeling and the hills, ascending up to 7,000 feet about the end of March, and breeding early in May. The nest is small and shallow, placed in the bifurcation of a small horizontal bough of some tall tree, and always high up; it is composed internally almost entirely of grey lichens and lined with bits of fine root fibres; it is completely covered on the outside with cobwebs. Eggs 2 in number, ·7 × ·6 in size, of a dull grey green, streaked with brown.

184. Campophaga intermedia, *Hume, Str. F.* v. 205, viii. p. 91. Campophaga saturata, *Sharpe, Cat. B. Br. Mus.* iv. p. 66; *Oates, B. Br. Burmah*, i. p. 230. Volvocivora saturata, *Swinh. Ibis*, 1870, p. 242; *David et Oust. Ois. Chine*, p. 103.—Swinhoe's Cuckoo-Shrike.

General colour dark slaty grey, paler below, the feathers of the crown with black shafts and the under tail coverts more or less fringed with white; lesser wing coverts like the back; remaining wing coverts and the whole wing deep glossy black; tail deep black, all the feathers tipped with white, broadly on the outermost, and decreasing in extent towards the middle rectrices.

The female is slightly paler in the adolescent stage, and a white patch is present on the fourth and fifth primaries. Bill and legs black; iris hazel-brown.

Length.—9·5 to 10 inches; wing 4·5 to 4·8; tail 4·5. (Oates.)

Hab.—British Burmah (Tennaserim) and Nepal. Hainan (Swinh.). Cochin-China (Tiraud). Mr. Davison found it all over the Tennaserim Division as far down as Mergui. It is, according to Oates, spread all over the Pegu Division where he found it, and *C. melanoptera* in much the same localities.

Swinhoe's Cuckoo-Shrike does not differ in its habits from the other species of the genus. All live almost entirely on insectivorous diet which they either pick off leaves, or capture on the ground.

185. Campophaga melanoptera, *Rupp. Mus. Senck.* iii. p. 25; *tab.* ii. f. 1.; *Sharpe, Cat. B. Br. Mus.* iv. p. 67. Campephaga melanoptera, *Bl. J. A. S. B.* xv. p. 307. Campephaga avensis, *Bl. Cat. B. Mus. As. Soc. Beng.* p. 327. Volvocivora avensis, *Bl. B. Burmah*, p. 123; *Hume, Str. F.* iii. p. 93; v. p. 205; viii. p. 91.—BLYTH'S CUCKOO-SHRIKE.

In every respect similar to *Campophaga intermedia*, except that the central tail feathers are washed with grey on the basal half, the vent and under tail coverts are pure white, and the white tippings to the tail feathers much broader.

The female is as pure grey above as the male, and the shafts of the feathers of the head are as black. Rump and upper tail coverts paler and indistinctly barred. Under surface greyish white, everywhere barred with ashy; primaries with a white patch basally; tail dark brown, the middle rectrices ashy; all the feathers tipped with white. Bill and legs black; iris hazel-brown.

Length.—9 to 9·5 inches; wing 4·3; tail 4·3 to 4·5; culmen 1·; tarsus ·9.

Hab.—British Burmah. Spread over the whole of Pegu. Common in Arrakan; also in Tennaserim, where Davison found it as far south as Moulmein.

186. Campophaga neglecta, *Hume, Str. F.* v. p. 203; viii. p. 91; *Sharpe, Cat. B. Br. Mus.* iv. p. 68; *Oates, B. Burmah*, i. p. 232. Campophaga polioptera, *Sharpe, Cat. B. Br. Mus.* iv. p. 69, pl. ii. Volvocivora neglecta, *Hume, Str. F.* v. p. 203.—DAVISON'S CUCKOO-SHRIKE.

Male.—In all respects the same as *Campophaga melanoptera*, but differs in having the upper parts a shade darker, and a white patch on the primaries. The female too is not unlike the female of *C. melanoptera*; the differences, if any exist, are so insignificant that really it cannot be separated from the latter. There is a difference in size, but when it is a remarkable fact that such differences are stretched in some families to as much as half an inch or more the same latitude should be permitted in the case of the Genus *Campophaga* with such nearly uniform colouring.

C. melanoptera has the wing	4·3;	tail 4·3;	length	9 inches.
„ *intermedia* „	4·8;	tail 4·5;	„	9·5 „
„ *neglecta* „	4· ;	tail 3·35;	„	8· „

Another species, which I do not admit, is Campophaga innominata, *Oates, B. Br. Burmah* i. p. 233. Volvocivora Vidua, (*Hartl.*) *Hume, Str. F.* v.

p. 206; vi. p. 508; viii. p. 91. Here again a paler colouring and size are allowed to make a species—wing 4·65 to 5·0.

Mr. Hume's remarks in regard to this latter are as follows:—

From the neighbourhood of Tavoy we have a series of *Volvocivora*, which cannot be referred to either *V. melaschista*, *V. neglecta*, *V. intermedia*, or *V. culminata* or even *V. avensis*. They are paler than *V. intermedia*, and *à fortiori* than *V. melaschista* * * * * Surely some allowance must be made for the colouring of the different stages of the birds, their habitat, the situation they affect as well as the nature of such. Then again climatic influences and the time of year in which the specimens were collected. I certainly hold that all the species here referred *intermedia*, *melanoptera*, *neglecta*, and *innominata* are simply races or varieties of *C. lugubris* with wings ranging from 4·0 inches to 5·0.

Gen. **Pericrocotus**.—*Boie.*

Bill short, rather broad at base, and high; culmen slightly curved; wing long, 4th and 5th quills longest; tail long, lateral feathers graduated; tarsi and feet short and feeble.

Mr. Sharpe has properly, like most authors, placed this group of brightly coloured birds next to the *Campephaginæ*. The Minivets form a group of species very similar to each other; the males being for the most part clothed in black and red (vermilion red), and the females in dusky and yellow. They associate in small flocks and are always found on trees, actively hopping from branch to branch in search of insects, upon which they feed.

187. Pericrocotus speciosus, *Lath. Bly. Cat. B. A. S. B.* 1158; *Jerd. B. Ind.* i. p. 419, No. 271; *Stray F.* ii. p. 208; *Oates, B. Br. Burmah*, i. p. 236; *Sharpe, Cat. B. Br. Mus.* iv. p. 72. Phœnecornis princeps, *Gould, Cent. Him. B.* pl. 7.—The LARGE MINIVET.

Male.—Head, neck, upper back, wings, and two central tail feathers, glossy black; lower back, rump, upper tail coverts and under wings coverts rich vermilion red; primaries black with a band of rich vermilion red across all but the first three; greater coverts black, very broadly tipped with vermilion; secondaries black, vermilion red at the base, the later ones with a vermilion spot near the tip of the outer webs; lateral tail feathers vermilion red.

The female has the head, neck, upper back and central tail feathers light ashy grey, tinged with greenish. Quills dusky black, with a deep yellow spot; four central tail feathers dusky, the outer pair tipped yellow, the others deep yellow with some blackish markings at the base; forehead, rump and upper tail coverts greenish yellow, also the whole lower plumage.

The young are like the female, but have the forehead tinged with orange. Bill and legs black; irides deep brown; eyelids grey.

Length.—9 inches; wing 4·25 to 4·5; tail 4·25; tarsus ·9; bill from gape 0·5 to ·8.

Hab.—Nepaul, the Himalayas down to the N.-W. Provinces, Oudh, Bengal, the Central Provinces, and Central India. Does not extend to Assam and British Burmah, as stated by Jerdon. The species found there, is the next, a slightly smaller bird, with some few not very material differences.

188. Pericrocotus elegans, *McLell. P. Z. S.* 1839, p. 156; *Hume, Str. F.* iii. p. 95; *Sharpe, Str. F.* iv. p. 206; *Hume, Str. F.* v. p. 194; *Anders. Yunnan Exped.* p. 648; *Sharpe, Cat. B. Br. Mus* iv. 73; *Hume, Str. F.* viii. p. 91; *Oates, B. Br. Burmah,* i. p. 236. Pericrocotus fraterculus, *Swinh. Ibis,* 1870, p. 244. Pericrocotus speciosus, *Bl. & Wald. B. Burm.* p. 123.—MACCLELLAND'S MINIVET.

In all respects the same as the preceding (*P. speciosus*), but differs in being smaller.

Length.—8 inches; wing 3·7; tail 3·6; tarsus ·75. The female is a trifle smaller, the outer webs of the central tail feathers are red, and not as in *speciosus* entirely black, or with only a patch of red on them.

Hab.—British Burmah. According to Oates it is found over the whole of Pegu. Common over the whole of Arrakan, got in Karenne by Capt. Wardlaw-Ramsay. Mr. Davison states it is common in Tennaserim as far south as Tavoy; thence occurring even down to Malewoon, but comparatively rare in the extreme southern portion. It has also been found at and around Bhamo, in Cachar, Tipperah and the whole of Assam and the Tributary Mehals.

This gorgeous species, like the rest of its tribe, goes about in small parties, and are generally seen about gardens and orchards, also heavy and thin forests, searching the leaves of trees for insects.

189. Pericrocotus andamanensis, *Tytler, Str. F.* ii. p. 208; v. 175, 194.—THE ANDAMAN MINIVET.

Allied to *P. elegans*; differs from it in size. Wing 3·6 to 3·75; the vermilion red of the back less in extent, the wing patch extending to only the outer web of the 4th primary. The difference in this latter extends in *speciosus* to the 3rd primary; *Andamanensis* to the 4th primary, and *flammifer* to the 5th primary.

Together with the slight differences in the amount of red on the back and in the habitat, the question is, whether these are sufficient to constitute good species. I would place *elegans* and *andamanensis*, as synonyms of *speciosus*.

190. Pericrocotus flammifer, *Hume, Str. F.* iii. p. 321; (footnote); v. p. 195; viii. p. 91; *Sharpe, Cat. B. Br. Mus.* iv. p. 74; *Oates, B. Br. Burmah,* i. p. 237.—DAVISON'S MINIVET.

Male.—Whole head, neck, back, scapulars, lesser wing and primary coverts deep glossy black; primaries black, all but the first three with a scarlet patch;

secondaries black, their bases scarlet; tertiaries black, their outer web near the tip with a scarlet spot; greater wing coverts black, broadly tipped with scarlet; rump, upper tail and under wing coverts and the whole lower plumage scarlet; tail scarlet, except the central tail feathers, which have the base of the outer and the whole inner web black.

The female has the front of the head, cheeks, lower back, rump, upper tail coverts and the whole of the under surface bright yellow; back, scapulars, back of head and lesser wing coverts ashy brown; greater coverts dark brown, tipped yellow; wings dark brown, the red patch replaced by yellow; central tail feathers black, with a margin of yellow on their outer webs, the next pair black, the terminal half of outer web and tip of the inner web yellow, the others yellow with black bases. Bill and legs black.

Length.—7·3 inches; tail 3·1; wing 3·4; tarsus 0·65; bill from gape ·85.

Hab.—British Burmah, in the extreme south of Tennaserim, at Bankasoon, and Pakchan. It also occurs in the Malay Peninsula.

191. Pericrocotus flammeus, (*Forst.*) *Sws. Zool. Ill.* p. 52; *Jerd. Ill. Ind. Orn.* pl. ii. *m.* and *f.*; *id. B. Ind.* i. p. 420, No. 272; *Str. F.* iii. p. 95; iv. pp. 207, 394; v. 175, 197; *Sharpe, Cat. B. Br. Mus.* iv. p. 75.—The ORANGE MINIVET.

Whole head, nape, neck, upper back, wings, and central tail feathers shining blue-black; lower back, rump, upper tail coverts, wing spot to the fifth primary, tips of some of the coverts, and entire under surface deep crimson; lateral tail feathers the same, but with black bases.

The Female has the forehead tinged with yellow, the head and back grey; the rump, wing spots, lateral tail feathers and entire under surface yellow; wings and tail dusky, the pair next the middle feathers edged narrowly with yellow. Bill and legs black; irides dark brown.

Length.—7·5 to 8 inches; 3·5 to 3·7; tail 3·9 to 4; culmen 0·37; tarsus 0·6.

Hab.—Southern India, in the Circars, along the Coromandel and Malabar Coasts, and Travancore to Ceylon, and in the Concan.

The Orange Minivet is abundant in all the more wooded parts of its habitat, and generally keeps to the topmost branches of high trees. It keeps continually flying from branch to branch, and is incessantly on the move, catching insects. It breeds on the Neilgherries during June and July. The nest is a comparatively massive little cup composed of fine twigs and plastered over with lichen like cobwebs. It is usually placed in the fork of a slender bough. Eggs a palish green, thickly streaked and spotted chiefly at the large end with pale yellowish brown and dingy purple.

192. Pericrocotus igneus, *Blyth, J. A. S. B.* xv. p. 309; *Sharpe, Str. F.* iv. p. 209; *Hume, Str. F.* v. p. 190; viii. p. 91; *Sharpe, Cat. B. Br. Mus.* iv. p. 78; *Wardlaw-Ramsay, Tweed. Mem. App.* p. 656; *Oates, B. Br. Burmah,* p. 239. Pericrocotus minutus, *Strickl. Contr. Orn.* 1849. pl. —The FIERY MINIVET.

Whole head, chin, throat, nape, neck, back, scapulars, tertiaries, and lesser wing coverts glossy black; rump and upper tail coverts crimson; greater wing coverts black, tipped with crimson; primaries black, all but the first four with a scarlet or crimson spot; secondaries orange at the base and black terminally; under wing coverts and axillaries yellow, tipped with red; central tail feathers black; the next pair black, tipped with red; and the others red, with black bases.

The female has the forehead, feathers round the eye, and entire under surface including the under wing coverts bright yellow; the crown of the head, nape, neck, back, scapulars and wing coverts, olivaceous or greenish ashy; rump and upper tail coverts scarlet; wing and tail as in the male, the crimson spot orange yellow instead; bill and legs black; irides dark brown.

Length.—6·5 inches; wing 3·0; tail 3; tarsus ·6; culmen ·7.

Hab.—South Tennaserim (Davison); also Malacca, Singapore, and China.

193. Pericrocotus cinereus, *Lafres. Rev. Zool.* 1845, p. 94; *Sharpe, Str. F.* iv. p. 211; *Hume, Str. F.* v. p. 175; *Sharpe, Cat. B. Br. Mus.* iv. p. 83; *Oates, Str. F.* x. p. 200. Pericrocotus modestus, *Strickl. P. Z. S.* 1846, p. 102. Pericrocotus motacilloides, *Swinh. P. Z. S.* 1860, p. 58.—The ASHY MINIVET.

Forepart of the head, cheeks, sides of the neck, chin and throat white; feathers round the eye, at the base of the bill, lores, top of the head and nape deep black; primary coverts also black; wing coverts blackish brown, edged with ashy; the greater coverts white-tipped; primaries dark brown, with an oblique pale ashy white bar across; secondaries brown with white bases; tertiaries ashy, the edges of the outer web white; entire under surface white, the flanks shaded with ashy and the breast and belly with buffy; tail black, the outermost feathers with a broad oblique white tip.

The female is marked similar to the male, except that the black is replaced everywhere with ashy, the tail is brown, and the under parts are suffused with brown; bill and legs black.

Length.—8 inches; wing 3·8; tail ·4; tarsus ·6; culmen ·8.

Hab.—British Burmah. Oates says he has met with this species near Pegu. It is also found in the Phillippines, Borneo, and Sumatra; also in China and Japan.

194. Pericrocotus peregrinus, *Lin. Syst. Nat.* i. p. 342; *Jerd. B. Ind.* i. p. 423; *Hume, Nests and Eggs*, p. 184; *Bl. and Wald. B. Burmah*, p. 124; *Hume, Str. F.* i. p. 177; iii. p. 96; *Sharpe, Str. F.* iv. p. 209; *Hume, Str. F.* v. 179; viii. p. 91; *Oates, Str. F.* viii. p. 166; *Legge, Birds, Ceylon*, p. 366; *Sharpe, Cat. B. Br. Mus.* iv. p. 76; *Murray, Vert. Zool. Sind*, p. 125. Pericrocotus malabaricus (*Gm.*) *Hume, Str. F.* v. p. 182; *Oates, B. Br. Burmah*, i. p. 245.—The SMALL MINIVET.

Upper surface of body ashy grey; a narrow frontal band, lores, chin, throat and ear coverts blackish; wing coverts black, the lesser series edged with dull grey, and the greater with a narrow orange tip; quills dusky black, duller toward the tips; the bases of the primaries, except the first three, orange red, forming a conspicuous wing patch; rump and upper tail coverts bright vermilion; tail black, the four outer feathers on each side widely tipped with orange; the breast vermilion, also the upper abdomen and flanks; fading on the lower abdomen, vent and under tail coverts to yellowish; under wing coverts and edge of the wing yellow; thigh coverts dusky black. Bill and legs black; irides brown.

Length.—6 inches; wing 2·55; tail 3; bill at front 0·45.

The female is light grey above, the throat white, also the eye streak; sides of forehead and lower parts whitish, tinged with yellow on the breast, abdomen, and under tail coverts; the flanks and under wing coverts brighter yellow; quills light brown; the primaries with narrow white edgings; the wing spot yellow; rump vermilion; colour of bill and legs as in the male.

Length.—6·25 inches; wing 2·75; bill 0·45; tail 3·1.

Hab.—India, Ceylon, Burmese countries, Andamans and Java. Occurs in the N.-W. Himalayas, South and Central India, Nepaul, the Punjab, N.-W. Provinces, Oudh, Bengal, Rajputana, Deccan, Kutch, Kattiawar, Jodhpore, and N. Guzerat. In Sind it is a winter visitant, arriving in August and remaining till about the end of December.

The Small Minivet is most abundant wherever it is found, and like the other species of the genus is a restless bird. It is usually found in small parties. Breeds from about the end of April to the end of June. The nest is a very neat cup, made of very fine twigs, and coated thickly with cobwebs, to which are attached dead leaves, &c. The cobwebs are the nests of a species of spider which build on trees an almost circular papery covering; with these this Minivet lines the outside, making the nest appear as if there were knotty excrescences growing on it. The nest is usually placed high up and in a fork at the end of a bough. Eggs three in number, pale green, marked with reddish brown.

195. Pericrocotus brevirostris, *Vigors. P. Z. S.* 1831, p. 43; *Jerd. B. Ind.* i. p. 421, No. 273; *Stolickza, J. A. S. B.* xxxvii. pt. ii. p. 27; *Beavan, Ibis,* 1870, p. 314; *Hume, Nests and Eggs,* p. 183; *Bl. B. Burmah,* p. 123; *Sharpe, Str. F* iv. p. 209; *Hume, Str.* v. p. 187; *id. and Dav. S. F.* vi. p. 211; *Hume,* viii. p. 91; *Sharpe, Cat. B. Br. Mus.* iv. p. 79; *Oates, B. Br. Burmah,* i. p. 240; *Murray, Vert. Zool. Sind,* p. 125.—The SHORT-BILLED MINIVET.

Head, nape, upper back, wings and middle tail feathers glossy blue-black; the lower back, rump and upper tail coverts deep crimson; lateral tail feathers crimson, the bases black; wing coverts glossy black; the greater coverts crimson, their bases black; wing spot crimson; chin, throat, and sides of face blue-black, rest of under surface crimson; wing coverts crimson, the greater series ashy black. The female has the head and back grey, the forehead tinged with yellow, the lower back, rump and upper tail coverts yellow; the tail yellow, the basal half of the feathers black; wings dusky, or black, the greater coverts tipped with yellow; wing spot yellow; forehead and lores yellowish white; chin, cheeks and feathers below the eye whitish; under surface of body yellow washed with orange on the breast. Bill and legs black; irides dark brown.

Length.—7·5 to 8 inches; wing 3·45; tail 4; tarsus 0·55.

Hab.—The Himalayas, Cashmere, Afghanistan, Bhootan, Shillong, Cachar, Assam, Chittagong, Arrakan, Upper Burmah, Punjab, Bengal, Oudh, Rajputana, Central India, and the N.-W. Provinces, visiting the Deccan, Concan, Kutch, Kattiawar, North Guzerat and Sind during the summer months.

The short-billed Minivet has all the habits of the other species of the genus. It breeds on the Himalayas during May and June. The nest is made of the same materials as those of other species. Eggs, 3—4 in number, moderately a broad oval in shape; dull white in colour, and richly spotted, blotched and streaked with brownish red and pale purple. Size 0·73 inch × 0·54,

196. Pericrocotus neglectus. *Hume, Str. F.* v. p. 189; *Sharpe, Cat. B. Br. Mus.* iv. p. 80; *Hume, Str. F.* viii. p. 91; *Oates, B. Br. Burmah* i. p. 241.

"A miniature representative of *P. brevirostris.*"

Length.—6·5 to 6·8; wing 3·25 to 3·3; tail 3·0 to 3·25.

The female has the chin and throat a brighter yellow than in *brevirostris*, and the upper plumage is a duller ash.

Hab.—Central Tennaserim.

197. Pericrocotus roseus, *Vieill. Nouv. Dict. d'Hist. Nat.* xxi. p. 486; *Jerd. B. Ind.* i. p. 422. No. 275; *Hume, Nests and Eggs*, p. 184; *Bl. B. Burmah*, p. 124; *Sharpe, Str. F.* iv. p. 210; *Armstrong, Str. F.* iv. p. 317; *Sharpe, Cat. B. Br. Mus.* iv. p. 81; *Hume, Str. F.* viii. p 91; *Reid. Cat. B. Prov. Mus. Oudh*, p. 55. Pericrocotus intensior, *Hume, Str. F.* v. p. 185.—The Rosy Minivet.

Head and neck ashy grey; back reddish cinereous; the feathers of the rump and upper tail coverts rosy red; wing coverts dark brown, the greater series tipped with rosy-scarlet; quills dark brown all but the first four primaries with a scarlet patch across them; later secondaries and tertiaries like the back, narrowly margined with scarlet, sides of the head ashy; chin and throat whitish. Entire under surface, including the under wing coverts and axillaries, rosy red; central tail feathers blackish, the others red with dark bases.

The female is paler ashy above; rump and other parts, which are red in the male, are pale yellow. Bill, legs and feet black, irides dark brown.

Length.—7·2 to 7·4 inches; wing 3·4 to 3·5; tail 3·5; tarsus ·6; culmen 0·6.

Hab.—The Himalayas, the Punjab, N.-W. Provinces, Oudh, Bengal, Assam, British Burmah and Afghanistan; also in South India, at Goomsur in Travancore, and the greater part of the Carnatic and the Malabar forests.

According to Oates, the Rosy Minivet is found abundantly over the whole of Pegu. It extends in Tennaserim down to Mergui, south of which point Mr. Davison does not appear to have met with it. It is recorded by Blyth from Arrakan, over which division it is probably common. North of British Burmah, it has been procured near Bhamo. It breeds during May and June on the Himalayas. Nests taken at Murree, are of the usual type. Eggs 3 in number, white with greyish brown spots and blotches at the larger end. Size, 0·82 × 0·6 inches.

198. Pericrocotus solaris, *Blyth, J. A. S. B.* xv. p. 310; *Jerd. B. Ind.* i. p. 422, No. 274; *Blanford, J. A. S. B.* 41, pt. ii. p. 47; *Sharpe, Str. F.* iv. p. 210; *Hume, Str. F.* v. p. 186; *Sharpe, Cat. B. Br. Mus.* iv. p. 82; *Hume, Str. F.* viii. p. 91.—The YELLOW-THROATED MINIVET.

Forehead, crown, nape, neck, back, scapulars and lesser wing coverts leaden black, darker on the wings and black on the tail; chin, cheeks and ear coverts grey; throat orange-yellow; rump and upper tail coverts, wing spot, greater portion of the three outer tail feathers, and entire under surface bright reddish flame colour; greater coverts black, tipped with scarlet; secondaries and tertiaries black with scarlet bases.

The female has the head dark ashy brown tinged with greenish beneath; wing spot, rump and lateral, tail feathers bright yellow; tail yellow. Bill, legs and feet black; irides deep brown.

Length.—7 inches; tail 4; wing 3·4; tarsus 0·6; bill from gape 0·6.

Hab.—N.-W. Provinces, Eastern Bengal, British Burmah and Nepaul. It is recorded from Pegu by Oates, and from Tennasserim near Thatone and round the base of Mooleyit Mountain; also from Kashmere, S.-E. Himalayas and Sikkim. Habits similar to the other species.

199. Pericrocotus erythropygius, *Jerdon, Birds, Ind.* i. p. 424, No. 277; *Jardine Contributions to Orn. fig.; Stray F.* v. 174, 177.—The RED-TAILED or WHITE-BELLIED MINIVET.

Male.—Plumage above, except the rump, glossy blue-back; rump and breast orange red; entire under surface, wing stripe, outer edges and tips of the lateral tail feathers white.

The female has the black of the male replaced by ashy; the tail black; forehead whitish; the rump and under surface of the body white, tinged with ashy on the breast.

Bill and legs black; irides brownish yellow.

Length.—6·5 to 6·8; wing 2·7; tail 3·3; bill at front 0·3; tarsus 0·5.

Hab.—The Punjab, N.-W. Provinces, Bengal, Central India, Hyderabad Deccan, and South India.

Jerdon says the white-bellied Minivet is extensively spread throughout India, but everywhere rare. He records it from near Jaulnah, Hydrabad in the Deccan, the foot of the Neilgherries, Bundelcund and the N.-W. Provinces. It frequents low and bushy jungles; also thin tree jungle, groves, gardens, and hedgerows, and lives in small flocks. Food various insects. Breeds in Khandeish at Dhoolia. Nest of the usual shape and structure. Eggs 3 in number, greenish-white with pale purplish streaks. Size 0·65 × 0·5 inch.

200. Pericrocotus albifrons, *Jerd. Ibis,* 1862, p. 20; *Bl. B. Burmah* p. 124; *Hume, Str. F.* iii. p. 96; *Sharpe, Str. F.* iv. p. 212; *Hume Str. F.* v. p. 178; *Sharpe, Cat. B. Br. Mus.* iv. p. 86; *Hume, Str. F.* viii. p. 91.—JERDON'S MINIVET.

Forehead, supercilium, cheeks, sides of the neck, chin and throat white lores, ear coverts, top of head, back, scapulars, upper tail and lesser wing coverts, also the primary coverts, glossy black; rump and breast orange red; greater wing coverts black, broadly tipped with white, forming a broad band on the wing; primaries black, with an oblique patch of white on all but the first five feathers; secondaries black, their bases white; tertiaries white, with a large black oblique patch in the centre of each feather; breast, belly and under tail coverts white; the two central pairs of tail feathers wholly black, the others black, broadly tipped with white. The female has the black of the male replaced by sooty brown; the white parts less pure; only a trace of red on the rump, and wholly wanting on the breast.

Bill and legs black; irides dark brown.

Length.—6·25 to 6·5 inches; wing 2·5 to 2·65; tail 3·25 to 3·4; tarsus 0·6; bill 0·54.

Hab.—British Burmah. According to Jerdon it is a very local species, and is the representative in Upper Burma of *P. erythropygius* of Southern and Central India. It was first procured at Thayetmyo. Oates got it at Palow, south of Thayetmyo, and Blanford traced it as far as Pagan on the Irrawady. It is found usually in couples or in small families, chiefly in low and thorny jungles, not frequenting the dense forests. It is active and restless, flitting about the smaller branches and feeding on various insects, which it usually picks up from a leaf or twig, now and then catching one in the air.

201. Pericrocotus immodestus, *Hume, Str. F.* v. p. 177; viii. p. 91; *Bingham, Str. F.* ix. p. 173; *Oates, B. Br. Burmah.* i. p. 243.—The WHITE-FRONTED MINIVET.

Female.—Forehead and front of crown, feathers round the eye, cheeks, sides of the neck, chin and throat whitish; rest of head, neck, scapulars and back earthy brown; lores dark brown; rump and upper tail coverts light brown, very much paler than the back; wings and wing coverts blackish brown, paler on the edges; the primaries with an oblique mark of yellowish white, and the secondaries with a yellow patch at their bases; under wing coverts and axillaries pale yellow; breast, belly, vent and under tail coverts pale buffy brown; tail feathers dark brown, the four outer pairs very broadly tipped with yellowish white, and the shafts of all hair brown. The male is similar, but the white of the head and throat is pure, the head and back dark ashy brown; wing spot white, that on the secondaries tinged with brown, and the lores very dark brown.

Bill and legs black; irides hazel.

Length.—8 inches; wing 3·5; tail 3·7; tarsus 0·55; bill from gape 0·75.

Hab.—British Burma, in the Pegu Division, and in the extreme south of Tenasserim, where Davison met with it.

Gen. **Lalage.**—*Boie.*

Shrike-like birds of soft plumage; feathers of the lower back and rump rather stiff; bill stout and moderately hooked; rictal bristles almost wanting; wings longer than the tail; under tail coverts long.

202. Lalage sykesi, *Strickl. Ann. Nat. Hist. Ser.* i., xiii. p. 36; *Legge, Birds, Ceylon,* p. 369; *Sharpe, Cat. B. Br. Mus.* iv. p. 89. Volvocivora sykesi, *Jerd. B. Ind.* i. p. 414, No. 268; *Hume, Nests and Eggs,* p. 179; *Bl. B. Burm.*, p. 123; *Hume, Str. F.* viii. p. 91. Campophaga sykesi, *Oates, B. Br. Burm.* i. p. 234.—The BLACK-HEADED CUCKOO-SHRIKE

Head, neck, upper back, chin, throat and upper breast black; lower breast and abdomen pale grey, gradually passing to white on the vent and lower tail coverts; lower back, scapulars, lesser wing coverts, rump and upper tail coverts grey, the latter margined paler; median wing coverts black, tipped and broadly margined for their terminal half on the outer webs with grey; greater wing coverts black, narrowly margined greyish; primaries and secondaries black, the primaries with a narrow white margin on their outer webs and a large white patch on their inner webs, the secondaries rather broadly margined and tipped with white; tail with the central feathers grey, the rest black, broadly tipped with white.

The female has the head and the upper plumage grey, paler on the rump and upper tail coverts, the latter barred with dusky; cheeks, sides of the neck and the whole of the lower plumage whitish or albescent, closely and narrowly barred transversely with black, the bars becoming obsolete on the abdomen; vent and under tail coverts white; quills and wing coverts dark brown, each feather margined with greyish white; ear coverts greyish, mottled with brown; the feathers white shafted; tail with the central pair of feathers grey, narrowly tipped with white, the rest blackish or dark brown, broadly tipped with white, the outermost with the white tippings, mottled with brown.

The young are similar to the adult female; adults have the bill black, also the legs and feet; iris brownish red.

Length.—7·5 inches; wing 4; tail 3; tarsus 0·8; bill from gape 0·85.

Hab.—The whole Peninsula of India and Ceylon, Central and Southern India, Bengal, the Concan and Deccan, and, according to Blyth, Upper Pegu. It hunts usually in small parties, and occasionally, according to Jerdon, singly or in pairs, flying from tree to tree, and slowly and carefully examining the foliage, prying searchingly all around and under the leaves to discover a suitable morsel. It continues its search, hopping and flying, from branch to branch till the tree has been well inspected, when the flock flies off together to another tree. Caterpillars and other soft insects are its favourite food. Dr. Jerdon adds that it is usually a silent bird but has a harsh call, and mentions having in June heard a male giving out a clear whistling call as it was flying from tree to tree. It affects wooded tracts, but not deep forests. Mr. Blewitt found the nest of this species in Bundelcund in July. It was placed at the end of two small out-shooting branches of a Mowa tree, and was slightly made of thin twigs and roots, and partially covered with spider's web. The eggs, two in number, were green, mottled with dark brown.

203. Lalage melanothorax, *Sharpe, Cat. B. Br. Mus.* iv. p. 90.—The BLACK-BREASTED CUCKOO-SHRIKE.

Closely allied to *L. sykesi* but differs in being larger and in having the black of the neck extending much further down on the breast and back.

Length.—7·5 inches; wing 4·2; tail 3·2; culmen 0·8.

Hab.—Madras (South India).

204. Lalage terat, *Bodd., Tab. Pl. Enl.* pl. 17; *Hume, Stray F.* i. p. 66; ii. p. 202; *Sharpe, Cat. B. Br. Mus.* iv. p. 91.—The NICOBAR CUCKOO-SHRIKE.

Adult Male.—Forehead, top and back of head, interscapulary region, scapulars and lesser wing coverts black, with a green metallic gloss; a broad streak from the nostrils over the eye and ear coverts, wing lining, edge of the wing, axillaries and entire lower parts including the sides of the neck, broad tips to the two external lateral tail feathers, a narrow tip to the next pair, the median wing coverts, broad margins to the outer webs of the greater coverts, the secondaries and the bases of the inner web of the primaries pure white; the breast and sides tinged with grey; the middle and lower back, rump and upper tail coverts grey, the two latter with faint traces of whitish bars; a streak from the gape through the eye black.

In the female the superciliary stripe is not so conspicuous and the greater wing coverts are only narrowly tipped with white. The forehead, top and back of the head and interscapulary region are iron grey, the breast is regularly and narrowly barred with darker grey.

Length.—6·75 to 7·25; wing 3·4 to 3·6; tail from vent 2·75 to 3·12; tarsus 0·65 to 0·82; bill from gape 0·8.

Hab.—Camorta Island (Nicobars), also in Acheen, the Malay Peninsula, Java, Sumatra, Borneo and the Philippine Islands.

Mr. Davison says it is not uncommon at Camorta, frequenting in small parties, of five or six or in pairs, the low scrubby under-growth and gardens, and feeding close to the ground. Nothing is known of its nidification.

Family.—MUSCICAPIDÆ.

Passerine birds of very varied form, embracing a large number of Genera, connecting the woodshrikes with the thrushes, with ample rictal bristles, wide, depressed or shallow-bills. They are all chiefly insectivorous. Their wings are moderate and not adapted for long and speedy flight, but are capable of rapid and powerful sallies.

Gen. Hemichelidon—*Hodgs.*

Bill much depressed and shallow, wide at base, slender and narrowed at tip, which is faintly hooked; gape wide; rictal bristles moderate; wings long; 3rd and 4th quills sub-equal and longest; 1st quill minute; tarsus feeble, lateral toes unequal.

Head of Hemichelidon ferruginea.

205. Hemichelidon sibirica, *Gm. Syst. Nat.* i. p. 936; *Hume, Nests and Eggs*, p. 206; *id. Str. F.* iii. p. 104; *David et Oust. Ois. Chine*, p. 122; *Hume, Str. F.* viii. p. 92; *Sharpe, Cat. Birds, B. Mus.* iv. p. 120. Hemichelidon fuliginosa, *Hodgs. P. Z. S.* 1845, p. 32; *Hume and Henders. Lah. to Yarkand*, p. 184, pl. iv.; *Jerd. B. Ind.* i. p. 458, No. 296; *Oates, B. Br. Burm.* i. p. 275. Butalis sibiricus, *Bl. B. Burm.* p. 104.—The Sooty Fly-Catcher.

Above brown, the feathers of the head with darker centres, the wings slightly edged pale rufous, broader after the autumnal moult; feathers round the orbits white; lores mixed whitish and brown; sides of the face brown; chin, throat, breast, sides of the body fuliginous or smoky brown, in some an indistinct whitish patch on the lower throat; abdomen, vent and under tail coverts white, the latter mixed with brown; tail brown.

The young are spotted with fulvous white above, and the margins of the wing feathers are broadly fulvous. Upper mandible of bill dark brown, lower mandible yellowish, iris brown, legs brownish black.

Length.—4·5 to 4·6 inches; wing 2.75 to 2·8; tail 1·75 to 2·0; tarsus 0·5; bill from gape 0·55.

Hab.—N. W. Provinces, Oudh, and probably Bengal. It is found throughout the Himalayas, common about Darjeeling, from 6,000 feet upwards, to Nepaul; spread over the whole of British Burmah as a winter visitant. Oates records it from the Pegu Hills near the frontier, and Dr. Armstrong got it at Elephant Point, but found it rare. Captain Wardlaw-Ramsay mentions his getting a young bird on the Tounghoo Hill in December. According to Davison, it is everywhere scarce in Tenasserim. Found also in the Malay Peninsula, and extends to China and Eastern Siberia.

The Sooty Fly-Catcher breeds in the Himalayas, making a nest of moss against the side of a tree trunk, or on the broken end of a branch, laying three eggs, which are dull green marked with reddish brown, They are long ovals, a good deal pointed and compressed at the smaller end; size 0·65, × 0·46. Jerdon says it is sedentary in its habits, darting on insects from a fixed perch on a low branch, and that he never saw it descend to the ground to feed,

206. Hemichelidon ferruginea, *Hodgs., P. Z. S,* 1845, p. 32; *Hume, Nests and Eggs,* p. 207; *Sharpe, Cat. B. Br. Mus.* iv. p. 122. Butalis ferruginea, *Bl. B. Burm.* p. 104; *David et Oust. Ois. Chine.* p. 121. Alseonax ferruginea, *Jerd. B. Ind.* I. p. 460, No. 299; *Hume and Dav., Str., F.* vi. p. 277; *Bingham, Str. F.* ix. p. 175; *Oates, Str. F.* x. p. 204; *Oates B. Br. Burm.* I p. 276.—The FERRUGINOUS FLY-CATCHER.

Forehead and crown of head dark brown; orbital feathers pale buff; lores and ear coverts rufescent brown; back, scapulars, lesser wing coverts, rump and upper tail-coverts, rusty or reddish brown, becoming deeper (chestnut) on the latter and on the rump; median and greater coverts brown, edged and tipped with chestnut; quills dark brown, the later secondaries and tertiaries edged with rusty brown; under surface of quills buffy; tail reddish brown; lower throat with a patch of white, the rest of the under surface chestnut; the throat rufescent brown; bill dusky, yellowish at base of lower mandible; legs pale fleshy; irides dark brown.

Length.—5 inches; wing 2·75; tail 2·0; tarsus 0·5; bill from gape 0·65.

Hab.—The Carnatic, N. W. Provinces, British Burmah, Nepaul, Sikkim, and Ceylon. The ferruginous flycatcher is a rare visitant to the plains of India. Jerdon says he did not hear of its occurrence away from the Himalayas. It is common in the neighbourhood of Darjeeling, from 4,000 to 8,000 feet. In Burmah it is a winter visitor. It is recorded from Bankasoon in Tenasserim; Oates procured specimens near Pegu, and Captain Bingham secured a specimen in the Thoungyeen Valley. It extends southwards through the Malay

Peninsula, and is found in Cochin-China. It frequents, according to Jerdon, dark, open forests without underwood, and pursues insects from a low branch, or the stump of a fallen tree.

It breeds in the Himalayas. The structure of the nest, as well as the number, size, and shape of the eggs, is the same as in the preceding species—colour a sort of buff, minutely and feebly freckled with brownish red; size 0·64 × 0·5.

Gen. **Alseonax.**—*Cabanis.*

Bill more lengthened than in *Hemichelidon*, less swallow like, being narrower in front and deeper vertically; 3rd and 4th quills subequal.

207. Alseonax latirostris, *Raffles, Trans. Lin. Soc.* xiii. p. 312; *Jerd. B. Ind.* i. p. 459, No. 297; *Hume and Henders. Lahore to Yark.* p. 185, pl. v.; *Hume, Str. F.* ii. p. 219; *Brooks, Str. F.* iii. p. 276, iv. p. 273, v. p. 470; *Sharpe, Cat. B. Br. Mus.* iv. p. 127; *Scully, Str. F.* viii. p. 276; *Legge, B. Ceylon*, p. 415; *Hume, Str. F.* viii. p. 92; *Brooks, Str. F.* ix. p. 225. Butalis terricolor, *Bl. J. A. S. B.* xvi. p. 120. Muscicapa cinereo-alba, *Tem. and Schleg. Faun. Jap-Aves*, p. 42. pl. 15. Alseonax terricolor, *Jerd. B. Ind.* i. p. 460, No. 298; *Brooks, Str. F.* iii. p. 234. Butalis latirostris, *Bl. B. Burm.* p. 104; *Oates, B. Br. Burm.* i. p. 277.—The Brown Fly-Catcher.

Above greyish brown or dark brown, the feathers of the crown centred darker; lores and orbital ring white. Scapulars, tertiaries, and secondaries dark brown; wing coverts the same; all but the primaries edged with rusty; tail dark brown, the outermost feathers narrowly tipped with whitish; under surface of body white, tinged with pale ashy on the breast, flanks, and sides of the throat.

Immature birds have broad fulvous margins to all the feathers of the upper plumage. Bill, legs and claws black; base of lower mandible yellow; in the immature, except the tip, which is dusky, the whole lower mandible is yellow.

Length.—5 to 5·2 inches; wing 2·75 to 2·85; tail 2·5 to 2·85; tarsus 0·5; bill from gape 0·7.

Hab.—N. W. Provinces, Oudh, Central India, the Concan, Deccan, South India, Malabar Coast, Ceylon, British Burmah, and Nepaul. Extends to Cochin-China.

The Brown Fly-Catcher is a winter visitor to Burmah. It is said to be a resident of Southern India and Ceylon, but nothing appears to be known of its nidification. Oates says that in Pegu some birds would appear to stay all the year round, or to nest close by, having shot both adult and young in July. It is abundant, according to him, in the southern half of Pegu. Captain Wardlaw-Ramsay got it at Tounghoo. Mr. Blyth received it from Arrakan, and Davison says he observed it in the southern half of Tenasserim. It extends down the

Malay Peninsula to the Archipelago, and is found spread over China in winter. Its habits are quite those of the other species. Jerdon says it is very sedentary, sitting motionless on a branch and darting out occasionally to capture an insect on the wing.

Gen. **Muscicapa,** *Linn.*; Butalis *Boie.*; Erythrosterna, *Bp.*

Wings pointed and long; bill rather long, depressed, wide throughout, except at tip; second primary longer than the secondaries and nearly the length of the third; nasal bristles scanty.

208. Muscicapa grisola, *Linn. Syst. Nat.* i. p. 328; *Tem. Man.* i. p. 152; *Naum. vogt. Deutch.* ii. p. 216; *MacGill. Br. B.* iii. p. 518; *Gray, Gen. B.* i. p. 262; *Gould. B. Eur.* ii. pl. 65; *Sharpe, P. Z. S.* 1873, p. 71; *id. Cat. Passerif. B. Br. M.* p. 151; *Blf. East Pers.* p. 143; *Str. F.* 1873, p. 377; *Murray, Vert. Zool. Sind,* p. 127. Butalis grisola, *Boie. Isis,* 1826, p. 973; *Cat. Mus. Heine. Th.* i. p. 52; *Sharpe, Cat. Afr. B.* p. 42, No. 391; *id. Ibis,* 1872, p. 70; *Hume, Str. F.* 1875, p. 467; 1877, p. 495. Butalis africana, *Bp. C. R.* xxxviii. p. 652.—The Spotted Grey Fly-Catcher.

Lores and feathers immediately above the nostrils dingy fulvous white; head, nape, cheeks, ear coverts, back and scapulars, pale earthy or greyish brown; the feathers of the head with darker brown central streaks not extending to the tips, and those of the forehead tinged with the fulvous colour of the lores; the rump, in some, uniform with the back, in others slightly darker; wings and tail brown, paler and greyer on the tertiaries and laterals, all the feathers margined with brownish white; the greater secondary coverts and tertials most broadly so; the tail feathers, except the exterior lateral ones, inconspicuously so; lower parts white, tinged with fawn colour towards the vent, and with narrow inconspicuous grey brown streaks on the breast; axillaries and wing lining very pale rufous fawn; sides and flanks tinged faintly with the same colour and dull fulvous.

"Bill black, dark fleshy at base of lower mandible; legs and feet blackish brown; iris deep brown; interior of mouth orange."—(*Hume, Str. F.*, vol. 3, p. 467.)

Length.—5·4 inches; bill at front 0.55; wing 3·4; tail 2·45; tarsus 0·6.

Hab.—The whole of Europe, extending in the winter into South Africa and N. W. India, Sind, Beloochistan, Afghanistan, Persia (Northern and Southern), Kutch, Kattiawar, Jodhpore, Sambhur. Visits Sind in the course of its migration in August and September, and at about the same time of the year in other parts of the Western Presidency.

All the species of this genus are quick and active birds, incessantly hopping about on the branches of trees, generally thin scrub or acacias, searching for insects, which are their chief food.

209. Muscicapa sordida (*Godw.-Austen*). *Sharpe, Cat. B. Br. Mus.* iv. p. 156. Erythrosterna sordida, *Godw.-Austen, J. A. S. B.* xliii., p. 158; *Hume, Str. F.* 1875, p. 692.—The OLIVE-BROWN FLY-CATCHER.

Above dull, olivaceous brown, ochraceous on rump and upper tail feathers; tail umber-brown, slightly tinged with ochre on outer web; quills the same as the tail and edged with olive; the primary and secondary coverts very slightly tipped pale, forming an inconspicuous bar on the wing; lores and a distinct ring round the eye dull whitish; ear coverts and sides of face olive brown, with buffy shaft streaks; cheeks and under surface of body ashy (lutescent, Hume), strongly washed with olive, the foreneck with an ochraceous tinge; under wing coverts and axillaries pale yellowish buff; quills ashy brown below, yellowish buff along the inner webs.

Length.—4·6 inches (5·25, Hume); wing 2·6 to 2·7; tail 2·2; tarsus 0·65. (Sharpe).

Hab.—Sudiya in Upper Assam, and the Naga Hills.

210. Muscicapa parva, *Bechst. Nat. Deutsch.* iv. p. 505; *Tem. Man.* i. p. 158; *Werner, Atlas, Insectivores*, pl. 10; *Gray, Gen. Birds*, i. p. 262; *Gould. B. Eur.* ii. pl. 64; *Dresser, Ibis*, 1876, p. 188; *Sharpe, Cat. B. Br. Mus.* iv. p. 161; *Murray, Vert. Zool., Sind*, p. 128. Erythrosterna parva, *Bp. Consp. List. B. Eur. and N. Amer.* p. 25; *id. Consp.* i. p. 318; *Blf. East. Pers.* p. 144; *Hume, Str. F.* 1873, pp. 179, 377, 405; 1875, p. 469; 1876, p. 273; 1877, p. 484; vol. v. p. 471; *Murray, Hdbk. Zool., &c., Sind*, p. 139. Muscicapa rufogularis, *Brehm. Vog. Deutsch.* p. 228.—THE RED-BREASTED FLY-CATCHER.

Forehead, sides of face and ear coverts grey; a circle of whitish feathers round the eye; crown of head, back, wing coverts and quills externally ashy brown; inner web of primaries dusky; upper tail coverts and tail dark brown, all, except the centre tail-feathers, white at their bases; the external web of the lateral ones on each side dusky; chin, cheeks, and foreneck orange, rest of under surface fulvous white or buffy white; thigh coverts ashy brown; under wing coverts fulvescent, as are also the margins of the inner webs of the under surface of the quills; bill brownish; legs dark brown.

Length.—5 inches; bill at front 0·4; wing 2·6; tail 2; tarsus 0·65; culmen 0·4.

The female has the quills and wing coverts, especially the greater series, edged with light brown; the chin, throat and breast deep buffy, and the abdomen and vent white.

Hab.—Europe, extending into N. W. India, the Himalayas, Cashmere and Nepaul. Extremely common in Beloochistan, Persia, and South Afghanistan; also in Sind, the Punjab, N. W. Provinces, Oudh, Rajputana, Central India, the Deccan, Concan, Kutch, and North Guzerat. A winter visitant in Sind and other parts of the Western Presidency.

211. Muscicapa albicilla, *Pall. Zoogr. Rosso-Asiat.* i. p. 462, *Aves, tab.* i.; *Sharpe, Cat. B. Br. Mus.* iv. p. 162; *Oates, B. Burm.* i. p. 278. Erythrosterna leucura, (*Gm.*) *Jerd. B. Ind.* i. p. 481, No. 323; *Bl. B. Burm.*, p. 103. Erythrosterna albicilla, (*Pall.*) *Anders. Yunnan Expedition*, p. 621; *Hume and Dav., Str. F.* vi. p. 233; *David et Oust. Ois Chine*, p. 120; *Scully, Str. F.* viii. p. 280; *Hume, Str. F.* viii. p. 93.—The WHITE-TAILED ROBIN FLY-CATCHER.

Male in summer plumage.—Upper plumage and wings olive brown, the latter margined paler; upper tail coverts black; tail black, the four outer pairs of feathers white for about two-thirds of their length from the base; lores mixed ashy and white; chin and throat orange; ear coverts, cheeks and a band passing round the orange of the throat pure ashy, extending on to the upper breast in some; rest of lower plumage ashy white.

In winter the male loses the orange on the chin and throat, and the plumage on the under surface of the body is tinged with buff; orbital ring white.

The female is like the male in summer; bill dark brown, yellowish at the gape; iris hazel brown; legs black.

Length.—5 to 5·1 inches; wing 2·75; tail 2·0 to 2·1; tarsus 0·65; bill from gape 0·6.

Hab.—N.-W. Provinces, Oudh, Bengal, also the Concan, and, perhaps, the Deccan, as well as British Burmah and Nepaul. Jerdon says it is found "throughout the whole of India." This statement is certainly incorrect. It is not known from South India, though it occurs in Ceylon. In Northern and Central India it is not uncommon, but everywhere, even in British Burmah, as a winter visitant. According to Oates it is common in Pegu, and spread over the whole division from November to March. It is recorded from Arrakan, and Mr. Shopland got specimens at Akyab. At Tounghoo Captain Wardlaw-Ramsay obtained specimens. It is spread over the whole of Tenasserim. It is said to summer in Eastern Siberia and North China.

The White-tailed Robin Fly-Catcher affects gardens, orchards, groves and low jungle chiefly. It appears to be strictly arboreal, playing about on the branches of trees searching for insects, and never descending to the ground.

212. Muscicapa hyperythra, *Cab. Journ. F. Ornith.* 1866, p. 391; *Sharpe, Cat. B. Br. Mus.* iv. p. 163. Erythrosterna hyperythra (*Cab.*) *Hume, Str. F.* vii. p. 376.—The WHITE-TAILED ROBIN OR RUFOUS-BREASTED FLY-CATCHER.

The upper surface is brownish grey, turning to a purer grey on the rump and upper tail coverts; tail black, with the basal halves of the lateral rectrices white, the upper tail coverts, especially the longest, are blackish in parts, especially on the outer webs. The lower surface is a bright red-brown or rusty-red, except on the middle of the abdomen, which is pure white. The red-brown colour is most intense on the throat and breast, lighter and mingled with albescent on the sides of the abdomen and lower tail coverts; tibial plumes grey; loreal region somewhat dotted with white; sides of the head and neck pure grey, separated from the red-brown of the throat and breast by an irregular blackish line; under wing coverts tinged with rusty yellow; feet and upper mandible brown, the lower yellow; 4th quill longest, fifth longer than the third, 2nd about equal to the 8th.

Length.—5·33 inches; wing 2·88; tail 3·3; tarsus 0·78 (Cabanis). The distinguishing characters of this species are the rich orange-brown of the throat and breast, and the black stripe running from the bill down the sides of the neck to the breast and terminating below the bend of the closed wing; bill dusky above, yellow beneath; irides dark brown. (Holdsworth.)

Hab.—Central India and the N.-W. Provinces. Also Ceylon and Cashmere.

The Rufous-breasted Fly-Catcher appears to have the usual habits of the other species. According to Brooks it breeds in Cashmere at from 6,000 to 7,000 feet elevation. There is no record of its nest having been found.

Gen. **Pratincola**, *Koch. Syst. d. Baier. Zool.* p. 190.

Bill short, straight, wider at the nostrils than high; nostrils hidden; second primary longer than the secondaries, the first not half the length of the second.

213. Pratincola macrorhyncha, *Stolickza, J. A. S. B.* xli. p. 238; *Hume, Str. F.* 1876, p. 40; 1877, p. 131, 241, 244; 1879, p. 53. *Sharpe, Cat. Birds, B. Museum.* vol. iv. p. 182; *Murray, Vert. Zool., Sind,* p. 138. Pratincola rubetraoides, *Jerd. B. Ind.* iii. *App.* p. 872 (*ex. Jameson MS. Desc Nulla*) *Dresser, B. Eur.* parts 23, 24; *Hume, Str. F.* 1877, p. 239. Pratincola rubetra, *Hume, Ibis,* 1869, p. 354. Pratincola Jamesoni, *Hume, Str. F* 1877, p. 239 (*nom emende*).—STOLICKZA'S BUSH-CHAT.

Adult Male.—A broad stripe over the eyes and over the greater portion of the ear coverts white, with a slight buffy tinge; lower parts of the lores dusky; chin, throat and entire lower parts, including lower tail coverts and tibial plumes, white with a yellowish tinge and a very feeble rufescent tinge on breast and flanks; wing lining and axillaries pure white, the former slightly mottled with dusky; forehead, crown, occiput, nape, back and scapulars light sandy buff, striated longitudinally with hair brown; rump and upper tail coverts white, most of the feathers tinged towards their tips with pale rusty buff; primaries and secondaries hair brown, margined on the outer webs with light buff and tipped with yellowish white, the primaries more narrowly, the secondaries more broadly; tertiary greater coverts, or perhaps I should call them lower scapulars, white; tertiaries and greater and median secondary coverts deep brown, broadly margined with pale, more or less rufescent buff;

entire visible portion of lesser coverts pale sandy buff; edge of wing and outer webs of earlier greater primary coverts pure white; tail hair brown, all the feathers margined on the outer webs with sandy buff or light yellowish brown; the outer web of the outermost feather almost entirely of this colour; all the feathers, except the central pair, with almost the entire inner webs, white, the outermost pair have an irregular subterminal brown band from 0·2 to 0.3 inch wide on this web, but the rest have only a small patch of brown near the shaft close to the tip, the pair next the centre have the patch rather larger; there are traces of a dark streak from the base of the lower mandible down either side of the throat, expanding on the sides of the breast; doubtless in breeding plumage this streak and patch are black or blackish; bill and feet black; iris brown.

Length.—6 inches; culmen 0·7; wing 3; tail 2·12; tarsus 0·7. (Hume.)

Breeding Plumage.—Two or three of both my males and females have the lower parts of the lores, cheeks, ear coverts and entire sides of the throat (leaving only a narrow pure white stripe down the centre of the throat) black; the feathers only a little tipped with pale sandy, which doubtless in the breeding season entirely disappears; also the lesser and median, and secondary greater wing coverts and the winglet have become nearly black, only very narrowly edged with sandy buff, which colour also seems in the course of disappearing. (Hume.)

Adult Female in winter plumage similar to the male, but smaller and showing the dark streak and patch much less.

Length.—5·5 inches; culmen 0·7; wing 2·9; tail 2; tarsus 0·93. (Hume.) *Ex. Sharpe, Cat. B. Br. Mus.* vol. iv. p. 188.

Hab.—Sind, Punjab, and N.-W. Provinces. Mr. Hume gives the following distribution of this species in vol. vii. of *Stray Feathers*, p. 55:—"Punjab (Goorgaon, Umballa, Sirsa, Hansi, Shahpoor and probably all western districts); Rajputana (Jodhpore, Biccaneer, Jeysulmere); North Guzerat, Kutch, Sind (Thurr and Parkur districts) and probably elsewhere." I got it at Chaman (Afghanistan), and in the Bolan Pass, Beloochistan.

214. Pratincola insignis, *Blyth, J. A. S. B.* xvi. p. 129; *Jerd. B. Ind.* ii. p. 127, No. 485; *Rainey, Str.* F. iii. p. 330; *Hume, Str. F.* v. pp. 132, 496; *id. Str. F.* vii. pp. 454, 519; *Sharpe, Cat. B. Br. Mus.* iv. p. 187.—The LARGE BUSH CHAT.

Male.—Entire cap, lores, cheeks and ear coverts black, many of the feathers faintly fringed at the tips with pale brown; nape dark brown; the feathers much fringed at the tips with the same pale brown; chin, throat, sides of the neck, behind the ear coverts, and a broad imperfect collar at the base of the neck, white; back and scapulars brown, all the feathers fringed with pale brown; rump greyish buffy, more distinctly tinged buffy at the tips; upper tail coverts white, with a buffy tinge towards the middle; wings dark brown;

the primaries white at the base on both webs so as to form a conspicuous wing spot; all the quills broadly white on their inner webs towards their base; tertiaries and all the coverts, and the greater and median coverts of the later secondaries, white; first and second primaries very narrowly margined white towards the tips; secondaries tipped inconspicuously with dull white; all the quills more or less margined paler on their outer webs; 3rd to 6th primaries conspicuously emarginate on their outer webs; tail dark brown, very narrowly margined and tipped with pale fulvous brown; breast rather pale ferruginous chestnut; rest of the lower parts very pale fulvous; axillaries white, grey on their inner webs; wing lining mingled with pale brown and fulvous white.

Length.—5·0 to 6·3 inches; wing 3·3 to 3·55; tail 2·3; bill from forehead 0·69; tarsus 0·97 to 1·1.

The above is Mr. Hume's description of a male specimen obtained by Mr. Mandelli in the lower hills of the Bhootan Doars in April.

A female obtained by Mr. Cleveland in October, a little west of the place where Hodgson got his type, is described by Mr. Hume as under:—

Upper parts grey earth-brown, the feathers centred with dark hair brown; upper tail coverts dull rather pale ferruginous buff; wings and tail blackish brown, the greater and median coverts broadly tipped, the greater coverts with dull rather creamy white, the rest with pale buff, forming two rather conspicuous wing bars; all the quills and coverts margined with creamy white; tail feathers similar; chin and upper throat creamy; rest of lower parts nearly uniform rufous buff, and paling somewhat on the lower tail coverts, flanks, axillaries and wing lining; the base of the quills on their inner web with a rufous white patch; irides brown; bill and legs black.

Length.—5·8; wing 3·42; tail 2·4; tarsus 1·08; bill 0·67.

Hab.—Bengal and Nepaul. Mr. Cleveland's specimen came from Captain Gunj, Zilla Bustee; Hodgson's type was from Segowlee. The species, according to Mr. Cleveland, affects the cane-fields.

215. Pratincola maura, (*Pall. Reis.* ii. *Anhang.* p. 708); *Gm. Syst. Nat.* i. p. 975. *Blyth, J. A. S. B.* xvi. p. 129; *id. Cat. Mus. A. S. B.* p. 170; *Bp. Consp.* i. p. 305; *Str. F.* 1873, p. 355; 1875, p. 138; t. c. p. 475; 1876, pp. 142, 259, 275, 327; 1877, p. 36; *Jerd. B. Ind.* ii. p. 124, No. 483; *Murray, Hdbk., Zool., &c., Sind*, p. 145; *Sharpe, Cat. Birds, Br. Mus.* vol. iv. p. 188. *Murray, Vert. Zool. Sind*, p. 139. Pratincola robusta, *Tristr. Ibis.* 1870, p. 497; *Brooks, Str. F.* 1876, p. 274; *Hume, Str. F.* 1877, p. 131; 1878, p. 335; vii. p. 55. Pratincola rubicola (*Pt.*), *Severtz. Turkst. Jevotn.* p. 65; *Dresser, B. Eur.* pt. 23, 24. *Hume, Nests and Eggs, Ind. B.* p. 316.—The Indian Bush Chat.

Adult Male.—Head, neck, chin, throat, sides of face, back, tail and wings black; the feathers of the back and scapulars (some of which are white tipped) edged with pale rufous, and the tail basally white; the quills dusky brown, margined with sandy brown, as are also the wing coverts and secondaries; a large wing patch, rump, upper tail coverts, and sides of neck forming a demicollar, white; foreneck and breast bright ferruginous; abdomen, vent and under tail coverts white, slightly tinged with fulvous; axillaries black. In winter plumage, the general colour above is brown, the rump and upper tail coverts rusty, also the entire under surface, but duller. The adult female is brown above with pale rufous edges to the feathers, and the edgings to the wing coverts and scapulars much lighter; the wing patch is much smaller and less distinct; the rump and upper tail coverts a rufescent buff; cheeks and throat fulvous ashy, and the entire under surface a sullied white or pale buff; the axillaries also buffy; the bases of the feathers brownish; bill and legs black; irides brown.

Length.—4·5 to 5·5 inches; wings 2·75; tail 1·75; tarsus 0·85.

Hab.—India generally during the winter, also China, Japan, Cashmere, Nepaul, N.-W. Himalayas, Upper Burmah, Eastern Turkistan, Abyssinia, Beloochistan (Bolan and Quetta), Afghanistan (Chaman and Gulistan). Occurs in Sind, Kutch, Kattiawar, Jodhpore, Jeypore, North Guzerat, the Deccan, Kamptee, in Central India and Darjeeling.

The Indian Bush Chat breeds throughout the lower ranges of the Himalayas, south of the first snowy range, at almost any elevation not exceeding 5,000 feet, from Afghanistan to Assam. Ocasionally, too, they breed in the salt range in the Suleiman Hills, in the plains district of the Punjab which skirt the bases of these lower hills, and there is one instance on record of the nest being taken at the extreme south of the Sharunpoor district. April and May appear to be the months in which they mostly lay, but they have two, and possibly three, broods, eggs having been taken at Kotegurh as early as the first week in March and as late as the middle of July. The situation of the nest varies according to locality. They have been found in low, thick, generally thorny, bushes or dense tufts of grass on or near the ground and in crevices of rough stone walls.

The nest is a more or less regular cup, composed of coarse grass and dried moss lined with fine grass, fur, hair, feathers, and the like. The eggs are 4 or 5 in number. The ground colour is dull pale green or greenish white, and they are finely and faintly freckled with pale brownish red; size 0·7 + 0·55.

216. Pratincola leucura, *Blyth, J. A. S. B.* xvi. p. 474; *Bp. Consp.* i. p. 305; *Jerd. B. Ind.* ii. p. 126, No. 484; *Hume, Str. F.* 1873, p. 183; 1874, p. 478; 1875, p. 135; *Murray, Hdbk., Zool., &c., Sind,* p. 145; *Sharpe, Cat. B. Br. Mus.* iv. p. 134; *Murray, Vert. Zool., Sind,* p. 140; *Oates, B. Br. Burm.,* i. p. 280.—The White-tailed Bush Chat.

Adult Male in Summer Plumage.—Above black; rump duller; upper tail coverts white; central tail feathers blackish brown, basally white, the others dark brown on the outer web and white on the inner; wings black; quills duller, margined pale brown; a white wing spot; breast bright rufous; sides of head and throat black; on the sides of the neck a white patch, broader at the lower throat; rest of under surface pure white, tinged with rufescent on the sides; under wing coverts black, edged with white. "In the winter plumage the male is nearly a sandy brown above, almost uniform, the black centres to the feathers being effectually concealed; upper tail coverts white, sandy rufous at their ends; tail feathers dark brown, edged with sandy colour; the inner webs white, slightly shaded with sandy buff at the tips; wings black, with broad sandy brown edges to the feathers; the inner secondaries margined with rufous, some of the feathers forming the white wing patch, edged with brown; a loral line of ashy white; feathers in front of and round the eye black, with sandy brown edgings; throat black, obscured by ashy white margins to the feathers; on each side of the lower throat a white patch half concealed by rufous tips to the feathers; breast and sides of body orange rufous, the feathers edged with sandy buff; plumes on the sides of the upper breast white, tipped rufous; under wing coverts and axillaries white with dusky bases."

"The *adult female* is earthy brown, with more or less distinct remains of sandy brown edges; upper tail coverts sandy buff; tail feathers brown, dull white along the basal portion of the inner web; wings brown, with buffy white tips to the greater coverts; wing patch smaller than in the males; lores fulvous, extending over the forepart of the eye; round the latter a ring of sandy buff; ear coverts brown with fulvous shaft-lines; cheeks and throat white; breast and sides of body paler orange buff; the centre of the abdomen buffy white; under wing coverts and axillaries pale sandy buff with dusky bases; quills brown below, whitish along the edge of the inner web; bill and feet brownish black; irides brown." (Sharpe.)

Length.—5 inches; wing 2·5; tail 2; bill at front 0·5.

Hab.—India and Burmah, N.-W. Himalayas, Sind, Punjab, at Mooltan, and the Gangetic Valley, where Jerdon states he found it most abundant from Rajmahal to Monghyr, frequenting fields and long grasses. It winters in Sind and the Punjab. In Burmah Oates collected specimens a few miles south of Thayetmyo, and Colonel Lloyd at Tonghoo. Mr. Blanford found it on the Irrawady, and Davison in the neighbourhood of Pahpoon. It frequents the neighbourhood of swamps and wet paddy fields.

217. Pratincola caprata (*Linn.*), *Blyth, J. A. S. B.* xvi. p. 129; *Bp. Consp.* i. p. 305; *Jerd. B. Ind.* ii. p. 123, No. 481; *Hume, Str. F.* 1873, pp. 182, 379; 1874, pp. 413, 477; 1875, p. 134; 1877, p. 229; 1876, p. 259; *Str. F.* 1875, p. 238; *Murray, Vert. Zool., Sind,* p. 141; *Oates, B. Br. Burm.* i. p. 281; *Blanfd. Eastern Persia,* p. 144; *Murray, Hdbk., Zool.,*

&c., Sind, p. 145. Motacilla caprata, (*Linn.*) *S. Nat.* i. p. 325. Œnanthe caprata, *Viell. N. Dict.* xxi. p. 433. Saxicola bicolor, *Sykes, P. Z. S.* 1832, p. 92. Pratincola atrata, *Blyth, J. A. S. B.* xx. p. 177; *Jerd. B. Ind.* ii. p. 124, No. 482. Pratincola bicolor, *Hume, Nests and Eggs, Ind. B.* p. 314. —The White-winged Black Robin.

Adult Male.—Head, neck all round, throat, breast, sides of the face, back, wings, tail and entire under surface black; under wing coverts black; vent, under tail coverts, rump, upper tail coverts and wing patch white; some of the feathers of the lower abdomen very slightly edged with white. The young male is dark brown, the feathers of the upper and lower surface with brownish edgings; the quills dark brown with whitish tips, and the lower abdomen, vent and upper tail coverts, as well as the wing patch, white. The female is dusky brown, the feathers edged pale, and with dark centres to the feathers of the head, scapulars and back; rump and upper tail coverts rufescent; tail dark brown, as also are the wing coverts and quills, but margined with lighter brown; beneath pale reddish or ochraceous brown, whitish on the throat; vent and under tail coverts white, with a slight rufous tinge; bill and legs black; irides dark brown.

Length.—5 to 5·4 inches; wing 2·75; tail 2·1; tarsus 0·8; bill at front 0·45.

Hab.—India generally, Ceylon, Southern India, Burmah, Java, and Philippines. In the Indian region it extends to the Himalayas, and is extremely common throughout Sind, the Punjab, Beloochistan, S. E. Persia and S. Afghanistan, at Chaman, Gulistan, Dubrai and Kandahar; also occurs all along the Western Coast, Kutch, Kattiawar, Jodhpore, North Guzerat, the Deccan and Concan. Breeds in Sind and the plains generally during March and April. Eggs usually three, pale greenish white, speckled finely with brown.

Gen. **Poliomyias**.—*Sharpe.*

Bill rather broad, with well defined culmen, broader at the nostrils than it is high; shorter than in *Pratincola* and not exceeding the inner toe and claw. General aspect and style of plumage of *Muscicapa*, but with long wings.

218. Poliomyias Hodgsoni, (*Verr.*) *Sharpe, Cat. B. Br. Mus.* iv. p. 203; *Oates, B. Br. Burmah*, i. p. 286. Siphia Hodgsoni, *Verr. N. Arch. Mus.* vi. *Bull*, p. 34, vii. p. 29; *David et Oust. Ois. Chine*, p. 115. Siphia erythaca, *Jerd. and Bl. P. Z. S.* 1861, p. 201; *Jerd. B. Ind.* i. p. 480, No. 322; *Hume, Str. F.* ii. p. 456; *Wald in Bl. B. Burm.* p. 103; *Hume, Str. F.* vi. p. 137; *Hume and Dav. Str. F.* vi. p. 233; *Hume, Str. F.* viii. p. 93.—The Rusty-breasted Fly-Catcher.

Male.—Above dull cyaneous, also the ear coverts; lores, feathers under the eye, the cheeks and upper tail coverts black; wing coverts brown, edged with cyaneous; quills black, edged with brown; tail black, the bases of all but the two central feathers white at the base; sides of the neck and a patch on either side of the breast dull cyaneous; chin, throat, breast and abdomen rich orange; lower abdomen, vent, flanks and under tail coverts pale ferruginous. Bill black; legs and feet dark reddish horny; irides very dark brown. (Dav.)

Length.—5·5 inches; tail 2·2 to 2·5; wing 2·95; tarsus ·65; bill from gape ·55.

Hab.—Darjeeling (Jerdon), British Burmah and Nepaul. According to Oates it has been procured in Karenne and in the Karin Hills, east of Tounghoo, at 4,000 feet elevation. Davison says it is confined to the higher hills of the northern and central portions of Tennaserim, and that he got it in the pine forests north of Pahpoon and near the summit of Mooleyit. It is found in the Himalayas, and extends its range to Western China.

The female of this species is not yet satisfactorily identified. There is a closely allied species *P. luteola*, which Oates says will probably be found in Burmah.

Gen. **Muscicapula**.—*Blyth.*

Bill feeble, narrow at tip, moderately wide at base, depressed, very slightly hooked and notched at the tip; rictal and nareal bristles moderately developed; 3rd quill nearly as long as 4th; 1st and 2nd primaries moderately developed; tarsus slightly lengthened.

219. Muscicapula superciliaris, (*Jerd.*) *Blyth, J. A. S. B.* xii. pp. 939, 962; *Jerd. B. Ind.* i. p. 470, No. 310; *Stol. J. A. S. B.* xxxvii. pt. ii. p. 30; *Hume, Nests and Eggs*, p. 213; *Ball, Str. F.* v. p. 415; *Hume, Str. F.* viii. p. 92; *Sharpe, Cat. B. Br. Mus.* iv. p. 204; *Oates, B. Br. Burm.*, i. p. 292. Muscicapa superciliaris, *Jerd. Madr. Journ.* xi. p. 16. Erythrosterna acornaus (*Hodgs.*), *Jerd. B. Ind.* i. p. 483, No. 325; *Beavan, Ibis*, 1870, p. 320; *Bl. and Wald., B. Burm.* p. 103; *Hume and Dav., Str. F.* vi. p. 233; *Hume, Str. F.* viii. p. 93.—The White-browed Blue Fly-Catcher.

Top of head, cheeks, ear coverts and sides of the neck dull blue; lores black; a broad distinct supercilium reaching behind to the nape white; back of the head, nape, entire upper plumage, including the lesser and median wing coverts, dull blue; greater wing coverts and quills dark brown, edged with pale bluish; tail black, edged with blue, the basal half of all, except the central ones, white; entire lower surface of body white, except a broad, dull-blue collar across the breast.

The female has the upper plumage brown, the feathers of the head centred darker, the forehead, rump and upper tail coverts tinged with rufous; wing coverts, quills and tail brown, edged paler; the lores mixed rufous and white;

ear coverts greyish brown with paler shafts; under surface of body sullied with brown on the breast and sides of the body.

Length.—4·25 to 4·75 inches; wing 2·4 to 2·5; tail 1·8 to 1·9; tarsus ·6; bill from gape ·6.

Hab.—Punjab, N. W. Provinces, Oudh, Bengal, Central Provinces, British Burmah and Nepaul. According to Jerdon it is found throughout the Himalayas, spreading to the plains of India in the cold weather, but is nowhere a common bird. Mr. Brooks reported its occurrence at Assensole; Ball says it is tolerably abundant in Sumbulpoor and in the adjoining districts on the south, and records it from Midnapoor, Lohardugga, Singhboom, Orissa, Nowagurh, and the Godavery Valley; and Oates has it from British Burmah, on the strength of two female specimens from Karenne, procured by Captain Wardlaw Ramsay.

The White-browed Blue Fly-Catcher nests in the Himalayas. The nest is a small cup made of moss, and lined with fine roots and hairs, and is either placed in a hole of a tree or wall. The eggs are 4 to 6 in number, pale green, and entirely covered with brownish red freckles.

220. Muscicapula astigma, (*Hodgs.*) *Sharpe, Cat. B. Br. Mus.* iv. p. 205; *Jerd. B. Ind.* i. p. 471, No. 311; *Gray, Cat. B. Nepaul; Hodgs. Coll. app.* p. 155; *Ball, Str. F.* vii. p. 212; *Oates, B. Br. Burm.* i. p. 293.—The LITTLE BLUE and WHITE FLY-CATCHER.

Differs from *M. superciliaris* in having the whole upper surface blue, the wings and tail black, margined with blue—the latter with no white at the base—no white supercilium, and in the under surface being pure white.

Length.—4·25 inches; wing 2·25; tail 1·8; tarsus ·5; culmen 0·45.

Hab.—N.-W. Provinces and Bengal to the Himalayas and Nepaul.

The females of the species of this small group of birds are so alike that they cannot be readily distinguished, especially of *M. superciliaris.*

221. Muscicapula maculata, *Tick. J. A. S. B.* ii. p. 574; *Sharpe, Cat. B. Br. Mus.* iv. p. 207; *Oates, B. Br. Burm.* i. p. 294. Erythrosterna maculata, *Jerd. B. Ind.* i. p. 483, No. 326; *Bl. B. Burm.* p. 103; *Brooks, Str. F.* iii. pp. 236, 277; viii. p. 470; *Hume, Str. F.* viii. p. 93. Erythrosterna pusilla, *Bl. J. A. S. B.* xviii. p. 813; *Jerd. B. Ind.* i. p. 482, No. 324; *Brooks, Str. F.* v. p. 471.—The LITTLE-PIED FLY-CATCHER.

Above, including the lores, cheeks, ear coverts and sides of the neck glossy black; a superciliary streak reaching to the nape white. Whole under surface also white; wings black; the later secondaries edged with white on their outer webs, the remaining secondaries and all the primaries with an interior lining of white; the greater upper wing coverts white, forming a bar across the wing; tail black, the basal two-thirds, except of the central tail feathers, white.

The female has the upper surface and lesser wing coverts olive brown, tinged with rufous; upper tail coverts ferruginous; greater wing coverts and quills brown, margined with pale rufous brown; lores and sides of the head fulvescent brown; under surface of body white, tinged with brown on the flanks and breast; tail dark brown, narrowly margined with rufous brown; no white bases to the feathers of the tail.

Bill black; legs brown; irides light brown.

Length.—4·4 inches; wing 2·4; tail 1·75; tarsus 0·6; bill from gape 0·55.

Hab.—N.-W. Provinces, Central India, Bengal, and British Burmah.

Taking Jerdon's notes on *Erythrosterna pusilla*, which is now identified with the female of this species, and the notes against *E. maculata*, the Little-pied Fly-Catcher occurs in the plains of Central India during the cold weather and retires to the Himalayas during the summer He says he obtained it near Darjeeling in summer dress, and quotes Blyth as to its occurrence in the Midnapoor District. It extends through Arrakan and Tenasserim into Western Malasia. It also occurs at Pegu in the cold weather. Jerdon saw this species in pairs, but generally in small parties, active and restless, capturing insects entirely on the wing. It has a pleasing little song.

222. Muscicapula sapphira, *Tickell, MSS.*; *Blyth, J. A. S. B.* xii. p. 939; *Jerdon, Illus. Ind. Orn.* pl. 32; *id. B. Ind.* i. p. 471, No. 312; *Str. F.* iii. p. 237; *Ball, Str. F.* ii. p. 405; *Sharpe, Cat. B. Br. Mus.* iv. p. 209.—The SAPPHIRE-HEADED FLY-CATCHER.

Male.—Above rich dark purplish blue, inclining to smalt blue on the rump and upper tail coverts; forehead and crown pale azure or sapphire blue (*vivid smalt blue*, Blyth), deepening on the hind head; lores black; foreneck and breast rich purple, with a broad median line of deep and bright ferruginous; flanks greyish; belly and forepart of the wings underneath, also the axillaries, white; quills and tail black, and the feathers edged externally with blue; there is no white at base of the feathers of the latter.

Bill and feet black; irides dark brown.

The female has the head, neck and interscapulars plain olive brown; forehead, lores and cheeks ferruginous; wings, rump and tail deep blue; throat, foreneck and breast bright ferruginous, much broader than in the male; belly and lower tail coverts bluish white.

Length.—4·75 inches; wing 2·5; tail 1·9; tarsus 0·6; culmen 0·35.

Hab.—N.-W. Provinces, Oudh, Bengal, also Sikkim and Nepaul. Jerdon says it is somewhat rare at Darjeeling, and that the species affects open forest, perches high up, and catches insects on the wing.

Gen. **Tarsiger.**—*Hodgs.*

Bill short, slender, straight; rictal bristles moderate; wings moderate; 4th and 5th quills equal and longest, 3rd and 6th subequal; tail slightly mucronate; tarsus extremely powerful, more than twice the length of the culmen; toes and claws long and slender; plumage of males blue above, and more or less rufous below.

223 Tarsiger rufilatus, *Hodgs. Icon. ined. Passeres*, pl. 88; *id. P. Z. S.* 1845, p. 27; *Gray, Gen. B.* i. p. 180; *Hume, Nests and Eggs, Ind. B.* p. 324; *Sharpe, Cat. B. Br. Mus.* iv. p. 256. Nemura cyanura, *Hodgs. Icon. ined. Passeres* pl. 76, fig. 3. Ianthina rufilata, *Bly. J. A. S. B.* xvi. p. 132, *id. Ibis*, 1867, p. 16; *Brooks, Str. F.* 1875, p. 240; 1876, p. 229; 1877; p. 470. Ianthina cyanura, *Jerd. B. Ind.* ii. p. 146, No. 508; *Godw.-Austen, J. A. S. B.*, 1870, p. 106. Nemura cyanura, (*Pall*) *Dresser. B. Eur.* pts. lxvii. lxviii. (♂ ad. desc. et. fig.) *nec. Pall.*—The WHITE-BREASTED BLUE WOOD-CHAT.

Adult Male.—General colour above dark ultramarine, brighter and inclining to deep cobalt blue on the rump and upper tail coverts; forehead also bright cobalt, extending backwards and forming a distinct eyebrow; shoulder patch bright cobalt blue; rest of wing coverts and quills blackish, edged with dark ultramarine, the margins of the primaries somewhat greyish blue; tail feathers blackish on their inner webs and dark blue on the outer; lores and feathers round the eye dusky blue black; the sides of the face dark blue, also the feathers bordering the throat for the whole extent of the latter; throat and centre of body below greyish white, pure white on the abdomen and under tail coverts; sides of the body bright orange; thighs dull blue; under wing coverts and axillaries white, slightly washed with fulvous; edge of the wing blue; bill dusky; legs brown; iris dark brown.

Length.—5·75 to 6·5 inches; wing 3·2; tail 2·5; tarsus 0·95; culmen 0·45.

The adult female is olive brown above, becoming ashy blue on the rump and bright cobalt on the upper tail coverts; the lesser and median wing coverts like the back; greater coverts and quills dark brown, margined with reddish olive; tail blackish on the inner webs and blue on the outer; throat, lores and round the eye buffy; eyebrow faint greyish; sides of the face, foreneck, breast and flanks olive brown; middle of abdomen and under tail coverts white; thighs dusky; sides of the body bright orange; axillaries yellowish buff; under wing coverts whitish with dusky bases.

Length.—5·2 inches; wing 3·15; tail 2·5; tarsus 0·95; culmen 0·45.

Hab.—The Himalayas, from the N. W. to Sikkim. Said to be common in China and Central and Northern Asia, also Japan. It is recorded from Nepaul and Cashmere, and from between Mussoorie and Gangaotri. Jerdon says it is a winter visitant at Darjeeling. It frequents thick brushwood and long grass. Found on the banks of the Ganges at Caragola Ghat. In Cashmere, according to Brooks, it is more numerous in the upper part of the valley. Its call-note and manners, he says, are like those of a robin. It is a very shy bird. It breeds very high up in the hills north of Simla, but in Cashmere they are said to breed as low as 6,000 feet during June and July, nesting in holes of banks. The normal number of eggs is 4, of a bluish white colour, faintly marked towards the larger end with pale reddish brown. Size 0·74 × 0·56.

224. Tarsiger hyperythrus, *Blyth, J. A. S. B.* xvi. p. 132; *id. Cat. B. Mus. A. S. B.* p. 170; *Jerd. B. Ind.* ii. p. 147, No. 509; *Sharpe, Cat. B. Br. Mus.* iv, p. 257; *Godw.-Austen, J. A. S. B.* 1870, p. 106. Nemura hyperythra, *Gray, Gen. B.* iii. *App.* p. 8; *Bp. Consp.* i, p. 300.—The RUSTY-THROATED BLUE WOOD-CHAT.

Adult Male.—Above dark purplish or indigo blue; the forehead brighter and more cobalt blue, *extending backward over the fore part of the eye*; *no white eyebrow*; shoulder patch deep cobalt; rest of wing coverts and quills dusky blackish, externally edged with purplish blue; lores, ear coverts, sides of the face, feathers round the eye and sides of the throat deep purplish black; entire under surface of body chestnut rufous; thighs brown; lower flanks whitish, forming a tuft on each side of the back; axillaries and under wing coverts yellowish buff; bill dusky; legs brown.

Length.—4·8 to 5·5 inches; wing 3·15; tail 2·3; tarsus 1; culmen 0·45.

The female is brown above, the lower back and rump greyish, the upper tail coverts and tail blue; median and greater wing coverts brown like the back; quills dark brown, edged lighter; a faint greyish blue eye streak on the side of the crown; ring round the eye fulvous; ear coverts, sides of face and under surface of body rufescent brown; middle of abdomen and under tail coverts whitish; under wing coverts and axillaries yellowish buff.

Length.—5 inches; wing 2·95; tail 2·2; tarsus 1; culmen 0·4.

Hab.—The Eastern Himalayas and Khasia Hills. Recorded from Nepaul and Darjeeling.

This is a rare species, and supposed to be a migrant. Nothing is known of its nidification.

225. Tarsiger hodgsoni, *Moore, P. Z. S.* 1854, p. 76, pl. 62. Nitidula campbelli, *Jerd. and Blyth, P. Z. S.* 1861, p. 201. Nitidula hodgsoni, *Jerd. B. Ind.* i. p. 472, No. 313. Niltava hodgsoni, *Gray, Hd.-L. B.* i. p. 327.—The PIGMY BLUE FLY-CATCHER.

Above deep ultramarine, brighter and more cobalt on the forepart of the crown and over the eye; a broad frontal line, lores, feathers round the eye, sides of face and ear coverts black, the latter with a bluish tinge; scapulars and wing coverts deep ultramarine blue like the back; the primary coverts and primaries narrowly edged with blue, their inner webs brown; cheeks and under surface of body rich orange yellow, slightly paler on the abdomen; the thighs and under tail coverts whitish; tail blackish, washed with blue externally; axillaries, sides of breast and under wing coverts pure white. (Sharpe.) Bill black; legs pale reddish; iris dark brown. (Jerd.)

Length.—3·6; wing 1·85; tail 1·4; tarsus 0·6; culmen 0·4.

The female is yellowish olive brown above, rather rufous on the rump and upper tail coverts; wings like the back; quills dark brown, edged externally with the same yellowish olive brown of the back; tail brown, washed externally with rufous brown; lores and sides of the face ochraceous buff, as also a ring of feathers round the eye; ear coverts washed with olive; cheeks and under surface of the body pale saffron yellow, deeper on the flanks; middle of abdomen, sides of the body, under wing and under tail coverts white.

Length.—3·7 inches; wing 1·8; tail 1·35; tarsus 0·65; culmen 0·4.

Hab.—The Eastern Himalayas, from Darjeeling to Sikkim and Nepaul, Entirely confined to the Himalayas.

226. Tarsiger indicus, *Vieill. N. Dict. d'Hist. Nat.* xi. p. 267. Nemura flavo-olivacea, *Hodgs. P. Z. S.* 1845, p. 27. Tarsiger superciliaris, *Hodgs. Icon. ined. Passeres, App.* pl. 57; *Moore, P. Z. S.* 1854, p 76; *Swinh, P. Z. S.* 1871, p. 359. Ianthina flavo-olivacea, *Blyth, J. A. S. B.* xvi. p. 133. Erythaca flavo-olivacea, *Gray, Cat. Mam, &c., Nepaul*; *Bly. Cat. B. Mus. A. S. B.* p. 171. Ianthina superciliaris, *Jerd. B. Ind.* ii. p. 148.—The RUFOUS-BELLIED BLUE WOOD-CHAT.

Adult Male.—Above dark slaty blue grey, some of the feathers on the sides of the rump tipped with yellowish buff; sides of the crown white, *forming a very broad white eyebrow*, extending from the base of the bill to the sides of the nape; lores, and sides of the face black, the latter slightly washed with slaty grey; wing coverts yellowish brown, the innermost of all the series slaty blue; greater coverts and quills blackish brown, externally edged with yellowish brown, the inner secondaries with slaty blue; tail dark slaty blue, blackish on the inner webs; under surface of body orange rufous, whiter on the middle of the abdomen; bill brownish; feet reddish grey; iris brown.

Length.—5 inches; wing 3·1; tail 2·5; tarsus 1·1; culmen 0·5.

The female differs from the male in being ochraceous brown above; the wings margined with rusty olive; eyebrow white, but not so distinct as in the male; sides of face olive brown, with fulvous shaft lines; under surface of body deep ochraceous brown; chin whitish.

Length.—5·3 inches; wing 2·85; tail 2·4; tarsus 1·1; culmen 0·45.

Hab.—S. E. Himalayas. Rare in Sikkim and Nepaul. Fairly common about Darjeeling.

227. Tarsiger chrysœus, *Hodgs. Icon. ined. Passeres,* pl. 80; *id. P. Z. S.* 1845, p. 28; *Jerd. B. Ind.* ii. p. 149; *Hume, Nests and Eggs, Ind. B.* p. 325.—The GOLDEN BUSH-CHAT.

Adult Male.—Above orange yellow, the scapulars and feathers of the lower back with olive brown tips; crown of the head, hind neck and mantle olive brown, inclining to rufous olive on the head; a narrow frontal band, *lores, feathers round the eye and ear coverts black;* supercilium orange yellow; lesser and median wing coverts black, with mesial streaks of golden yellow near the tips of the feathers; greater series and quills black, externally edged with orange brown; the innermost greater series entirely orange yellow; *tail particolored,* yellow with a broad terminal band of black on all but the two centre feathers, which are entirely black, and orange yellow only at the base; entire under surface of body orange yellow, some of the feathers on the sides of the breast edged with black; under wing coverts yellow; under surface of quills brown, yellowish buff along the inner webs; bill blackish above; lower mandible yellow; iris dark brown.

Length.—5 to 5·75 inches; wing 2.75 to 2·8; tail 2·25; tarsus 1·3; culmen 0·6.

The female is olive yellow, or olivaceous above; orbital ring whitish; supercilium and lores dull yellow; ear coverts olive brown, with whitish shaft streaks; cheeks and under surface of body deep ochraceous yellow; lower abdomen whitish.

Length.—5 inches; wing 2·6; tail 2; tarsus 1·2.

Hab.—The Himalayas. Recorded from Nepaul and Sikkim, and also Darjeeling, where Jerdon says it is not uncommon and is a permanent resident. It keeps to the forest in the valleys amongst thick underwood. Hodgson says it is shy, solitary, and bush-loving. It breeds in the central regions of the mountains of Nepaul, making a compact saucer-like nest of moss on the ground under the roots of a tree, under stone, or in holes in banks. The breeding season is from May to August. Eggs, 3—4 in number, of a verditer-blue colour; size 0·72 × 0·5.

Gen. **Hypothymis.**—*Boie.*

Bill of moderate length, broad, triangular, suddenly narrowed, straight, tip hooked, and with a distinct notch; rictal bristles numerous; nostrils with a few hairs above it; 4th and 5th quills of wing subequal and longest; tarsus short; head with scale-like velvetty plumes.

228. Hypothymis azurea, *Bodd, Tab. Pl. Enl.* p. 41; *Sharpe, Cat. B. Br. Mus.* iv. p. 274; *Oates, B. Br. Burm.* i. p. 265. Myiagra azurea, *Jerd. B. Ind.* i. p. 450, No. 290; *Hume, Nests and Eggs*, p. 198; *id. Str. F.* ii. p. 217, iii. p. 103; *Fairbank, Str. F.* 1876, p. 257; *Armstrong. l. c.* p. 322; *Hume, l. c.* p. 395; *Bl. and Wald., B. Burm.* p. 131.—The BLACK-NAPED BLUE FLY-CATCHER.

Adult Male.—A patch on the nape, a narrow frontal line, chin and a crescentic band across the fore neck black; sides of the face, throat and fore-neck light azure blue; rest of under surface white, washed with bluish; the whole remaining plumage with the lesser wing coverts blue; greater wing coverts black, externally edged with blue; wings brown, narrowly edged with blue; tail brown, suffused with blue on the central pair of feathers and on the outer webs of the others; and with either a very narrow nearly obsolete white tip, or this is wanting; bill dark blue or plumbeous, the edges and tip black; inside of mouth yellow; legs plumbeous; iris dark brown; edges of eyelids blue.

Length.—5·8 to 6·4 inches; wing 2·8; tail 2·85 to 3; tarsus 0·7; culmen 0·55 to 0·75.

The female has the head above azure blue, the sides of the head, chin and throat duller; breast greyish brown; abdomen, flanks and under tail coverts white, tinged with grey; wings, black; rump and upper tail coverts brown; tail darker brown, the outer edges washed with blue and all but the central feathers tipped with white.

Length.—6·5 inches; wing 2·95; tail 3; tarsus 0·7.

Hab.—India generally, ranging through the Burmese countries to Pegu, Tenasserim, and the Malay Peninsula; also China, Cochin-China, and the Indo-Burmese countries and Ceylon. Occurs in the Punjab, N. W. Provinces, Oudh, Bengal, Central India, the Concan, Deccan, South India, Pegu, British Burmah generally, and Nepaul. It affects every description of jungle, also gardens orchards, and bamboo groves. It is an active bird and ever on the move, darting on insects and capturing them on the wing. Jerdon says it is almost always solitary, flying from tree to tree. It breeds in the low, warm, well-wooded valleys of the sub-Himalayan ranges up to 3,000 feet, from May to August. The nest is a delicate cup, made of green grass and coated with cobwebs, and is generally placed in the fork of a tree, or a bamboo, not far from the ground. The eggs, 3 to 4 in number, are white, or white with a salmon tinge, speckled and spotted with pale red and purple, or reddish pink; size 0·69 × 0·53.

229. Hypothymis occipitalis, *Vigors, P. Z. S.* 1831, p. 97; *Sharpe, Cat. B. Br. Mus.* iv. p. 275. Myiagra tytleri, *Beavan Ibis*, 1867, p. 324; *Hume, Str. F.* 1874, p. 217. Hypothymis azurea (*nec. Bodd*) *Walden, Ibis*, 1872, p. 102; *Oates, Str. F.* 1877, p. 149; *Sharpe, Ibis*, 1887, p. 18; *id. Tr. Lin. Soc. n. s.* i. p. 235; *Tweedale, P. Z. S.* 1877, pp. 693, 760, 825 *et.* 1878, p. 284.—The ALLIED BLACK-NAPED BLUE FLY-CATCHER.

Adult Male.—Above rich deep azure blue, brighter on the head, where the feathers are of a velvetty texture; a frontal line, chin and a nuchal patch black; wing coverts like the back; quills and tail and the remaining plumage as in *H. azurea*, except that the under surface is greyish purple instead of white on the breast, abdomen, and under tail coverts; bill blackish blue; iris dark brown.

Length.—5·8 inches; wing 2·7; tail 2·6; tarsus 0·6; culmen 0·5.

The adult female differs from the male, as does the female of *H. azurea*, i.e., it has the back brown, with the head dull azure, the black nape spot being absent; the abdomen is whitish and overspread with a shade of bluish grey.

Hab.—The Andaman and Nicobar Islands, Malay Peninsula, Sumatra, Borneo, Philippine Islands, and Port Blair. Occurs also probably in Tenasserim.

Having had before me a series of skins of both *H. azurea* and *H. occipitalis*, I am inclined to give the present form specific distinction. Call it a race or a subspecies, but the constancy of the markings of the under surface and the brighter colouring of the upper parts are sufficient characters. *Hume* (*Str. F.* ii. p. 217) says the Andamans birds do not differ from the Indian ones in dimensions, but that the typical adult male of this species has not a particle of white about the abdomen, vent and under tail coverts. The female, too, has a dingy lilac grey abdomen, instead of the pure white of the female of *H. azurea.*

A nest of this species was found at Aberdeen, South Andamans, on the 23rd April. "It was fastened to the branch of a small tree that overhung the path. In shape it was an inverted cone, three inches in depth exteriorly and two and a half inches in diameter; the cavity, which is nearly hemispherical, was two inches in diameter and 1·1 in depth. The nest is very compactly woven, of soft vegetable fibre, with which also it is firmly bound against the slender stem to which it is attached. Towards the exterior of the nest a good deal of green moss, a number of satiny white cocoons, and a little bright ferruginous fern root have been incorporated in the nest, and the whole carefully coated, though not thickly so, with gossamer threads and spider's webs, and the cavity of the nest is neatly lined with black hair-like moss roots.

The eggs were three in number, very similar to those of *H. azurea*, but perhaps more strongly marked; in shape they are regular broad ovals; the shell is smooth and fine, and has a faint gloss. The ground colour varies from pinky to creamy white, and towards the larger end there is a broad irregular zone of red or brownish red specks or spots. The eggs measured 0·67 to 0·68 × 0·52 to 0·53."

Gen. **Xanthopygia**.—Sharpe

Bill broad, the culmen equal to only twice the breadth of the bill at nostrils; tarsus moderate; tail long; 1st primary short, about one-third the length of the 4th; the 5th and 6th quills subequal; feet moderate; claws slender, moderately curved.

230. Xanthopygia fuliginosa, (*Vig.*) *Sharpe, Cat. B. Br. M.* iv. p. 253. Phœnicura fuliginosa, *Vig. P. Z. S.* 1831, p. 35; *Blyth, J. A. S. B.* xi. p. 190. Phœnicura rubicauda, *Hodgs. in Gray's Zool. Misc.* p. 82. Ruticilla fuliginosa, *Gray, Gen. B.* i. p. 180; *Blyth, J. A. S. B.* xvi. p. 134; *Moore, P. Z. S.* 1854, p. 29; *Jerd. B. Ind.* ii. p. 142. Ruticilla plumbea, *Blyth, J. A. S. B.* xvi. p. 134. Rhyacornis fuliginosa, *Blanford, J. A. S. B.* xli. pt. i. p. 51; *Bl. and Wald. B. Burm.* p. 101; *Brooks, Str. F.* 1875, p. 240; *Inglis, Str. F.* 1877, p. 37. Nymphæus fuliginosus, *Hume, Nests and Eggs, Ind. B.* p. 322; *Oates, B. Br. Burm.* i. p. 284.—The Plumbeous Water-Robin.

Male.—The whole plumage dull cyaneous; upper and lower tail coverts, vent and tail bright chestnut; wings black, edged externally with bluish or light slaty grey; a frontal line and feathers in front of the eye blackish; bill black; gape fleshy white; irides dark brown; feet dark horny brown; claws black.

Length.—4·5 inches; wing 3·05; tail 2·1; tarsus 0·9; culmen 0·45.

The female is dull bluish brown above, the upper and under tail coverts white; tail feathers white at base, brown at the tips, the white increasing obliquely toward the outer tail feather, which is entirely white, except a narrow edging along the outer web and a small brown tip to the inner one; two centre tail feathers rufous brown; wing coverts like the back, and tipped with a small spot of ashy white; primary coverts dark brown; lores buffy white, mottled with dusky bases to the feathers; orbital ring of feathers dull rufous; ear coverts dull ashy brown, with broad white shaft streaks; whole lower plumage ashy brown, each feather centred with whitish and margined with paler ashy; tertiaries brown, edged with rufescent and tipped with whitish.

Length.—4·5 inches; wing 2·6; tail 1·9; tarsus 0·85; culmen 0·45.

Hab.—The Himalayas, ranging to China and Mongolia. It is found in South China, the hill tracts of Eastern Bengal, and along the whole range of the Himalayas from Assam to the North-West.

According to Jerdon it lives entirely along rivers and mountain-torrents, and may often be seen on a wet and slippery rock just above a boiling rapid; it climbs up the wet rocks with great facility, and, every now and then alighting on a rock, it spreads its tail, but does not vibrate it like some of the Redstarts. Its flight is rapid and direct. It feeds on various aquatic insects and larvæ, some kinds of which are always found just at the edge of the water, and which a wave often leaves behind it on a rock. The nest, made chiefly of moss, is placed on the shelf of a rock, or in a hole in a bank, and the eggs, 3 to 5 in number, are faint green, marked with pale reddish brown.

Gen. **Oreicola**.—*Bonap.*

Bill much as in *Pratincola*, but longer and deeper, and barely depressed at base; nostrils rounded, situated in a groove, with a few nareal bristles covering them; rictus strongly bristled; second primary longer than the secondaries; wing rounded, about equal to the tail in length; 1st quill short; 2nd, 3rd and 4th graduated, the 4th longest.

231. Oreicola Jerdoni, *Blyth, Ibis*, 1867, p. 14; *Beavan, l. c.* p. 449; *Blanford, Ibis*, 1870, p. 466; *Blyth and Walden, B. Burm.*, p. 101; *Sharpe, Cat. B. Br. Mus.* iv. p. 264. Rhodophila melanoleuca, *Jerd. B. Ind.* ii. p. 128; iii. p. 872, No. 487.—The Black and White Bush-Chat.

Entire plumage above, including the thighs, glossy black; entire under surface pure white; under wing coverts and axillaries black, with broad white edgings; bill and legs black; iris dark brown.

Length.—5·4 inches; wing 2·55; tail 2·6; tarsus 0·8; culmen 0·5.

The female is brown above, tinged with rufous, especially on the rump and upper tail coverts; tail brown, edged paler; wings and their coverts brown, edged with rufous; sides of the head mixed ashy and brown, the top of head with dark centres; under surface of body uniform pale fulvous; thighs brown; under wing coverts brown; axillaries ashy, tinged with fulvous.

Length.—5·2 inches; wing 2·5; tail 2·5; tarsus 0·8; culmen 0·5.

Hab.—N. W. Provinces, Oudh, Bengal, and British Burmah. Jerdon procured this species in Purneah, near the banks of the Ganges, and subsequently along the reedy edge of some of the rivers in Eastern Bengal and Cachar. Mr. W. Blanford obtained it in Burmah in long elephant grass, and Dr. Anderson found it near Bhamo in Upper Burmah.

232. Oreicola ferrea, *Hodgs. in Gray's Misc.* p. 83; *Sharpe, Cat. B. Br. Mus.* iv. p. 266; *Oates, B. Br. Burm.* i. p. 283. Saxicola ferrea, *Hodgs. Icon. ined. Passeres*, pl. 97. Pratincola ferrea, *Bly. J. A. S. B.* xvi. p. 129; *Jerd. B. Ind.* ii. p. 127, No. 486; *Hume, Nests and Eggs*, p. 318; *Hume and Henderson, Lahore to Yarkand*, p. 205, pl. xii; *Bl. B. Burm.* p. 101; *Hume, Str. F.* iii. p. 135; *Brooks, Str. F.* iii. p. 239; *Hume, Str. F.* viii. p. 99; *Scully, Str. F.* iii. p. 301.—The Dark-grey Bush-Chat.

Male.—Entire head above, back and scapulars black, each feather with a broad edging of deep grey; sides of the head and chin black; rump grey without any black; upper tail coverts black, edged with grey; wings black, each feather of the coverts and tertiaries broadly, and the primaries and secondaries narrowly edged with grey, the inner median coverts tipped with white, the inner greater coverts wholly white; tail black, edged with grey on both webs; supercilium whitish; lower plumage white, with a greyish tinge on the breast and flanks. *In winter dress* males have the feathers of the upper plumage fringed with rusty, and the black centres to the feathers indistinct; rump grey; rest of plumage as in summer. The female is the same throughout the year. The whole upper plumage is reddish brown, turning to chestnut on the upper tail coverts; the wings and tail are brown, broadly edged with chestnut brown; the sides of the head are reddish brown, mottled with black; the chin and throat are whitish; the remainder of the lower plumage buffy, more or less pure, according to the age of the plumage.

Length.—5·2 inches; wing 2·55; tail 2·45; tarsus 0·85; culmen 0·55.

Hab.—India and the Burmese countries, ranging eastward into China. (Sharpe.) According to Jerdon it is found throughout the whole extent of the Himalayas, and is tolerably common about Darjeeling. It has been recorded from Arrakan, from Prome in Pegu, and Tounghoo in the hills, also from Karin. Davison says it is rare in the northern portions of Tenasserim. He procured specimens in the pine forests of Salween, and Captain Bingham in the Thoungyeen Valley. It is also recorded from the N. W. Provinces of India, Oudh, Bengal, and Nepaul.

The Grey Bush-Chat is said to affect the outskirts of forests and brushwood. It has a pleasing song. Breeds throughout the Himalayas from Murree to Bhootan during April and May, also June and July, two broods being rared in the same nest. The nest is placed on the ground under a dense bush, or in a hole in a bank; it is cup-shaped, and is composed of grass, twigs or moss, and lined with fine grass roots, horse-hair or fur. Eggs 4 to 5 in number, similar to those of *Pratincola maura.*

Gen. **Chelidorynx**.—*Hodgs.*

Bill short, broad, suddenly compressed at tip, much deflected and barely notched; nostrils covered by long and fine nareal bristles; gape with long rictal bristles; wings rounded; the 1st four quills graduated; tail long, rounded, firm; tarsus rather short; feet feeble; lateral toes slightly unequal. (Jerd.).

233. Chelidorynx hypoxantha, *Blyth, J. A. S. B.* xii. p. 935; *Hodgs., Drawing*, No. 386; *Jerd. B. Ind.* i. p. 455, No. 294; *Hume, Nests and Eggs*, p. 204; *Wald. in Blyth, B. Burm.* p. 132; *Hume, Str. F.* viii. p. 93; *Scully, Str. F.* viii. p. 275; *Sharpe, Cat. B. Br. Mus.* iv. p. 279; *Oates, B. Br. Burm.* i. p. 269.—The YELLOW-BELLIED FANTAIL.

Forehead, a broad supercilium, and the whole lower plumage bright yellow; lores, feathers round the eye, cheeks and ear coverts dark brown, tinged with green, the shafts of the latter whitish; tail brown with conspicuous white shafts, and all the feathers, except the central ones, tipped with white; upper plumage and wing coverts olive brown; wings brown, narrowly margined with olive brown; bill black above, the lower mandible yellow; irides brown; gape orange; feet brownish reddish. (Jerd.)

Hab.—Eastern Himalayas, Khasia Hills, and Burmah.

The Yellow-bellied Fantail has been found at Darjeeling, in Bhootan, between Simla and Mussoorie, and throughout the Indo-Burmese countries. Dr. Jerdon says: "This pretty little Fantail is found in Nepaul, Sikkim, and Bhootan. It affects high altitudes from 6,000 to 8,000 feet and upwards. It frequents the skirts of large woods and low trees by the roadsides, either in pairs or small flocks. It is very lively and active, making short sallies after insects with a low pleasant twitter." A nest brought to him after the young had flown was an exceedingly neat deep cup, made of moss and lichens, also hair and wool, well carded into a compact structure. The breeding season (*vide Hume, Nests and Eggs*) is May and June. Eggs white, faintly speckled.

Gen. **Rhipidura**.—*Vig. and Horsf.*

Plumage of the head full, no elongated crest; bill rather long, depressed, wide, except at tip, which is slightly hooked and notched; nostrils overhung by long nareal bristles; rictal bristles long and slender; wings with the first 4 quills unequally graduated; tail lengthened, rounded or graduated; tarsus moderate; lateral toes unequal.

234. Rhipidura albicollis, *Vieill N. Dict. d'Hist. Nat.* xxvii. p. 130; *Sharpe, Cat. B. Br. Mus.* iv. p. 317; *Oates, B. Burm.* i. p. 266. Rhipidura fuscoventris, *Frankl. P. Z. S.* 1831, p. 117; *Jerd. Ill. Ind. Orn.* (text to pl. ii.); *Blyth, J. A. S. B.* xii. p. 935, xv. p. 290; *Jerd. B. Ind.* i. p. 451, No. 291; *Cock. and Marsh., Str. F.* 1873, i. p. 352; *Ball, Str. F.* 1874, p. 404; *Brooks, Str. F.* 1875, p. 235. Leucocerca fuscoventris, *Hume, Nests and Eggs, Ind. B.* p. 200, No. 291. Leucocerca albicollis, *Wald. in Blyth, B. Burm.* p. 132; *Hume, Str. F.* iii. p. 103; *Cripps, Str. F.* vii. p. 276; *Hume, Str. F.* viii. p. 92; ix. p. 174 (footnote).—The WHITE-THROATED FANTAIL.

Crown, lores, sides of the head, face and chin deep black; supercilium white; throat extending to the sides of the neck white, the bases of the feathers black, causing the white to appear dull; rest of the plumage dark sooty brown, paler on the wing; tail dark brown, all but the central pair of feathers broadly tipped with white; bill and legs black.

Length.—7·5 inches; wing 2·9 to 3·1; tail 4; tarsus 0·7 to 0·75; culmen 0·7.

The young are browner in colour, the feathers tipped with rufescent, the under surface washed with the same at the edges of the feathers.

Hab.—India and Burmah, also Cashmere and throughout the Himalayas.

The White-throated Fantail is spread over nearly all India. It is found in the Punjab, N. W. Provinces, Oudh, Bengal, Central India, the Deccan, parts of South India, in British Burmah and Nepaul. Jerdon says: "It is very abundant at Darjeeling in the spring and summer, descending to the valleys and plains in winter. According to Oates it is spread sparingly over the whole of Pegu, and as in India generally a permanent resident. It has been procured in the

Karin Hills. Davison got it in Tenasserim, where he says it is apparently confined to the forests of the outer Tenasserim range and adjacent spurs. It is said to occur commonly in Arrakan, also in Sikkim. It is generally seen in pairs flitting restlessly about trees, catching small insects on the wing; has a sharp twittering note not unlike that of *M. paradisi,* and is continually snapping its beak, going from branch to branch with a short, jerky, tumbling flight. It has the peculiar habit of dancing about with tail outspread.

The Fantail breeds throughout India and in the wooded sub-Himalayan tracts, also in all the warmer valleys of the outer Himalayan ranges from Debroo-ghur to Murree, in Eastern and lower Bengal, and in the forest districts of Central India, in Raipoor, and the tributary mehals, and doubtless in suitable localities throughout Southern India. The breeding season lasts from May to July. The nest is a solid, compact, tiny structure, made of grass and coated with cobwebs, and placed in a fork of a tree not far from the ground. In shape it is like an inverted cone. The eggs, three in number, are oval, fawn-yellowish or greenish white, marked with grey specks and spots; size 0·65 × 0·49.

Rhipidura perlata (S. Mull.) is described from Borneo and Sarawak, but as it is not certain whether the specimens were from the portions of country belonging to the British, it is not included in the Avifauna. The upper surface is of a dark slate colour, duller on the external edges of the wing coverts; upper tail coverts black; cheeks, throat and breast slaty grey spotted with white, the latter with large ovate spots; centre of abdomen and under tail coverts white.

Hab.—The Malay Peninsula, Java, Sumatra and Borneo.

235. Rhipidura javanica, *Sparrm., Mus. Carls.* iii. pl. 75; *Sharpe, Cat. B. Br. Mus.* vi. p. 332; *Oates, B. Br. Burm.* i. p. 267. Leucocerca javanica, *Salvad. Ucc. Borneo,* p. 135; *Bl. B. Burm.* p. 132; *Hume and Dav., Str. F.* vi. p. 226; *Hume, Str. F.* viii. p. 92; ix. p. 175 (footnote). Leucocerca infumata, *Hume, Str. F.* i. p. 455; *Tweedd. Ibis,* 1877, p. 316.—The Javan Fantail.

Male.—Forehead, crown and sides of the head sooty brown; the whole upper plumage and the wings brown, washed with rufous; tail dark brown, the four outer pairs of feathers broadly tipped with white, the pair next these narrowly tipped white; supercilium white; chin and a band across the upper breast blackish brown; flanks, thighs and axillaries brown, the latter broadly edged with white; under wing coverts mixed black and white; the rest of the lower plumage white; bill black, fleshy at base of lower mandible; irides brown.

Length.—7·5 inches; wing 3; tail 3·6; tarsus 0·75; culmen 0·7.

The female has the lower plumage from the breast downwards tinged with buff; tail dark brown with reddish shafts, all but the two centre feathers tipped with white; supercilium as in the male.

Length.—7·2; wing 2·85; tail 3·5; tarsus 0 75, culmen 0·6.

Hab.—Indo-Chinese countries, Tenasserim and Cochin-China, ranging down the Malayan Peninsula to the Sunda Islands. (Sharpe.) The British Museum possesses specimens from East and West Java, Sumatra, Labuan, Sarawak, Penang, Malacca, Tenasserim and Saigon (Cochin-China). Oates says it was recorded from Mergui by Blyth. Davison met with it in Tenasserim in the neighbourhood of the sea coast from Tavoy southwards. It extends also to Siam.

236. Rhipidura pectoralis, *Jerd. Ill. Ind. Orn.* (text to pl. ii.); *Sharpe, Cat. B. Br. Mus.* iv. p. 335. Leucocerca pectoralis (*Jerd.*), *Blyth, J. A. S. B.* xii. p. 935; *Jerd. B. Ind.* i. p. 453, No. 293; *Butler, Str. F.* 1875, p. 466; *Hume, Nests and Eggs, Ind. B.* p. 203; *id. Str. F.* 1876, pp. 415-421. Rhipidura fuscoventris, *Sykes, P. Z. S.* 1832, p. 85. Leucocerca leucogaster, *Blyth, Ibis,* 1866, p. 371; *Fairbank, Str. F.,* 1876, p. 257.—The White-spotted Fantail.

Whole head, sides of the face and ear coverts, also chin and collar across the lower throat, black; sides of the breast blackish, the lower part barred with half concealed ovate spots of white; supercilium from the base of the bill white; quills ashy brown on their edges, tail the same, but paler towards the tips of the feathers, which are buffy white; under surface, except the black collar, creamy buff, deeper on the under tail coverts; thighs brown, also the axillaries, which are ochraceous externally; bill and feet black; iris dark brown.

Length.—7 inches; wing 2·85; tail 3·85; tarsus 0·75; culmen 0·45.

Hab.—South India and Guzerat, also the Deccan (Fairbank), Egutpoora. Mr. Blanford notes it from the Godaveri Valley, and Jerdon from the Neilgherries. It has the usual habits of the genus, and utters a feeble warbling song. Captain Butler says it is very common at Mount Aboo. It breeds in March and April, during which months he took many nests. The nest is described as a very neat cup, made of fine dry grass stems, thickly coated exteriorly with cobwebs, many of which are fastened to neighbouring twigs to support the nest. The lower part often terminates in a fine tapering point. The nest is usually placed in the fork of one of the small branches of some low thick bush, about three feet from the ground (sometimes 6 or 7 feet), often overhanging a small stream or dry nulla. The eggs, usually three in number, are rather round ovals of a buffy white color, surrounded at the large end with a zone of lavender and olive brown spots and blotches. When the nest is being robbed the parents evince the greatest possible anxiety, and fly in great excitement about the nest, near enough to be caught by the hand.

237. Rhipidura albifrontata, *Sharpe, Cat. B. Br. Mus.* iv. p. 338; *Oates, B. Br. Burm.*, i. p. 268; *Murray, Vert. Zool. Sind,* p. 129. Rhipidura albofrontata, *Frankl., P. Z. S.* 1831, p. 116; *Blyth, J. A. S. B.* xii. p. 935. Leucocerca albofrontata, *Jerd., Madras Journ.*, xi. p. 12; *id. B. Ind.* i. p. 452; *Hume, Nests and Eggs,* p. 201; *Blyth and Wald, B. Burm.* Leucocerca aureola, *Hume, Str. F.* i. p. 436; iii. p. 104; viii. p. 92. Leucocerca burmannica, *Hume, Str. F.* ix. p. 175 (footnote).—The WHITE-BROWED FANTAIL.

Head, neck, lores, and sides of the face slaty black; a broad frontal band, extending over the eyes to the nape, white; throat white, the feathers black at their bases; lower throat black, slightly edged with white; back and wing-coverts ashy brown, the latter, including the primary coverts, tipped with triangular spots of white; axillaries dark brown, edged with whitish; breast, abdomen, under tail and thigh coverts white, the feathers of the latter with black bases; tail dark brown, all, except the centre ones, broadly tipped white; bill and legs black; irides deep brown.

Length.—6 to 6·7 inches; bill at front 0·5; wing 3·3 to 3·15; tail 3·6; tarsus 0·75.

Hab.—India generally and Ceylon to Burmah, Pegu and N. W. Himalayas. Common in the Punjab, N. W. Provinces, Oudh, Central India, Rajputana, Kutch, Kattiawar and Jodhpore; also in Southern India, the Concan and Deccan, especially in gardens. Breeds in Sind from March to August. The nest is a very neat cup, made of fine fibres, &c., covered on the outside and inside with cobweb, and usually attached towards the end of a low branch. Eggs 2 to 3 in number, not unlike those of the preceding.

Gen. Terpsiphone.—*Gloger.*

Bill long, wide, depressed at base, narrowing at tip, hooked and notched; the culmen keeled; rictal bristles numerous, long and stout, not reaching beyond half the length of the bill; wings rather long and somewhat pointed; tail long, cuneate, with the central feathers greatly elongated in the males. Head crested.

238. Terpsiphone paradisi, *Linn. Syst. Nat.* i. p. 224; *Sharpe, Cat. Passerif.* p. 347; *Cat. Mus. Heine. Th.* i. p. 58. Muscicapa paradisi, *Cuv. Regne. Anim.* 1817, i. p. 344; *Sykes, P. Z. S.* 1832, p. 84; *Jerd. Ill. Ind. Orn.* pl. 7. Tchitrea paradisi, *Less. Traité,* p. 386; *Gray, Gen. B.* i. p. 259; *Hume, Ibis,* 1869, p. 9; *Jerd. B. Ind.* p. 444, No. 288; *Str. F.* 1873, pp. 403, 474; 1875, p. 102; *Murray Hdbk. Zool., &c.* p. 138.—THE PARADISE FLY-CATCHER.

Adult Male.—Head with a long occipital crest; sides of face, neck, and entire throat glossy steel green; above and below pure white, some of the feathers more or less black shafted; quills black, externally white; the edges of the innermost quills white, with a longitudinal dark mark down the centre; tail white, with black shafts and narrow blackish edgings to the feathers; middle tail feathers elongated; 12-13 inches in length.

Adult Female.—Crown of head and crest glossy greenish black; lores, sides of face, sides of neck, and throat greyish; rest of under surface of body white; the flanks greyish and tinged with rufous; back, wing coverts and inner secondaries bay; tail light chestnut; bill bluish; legs and feet pale blue; irides dark brown.

Length of Male.—Including elongated tail feathers 17 inches; bill 0·85; wing 3·65; tail 5·5; middle-feathers 13. *Female, length* 7·5; wing 3·45; tail 4.

Hab.—India and Ceylon to Nepaul and Cashmere. Abundant on the Malabar Coast and in Southern India. Occurs in the Punjab, N. W. Provinces, Oudh, Bengal, Rajputana, Central India, Kutch, Kattiawar, Jodhpore and N. Guzerat. In Sind it is a winter visitant, arriving in September.

The Paradise Fly-Catcher is more or less a permanent resident of forest and wooded districts of India, and although it occurs in open districts as Sind and Rajputana, it is only a winter visitant in those parts. The highest elevation it has been found at is about 5,500 feet. Jerdon says it is very partial to bamboo jungle. In its habits it is restless and wandering, flitting continually from branch to branch and tree to tree, and feeds on flies and other insects, always capturing them on the wing, sometimes picking them off a leaf or bough. It breeds throughout the outer ranges of the Himalayas, in the warmer valleys, up to 5,500 feet, also in the Dhoon Terai, Oudh, and the Central Provinces. The season lasts from May to July. The nest is cup-shaped, and composed of moss, fibres, and grass, ornamented on the outside with white silky cocoons. Eggs 3 to 4 in number, longish oval in shape; in color pinkish white, speckled with brownish red; size 0·81 × 0·6.

In regard to the change of plumage of the Paradise Fly-Catcher, I entirely agree with Mr. Sharpe's views, viz., that the changes are not seasonal but due to age.

The nestlings in their first dress has a dull chestnut plumage, with the under surface of the body (abdomen) white, and this is the plumage of the females of the first year, except that the sides of the breast are greyish. In the second year the chestnut becomes duller, and this is the first stage of the males, which also have the steel green crown, crest and throat. In the following stage the long red tail is acquired, the quills and primary coverts are edged with white, and the inner secondaries only retain some of the rufous of the back. This is certainly the breeding plumage of the male in the second year. It is during the third year that the male changes to the full white plumage during autumn. Once the white plumage is assumed there is no further change, either by moult or other means, and the birds are said to breed and live throughout the rest of their lives in their white plumage.

239. Terpsiphone affinis, (*A. Hay*), *Bl. J. A. S. B.* xv. p. 292; *Sharpe, Cat. B. Br. Mus.* iv. p. 349; *Oates, B. Br. Burm.* i. p. 261. Tchitrea affinis (*A. Hay*), *Jerd. B. Ind.* i. p. 448, No. 289; *Hume, Str. F.* ii. p. 216. Tchitrea paradisi (*Lin.*), *Hume, Str. F.* iii. p. 102. Muscipeta affinis, *Hume and Dav., Str. F.* vi. p. 223, viii. p. 92; *Scully, Str. F.* viii. p. 274.—The BURMESE PARADISE FLY-CATCHER.

Male.—The whole head and neck black, glossed with blue; lower plumage, axillaries and under wing coverts pure white; back, scapulars, rump and upper wing coverts white, with indistinct blackish shaft stripes; lesser and median wing coverts white, the shafts conspicuously black; greater coverts and the tertiaries white, the shafts and a portion of the webs on either side black; primaries black, edged with white; secondaries black, very broadly edged with white on both webs, the white increasing in extent as the feathers approach the body; tail white; the shafts black, except on the central pair, where the shafts turn white towards the tip; all the tail feathers finely margined with black. The female has the forehead and crown black; the sides of the head, the chin, throat, breast and a collar round the neck ashy; the abdomen white, tinged with buff; the flanks and under tail coverts buff; the whole upper plumage, lesser wing coverts and tail chestnut; the median and greater coverts and all the quills brown edged with chestnut; the long tail feathers are wanting at all seasons. Young birds of both sexes are similar to the female. The young male in its second year loses the buff tinge on the abdomen, the ashy parts become darker, and the central tail feathers are replaced by long ones. In this plumage the male probably breeds for the first time; subsequently the chin and throat, as well as the sides of the head, turn black, and the white plumage of the adult is assumed either by a moult or, as is very probable, a change in the colour of the feathers only.

Iris hazel-brown; eyelids plumbeous, the edges tumid and rich blue; inside of mouth yellow; bill blue; the tip and anterior half of the margins black; legs plumbeous blue, claws dark horn colour.

Length of breeding males as much as 18 inches; of females and non-breeding males about 8 to 9; tail 4; wing 3·6; tarsus 0·68; bill from gape 1.

The tail in adult males is frequently 14 inches in length. (Oates.)

The Burmese Paradise Fly-Catcher is generally distributed over Burmah. In the plains of Pegu it occurs in large numbers in September and October, in which months it appears to be migrating locally. To the south it extends down the Malay Peninsula to the islands of Sumatra, Java, and Borneo, also Flores, and Dr. Tiraud mentions that it is found in Cochin-China. To the north it occurs in the Indo-Burmese countries, ranging into the Himalayas as far as Nepaul. It affects the well-wooded parts of the country, and is more abundant in heavy forest and bamboo jungle than elsewhere. Like *T. paradisi* it is generally seen in pairs. At the period of local migration considerable numbers associate together for a short time. Oates says its nest has not yet been found.

Gen. **Philentoma**.—*Eyton.*

General characters of *Terpsiphone.*

Wing longer than the tail; second primary shorter than the secondaries, the third equal to the latter; wing rounded; the distance between the primaries and the secondaries not so great as the length of the culmen.

240. Philentoma velatum (*Tem.*) *Sharpe, Cat. B. Br. Mus.* iv. p. 365; *Blyth, Cat. B. Mus. A. S. B.* p. 204; *Jerd. B. Ind.* i. p. 449; *Walden, Ibis,* 1872, p. 373; *Sharpe, Ibis,* 1877, p. 191; *Hume and Dav.* 1878, p. 224; *Hume, Str. F.* viii. p. 92; *Oates, B. Br. Burm.* i. p. 263.—The Maroon-breasted Fly-Catcher.

Male.—General colour bright greyish or indigo blue; forehead, lores, chin, cheeks and a narrow supercilium black; ring round the eye, ear coverts and upper half of the throat also black; lower half of throat and breast rich maroon; quills black; the outer webs broadly margined with indigo blue; tertiaries like the back and with black shafts; central tail feather indigo blue, the rest black on the inner web and blue on the outer; bill black; feet dark greenish black; iris crimson.

Length.—7·5 inches; wing 3·85; tail 3·3; tarsus 0·75; culmen 0·75.

The female is dull indigo blue throughout, except on the wings and tail, which are as in the male. The base of the forehead, lores, cheeks, throat and breast black.

Length.—7·9 inches; wing 3·8; tail 3·5; tarsus 0·7; culmen 0·7.

The following is a description by Mr. Hume of a young male: "Entire head and neck all round, chin, throat, breast and, in fact, all the lower parts, a dull chestnut, with only here and there on the lower parts patches of new dull cyaneous feathers appearing; median and the secondary and tertiary greater coverts tipped with chestnut."

Hab.—Southern half of the Tenasserim Provinces, Malayan Peninsula, Sumatra, and Borneo. (Sharpe.) Recorded by Mr. Sharpe as from Malacca, Sumatra, Sarawak, and Bintulu (N. W. Borneo).

Oates says the Maroon-breasted Fly-Catcher occurs in Tenasserim, and that Mr. Davison met with it at numerous places from Meetan, at the foot of the Mooleyit, to Malewoon at the extreme south. It is a constant resident. According to Davison it keeps entirely to the evergreen forests, never straying even to their outskirts. It has always been met with in pairs. It has a harsh, grating, metallic-sounding note. Mr. Hume in vol. ix., p. 113, describes an allied species from the Malayan Peninsula as *P. intermedium.*

241. Philentoma pyrrhopterum (*Tem.*) *Sharpe, Cat. B. Br. Mus.* iv. p. 366; *Jerd. B. Ind.* i. p. 449; *Salvad, Ucc. Born.* i. p. 138; *Hume and Dav.*, vi. p. 223; *Hume, Str. F.* viii. p. 92; *Oates, B. Br. Burm.* i. p. 264. Philentoma castaneum, *Eyton, Ann. Nat. Hist., Ser.* i. xvi. p. 220; *Sharpe, Ibis,* 1877, p, 19.—The Chestnut-winged Fly-Catcher.

Male.—Whole head and neck, the breast, back, and lesser wing coverts bluish grey or indigo blue, less deep on the forehead and over the eye; lower back and rump rufescent grey; upper tail coverts, tail, some of the outer webs of the scapulars, the tertiaries and most of the outer webs of the secondaries bright chestnut; remainder of the quills dark brown; the outer webs of the primaries margined with greyish blue, in some with a reddish tinge; primary coverts blue centred with blackish; greater wing coverts chestnut; lower plumage pale buff, becoming paler on the vent and under tail coverts; bill black; irides crimson.

Length.—6·8 to 7·5; wing 3·12 to 3·87; tail 2·75 to 3·3; tarsus 0·75.

The female has the forehead, crown, nape and sides of the head dull bluish or greenish grey; the back, scapulars, lesser and median wing coverts, rump and upper tail coverts dull earthy brown; chin, throat and breast fulvous white, more distinctly buffy at the base of the throat; rest of under surface sordid white, with more or less of a creamy tinge, washed with fulvescent; wings and tail as in the male; edge of the wing and coverts immediately under it blue; wing lining pale pinkish buff; legs dark greenish black; irides crimson.

Length.—6·75 to 7·9; wing 3·8 to 3·12; tail 2·62 to 3; tarsus 0·65 to 7; culmen 0·72 to 0·95.

Hab.—The Chestnut-winged Fly-Catcher occurs in the extreme south of Tenasserim, where it was observed by Davison in the evergreen forests about Bankasoon and Malewoon. It extends down the Malay Peninsula to Sumatra, Malacca, and Borneo, and Dr. Tiraud records it from Cochin-China. Davison says its habits are similar to those of *P. velatum.*

Gen. Culicicapa.—*Swinhoe.*

Head subcrested; bill moderately broad, flattened, outline bowed in towards the tip; nareal bristles long and strong; rictal bristles slightly shorter; wing rather pointed; 1st quill shorter than the second; 4th and 5th very little longer than the third; tarsus short, feeble; tail nearly even.

242. Culicicapa ceylonensis, *Swainson, Zool. Ill. Ser.* i. pl. xiii.; *Sharpe, Cat. B. Br. Mus.* iv. p. 369; *Oates, B. Br. Burm.*, i. p. 274, *Hume, Str. F.* viii. p. 92; *Scully, Str. F.* viii. p. 275; *Legge, B. Ceylon,*

p. 410. Cryptolopha cinereocapilla, (*Hutton*) *J. A. S. B.* xvii. p. 689; *Jerd. B. Ind.* i. p. 455, No. 295. Myiolestes cinereocapilla (*Vieill.*), *Hume, Nests and Eggs, Ind. B.* p. 205; *Ball, Str. F.* 1874, pp. 404, 406; *Wald, B. Burm.* p. 132. Culicicapa cinereocapilla, *Hume, Str. F.* iii. p. 104.—The Grey-headed Fly-Catcher.

Head, neck and breast ashy, darker on the crown, where the feathers are dark centred; under surface bright yellow; the under wing coverts slightly paler; lores and edges of the eyelids whitish; back, rump, scapulars and upper tail coverts greenish yellow; wings and their coverts dark brown; the outer webs of all the feathers, except the first two primaries, edged with bright greenish yellow; the lesser wing coverts more broadly edged with the same on both webs; tail dark brown, the outer webs of all except the outer pair edged with greenish yellow; bill brown, paler at gape; mouth yellow; iris dark hazel; legs yellowish brown.

Hab.—The greater portion of India and Ceylon, extending through the Burmese countries down the Malay Peninsula to the islands of Java, the Philippines, and Celebes. (Sharpe.) According to Jerdon the Grey-headed Fly-Catcher is dispersed from the Himalayas to the Neilgherries, and spreads on the other side of the Bay through Assam, into Arrakan, Burmah, and Tenasserim. In South India, on the summit of the Neilgherries, it is very common. Towards the north and in Central India it is occasionally met with, and is not rare in Lower Bengal. Oates found it spread over the whole of Pegu as a winter visitor, both in the hills and plains. Davison states it is generally distributed throughout the whole of Tenasserim. Captain Bingham found it in the Thoungyeen Valley, and Captain Wardlaw-Ramsay in the hills in Karin. It prefers rather dense jungle in general, or shady groves and tangled thickets, is tolerably active and lively, making frequent sallies after small insects. It is often seen in small parties, occasionally singly or in pairs, and has a pleasant, but feeble, chirping song. It breeds in the Himalayas and in the Neilgherries at considerable elevations. Hutton obtained a nest at Mussoorie. It was placed against the trunk of a tree. It is sometimes placed against a rock. In shape the nest is like a watch-pocket, made of moss, and fixed to the moss of the tree by spider's web and lined with fine fibres. It breeds during April and May. The eggs, 4 in number, are dingy yellowish white, minutely spotted with pale greenish brown, or purplish grey, with a broad ring of the same near the large end; size 0·62 × 0·48.

Gen. **Cryptolopha**.—*Swains.*

Bill depressed, rather wide; culmen moderately keeled; rictal bristles well developed; nostrils concealed by bristles.

243. Cryptolopha burkii, *Sharpe, Cat. B. Br. Mus.* iv. p. 395. Sylvia burkii, *Burton, P. Z. S.*, 1835, p. 153. Culicepeta burkii, *Blyth, J. A. S. B.* xii. p. 968; *Jerd. B. Ind.* ii. p. 199, No. 569; *Blyth and Walden, B. Burm.* p. 107; *Str. F.* iii. p. 140.—The Black-browed Warbler.

Above bright yellowish olive green, rather brighter on the rump and upper tail coverts; wing coverts like the back, the greater series tipped with yellow, forming an indistinct bar across the wing; the quills ashy brown with yellowish green margins, less distinct on the secondaries; tail feathers ashy brown, margined with yellowish green, the inner web of the outermost nearly all white, also the terminal half of the next; crown of the head yellowish green, on each side of which is a broad black band slightly shaded with grey below; lores, eyebrow and sides of face olive yellow; round the eye a circlet of bright yellow feathers; cheeks, sides of the neck, under wing coverts and *under surface of the body bright yellow*; bill dusky above, beneath amber; legs brownish yellow; irides dark brown.

Length.—4 to 4·3 inches; wing 2·2; tail 1·75 to 1·85; tarsus 0·7; culmen 0·5.

The female is much duller in colour.

Hab.—Northern India, ranging to Nepaul.

The Black-browed Warbler occurs in the N. W. Provinces of India, also in Oudh. The specimens in the National Collection are from between Simla and Mussoorie, Nepaul, Behar, Darjeeling, and Bhootan. Jerdon, quoting Blyth, says "it is not uncommon in the neighbourhood of Calcutta during the cold season, and, like the rest of its tribe, retires to the sub-Himalayan region to breed." Of its nidification there is no record.

244. Cryptolopha cantatrix, *Sharpe, Cat. B. Br. Mus.* iv. p. 397. Motacilla cantator, *Tick, J. A. S. B.* ii. p. 576. Culicepeta cantator, *Jerd. B. Ind.* ii. p. 200, No. 570; *Seebohm, Ibis*, 1878, p. 490. Abrornis cantator, *Hume, Nests and Eggs, Ind. B.* p. 370; *id. Str. F.* viii. p. 102; *Ball, Str. F.* 1874, p. 415. Abrornis chrysea, *Wald. in Blyth's B. Burm.* p. 106; *Hume, Str. F.* 1877, p. 56. Cryptolopha cantator, *Oates, B. Burm.* i. p. 270.—The Lesser Black-browed Fly-catcher.

Olive green above, yellower on the rump and upper tail coverts; chin, lores, throat, cheeks, supercilia, sides of neck, lower tail coverts and edge of the wing bright yellow; quills dusky brown, externally edged with bright yellow, greyish at the end of the primaries; greater wing coverts edged and tipped with yellow, forming a bar across the wing; tail feathers light brown, externally edged with olive yellow; the outer feathers edged with white towards the tip of the inner web; crown of head olive yellow, on each side of which a broad black band extending from the base of the bill to the sides of the nape; feathers round the eye bright yellow; a dusky spot in front of the eye; breast yellow; abdomen and flanks *greyish white, or silky white;* vent, thighs and under tail coverts bright yellow; bill brown; the lower mandible yellowish white; legs brown or fleshy yellow; irides hazel.

Length.—3·7 to 4 inches; wing 2·25; tail 1·7 to 1·8; culmen 0·45 to 0·55; tarsus 0·65.

Hab.—Bengal, Central India, Assam, Nepaul and British Burmah. In the latter it has been obtained in the Karin Hills, near Tounghoo, by Captain Wardlaw-Ramsay. Breeds in the Himalayas and Sikkim during May, and probably June also. A nest, containing a single egg, was sent to Mr. Hume in May from Sikkim. The egg was pure glossy white, oval in shape, and in size 0·6 × 0·49.

245. Cryptolopha affinis (*Hodgs.*) *Sharpe, Cat. B. Br. Mus.* iv. p. 398. Culicepeta tephrocephala, *Anders., P. Z. S.* 1871, p. 213; *Bl. and Wald., B. Burm.* p. 107; *Anders. Yunnan Exped.* p. 626, pl. 50; *Hume, Str. F.* 1874, p. 479; *Hume and Dav., Str. F.* 1878, p. 358; *Seebohm. Ibis,* 1878, p. 490; *Hume, Str. F.* viii. p. 102; *Dav. et. Oust. Ois Chine,* p. 273; *Oates, B. Burm.* i. p. 271. Abrornis affinis (*Hodgs.*), *Jerd. B. Ind.* ii. p. 204, No. 576.—The Allied or Anderson's Warbler.

Forehead, lores, cheeks, feathers above the eyes, the ear coverts, sides of the neck, back, rump and upper tail coverts yellowish green; a broad supercilium and a streak on each side of the crown slate coloured; *crown of head and nape ashy grey*; wing coverts broadly margined with yellowish green; feathers on the edges of the eyelids and the whole lower plumage, also the under wing and tail coverts, bright yellow; primaries and secondaries sepia-brown, the outer webs margined with yellowish green; wing coverts concolorous with the back; tertiaries the same; tail feathers sepia brown, the four central pairs washed with the same yellowish green as the back, the two outer pairs white for the whole extent of the inner web; upper mandible brown, lower yellow; mouth yellow; feet and claws yellowish horn; legs yellow.

Length.—3·8 to 4·25; wing 2·1 to 2·2; tail 1·8; tarsus 0·7 to 0·75; bill from gape 0·65.

Hab.—Eastern Himalayas, extending to Nepaul, the Burmese countries and Western China. (Sharpe.)

This Warbler, according to Oates, is very abundant throughout Pegu in the winter months. It has been obtained in the Karin Hills at 3,500 feet elevation. In Tenasserim, Davison states that it is sparingly distributed throughout the northern and central portions of the division. Captain Bingham found it in the Thoungyeen Valley. Dr. Anderson described it under the name of *C. tephrocephalus* from the hills to the east of Bhamo. He also found it in Yunnan and in Western China. It leaves Burmah during March and April, but where it goes to is not known; it is, however, suggested that its breeding haunts are in some part of China.

246. Cryptolopha xanthoschista (*Hodgs.*) *Sharpe, Cat. B. Br. Mus.* iv. p. 398; *Oates, B. Br. Burm.* i. p. 272. Phyllopneuste xanthoschistos, *Hodgs. in Gray's Zool. Mis.* p. 82. Abrornis xanthoschistos, *Jerd. B. Ind.* ii. p. 202, No. 572; *Hume, Nests and Eggs,* p. 370; *Hume and Henderson,*

Lah to Yarkand, p. 220 pl. xx. fig. 2; *Hume, Str. F.* i. p. 493; *Brooks, Str. F.* iii. p. 245; viii. p. 483; *Hume, Str. F.* viii. p. 102; *Scully, Str. F.* vii. p. 309. Abrornis albosuperciliaris (*Bl.*) *apud. Jerd. B. India*, ii. p. 202, No. 573; *Hume and Henders. Lah tô Yark.* pl. xx. fig. 1; *Hume, Str. F.* i. p. 493; *Brooks, Str. F.* iii. p. 245; *Hume, Str. F.* vii. p. 245.—Hodgson's Grey-headed Fly-Catcher.

Head, nape and back dark ashy grey in some, the latter washed with yellowish; wing coverts, rump and upper tail coverts olive yellow; quills dusky brown, externally edged with olive yellow, brighter on the primaries; tail dark ashy brown, edged narrowly with white on the inner web, increasing in extent towards the two outermost, which are almost entirely white, except at the base and towards the tip of the outer web; outer web of rest of tail feathers edged with olive yellow; a white supercilium from the nostril to the nape; lores dark grey; ear coverts greyish white; feathers below the eye the same; cheeks and entire under surface of body bright yellow; the feathers on the flanks with a subterminal shade of white; under wing coverts and edge of the wing yellow; axillaries whitish, washed with yellow; bill, the upper mandible, brownish black; the lower horny yellow; irides blackish brown.

Length.—3·8 to 4·2 inches; wing 2·1 to 2·2; tail 1·7 to 1·8; tarsus 0·75; culmen 0·4; from gape 0·5.

Hab.—The Himalayas extending to Assam, Arrakan, British Burmah and Nepaul. It occurs in the Punjab, N. W. Provinces, Bengal, Central India, the Khasia Hills, Burmah and Nepaul, also Bhootan. Mr. Sharpe, under "Obs." (*Cat. B. Br. Mus.* vol. iv. p. 399), says: "The specimens of this bird from the North Western Himalayas are generally rather more ashy brown on the head and are rather larger; in this state they are *Cryptolopha albosuperciliaris* of Indian authors. These birds can, however, be matched by some Nepaulese examples. In the Eastern Himalayas, the specimens have the head rather clearer blue grey, and are smaller in dimensions.—(*Cryptolopha xanthoschista, Hodgs. and* C. Jerdoni, *Brooks*)." Hodgson's Grey-headed Warbler breeds in Nepaul and Sikkim up to 6,000 or 7,000 feet during April and May. It nests on the ground under thick bushes, under roots of trees, or in holes in banks. Mr. Gammie found a nest in Sikkim: it was a domed structure made of moss. The eggs are pure white, four in number, and in size 0·56 × 0·47.

247. Cryptolopha schisticeps, (*Hodgs.*), *Sharpe, Cat. B. Br. Mus.* iv. p. 400. Abrornis schisticeps, *Hodgs. Icon. ined. Passeres*, pl. 57, fig. 6; pl. 28, fig. 2; pl. 64, fig. 1; *Seebohm, Ibis*, 1878, p. 490; *Jerd. B. Ind.* ii. p. 201, No. 571. Abrornis melanotis, *Jerd. and Blyth, P. Z. S.* 1861, p. 200.—The Black-eared Warbler.

Head and hind neck dark slaty grey; a narrow frontal line, lores, feathers in front of and below the eye, ear coverts and sides of the neck slaty grey; forehead and a very broad eye-brow brilliant yellow; the cheeks, throat, foreneck and upper breast dull yellow; sides of the breast dull greenish; lower breast and abdomen white; thighs and under tail coverts dull olive yellow, also the wing coverts; quills dusky blackish; the primaries narrowly edged with yellow, and the secondaries broadly washed with the same; tail feathers dusky brown, with olive yellow on the outer web, and whitish on the inner web; the inner web of the outermost entirely white; under wing coverts and edge of wing bright yellow; axillaries very pale yellow; bill and legs horny.

Length.—3·5 inches; wing 1·75; tail 1·55; tarsus 0·6; culmen 0·35.

Hab.—The Himalayas, extending to Sikkim and Nepaul. Dr. Jerdon records it from Nepaul, Mussoorie, and Sikkim. Hutton found the nest at Mussoorie in March and May, and says that it breeds at about 5,000 feet. It makes a round ball-like nest, with a lateral entrance. The nest is composed of grass, moss, wool, cotton, feathers, thread, and hair. The eggs, three in number, are oval and glossy white, and in size 0·82 × 0·48.

248. Cryptolopha superciliaris. *Tick, J. A. S. B.* xxviii. p. 414; *Sharpe, Cat. B. Br. Mus.* iv. p. 402; *Oates, B. Br. Burm*, i, p. 273. Abrornis superciliaris (*Tick*), *Jerd. B. Ind.* ii. p. 203; *Hume, Str. F.* iii. p. 140; *Hume and Dav.*, *Str. F.* vi. p. 359; *Anders., Yunnan Exp.* p. 626; *Hume, Str. F.* viii. p. 102; *Bingham, Str. F.* ix. p. 188. Abrornis albigularis, *Jerd. and Blyth, P. Z. S.* 1861, p. 200 (*nec. Moore*). Abrornis flaviventris, *Jerd. B. Ind.* ii. p. 203, No. 574.—The Yellow-bellied Warbler.

Forehead and crown light ashy brown, slightly washed with olive; rest of upper plumage dull olive brown; supercilium from the bill over the eye to the nape white; lores and behind the eye brown; cheeks and ear coverts greyish white; chin, throat, foreneck and upper breast white, rest of lower surface bright yellow, paler on the abdomen; under wing coverts whitish, washed with yellow; quills and wing coverts dark brown, edged with olive green; tail brown, edged on the outer web with olive, and on the inner with pale rufous for the greater part of the web; bill more or less of a dark olive brown or horn colour, plumbeous at the base of the lower mandible; inside of mouth yellow; eyelids grey; iris dark brown; legs yellow.

Length.—4·2 to 4·4 inches; wing 2·05 to 2·1; tail 1·75 to 1·8; tarsus 0·75; culmen 0·45.

Hab.—The Himalayas, British Burmah and Java; also Sikkim and Nepaul.

Jerdon found this species at Darjeeling. It also occurs in Upper Bengal. Oates obtained it in various parts of Pegu, both on the hills and in the plains. Captain Wardlaw-Ramsay procured it in the Tounghoo Hills, and also in Karin, while in Tenasserim Davison states it is sparingly distributed throughout the country. Captain Bingham found the nest in March near the Zammee River in Tenasserim. It consisted of a mass of fibres placed in a bamboo which had been cut down, and then left leaning against a bush. The eggs, three in number, are white, speckled with pinkish claret colour.

249. Cryptolopha poliogenys, *Blyth, J. A. S. B.* xvi. p. 441; *Sharpe, Cat. B. Br. Mus.* vol. iv. p. 403. Abrornis poliogenys, *Blyth, Cat. B. Mus. A. S. B.* p. 183; *Jerd. B. Ind.* ii. p. 203, No. 575; *Seebohm, Ibis,* 1878, p. 490.—The GREY-CHEEKED WARBLER.

Above yellowish green, brighter yellow on the rump; tail dark brown, edged with olive green; the three outermost feathers greenish dusky on the terminal half of the outer web; the basal half and whole of the inner web white; quills and wing coverts dark brown, narrowly edged with yellowish green; the greater coverts tipped with bright yellow, and forming a bar across the wing; head slaty grey; the sides of the crown blackish, forming a broad stripe reaching to the nape; sides of the face ashy grey; the ear coverts slightly streaked with black; orbital ring of feathers white; lores and fore part of cheeks ashy white, the feathers with dusky bases; chin white; rest of under surface, including under wing coverts, bright golden yellow; sides of the breast washed with olive green; bill blackish, horny above, yellowish beneath; feet yellowish horny.

Length.—3·8 to 4·25 inches; wing 1·9 to 2; tail 1·75; tarsus 0·7; culmen 0·4.

Hab.—The Himalayas, extending to Nepaul and Sikkim.

Dr. Jerdon found this species near Darjeeling and in the Khasia Hills, where, he says, it probably breeds. There is no record of its habits, nor of its nidification. It is is also found in Upper Bengal.

250. Cryptolopha castaneoceps, (*Bp.*) *Sharpe, Cat. Birds Br. Mus.* iv. p. 404. Abrornis castaneoceps, *Hodgs. Icon. ined. Passeres.* pl. 57, fig. 7; *Jerd. B. Ind.* ii. p. 205, No. 578; *Seebohm, Ibis,* 1878, p. 490. Culicepeta castaneoceps, *Blyth, J. A. S. B.* xvi. p. 442. Reguloides castaneoceps, *Bp. Consp.* i. p. 202; *Jerd. and Blyth, P. Z. S.,* 1861, p. 200.—The CHESTNUT-HEADED WARBLER.

Crown of head chestnut, with a black stripe running down the sides of the nape from above and behind each eye; lores white, tipped with black; orbital ring of feathers white; sides of the face grey, as also the sides of the neck; a white stripe below the black streak on the sides of the nape; cheeks, throat and upper breast light greyish; the middle of the abdomen whitish; rest of under surface, including the under wing coverts, axillaries and edge of the wing bright yellow; back olive yellow; rump and upper tail coverts bright yellow, the least wing coverts the same but rather brighter; median and greater coverts dark brown, edged and tipped with bright yellow, forming a double bar across the wing; quills dark brown, externally edged with olive yellow; tail light brown, edged with olive yellow, the two outermost feathers white, brown only along the tip of the outer web; bill dark horn brown, the lower mandible paler; legs pale.

Length.—3·5 to 4 inches; wing 1·85 to 1·95; tail 1·5 to 1·6; tarsus 0·65; culmen 0·4.

Hab.—The Himalayas, Upper Bengal, Nepaul and Sikkim.

Very little is known of the habits of this species. It is said to breed in Nepaul.

251. Cryptolopha albigularis, (*Hodgs. ?*) *Sharpe, Cat. B. Br. Mus.* iv. p. 405. Abrornis albogularis, *Hodgs. Icon. ined. Passeres, App.* pl. 46; *Jerd. B. Ind.* ii. p. 204, No. 577; *Seebohm, Ibis.*, 1878, p. 490.—The WHITE-THROATED WARBLER.

Forehead, eyebrow, lores, sides of the face, hind-crown and nape rufous fawn colour; crown dusky, the feathers tipped with black, and forming, as it were, a double row or band down the crown; throat whitish; back yellowish green; the rump whitish, washed with yellow; upper tail coverts olive yellow; wing coverts and quills dark brown, edged with yellowish green; tail light brown, margined with olive yellow; along the outer webs, breast and sides of the body pale olive yellow; the middle of the abdomen white; thighs and under tail and under wing coverts, also the edge of the wing, olive yellow; axillaries white, washed with yellow; rictal bristles as long as the bill; bill and legs pale fleshy.

Length.—3·3 to 3·5 inches; wing 1·75; tail 1·5; tarsus 0·6; culmen 0·35.

Hab.—Nepaul and Darjeeling.

Nothing is on record of its habits and nidification.

252. Cryptolopha hodgsoni, *Moore, App. to Horsf. and Moore, Cat. B. Mus. E. I. Co.* i. p. 412; *Sharpe, Cat. B. Br. Mus.* iv. p. 406. Tickellia hodgsoni, *Jerd. and Blyth, P. Z. S.*, 1861, p. 199; *Jerd. B. Ind.* ii. p. 206; *Seebohm, Ibis*, 1878, p. 490.—The BROAD-BILLED WARBLER.

Above olive green, yellowish on the rump and upper tail coverts; forehead and crown deep ferruginous; lores white with blackish tips; sides of the head, eyebrow, and sides of the neck dull grey; throat lighter ashy grey, nearly white on the chin; rest of under surface bright yellow; under wing coverts and axillaries light yellow; tail brown, margined with olive, the two outermost feathers white along the inner web and brown on the outer; quills and wing coverts dull brown, edged with olive green; bill horny yellowish at base below; legs yellowish.

Length.—3·5 to 3·75 inches; wing 1·75 to 1·95; tail 1·5; tarsus 0·65; culmen 0·3.

Hab.—The Eastern Himalayas.

Jerdon says he procured one specimen only of this pretty Warbler at Darjeeling. He thinks Hodgson's specimens were probably from Sikkim, and not Nepaul.

253. Cryptolopha flavigularis, *Godw.-Austen, J. A. S. B.* xlvii. p. 19, 1878; *Sharpe, Cat. B. Br. Mus.* iv. p. 474, *App.*—The YELLOW-THROATED WARBLER.

Above ashy grey, purer grey on rump, rather darker on the head; wings pale amber brown; tail ash brown; the two outer feathers white on the inner web, the next with a narrow edging of white; lores white; ear coverts white and grey; chin pure yellow, fading on the throat; breast, nape, flanks and thighs greyish white; whitish on the breast; a very faint yellow tinge on the abdomen; under tail coverts white; a small patch of white on the inner shoulder of the wing; bill dark brown, buff below.

Length.—3·6 to 3·8 inches; wing 1·84; tail 1·8; tarsus 0·67; bill from front 0·3. (Godwin-Austen and Sharpe.)

Hab.—Sadiya near Brahmakhund, and hills of Eastern Bengal.

Gen. Stoparola.—*Blyth.*

Bill short, depressed; the culmen not equal to twice its breadth at the gape; tip-hooked; rictal bristles numerous; wing rather long; 3rd, 4th and 5th quills subequal; tail moderate; tarsus short.

254. Stoparola albicaudata, *Jerd. Madras, Journ.* xi. p. 16; *id. Illust. Ind. Orn.* pl. 14; *Blyth, J. A. S. B.* xvi. p. 125; *id. Cat. B. Mus. A. S. B.* p. 175; *Hume, Nests and Eggs, Indian B.* p. 210; *Fairbank, Str. F.* 1877, p. 402. Eumyias albicaudata, (*Horsf. & Moore*) *Jerd. B. Ind.*, i p. 464, No. 302; *Hume, Str. F.* 1876, p. 396.—The NEILGHERRY BLUE FLY-CATCHER.

Above deep indigo blue, with a slight lazuline blue eyebrow; forehead and head also inclining to lazuline blue; wing coverts and quills dusky black, externally edged with lazuline blue; primary coverts dark brown, edged externally with blue; tail the same, the base of all the feathers, except the two centre ones, white; central tail feathers white-shafted; under surface of body indigo blue, rather greyish on the lower flanks and abdomen; the lower abdomen and vent slightly whitish; under tails coverts dusky, with whitish edges to the feathers; bill and legs black; irides dark brown.

Length.—6 to 6·5 inches; wing 3·05 to 3·2; tail 2·3 to 2·10; tarsus 0·75; culmen 0·45.

Hab.—South India.

This species is confined to Southern India, nearly throughout the high mountain ranges of which it is found. The Neilgherries and Travancore, also Madras, are noted as localities.

In Travancore, Mr. Bourdillon says it is common, though not abundant, up to 2,000 feet elevation, and is frequently observed in the forest wherever there are heaps of unburnt brushwood lying about. It is a winter visitor there from December to March. In the Neilgherries Jerdon says it is very common, generally in parties of five or six, capturing insects in the air. It makes its nest in a slight hole in a bank. The eggs are three in number, longish ovals, in colour varying from creamy white to warm *cafe au lait* with brown, red or very obscure markings; size 0·81 × 0·59.

255. Stoparola melanops, *Vigors., P. Z. S.* 1831, p. 171; *Gould., Cent. Him. B.* pl. 6; *Blyth, J. A. S. B.* xvi. p. 174; *Hume, Nests and Eggs, Ind. B.* p. 208; *Adams, Str. F.* 1874, p. 338; *Ball* t. c. p. 405; *Butler, Str. F.* 1877, p. 230; *Hume and Dav., op. cit.* 1878, p. 227; *Sharpe, Cat, B. Br. Mus.* iv. p. 438; *Oates, B. B. Burm.* i. p. 285. Eumyias melanops (*Vig.*), *Jerd. B. Ind.* i. p. 463, No. 301; *Armstrong, Str. F.* iv. p. 323; *Anderson Yunnan Exped.* p. 622. Glaucomyias melanops, *Scully, Str. F.* viii. p. 277.—The VERDITER FLY-CATCHER.

Lores, feathers in front of the eye and at the base of the upper mandible black, rest of the plumage verditer-blue, brightest on the forehead, chin, throat, breast and upper tail coverts; under tail coverts broadly tipped with white; tail blue, the shafts black and the inner webs edged with brown; primaries and secondaries blue on the outer and black on the inner webs; tertiaries and upper wing coverts blue; bill and legs black; irides deep brown.

Length.—6 inches; wing 3·2 to 3·4; tail 2·75 to 2·8; tarsus 0·65; culmen 0·45.

The female is like the male, but has the blue of the head and body much duller, and the chin and throat are mottled with whitish.

Hab.—Indian Peninsula, Burmese countries, and Sikkim, ranging into Southern China. (Sharpe.) It visits the plains of India and Burmah during winter, and is generally spread throughout the better-wooded parts of the country. It also occurs in Arrakan. Oates found it in Pegu, Blanford got it at Bassein; Captain Wardlaw-Ramsay on the Karin Hills, Mr. Davison in Tenasserim, and Captain Bingham in the Thoungyeen Valley. It breeds in the Himalayas, making a neat cup-shapped nest, composed of moss, lined with fibres and hair, which is generally placed under a wooden bridge, or under the eaves of roofs. The eggs, four in number, are oval, in colour dull white, and with rufous spots.

Gen. **Siphia**.—*Hodgs.*

Bill moderately wide; length of culmen equal to twice the breadth of the base at gape, slightly hooked at tip and notched; nostrils covered by bristles and frontal plumes; wings pointed and long, but not reaching to the tip of the tail; 4th quill longest; hind claw moderate and curved, not as long as the hind toe; toes scutate at base of claws; tarsus as long as hind toe and claw.

256. Siphia pallidipes, *Sharpe, Cat. B. Br. Mus.* iv. p. 444; Muscicapa pallipes, *Jerd., Madras Journ.* xi. p. 15. Cyornis pallipes (*Blyth*), *Jerd. B. Ind.* 1. p. 469, No. 309; *Fairbank, Str. F.* 1876, p. 357; *Hume*, t. c. p. 397.—The WHITE-BELLIED BLUE FLY-CATCHER.

Above dull blue, the forehead and eyebrow inclining to cobalt; lores and feathers in front of the eye black; sides of face, throat and breast deep blue; wing coverts blue, the least series brighter and more cobalt; quills blackish, externally dull blue; tail blue, the feathers dusky on their inner webs; under surface of body pure white, shaded with ashy on the upper breast and bluish grey on the flanks; thighs dull blue; *under wing coverts and axillaries white*; edge of wing blue; bill black; legs and feet flesh colour; iris brown.

Length.—5·7 to 6·5 inches; wing 2·9 to 3; tail 2·5; culmen 0·6; tarsus 0·75.

Hab.—Southern India and the Concan. It is recorded from Coorg in Mysore, Sirci above Honore and the Coonoor Pass of the Neilgherries, and Dr. Fairbank got it in deep ravines near (Parwar?) Carwar on the Goa frontier. Jerdon says it is probably an inhabitant of the upland forests of the Western Ghauts; he observed it on the Neilgherries darting on insects from its perch on a low branch. Mr. Bourdillon also records it from the Travancore Hills.

257. Siphia unicolor, (*Blyth*) *Sharpe, Cat. B Br. Mus.* iv. p. 444. Cyornis unicolor, *Blyth. J. A. S. B.* xii. pp. 941, 1007; *id., Cat. B. Mus., A. S. B.* p. 173; *Jerd. B. Ind.* i. p. 465, No. 303; *Hume, Str. F.* 1875, p. 401; 1876, p. 398; 1877, p. 489; *Sharpe, Ibis*, 1878, p. 418; *Godw.-Austen, J. A. S. B.* 1878, p. 15.—The PALE BLUE FLY-CATCHER.

Above light blue, inclining to cobalt on the rump; forehead, over the eye, as also the feathers round the eye, cobalt; sides of the face deep blue, paler under the eye and fore part of the cheeks; lores blue black; wing coverts bright blue; the greater series and quills blackish, edged externally with bright blue; tail deep blue, all, except the two centre feathers, blackish on the inner webs; throat and breast light greyish blue, centre of abdomen and under tail coverts whitish; rest of the under surface of body very pale blue; *under wing coverts fulvous or yellowish fawn*; edge of the wing blue; bill and legs black.

Length.—6 to 6·75 inches; wing 3·2; tail 2·8; tarsus 0·7; culmen 0·5.

The female is dark ashy brown above, all the parts which are blue in the male are rufous brown; lores fulvescent; ear coverts and sides of face and neck dark ashy brown, with hair-like shaft streaks; chin and throat pale rufous; fore neck and breast ashy brown; abdomen dull white; flanks and under tail coverts fulvous; under wing coverts buffy brown.

Length.—6·2 inches; wing 3·1; tail 2·6; tarsus 0·65.

The young are mottled all over with ochraceous spots.

Hab.—The Eastern Himalayas, extending to the Malay Peninsula, Java and Borneo. (Sharpe.) Recorded from Darjeeling and Sikkim.

258. Siphia rubeculoides, (*Vigors*), *Sharpe, Cat. B. Br. Mus.* iv. p. 445; *Oates, B. Br. Burm.* i. p. 287. Phœnicura rubeculoides, *Vig. P. Z. S.* 1831, p. 35; *Gould., Cent. Him. B.* pl. 25, fig. 1. Cyornis rubeculoides, *Blyth, J. A. S. B.* xii. p. 941; *Jerd. B. Ind.* i. p. 466, No. 304; *Blyth and Wald., B. Burm.* p. 103; *Hume, Nests and Eggs, Ind. B.* p. 211; *id. Str. F.* iii. p. 104; *Hume and Dav., Str. F.* vi. p. 227; *Anders. Yunnan Exp.* p. 619; *Hume, Str. F.* vii. p. 92.—The BLUE-THOATED REDBREAST.

Male.—Forehead and streak over the eye glistening blue; lores and feathers at the base of the bill black; ear coverts dusky blue; cheeks, sides of the neck, *throat and chin dusky blue black*; whole upper plumage dark blue; tail black-shafted, the feathers brown on their inner webs; wing dark brown, the feathers narrowly edged with dark blue; lesser wing coverts bright blue; the larger coverts brown, edged with dark blue, breast and abdomen bright ferruginous, running up to a point on the throat; lower abdomen and under tail coverts white; under wing coverts pale ferruginous; bill black; iris brown.

The female has the upper plumage olive brown, tinged with ferruginous, strongly so on the forehead, feathers, round the eye and upper tail coverts; lores albescent; *chin, throat and breast ruddy ferruginous*; abdomen and under tail coverts white.

Length.—5·7 inches; tail 2·4; wing 2·75; tarsus 0·75; bill from gape 0·7.

Hab.—India generally, extending to the N. W. Himalayas, Nepaul, Sikkim, and the Burmese countries.

The Blue-throated Redbreast visits the plains of India during the winter months. It is rare in the south of India, and occurs both on the Eastern and Western Coasts. In the Punjab, N. W. Provinces, Oudh and Bengal it is tolerably common. At Darjeeling it is found at from 4,000 to 6,000 feet elevation. In British Burmah it is also a winter visitor. It is recorded from Arrakan, and is found both in the hills and plains of the Pegu District from October to April. Mr. Davison says it is common throughout Tenasserim and is a permanent resident. It breeds in holes in banks. Captain Hutton found two nests at Mussoorie: they were made of moss and hair-like fibres. The eggs, four in number, were dull pale olive, or olive green, faintly clouded with clay colour and marked with dull rufous; size 0·72 × 0·52.

259. Siphia tickelliæ, (*Blyth*). *Sharpe, Cat. B. Br. Mus.* iv. p. 448; *Oates, B. Burm.* i. p. 289. Cyornis tickelliæ, *Blyth, J. A. S. B.* xii. p. 491; *Jerd. B. Ind.* i. p. 367, No. 306; *Hume, Nests and Eggs,* p, 212; *id., Str. F.* i. p. 436; *Ball, Str. F.* ii. p. 405; *Hume, Str. F.* iii. p. 468; *Wald. in Bl. B. Burm.* p. 103. Cyornis banyumas (*nec. Horsf.*), *Jerd. B. Ind.* i. p. 466, No. 305.—TICKELL'S BLUE REDBREAST.

Above light blue; forehead cobalt; a narrow frontal line and space in front of the eye blue black; cheeks, ear coverts and a narrow line across the chin at the base of the bill dark blue; the ear coverts washed with lighter blue; wing coverts cobalt blue; quills and tail light blue externally and dusky brown on the inner webs; two centre feathers and inner secondaries nearly entirely blue; entire throat and breast orange rufous; under wing coverts and axillaries, the lower abdomen and under tail coverts, white; sides of the breast, edge of the wing and thighs blue.

Length.—5·3 to 5·8 inches; wing 2·8 to 2·9; tail 2·3 to 2·5; tarsus 0·7; bill from gape 0·75.

The female is similar to the male, but paler, and has no black on the chin and face; the frontal line and lores are dull white; the ear coverts greyish blue, with whitish shaft streaks.

Hab.—India and Ceylon, ranging to British Burmah.

Tickell's Redbreast is recorded from the N. W. Provinces and Oudh, also Bengal, Kattiawar, Rajputana, Central India, the Central Provinces, the Carnatic, Malabar Coast, Guzerat, Concan, Deccan, South India and British Burmah. It breeds during May and June throughout Central India, the Neilgherries, and the Western Ghauts, nesting in the hole of a tree or wall. The nest is made of moss and dry leaves. The eggs are greyish white (dull brownish pink? Hume), speckled with dull reddish brown; size 0·61 × 0·48. It affects open forests, groves, and gardens.

260. Siphia magnirostris, (*Blyth*), *Sharpe, Cat. B. Br. Mus.* iv. p. 453; *Oates, B. Br. Burmah,* i. p. 290. Cyornis magnirostris, *Blyth, J. A. S. B.* xviii. p. 814; *Jerd. B. Ind.* i. p. 469, No. 308; *Godw.-Austen, J. A. S. B.* xxxix. p. 100; *Hume, Str. F.* viii. p. 92; 1876, p. 223; 1877, pp. 339, 489; *id., Hume and Dav., Str. F.* 1878, p. 229.—The LARGE-BILLED REDBREAST.

Whole upper plumage, cheeks, ear coverts, sides of the neck and wing coverts dull deep blue; brilliant on the forehead and over the lores and eyes; base of lower mandible and lores black; chin, throat and breast chestnut; sides of the breast blue; sides of the abdomen and flanks fulvous; centre of abdomen and under tail coverts white; under wing coverts and axillaries buff; tail, quills and greater wing coverts dark brown, externally edged with blue; bill dusky; legs pale whitish; irides dark brown.

Length.—6 inches; wing 3·1 to 3·2; tail 2·5; tarsus 0·7; culmen 0·55.

The female is ashy above, tinged with fulvous; lores, a ring of feathers round the eye, chin, throat and under tail coverts white; rest of the under surface pale buff; quills dusky brown, edged with fulvous; tail fulvous.

Length.—5·5 inches; wing 2·75; tail 2·3; tarsus; 0·7.

Hab.—Eastern Bengal, on the Hills; Cachar and throughout the Eastern Himalayas, ranging to South Tenasserim, also Darjeeling and in Sikkim.

Oates says it is rare in South Tenasserim, and that it will be found generally distributed throughout British Burmah.

261. Siphia nigrorufa, (*Jerd.*) *Sharpe, Cat. B. Br. Mus.* iv. p. 455. Saxicola nigrorufa, *Jerd., Madras Journ.* x. p. 266. Ochromela nigrorufa, *Blyth, J. A. S. B.* xvi. p. 129; *Jerd. B. Ind.* i. p. 492, No. 300; *Hume, Nests and Eggs, B. Ind.* p. 207; *id, Str. F.* 1876, p. 396; *Fairbank, Str. F.* 1877, p. 401.—The BLACK and ORANGE FLY-CATCHER.

Head, nape and back of neck dusky black; cheeks and upper surface of body orange-rufous; wings black, the quills browner, white edged along the inner web; tail orange, thighs dusky, under wing coverts pale orange; rest of under surface of body orange-rufous, rather buffy on the middle of the abdomen; bill black; legs dirty reddish; irides hazel brown.

Length.—4·7 to 4·9 inches; wing 2·4; tail 1·9; tarsus 0·8.

The female is dusky on the head, also on the wings; wing coverts washed with orange.

Hab.—Southern India and Ceylon.

Jerdon says it has only been found on the summit of the Neilgherries and in Ceylon.

It frequents the dense forests, preferring shady, damp and swampy places. Breeds on the Neilgherries. Eggs, 2 to 3, pale salmon in colour, 0·7×0·53; nest a large ball of dry sedges placed in a bush.

262. Siphia strophiata, *Hodgs., Ind. Rev.* i. p. 651; *Jerd. B. Ind.* i. p. 479, No. 319; *Godw.-Austen, J. A. S. B.* 1870, p. 101; *Sharpe, Cat. B. Br. Mus.* iv p. 455; *Oates, B. Br. Burm.* i p. 290; *Hume, Str. F.* viii. p. 92; *Scully, Str. F.* viii. p. 278.—The ORANGE-GORGETED FLY-CATCHER.

Above olive brown, the back and rump slightly tinged with fulvous, the feathers of the latter long and silky and with a white subterminal bar; upper tail coverts black; a narrow frontal line at base of upper mandible; lores, cheeks, chin, feathers round the eye and throat black; forehead and a line extending backwards over the fore part of the eye white; sides of face and ear coverts deep slaty; a bright chestnut patch on the throat; breast and sides of the neck slaty; abdomen, vent and under tail coverts white; flanks olive brown; thighs slaty grey; lesser wing coverts slaty grey, the other coverts and all the quills brown, edged externally with fulvous; tail feathers blackish, the two centre feathers entirely blackish, the next feather on each side with a white bar on the outer web, all the others white for the basal half and blackish terminally; under wing coverts and axillaries light buff; bill black; legs brown; iris dark brown.

Length.—5 to 5·3 inches; wing 2·9 to 3; tail 2·15 to 2·3; tarsus 0·8; culmen 0·45.

The female is similar, but the orange patch on the throat is smaller and much paler chestnut, and the white frontal band is nearly obsolete. The young bird is brown above and below, each feather streaked with fulvous, the throat patch of chestnut is absent.

Hab.—The Himalayas, from Nepaul to Sikkim, also Assam and the Naga Hills, ranging into British Burmah.

The Orange-throated Fly-Catcher is recorded from Mussoorie and Nepaul, and also from Darjeeling, where Jerdon says it is very common, and may often be seen on the roadside seated on a fallen tree or stone, frequently alighting on the ground to pick up an insect, and occasionally making a dart in the air and returning to its perch. In British Burmah it has been met with in South Tenasserim on the Mooleyit Mountains.

263. Siphia ruficauda, (*Swains.*) *Sharpe, Cat. B. Br. Mus.* iv. p. 457. Muscicapa ruficauda, *Sws., Nat. Libr. Flyc.* p. 251. Cyornis ruficauda, *Jerd. B. Ind.* i. p. 468, No. 307; *Godw.-Austen, J. A. S. B.* 1870, p. 268; *Brooks, Str. F.*, 1875, p. 235; *Fairbank, Str. F.* 1876, p. 257; *Hume*, t. c. p. 396; *Butler, Str. F.* 1877, p. 228; *Brooks*, t. c. p. 470.—The RUFOUS-TAILED FLY-CATCHER.

Above olivaceous or ashy brown, somewhat buffy on the rump; the upper tail coverts and external edge of the tail feathers rufous, the centre tail feathers and inner webs of the others ashy brown; wing coverts and quills dusky, the latter externally edged with ashy brown, the greater series with narrow pale tips; lores and a conspicuous ring round the eye whitish; ear coverts ashy brown, with narrow whitish shaft streaks; under surface of body dull whitish, ashy on the breast and flanks; under wing and tail coverts fulvescent; bill dusky; irides deep brown.

Length.—4·5 inches (5·5 Jerd.); wing 2·6 to 3·1; tail 2·15; tarsus 0·65; culmen 0·55.

Hab.—The Indian Peninsula generally. Recorded from the Punjab and N. W. Provinces, also Guzerat, the Concan, Deccan, and South India. It is fairly common in the Kumaon, also Mussoorie between where and Gungotri it was procured by Brooks. Jerdon obtained it in the Carnatic at Nellore and the Coonoor Pass of the Neilgherries. Its habits are those of the last.

264. Siphia mandelli, *Hume, Str. F.* 1874, p. 510; *id.* 1876, p. 396; *Sharpe, Cat. B. Br. Mus.* iv. p. 453.—MANDELL'S FLY-CATCHER.

Forehead, crown, occiput, cheeks, ear coverts and nape brown; lores, a ring round the eye and a patch at the base of the lower mandible white; upper surface of body brown, tinged with rufous near the rump; wings hair brown, darker on the primaries; the secondaries, tertiaries, greater and median wing coverts margined with pale ferruginous on the outer webs; breast, sides and flanks pale brown, margined very narrowly with pale rufous buff; under wing

1. DIGENEA LEUCOMELANURA. ♂
2. DIGENEA MONILIGER. ♂

Mintern Bros. lith.

coverts and axillaries rufous buff; abdomen, vent and under tail coverts white; bill blackish brown, paler at tip; lower mandible yellowish horny; legs and feet fleshy.

Length.—5·25 inches; wing 2·9; tail 2; bill at front 0·45; tarsus 0·6. (Hume.)

Hab.—Sikkim. Nothing is known of its habits and nidification.

265. Siphia olivacea, (*Hume*) *Sharpe, Cat. B. Br. Mus.* iv. p. 457. Cyornis olivacea, *Hume, Str. F.* 1877, p. 338; *id. Dav. and Hume, Str. F.* 1878, p. 229.—The OLIVE-BACKED FLY-CATCHER.

Above dull olivaceous, the head and nape very slightly tinged greyish; sides of the head, cheeks and ear coverts ashy grey, with paler shaft streaks; under surface whitish; the breast and flanks tinged grey; tail rufous brown, brighter on the outer webs of the quills, edged with fulvous brown and tinged with rufous brown externally; bill black; iris brown; legs pinkish white.

Length.—5·8 inches; wing 3; tail 2·5; tarsus 0·75; culmen 0·8.

Hab.—Tenasserim, Java, and Borneo. According to Mr. Davison, this species, like its other congeners, keeps to the forests or its outskirts, and is usually seen singly. They perch on commanding twigs, whence they capture passing insects with short sharp flights, returning to the same perch.

Gen. **Digenea.**—*Hodgs.*

Bill narrow, not as long as hind toe and claw; nostrils covered by rictal bristles and frontal plumes; wings pointed and long, but not reaching to the tip of the tail; hind claw moderate and curved, about equal in length to the hind toe.

266. Digenea leucomelanura, (*Blyth*). *Sharpe, Cat. B. Br. Mus.* iv. p. 459. Siphia leucomelanura, *Blyth, J. A. S. B* xvi. p. 126; *Jerd. B. Ind.* i. p. 479, No. 320; *Hodgs., icon. ined. Passeres App.* pl. 113. Siphia tricolor, *Blyth, J. A. S B.* xvi., p. 126; *Jerd. B. Ind.* i. p. 478, No. 318; *Brooks, Str. F.* 1877, p. 471.—The SLATY FLY-CATCHER.

PLATE, *Fig.* 1.

Above dull slaty blue, brighter and more ashy blue on the forehead and crown; ear coverts dark slaty blue; a narrow frontal line, lores and feathers in front of and below the eye and the fore part of the cheeks slaty black; wing coverts slaty blue; the greater series blackish brown externally, washed with slaty blue; secondaries the same; primaries brown, edged with ochraceous brown; upper tail coverts darker than the back; tail black, white at base, the two centre feathers entirely black; throat white, rest of under surface of body ashy grey, the flanks dull greyish; sides of upper breast slaty blue; the centre of abdomen white; under tail coverts dusky blackish, with longitudinal white central streaks; under wing coverts and axillaries pale ochraceous, with blackish bases to the feathers; bill dusky; feet brown; iris dark brown.

Length.—4·6 inches; wing 2·45; tail 2·2; tarsus 0·75; culmen 0·4.

The female is olive brown, rather more rufous on the forehead, and inclining to fulvescent brown on the rump; upper tail coverts and tail chestnut, the latter brown at the tip and having indistinct transverse lines under certain lights; lesser wing coverts olive brown like the back, the median and greater series dark brown, edged with rufous and tipped with a light rufous spot on each; quills dark brown, externally edged with rufous, more broadly on the secondaries; in front of the eye a dull whitish spot; sides of face olive brown, darker on the ear coverts; the feathers round the eye fulvescent, the cheeks and fore part of the ear coverts mottled with spots of ochraceous buff; throat light ochraceous brown, lighter in the centre; breast, sides of body, and under tail coverts light ochraceous brown, washed with olive on the sides of the upper breast; the centre of the abdomen whitish; thighs brown; under wing coverts and axillaries light ochraceous buff; quills sepia brown below, rufescent along the edge of the inner webs.

Length.—4·5 inches; wing 2·35; tail 2; tarsus 0·7; culmen 0·4.

Hab.—The Himalayas from Nepaul to Sikkim. Has been recorded from Mussoorie and Darjeeling. Breeds throughout the Himalayas, from Nepaul to Cashmere, during June, laying 4 eggs of a pale buff colour, clouded with dull rufous towards the larger end; size 0·62 × 0·48.

267. Digenea cerviniventris, *Sharpe, Cat. B. Br. Mus.* iv. p. 460; Siphia tricolor, *Godw.-Austen, J. A. S. B.* 1872, p. 142 (*nec. Hodgs*). Siphia leucomelanura, *Godw.-Austen, J. A. S. B.* 1878, p. 15 (*nec. Blyth*).—The FAWN-BELLIED FLY-CATCHER.

"Similar to *D. leucomelanura*, but deep fawn-coloured underneath instead of white."

Length.—4 inches; wing 2·2; tail 1·9; culmen 0·35.

Hab.—Khasia and neighboring range of hills (Munipoor). (Sharpe.)

268. Digenea moniliger, (*Hodgs.*) *Sharpe, Cat. B. Br. Mus.* iv. p. 460; *Oates, B. Br. Burm.* i. p. 300. Dimorpha? moniliger, *Hodgs. P. Z. S.*, 1845, p. 26. Anthipes moniliger, *Blyth, Cat. B. Mus. A. S. B.* p. 172; *Jerd. B. Ind.* i. p. 477, No. 317; *Hume, Str. F.* 1877, p. 113.—The WHITE GORGETED FLY-CATCHER.

PLATE, *Fig.* 2.

Forehead and a broad but short superciliary band fulvous; upper plumage olive brown, tinged with rufous on the rump; upper tail coverts and tail reddish brown; wing coverts and wings brown, edged with rufous; sides of the head olive brown; chin and throat white, surrounded by a distinct line of black; lower plumage brown, becoming albescent on the abdomen; bill black; legs pale fleshy; irides dark brown.

SINCE the publication of the 2nd part of the 1st Voume of this work, the following species of *Digenea* has been described by Mr. Sharpe of the British Museum :—

269a. Digenea leucops, *P. Z. S.* 1888, pt. ii., p. 246:—

General colour above light olive brown, with somewhat of an ashy tinge; wing coverts like the back, the greater series somewhat more ruddy brown externally; bastard wing, primary coverts and quills dusky brown, externally ruddy olive; upper tail coverts rather more reddish brown than the back; tail feathers dusky brown, externally reddish brown; crown of the head like the back; a white line across the base of the forehead widening into a large supra-loral spot; feathers about the eye washed with ashy grey; lores ashy, as also the feathers round the eye; ear coverts and cheek ashy washed with olive; throat white; the chin and a broad band on each side of the throat black, continued downwards, and forming a collar on the foreneck; chest and breast pale ashy, with a slight tinge of olive brown; abdomen white; sides of body and flanks olive brown; thighs olive brown; under tail coverts white, also the under wing coverts and axillaries. "Bill slaty brown; feet white tinged fleshy; iris bright dark brown." (*R. G. Wardlaw-Ramsay.*)

Length.—4·3 inches; wing 2·5; tail 1·75; tarsus 0·8; culmen 0·45.

Hab.—Shillong and Karenne, B. B.

An allied species (*D. malayana*) is also described from Perak.

VOL. I., p. 231.

Length.—4·2 to 5 inches; wing 2·3 to 2·4; tail 2; tarsus 0·8; culmen 0·5 to 0·6.

Hab.—Eastern Himalayas, Arrakan, Naga Hills, and Karin Hills in Burmah, also Nepaul.

Jerdon says this species is common in the hilly regions of Arrakan and Tenasserim, and probably occurs also in Assam. It is not uncommon about Darjeeling, frequenting open forests, and may be often seen seated on a low branch or the stump of a tree, sometimes catching insects in the air or descending to the ground to pick one up.

269. Digenea submoniliger, (*Hume*) *Sharpe, Cat. B. Br. Mus.* iv. p. 461. Anthipes moniliger, *Hume, Str. F.* 1874, p. 475 (*nec. Hodgs.*). Anthipes submoniliger, *Hume, Str. F.* 1877, p. 105; *id. Dav., Str. F.* 1878, p. 232.—HUME'S WHITE GORGETED FLY-CATCHER.

Upper plumage fulvous brown; forehead, lores, a broad supercilium and a circle of feathers round the eye rich golden fulvous; chin and throat white, with a few black feathers on the sides of the chin; a narrow, scarcely noticeable brown line bounds the white on the throat; lower breast and flanks olive brown; abdomen, vent and under tail coverts white; wings and coverts brown, edged with rufous; tail ferruginous; bill black, yellowish on lower mandible; legs and feet pale fleshy white.

Length.—5·2 inches; wing 2·45; tail 2; tarsus 0·87; culmen 0·6.

Hab.—Tenasserim, where Mr. Davison met with it, about Mooleyit and its spurs.

Gen.—**Niltava.**—*Hodgs.*

Bill rather short and stout, slightly depressed at base; tip deflected and strongly notched; nostrils hidden by frontal plumes; rictal bristles feeble; wings very short, the distance between wings and tail more than twice the length of the tarsus; quills unequally graduated; 5th longest; tail moderate.

270. Niltava sundara, *Hodgs., Ind. Rev.* i. 658; *Jerd. B. Ind.* i. p. 473, No. 314; *Hume, Nests and Eggs, Ind. B.* p. 213; *Bl. B. Burm.* p. 102; *Hume and Dav., Str. F.* p. 231; *Hume, Str. F.* vii. p. 93; *Sharpe, Cat. B. Br. Mus.* iv. p. 463; *Hume, Str.* ix. p. 234; *Oates, B. Br. Burm.* i. p. 295.—The RUFOUS-BELLIED FAIRY BLUE-CHAT.

Forehead, lores, sides of the head, chin, and *throat deep black*; crown of head, nape, rump, upper tail coverts and a spot on either side of the neck glistening blue; lesser wing coverts the same; median and greater coverts and quills dark brown, edged with purplish blue; back and scapulars purplish black; tail black, the outer webs tinged with bright blue; lower plumage and under wing coverts chestnut; edge of wing blue black; bill black; legs brown; iris dark brown.

Length.—6·5 inches; wing 3·1; tail 2·8; tarsus 0·85; culmen 0·45.

The female has the upper plumage olive brown, tinged with fulvous; the tail is rufous, the forehead and sides of the head are mingled buff and ashy brown; ear coverts paler shafted; neck spot blue; under surface ashy brown, becoming whitish on the abdomen; front of neck with a white patch.

The young are dark brown, streaked above and below with fulvous; outer webs of wings and tail tinged with blue. No blue neck spot.

Length.—6·0 inches; wing 3·1; tail 2·8; tarsus 0·85.

Hab.—The Himalayas, extending to the Burmese countries and Western China. (Sharpe). The Rufous-bellied Fairy Blue-Chat occurs in the Punjab, N. W. Provinces, Oudh, British Burmah and Nepaul. It inhabits the whole extent of the Himalayas, being common at Simla, and extending to Assam. About Darjeeling, Jerdon adds it is not rare. It has been recorded from Arrakan and Tenasserim, and Captain Wardlaw-Ramsay procured it in Karin. It frequents thick bushy ground, often near water, is shy and wary, seldom showing itself. It feeds chiefly on insects, which it captures on the ground or picks off leaves and branches.

It breeds in the Himalayas during April and May. The nest is usually placed on some rocky ridge or crevice, or in some decayed stump of a tree. The eggs are 4 in number, and longish oval, in color pale reddish buff, faintly freckled with dingy; size 0·93 × 0·71.

271. Niltava vivida, (*Swinhoe*). *Sharpe, Cat. B. Br. Mus.* iv. p. 463; *Oates, B. Burm.* i. p. 297. Cyornis vivida, *Swinhoe, Ibis,* i. 864, p. 363; *Hume and Dav., Str. F.* 1878, p. 229; *Hume, Str. F.* viii. p. 92.—SWINHOE'S RUFOUS-BELLIED BLUE-CHAT.

Whole upper plumage, lesser wing coverts and sides of the neck deep purplish blue, becoming ultramarine on the head, rump and upper tail coverts; a narrow frontal line, lores, and feathers in front of the eye black; cheeks and ear coverts blue-black; *chin and throat bluish black,* the rest of under surface chestnut; central tail feathers blue, the rest black, broadly margined on the outer web with blue; quills black, washed externally with purplish blue; lesser and median wing coverts the same; under wing coverts chestnut; bill black; legs and feet dark brown or purplish plumbeous; irides deep brown.

Length.—5·7 to 6 inches; wing 3·25 to 3·5; tail 2·65 to 3; tarsus 0·75; culmen 0·5.

The female is olive brown above, with a grey shade on the mantle; the lores, feathers at the base of the upper mandible and round the eye are mixed ferruginous and grey; crown olive brown washed with blue; median and greater coverts and quills are brown, margined externally with a shade of blue; tail brown, margined externally with ferruginous; chin and throat ochraceous buff; under wing and under tail coverts the same; rest of under surface ashy, tinged with ochraceous; the centre of abdomen whitish.

Hab.—Formosa and the Tenasserim Province of British Burmah.

Swinhoe's Rufous-bellied Chat was obtained by Davison on the Mooleyit Mountain in Tenasserim. It extends to China. According to Davison this species moves about on the tops of trees by short flights. He always saw them singly.

272. Niltava grandis, (*Blyth*). *Jerd. B. Ind.* i. p. 476, No. 316*; *Hume, Nests and Eggs*, p. 215; *Bl. B. Burm.* p. 102; *Hume, Str. F.* v. p. 103; *Hume and Dav.* vi. p. 232; *Sharpe, Cat. B. Br. Mus.* iv. p. 464; *Hume, Str. F.* viii. p. 93; *Oates, B. Burm.* i. p. 297. Chaitaris grandis, *Blyth, J, A. S. B.* xi. p. 189.—The LARGE FAIRY BLUE-CHAT.

Above dark purplish blue; the forehead, crown, nape, rump, upper tail coverts, lesser and median wing coverts and a large spot on each side of the neck brilliant smalt-blue; lores, feathers above the eye, sides of face and entire throat and fore neck black; greater coverts and quills black, narrowly margined externally with blue. Central tail feathers purplish blue; rest brown, margined externally with blue; under surface of body dusky black, tinged with purplish, the under tail coverts edged with white; bill black; legs reddish black; iris dark brown.

Length.—7·5 to 8 inches; wing 4·2; tail 3·6; tarsus 0·9; culmen 0 7.

The female is brown above, tinged with fulvous; the tail is chestnut brown; forehead, sides of the head, chin and throat bright fulvous brown, mottled with dusky; under surface ochraceous brown, tinged with ashy on the abdomen.

Hab.—The Himalayas, extending into the Burmese countries and to Sikkim and Nepaul.

The Large Fairy Blue-Chat is found in the hill tracts of Eastern Bengal. Jerdon says it is common about Darjeeling, and Mr. Davison says it is not uncommon on the Mooleyit Mountain and its spurs. In Assam, too, it is fairly common. It is quite a forest bird, seen only on trees, dry brushwood, and even fallen trees. It occasionally catches insects on the wing. According to Hodgson it lays during April and May. Nest massive, composed of green moss and lichen, and lined with fine moss roots. Eggs, four in number, of a buffy color. In size they average 1·0 x 0·73.

273. Niltava leucoprocta, (*Tweed.*) *Wardlaw-Ramsay, Tweed. Mem. App.* p. 668; *Oates, B. Br. Burm.* i. p. 298. Trichastoma leucoproctum, *Tweed. P. Z. S.* 1877, p. 366; *Hume, Str. F.* vii. p. 318. Niltava leucura, *Ann. Nat. Hist. Ser.* 4, xx. p. 95. Muscitrea cyanea, *Hume, Str. F.* v. p. 101; *Hume, Str. F.* vi. p. 207; *id. Str. F.* vii. p. 318, viii. p. 91.—The WHITE-TAILED BLUE-CHAT.

Nasal plumes and lores black; forehead, crown, nape and a small patch on the wing coverts near the edge of the wing cobalt blue; upper plumage and wing coverts deep blue; quills dark brown, edged with blue; four central feathers dull blue; the next pair dark brown, edged with blue and with a long streak of white on the outer web; the next two pairs brown on the outer webs and almost entirely white on the inner webs; the outermost pair brown, merely white at the base; sides of the head and neck, chin and throat, dull blue; *abdomen and sides of the body bluish grey;* vent and under tail coverts pure white; under wing coverts ashy.

The female has the nasal plumes and lores reddish brown; the upper plumage olive brown tinged with rufous; wing coverts and quills dark brown, margined with rufous; tail the same, the white on the feathers the same as in the male, except that the outermost feathers are broadly edged with white on the inner web; chin, throat, breast and sides of the body rufous olive; foreneck with a large patch of white; centre of abdomen whitish; vent and under tail coverts white; under wing coverts and axillaries rufous ashy; bill black; legs light brown; irides deep brown. (Limborg.)

Length.—7 inches; tail 3; wing 3·6; tarsus 0·9; bill from gape 1. (Oates.)

Hab.—Tenasserim, where it was procured by Mr. Limborg; at Taoo and on the Mooleyit Range at elevations of 5,000 and 2,000 feet. It is, according to Davison, an eminently forest bird. It has the habit of rapidly expanding its tail, thus showing the white on it.

274. Niltava macgrigoriæ, (*Burton.*) *Jerd. B. Ind.* i. p. 475, No. 315; *Hume, Nests, and Eggs*, p. 214; *Wald in Bl. B. Burm.* p. 102; *Hume and Dav., Str. F.* vi. p 231; *Sharpe, Cat. B. Br. Mus.* iv. p. 465; *Hume, Str. F.* viii. p. 93; Phœnicura macgrigoriæ, *Burton, P. Z. S.* 1835, p. 152. Niltava vivida, *Hume, Str. F.* ii. p. 475.—The SMALL FAIRY BLUE-CHAT.

Above rich purplish blue; forehead, eyebrow, rump, upper tail coverts and a spot on each side of the neck brilliant rich cobalt; lores, sides of face, feathers above the eye and entire throat deep purple; lesser wing coverts purplish blue; median coverts and quills black, edged externally with purplish blue; tail feathers deep purplish blue, all but the centre feathers black on the inner web; lower plumage ashy, becoming albescent on the abdomen and under tail coverts; under wing coverts and axillaries pure white; bill black; legs reddish black; iris dark brown.

The adult female is plain olivaceous above, lighter below, with a neck patch of light lavender blue.

Length.—4·6 to 4·8 inches; wing 2·6; tail 2·15; tarsus 0·7; culmen 0·6.

Hab.—The Himalayas up to Simla in the N. W. Provinces, also Oudh, the hills of Eastern Bengal, Assam, Sikkim, British Burmah and Nepaul.

Jerdon says it is common at Simla and about Darjeeling, and, according to Oates, has been recorded from Arrakan and Tenasserim by Blyth. According to Hume (Nests and Eggs) it breeds in Nepaul and Sikkim from April to June at from 3,000 to 5,000 feet. The nests are placed on the ground and are composed of soft moss of different kinds. Eggs 3 to 4 in number.

Family.—TURDIDÆ.

Bill slender but rather wide and depressed; *wing long and flat, with a very small bastard primary not more than half the length of the second,* the latter generally longer than the secondaries. Composed of birds generally migratory.

Sub-family.—SYLVIINÆ—Grey Warblers.

The young in first plumage differ very slightly in color from the adult, both being unspotted both above and below. In rare instances in which the upper parts are spotted in the adult the spots are less conspicuous in the young. (Seebohm.)

Gen. Sylvia.—*Scop.*

Bill Sylviinæ, generally with more or less dark underneath; nostrils in a groove. Tail nearly even, generally with white on the outermost tail feathers; bastard primary not extending beyond the primary coverts, or not more than 0·3; 2nd primary generally shorter than the 3rd and 4th; feet and tarsus stout, latter scutellated in front. The males of many have dark heads.

275. Sylvia cinerea, *Bechst. Orn. Taschenb.* i. p. 170; *Tem. Man. d'Orn.* p. 112; *Gray Gen. B.* i. p. 174; *Heugl. Orn. N. O. Afr.* i. p. 307; *Blf. Geol. and Zool. Abyss.* p. 379; *Shelley, B. Egypt,* p. 111. Curruca cinerea (*Bechst.*) *Gould B. Eur.* ii. pl. 125. Sylvia rufa, (*Bodd*) *Pl. E.* p. 35; *apud. Newt. ed. Yarr. B. Eur.* pt. I; *Hume, Str. F.* iii. 488; *Murray, Hdbk. Zool., &c., Sind,* p. 163; *Murray, Vert. Zool., Sind,* p. 162.—The European White-Throat.

"*Male.*—Over the eye is a streak of yellowish white. Head on the crown slate grey with a tinge of brown; neck on the sides pale brownish grey; on the back and nape, lighter greyish brown than the head; chin and throat silvery white, the latter has the feathers somewhat puffed out as when it is inflated in singing; breast above pale dull white, tinged with rose colour, and on the sides shaded off to yellowish white, and into greyish white below; back reddish brown, but tinged with olive on its lower part. The wings extend to within an inch and a half of the end of the tail. Expanse 8½ inches. The first primary extremely short; the 2nd and 3rd of equal length and the longest; edge of outer quill white; underneath grey; greater and lesser wing coverts reddish brown; primaries pale brown, narrowly edged with chestnut; the secondaries and tertiaries also pale brown, broadly edged with brighter chestnut than the former; tail somewhat rounded, graduated and brown; middle feathers margined lighter; outer feather on each side dull white over the greater portion or the whole of outer web, and often a portion of the inner; next two feathers tipped with the same. Tail underneath grey; upper tail-coverts inclining to olive brown; under tail coverts pale brownish white, with a tinge of faint rose red; legs pale rusty brown; toes darker with more of an olive tinge; claws dusky brown.

"*Length.*—5½ to 6 inches; bill bluish brown, base of under mandible yellowish brown, and the corners of the mouth yellowish green; iris brownish yellow. A winter visitant."—*Morris, Br. Bird*, vol. iii. p. 227.

Hab.—Europe, extending to Persia, Siberia and Turkestan; Sind, Punjab, N. W. Provinces, Bengal, Guzerat, Western, Central and Southern Africa.

276. Sylvia jerdoni, *Blyth, J. A. S. B.* xvi. p. 439; *Blf. East. Persia*, ii. p. 172; *Hume, Str. F.* i. p. 197, ii. 330; *Seebohm Monog. B. Br. Mus.* v. p. 16; *Murray, Vert. Zool., Sind*, p. 161.—THE EASTERN ORPHEAN WARBLER.

Adult Male.—General colour slaty grey; head, lores, and feathers behind the eye, ear coverts and nape sooty black; primaries and secondaries brown, their outer margins whitish, the secondaries edged at the tips with greyish white, as also some of the tertiaries; tail darker brown than the wings, the outermost feathers white on the outer web, and nearly one-half of the inner, the next two tipped white; in some specimens the centre feathers are margined very narrowly and tipped with fulvescent white; chin and throat white; belly, flanks, vent and under tail coverts greyish white, darker on the under tail coverts; bill dark brown; the base of the lower mandible pale yellowish; legs and feet dusky brown; irides hazel.

Length.—6·75 to 7 inches; wing 3 to 3·25; tail 2·75. The *Female* differs from the male in having the brown of the head less darker than the back.

Hab.—Northern, Southern and Western India, Sind, Punjab, N. W. Provinces, Beloochistan, S. E. Persia, Afghanistan, Turkestan, Kutch, Kattiawar; Jodhpore, Jeypore, North Guzerat, Mount Aboo and Deccan. Breeds in Persia and Turkestan; winters in Arabia and the plains of India.

277. Sylvia affinis, *Blyth, Cat. B. Mus. As. Soc.* p. 187; *Hume, Str. F.* vii. p. 60; i. 197; ii. 332; iii. 272; *Jerd. B. Ind.* ii. 209, No. 582; *Murray, Hdbk., Zool., &c., Sind*, p. 163. Sylvia curruca, *apud. Jerd. B. Ind.* ii. p. 209; *apud. Blf. East. Persia*, ii. p. 175; *Murray, Vert. Zool., Sind*, p. 161.—THE ALLIED GREY WARBLER.

General colour pale slaty or brownish grey; supercilium indistinct; wings and tail brownish; outermost tail feather on each side white on their outer webs; chin, throat, belly, and under tail-coverts, also axillaries and under wing coverts, white, tinged greyish brown on the breast and flanks; bill and legs brown; irides light brown.

Sylvia minuscula.

Mintern Bros. lith.

Length.—6 inches; wing 2·5; tail 2·25; bill at front 0·51.

Hab.—Nearly all India and Ceylon, Sind, Punjab, N. W. Provinces, Behar, Deccan, Kutch, Guzerat, Kattiawar, Jodhpore and Sambhur; also Beloochistan, Persia, S. Afghanistan and Turkestan. Seebohm says it breeds throughout Siberia, extending northwards almost to the limit of forest growth.

278. Sylvia althea, *Hume, Str. F.* vii. p. 60; *Seebohm, Cat. B. Br. Mus.* vol. v. p. 20; Sylvia affinis, *Blyth apud. Jerd. B. Ind.* vol. ii. p. 209; *apud. Legge, B. Ceylon,* p. 538; *Murray, Vert. Zool., Sind,* p. 162.—THE HIMALAYAN LESSER WHITE-THROAT.

Upper surface darkish grey, slightly tinged with brown on the back. Under surface white; 2nd primary intermediate in length between, or equal to 6th and 7th, or 7th and 8th; wing 2·7 to 2·8; culmen 0·56 to 0·51; tarsus 0·8 to 0·75.

Hab.—Sind, Punjab, N. W. Provinces, Oudh, Deesa, Concan and Deccan. A winter visitant.

279. Sylvia minuscula, *Hume, Str. F.* i. 198; vii. 58 *et seq.*; viii. pp. 103, 388, 498; *Seebohm, Cat. B. Br. Mus.* vol. v. p. 20, pl. 1; *Murray, Vert. Zool., Sind,* p. 161.—HUME'S LESSER WHITE-THROAT.

PLATE.

Forehead and crown pale bluish grey; back, rump and upper tail coverts isabelline fawn, or pale sandy brown; chin, throat and under surface white; 2nd primary equal to the 7th, in some intermediate between 7th and 8th; wing 2·3 to 2·45.

Hab.—Sind, Beloochistan, Afghanistan, Punjab, N. W. Provinces, Rajputana, Kutch and Guzerat.

280. Sylvia nana, *Hempr. et Ehr. Symb. Phys. Aves.* fol. c. c.; *Gray, Handlist B.* p. 212; *Heugl. Orn. N. O. Afr.* i. p. 306; *Dresser, Ibis,* 1876, p. 80; *Blf. East. Pers.* ii. p. 187; *Str. F.* i. 199; ii. 330; *Murray, Hdbk., Zool. &c., Sind,* p. 164; *Seebohm, Cat. B. Br. Mus.* v. p. 26. Sylvia delicatula, *Hartlaub. Ibis,* 1859, p. 340, pl. x. fig. i.; *Blyth, Ibis,* 1867, p. 28; *Hume, Ibis,* 1869, p. 355; *Str. F.* i. p. 199; *Murray, Vert. Zool., Sind,* p. 163.—THE DESERT WARBLER.

"The lores are greyish white; from the nostrils to the upper margin of the eye runs a very narrow yellowish streak, whiter and less grey than the lores; this line ceases to be visible in nine out of ten skins, but is sufficiently apparent in the freshly killed bird. A circle of yellowish white feathers surrounds the eye; forehead, crown, occiput, nape, back and scapulars pale fawn brown; rump and upper tail coverts pale rufous; central tail feathers pale rufous, with dark shafts; external lateral feathers wholly white; next pair white on the outer webs, and with a moderately broad white tip to both webs, the rest of the inner webs dark hair brown; the rest of the feathers dark hair brown, margined on the outer webs with pale rufous. The whole of the lower parts white, with, in the freshly-killed birds, a just perceptible rufescent tinge; wing lining and axillaries pure white; wing pale brown, narrowly margined and tipped with rufescent white; the tertiaries pale dingy rufescent with brown shafts.

"*Length.*—4·8 to 4·9 inches; expanse 7 to 7·2; tail from vent 1·8 to 2; wing 2 to 2·2; wing when closed reach to within 1 to 1·2 of end of tail; bill at front 0·3 to 0·33; tarsus 0·8; irides yellow to orange yellow; legs and feet pale yellow, in some very pale lemon yellow; claws dusky; bill pale yellow, dusky, or horny grey on culmen and at tip." (*Hume, Str. F.* i. p. 199.)

Hab.—Sind, Beloochistan, Kokand, Southern Persia and Algiers; also Punjab, N. W. Provinces and Rajputana. Breeds in Turkestan. In Sind it is a winter visitant, affecting arid plains, and sides of hills wherever there is an abundance of scrubby vegetation.

281. Sylvia familiaris, *Menetries, Cat. Rais. Cauc.* p. 32; *Seebohm. Monog. B. Br. Mus.* v. p. 36. Aedon familiaris (*Menetr.*) *Gray, Gen. B.* i. p. 173; *id. Handlist B.* i. p. 211; *Dresser, B. Eur.* pt. xxxii.; *Hume, Str. F.* iii. p. 476; *Murray, Hdbk., Zool. &c., Sind,* p. 151; *Murray, Vert. Zool., Sind,* p. 163;—The Grey-backed Warbler.

The following is Mr. Hume's description of Indian specimens, *ex* "*Stray Feathers,*" vol. iii. p. 477.

"A broad superciliary stripe from the nostrils over and for some little distance behind the eyes dull white or yellowish white; a brown stripe from the nostrils to the anterior angle of the eye, continued backwards, though not conspicuous, for some distance from the posterior angle; forehead, crown, occiput, sides of the neck, entire back and wing dull earthy brown, paler and more drabby in some; quills and coverts margined and narrowly tipped with dull yellowish or brownish white, with usually a slight rufescent tinge on the margins of the primaries. Rump brownish chestnut; upper tail coverts and tail chestnut; central tail feathers more or less brown on one or both webs; all the other tail feathers with a conspicuous subterminal dark brown band (which in the outer feathers runs some distance down the outer web) and tipped, the two pairs next the centre narrowly with rufescent, and the other three successively more and more broadly with pure white. Chin and throat sordid white, with an indication of a darker line at the angle of the gape; ear coverts and the rest of the lower parts similar, but tinged with a faint brownish shade usually; wing lining and axillaries with a very faint yellowish salmon tint; inner margins of quills, on the lower surface, with a decided buffy salmon tinge.

Length.—Male, 6·5 inches; expanse 9·75; tail from vent 2·62; wing 3·3; tarsus 0·97; bill at front 0·77; bill at gape 0·87.

Length.—Female, 7·5 inches; expanse 10·62; tail 2·62; wing 3·5; tarsus 1·03; bill at front 1·08; bill from gape 0·93; mid-toe and claw 0·87; hind-toe and claw 0·56.

"The first quill is about 0·75 long; the third quill is longest; the second and fourth, which are nearly equal, about 0·06 shorter; the fifth about 0·25 shorter, tail somewhat rounded; outer tail feathers about 0·35, shorter than those next the central pair, which latter are shorter than those next them by about 0·15; the frontal feathers are prolonged over the base of the bill, extending laterally quite to the nostrils; legs and feet dusky or livid fleshy; irides dark brown; bill dusky brown; lower mandible yellowish, fleshy at the base."

Hab.—Afghanistan, Beloochistan, Persia, Sind, Kutch, Jodhpore and North Guzerat, visiting Sind in the course of its migration about the middle of September.

Gen. **Phylloscopus.**—*Boie*; Willow-Warblers.

Bill Acrocephaline, pale underneath, slender, small, straight, with a few short rictal bristles; wings long, flat, and pointed, or short and rounded as in those which inhabit the plains and breed in the mountains near by; bastard primary small; greater wing coverts with pale tips in the spring plumage; *axillaries and under wing coverts yellow.*

This genus comprises a group of birds, mostly of small size, familiarly known as Willow or Tree Warblers, tolerably abundant throughout India during winter—a very few only of which are known to breed in the Himalayas. They are exclusively fly-catchers or insectivorous, feeding on minute insects and flies, which they pick off leaves and branches or capture in the air, and may be said to be strictly arboreal. The majority have their summer residence in Europe or Western Asia, and migrate thousands of miles in winter. Seebohm says: "In their breeding range these birds are palæarctic, ranging from the Atlantic to the Pacific, one species being known even to cross Behring's Straits into Alaska." Those which breed in the Himalayas ascend till they reach a palæarctic climate.

No mesial line on the crown.

282. Phylloscopus borealis, (*Blas.*) *Seebohm, Ibis*, 1877, p. 69; *Dresser, B. Eur.* ii. p. 509; *Hume and Dav.*, vi. p. 352; *Hume, Str. F.* viii. p. 102; *Seebohm, Ibis*, 1879, p. 9; *id. Cat. B. Br. Mus.* v. p. 40; *Oates, Str. F.* x. p. 222; *id. B. Burm.* i. p. 77. Phyllopneuste borealis, *Blas. Naum.* 1858, p. 313.—The Arctic Willow-Warbler.

Above olive green, lighter or somewhat yellow on the rump; wing coverts brown, the outer webs margined with olive greeen; median and greater coverts with yellowish white tips forming two bars, a well-defined narrow yellow or greyish white eye stripe extending to the nape; lores and feathers behind the eye brown; ear coverts olive mingled with yellowish; under wing coverts and axillaries, also the thighs, pale yellow; tail brown, the outer webs olive green, the inner webs except the central feathers brown, margined with greyish white; under surface of body white, slightly suffused with yellow; bill Acrocephaline; upper mandible dark brown, under mandible pale; iris dark brown; legs and feet brown; 2nd primary intermediate in length between the 5th and 6th; 3rd and 4th longest; 1st primary 0·3 to 0·45.

Length.—4·8 inches; wing 2·5 to 2·7; tail 2; tarsus 0·8; culmen 0·68.

In summer the upper parts become greyer, the olive green margins to the wing and tail feathers and the tips to the wing coverts disappear, and the under surface is nearly pure white.

Hab.—The Arctic Willow-Warbler is a winter visitor to Burmah. It has been found in Pegu and Kyeikpadien and in the southern half of Tenasserim at Bankasoon and Malewoon. It extends down the Malay Peninsula and Archipelago as far as Timor and Flores, also Cochin-China. On the Andaman Island it has also been procured, but no where north or west of Burmah.

Mr. Seebohm found the nest in Siberia. It was built on the ground in a wood thinly scattered with trees, and was placed in a recess on the side of a tussock or mound of grass. It was semi-domed, the outside being composed of moss and the inside of fine dry grass. The eggs, five in number, were white, profusely spotted all over with pale pink.

283. Phylloscopus nitidus, *Blyth, J. A. S. B.* xii. p. 965; xiv. p. 591; *Jerd. B. Ind.* ii. p. 193, No. 559; *Hume, Str. F.* 1873, p. 197; *Legge, Ibis,* 1874, p. 22; *Seebohm, Ibis,* 1877, p. 72; *id. Cat. B. Br. Mus.* v. p. 43; *Murray, Hdbk., Zool. &c., Sind,* p. 162; *Murray, Vert. Zool., Sind,* p. 159. Phyllopneuste nitida, (*Blyth*) *Adam, Str. F.* 1873, p. 382.—The GREEN WILLOW-WARBLER.

Head, nape, back, scapulars, rump and upper tail coverts yellowish green; supercilium extending to the nape yellow; lesser wing coverts and tips and edges of the median ones like the back; greater wing coverts brown, edged with yellowish green and tipped yellow, forming a conspicuous wing band; primaries, their coverts and secondaries brown, edged on their outer webs with yellowish green; 2nd primary intermediate in length between 6th and 7th; exposed 1st primary 0·55 to 0·6; edge of the wing, under wing coverts and *entire under surface yellow or yellowish green*; in some specimens albescent on the chin; bill dusky brown; the lower mandible pale; legs light brown; irides dark brown.

Length.—4·5 to 4·75 inches; wing 2·5; bill at front 0·5.

Hab.—Sind, Punjab, N. W. Provinces, Oudh, Bengal, Concan, Deccan, Southern India, Ceylon, and Nepaul; breeding in the Himalayas and wintering in the plains.

284. Phylloscopus viridanus, *Blyth, J. A. S. B.* xii. p. 967; *Jerd. B. Ind.* ii. p. 193, No. 560; *Brooks, Ibis,* 1872, p. 31; *Scully, Str. F.* iv. p. 148; *Seebohm, Ibis,* 1877, p. 73; *Hume, Str. F.* vi. p. 356. Phyllopneuste viridanus, *Blyth and Wald., B. Burm.* p. 105. Phylloscopus seebohmi, *Hume, Str. F.* v. p. 355.—The INDIAN WILLOW-WARBLER.

Similar to *Phylloscopus nitidus,* except that the quills are narrowly tipped with pale white and that the *greater coverts only are tipped with pale yellowish white,* and so forming only one wing bar; 3rd, 4th and 5th primaries longest; 2nd intermediate in length between 7th and 8th, sometimes between 6th and 7th; 2nd primary 0·5 to 0·65.

Length.—4 inches; wing 2·3 to 2·5; tarsus 0·75; culmen 0·45 to 0·5.

Hab.—The Himalayas up to Cashmere, where it breeds. In winter it is found all over India nearly. It has been recorded from Arrakan, in Tenasserim at Thatone, Moulmein, and Tavoy, and extends through the Indo-Burmese countries to Cochin-China. In India proper it is recorded as having occurred in the N. W. Provinces, Oudh and Bengal, also Rajputana and Southern India; also from Nepaul. Mr. Brooks found its nest in Cashmere at an elevation of 11,000 feet. It was a domed structure, placed on the steep bank side of a ravine full of birch trees, but it did not contain eggs.

285. Phylloscopus plumbeitarsus, *Swinh., Ibis,* 1861, p. 330; *Seebohm, Ibis,* 1877, p. 76; *Hume and Dav.* vi. p. 355; *Brooks, Str. F.* vii. p. 508; *Hume, Str. F.* viii. p. 385; *Bingham, Str. F.* ix. p. 187; *Seebohm, Cat. B. Br. Mus.* v. p. 45. Phyllopneuste plumbeitarsus, *David et. Oust. Ois Chine,* p. 270.—MINDENDORFF'S WILLOW-WARBLER.

Similar to *Phylloscopus viridanus,* except that the greater and median coverts are pale tipped and form two bars on the wing; the ear coverts are greenish yellow, and the under plumage *pale greyish yellow;* bill pale yellow on lower mandible, brown on the upper.

Length.—4·2 inches; wing 2·2; tail 1·7; tarsus 0·7; culmen 0·6; 2nd primary intermediate in length between 7th and 8th, occasionally equals the 8th; 1st primary 0·5 to 0·7. *Legs plumbeous.*

Hab.—British Burmah. According to Oates it is a very common winter visitor to Pegu.

Mr. Davison obtained it in December near Moulmein, and Captain Bingham observed it in the Thoungyeen Valley. It passes through China on migration, and appears to summer in Turkestan and Southern Siberia. It frequents thickly foliaged trees. Nothing is known of its nidification.

286. Phylloscopus tenellipes, *Swinh.*, *Ibis*, 1860, p. 53; *Seebohm*, *Ibis*, 1877, p. 75; *Brooks*, *Str. F.* iv. p. 276; *Hume and Dav.*, *Str. F.* vi. pp. 354, 517; *Hume*, *Str. F.* viii. p. 102; *Seebohm*, *Cat. B. Br. Mus.* v. p. 46; *Oates*, *Str. F.* x. p. 222; *id. B. Br. Burm.*, i. p. 81.—The Pale-legged Willow-Warbler.

Above olive brown, suffused with buff, especially on the rump; a buffish white narrow eye streak extending to the nape; lores and feathers behind the eye blackish; ear coverts mingled buff and brown; wings brown, edged with olive brown; the median and the greater coverts tipped with buff, forming two distinct wing bars. Under surface of body white, suffused with buff, especially on the flanks and vent.

Tail feathers brown, externally margined with pale buffish brown, and the inside webs with buffish white.

Bill Acrocephaline; upper mandible dark brown, lower mandible pale iris brown; *legs, feet and claws pale flesh colour*; 3rd, 4th and 5th primaries longest; 2nd equal to the 7th; 1st primary 0·5 to 0·53.

In autumn plumage the olive brown of the upper parts is replaced by russet brown, the eye stripe and under surface more suffused with buff.

Length.—5·15 inches; wing 2·2 to 2·67; tail 2; tarsus 0·73; bill from gape 0·65.

Hab.—British Burmah and southwards in the Malay Peninsula. It is also recorded from Cochin-China, Amoy, and Pekin. Oates says the Pale-legged Willow-Warbler is a winter visitor to Burmah, but a comparatively rare one. It was obtained by Davison in various parts of Tenasserim. It is said to breed in Japan. Habits the same as other *Phylloscopi.*

287. Phylloscopus magnirostris, *Blyth*, *J. A. S. B.* xii. p. 966; *Jerd. B. Ind.* ii. p. 191, No. 556; *Brooks*, *Str. F.* iii. p. 243; *Seebohm*, *Ibis*, 1877, p. 77; *Hume and Dav.*, *Str. F.* vi. p. 355; *Hume*, *Str. F.* viii. p. 102; *Seebohm*, *Cat. B. Br. Mus.* v. p. 47; *Oates*, *B. Br. Burm.* i. p. 82. Phyllopneuste magnirostris, *Bl. B. Burm.* p. 105.—The Large-billed Willow-Warbler.

Above dark olive green, slightly darker on the head and somewhat greener on the rump; eye stripe pale yellowish white; lores and feathers behind the eye brown; ear coverts yellowish white, suffused with brown; wing coverts and wings brown, edged with olive; the median coverts with small and the greater coverts with large yellowish white tips, forming two distinct wing bars; tail brown, edged with olive green on the outer webs and tipped paler beneath; the inner webs, except those of the central tail feathers, with a narrow greyish white margin. Under surface of body pale greyish yellow, greyest on the breast and flanks; axillaries, under wing coverts and thighs greyish yellow. Bill much decurved at tip, the rictal bristles well developed; upper mandible dark brown, under mandible pale, darker towards the tip; legs, feet and claws bluish brown; 4th and 5th primaries longest; 2nd intermediate between 7th and 8th, 1st primary 0·6 to 0·75.

Length.—5.4 inches; wing 2·7; tail 2·2; bill from gape 0·65.

Hab.—The Punjab, N. W. Provinces, Oudh, Bengal, Central India, the Central Provinces, Deccan, and South India, also British Burmah, Cashmere and Nepaul. It has been recorded from Arrakan by Blyth. Davison procured it in Tenasserim, and Mr. Hume records it from the Malay Peninsula. It is generally spread over the whole Peninsula of India, Ceylon, and the Andamans, and summers in the Himalayas up to Cashmere, where it breeds.

Mr. Brooks, who met with this species in the Himalayas, says: "The conditions this bird require are wooded cliffs or very steep rocky banks impracticable for man, and plenty of flowing water below. Above a roaring torrent it is in its element and sings most vigorously.

288. Phylloscopus lugubris, *Blyth, Ann. Nat. Hist.* xii. p. 98; *Blyth and Walden, B. Burm.*, p. 105; *Blyth, J. A. S. B.* xii. p. 968; *Jerd. B. Ind.* ii. p. 192, No. 558; *Seebohm, Ibis*, 1877, p. 78; *Hume, Str. F.* vi. p. 355; *Anders. Yunnan. Exped.* p. 624; *Hume, Str. F.* viii. p. 102; *Seebohm, Cat. B. Br. Mus.* v. p. 48; *Oates, B. Br. Burm.*, i. p. 83.—BLYTH'S WILLOW-WARBLER.

Closely allied to *Phylloscopus magnirostris*, being absolutely identical in colour and in its seasonal changes, and would scarcely be entitled to specific rank were it not that it appears to have a more eastern geographical range. It is somewhat smaller, with a more rounded wing; the 4th and 5th primaries are longest and the 2nd is equal to the 10th; 1st primary 0·7 to 0·8 inch.

Length.—5 inches; wing 2·4 to 2·6; tail 2·0 to 2·1; tarsus 0·75; culmen 0·45 to 0·62.

This is one of the most abundant species of the genus. It is found in the Eastern Himalayas, where it breeds, and as far west as Nepaul. It extends in winter to Assam and Lower Bengal. Jerdon records it from the Neilgherries, the Wynaad, Bengal and Sikkim. Round Pegu Oate's says it is very common. Dr. Armstrong got it at Elephant Point, Mr. Davison in the northern half of the Tenasserim Division, and Dr. Anderson procured it near Bhamo. Seebohm says it straggles in the winter to the Philippine Islands.

Like the last this species is entirely arboreal in its habits, affecting the high tree tops.

A pale mesial line on the crown.

289. Phylloscopus occipitalis, (*Blyth*). *Seebohm, Cat. B. Br. Mus.* v. p. 150. Phyllopneuste occipitalis, (*Jerd.*) *fide. Blyth J. A. S. B.* xiv. p. 593. Reguloides occipitalis, (*Jerd*). *fide Jerd., B. Ind.* ii. p. 196, No. 563; *Brooks, Ibis,* 1869, p. 457; *Cock and Marsh, Str. F.* 1873, p. 355; *Hume, Nests and Eggs, Ind. B.* p. 362. Phylloscopus occipitalis, (*Jerd*). *fide Seebohm, Ibis,* 1877, p. 80.—JERDON'S CROWNED WILLOW-WARBLER.

Above olive green, slightly yellower on the rump and upper tail coverts; a well-defined narrow yellowish white eye stripe from the base of the bill to the nape on each side, and a pale rather broader mesial one on the crown, the interspaces dark olive green; wing coverts olive green; the median and greater series with greyish white tips, forming two pale bars across each wing; quills brown, tipped narrowly with greyish white, externally edged with yellowish green and emarginated as far as the sixth primary; tail brown, externally edged with yellowish green, and, except the two central feathers, the inner webs have a narrow well-defined greyish white margin; under surface greyish white, very slightly suffused with yellow, greyest on the breast and flanks; axillaries, under wing coverts and thighs pale yellow; bill Acrocephaline; upper mandible dark brown; under mandible pale, slightly darker towards the tip; legs, feet and claws dark brown; 3rd, 4th and 5th primaries nearly equal and longest; 2nd intermediate between 7th and 8th; 1st primary 0·55 to 0·7.

Length.—4·75 to 5 inches; wing 2·65 to 2·7; culmen 0·5 to 0·6.

The summer plumage is greyer on the upper parts, the lower parts become abraded, the light tips to the quills and wing coverts also become abraded, and the yellowish green edgings greyer. The autumn plumage is rather brighter everywhere, otherwise it is similar to that of the summer.

Hab.—The Punjab, N. W. Provinces, Oudh and Bengal, also British Burmah (Tenasserim Province), Cashmere and Nepaul.

Jerdon's Willow-Warbler breeds in Cashmere and throughout the Himalayas generally during the latter half of May, June and the first half of July from 4,000 to 8,000 feet. The nests are placed in holes under the stump of a tree, or steep bank sides. Eggs 4 to 5 in number, pure white, 0·65 × 0·5 inch.

290. Phylloscopus coronatus, (*Temm.*) *Swinhoe, Ibis,* 1863, p. 93; *Seebohm, Ibis,* 1877, p. 79; *id. Cat. B. Br. Mus.* v. p. 49; *Oates, B. Br. Burm.*, i. p. 84. Ficedula coronata, *Tem. et Schleg. Faun. Jap. Aves.* p. 48, pl. xviii. Phyllopneuste coronata, *David. et Oust. Ois Chine,* p. 269. Reguloides coronata, *Hume and Dav., Str. F.* vi. p. 356; *Hume, Str. F.* viii. p. 102.—TEMMINCK'S CROWNED WILLOW-WARBLER.

Upper plumage olive green, the head suffused with dusky; a yellowish white mesial line on the crown, and another on each side from the base of the bill to the nape; lores and feathers behind the eye brown; ear coverts mixed yellowish and dusky; wings and wing coverts brown, externally margined with yellowish green; the median and greater coverts tipped with yellowish, forming two wing bars; tail olive brown, externally margined with yellowish green, and, except the two centre feathers, narrowly margined on the inner webs with greyish white; under surface white suffused with yellow, the breast and flanks greyish; under wing coverts, axillaries, thighs and *under tail coverts pale yellow.* The summer plumage is duller. Upper mandible brown, lower mandible yellowish; mouth yellow; legs and feet plumbeous.

Length.—5·2 inches; tail 2·1; wing 2·4; tarsus 0·7; bill from gape 0·6; 1st primary 0·5 to 0·55 inch; 2nd primary longer than the 7th and shorter than the 6th.

Hab.—British Burmah, in the Pegu and Tenasserim Provinces; southwards down the Malay Peninsula as far as Java and Cochin-China. According to Seebohm it breeds in Japan in the valley of the Ussuri and in the sub-alpine districts of South East Persia. Its habits are not known.

291. Phylloscopus reguloides, *Blyth, J. A. S. B.* xi. p. 191; xii. p. 963; *Seebohm, Cat. B. Br. Mus.* v. p. 5. Reguloides trochiloides, (*Sund.*) *Jerd. B. Ind.* ii. p. 196, No. 564; *Hume, Str. F.* iii. p. 139; *Bl. and Wald. B. Burm.* p. 105; *Hume and Dav., Str. F.* vi. p. 358; *Hume, Str. F.* viii. p. 102; *Scully, Str. F.* viii. p. 307; *Brooks, Str. F.* x. p. 169. Reguloides viridipennis, (*Bl.*) *Jerd. B. Ind.* ii. p. 198, No. 567. Phylloscopus viridipennis, (*Bl.*) *Seebohm, Ibis,* 1877, p. 82. Phylloscopus flavolivacea, *Hume, Str. F.* v. p. 504; *Hume and Dav., Str. F.* vi. p. 358. Reguloides flavolivaceous, *Hume, Str. F.* viii. p. 102; ix. p. 291.—Blyth's Crowned Willow-Warbler.

An ill-defined coronal streak from the forehead to the nape, and a well-defined superciliary streak on each side pale yellowish. Upper parts olive green, slightly yellower on the rump and upper tail coverts; the interspaces on the crown dark olive; wings and wing coverts brown, edged externally with bright olive green; the median and greater coverts with yellow tips forming two conspicuous wing bars; quills brown, very narrowly tipped paler, and the outer webs margined with bright olive green; lores and feathers behind the eye brown; ear coverts mixed brown and yellowish; lower plumage greyish white, whiter on the belly, and more or less suffused with yellow; under wing coverts, axillaries and thighs bright yellow. In summer, as in all the *Phylloscopi*, the plumage is duller. Upper mandible dark brown; lower one with the gape and the edges of the upper mandible yellow; iris dark hazel; legs yellowish brown.

Length.—4·6 inches; wing 2·25 to 2·4 inches; tail 1·85 to 2·0; tarsus 0·7; bill from gape 0·6; 1st primary 0·6 inches in length, the 2nd about equal to the 10th; 3rd, 4th and 5th about equal and longest.

Hab.—The Himalayas from Nepaul eastwards, in the alpine districts of which it is supposed to breed. It winters in both the Indian and Burmah Peninsulas.

It has been recorded from the N. W. Provinces of India, also from Oudh, Bengal, British Burmah and Nepaul. Oates says it is common throughout Southern Pegu, and, quoting Davison, that it has been met with in Tenasserim. Dr. Armstrong procured it at Amherst. It is said to be common also from Cashmere eastwards, and to have occurred in China. Jerdon, under *R. trochiloides*, says he got it at Calcutta, and that Mr. Blyth has seen it from Dehra Doon, and again, under *R. viridipennis*, that he obtained it at Darjeeling. It is found on trees, searching the leaves for insects.

292. Phylloscopus viridipennis, *Blyth*, *J. A. S. B.* xxiv. p. 275; *Hume, Str. F.* v. p. 330; *Brooks and Hume, Str. F.* ix. pp. 290, 291; *Seebohm, Cat. B. Br. Mus.* v. p. 53. Phylloscopus presbytis, (*Mull.*) *Seebohm, Ibis*, 1877, p. 883. Reguloides viridipennis, (*Bl.*) *Hume, Str. F.* viii. p. 202.—WALLACE'S CROWNED WILLOW-WARBLER.

Similar to *Phylloscopus reguloides*, except that it is smaller and that the inner webs of the three outermost tail feathers on each side are white. The lower plumage, too, is more suffused with yellow. Bill dark brown, the lower mandible pale.

Length.—4·3 inches; wing 2·05 to 2·1; tail 1·7, tarsus 0·75; bill from gape 0·55; 2nd primary equal to the 10th; 1st 0·55 inch to 0·7; 4th and 5th primaries longest.

Hab.—British Burmah and southwards down the Malay Peninsula. Seebohm says it breeds in the mountains of British Burmah and winters in the plains, ranging also as far as Timor and probably also Sumatra. Mr. Davison procured it on the Mooleyit Mountain in Tenasserim, and he also found a nest in February. It was a globular structure, made of moss mingled with dry leaves and fibres, and lined with vegetable down. The nest was placed in a mass of creepers on the face of a rock, and contained 3 pure white eggs.

No bar across the wings; bill slender, depressed at base.

293. Phylloscopus tristis, *Blyth, J. A. S. B.* xii. p. 966; xiv. p. 59; *Jerd. B. Ind.* ii. p. 190, No. 554; *Dresser, B. Eur.* pt. lxvi. 1875; *Blf. East. Pers.* ii. p. 180; *Scully, Str. F.* iv. p. 148; *Seebohm, Ibis*, 1877, p. 97; 1879, p. 10; *id. Cat. B. Br. Mus.* v. 63; *Murray, Hdbk. Zool. &c., Sind*, p. 161. Phyllopneuste tristis, (*Blyth*) *Gould. B. Asia*, pt. xvii. Phylloscopus brehmi, *Homeyer, apud. Blf. East Persia*, ii. p. 182.—The SIBERIAN WILLOW-WARBLER.

Above dull earthy brown, with an olive green tinge on the lower back and rump; lores and behind the eye and ear coverts like the back; supercilium pale buffy white; wings brown, their coverts with pale margins, and the primaries and secondaries edged on their outer webs with greenish; edge of wing and under wing coverts yellow; tail brown, the feathers edged on their outer webs with yellowish green; the inner web faintly and narrowly margined with whitish; under surface albescent; bill dark brown; legs black; irides brown.

Length.—5 inches; wing 2·5; tail 2 to 2·3; culmen 0·45 to 0·48.

Hab.—Sind, Punjab, N. W. Provinces, Oudh, Bengal, Beloochistan, S. E. Persia, Afghanistan, and East Turkistan; Deccan, Kutch, Kattiawar, Jeypore, Jodhpore, and North Guzerat. In Sind, as in other parts of India, it is a winter visitor. According to Seebohm "The Siberian or Brown Tree Warbler breeds in the valleys of Petchora, the Obb and the Yennessee, extending northwards beyond the limits of forest-growth, and southwards as far as Perm in the west and Yennasaisk in the east. It passes across the Khirgiz steppes and Turkestan on migration, and winters in Beloochistan and the plains of India. It also breeds abundantly at Cashmere and in the mountains near Lake Baical."

294. Phylloscopus affinis, (*Tick.*) *Bly. J. A. S. B.* xvi. p. 442; *Jerd. B. Ind.* ii. p. 194, No. 561; *Blanf. J. A. S. B.* xli. pt. 2, p. 81; *Brooks, Ibis*, 1872, p. 31; *Godw.-Austen, J. A. S. B.* xlv. pt. 2, p. 80; *Hume and Dav., Str. F.* vi. p. 356; *Seebohm, Ibis*, 1877, p. 100; *id. Cat. B. Br. Mus.* v. p. 65. Motacilla affinis, *Tick., J. A. S. B.* ii. p. 576.—TICKELL'S WILLOW-WARBLER.

Upper parts olive brown, very slightly darker on the head; superciliary stripe deep yellow; wing and tail feathers brown, externally washed with olive brown, the former emarginated as far as the 6th quill; *under surface deep yellow*, shading into buffish yellow on the breast and flanks; axillaries and under wing coverts deep yellow. Bill Phylloscopine; upper mandible dark brown, lower pale brown; legs and feet brown; 3rd, 4th and 6th primaries longest, 2nd equal to the 9th or 10th; 1st primary about half the length of the second (0·7 to 0·8 inch).

Length.—4·5 inches; wing 2·2 to 2·4; tail 1·95 to 2·23; bill 0·46; tarsus 0·7.

Hab.—The Himalayas, from Cashmere to Sikkim and British Burmah. It is recorded from the N. W. Provinces, Bengal, South India, British Burmah and Nepaul. Jerdon says it is spread over all India; but this is not accurate, being absent from the Concan and Deccan and the drier parts of the Peninsula. He adds that a specimen was procured at Sikkim.

Tickell's Willow-Warbler is said to breed in the Himalayas from Cashmere to Burmah.

295. Phylloscopus tytleri, *Brooks, Ibis,* 1872, p. 237; *Hume, Nests and Eggs, Ind. B.* p. 362; *id. Str. F.* iii. p. 279; *Seebohm, Ibis,* 1877, p. 101; *id, Cat. B. Br. Mus.* v. p. 66.—TYTLER'S WILLOW-WARBLER.

Above olive brown, shading into greenish olive on the rump; superciliary stripe narrow, greyish white, not extending quite to the nape; quills and tail feathers brown, externally margined with greenish olive; under surface yellowish white, greyish on the breast and flanks; axillaries and under wing coverts yellow; *bill very long and slender,* dark brown, paler on the under mandible; legs dark brown; 3rd, 4th and 5th primaries longest; second intermediate between 8th and 9th; 1st less than half the length of the 2nd; 0·55 to 0·68.

Length.—4·5 to 4·7 inches; wing 2·35 to 2·43 inches; tail 1·7 to 1·9; culmen 0·5.

Hab.—South India (?) Nepaul. It breeds in Cashmere and winters in India. The nest is deep and solidly built, composed of grass, fibres, moss, and lichen, thickly lined with hair and feathers; eggs 4, pure white, 0·58 × 0·45.

Two bars across the wings; upper mandible dark; generally a pale mesial line on the crown.

296. Phylloscopus humii, *Brooks, Str. F.* vii. p. 131; *Seebohm, Cat. B. Br. Mus.* v. p. 67; Abrornis tenuiceps, *Hodgs. MSS. B. of Nepaul.* Reguloides superciliosus (*Gmel.*), *Brooks, Ibis,* 1869, p. 236; *id. Ibis,* 1872, p. 24.—HUME'S BARRED WILLOW-WARBLER.

Above olive, browner on the head and greener on the rump; *a well defined buff eye stripe extends from the base of the bill to the nape*; sometimes (rarely) slight traces of a mesial line are visible; lores and the space behind the eye brownish olive; wing coverts brown, the lesser wing coverts with broad olive green margins; the median wing coverts with obscure pale tips and the greater series with broad well defined buffish yellow tips forming a conspicuous pale bar across each wing; quills brown; all the secondaries and four or five of the primaries narrowly tipped with greyish white; outside webs of the quills edged with yellowish green and emarginated as far as the sixth; tail feathers the same, but the inner webs with a narrow greyish white margin; under parts greenish yellow, nearly white on the throat and shading into buff on the flanks; inner margin of quills nearly white. Bill dark brown, under mandible paler at base; legs and feet dark brown; 4th primary slightly the longest; second intermediate between 8th and 9th, occasionally between the 7th and 8th, or 9th and 10th; 1st primary 0·45 to 0·55 inch.

Length.—2·38 to 2·45 inches; wing 2·01 to 2·3; tail 1·5 to 1·8; culmen 0·4 to 0·45.

Hab.—Afghanistan, Punjab, N. W. Provinces, Oudh, Bengal, Rajputana, Central India and the Central Provinces to Nepaul and Cashmere, and probably also British Burmah.

Wherever Hume's Barred Willow-Warbler occurs it is fairly numerous, affecting both high trees and shrubby jungles. It breeds in Cashmere at 8,000 feet. The nest is globular, composed of coarse grass, and placed on the side of a bank: it is usually lined with hair. Eggs, 4 or 5 in number, 0·56 × 0·44, white, and profusely spotted with red.

297. Phylloscopus superciliosus, (*Gmel.*) *Seebohm, Cat. B. Br. Mus.* v. p. 68; *Dresser, B. Eur.* pt. xxx. 1874; *Seebohm. Ibis,* 1877, Motacilla superciliosus, *Gmel. Syst. Nat.* i. p. 975; *Oates, B. Br. Burm.* i. p. 87. Reguloides superciliosus, *Bl. B. Burm.* p. 106; *Armstrong, Str. F.* iv. p. 329; *Hume and Dav., Str. F.* vi. p. 358; *Brooks, Str. F.* vii. pp. 128, 236, 475; *Hume, Str. F.* viii. p. 102; *Brooks, Str. F.* viii. p. 393. Reguloides proregulus, (*Pall.*) *Jerd. B. Ind.* ii. p. 197, No. 566.—The YELLOW-BROWED BARRED WILLOW-WARBLER.

Upper plumage olive green, yellower on the rump and upper tail coverts; a well defined supercilium reaching to the nape pale yellow; an indistinct pale yellow coronal streak also present and reaching to the nape; crown of the head slightly darker than the back, also the space before and behind the eye; wings and wing coverts dark brown, edged with yellowish green, the median and greater wing coverts tipped with yellow, forming wing bars; quills tipped with whitish; tail brown, edged with yellowish green on the outer webs and margined with greyish white on the inner; under surface white, suffused with yellowish green; axillaries yellow; under wing coverts and thighs greyish yellow; bill slender, dark brown, paler at base of lower mandible; legs, feet and iris brown; 3rd, 4th and 5th primaries longest; second primary intermediate in length between 7th and 8th; 1st primary 0·5 to 0·55 inches.

Length.—4 inches; wing 2·1 to 2·35; tail 1·7 to 1·8; culmen 0·4.

Hab.—The Punjab, N. W. Provinces, Oudh, Central India, Assam, Bengal, British Burmah and Sikkim.

According to Jerdon the Yellow-browed or, as he calls it, the "Crowned Tree Warbler" is common in most parts of India during the cold weather and at all times on the Himalayas. He got it at Nellore on the Malabar Coast, in Central India, and at Darjeeling. Oates says it is one of the commonest birds in Burmah during winter. It is found abundantly in every portion of Pegu. Blyth records it from Arrakan. Davison found it in Tenasserim as far south as Mergui, and Captain Bingham observed it in the Thoungyeen Valley. In the Karin Hills it has been procured up to altitudes of 2,500 feet. It is found throughout the Indo-Burmese countries, also in Sikkim and Assam. According to Blyth it is a solitary bird. It is a cheerful and active bird, frequenting alike large trees and low hedges in pursuit of its insect food. Mr. Seebohm says it breeds in North Siberia and at a high elevation in the mountains of South Siberia. The nest he found was composed of dry grass and moss, and lined with reindeer hair. The structure is semi-domed and built usually in a small tuft of grass, moss, and bilberries. The nest contained six white eggs, spotted with reddish.

298. Phylloscopus maculipennis, (*Blyth*) *Seebohm, Cat. B. Br. Mus.* v. p. 70; *id. Ibis,* 1877, p. 107. Abrornis chloronotus, *Hodgs. MS. Drawings B. Nepaul*; *Hume, Nests and Eggs, Ind. B.* p. 372.—HODGSON'S BARRED WILLOW-WARBLER.

Upper parts yellowish green, the rump with a broad yellow band. Head, nape, hindneck, lores and space behind the eye dark olive brown; mesial line on crown and eye stripe pale buff; wing coverts and quills brown, margined with yellowish green; the median and greater coverts tipped with yellow and forming two bars across the wing; innermost secondaries tipped with white on the outer web; tail brown, externally edged with yellowish green; 2 to 3 outermost feathers on each side white, the basal third of the outer web yellow and the terminal third of the same brown; under surface greyish white; the axillaries and under wing coverts, also the middle of the abdomen, greyish yellow; legs and claws brown; 1st primary half the length of 2nd; 2nd equal to 10th; 4th and 5th longest.

Length.—3·3 inches; wing 1·8 to 2·0; tail 1·3 to 1·6; culmen 0·35 to 0·4.

Hab.—The Himalayas from Nepaul to Sikkim. Breeds probably in the pine districts.

299. Phylloscopus proregulus, (*Pall.*) *Seebohm, Ibis,* 1877, pp. 104, 162; *id. Cat. B. Br. Mus.* v. p. 72. Motacilla proregulus, *Pall. Zool. Rosso. As.* i. p. 499. Abrornis chloronopus, *Hodgs. Gray, Zool. Misc.* p. 82. Reguloides chloronotus (*Hodgs.*) *Jerd. B. Ind.* ii. p. 197, No. 566. Reguloides proregulus (*Pall.*) *Seebohm, Ibis,* 1863, p. 307 et sub-seq.; *Blanf. J. A. S. B.* xli. pt. 2, p. 53; *Hume, Nests and Eggs, Ind. B.* p. 368; *id. Str. F.* vi. p. 368; *Hume and Dav., Str. F.* viii. p. 102; *Scully, Str. F.* viii. p. 309; *Brooks, Str. F.* viii. p. 392.—PALLAS'S BARRED WILLOW-WARBLER.

Upper parts dark green, the head slightly darker; coronal stripe and supercilia pale yellow; rump yellowish green to bright yellow; wings and wing coverts brown, the outer webs of all margined with greenish yellow, and the median and greater coverts broadly tipped with pale yellow forming two wing bars; quills margined with greyish white on their inner web; tail olive brown, edged with greenish yellow externally; the inner webs and shafts of the three outermost feathers on each side pure white, and the outer webs of these yellowish white tinged with greenish basally and brown terminally; under surface dull greenish yellow, brighter on the middle of the abdomen; axillaries, under wing and tail coverts and thighs yellow; legs light brown; bill dark brown; the lower mandible dusky; irides dark brown.

Length.—3·5 inches; wing 1·95 to 2·05; tail 1·4 to 1·6; tarsus 0·7; culmen 0·3 to 0·4.

The female is smaller. In the summer plumage the coronal and superciliary stripes, also the yellow tips to the coverts, are pale by abrasion.

Hab.—The Himalayas, Cashmere, Nepaul, N. W. Provinces, Bengal and British Burmah during winter.

Pallas's Willow-Warbler was got in Tenasserim by Mr. Davison in the pine forests of the Salween near Pahpoon. Captain Cock found its nest in Cashmere in May and June. The nest is placed high up on the bough of a tree (pine). It is domed or roofed, and made of moss with a lining of feathers. The eggs appear to be usually 5 in number, are white, and richly marked with brownish red, particularly at the larger end, where they form a zone. Size 0·54 × 0·43.

300. Phylloscopus pulcher, (*Hodgs.*) *Seebohm, Cat. B. Br. Mus.* v. p. 73. Abrornis erochroa, (*Hodgs.*) *Gray's Misc.* p. 82. Reguloides erochroa (*Hodgs.*) *Jerd. B. Ind.* ii. p. 199, No. 568; *Wald. in Bl. B. Burm.* p. 106; *Hume and Dav.* vi. p. 358; *Hume, Str. F.* viii. p. 102; *Brooks, Str. F.* viii. pp. 392, 482; *Scully, Str. F.* viii p. 309. Phylloscopus erochrous, *Seebohm, Ibis*, 1877, p. 106. The ORANGE-BARRED WILLOW-WARBLER.

Upper parts dark green; rump with a yellowish green terminal band covering the upper tail coverts; superciliary stripe and coronal streak not well defined, the latter nearly obsolete; the interspaces on the crown dark olive green, also the lores and space behind the eye to the nape; wing coverts brown, the lesser series with broad green margins, the median with green tips, and the greater series with broad well-defined orange tips forming a conspicuous lower wing-bar; quills brown, margined externally with greenish, fading into yellowish white, and becoming broad and conspicuous on the terminal portion of the innermost secondaries; tail with the central feathers brown, edged externally with greenish; the inner webs and shafts of the three outermost feathers on each side pure white, the outer webs of the same greenish yellow on the basal half and terminated with brown; under surface of body dull greenish yellow, brighter on the middle of the abdomen; legs, bill and irides dark brown; 4th, 5th and 6th primaries longest; 2nd about equal to the 10th; the 1st, or exposed portion of bastard primary 0·55 to 0·65 inch.

Length.—4·2 inches; wing 2·4; tail 1·75, tarsus 0·8; culmen 0·5; from gape 0 8.

Hab.—The Himalayas, from Nepaul and Simla to Bhootan. Recorded from the N. W. Provinces of India, Darjeeling, Sikkim and Simla, also Burmah; in the latter a winter visitor. It has been found on the Mooleyit Mountains in Tenasserim and at Karin at 3,000 feet elevation. It is said to breed in the pine regions of the Himalayas, in Nepaul and Sikkim, coming down into the valleys during winter, but rarely, or never, descending into the plains of India. Brooks says its note is a Thrush-like *zip*, and Dr. Scully that in Nepaul it is always found hunting about in the bushes at from 6,000 to 7,500 feet elevation.

301. Phylloscopus subviridis, *Brooks, Proc. As. Socy. Bengal*, 1872, p. 148; *Hume, Str. F.* iv. p. 494; *Seebohm, Cat. B. Br. Mus.* v. p. 74; vii. 417.—BROOK'S BARRED WILLOW-WARBLER.

PLATE.

Upper parts olive green, shading into light yellowish green on the rump; coronal and superciliary streaks *ill* defined; lores, behind the eye and interspaces on the crown olive; wings and wing coverts brown, margined with olive green; the median coverts with slightly paler tips, and the greater series with broad well defined pale tips forming a conspicuous dirty yellowish white bar across the wing; tail brown, margined externally with yellowish green; under surface of body nearly uniform greenish yellow; legs, feet, claws and irides brown; 4th primary slightly the longest; 2nd generally intermediate between 8th and 9th, 7th and 8th, or 9th and 10th.

Length.—3·6 inches; wing 2·3, tail 1·9; culmen 6·45.

Hab.—Punjab, N. W. Provinces, Oudh and Nepaul. Has been recorded from Moorshedabad, Etawah, Cawnpore, and N. W. Himalayas. Breeds in the highlands of N. W. Cashmere.

302. Phylloscopus sindianus, *Brooks, Str. F.* viii. p. 476; *Murray, Vert. Zool., Sind*, p. 160.—THE SIND BARRED WILLOW-WARBLER.

"Above uniform dull brown, rather lighter than in *P. tristis*, and much the colour of the upper surface of *Hypolais rama*; below albescent, with a ruddy tinge on the pale supercilia, sides of face, neck, breast and flanks; axillaries and edge of wing yellowish white, sometimes almost quite white, and not pure sulphur yellow as in *P. tristis*; no greenish on bend or shoulder of wing, nor any green edging to the primaries, secondaries and tail feathers generally observable in *P. tristis*; no greenish tinge on rump; like *P. neglectus* and *H. rama*, the uniform light greyish brown upper surface is characteristic; bill *Phylloscopine*, like *tristis*, dark brown; the base of lower mandible yellowish."

Male, length.—4·40 to 4·70; wing 2·22 to 2·4; tail 1·85 to 2·05; bill at front ·3 to ·35.

Female, length.—4·20 to 4·45; wing 2·05 to 2·15; tail 1·75 to 1·9.

Hab.—Sukkur, Sind.

Gen. **Hypolais.**—*Brehm.*

Bill slender, wide basally; rictal bristles few; wings moderate axillaries buff, white or grey; greater wing coverts without pale tips; bastard primary extending beyond or shorter than the primary coverts or considerably less than half the length of the second; 3rd and 4th quills longest; tail even or rounded; no white on outermost feather; tarsus scutellated in front.

Phylloscopus subviridis.
~~*Phylloscopus humii*~~.

Mintern Bros. lith.

303. Hypolais pallida, *Hemp. et Ehr. Symb. Phys. Aves.* fol. b. b. Hypolais pallida (*Ehr.*) *Dubois, Ois. Eur.* pl. 71.; *Dresser, B. Eur.* pt. xxxi.; *Blf. East. Pers.* ii. p. 187; *Hume, Str. F.* vol. vii. pp. 398, 504; *Murray, Zool., &c., Sind,* p. 160; *Seebohm, Cat. B. Br. Mus.* vol. v. p. 82; *Murray, Vert. Zool., Sind,* p. 156. Hypolais elæica, (*Lindern*) *Gerbe, Rev. Zool.,* 1844, p. 440; *Heugl. Orn. N. O. Afr.* i. p. 297; *Blanf. Geol. and Zool., Abyssinia,* p. 380; *Sharpe, Cat. Afr. B.* p. 33; *Shelly, B. Egypt,* p. 100.—The Olivaceous Tree-Warbler.

Adult Male.—Upper parts pale dull olive brown, clearer on the back in colour, and rather lighter on the rump; from the base of the bill over the eye a rather indistinct yellowish stripe; wings dark brown; the inner secondaries lighter in colour, all the feathers having lighter margins; tail dark brown, very narrowly edged with lighter brown; under parts buffy white; the throat and centre of the abdomen almost pure white; flanks washed with pale brownish; bill horn brown, dull yellowish at the base of the lower mandible; legs pale horn brown; iris dark brown.

Length.—About 5 inches; culmen 0·62; wing 2·63; the first primary extending 0·27 beyond the wing coverts and 1·15 shorter than the 2nd; 2nd 0·2 shorter than the 3rd; 3rd and 4th equal; tail 2·2; tarsus 0·83.—(*Dresser, Birds Europe*) *ex. S. F.* vol. vii. p. 398.

Hab.—Europe, Africa, Greece, Constantinople, Palestine, Egypt, Sind, Beloochistan, Persia, S. Afghanistan, Turkestan. This species and the next two (*caligata* and *rama*) are winter visitants in Sind and affect the same situations. All appear to be varieties of *Hypolais languida,* a species found in S. E. Persia, at Quetta in Beloochistan (Chaman), S. Afghanistan, and probably also in Sind. Mr. Seebohm, grouping *H. opaca, pallida, rama, caligata* and *obsoleta,* says that an unbroken series may be found from the largest *opaca* from Spain, through the smaller *H. pallida* from Greece and Asia Minor, and the still smaller *H. pallida* and *H. rama* from Persia down to the small skins of *H. rama* from India, and the still smaller *H. caligata* from Turkestan and India. Skins from Sind of these three last do not appear to have been in the British Museum collection. In reference to *H. pallida,* comparing Indian skins, Mr. Hume observes (*Str. F.* vol. vii. pp. 396, 398) that it is very close to *rama,* but is somewhat larger, with a longer and decidedly larger bill; and that the two forms, *rama* and *pallida,* quite run into each other, many of the Sind and Beloochistan specimens being quite intermediate. There does not appear to be any very appreciable difference in colour in the series I possess of these species from Sind, Beloochistan, Afghanistan and the Deccan, except the seasonal abrasion of feathers; this is also remarked by Mr. Seebohm. *H. languida,* he says, has apparently only just succeeded in isolating itself, and adds that he is not sure whether in a large series of the species intermediate forms might not occur between it and *H. pallida.* I extract the following key to the species from Mr. Seebohm's *Cat. B. Br. Mus.* vol. v. p. 76.

(*Subgeneric Group—Idunæ.*)

A. General colour of the upper parts brown or grey; under parts white or pale brown; outside tail feathers 0·15 to 0·2 inch shorter than the longest.

(*a*) 2nd primary intermediate between the 5th and 6th, bastard primary falling short of the primary coverts by 0·1 inch, or extending 0·05 beyond them. Length of wing 3·05 to 2·8 inches..*H. languida.*

B. Bastard primary exceeding the primary coverts by at least 0·1 inch.

(*a*) General colour of the upper parts pale sandy brown or isabelline brown....................................*H. obsoleta.*

C. General colour of the upper parts darkish rufous brown or grey.

(*a*) 2nd primary generally intermediate between the 5th and 6th; bastard primary exceeding the primary coverts from 0·1 to 0·3 inches. Length of wing 2·75 to 2·5 inches; culmen 0·7 to 0·6 ....*H. pallida.*

(*b*) 2nd primary generally intermediate between the 7th and 8th, or 8th and 9th; bastard primary exceeding the primary coverts from 0·2 to 0·4 inch. Length of wing 2·53 to 2·3 inches; culmen 0·6 to 0·53 ....*H. rama.*

(*c*) 2nd primary generally intermediate between 6th and 7th; bastard primary exceeding the primary coverts 0·15 to 0·26. Length of wing 2·38 to 2·28 inches; culmen 0·51 to 0·5 ....*H. caligata.*

304. Hypolais rama, *Sykes P. Z. S.* 1832, p. 89; *Blf. East. Pers.* ii. p. 187; *Hume, Str. F.* vol. vii. 183, 396; *Murray, Hdbk. Zool., &c., Sind,* p. 160; *Seebohm, Cat. B. Br. Mus.* vol. v. p. 84. Phyllopneuste rama, (*Sykes*) *Jerd. B. Ind.* ii. p. 189, No. 553; *Murray, Vert. Zool., Sind,* p. 157.—SYKES' TREE-WARBLER.

Seebohm (*Cat. B. Br. Mus.*) describes this as "a shade darker in colour, both above and below, than typical, *H. pallida.* It is on an average a somewhat smaller bird, with a shorter second primary and a longer bastard primary. The 3rd, 4th and 5th primaries are nearly equal and longest; the second is usually intermediate in length between the 7th and 8th, and not infrequently between the 8th and 9th, and in rare instances between the 6th and 7th. The bastard primary exceeds the primary coverts by 0·2 to 0·4 inch."

Length.—Of wing 2·53 to 2·3 inches; tail 2·25 to 1·9; culmen 0·6 to 0·53; tarsus 0·85 to 0·8; outside tail feathers 0·25 to 0·15 inch shorter than longest. After the autumn moult the under parts are somewhat more suffused with pale buffish brown than appears to be the case after the spring moult; otherwise, I can discover no differences attributable to age, sex, or season, beyond the usual wear and tear of abrasion.

Hab.—Sind, Beloochistan, S. E. Persia, Afghanistan, East Turkestan, Punjab, N. W. Provinces, Oudh, Cashmere, Kutch, Kattiawar, N. Guzerat, Jodhpore, Concan, Deccan and South India.

305. Hypolais caligata, (*Licht.*) *Eversm. Reis. Buchara,* p. 128; *Degle et Gerbe. Orn. Eur.* i. p. 510; *Dresser, B. Eur.* pt. xxxviii. 1875; *Dresser, Ibis,* 1876, p. 88; *Murray, Hdbk. Zool., &c., Sind,* p. 160; *Seebohm, Cat. B. Br. Mus.* vol. v. p. 86. Phyllopneuste rama, (*Sykes*) *apud. Jerd. B. Ind.* vol. ii. p. 189 (*partim*). Jerdonia agricolensis, *Hume, Ibis,* 1870, p. 182. Calamodyta agricolensis (*Hume*) *Tristram, Ibis,* 1870, p. 494. Salicaria microptera, *Severtz., Str. F.* iii. p. 425; *id.* vii. p. 397; *Murray, Vert. Zool., Sind,* p. 158.—The Booted Tree-Warbler.

Male.—Head, hindneck, back, scapulars, ear coverts and sides of the neck a greyish brown; supercilium, extending from the base of the bill to the ear coverts, whitish buff; rump and upper tail coverts brownish, the feathers of the rump tinged very slightly with a shade of rufescent; wings concolorous with the tail; their coverts, as well as the primaries, secondaries and tertiaries, margined with rufescent brown, in some specimens greyish white, more broadly on the tertiaries and wing coverts; edge of wing and under wing and thigh coverts pale buffish white; tail brown, the feathers narrowly margined with fulvescent in some specimens; the outer web of the outermost feather on each side indistinctly fulvous white, the others, except the centre feathers, tipped greyish white or fulvous; under surface pale buffy white, albescent on the chin, belly and lower tail coverts, and tinged brownish on the flanks; bill dark brown; the lower mandible pale fleshy, dusky near the tip; legs and feet fleshy or pale brownish yellow; irides brown.

Length.—4·5 to 5 inches; wing 2·2 to 2·38; tail from vent 1·95 to 2; bill at front 0·35; tarsus 0·8.

Hab.—India to Nepaul and Cashmere, Sind, Punjab, N. W. Provinces, Deccan, Concan, Khandesh, Behar and Madras; wintering in the plains of India and breeding in Cashmere, Turkestan and Southern Siberia.

306. Hypolais obsoleta, (*Severtz.*) *Seebohm, Cat. B. Br. Mus.* vol. v. p. 86. Salicaria obsoleta, *Severtz. Turkest. Jevotn.* pp. 66, 129; *Dresser, Ibis,* 1876, p. 87; *Murray, Vert. Zool., Sind,* p. 158.—The Desert Tree-Warbler.

The following is Mr. Seebohm's description of this species: "The general colour of the upper parts is a sandy brown or pale isabelline brown. In other respects the colouration is the same as that of the two or three preceding sub-species; 3rd and 4th primaries nearly equal and longest; 2nd primary in a skin from Turkestan intermediate in length between the 6th and 7th, and in one from Sind between the 7th and 8th; the bastard primary exceeds the primary coverts by 0·35 inch in both skins.

Length.—Of wing 2·4 inches; tail 2·0; culmen in the Turkestan skin 0·51; in the Sind skin 0·8, darkish brown." The colour of the soft parts are not given. This has been included on Mr. Seebohm's authority, who says he has a skin from Sind as well as from Turkestan. Comparing my small series, I cannot find any to agree with the colouration as above.

Hab.—Turkestan; wintering in Sind.

Gen. **Acrocephalus.**—*Naum.*

Bill large, depressed and broad at the base, with moderately developed rictal bristles in two species only; the bill is as slender as in *Locustella*; wings moderately long; 3rd and 4th quills generally longest; bastard primary minute in one or two species only, extending in length beyond the primary coverts; tail more rounded than in *Hypolais.*

307. Acrocephalus bistrigiceps, *Swinh. Ibis*, 1860, p. 51; *Wald, in Bl. B. Burm.* p. 104; *Hume and Dav., Str. F.* vi. p. 338; *Hume, Str. F.* viii. p. 100; *Seebohm, Cat. B. Br. Mus.* v. p. 94; *Oates, Str. F.* x. p. 214; *Oates, B. Br. Burm.* i. p. 97; Salicaria maackii, *Schrenck, Vog. Amurland,* p. 370.—SCHRENCK'S REED-WARBLER.

Upper parts russet-brown, slightly brighter on the rump and upper tail coverts, and greyer on the head, quills and tail feathers; a distinct black streak on either side of the crown of the head, below which is a broad supercilium running from the base of the bill; lores dark brown; ear coverts hair brown; breast and flanks pale rufous brown, shading into pale buff on the middle of the abdomen and into white on the chin and throat; wings and tail brown, edged with russet brown on the outer webs; axillaries, thighs, under wing coverts and the inner edgings of the quills pale brownish buff; bill slender, locustelline; upper mandible dark, lower mandible pale; legs, feet and claws horn-colour; iris brown; mouth pale yellow.

Length.—5 to 5·1 inches; wing 2·1 to 2·2; tail 1·85 to 2·1; culmen 0·52 to 0·67; from gape 0·7; tarsus 0·8; *2nd primary shorter than the 6th, generally intermediate between the 6th and 7th,* or equals the 7th; the first primary is 0·5 inch, or exceeds the primary coverts by 0·15 to 0·25 inch.

Hab.—The Amoor Valley, where it breeds; also Japan, China, and Tenasserim.

Schrenck's Reed-Warbler, Oates says, occurs commonly in the neighbourhood of Kyeikpadein in Pegu. Mr. Davison procured it at Tavoy in Tenasserim. It occurs in China. Mr. Swinhoe met with it in Amoy and Pekin. It affects inundated rice and paddy fields, grass jungles, and low brushwood.

308. Acrocephalus orientalis, *Tem. et. Schleg. Faun. Jap. Aves.* p. 50, pl. xx. *B.*; *Seebohm, Cat. B. Br. Mus.* v. p. 97; *Oates, Str. F.* iii. p. 337; *Hume and Dav., Str. F.* vi. p. 338; *Hume, Str. F.* viii. p. 100; *Oates, Str. F.* x. p. 213. Acrocephalus magnirostris, *Swinh., Ibis,* 1860, p. 51.—The EASTERN GREAT REED-WARBLER.

Upper plumage olive brown, tinged with fulvous, especially on the rump and upper tail coverts; wings and tail brown edged on the outer web with fulvous brown; lores darker; a pale indistinct supercilium buffish white; ear coverts and sides of the neck like the back; chin and throat white, rest of under plumage fulvous, paler on the abdomen; throat and breast generally streaked with brown; bill dark brown, the lower mandible dusky or pale flesh colour; *legs and feet slaty*; *2nd primary between 3rd and 5th generally equalling the 4th*; the first is minute; irides yellowish brown; eyelids plumbeous.

Length.—7·7 inches; wing 3·0 to 3·5; tail 3; tarsus 1·15; culmen 0·8 to 0·95; from gape 1·0.

Hab.—The valley of the Amoor, North China and Japan, passing through South China on migration, and wintering in the islands of the Malay Archipelago and the Burmah Peninsula.

This species occurs in the grassy plains of Southern Pegu during winter, also in Tenasserim, at Tavoy and Malewoon. It has a very wide range, being found in the Malay Peninsula and Philippine Islands; also in Batchian, Morty and Lombock. It frequents large grassy tracts, bamboo thickets, and bushy jungles.

309. Acrocephalus stentoreus, *Hemp. et Ehr. Symb. Phys. Aves.* fol. b.b; *Heugl. Orn. N. Afr.* i. p. 287; *Shelley, B. Egypt,* p. 95; *Blf. East Persia,* ii. p. 194. Agrobates brunnescens, *Jerd. Madr. Journ.* x. p. 269. Acrocephalus brunnescens, (*Jerd.*) *Blyth, Cat. B. Mus. As. Soc.* p. 181; *Jerd. B. Ind.* ii. p. 154, No. 515; *Hume and Henderson, Lahore to Yarkand,* p. 214, pl. xvi.; *Murray, Hdbk. Zool., &c., Sind,* p. 152; *Str. F.* vol. ii. 330; iii. 369.—The INDIAN GREAT REED-WARBLER.

Above light olive brown, with a very slight ferruginous tinge, paler on the rump; wings and tail dark brown; the quills and lateral tail feathers pale edged; supercilium buffy white; chin white; throat greyish white, as also is the breast, but with a fulvous tinge; rest of under surface yellowish or fulvous white; bill dark brown, fleshy at base of lower mandible; irides yellowish; legs slaty brown.

Length.—7·5 to 8·5 inches; wing 3 to 3·35; tail 3; tarsus 1 to 1·1.

Hab.—India generally, extending to Nepaul. Appears to be a resident in Egypt; breeds in Turkestan and the highlands of Persia, also in Cashmere and Nepaul. (Seebohm.) In Sind it breeds in August. Probably also a resident of Beloochistan and Afghanistan, where it occurs in some numbers. Recorded from Rajputana, North Guzerat and Kutch.

310. Acrocephalus dumetorum, *Blyth, J. A. S. B.* xviii. p. 815; *Jerd. B. Ind.* ii. p. 155, No. 516; *Dresser, B. Eur.* pt. liii.; *Seebohm, Cat. B. Br. Mus.* v. p. 96. Calamodyta dumetorum (*Blyth*), *Gray. Handlist, B.* p. 207. Salicaria eurhyncha, *Severtz. Turkest. Jevotn.* pp. 66, 128; *id. Str. F.* 1875, p. 425.—BLYTH'S REED-WARBLER.

Upper parts olive brown; supercilium very pale, nearly obsolete; wings and tail slightly darker brown, narrowly edged paler on the outer webs; beneath brownish buff, paler on the chin and throat; under wing coverts buffy white; bill dusky, fleshy at base of lower mandible; legs pale horn brown; irides yellowish.

Length.—6 inches; wing 2·5; tail 2·3; bill 0·7.

Hab.—Europe, breeds in the Himalayas, and winters in Sind, Punjab, N. W. Provinces, Deccan, Travancore, Ceylon, Neilgherries, the Carnatic, Central India, Bengal to Assam, and Nepaul.

311. Acrocephalus agricola, *Jerd., Madras Journ.* xiii. pt. ii. p. 131; *Blyth, Cat. B. Mus. As. Soc.* p. 182; *Jerd. B. Ind.* p. 156, No. 517; *Murray, Hdbk. Zool., &c., Sind,* 153; *Seebohm, Cat. B. Br. Mus.* vol. v. p. 105; *Dresser, B. Eur.* pt. liii. Salicaria capistrata, modesta *et* gracilis, *Severtz. Str. F.* 1875, pp. 425, 426.—The PADDY-FIELD WARBLER.

Above from pale rufous brown to earthy brown; supercilium faint, nearly obsolete; wings, wing coverts and tail feathers slightly darker, the feathers edged rufescent or earthy brown; beneath whitish with a fulvous tinge; bill brown, fleshy at the base of the lower mandible; legs horn brown; irides yellowish.

Length.—5·25 to 5·5 inches; wings 2·25; tail 2·25; bill at front 0·55.

Hab.—According to Seebohm, this little Warbler breeds in the valley of the Lower Volga and extends its range eastward in the Palæarctic region, at least as far Turkestan, and probably to China. It also breeds in the Himalayas from Cashmere to Nepaul, and winters in the plains of India. Occurs as a migrant in Southern India, Sind, Deccan, Punjab, Beloochistan and Afghanistan.

Gen. **Locustella**.—*Kaup.*

Bill of moderate length, slender, straight, compressed, barely deflected at the tip, which is slightly notched; rictal bristles nearly obsolete; wings long; the 1st quill minute, rarely extending beyond the primary coverts; 2nd nearly equal to the third, which is longest; tail of 12 feathers rounded, the outermost feather, except in one species, shorter than the under tail coverts; tarsus scutellated in front; hind claw curved; plumage lark-like, striped or spotted.

312. Locustella certhiola, (*Pall.*) *Seebohm*; *Cat. B. Br. Mus.* v. p. 114; *Hume, Str. F.* viii. p. 100; *Oates, B. Br. Burm.* i. p. 102. Motacilla certhiola, *Pall. Zoogr., Rosso-Asiat.* i. p. 509. Locustella rubescens, *Blyth, J. A. S. B.* xiv. p. 582; *Jerd. B. Ind.* iii. p. 160. Locustella temporalis, *Jerd. B. Ind.* ii. p. 160. Calamodyta doriæ, *Salv. Atti. R. Ac. Sc. Tor.* iii. p. 531; *Sharpe, Ibis,* 1876, p. 41, pl. ii., fig. 2.—The LESSER REED-WARBLER.

Upper parts russet brown, greyer on the head, more tawny on the rump and upper tail coverts, and paler on the edges of the wing coverts; tail feathers blackish brown, irregularly margined with rufous brown, and broadly terminated with whitish; stripe over the eye and a streak from the bill under the cheeks and ear coverts yellowish buff; ear coverts hair brown; under wing coverts whitish; primaries and secondaries dark brown, narrowly edged with rufous brown; under surface buff, paler on the throat and upper breast, which and the whole breast are spotted with black brown. In the next stage the throat and breast are unspotted, and the whole under surface, including these, are brighter yellow; the rump is also unstreaked or almost so; the rectrices are not so broadly tipped white, and the eye streak, chin, throat, and the whole lower plumage are yellowish buff. In spring the adult birds have the head blackish brown, each feather narrowly edged with pale reddish brown. An unmarked reddish brown collar is present in some; the back, scapulars, and wing coverts dark blackish brown, rather broadly edged with reddish brown; the rump is also reddish brown; the upper tail coverts reddish brown with a central spot of black; outer tail feathers nearly all black, with scarcely any rufous margins; towards the middle the feathers become less black and more margined with rufous, the central pair being rufous with only a black shaft line; all the feathers are tipped with white; chin, throat and centre of abdomen whitish; rest of the under parts delicate buff; bill dark brown; legs whitish; irides sepia brown.

Length.—5·5 inches; wing 2·3; tail 2·2; tarsus 0·85; bill from gape 0·7.

Hab.—Central and Eastern Siberia, where it breeds. It passes through China on migration, and winters in India, Ceylon, the Burmah Peninsula, and the Islands of the Malay Archipelago. In India it is found in the N. W. Provinces, Oudh, Bengal, and Central India, also Assam. It is also recorded from the Khasia Hills. In Burmah Oates says it occurs in Pegu, and probably also in Arrakan and Tenasserim. It summers in Siberia and occasionally straggles into Europe. It is shy, and never by any chance seen except by accident. Oates says it swarms in inundated paddy fields to an incredible extent. After the 16th December the bird disappears entirely. Quoting Dybowsky, Oates has it that it makes its nest in a tuft of grass close to the ground, and lays five or six eggs, which are rosy white, speckled with reddish brown.

313. Locustella straminea, (*Severtz*). *Seebohm, Cat. B. Br. Mus.* v. p. 117. Acridiornis straminea, *Severtz, Turkest., Jevotn.* p. 66, 1873. Locustella lanceolata, (*Tem.*) *apud. Dresser, Ibis,* 1876, p. 90. Locustella Hendersoni, (*Cass.*) *apud. Hume, Str. F.* vi. p. 340, 1878.—The SIBERIAN GRASSHOPPER WARBLER.

Upper parts pale olivaceous brown, each feather having a well defined dark brown centre; lores and feathers behind the eye olivaceous brown, obscurely streaked, supercilium nearly obsolete; wings brown, the outside webs edged with pale olivaceous brown; tail brown, also edged paler externally and tipped obscurely with the same; chin, throat, and centre of abdomen white, shaded with brownish on the flanks and breast, and greyish white on the under tail coverts, which are centred brown; upper mandible dark brown, the lower pale horn; rictal bristles obsolete.

Legs, feet, and claws pale horn. (Seebohm.)

Length.—4·95 inches; wing 2·4 to 2·05; tail 1·9 to 2·2; culmen 0·48 to 0·55; *2nd primary between 4th and 5th or 5th and 6th.*

Hab.—N. W. Provinces (Etawah).

Seebohm says it is supposed to breed in South-Western, Siberia from the Ural Mountains to Turkestan, and to winter in the plains of India.

314. Locustella lanceolata, (*Tem.*) *Wald. Ibis,* 1874, p. 139; *id. in Blyth, B. Burm.* p. 121; *Dresser, B. Eur.* ii. p. 617; *Seebohm, Cat. B. Br. Mus.* v. p. 118; *Oates, B. Br. Burm.* i. p. 104; *Hume and Dav., Str. F.* vi. p. 118. Sylvia lanceolata, *Tem. Man. d'Orn.* iv. p. 614. Lusciniopsis hendersoni, *Cass. in Proc. Phil. Ac. Sc.* 1858, p. 194. Locustella minuta, *Swinh., P. Z. S.* 1863, p. 93. Locustella macropus, *Swinh., P. Z.* 8, 1863, p. 93. Locustella subsignata, *Hume, Str. F.* i. p. 409.—TEMMINCK'S GRASSHOPPER WARBLER.

Upper parts russet brown, each feather centred with dark brown; quills brown, the primaries and secondaries externally edged with russet brown, and the tertiaries on both webs; tail brown, obscurely edged paler; ear coverts hair brown; sides of the head streaked with russet and dark brown; chin, throat, and centre of abdomen ochraceous white; rest of under surface darker ochraceous, streaked with blackish brown; under wing coverts pale vinaceous; legs fleshy white; claws pale horn; upper mandible dark brown, the lower yellow at base and brown at tip; iris brown; *2nd primary generally between the 3rd and 4th.*

Length.—5·2 inches; wing 2·1 to 2·25; tail 1·8 to 2; tarsus 0·75 to 0·78; culmen 0·55; from gape 0·6.

Hab.—British Burmah and the Andaman Islands during winter. In Pegu Oates found it abundant from October to February. Mr. Davison procured it at various places in Tenasserim quite down to the extreme southern portion of the Division. It is diffused over China, and possibly in the Islands of the Malay Archipelago. It summers in Siberia. Its habits are not unlike those of *L. straminea*.

Gen. **Lusciniola**,—*Gray*.

General characters of *Locustella*; wing rather short; 1st quill longer than the primary coverts, and never more than half the length of the 2nd, which is a little shorter than the 3rd and 4th, which are equal; tail graduated; tarsus moderate, more or less distinctly scutellated in front.

315. Lusciniola ædon, (*Pall.*) *Seebohm, Cat. B. Br. Mus.* v. p. 121. Muscicapa ædon, *Pall. Reis. Russ. Reichs*, iii. p. 695. Phragmaticola olivacea, (*Blyth*) *Jerd., Madr. Journ.* xiii. pl. ii. p. 129. Arundinax olivaceus, *Jerd., B. Ind.* ii. p. 157, No. 518. Arundinax ædon, *Hume, Str. F.* ii. p. 234; *Armstrong, Str. F.* iv. p. 328; *Hume and Dav.*, vi. p. 339; *Hume, Str. F.* viii. p. 100. Arundinax ædon, *Blyth, B. Burm.* p. 104; *Oates, Str. F.* x. p. 215; *Oates, B. Br. Burm.* i. p. 98.—PALLAS'S GRASS-WARBLER.

Upper parts fulvous olive brown, brightest on the rump; wing coverts, quills, and tail brown, all edged with fulvous olive brown externally; lores brown; ear coverts and sides of the neck fulvous olive brown; no superciliary streak; under surface buffish white, lighter on the chin, throat, and abdomen and suffused with russet brown on the flanks, vent and under tail coverts; axillaries and under wing coverts buff; upper mandible dark horny brown, lower flesh colour tipped with orange; legs and feet plumbeous; claws horn colour.

Length.—7·7 inches; wing 3· to 3·3; tail 3·1 to 3·5; tarsus 1·1; culmen 0·7 to 0·8; from gape 0·88; 2nd primary intermediate between 7th and 8th or equal to 7th.

Hab.—Punjab, N.-W. Provinces, Oudh, Bengal, the Carnatic, also Nepaul and British Burmah during winter. It is spread well over the whole of Northern India and British Burmah. In the latter, it has been found over the whole of Pegu, also in Arrakan, Tenasserim, and the Andamans. Breeds in S.-E. Siberia and North China. It is usually seen on reeds, in marshes, ponds, &c.

316. Lusciniola thoracica, (*Blyth*) *Seebohm, Cat. B. Br. Mus.* v. p. 124. Dumeticola thoracica, *Blyth, J. A. S. B.* xiv. p. 584; *id. Cat. B. As. Soc.* p. 183. Dumeticola affinis, (*Hodgs.*) *Jerd. B. Ind.* ii. p. 158; *Brooks, Str. F.* 1875, p. 286.—HODGSON'S GRASS-WARBLER.

Upper parts dark russet brown, tinged slightly with olive; lores and feathers behind the eye dark brown; eye stripe pale ashy white, rather indistinct; wings and tail like the back; chin and centre of abdomen nearly white, shading into pale ashy grey on the throat and breast, and olive brown on the flanks and under tail coverts, which latter are broadly tipped with whitish; throat spotted with dark brown; bill dark brown; *2nd primary* equal to the 9th or 10th, the first, half the length of the 2nd; legs, feet, and claws pale horn colour; axillaries greyish white.

Length.—4·95 inches; wing 2 to 2·3; tail 1·8 to 2·5; culmen 0·52; tarsus 0·78 to 0·83.

Hodgson's Grass-Warbler is said to breed in South Siberia and N.-W. China. It is known only from N.-W. India, in the Himalayas, and between Simla and Mussoorie. It is also recorded from Nepaul.

317. Lusciniola luteiventris, (*Hodgs.*) *Seebohm, Cat. B. Br. Mus.* v. p. 125. Tribura luteoventris, *Hodgs. M. S. Drawings Nepaul Birds.* Dumeticola mandelli, *Brooks, Str. F.* 1875, p. 286. Dumeticola luteoventris, (*Hodgs.*) *Brooks, Str. F.* 1875, p. 286.—The BROWN GRASS-WARBLER.

Upper parts russet brown, inclining to olive; lores and behind the eye dark brown; eye stripe pale chestnut, very indistinct; wings and tail slightly darker than the back; chin, throat, and centre of abdomen nearly white, shading into pale chestnut on the breast, flanks, thighs, and under tail coverts; axillaries and under wing coverts buffish white, mottled with brown on the shoulder; inner margin of quills pale brown; upper mandible dark brown, under mandible pale horn colour; wing short; *2nd primary equal to the secondaries*; legs, feet, and claws pale brown. (Seebohm.)

Length.—4·9 to 5·5 inches; wing 1·95 to 2·25; tail 2·2 to 2·6; culmen 0·5; tarsus 0·7 to 0·8.

Brooks under *Dumeticola mandelli* (*Str. F.* 1875, p. 284,) gives the measurements of two skins of this species as 5·4 and 5·5 inches, both from Native Sikkim. Under *Tribura luteoventris* (t. c.) from the same locality and the Bhootan Doars, he gives the length as 5·10 to 5·25; wing 1·97 to 2·23.

The Brown Grass-Warbler is confined to the Himalayas, having hitherto only been found in Nepaul, the N.-W. Provinces, and Sikkim. It is recorded by Seebohm from Darjeeling.

318. Lusciniola indica, (*Jerd.*) *Seebohm, Ibis,* 1880, p. 277; *id. Cat. B. Br. Mus.* v. p. 126. Sylvia indica, *Jerd., Madr. Journ.* xi. p. 6. Phyllopneuste indicus, (*Jerd.*) *Jerd. B. Ind.* ii. p. 194; *Brooks, Ibis,* 1869, p. 56; *Godw.-Austen J. A. S. B.* xli. pt. 2, p. 142; *Seebohm, Ibis,* 1877, p. 87.—JERDON'S GRASS-WARBLER.

Upper parts earthy brown with a slight tinge of ochraceous on the rump; *eye stripe deep yellow,* shading into buffy from behind the eye; lores and feathers behind the eye earthy brown; quills brown, very narrowly tipped with pale; tail brown, the feathers narrowly tipped and margined with greyish white on the inner web; *under surface of body buffish yellow;* axillaries and wing coverts buff; bill Phylloscopine; upper mandible dark brown, the under mandible pale horn colour; legs, feet, and claws brown; irides dark brown.

Length.—5·25 inches; wing 2·2 to 2·65; tail 1·75 to 2·2; culmen 0·55; tarsus 0·8; 4th and 5th primaries nearly equal and longest; 2nd about equal to 10th; 1st 0·65 to 0·85 inch.

Hab.—N.-W. and Central Provinces, Oudh, Bengal, Central India, and the Concan; at Matheran and Deccan.

Jerdon's Grass-Warbler has been obtained near Jaulnah in Central India, also on the Northern Ghauts and at Mhow, Saugor, and Khandeish. Jerdon says it frequents trees, but is more common in bushes and shrubs near rocks, and especially on rocky cliffs, which it appears to affect much. It probably breeds in the alpine districts of the Himalayas.

319. Lusciniola fuscata, (*Blyth*) *Seebohm, Cat. B. Br. Mus.* v. p. 127. Phyllopneuste fuscata, *Blyth, J. A. S. B.* xi. p. 113; *Blyth and Wald. B. Burm.* p. 105. Horornis fulviventris, *Hodgs. MS. Drawings B. Nepaul*, pl. 63; *id. P. Z. S.* 1845, p. 31. Phylloscopus brunneus, *Blyth, J. A. S. B.* xiv. p. 591. Phylloscopus fuscatus, (*Blyth*) *Jerd. B. Ind.* ii. p. 191; *Seebhom, Ibis*, 1877, p. 85; *Armstrong, Str. F.* iv. p. 329; *Hume and Dav., Str. F.* vi. p. 352; *Cripps, Str. F.* vii. p. 285; *Hume, Str. F.* viii. p. 102. Herbivocula fuscata, (*Blyth*) *Oates, B. Br. Burm.* i. p. 92.—The Brown Bush-Warbler.

Upper parts brown; wing and tail the same, but edged exteriorly with olive brown, and on the inner webs with pale buff or olive brown; supercilium, reaching to the nape, buff; cheeks and ear coverts buff, tinged with brown. Chin, throat, and abdomen buffy white; breast, flanks, axillaries, vent, and under tail coverts rich buff; bill Phylloscopine; upper mandible dark brown; under mandible pale; rictal bristles fairly developed; iris brown; legs and feet dusky flesh colour; claws yellowish horn colour.

Length.—5·3 inches; wing 2·3 to 2·55; tail 2·2 to 2·4; culmen 0·45 to 0·49; tarsus 0·8 to 0·9.

Hab.—N.-W. Provinces, Oudh, Bengal, Assam, British Burmah, and Nepaul. In India it is a winter visitor. Oates says during this season it is common to every portion of Pegu. Mr. Davison got it at Tenasserim as far south as Tavoy. It also winters in South China. In summer it is found in Eastern Siberia and Japan. According to Seebohm it breeds in South-Eastern Siberia.

The Brown Bush-Warbler confines itself to low jungle and grass land, and, according to Seebohm, is especially fond of wet localities and the banks of nullahs and ditches. It has a low single note, which it frequently utters while flitting from spot to spot.

320. Lusciniola schwarzi, (*Radde*) *Seebohm, Ibis*, 1880, p. 277; *id. Cat. B. Br. Mus.* v. p. 128. Sylvia (Phyllopneuste) schwarzi, *Radde, Reis. Sibir. Voy.* p. 260. Herbivocula schwarzi, *Swinh. P. Z. S.* 1871, p. 354; *Oates, B. Br. Burm.* i. p. 9. Phylloscopus brooksi, *Wald. in Bl.*

B. Burm. p. 105. Neornis flavolivacea, *Hodgs.? apud. Hume, Str. F.* iii. p. 139; *Oates, Str. F.* x. p. 221. Phylloscopus schwarzi, *Brooks, Str. F.* iv. p. 277; *Seebohm, Ibis,* 1877, p. 84; *Hume and Dav., Str. F.* vi. p. 353; *Hume, Str. F.* viii. p. 102; *Bingham, Str. F.* ix. p. 186.—RADDE'S BUSH-WARBLER.

Upper parts olive brown tinged with tawny, especially on the rump; wings and tail brown, edged on the outer web with the colour of the back; supercilium, reaching to the nape, buff; lores and feathers behind the eye dark brown; ear coverts buff and brown; under surface rich tawny buff, paling on the throat and abdomen; axillaries and under wing coverts buff; bill short, thick, and wide at base; upper mandible dark brown, under mandible pale; 4th and 5th primaries longest; 2nd intermediate in length between 7th and 8th; the 1st frequently more than half the length of the 2nd; legs and feet pale horn colour.

Length.—5·6 inches; wing 2·35 to 2·5; tail 2·2 to 2·05; culmen 0·48 to 0·5.

In summer the lower parts are nearly white with, in some, a slight tinge of yellowish white or buff.

Hab.—British Burmah, where Oates says it has been frequently met with in winter, and in North Pegu. It has also been obtained at Kyeikpadien, and by Davison in the northern half of the Tenasserim Division, at Pahpoon, and other places. Captain Bingham got it in the Thoungyeen Valley. It also winters in South China. Breeds in South-Eastern Siberia. Affects low bushes and dense jungle.

321. Lusciniola fuliginiventris, (*Hodgs.*) *Seebohm, Ibis,* 1880, p. 277. Horornis fuliginiventer, *Hodgs. P. Z. S.* 1845, p. 31. Phylloscopus fuliginiventer, (*Hodgs.*) *Blyth, Ibis,* 1867, p. 28.—The SMOKY GRASS-WARBLER.

Upper parts dark olive brown; wings and tail dull chocolate brown; an indistinct supercilium and the whole of the under surface of the body, including the axillaries and under wing coverts, pale olive brown, yellowish on the throat and middle of abdomen; bill Phylloscopine; both mandibles dark brown, the under mandible slightly paler at base; legs and feet brown.

Length.—5·3 inches; wing 2·1 to 2·3; tail 1·75 to 2·0; culmen 0·45 to 0·5.

Hab.—Nepaul and Sikkim.

322. Lusciniola neglecta, *Hume, Ibis,* 1870, p. 143; *Blanf. East. Persia,* ii. p. 182; *Seebohm, Ibis,* 1877, p. 99; *id. Cat. B. Br. Mus.* v. p. 131. Phylloscopus neglectus, (*Hume*) *Hume, Str. F.* p. 195. Lusciniola neglectus, (*Hume*) *Murray, Vert. Zool., Sind,* p. 150.—HUME'S GRASS-WARBLER.

The following is Mr. Hume's description of the species:—

"The lores are brownish white; a comparatively pure and very narrow white streak runs from the nostrils over the lores and eyes, but not beyond;

the whole upper surface is dull earthy brown, with, in some, a faintly olivaceous rufescent tinge on the back, most conspicuous on the rump; the quills and tail are a moderately dark hair brown, narrowly margined on the outer webs with pale olivaceous brown, much the same colour as the upper parts; the secondaries are very narrowly margined at the tips with albescent; the whole lower surface is albescent, tinged with very pale fulvous fawn, or earthy brown, more strongly so in some specimens than in others; the sides and flanks are pale earthy brown; the wing lining and axillaries are white with, at times, the faintest possible fulvous or brownish tinge.

"*Length.*—4 to 4·2 inches; expanse 6·25 to 6·4; tail from vent 1·4 to 1·6; wing barely 2 to 2·15; bill at front 0·27 to 0·3; tarsus 0·68 to 0·71. The 4th primary the longest, the 3rd and 5th a hair's breadth shorter, the 2nd 0·26 to 0·3, and the 1st 1 to 1·1 shorter than the 4th; the irides are brown; the legs and feet black; the bill black, paler or horny greenish in some at the base of the lower mandible."—*Str. F.* i. p. 196.

Hab.—Sind, Punjab, N.-W. Provinces, Beloochistan, and Persia. A winter visitant; chiefly affecting acacia groves.

323. Lusciniola melanopogon, (*Tem.*) *Gray. List. Gen. B.* p. 28; *Heuglin, Orn. N. D. Afr.*; *Salvad. Faun. Ital. Ucc.* p. 116; *Hume, Str. F.* 1873, p. 190; *Seebohm, Cat. B. Br. Mus.* v. p. 132; *Murray, Vert. Zool., Sind,* p. 149. Sylvia melanopogon, (*Tem.*) *pl. Col.* 245, fig. 2. Calamodus melanopogon, (*Tem*). *Blanf. E. Persia* ii. p. 198.—The Moustached Grass-Warbler.

A broad conspicuous white stripe from the nostrils over the eyes and ear coverts; a dark brown stripe from in front of, under, and through the eyes, enveloping the upper portion of the ear coverts, darker in the males than in the females; the chin, throat, and lower parts, including the lower tail coverts, white, faintly tinged rufescent on the breast, more strongly so on the flanks, about the vent, and in some specimens the lower tail coverts also; the sides both of the neck and of the body tinged with greyish or, in some, olivaceous brown; forehead, crown, occiput, and nape very dark brown, the feathers tipped and margined a paler yellowish olive brown; in some specimens these tippings entirely obscure the base, except on a narrow line immediately above the white eye streak; in others these parts appear to be very dark brown regularly striated with a pale olive brown, while in some the tippings are almost wanting; the back, scapulars, rump, and upper tail coverts, the same yellowish olive brown, becoming more rufescent on the lower back, rump, and upper tail coverts; the feathers of the centre of back with more or less conspicuous dark central shaft-streaks; in some birds the whole back seems regularly streaked with dark lines, in others only a few faint darker streaks are visible in the very centre of the back; in some again the lower back is much more decidedly rufous; the wings are hair brown; the primaries very narrowly margined and tipped on the outer web paler; the secondaries and tertiaries and most of the coverts more distinctly margined with a sort of rufescent olive, the wing lining and axillaries pure or nearly pure white; tail feathers somewhat pale hair brown, obscurely margined with rufescent olive; the shaft dull white below. "The plumage," Mr. Hume says, "is rather variable, and in some specimens the flanks and tail coverts are much browner than above described; the upper surface, too, varies a good deal in its general appearance * * * ; all the quills are margined on their inner webs albescent."

Dimensions from the fresh bird—sexes not differing appreciably in size.

Length.—5·7 to 5·8 inches; expanse 7·3 to 7·5; tail from vent 2 to 2·2; wing 2·4 to 2·5; wing, when closed, reach to within 1·25 to 1·4 of end of tail; bill at front 0·42 to 0·47; tarsus 0·82 to 0·87; hind toe and claw 0·55, claw only from root to point 0·3; weight 0·35 to 0·4 oz.; irides brown to pale brown; feet dark horny grey, in some dusky brown; legs dusky brown; soles pale yellowish; bill very dark brown, almost black, paler on lower mandible.—*Hume, Stray Feathers*, vol. i., p. 191.

Hab.—Sind, Punjab, N.-W. Provinces, Beloochistan, Persia, and Afghanistan. A winter visitant.

Seebohm says it appears to be a resident on both shores of the Mediterranean, extending eastwards into Persia. In Sind and the N.-W. Provinces it is only a winter visitor. Probably breeds in Turkestan.

Gen. **Cettia.**—*Bonap.*

This genus contains a small group of Bush-Warblers, distinguished by having only ten tail feathers. The wing is generally rounded; the 1st primary always half the length of the 2nd or a little more; the 2nd is nearly equal to the secondaries; tail rounded, the outermost feathers two-thirds to five-sixths the length of the longest; tarsus and feet robust, the former scutellated in front. The predominant colours are russet brown and olive brown. (Seebohm.)

324. Cettia cetti, (*Marm.*) *Degl. Orn. Eur.* i. p. 518; *Murray, Vert. Zool., Sind,* p. 151; *Seebohm, Cat. B. Br. Mus.* v. p. 135. Sylvia cetti, *Marm. Mem. Acc. Tor.* xxx. p. 254; *Tem. Man. d'Orn.* i. p. 194. Bradypterus cetti, (*Marm.*) *Cat. Mus. Hein.* i. p. 43; *Shelley, B. Egypt,* p. 89; *Dresser, Ibis,* 1876, p. 89. Cettia orientalis, *Tristram, Ibis,* 1867, p. 79. Cettia stolickza, *Hume, Str. F.* ii. p. 520. Cettia cettioides, *Hume, Str. F.* i. p. 194. Bradyptetes cetti, (*Marm.*) *Blanf. East Persia* ii. p. 200.—CETTI'S BUSH-WARBLER.

"A spot in front of the eyes dusky; a streak from the nostrils over the eye and a circle round the eye fulvous white; the forehead, crown, and whole upper surface a warm rufous or ferruginous brown, more rufous on the rump and upper tail coverts; the quills and tail hair brown, margined with rufescent olive; ear coverts, sides of the neck, body, flanks and vent feathers a pale dull greyish or earthy brown; chin, throat, breast, and abdomen white, lower tail coverts slightly rufous brown (webs very lax and much disunited) narrowly tipped with white; axillaries and wing lining slightly greyish white; the edge of the wing just above the base of the primaries is white; in some few specimens the eye streak extends beyond the eye to more than half of the ear coverts, but in most it ceases just beyond the posterior angle of the eye; irides brown; legs and feet pale brown or fleshy brown, darker on toes and claw; bill dark horny brown, but paler on lower mandible.

"*Length.*—5·8 to 6·5 inches; expanse 7·5 to 8·4; tail from vent 2.4 to 3; wing 2·5 to 2·8; wings, when closed, reach to within from 1·2 to 2 of end of tail; bill at front 0·4 to 0·5; tarsus 0·8 to nearly 0·9; weight 0·4 oz."—*Stray Feathers*, vol. i. p. 191.

Hab.—Sind, Beloochistan, Persia, and Afghanistan. Found in France, Spain, Algeria, Greece, Asia Minor, Palestine and Turkestan.

It is found on both shores of the Mediterranean, extending eastwards as far as Turkestan. It winters in Sind. Mr. Blanford obtained it in the Elburz Mountains north of Tehran, where it abounded in bushes on the sides of the valleys. Menetries found it on the Talish Mountains south of Lankoran. Mr. Blanford found its nest near Asupas. He describes it as cup-shaped, deep, rather roughly constructed of dried grass and lined with a little down of plants. Eggs, two in number, uniform dull brick red in colour. Size 0·75 inch × 0·57.

Mr. Hume gives an interesting account of its skulking habits among the almost impenetrable rushes.

325. Cettia fortipes, (*Hodgs.*) *Seebohm, P. Z. S.* 1878, p. 980; *id.*, *Ibis*, 1879, p. 36; *id.*, *Cat. B. Br. Mus.* v. p. 137. Horornis fortipes, *Hodgs. MS. Drawings B. Nepaul*, pl. 63; *Blyth, J. A. S. B.* xiv. p. 584; *Jerd. B. Ind.* ii. p. 162; *Hume, Nests and Eggs*, p. 329; *Brooks, Str. F.* viii. p. 475. Drymoica brevicauda, *Blyth, J. A. S. B.* xvi. p. 459. Horornis assimilis, (*Gray*) *Brooks, Str. F.* x. p. 170. Neornis assimilis, *Bl. Ibis*, 1867, p. 22; *Godwn.-Austen, J. A. S. B.* xliii. pt. ii. p. 167; *Wald. in Bl. B. Burm.* p. 105; *Hume and Dav.*, vi. p. 351; Schœnicola fortipes, *Hume, Str. F.* viii. p. 101.—HODGSON'S HILL-WARBLER.

Upper surface rich russet brown; lores and ear coverts darker russet; eye streak indistinct pale brown, in some with a yellowish tinge; wings and tail brown, the outer webs edged with russet brown; under surface of body buffish brown; axillaries and under wing coverts pale yellow; bill dark brown, the base of lower mandible paler; legs and feet pale brown; irides pale brown.

Length.—4·5 inches; wing 1·88 to 2·28; tail 1·86 to 2·21; culmen 0·48 to 0·56; from gape 0·62; tarus 0·83.

Hab.—The Himalayas from Cashmere to Assam, Sikkim, Eastern Bengal, Western China, Burmah and the Island of Formosa. Recorded from Nepaul, Darjeeling, Kashgar and British Burmah. It has been procured in Karin by Captain Wardlaw-Ramsay, and by Dr. Anderson in the hills east of Bhamo. Colonel Godwin-Austen got it in the hill tracts of Eastern Bengal. Seebohm says "in all localities it is doubtless a partial migrant, breeding at high elevations above the level of winter snow, and descending lower into the valleys during the cold season.

326. Cettia flavolivacea, (*Hodgs.*) *Seebohm, Ibis,* 1879, p. 36; *id. Cat. B. Br. Mus.* v. p. 138. Neornis flavolivacea, *Hodgs., MS. Drawings B. Nepaul,* pl. 61 fig. 1; *Jerd. B. Ind.* ii. p. 188, No. 552. Neornis cacharensis, (*Hodgs.*) *Gray, Cat. Mam. & B. Nepaul,* p. 67.—The HIMALAYAN BUSH-WARBLER.

Upper parts dark brownish green, paler on the rump; lores and feathers behind the eye brown; supercilium rather indistinct, buffish yellow; wings and tail brown, the outer webs of the feathers edged with brownish green. Chin, throat and centre of abdomen deep yellow, with a brownish tinge on the breast, flanks, thighs and under tail coverts; axillaries and under wing coverts bright yellow; inner margins of quills nearly white; bill dark brown, paler at base of lower mandible; 4th, 5th and 6th primaries nearly equal and longest; legs and feet brown.

Length.—4·5 inches; wing 1·9 to 2·15; tail 1·9 to 2·2; culmen 0·51 to 0·48; tarsus 0·9.

Hab.—The Himalayas from Nepaul to Assam. Breeds at high altitudes.

327. Cettia pallidipes, (*Blanf.*) *Seebohm, Ibis,* 1879, p. 36; *id. Cat. B. Br. Mus.* v. p. 139. Phylloscopus pallidipes, *Blanf., J. A. S. B.* xli., pt. ii. p. 162; pl. vii. (1872). Horeites sericea, *Walden, Blyth, Wald. in B. Burm.* p. 119; *Tweed., Ibis,* 1877, p. 487; *Hume, Str. F.* v. p. 57. Horeites pallidipes, *Hume and Dav., Str. F.* vi. p. 344; *Hume, Str. F.* viii. p. 101; *Oates, B. Br. Burm.,* i. p. 122.—BLANFORD'S HILL WARBLER.

Upper plumage, tail, and wings olive brown; a broad supercilium greyish white; lores and feathers behind the eye olive brown; ear coverts greyish white; under surface white, very slightly tinged with brownish on the breast, flanks, and under tail coverts; axillaries and under wing coverts white. Bill Phylloscopine, yellow, the under mandible pale brown; 4th, 5th, and 6th primaries nearly equal and longest; 2nd shorter than the secondaries; 1st more than half the length of the second; iris dull brown; legs fleshy white.

Length.—4 inches; tail 1·7; wing 2·05 to 2·2; bill from gape 0·55.

Hab.—Sikkim and Assam, also Tenasserim. Oates says, "Blanford's Hill-Warbler was procured at Pahpoon in Tenasserim by Mr. Davison, and on the

Karin Hills east of Tounghoo by Captain Wardlaw-Ramsay. It was first discovered by Blanford in Sikkim, where it is probably a partial migrant, ascending to a considerable elevation to breed.

328. Cettia brunneifrons, (*Hodgs*). *Seebohm, Ibis*, 1879, p. 36; *id., Cat. B. Br. Mus.* vi. p. 143. Horeites brunneifrons, *Hodgs., M. S. Drawings, B. Nep. Passeres*, pl. 62, a fig 1; *Bly., J. A. S. B.* xiv. p. 585; *Jerd. B. Ind.* ii. p. 163, No. 527; *Brooks, J. A. S. B.* xli. pt. ii. p. 78, (1878). Horeites pollicaris (*Hodgs.*), *Jerd. B. Ind.* ii. p. 163, No. 528.—The NEPAULESE BUSH-WARBLER.

Upper surface dark russet-brown, shading into brownish red on the nape and head; supercilium buffish white, extending to the nape; wings and tail dark russet-brown, their outer webs edged with the same; chin and centre of belly nearly white, shading into ashy grey on the sides of the neck and breast and into russet-brown on the flanks, thighs, and under tail coverts; axillaries and under wing coverts nearly white. Bill Phylloscopine, upper mandible dark brown, the under mandible pale brown; primaries, secondaries, and 1st quill as in the last; legs, feet, and claws pale brown.

Length.—4·37 inches; wing 1·7 to 1·95; tail 1·5 to 1·8; tarsus 0·73 to 0·75; culmen 0·4 to 0·45.

Hab.—The Himalayas from Nepaul, the Mountains of Chinese Thibet to Sikkim, as low as Darjeeling. Breeds at high elevations.

329. Cettia major, (*Moore*), *Seebohm, Ibis*, 1879, p. 36; *id., Cat. B. Br. Mus.* v. p. 145, pl. vii. Horeites major, *Moore, P. Z. S.*, 1854, p. 105; (*descr. prem.*); *Jerd. B. Ind.* ii. p. 164, No. 529.—MOORE'S BUSH or LARGE HILL-WARBLER.

Upper surface olive brown, shading into russet on the wings and tail, which are edged with dark olive brown, and into rich dark russet-brown colour on the nape and head; supercilium yellowish ferruginous, extending over the ear coverts, which are brown tinged with ruddy; chin and abdomen white; throat, sides of neck, and centre of breast olive brown, deeper on the flanks, thighs, and under tail coverts. Bill Phylloscopine, dark brown; under mandible paler at base; 5th and 6th primaries nearly equal and longest; 2nd shorter than the secondaries; 1st more than half the length of the second; legs, feet, and claws pale brown.

Length.—3·9 to 4·5 inches; wing 2·41 to 2·63; tail 2·2 to 2·4; tarsus 1·02; culmen 0·55.

Hab.—The Himalayas, from Nepaul to Sikkim, and the Mountains of Chinese Thibet, descending into the valleys in the cold season. Seebohm adds that it is probably a partial migrant breeding at or near the limit of forest growth on the Himalayas.

GROUP—BRADYPTERI.

Aberrant Reed Warblers with 10-12 tail feathers, allied to the Grass-Warblers.

Gen. **Schœnicola.**—*Blyth.*

Bill moderate, rather deep, much compressed; culmen slightly curved; rictal bristles moderate, few; wings moderate, slightly rounded; 4th quill longest, 3rd equal to the 5th; tail moderate, the feathers broad; under tail coverts long, reaching to more than half the length of the tail; tarsus long; plumage lax.

330. Schœnicola platyura, (*Jerd.*) *Blyth, J. A. S. B.* xiii. p. 374; *Jerd. B. Ind.* ii. p. 73, No. 442; *Hume, Str. F.* 1878, p. 37; *id. Str. F.* 1879, p. 97; *Brooks, Str. F.* 1881, p. 209; *Hume,* t. c. p. 211; *Legge, Birds, Ceylon,* p. 532; *Hume, Str. F.* 1880, pp. 234-260; *Butler, Cat. B. Bom. Pres.* p. 43; *Sharpe, P. Z. S.* 1881, p. 920; *id. Cat. B. Br. Mus.* vii. p. 110. Timalia platyura, *Jerd. Madr. Journ.* xiii. p. 170.—The BROAD-TAILED REED-BIRD.

Upper surface russet or rufous brown, including the ear and wing coverts; quills dusky, externally margined with russet-brown, the innermost secondaries the same on both webs; tail russet-brown, obscurely banded with dusky brown under certain lights; the outer feathers darker and tipped with ashy; lores whitish; supercilium fulvous, also the cheeks and sides of the neck; throat, centre of breast, and abdomen whitish, the former washed with fulvous on the lower parts, also the sides of the body, flanks, thighs, and under tail coverts—the latter washed with ashy at the tips; under wing coverts and axillaries buffish white. Bill horny yellow, 0·4; legs fleshy yellow; irides yellowish brown.

Length.—5·8 to 6·3 inches; wing 2·5 to 2·65; tail 2·6 to 2·8; tarsus 0·8 to 0·85.

Hab.—Southern India (Belgaum, Travancore, Wynaad, at the foot of the Neilgherries, and Ceylon). According to Jerdon the Broad-tailed Reed-Bird affects reeds in swampy places. In their actions and habits, Captain Butler says: These birds resemble *Chætornis striata* and in the breeding season rise constantly into the air, chirruping like that species, and descending afterwards in the same way on to some low bush or tussock of grass, sometimes even on to the telegraph wires. They are fearful little skulks. If you attempt to pursue them, at once they disappear into the grass, from whence it is almost impossible to flush them again unless you all but tread on them. They breed in September. The food of the Broad-tailed Reed-bird consists chiefly of insects. Captain Butler's notes, in *Str. F.* ix. p. 262, quoted by Mr. Hume, in regard to the nidification of this species are to the effect that the nest is composed of coarse grass, with an entrance on one side, built in long grass, and about a foot from the ground; the eggs, he says, have 'a purplish white ground, sprinkled all over with numerous small specks and spots of purplish brown and purple (brownish red, almost black in some), with a cap of the same at the large end. They are moderately broad ovals, with but little gloss. Size 0·73 × 0·6.

Gen. **Laticilla**.—*Blyth.*

Bill of moderate length, compressed and slender; the culmen slightly curved; wings short, rounded; 5th and 6th quills longest; second primary shorter than secondaries; tail strongly graduated, long and broad, the outer tail feathers just reaching beyond the under tail coverts, beyond which the outstretched feet do not reach. This genus comprises two species only—both found in India.

331. Laticilla burnesi, (*Blyth*) *Blyth, J. A. S. B.* xiv. p. 596; *Hume, Str. F.* 1873, p. 180; 1879, p. 97; *Doig,* t. c. p. 370; *Murray, Vert. Zool., Sind,* p. 134; *Sharpe, Cat. B. Br. Mus.* viii. p. 118; Eurycercus Burnesii, *Blyth. J. A. S. B.*, xiii. p. 374; *Jerd. B. Ind.* ii. p. 74, No. 443.—The LONG-TAILED REED-BIRD.

Above olive brown, paler on the head, rufescent on the back and sides of the neck; the feathers, including the scapulars, mesially streaked with dark brown; rump and upper tail coverts unstriped; lores and round the eye white; ear coverts greyish white; tail olive brown, with faint transverse striæ, the lateral feathers narrowly margined at the tips with whitish; a double line of dark spots from the base of the lower mandible on either side of the throat; under surface white; the flanks and sides brownish, the feathers with fulvous mesial streaks; under tail coverts ferruginous; bill horny brown, paler on lower mandible; irides brown; legs pale horny.

Length.—7 to 7·7 inches; wing 2 to 2·3; tail 4; bill at front 0·4.

Hab.—Sind, the Punjab, N.-W. Provinces and Bengal. Breeds in Sind from July to September.

Affects high grass jungles, from inside which it is most difficult to flush. When once disturbed, it climbs about in the interior of the reeds and grass, and seldom affords a chance of a shot. It requires much patience and trouble to secure specimens. Hume adds that they cost him more trouble than any other bird he met with in Sind. This is certainly the experience of every one desirous of forming a collection of the species.

332. Laticilla cinerascens, (*Wald.*) *Hume, Str. F.* 1879, p. 97; *Sharpe, Cat. B. Br. Mus.* vii. p. 119. Eurycercus cinerascens, *Walden, Ann. and Mag. Nat. Hist.* (4), xvi. p. 156 (1874.—The CINEREOUS LONG-TAILED REED-BIRD.

Adult Male.—Above olive brown, washed with ashy and streaked with dark brown down the centre of the feathers, a little more ashy on the rump and upper tail coverts, and also on the forehead and sides of crown; wing coverts like the back, ashy on the least series; bastard wing feathers dark brown, externally like the back; primary coverts dark brown, edged with olive; quills the same; tail feathers brown, washed with olive on the outer web, the centre of the feathers darker brown; lores, feathers in front of the eye and eyelid white; cheeks and under surface of body white, ashy on the sides of the breast and flanks, the latter washed with brown, as also the thighs externally; under tail coverts yellowish white or pale fulvous; axillaries and under wing coverts white, with a dusky spot near the edge of the wing.

Length.—6 inches; wing 2·1; tail 3·15, tarsus 0·8; culmen 0·55.

Hab.—Bengal. Has not been recorded from any other part of India.

Gen. **Megalurus**.—*Horsf.*

Bill slender, compressed and of moderate length; nostrils apert; rictal bristles few, strong, 3rd quill longest; 4th and 5th nearly equal to it; tarsus long, scutellated; mid toe long.

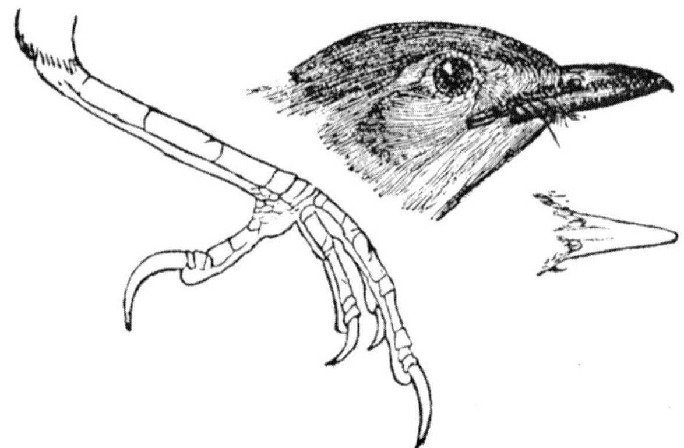

333. Megalurus palustris, *Horsf.*, *Trans.*, *Lin. Soc.* xiii. p. 159; *Blyth*, *Cat. B. Mus. As. Soc.* p. 139; *Jerd.*, *B. Ind.* ii. p. 70; *Hume, Nests and Eggs*, p. 276; *Blyth*, *B. Burm.* p. 118: *Wald.*, *Tr. Z. S.* ix. p. 189; *Oates*, *Str. F.* v. p. 156; *Tweed*, *P. Z. S.* 1877, p. 694; *Hume and Dav.*, *Str. F.* vi. p. 295; *Anderson*, *Yunnan Exp.* p. 639; *Hume*, *Str. F.* viii. p. 97; *Oates*, *Str. F.* x. p. 209; *Sharpe*, *Cat. B. Br. Mus.* vii. p. 123.—The STRIATED MARSH WARBLER.

Upper surface fulvous brown, the head rather rufous, and each feather with a mesial dark brown shaft streak; wing coverts and quills blackish brown, broadly edged with the colour of the back; tail fulvous brown, the shafts and the portion of each feather near them dusky; supercilium greyish white; chin and throat white; sides of the neck and all the lower plumage earthy brown, tinged with buff on the flanks; vent and undertail coverts, also the breast, with a few brown streaks.

The young are distinguished from the adult by the yellow colour of the under surface and lores, the streaks on the throat are absent, and only slightly indicated; the flanks and under tail coverts uniform light rufescent brown; bill black, pale horn on the lower mandible; iris pale brown; eyelids plumbeous.

Length.—9 to 10 inches; wing 3·2 to 4; tail 4·5 to 4·9; tarsus 1·3; bill from gape 0·95.

Hab.—Punjab, N.-W. Provinces, Bengal, Central India, Assam, and British Burmah.

The Striated Marsh Warbler has a very wide range. It is found in the Malayan Peninsula and Java. In Pegu, according to Oates, it is locally distributed, being found only where there is long grass. It occurs on the banks of the Irrawady and tributaries of the Godavery, also on the Nerbudda, but is most abundant in lower Bengal, where the country is intersected by rivers, and where long grass and reeds cover it for miles. It generally keeps in couples, and seldom moves away from the spot it selects for its feeding ground. During the cold weather, and up to the end of the breeding season, this bird has a fine song, which it utters while flying from one patch of grass to another, and which Blyth calls a fine flute-like voice. In doing this, it is said to mount 30 or 40 feet into the air, and to come down with motionless outspread wings. It breeds in May, making a partially domed structure of coarse grasses, in tufts of grass not very high from the ground. The eggs are usually 4 in number, white and speckled with purplish brown.

Gen. **Chætornis.**—*Gray.*

Bill short, about one-half the length of that of *Megalurus*, strong, high, compressed, curved on the culmen, hooked at the tip and notched. Five strong bristles on each side between the gape and the eye; wings long, the 3rd quill longest; legs and feet strong.

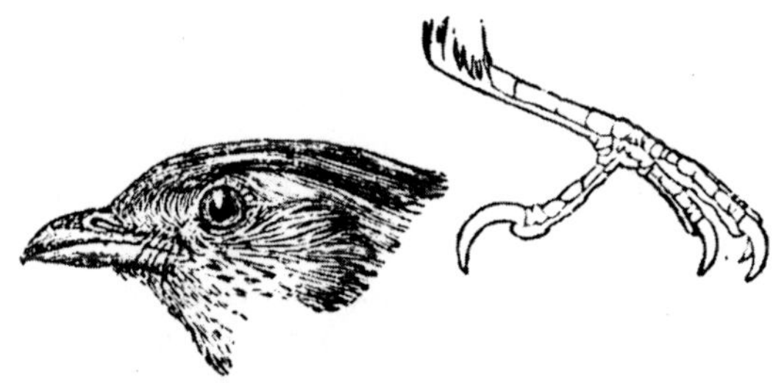

334. Chætornis locustelloides, (*Blyth*), *Blyth*, *J. A. S. B.* xi. p. 602; *Sharpe, Cat. B. Br. Mus.* vii. p. 130. Dasyornis collurioceps, *Blyth tom. cii.* p. 603. Chætornis striata, *Gray, Gen. B.* i. p. 167, pl. 48, fig. 9; *Jerd., B. Ind.* ii. p. 72, No. 441; *Ball, Str. F.* 1875, p. 288; *Butler, Str. F.* 1877, p. 209; *Ball*, t. c. p. 416; *Hume, Str. F.* 1878, p. 215; *Cripps*, t. c. p. 279; *Butler, Cat. B. Sind, &c., Str. F.* 1879, p. 29.—The GRASS WARBLER.

Upper surface brown, the feathers streaked mesially with dark brown, and edged with fulvous or whity-brown; lower back, rump, and upper tail coverts less broadly streaked; quills dark brown; broadly edged externally with rufescent or tawny buff; centre tail feathers dark brown, darker along the middle from where dusky bars radiate, forming dusky bands; rest of the feathers dark brown externally washed with lighter brown and tipped with white; forehead fulvous brown; lores dull whitish; supercilium buffy white; throat and centre of body dull white, yellowish buff on the chest, sides of the body, thighs, and under tail coverts; axillaries and under wing coverts buffy white; bill dusky brown above, fleshy brown beneath; legs brownish fleshy; irides dull greyish brown.

Length.—7·75 to 8 inches; wing 3·3 to 3·5; tail 3·3 to 3·75; tarsus 1·1; bill at front 0·46 to 0·5.

Hab.—Bengal, Southern India, and Central India. It has been found on the Neilgheries and at Nellore during the cold season in long grass and rice-fields, also in thickets of reeds. Its habits are quite those of *Megalurus*.

Group.—CISTICOLÆ.

The position of this group of birds has not been anywhere well defined. There can, however, be no doubt as to its position being next the *Badypteri*, with 10-12, tail feathers strongly graduated or round. The shape and form of the bills of the different Indian genera comprising it show a general affinity, as also the thick orbital bristles, which serve to protect the eyes of the members forming the group, when forcing their way through tufts of grass.

Gen. Suya.—*Hodgs.*

Bill stout and compressed, slightly (generally 0·1) shorter than that of *Chætornis striata*, and proportionately less in width; nostrils apert; gape with *two* strong rictal bristles on each side; tail of 10 feathers very long and much graduated.

335. Suya crinigera, *Hodgs., As. Res.* xix. p. 183; *Jerd., B. Ind.* ii. p. 183; *Hume, Nests and Eggs*, p. 353; *Wald. in Bl. B. Burm.* p. 120; *Hume, Str. F.* ix. p. 138; *id., Str. F.* vii. p. 1; viii. p. 151; *Scully, Str. F.*

viii. p. 305; *Sharpe, Cat. B. Br. Mus.* vii. p. 177. Suya fuliginosa, *Hodgs. in Gray's Zool., Misc.*, p. 82; *Jerd., B. Ind.* ii. p. 184; *Hume, Nests and Eggs*, p. 355; *id., Str. F.* viii. p. 101. Prinia striata, *Swinh., Journ. N. China, As. Soc.* 1859, p. 227. Suya obscura, *Hume, Str. F.* ii. p. 507; vii. p. 2. Suya striata, *Dav.* et. *Oust Ois. Chine*, p. 259; *Hume, Str. F.* vii. p. 1. Blanfordius striatulus, *Hume, Str. F.* 1873, p. 300; *id.*, 1879, p. 101; *Murray, Hdbk. Zool., &c., Sind*, p. 157; *id., Vert. Zool., Sind*, p. 153.—The BROWN HILL WARBLER.

Adult in breeding plumage. Above dull brown with a slight olive tint, the feathers margined with greyish olive, causing a somewhat mottled appearance; lower back and rump more uniform; wing coverts brown with greyish olive edges, the outer coverts of the lesser series margined with yellowish white as also the bastard wing and primary coverts; quills brown with hoary olive margins and tips; before the latter a dusky brown subterminal spot; crown of the head like the back, and mottled in the same manner; lores yellowish; *no supercilium*; ear coverts and cheeks yellowish buff, the former dusky along their upper margins; throat and under surface yellowish buff; sides of the breast brown or mottled with dark brown bases to the feathers; abdomen a little clearer yellowish buff; sides of the body and flanks light olivaceous; thighs a little more tawny like the abdomen; under wing coverts and axillaries light tawny. (Sharpe.)

Bill black; tarsus fleshy; claws brown and dusky; iris straw or golden yellow. (Scully.)

Length.—5·8; wing 2·1; tail 2·3; tarsus 0·8; culmen 0·6.

In non-breeding plumage, Dr. Scully says the bill is brown above; the lower mandible pale yellowish or pinkish horny, the head and upper back more or less rufescent, and more or less deep brown, conspicuously striated with pale more or less rufescent fawn or yellowish brown; the quills margined with bright ferruginous, the supercilium small and inconspicuous and of a creamy colour.

The young female (*Suya obscura*, Hume,) is described by Sharpe as being brown above, with dusky centres to the feathers of the head and back, causing a mottled appearance, less distinct on the back; rump uniform brown; lesser and median wing coverts like the back; greater coverts, bastard wing, primary coverts and quills light brown, with reddish buff margins to the feathers, more distinctly rufous on the outer edge of the primaries; upper tail coverts darker brown; tail feathers brown; with dusky cross bars under certain lights, the edges and tips paler and more fulvous brown; the tips plainer on all but the two centre tail feathers and having a distinct subterminal spot of dusky brown; lores dull whitish, obscured by blackish tips; no distinct eyebrow, but the superciliary feathers, a little paler than the crown; eyelid whitish; ear coverts light brown, washed with yellowish buff; cheeks, throat, foreneck and chest buffy whitish; breast and abdomen pure white; sides of the breast washed with olive brown; sides of the body, flanks, thighs, and under tail coverts clear fulvous brown; under wing coverts and axillaries pale tawny buff, whiter near the edge of the wing.

Length.—5·9 inches; wing 2·15; tail 2·8; tarsus 0·85; culmen 0·45.

A young bird in its first winter dress is described by Hume as *Blanfordius striatulus.* The following is his description:—

"An obscure rufous white streak from the nostrils to the upper part of the eye. The whole upper parts dull greyish olive brown (the grey preponderating on the head), all the feathers except those of the upper tail coverts conspicuously centred with dark brown; wings pale hair brown, all the feathers margined with pale rufescent olive; tail feathers a sort of olive brown, the feathers conspicuously darker, very stiff-looking, and with glistening shafts, all the feathers obsoletely transversely rayed, the central ones most strongly so. All but the central ones narrowly tipped fulvous white, and with an obscure subterminal dark band; on the under surface, the shafts are white; the ear-coverts mingled fulvous and pale rufous brown; the sides of the neck streaked like the back; on either side of the throat descends from the gape, for about half an inch, a band of tiny white feathers, with minute dark centres, so as to produce the appearance of two or three regular rows of little spots on each side of the throat; the chin and the centre of the throat, breast and abdomen white, tinged buffy on the two latter, and with all the feathers of the throat and breast very faintly and narrowly tipped with brown, so as to produce the appearance of a number of narrow, faint, transverse bars. The flanks, sides, vent and lower tail coverts are tinged with dull olive brown mingled with fulvous buff; the wing lining is buffy white, and so are the inner margins of the inner webs of the quills as seen from below.

"*Length.*—(Of the dry skin; female) about 6 inches, wing 1·9, tail from vent 2·75, bill at front about 0·45, tarsus 0·7, tail from vent 2·75, legs and feet, fleshy, bill brown, pale fleshy on lower mandible."—(*Hume, Str. F.* i. p. 300.)

Hab.—From Sind, throughout the Himalayas from Cashmere to Bhootan, and thence through Yunnan to South China and Formosa. Occurs also in the Burmese countries. Recorded from Cashmere, Nepaul, Darjeeling, Sikkim, Bhootan, Momein, Thayetmyo, and Sind. There has been much confusion in regard to the identity of the Brown Hill Warbler, owing to the very material difference in the plumage of the species in its various stages, from nestling to adult. The same remarks apply to all the species of the genus. This circumstance has led to the long full descriptions given of this little species. It is a resident species wherever it is found. It frequents brushwood, and may occasionally be seen on low trees. It seeks its food on the ground, and lives on small insects and larvæ. On tall grass it delights to sit, so Hutton says, from whence it pours forth a loud and long-continued grating note like the filing of a saw. The nest is large, and loosely constructed of fine grass, with an opening on one side. It breeds in May, June, and July. The eggs, 5 to 7 in number, are white and densely speckled with red.

336. Suya atrigularis, *Hodgs. Icon. ined. in Br. Mus. Passeres, App.* pl. 36, No. 893; *Moore, P. Z. S.* 1854, p. 77; *Jerd., B. Ind.* ii. p. 184, No. 549; *Beavan, Ibis.,* 1867, p. 455; *Hume, Str. F.* 1878, p. 4; *Sharpe, Cat. B. Br. Mus.* vii. p. 180. Prinia atrigularis, *Gray, Hand—L. B.* i. p. 197.—The BLACK-BREASTED HILL or WREN-WARBLER.

Above dark olive brown, lighter on the rump and upper tail coverts; crown of the head, nape, occiput, and hind neck distinctly dusky, with darker centres to the feathers of the forehead and sinciput; lores and sides of crown dusky, with a slight indication of a narrow white eyebrow; ear coverts dark ashy, with whitish shaft lines; feathers under the eye dusky; cheeks whitish, the feathers tipped with black forming a distinct moustache; sides of the neck, throat, foreneck and breast black; abdomen whitish; the sides of the body and flanks olive brown; thighs reddish olive; scapulars and wing coverts like the back; the greater coverts dusky, externally edged with olive; primary coverts dusky brown with olive margins; quills brown; the secondaries externally reddish near the base, the primaries edged with ashy olive or buffish; tail light brown, paler on the edges of the feathers, which are narrowly tipped with paler brown; under tail coverts pale olive; under wing coverts and axillaries pale tawny buff; bill horny brown; legs pale fleshy; irides yellow brown.

Length.—6 to 6·5 inches; wing 1·85; tail 3·6; tarsus 0·85; culmen 0·55.

During winter the black of the throat is wanting, the wing coverts and quills are broadly margined with tawny buff, a distinct white eyebrow is present, and the feathers of the cheeks, throat and breast have slight blackish margins.

Hab.—The Eastern Himalayas generally. Is recorded from Nepaul, Darjeeling, and Sikkim. Like its congeners it frequents brushwood. The nest is globular, and made of the same materials as that of the preceding, but with an opening on the top. Eggs, 4 to 5, of a dull Indian red colour.

337. Suya khasiana, *Godw.-Austen, Ann. and Mag. Nat. Hist.* (4) xviii. p. 412, 1876; *Hume, Str. F.* 1877, p. 59; *id., Hume, Str. F.* 1878, p. 3; 1879, p. 101; *Sharpe, Cat. B. Br. Mus.* vii. p. 181.—The KHASIA WREN-WARBLER.

Above rufescent brown, the head like the back, the rump rather more fulvous; wing coverts like the back; primary coverts and quills washed with olive brown on the margins; lores blackish, with a narrow line of white above; ear coverts and a line along the sides of the crown in continuation of the white streak dark ashy grey, extending on to the sides of the neck; cheeks white, forming a long moustachial streak; throat, foreneck and breast black, the latter mottled with subterminal spots of white; breast and abdomen white, with a few blackish margins to the breast feathers; sides of the body and flanks olive brown; thighs tawny buff; under tail coverts olive brown; under wing coverts and axillaries light tawny buff, white near the edge of the wing.

Length.—6·2 inches; wing 1·9; tail 3·5; tarsus 0·95; culmen 0·6.

In the non-breeding plumage, according to Hume, the bill is paler, the white supercilium conspicuous, the lores white; chin, throat and upper breast nearly pure white; no mandibular stripes; forehead, crown, and occiput clear rufous; tail feathers much broader and unabraded.

Hab.—Khasia Hills.

Nothing is known of its habits nor of its nidification.

338. Suya albigularis. *Hume, Str. F.* 1873, p. 459; *id., Str. F.* 1880, p. 227; *Sharpe, Cat. B. Br. Mus.* vii. p. 182.—The WHITE-THROATED HILL WREN-WARBLER.

Adult ♀.—*Above olive brown*; lesser wing and median coverts like the back; greater coverts slightly more rufous on the outer margins; bastard wing dusky, narrowly edged with whitish on the outer web; primary coverts and quills dusky brown, margined with fulvous brown, a little more rufescent on the primaries; upper tail coverts like the back; tail feathers brown, edged with fulvous brown, the outer feathers narrowly tipped with fulvous; *crown of the head dull ashy grey*, slightly washed with olive; lores dusky, surmounted by a narrow white line; ear coverts dark ashy, the lower portion mottled with whitish shaft lines; cheeks white, slightly mottled with blackish tips to the feathers; sides of the neck dark ashy with a wash of olive; *throat, foreneck and breast yellowish white*, the feathers at the sides of the throat and chest margined with black forming a black line; abdomen whitish; sides of the body, flanks, thighs and under tail coverts fulvous brown, washed with olive; under wing coverts and axillaries pale tawny buff, whiter near the edge of the wing; bill greyish black; tarsus pale flesh colour; iris greenish grey.

Length.—5·5 inches; wing 2; tail 2·7; tarsus 0·85; culmen 0·5. (Sharpe.)

Hab.—British Burmah (?), ranging to Sumatra.

The evidence as to the identity of this species with *Suya superciliaris* is not satisfactory. Oates places it as a synonym of *superciliaris*, simply on the assertion of Mr. Hume that the Sumatra bird, which he named *S. superciliaris*, is identical with the present species. Mr. Sharpe, however, says that a skin of the species under notice was lent to him by Mr. F. Nicholson, and that it agrees with Hume's description. He does not follow Mr. Hume in uniting *superciliaris* and *albigularis*. *S. albigularis*, he says, "*may* have, to judge from analogy, a black-throated breeding dress; but in its non-breeding dress it is very distinct from the Burmese, *S. superciliaris*, which never has a grey head." In its habits *S. albigularis* does not differ from its congeners.

339. Suya superciliaris, *Anderson, P. Z. S.* 1871, p. 212; *Swinh. P. Z. S.* 1871, p. 351; *Hume and Dav., Str. F.* 1878, vi. p. 350; *id., Str. F.* vii. p. 3; viii. p. 101; *Sharpe, Cat. Br. B. Mus.* vii. p. 182. Suya erythropleura, *Wald. in Bl. B. Burm.* p. 120; *Hume, Str. F.* v. p. 58; *Hume and Dav., Str. F.* vi. p. 351; *Hume, Str. F.* viii. p. 101.—ANDERSON'S HILL-WARBLER.

Adult ♀.—Head uniform brown; back, rump, upper tail coverts and tail rufescent brown; rectrices tipped pale; supercilium broad, white, extending from the nostrils to the nape; lores black; ear coverts pale brown with whitish shaft streaks; chin, throat, breast and abdomen white, tinged with fulvous; sides of the body, vent, thighs and under tail coverts ferruginous; wings brown, edged with dark rufous; iris greenish brown; legs flesh colour; bill black above.

Length.—7 to 7·4 inches; wing 1·95 to 2; tail 3·8 to 4·5; tarsus 0·85; culmen 0·5.

Hab.—British Burmah. Nothing is known of its habits, nor of its nidification.

Gen. **Prinia**.—*Horsf.*

Bill of moderate length, stoutish, slightly deeper than broad at nostrils; culmen moderately curving, and not exceeding the length of hind toe and claw; rictal bristles well developed, 2 to 3 on each side; wings short and rounded, the first three primaries nearly equal; 4th and 5th generally longest; tail graduated, long, and of 10 feathers; tarsus long; claws moderately curved.

340. Prinia inornata, *Sykes, P. Z. S.* 1837, p. 89; *Jerd., Mad. Journ.* xi. p. 4; *Blyth, J. A. S. B.* xiii. p. 376; *Sharpe, Cat. B. Br. Mus.* vii. p. 195; *Oates, B. Br. Burm,* i. p. 114. Sylvia longicaudata, *Tick., J. A. S. B.* ii. p. 576. Prinia fusca, *Hodgs., Gray's Zool., Misc.* p. 82; *id., P. Z. S.* 1845, p. 29. Prinia adamsi, *Jerd., B. Ind.* ii. p. 170, No. 533; *Hume, Nests and Eggs,* p. 335; *id., Str. F.* viii. p. 101. Drymoipus inornatus, *Jerd., B. Ind.* ii. p. 178, No. 543; *Hume, Nests and Eggs,* p. 346; *Hume and Henderson, Lahore to Yarkand,* pl. xvii. fig. 1; *Brooks, Str. F.* iii. p. 495; vii. p. 468. Drymoipus longicaudatus, *Jerd., B. Ind.* ii. p. 180, No. 544; *Butler, Str. F.* iii. p. 483; *Brooks, Str. F.* iv. p. 229; *Hume, Str. F.* iv. p. 407. Drymoipus fuscus, *Hume, Nests and Eggs,* p. 348. Drymoipus terricolor, *Hume, Nests and Eggs,* p. 349; *Brooks, Str. F.* iv. p. 229; *Hume, Str. F.* iv. p. 407. Drymoipus longicaudus, *Hume, Nests and Eggs,* p. 350. Drymœca longicaudata, *Bl. B. Burm.* p. 118; *Hume, Str. F.* viii. p. 101. Drymoica fusca, *Hume, Str. F.* viii. p. 101. Drymœca insularis, *Legge, Birds, Ceylon,* p. 529, pl. xxv. fig. 2. Prinia blanfordi, *Wald. in Bl. B. Burm* p. 118; *Oates, B. Br. Burm.* i. p. 112. Drymoipus extensicauda, (*Swinh.*), *apud. Oates, Str. F.* iii. p. 340. Drymoica blanfordi, *Hume and Dav., Str. F.* vi. p. 349.—The INDIAN WREN-WARBLER.

Winter.—Upper plumage and tail rufous brown, the feathers on the crown dark centred—the tail feathers tipped pale ashy, with a black subterminal spot more distinct when seen from below; wings brown, edged with bright rufous; under surface of body fulvous, rather darker on the breast, flanks, and under tail coverts; thighs dark rufous. The young in first plumage are very rufous.

In breeding plumage, the upper surface is ashy or greyish brown, with indications of dark centres to the feathers, especially of the head; wings dark brown, edged with ashy white or brownish ashy; the primary coverts and quills with narrow rufous brown edges, and the inner secondaries with fulvous brown; tail pale brown with dusky cross bars under certain lights; all, except the centre feathers, white at the tip, and a tolerably well defined subterminal bar of blackish; lores, supercilium, cheeks and ear coverts white, the latter tinged with fulvous; under surface of the body pale yellowish buff, whiter on the throat; thighs tawny rufous; sides of upper breast ashy; axillaries and under wing coverts yellowish white; bill black; legs and feet pale yellowish fleshy; iris hazel brown (Brooks), orange yellow (Oates).

Length.—In summer 5·25; in winter 6 inches; wing 1·9 to 2; tail in summer 2·25; winter 3 inches; culmen 0·4; tarsus 0·8.

Hab.—The whole of India and Ceylon, ranging westward into Sind, eastward through Assam, the Burmese countries, Southern China, Formosa, and Hainan. Occurs throughout Sind, parts of Beloochistan and Southern Afghanistan, Punjab, N. W. Provinces, Oudh, Bengal, the Concan, Deccan, South India, Behar, Khandesh, Cachar, all Burmah and Nepaul. Oates says it is an amusing little bird. Perched on the summit of a stalk of elephant grass, it gives out its monotonous song, consisting of one note repeated some twenty times; then, with its ample tail held at right angles to the back, it skips away to the bottom of the next tuft only to reappear on the summit with its persistent little song. These birds seem hardly able to regulate their flight. They seldom fly more than twenty yards, and in this short space they appear in imminent peril of turning sundry somersaults, for the bill on these occasions points to the ground, while the tail bent well over the back is nearly horizontal. The Indian Wren-Warbler breeds wherever it is found. The nest is cylindrical or oval in shape, made entirely of fine grasses most strongly woven together; although the walls can be seen through, yet they resist any ordinary efforts to tear them asunder. Altogether the nest is a beautiful specimen of bird architecture. The eggs, usually 4 in number, are pale blue, marked with spots and scrawls of purplish brown.

341. Prinia sylvatica, *Jerd., Madr. Journ.* xi. p. 4; *Blyth, J. A. S. B.* xiii. p. 376. Prinia neglecta, *Jerd., Madr. Journ.* xiii. p. 130. Drymoica sylvatica, *Blyth, J. A. S. Beng.* xvi. p. 458; *id., Cat. B. Mus. As. Soc.* p. 142. Drymoica jerdoni, *Blyth, J. A. S. B.* xvi. p. 459. Drymoica neglecta, *Gray, Gen. B.* i. p. 164; *Ball, Str. F.* ii. p. 218, Drymoipus validus, *Jerd. B. Ind.* ii. p. 182. Drymoipus sylvaticus, *Jerd.* t. c. p. 181. No. 545; *Hume, Nests and Eggs, Ind. B.* p. 351. Drymoipus jerdoni, t. c. p. 180; *Hume, Str. F.* 1873, p. 437; 1874, p. 453. Drymœca valida, *Blyth, Ibis.*, 1867, p. 302; *Hume, Str. F.* 1879, p. 101; *Legge, B. Ceylon.* p. 525. Suya gangetica, *Blyth, Ibis.*, 1867, p. 23; *Hume, Str. F.* 1877, p. 138; 1878, p. 6; 1879, p. 101. Drymoipus rufescens, *Hume, Nests and Eggs, Ind. B.* p. 351; *Butler, Str. F.* 1875, p. 484; *Hume,* t. c. p. 484; *Brooks, Str. F.* 1876, p. 229. Drymoipus insignis, *Hume, Nests and Eggs, Ind. B.* p. 351. Drymœca rufescens, *Hume, Str. F.* 1879, p. 101. Drymœca neglecta, *Hume,* t. c. p. 101; *Dav. and Wenden.* t. c. p. 407; *Vidal, Str. F.* 1880, p. 480.—The JUNGLE WREN-WARBLER.

Breeding Plumage.—Above dark brown, slightly paler on the lower back and rump; head and hindneck dusky ash brown; lores dull white; no supercilium present; ear coverts dusky brown, with obscure yellowish shaft lines; cheeks and under surface of body yellowish white, the abdomen pure white; sides of breast ashy; flanks fulvescent; thighs tawny brown; under tail coverts pale yellowish white; upper tail coverts and centre tail feathers pale reddish brown, crossed with obscure dusky bars under certain lights; the next feathers brown along the outer web and white on the inner, shaded more or less with pale sooty brown; external tail feather almost entirely white; lesser and median wing coverts, also scapulars, dark brown with ashy margins; greater coverts margined with reddish brown, also the quills. *In the winter plumage,* the tail feathers have no white on the inner web, but the external feathers are tipped with white, and have a tolerably distinct subterminal black bar; bill brown black; irides hazel; legs and feet yellowish.

Length.—6·3 to 6·5 inches; wing 2·55 to 2·6; tail 2·85 to 3·3 in winter plumage; tarsus 0·9; culmen 0·55.

Hab.—The whole of India, south of the Himalayas, and Ceylon. Recorded from the N. W. Provinces, Bengal, Assam, Concan, Deccan, Central and Southern India, Malabar Coast, Travancore, Nepaul and Cashmere.

Habits same as the last. Mr. Hume in his *Nests and Eggs, Indian Birds,* refers to the nidification of this species under all the synonyms quoted above. Generally it may be said that the nest is a deep cup, made of grass, well woven and neat, usually fixed in a thorny shrub, and lined with a little soft down. Eggs, 2 to 4, pale blue, with large purplish brown blotches, or unmarked.

Gen. **Burnesia.**—*Jerd.*

Bill longer and more slender than in Prinia. Culmen exceeding the length of hind toe and claw; rictal setæ fine and minute, not reaching beyond nostrils; plumage streaked; tail, of 10 feathers, strongly graduated.

342. Burnesia flaviventris, (*Deless.*), *Sharpe, Cat. B. Br. Mus.* vii. p. 204. Orthotomus flaviventris, *Deless., Rev. Zool.* 1840, p. 101; *id. Voy. Inde*, part ii. p. 30. Prinia flaviventris, *Blyth, J. A. S. B.* xiii. p. 376; xvi. p. 455; *Bp. Consp.* i. 284; *Jerd. B. Ind.* ii. p. 169, No. 532; *Hume, Nests and Eggs*, p. 334; *Bl. and Wald., B. Burm.* p. 118; *Oates, Str. F.* v. p. 158; *Wardlaw-Ramsay, Ibis.*, 1877, p. 466; *Hume and Dav., Str. F.* vi. p. 347; *Hume, Str. F.* viii. p. 101; *Doig, Str. F.* viii. p. 378; *Butler, Str. F.* ix. p. 386; *Oates, Str. F.* x. p. 219; *Oates, B. Br. Burm.* i. p. 111. Prinia rafflesi, *Tweed, Ibis.*, 1877, p. 311, pl. vi. fig i.—The YELLOW-BELLIED WREN-WARBLER.

Forehead, crown, lores and ear coverts dark ashy; nape, back, scapulars, rump and upper tail coverts olive or yellowish green; tail brown, tinged with fulvous and margined with olive yellowish; quills and wing coverts brown, edged with olive or yellowish green; cheeks, chin, throat and breast white, tinged with yellowish; abdomen, sides of the body, vent, and under tail coverts bright yellow; thighs olive brown; under tail coverts, axillaries and under wing coverts pale yellow.

In new plumage the tail is tipped with pale yellow, which, however, soon wears off; mouth black; irides reddish yellow; eyelids plumbeous; bill black; legs orange fleshy; claws yellowish.

Length.—5·4 to 5·7 inches; wing 1·75 to 1·8; tail 2·5 to 3·0; tarsus 0·85; culmen 0·55. Females are a little smaller.

Hab.—Bengal and N. W. Provinces, and westward into Sind; eastward along the Terai to near Calcutta and the Bengal Soonderbuns, and through the Burmese countries to Malacca and Sumatra. (Sharpe). Extends also into Assam, and Sylhet. It does not occur in the Concan or Deccan, nor in Southern India. In Lower Bengal, Jerdon says it is abundant in high grass, especially near the Ganges. It makes its way through the thick reeds with great facility in seeking food. Oates says, at frequent intervals it mounts to the top of a tall reed and utters a short merry song, and then suddenly plunges into cover again with a peculiar long-sounding snap of the bill. During May and up to September it breeds among the tall elephant grass in which it lives, attaching its nest to two or three stems. The nest is an oval cup-like structure, made of vegetable down and the flowering end of fine grass, held together by other strong grass. Eggs brick red, generally four in number.

343. Burnesia socialis, (*Sykes*), *Sharpe, Cat. B. Br. Mus.* vii. p. 208. Prinia socialis, *Sykes, P. Z. S.* 1832, p. 89; *Jerd., Madr. Journ.* xi. p. 3; *id., Birds Ind.* ii. p. 170. No. 534; *Blanf., Ibis*, 1867, p. 464; *Butler, Str. F.* 1875, p. 479; *Fairbank, Str. F.* 1876, p. 259; *id*, 1877, p. 406; *Vidal, Str. F.* 1880, p. 67. Prinia stewarti, *Blyth, J. A. S. B.* xvi. p. 455; *Jerd. B. Ind.* ii. p. 171, No. 535; *Hume, Str. F.* 1875, p. 480; *id. Str. F.* 1876, p. 497; 1878, p. 319; 1879, p. 101. Prinia brevicauda, *Legge, B. Ceylon*, p. 521.—The DARK-ASHY WREN-WARBLER.

Crown of the head and back, also upper tail coverts, dark slaty grey; lores and a streak above the eye buffy white; a dark spot in front of the eye; ear coverts and cheeks light tawny buff, slaty grey along the upper margin of the former; rump with a few tawny buff feathers on each side; lesser and median coverts like the back; greater coverts dusky brown, externally edged with light brown; tail feathers light brown, with a subterminal broad bar of black and tipped white; throat whitish, slightly washed with fulvous; lower throat, foreneck, chest, breast, sides of the body, flanks, thighs and under tail coverts tawny buff, paler on the latter; abdomen white; under wing coverts and axillaries light tawny buff, upper mandible black; lower, pale horny; legs dull yellowish brown; iris brown.

Length.—4·6 to 5 inches; wing 1·8; tail 1·8; tarsus 0·8.

The young bird is rufous brown above, a little more dusky on the head; rump and upper tail coverts brighter rufous; tail rufous brown, tipped with fulvous white, and with a subterminal black bar; an ochraceous superciliary streak present.

Hab.—Nepaul to Assam, Northern, Southern, Central and Western India generally. Recorded from north of the Godavery, the N. W. Provinces, at Agra, Cashmere, Punjab, the Deccan, Concan, Kattiawar, Saugor, the Neilgherries, Khandeish, and Dehra Doon.

Its habits are those of *Burnesia flaviventris*, except that, unlike *flaviventris*, it also frequents gardens, hedges, and vegetable crops. Eggs usually reddish white or brick red, with numerous darker red spots at the large end. Nest similar to that of *P. flaviventris*.

344. Burnesia lepida (*Blyth*), *Jerdon, B. Ind.* ii. p. 185, No. 550. Prinia lepida, *Blyth, J. A. S. B.* xiii. p 376. Drymoica lepida, *Blyth, J. A. S. B.* xvi. p. 460. Burnesia gracilis (*Non. Rupp*), *Hume, Nests and Eggs, Ind. B.* p. 356; *id., Str. F.* 1873, p. 195; *Adam*, t. c. p. 382; *Butler, Str. F.* 1875, p. 485; *Hume*, t. c. p. 485; *id. Str. F.* 1878, p. 58; *id., Str. F.* 1879, p. 102; *Doig*, t. c. p. 371; *Murray, Hdbk., Zool., &c., Sind*, p. 158; *id., Vert. Zool. Sind*, p. 154. Burnesia lepida, *A. Anderson, Ibis.*, 1872, p. 237. *Brooks, Str. F.* 1879 p. 476; 1880, p. 228; *Sharpe, Cat. B. Br. Mus.* vii. p. 211. Drymoeca gracilis, *Blanf., East Pers.* ii. p. 206. Drymoipus lepidus, *Brooks, Str. F.* 1876, p. 274.—The STREAKED WREN-WARBLER.

Head, back, scapulars and upper tail coverts light olive grey, each feather mesially streaked with dusky brown; quills dusky brown, the feathers margined on their outer webs with the colour of the back; lores and supercilium whitish; tail olive grey, the feathers with distinct but obsolete transverse dusky bars, a subterminal dark spot on the inner web of each feather and tipped white; chin, throat, breast, belly and vent greyish white; bill dusky brown; the lower mandible pale fleshy; irides yellowish brown.

Length.—5·25 to 5·5 inches; wing 1·75; tail 2·5; bill at front nearly 0·5.

Hab.—Sind, Punjab, N. W. Provinces, Beloochistan and Persia; also Bengal, Deccan, Kutch, Kattiawar, Jeypore, Jodhpore, and North Guzerat. As in most parts of Western India, it is a resident in Sind, breeding from May to July.

Blyth has well described the habits of this species. Jerdon quotes him too. He says it is an inhabitant of low scrub, intermixed with tufts of coarse sedgy grass growing in sandy places by the river side, and it frequently flies out to feed among the herbage growing along the margin of the sand dunes. Tamarisk scrub, too, it delights to hop about in, also sedges, &c., growing at the seaside. It is a very difficult bird to shoot, as, like *Cettia cetti*, it is a great skulk, only occasionally coming up from among the roots and uttering a feeble song. It breeds amongst thickets of flexible grass, making a neat nest, almost always in the vicinity of water. Eggs spotted with red brown.

Gen. **Scotocerca,** *Sundev.*

General characters of *Burnesia*; tail nearly square and not graduated.

345. Scotocerca inquieta, *Rupp. Syst. Uebers,* p. 56; *Hengl. Ibis.,* 1869, p. 129; *id., Orn. N. O. Afr.* i. p. 244; *Sund. Meth. Nat. Av. Tent.* p. 7; *Blf. Ibis.,* 1874; *id., East Persia* ii. p. 207, pl. xiii. f. 2; *Str. F.* i. 200; ii. 329; *Murray, Hdbk., Zool., &c. Sind,* p. 159; *id. Vert. Zool., Sind,* p. 154. Malurus inquietus, *Rupp. Atl. Reise. N. Afr. Aves.* p. 55. Curruca famula, *Hemp. et Ehr. Symb. Phys. Aves.* fol. b. b. Melizophilus striatus, *Brooks, Proc. A. S. B.* 1872, p. 66; *id., Ibis.,* 1872, p. 180; *Hume, Str. F.,* i. p. 200.—RUPPEL'S WREN-WARBLER.

PLATE.

Above light brownish grey, with narrow dark brown streaks on the head as far as the shoulders; a broad pale rufous brown supercilium; the cheeks and ear coverts are also of this colour, which extends down the sides of the neck and breast, becoming very pale and diluted under the wings and on the flanks; wings light brown; the edges of the quills and coverts greyish; tail a very much darker or rather blackish brown; the outer feather on each side is rather lighter, and tipped with white; the tail feathers are cross rayed, particularly the outer ones.

Lower surface of body, except sides of neck, breast, and flanks, white, with narrow brown streaks from chin to upper breast. These streaks are well defined in one specimen, and faint in another. Lining of wing and edge of the same reddish white. Bill dark brown, except basal half of lower mandible, which is dull brownish orange; legs and feet yellowish brown; claws brown.

Length.—4·55 to 4·8 inches; wing 1·93 to 1·95; tail 2·14 to 2·33; tarsus ·77 to ·82; bill at front ·35; from gape ·46. The bill is excessively like that of

Scotocerca inquieta.

Mintern Bros. lith.

Melizophilus provincialis; the wing also resembles that bird, except that the first primary is larger in proportion. Tail of similar form, but proportionately shorter; the outer feathers are ·35 shorter than the central ones; *length* 4·7, expanse 6·2, tail from vent 2, wing 1·9; wings, when closed, reach to within 1·6 of end of tail, bill at front 0·35, tarsus 0·8, weight 0·3 of an oz. (*Brooks*) *Ex. Str. F.* i. p. 200.

Hab.—Sind, Punjab, N. W. Provinces, Beloochistan, S. E. Persia, S. Afghanistan. Ruppel's Streaked Wren Warbler is a resident of the bare stony hills which run down from the Khyber Pass to the sea. It breeds from February to April, building in low thorny scrub a globular nest of thin dry grass stems, with an opening on the side and lined with fine down. Eggs pure to pinky white, speckled and streaked with bright red, most dense towards the larger end. Size 0·6 by 0·5 inch.

Gen. **Sutoria.**—*Nicholson.*

Bill long and slender, rather wide at base; rictal bristles few; culmen exceeding the hind toe and claw in length; 5th and 6th quills longest and equal; tail of 12 feathers, strongly graduated or rounded, with the middle tail feathers elongated beyond the rest and pointed. The birds of this genus, also of *Orthotomus*, are remarkable for the beautiful nests they make.

346. Sutoria sutoria. (*Forst.*), *Sharpe, Cat. B. Br. Mus.* vii. p. 215; *Oates, B. Br. Burm.* i. p. 107. Motacilla sutoria, *Forst., Ind. Zool.*, p. 17. Motacilla longicauda, *Gm. Syst. Nat.* i. p. 954. Orthotomus longicauda, *Moore, P. Z. S.* 1854, p. 81; *Jerd., B. Ind.* ii. p. 165, No. 530; *Hume, Nests and Eggs*, p. 331; *Hume, Str. F.* iii. p. 135; *Bl. and Wald., B Burm.* p. 120; *Murray, Vert. Zool., Sind*, p. 151. Orthotomus edele (*Tem.*) *apud. Bl. and Wald., B. Burm.* p. 120. Orthotomus sutorius, *Sharpe, Ibis.* 1877, p. 109; *Oates, Str. F.* v. p. 158; *Hume and Dav., Str. F.* vi. p. 345; *Hume, Str. F.* viii. p. 101; *Scully, Str. F.* viii. p. 305.—The Indian Tailor Bird.

Forehead and crown rufous; back of head and neck ashy, with a very faint rufous tinge; sides of nape with two dark brown setæ on each side; back, scapulars, rump and upper tail coverts yellowish green; edge of wing white; primaries and secondaries brown, edged with olive green, more distinct on the secondaries; all, for two-thirds their length, narrowly margined basally on the inner webs with whitish; under wing coverts buffy white; tail light brown, the central feathers greenish, and the lateral ones edged on the outer web with the same and tipped with white; chin, throat, breast, belly and under tail coverts white; the flanks cinereous; a dark spot on each side of the throat; bill horny brown, paler on the under mandible; legs brown; irides reddish yellow.

Length.—6 to 6·5 inches; wing 1·9 to 2; tail 3·5; bill at front 0·5.

Hab.—Throughout India to Nepaul and Cashmere, Ceylon and British Burmah. Common in the Deccan, Concan, Kutch, Kattiawar and North Guzerat, also the Punjab, N. W. Provinces, Oudh, Bengal, and Central India. In Sind it is common in all the open country studded with trees, and affects the acacias chiefly. Breeds in July and August. Eggs, 2 to 4, white, spotted with reddish brown, thicker and closer at the larger end. Nest made of leaves, stitched with cotton or fibre, and lined with wool and cotton.

Gen. **Orthotomus**.—*Horsf.*

General characters of *Sutoria*. *Middle tail feathers not elongated beyond the rest.*

347. Orthotomus atrigularis, *Tem. Pl. Col. livr.* 101; *Moore, P. Z. S.* 1854, p. 78; *Sharpe, Ibis.*, 1877, pp. 16, 113; *Hume and Dav., Str. F.* vi. p. 345; *Hume, Str. F.* viii. p. 101; *Oates, Str. F.* x. p. 219. Orthotomus flaviviridis, *Moore, P. Z. S.* 1854, p. 70; *Wald. in Blyth, B. Burm.* p. 121. Orthotomus nitidus, *Hume, Str. F.* ii. pp. 478, 507; iii. p. 525.—The BLACK-NECKED TAILOR BIRD.

Lores and whole top of the head from the nostrils to the nape bright chestnut; ear coverts rufous white; chin, throat and *cheeks dull white*, the black bases of the feathers showing through a good deal; *under side of neck black*, with a few narrow broken white bars; breast, abdomen and vent white; under tail coverts bright yellow; flanks white, suffused with yellow; back, scapulars, rump and upper tail coverts yellowish green, brighter on the latter; tail brown, edged externally with yellowish green; under surface of tail yellowish; under wing coverts pale yellow, edge of wing bright yellow; quills brown, margined externally with bright greenish yellow; the wing coverts brown, margined on both webs with greenish yellow; thighs yellowish tawny.

The *female* is like the male, but has no black on the throat, and the yellow on the edge of the wing is duller; generally the tail feathers show a distinct subterminal bar of blackish brown, which is scarcely visible in the males. Bill pale brown above, the lower mandible and gape flesh colour; irides orange brown; eyelids plumbeous; legs flesh colour.

Length.—4·5 inches; tail 1·6; wing 1·8; tarsus 0·8; bill from gape 0·7; culmen 0·6.

Hab.—Borneo and Sumatra, extending throughout the Malay Peninsula to British Burmah and to Eastern Bengal.

The Black-necked Tailor Bird is common in Southern Pegu, from Rangoon to up the Valley of the Pegu River. Mr. Davison found it in Tenasserim, and Colonel Godwin-Austen procured it in the hill tracts of Eastern Bengal. It frequents thick forest and brushwood, and is not found much on cultivated land. It is strictly arboreal in its habits.

348. Orthotomus ruficeps, (*Lesson*) *Moore, P. Z. S.* 1854, p. 79; *Salvad. Ucc. Borneo,* p. 248; *Sharpe, Ibis.,* 1877, p. 114; *Tweed. P. Z. S.* 1878, p. 619; *Hume and Davison, Str. F.* 1878, p. 346; *id.* 1879, pp. 64, 101; *Sharpe, P. Z. S.* 1879, p. 341; *id. Cat. B. Br. Mus.* vii. p. 224. Edela ruficeps, *Less., Tr. d' Orn.* p. 309. Orthotomus sericeus, *Tem. pl. col., text to* 101.—The RED-HEADED TAILOR BIRD.

Forehead, crown and nape bright chestnut, also the lores; rest of sides of the face yellowish buff; upper margin of ear coverts bright chestnut like the crown; back, scapulars and rump ashy brown, inclining to ashy grey on the rump; upper tail coverts ashy rufous; tail chestnut; wing and coverts brown, edged with ashy or ashy grey, the quills very slightly washed with rufous towards the tip of outer web; cheeks, lower half of ear coverts and entire under surface of body yellowish buff; thighs chestnut; under wing coverts fulvous; iris yellow, salmon, or pale brown.

Length.—5·12 to 5·2 inches; tail 1·5 to 1·75; wing 1·82 to 2·0; tarsus 0·8 to 0·85. Females are very slightly smaller.

Hab.—The Indo-Malayan Islands, the Malay Peninsula, and the southern boundary of Tenasserim.

Of its habits nothing is on record; but there can be little doubt of its being the same as those of its other congeners.

Gen. Phyllergates.—*Sharpe.*

Tail of 12 feathers; the outermost much longer than in *Orthotomus,* and falling short of the remainder by 0·4 to 0·5 inches; bill more equilateral. Other characters as in *Orthotomus.*

349. Phyllergates coronatus, (*Jerd. and Blyth*), *Sharpe, Cat. B. Br. Mus.,* vii. p. 230. Orthotomus coronatus, *Jerd. and Blyth, P. Z. S.* 1861, p. 200. *Jerd. B. Ind.* ii. p. 168, No. 531; *Hume, Nests and Eggs, Ind. B.* p. 334; *Wald. in Blyth, B. Burm.* p. 121; *Sharpe, Ibis.,* 1877, p. 115; *Hume and Dav., Str. F.* vi. p. 346; *Hume, Str. F.* viii. p. 101. Phyllobates* coronatus, *Oates, B. Br. Burm.* i. p. 110.—The GOLDEN-HEADED TAILOR BIRD.

Forehead and fore part of crown bright orange, the nape greenish, the hind-neck and sides of neck grey; round the eye a ring of yellow feathers, also a short yellow supercilium; lores and sides of the face grey, the ear coverts whitish on their lower margin; cheeks, throat and foreneck white, rest of

* Evidently a misprint for *Phyllergates.*

nder surface bright yellow, including the thighs and under wing and under tail coverts; wings brown, edged with yellowish green; tail brown, narrowly edged with yellowish green, the outermost feather white along the entire inner web and the penultimate one for the greater part of its extent; legs and feet yellowish fleshy; upper mandible, tip and edges of lower mandible along commissure black; rest of bill yellowish fleshy; irides brown.

Length.—4 to 4·5 inches; wing 1·8 to 1·9; tail 1·7 to 1·8; tarsus 0·75 to 0·8; culmen 0·6.

Hab.—Eastern Himalayas. Common east of Tounghoo in British Burmah, also on the higher slopes of the Mooleyit in Tenasserim. It occurs in Darjeeling and in Nepaul, and in the hills of North Cachar and hill tracts of E. Bengal.

In habits it does not differ from the Indian Tailor Bird. Mr. Davison observes that they are not easily overlooked, as on the approach of danger they utter a low buzzing note of alarm.

Gen. **Graminicola.**—*Jerd.*

Bill moderate, rather stout and compressed; culmen curved; four rictal bristles on each side curving outwards; wings short and rounded; tail of 12 feathers, much graduated and broad; tarsi stout, of moderate length.

350. Graminicola bengalensis, *Jerdon, B. Ind.* ii. p. 177; *Godw.-Austen, J. A. S. B.* xliii. p. 167; *Hume, Str. F.* 1879, p. 101; *id.*, 1880, p. 255. Drymœca bengalensis, *Hume, Nests and Eggs, Ind. B.* p. 345; *Sharpe, Cat. B. Br. Mus.* vii. p. 234.—The LARGE GRASS-WARBLER.

Crown of the head, occiput and nape black, dark or tawny brown, the feathers being with tawny or fulvous margins; hindneck much paler, the edges being buffy whitish; lores and eyebrow white, narrowly streaked with black; ear coverts and cheeks whitish; back also streaked, black, and tawny, the latter forming broad margins to the feathers; rump uniform tawny buff; the lesser, median and greater wing coverts tawny buff, streaked with blackish mesially; bastard wing and primary coverts dusky brown, edged with tawny; quills the same; upper tail coverts streaked black in the centre and edged with tawny rufous; tail blackish, the feathers washed with ashy olive on the margins, which gradually change to tawny on the extreme edge; under surface of body dull white, purer white on the abdomen; sides of the body, flanks, thighs and under tail coverts tawny buff, the sides of the breast with narrow black shaft lines; under wing coverts and axillaries pale tawny; bill reddish horny; tarsus fleshy yellow; iris yellow brown.

Length.—5·8 to 6·25 inches; wing 2·25; tail 3; culmen 0·5; tarsus 0·9.

Hab.—Eastern Bengal, extending into Assam. Affects high grass.

Gen. Cisticola.—*Kaup.*

Bill shorter and slightly more slender than that of *Phyllergates* and *Prinia*; rictal bristles two on each side and well developed; wings short; 1st quill short, 2nd generally equal to 7th and shorter than the 6th; tail of 12 feathers, shorter than in *Prinia*, broader than in both *Prinia* and *Phyllergates* and somewhat rounded; tarsus long; feet proportionally large, with the lateral toes nearly equal and the claws not so much curved as in *Prinia*.

The genus *Cisticola* forms a small group of small birds averaging in total length 3 to 4·5 inches, nearly all possessing a streaked plumage, and frequenting chiefly grass and reeds. In respect to the changes of plumage of this group, after examining all the available material in different Museums and in the collections of Naturalists, Mr. Sharpe gives his conclusions in Vol. VII. of the *Cat. B. Br. Mus.* p. 235. He says: "(1). The male and female are more or less different in the breeding plumage, the tendency being in the male to have a uniform coloured head, while the female's is striped. (2). The female's winter plumage resembles her summer dress, but is rather more mealy and the tail is longer. (3). In the autumn moult the male passes into a winter plumage, when he resembles the female. (4). The first winter plumage of the young bird resembles that of the old female, and that they have longer tails. (5). The male is always larger than the female." "There are," he adds, "probably some exceptions among the plain backed species." The range is given as the whole of Africa and Madagascar, South Europe and countries bordering the Mediterranean, eastwards to India, Ceylon, the Burmese countries and China, as well as Japan, the Malayan Peninsula, and throughout the whole of the Indo-Malayan sub-region.

351. Cisticola buchanani, (*Blyth*), *Sharpe*, *Cat. B. Br. Mus.* vii. p. 246. Drymœca buchanani, *Blyth*, *J. A. S. B.* xiii. p. 376. Franklinia buchanani, (*Blyth*) *Jerd. B. Ind.* ii. p. 186, No. 551; *Blyth*, *Ibis.*, 1867, p. 24; *Hume*, *Nests and Eggs*, *Ind. B.* p. 359; *id.*, *Str. F.* 1873, p. 195; *Adam*, t. c. p. 382; *Butler*, *Str. F.* 1878, p. 183; *Hume*, *Str. F.* 1879, p. 102; *Doig.* t. c. p. 371; *Murray*, *Handbk. Zool.*, *&c.*, *Sind*, p. 159; *id.*, *Vert. Zool.*, *Sind*, p. 155.—The Rufous-fronted Wren-Warbler.

Forehead and crown pale rufous; back, scapulars, wings, rump and upper tail coverts greenish ashy; tail brown, all the feathers, except the two central ones, broadly tipped with white; chin, throat, breast, belly, vent and under tail coverts white; bill brown; lower mandible yellowish; legs dusky; irides orange.

Length.—5 to 5·25 inches; wing 2 to 2·25; tail 2 to 2·25.

Hab.—Western India, Sind, Punjab, N. W. Provinces, Oudh, Central and South India, Deccan, Kutch, Kattiawar, Jeypore, Jodhpore, and North Guzerat. Breeds from May to August.

Nest a roundish ball of dry grass, with a circular entrance on one side near the top. Eggs, 3 to 4, white, speckled all over with reddish brown and pale lavender, rather densely at the larger end. It is like the *Malacocerci*, nearly always seen in flocks of half a dozen or more flying from bush to bush, scarcely ever leaving a bush without having examined it from the top to the root stalks.

352. Cisticola gracilis, (*Franklin*) *Sharpe, Cat. B. Br. Mus.* vii. p. 253; *Oates, B. Br. Burm.* i. p. 119. Prinia gracilis, *Frankl. P. Z. S.* 1831, p. 119; *Jerd., Madr. Journ.* xi. p. 3; *id., Birds Ind.* ii. p. 172, No. 536; *Hume, Nests and Eggs, Ind. B.* p. 341; *Wald. in Blyth, B. Burm.* p. 119; *Hume, Str. F.* iii. p. 136; viii. p. 101; *Brooks,* t. c. p. 476. Prinia hodgsoni, *Blyth, J. A. S. B.* xiii. p. 376; *Jerd., B. Ind.* ii. p. 173, No. 538; *Hume, Nests and Eggs*, p. 342; *Wald. in Blyth, B. Burm.* p. 119; *Hume, Str. F.* iii. p. 136; *Legge, Str. F.* iii. p. 203; *Oates, Str. F.* vii. p. 480. Prinia albogularis, *Wald., Ann. Nat. Hist.*, Series 4, vol. v. p. 219. Drymœca gracilis, *Dresser, B. Eur.* iii. p. 13. Prinia rufula, *Godw.-Austen, P. Z. S.* 1874, p. 47; *id., J. A. S. B.* xliii. pt. ii. 165; *Hume, Str. F.* iii. p. 397; *id.* t. c. viii. p. 101.—FRANKLIN'S GRASS-WARBLER.

Above, including the wings and tail, ashy grey, the wings edged with pale rufous; tail with a subterminal patch of brown on each feather *tipped with whitish,* and obsoletely across with dusky under certain lights; ear coverts whitish in front, greyish behind; lores and feathers above the eye dusky; cheeks, chin, throat, abdomen, vent and under tail coverts white or yellowish white; *breast ashy, forming a band across*; under wing coverts and axillaries white or yellowish white; sides of the body and flanks slightly tinged with ashy; bill black; legs and feet yellowish fleshy; irides reddish yellow.

In winter plumage the upper parts, including the tail, are rufous brown; the wings brown, broadly edged with rufous; the tail with subterminal dark patches and white tips; lower plumage white, tinged with fulvous; supercilium whitish.

Length.—3·7 to 4·2 inches; wing 1·75; tail 1·55 to 2·15; tarsus 0·7; culmen 0·5; from gape 0·55.

Hab.—Nepaul to Bhootan and throughout the more moist regions of India and Ceylon, ranging eastwards into the Burmese countries as far south as Pegu. It is also recorded from Malayana. It occurs also in the Concan, Deccan, and Bengal. In Central and Northern India, and on the Vindhian hills near Mhow and at Saugor, it is said to be not uncommon, also in the Nepaul Terai and lower hills. In Southern India it is recorded from the Malabar Coast, the Wynaad, the slopes of the Neilgherries and on the Eastern Ghauts, while in British Burmah it occurs throughout Pegu and Arrakan. It has been met with in Tenasserim also, and has been got in Karin by Captain Wardlaw-Ramsay.

Franklin's Wren-Warbler affects brushwood and the outskirts of tree forests where there is a plentiful undergrowth of grass. In such localities it is abundant. It breeds throughout the rains, making a nest very like that of the Tailor Bird but smaller, sewing the leaves together with cotton, and with the same material, wool and soft vegetable fibres lining the nest. The eggs, 3 to 4 in number, are pale blue with some brown or reddish spots.

353. Cisticola beavani, (*Wald.*) *Sharpe, Cat. Birds Br. Mus.* vii. p. 255. Prinia Beavani, *Wald. P. Z. S.* 1886, p. 551; *Beavan, Ibis.* 1867, p. 454; *Hume, Str. F.* iii. p. 136; *Oates, Str. F.* v. p. 158; *Hume and Dav., Str. F.* vi. p. 349. *Hume, Str. F.* viii. p. 101; *Oates, B. Br. Burm.* i. p. 120. Prinia rufescens, *Blyth, J. A. S. B.* xvi. p. 456; *Blyth and Wald., B. Burm.* p. 119; *Hume, Str. F.* iii. p. 136; *Anderson, Yunnan Exped.* p. 640; *Hume, Str. F.* viii. p. 101.—Beavan's Grass-Warbler.

Above brown with tufts of fulvous white feathers on each side of the rump and indications of dusky cross bars on the lower back and rump; lesser and median wing coverts like the back; bastard wing and primary coverts dusky brown, with narrow rufous edgings; quills and tail the same, all, except the centre feathers of the tail, with a subterminal spot of black and a white tip; *crown, occiput and nape slaty grey;* lores white, also *a small but distinct streak over the eye;* ear coverts slaty grey with pale shaft lines; cheeks, throat and foreneck white, tinged rather with fulvous; breast fulvous, also the sides of the body and flanks; under tail coverts buffish white; under wing coverts and axillaries light tawny buff. (Sharpe.) Bill black; legs and feet pale or dark pinkish fleshy; irides orange brown, light wood brown, or reddish yellow (W. Davison.)

Length.—3·8 to 4 inches; wing 1·8; tail 1·65 to 1·5; tarsus 0·7 to 0·75; bill from gape 0·6. In winter the length is 4·6, the tail 2·1. The head and upper surface of the body is reddish brown; the tail more rufous; the under surface of the body yellower; and the eye brown, distinct in some skins.

Hab.—From Nepaul through the Eastern Himalayas and the Burmese countries as far as Malacca. It has been recorded from Bhamo, Pegu, Tenasserim, the Arrakan Hills, Nepaul, the Bhootan Doars, and Sikkim.

Abundant in grassy situations on the outskirts of wooded forests. Breeds in Burmah. Nest and eggs are similar to those of the preceding species.

354. Cisticola cinereicapilla, (*Moore*) *Sharpe, Cat. B. Br. Mus.* vii. p. 256. Prinia cinereicapilla, *Moore, P. Z. S.* 1854, p. 77 (*ex. Hodgs. MSS.*) *Jerd. B. Ind.* ii. p. 172, No. 537; *Hume, Nests and Eggs, Indian Birds,* p. 341; *Brooks, Str. F.* 1875, p. 242; *A. Anderson, P. Z. S.* 1878, p. 370; *Hume, Str. F.* 1878, p. 320; *id.* 1879, p. 101; *id.* 1880, p. 286.—The Grey-headed or Hodgson's Wren-Warbler.

Crown of the head bluish grey; occiput and nape, also the back and wing coverts, reddish brown; a line across the forehead, extending back in a narrow eyebrow, pale tawny buff; an ashy spot in front of the eye; ear coverts tawny buff, the upper edge ashy; cheeks and under surface of body, also the thighs and under tail coverts, tawny buff; sides of the body and flanks rich fulvous; under wing coverts and axillaries pale tawny buff; bill black; legs pale horny; irides buff.

Length.—3·7 inches; wing 1·65; tail 1·95; tarsus 0·8; culmen 0·45.

Hab.—Himalayas from Nepaul to Gungaotri and Mussoorie.

Habits similar to those of the preceding species, also nest and eggs.

355. Cisticola poliocephala, (*A. Anderson*) *Sharpe, Cat. B. Br. Mus.* vii. p. 257. Prinia poliocephala, *A. Anders. P. Z. S.* 1878, p. 370, pl. 19; *Hume, Str. F.* 1878, ii. p. 319; *id. Str. F.* 1879, p. 101.; *id.* 1880, p. 286.—The GREY-HEADED WREN-WARBLER.

Differs from *Cisticola Beavani* in having a slaty grey head and no supercilium.

Length.—3·8 inches; wing 1·75; tail 1·8; tarsus 0·8.

Hab.—Himalayas, Nepaul, and Kumaon.

356. Cisticola cisticola, (*Tem.*) *Sharpe, Cat. B.* vii. p. 259; *Oates, B. Br. Burm.* i. p. 115. Sylvia cisticola, *Tem. Man. d'Orn.* i. p. 228; *id.* pl. col. 6, fig. 3. Prinia cursitans, *Frankl. P. Z. S.* 1831, p. 118. Cisticola schœnicola, *Bonap. Comp. List. B. Eur. and N. Am.* p. 12; *Jerd. B. Ind.* ii. p. 174, No. 539; *Hume, Nests and Eggs*, p. 343; *id.*, *Str. F.* i. p. 439, iii. 137; *Blyth, B. Burm.* p. 119; *Oates, Str. F.* v. p. 158. Salicaria brunniceps, *Tem.* et *Schleg. Faun. Jap. Aves.* p. 134, pl. 20. Cisticola munipurensis, *Godw.-Austen, P. Z. S.* 1874, p. 47; *id. J. A. S. B.* xiii. pt. ii. p. 165, pl. ix., fig. 2; *Hume, Str. F.* iii. p. 397; viii. p. 101. Cisticola cursitans, *Dresser, B. Eur.* iii. p. 3; *Hume, Str. F.* v. p. 90; *Hume and Dav., Str. F.* vi. p. 349; *Hume, Str. F.* viii. p. 101. Cisticola homalura, *Hume, Str. F.* v. pp. 93, 350; viii. p. 101.—The RUFOUS GRASS-WARBLER.

Forehead rufescent; crown, hindneck and back dark brown, all the feathers margined and edged with rufous; rump and upper tail coverts rufous; primaries and secondaries dusky brown, edged on their outer webs with pale rufous; tertiaries dark brown, edged and tipped with pale rufous; edging near the tips and the tips whitish; tail dusky brown above, pale brown below, the feathers with a broad subterminal band of black tipped with white; the dark spots and white tips more distinct on the under surface; chin and throat whitish or rufescent white; breast and belly rufescent; vent and under tail coverts paler; bill dusky brown; the under mandible paler; irides brownish.

Length.—4·5 to 4·75 inches; wings 2 to 2·25; tail 1·75 to 2; bill at front 0·25.

Hab.—India generally to Nepaul; British Burmah, S. W. Europe, Africa, Egypt, Arabia, Deccan, Concan, Kutch, Kattiawar, Jodhpore, and N. Guzerat, also Bengal and Central India.

In Sind it affects the tamarisk jungles along the banks of the Indus, and breeds in July and August. Nest a deep purse, beautifully made of vegetable down, and placed in a tuft of soft grass. Eggs, usually five, white, speckled with reddish.

357. Cisticola exilis, (*Vig. and Horsf.*) *Sharpe, Cat. B. Br. Mus.* vii. p. 269. Malurus exilis, *Vig. and Horsf. Trans. Linn. Soc.* xv. p. 223. Cisticola isura, *Gould, P. Z. S.* 1847, No. 32. Cisticola erythrocephala (*Jerd.*) *Blyth, J. A. S. B.* xx. p. 523; *Jerd. B. Ind.* ii. p. 174, No. 540; *Hume, Str. F.* v. pp. 94, 351, 406; viii. p. 101. Cisticola Tytleri, *Jerd. B. Ind.* ii. p. 196, No. 541. Cisticola delicatula, *Blyth, Ibis.,* 1870, p. 170. Cisticola melanocephala, *Godw.-Austen, J. A. S. B.* xliii. pt. 2, p. 165, pl. x. fig. 1; *Hume, Str. F.* viii. p. 101. The GOLDEN-HEADED GRASS-WARBLER.

Adult ♂. *In breeding plumage.* Forehead and crown golden fulvous; nape and hind-neck dusky fulvous; lower plumage pale yellowish buff; back and scapulars dark brown, each feather broadly edged with grey; wing coverts and quills brown, edged with rufescent grey; rump and the upper tail coverts fulvous; tail black, each feather narrowly tipped with ashy; centre of the abdomen and vent white.

In the female in breeding plumage the head is streaked with dark brown, and the tips to the tail feathers are about double the width they are in the male.

In winter plumage both sexes have much longer tails, the upper plumage is streaked with black and margined with rufous, the tail feathers are blackish along the shaft, and the tips are rufescent white. Iris light brown; upper mandible dark brown; lower mandible and gape fleshy pink.

Length.—4 to 4·8 inches; wing 1·75; tail 1·25 to 2; tarsus 0·7.

Hab.—Indo-Burmese countries, Eastern Bengal, and Western India, extending into China and Australia. Habits same as the last, also the mode of nidification, number, size, shape and colour of eggs.

Sub-family.—TURDINÆ.

Gen. Geocichla.—*Kuhl.*

This genus, as now revised, includes a number of well-known and very familiar genera, such as *Zoothera, Oreocincla, Turdulus, Cichlopasser, Chamœtylus* and *Psophocichla*, and forms a well-defined group of a number of birds commonly known as Ground-Thrushes. The characters of this group as given by Seebohm in the Vth Vol. of the British Museum Catalogue are briefly these: "basal portion of the outside web of all the secondaries and of many of the primaries white, occasionally tinted with buff, but abruptly defined from the brown of the rest of the quills. Axillaries parti-coloured, the basal half white, the terminal half black, slaty grey or brown; under wing coverts the same, the basal portion, however, *being black and the terminal* half white. Young generally spotted on the back and breast. Bill moderately stout, somewhat wide at base, gently arched throughout, and moderately hooked at the tip; rictal bristles more or less developed; wing more or less rounded; tail of 12 to 14 feathers (14 in three species only); toes long; plumage generally soft and silky, usually mottled above and spotted beneath, and dull blue and ferruginous in colour. Peculiar to the Indian region."

Twelve tail feathers.

358. Geocichla dauma, (*Lath.*) *Seebohm, Cat. B. Br. Mus.* vol. v. p. 154; *Oates, B. Br. Burm.* i. p. 6. Turdus dauma, *Lath., Ind. Orn.* i. p. 362. Oreocincla dauma, *Jerd. B. Ind.* i. p. 533; *Hume, Nests and Eggs, Ind. B.* p. 236; *Ball, Str. F.* ii. p. 408; *Hume, Str. F.* iii. p. 115; *Wald. in Blyth, B. Burm.* p. 100; *Hume and Dav., Str. F.* vi. p. 256; *Hume, Str. F.* viii. p. 94; *Bingham, Str. F.* ix. p. 178.—The Himalayan Ground-Thrush.

The plumage of the body above rich olive, each feather tipped black with an interior pale fulvous spot; scapulars the same, the black tipping larger and extending more on the inner than on the outer web; wing coverts dark brown or blackish brown, tipped with large fulvous spots; greater coverts to primaries blackish brown; the central portion of the outer webs tawny; quills brown, their outer webs suffused with tawny fulvous, the tertials partly tipped with the same; base of under webs fulvous white; central two pairs of tail feathers olive brown, the next two pairs tipped with white, the outer pair brown on basal half, whitish brown terminally, and margined with pale olive brown on the outer web; lores brown, shafted and tipped with white; cheeks and ear coverts white, terminated by black tips and with subterminal fulvous marks; chin white; throat and breast white, terminally fulvous and tipped with black crescentic marks; belly and flanks white, with subterminal fulvous spots and black tips; the centre of the abdomen pure white, also the under tail coverts, a few of the feathers of which are obsoletely tipped with brown; under wing coverts white, with a broad black band across the middle; thighs white, barred with brown; bill pale brown, the upper mandible and centre of lower dark brown; irides dark hazel brown; legs and claws fleshy white; 3rd and 4th primaries nearly equal and longest, *the second generally half an inch longer than the sixth.*

Length.—10·4 to 10·5 inches; wing 5·5 to 5·6; tail 3·75 to 3·8; bill at gape 1·2; culmen 1·0 to 1·1.

Hab.—The Himalayas from Kumaon to Assam, descending to the plains in Central and Southern India during winter, also in British Burmah.

The Himalayan or Small-billed Mountain-Thrush is said not to be uncommon in Lower Bengal also. It has been obtained in the N. W. Himalayas, at Almorah, Kumaon, Darjeeling, Kamptee, Nepaul, Cashmere, the Khasia Hills, Wynaad, the jungles south of Cuttack, on the Chilka Lake and in Saugor. It is not uncommon on the Pegu Hills, and also in the plains at Kyakpadein. Captain Ramsay got it at Tounghoo and Mr. Davison in Tenasserim. According to Jerdon it is very partial to bamboo jungles. It feeds on the ground; fruit and seeds, and also insects, being its food. It breeds in Cashmere during June and July. The eggs are broad ovals, somewhat compressed and pointed towards the small end. The ground colour is a pale greenish white, minutely and densely freckled with and mottled with pale brownish or reddish purple. Size from 1·2 to 1·26 in length, and in breadth 0·9 to 0·93.

359. Geocichla nilgiriensis, (*Blyth*) *Seebohm, Cat. B. Br. Mus.* v. p. 157. Oreocincla Neilgherriensis, *Blyth, J. A. S. B.* xvi. p. 141; *Jerd. B. Ind.* i. p. 534, No. 372; *Hume, Str. F.* 1876, p. 399. Turdus Neilgherriensis, (*Blyth*) *Gray, Gen. B.* i. p. 254.—The Neilgherry Ground Thrush.

Intermediate between *G. dauma* and *G. heinii*. Upper parts russet brown; head with subterminal chestnut brown spots; base of inside webs of secondaries and primaries white; abdomen and flanks as in *G. dauma*; 3rd, 4th and 5th primaries nearly equal and longest; 2nd primary between 5th and 6th.

Length.—10·75 inches; wing 5·5; tail 3·75; tarsus 1·2; bill at front 1·1.

Hab.—Neilgherries (South India). Occurs in the higher wooded tracts, and has a rich, charming song. In Travancore Mr. Bourdillon says it is rather scarce and solitary, and is found in thick jungle from the summit of the hills down to 2,000 feet elevation.

360. Geocichla mollissima, (*Blyth*) *Seebohm, Cat. B. Br. Mus.* v. p. 159. Turdus mollissimus, *Blyth, J. A. S. B.* xi. p. 188; *Gray, Cat. Mam., &c. Nepaul Coll. Hodgs.* p. 80. Oreocincla rostrata, *Hodgs. Ann. Nat. Hist.* xv. p. 326. Oreocincla mollisima, *Blyth, J. A. S. B.* xvi. p. 141; *Jerd. B. Ind.* i. p. 533, No. 370; *Godw.-Austen, J. A. S. B.* xxix. p. 103; *Hume and Dav., Str. F.* vi. 256.—The Short-tailed or Plain-backed Oreocincloid Ground-Thrush.

Upper parts brownish olive; inside web and tip of primary coverts black; lores buff; quills brown, margined exteriorly with ochraceous brown; four central tail feathers olive brown; three next on each side dark brown, the outer ones dark brown at base, fading to pale brown, with an obscurely defined white wedge-shaped terminal mark; ear coverts and lower surface generally white, with an ochraceous tinge on the breast and flanks; each feather with a transverse terminal crescent-shaped black band nearly obsolete on the chin and centre of belly; under tail coverts white, with obscure brown edges; axillaries white, tipped with black; under wing coverts white, with black bases; basal half of inner web of secondaries and of many primaries buff. Bill dark brown, paler at base of under mandible; 3rd and 4th primaries nearly equal and longest; 2nd between 5th and 6th and 7th.

Length.—9·5; wing 5·1 to 5·6; tail 4 to 4·1; culmen 0·92 to 1·1; tarsus 1·25 to 1·45.

Hab.—The Himalayas from Nepaul to Darjeeling and Sikkim, descending into the valleys during winter.

The Plain-backed Mountain-Thrush feeds like its other congeners on the ground in small parties on the summit of some high hill, flying into brushwood when disturbed. Food—insects and berries.

361. Geocichla dixoni, *Seebohm, Cat. B. Br. Mus.* v. p. 161; *Oates, B. Br. Burm.* i. p. 7.—DIXON'S THRUSH.

Similar to *G. mollissima* except that the tail is longer, 4·3 to 4·7 inches; the general colour of the upper parts olive brown instead of russet brown, and the greater and median wing coverts dark brown, edged with buffy brown and tipped with large fan-shaped buff spots; iris brown; bill brown; legs dull brownish yellow.

Length.—10·5 inches; wing 5·5; tail 4·7; tarsus 1·45; bill from gape 1·2.

Hab.—The Himalayas, where it is said to breed, to Darjeeling. Descends to the plains during winter as far as Central India. Occurs also in Nepaul and Tenasserim.

Group.—ZOOTHERÆ.

362. Geocichla monticola, (*Vigors*) *Seebohm, Cat. B. Br. Mus.* v. p. 161. Zoothera monticola, *Vig. P. Z. S.* 1831, p. 172; *Gould, Cent. Him. B.* pl. xxii.; *Blyth, J. A. S. B.* xvi. p. 140; *Jerd. B. Ind.* i. p. 509, No. 350; *Godw.-Austen J. A. S B.* xli. pt. 2. p. 142; *Blanford, J. A. S. B.* xli. pt. 2, p. 49.—The SAW-BILLED GROUND-THRUSH.

Upper parts dark olive brown, each feather obscurely barred with slate grey; wings and wing coverts darkish brown, with obscure paler tips to the median and greater coverts; tail brown, the outermost feathers obscurely tipped with white; cheeks, sides of the neck and breast brown, with obscure subterminal dark spots on each feather; chin and throat white with dark brown fan-shaped terminal spots on some of the feathers; flanks brown, the feathers obscurely barred with dark brown; centre of belly white; under tail coverts dark brown, tipped with white; axillaries basally white, terminally dark brown, and narrowly edged with white; under wing coverts dark brown basally and white terminally; the basal half of secondaries (inner webs) and of many primaries buffish white; 4th primary slightly the longest, 2nd between the 6th and 7th; bill abnormally long, longer than the tarsus; both mandibles obscurely serrated; rictus strongly bristled; legs and feet darkish brown; irides dark brown.

Length.—10 to 12 inches; wing 5·1 to 6·0; tail 3 to 3¼; culmen 1·3 to 1·6; tarsus 1·25 to 1·4.

Hab.—Throughout the Himalayan Range to Assam. Common from Mussoorie to Darjeeling. Recorded from Cashmere, Nepaul, Simla, Bootan, Mussoorie, Assam, and Darjeeling. It is said by Seebohm to breed in the Himalayas.

363. Geocichla marginata, (*Blyth*) *Seebohm, Cat. B. Br. Mus.* v. p. 162. Zoothera marginata, *Blyth, J. A. S. B.* xvi. p. 141, n.; *Hume, Nests and Eggs*, p. 226; *Blyth and Wald. B. Burm.*, p. 100; *Hume and Dav.*. *Str. F.* vi. p. 246; *Hume, Str. F.* viii. p. 94; *Bingham, Str. F.* viii. p. 195; *Oates, B. Br. Burm.* i. p. 8.—The LONG-BILLED GROUND-THRUSH.

Upper plumage rufescent olive brown, dark and dull on the head, bright on the outer webs of the feathers of the wings, the coverts with buff tips; inner webs of quills and primary coverts dark brown; lores and sides of the head mixed white and black, the black preponderating on the ear coverts; chin, throat and a line down the neck pure white, bounded on each side by a brown moustachial line; breast and abdomen brown, each feather with a large white spot in the centre; sides of breast, body and flanks brown, with broad white shaft lines, becoming broader towards the abdomen; under tail coverts buffy white, broadly margined with brown; axillaries buffy white at base and brown at tips; tail uniform rufescent olive-brown; bill dark or pale bluish brown; legs and feet the same; irides deep hair-brown. (Dav. *ex.* Oates).

Length.—10 inches; wing 4·9; tail 3; tarsus 1·1; bill from gape 1·5.

Hab.—The Himalayas from Sikkim to Assam. It is also found in the north and central portions of the Tenasserim Provinces, as well as Siam. Recorded from Afghanistan. Oates says it appears to be sparingly distributed over the whole of British Burmah. It has been got on the Arrakan Hills, also in Karin, while in Tenasserim Davison met with it near Pahpoon and on the Mooleyit Mountain. Captain Bingham has recorded it from the Thoungyeen Valley.

Wherever it occurs it is probably a resident. Its food consists of insects and berries. The eggs are said to be like those of *Pitta*, white, with a few rusty brown spots.

364. Geocichla cyanonotus, (*Jard. and Selby*) *Seebohm, Cat. B, Br. Mus.* v. p. 172. Turdus cyanotus, *Jard. and Selby, Ill. Orn.* i. pl. xlvi;

Sykes, P. Z. S. 1832, p. 87. Geocichla cyanota, (*Jard. and Selby*) *Blyth, J. A. S. B.* xvi. p. 145; *Jerd. B. Ind.* i. p. 517, No. 354; *Hume, Nests and Eggs, Ind. B.* p. 229; *Ball, Str. F.* 1874, p. 407; *Hume, Str. F.* 1876, p. 398.—The White-winged Ground-Thrush.

Head, nape, hindneck and sides of the neck ferruginous; general colour of the rest of the upper parts dull cyaneous or pale slaty grey, each feather rather darker in the centre. Cheeks, chin, throat and neck white; breast, abdomen and flanks bright ferruginous or orange chestnut; vent and under tail coverts white; lores white. A dark brown band extends from the eye half way to the shoulder; behind this is a white band extending nearly to the shoulder; behind this again is another shorter dark brown band, leaving a small white spot at the junction of the ear coverts and the nape. Quills and innermost secondaries brown with the unemarginated portions of the outside webs slate grey; median wing coverts broadly tipped with white; greater wing coverts and primary coverts dark brown on inside web and slate grey on outside web; axillaries white basally, dark slate grey terminally; under wing coverts dark slate grey basally, terminally white; bill dark brown; legs and feet flesh colour; irides dark brown.

Length.—8·5 to 8·6 inches; wing 4.3; tail 2·8 to 3·1; culmen 0·8 to 0·95; tarsus 1·15 to 1·2. The female differs in having the colours less pure.

Hab.—Central, Southern and Western India.

The White-winged Ground-Thrush has not been found outside the above limits. Jerdon says "it is peculiar to the jungles of Southern India, extending as far as Goomsoor on the east coast and to Bombay on the west side of India. It is most abundant in the forests of Malabar and Wynaad, but it is not rare in the jungle of the Eastern Ghauts. It has also been got in North Canara. Recorded from Travancore, the Neilgherries, Matheran, Malabar Coast, and Behar. It prefers bamboo jungles, feeds on the ground, and generally perches low. Its food consists of insects, as ants, cockroaches and beetles, and not unfrequently stony fruit. Mr. Ward procured the nest in North Canara, made of roots and grass, placed at no great height from the ground. The eggs, three in number, were pale bluish, speckled with brown.

365. Geocichla citrina, (*Lath.*) *Seebohm, Cat. B. Br. Mus.* v. p. 172. Turdus citrinus, *Lath. Ind. Orn.* i. p. 350. Geocichla citrina (*Lath.*) *Jerd. B. Ind.* i. p. 517, No. 355; *Hume, Nests and Eggs, Ind. B.* p. 229; *Blyth, B. Burm.* p. 99; *Oates, Str. F.* v. p. 151; *Hume and Dav., Str. F.* vi. p. 250; *Hume, Str. F.* viii. p. 94; *Legge, B. Ceylon* p. 457; *Scully, Str. F.* viii. p. 283; *Hume, Str. F.* ix. p. 101; *Oates, B. Br. Burm.* i. p. 3. Geocichla andamanensis, *Wald. Ann. and Mag. Nat. Hist.*, 1874, p. 56. Geocichla albogularis, *Blyth, J. A. S. B.* xvi. p. 146. Geocichla innotata, *Blyth, J. A. S. B.* xv. p. 370.—The Orange-headed Ground-Thrush.

Whole head, neck, breast, belly and flanks orange buff, darkest on the head and albescent on the chin and throat; vent, thighs and under tail coverts pure white; back, rump, upper tail coverts, scapulars and smaller wing coverts dark bluish grey; some of the wing coverts near the edge of the wing tipped white, the larger wing coverts, primaries and primary coverts dark brown, exteriorly edged with ashy; inner webs of primaries white at their bases; under wing coverts dark slate grey basally and white terminally; the bases of the secondaries and some of the primaries white on their inner webs; two centre tail feathers and most of the outside web of the remainder dark slate grey, the rest dark brown; outermost feathers generally paler at tip and frequently tipped with white; bill dark brown or horny black; iris dark hazel; legs and feet fleshy.

Length.—8·5 to 8·8 inches; wing 4·6; tail 3; tarsus 1·3; bill from gape 1·1

Young birds differ in having the feathers of the upper parts edged with pale yellowish instead of ashy.

Hab.—Throughout the whole range of the Himalayas from Nepaul to Assam up to about 5,000 feet elevation, descending to the plains during winter, being then found in Northern, Central and Southern India, and Burmah, straying also as far south as Ceylon. Jerdon says it is found in most of the forests and well-wooded districts of Northern and Central India, extending rarely as low as N. lat. 16°. In the neighbourhood of Calcutta it is not uncommon, also at Darjeeling and in the warmer valleys in Sikkim. In British Burmah, according to Oates, it is a constant resident.

It keeps to woods and shady gardens, and, like the last, prefers bamboo jungle. Like others of its kind, it feeds on the ground. It is not a shy bird, and does not retreat far from villages. It is said to have a pretty song during the breeding season, but otherwise is silent. The nest is usually built in the forks of high trees, made of grasses, moss, stalks, and roots. Eggs, 3 to 4, pale greenish, freckled with rufous, forming a patch at the larger end. Size 0·8 to 1·1 inch in length by 0·7 to 0·82 in breadth.

It will be seen that *Geocichla andamanensis, albogularis,* and *innotata* are not admitted in this work, these being, in my opinion, only varieties of *G. citrina.* All agree generally in the wing formula of *citrina,* and the only difference upon which these species have been founded is the tone of colouration of the upper plumage and scarcely appreciable difference in size. Considering that the autumnal and first year plumage of the majority of the species of *Geocichla* are either quite unknown or very little known, and that the species have been founded on single or two skins, it is open to doubt whether these Andaman and Nicobar skins are not of birds in partial *autumnal* moult. Presumptions cannot be tolerated in making new species.

366. Geocichla wardi, (*Jerd.*) *Seebohm, Cat. B. Br. Mus.* v. p. 178. Turdus wardi, *Jerd. J. A. S. B.* xi. p. 882. Merula wardi, (*Jerd.*) *Blyth, J. A. S. B.* xvi. p. 146. Cichloselys wardi, (*Jerd.*) *Bp. Compt. Rend.* xxxviii. p. 5; *Hume, Nests and Eggs*, p. 231. Turdulus wardi, (*Jerd.*) *Jerd. B. Ind.* i. p. 520, No. 357. Turdus (Cichloselys) wardi, *Brooks, Str. F.* 1875 p. 237. Oreocincla pectoralis, *Legge, Str. F.* 1876, p. 244; *Hume, Str. F.* 1877, p. 202.—WARD'S PIED GROUND-THRUSH.

Upper parts black; whole head, neck, lores, chin, throat, breast and ear coverts black; wing coverts, innermost secondaries, upper tail coverts and most of the tail feathers more or less conspicuously tipped with white; quills dark brown, their outer webs black and edged with white for some distance, where they cease to be emarginated; under surface white, the flanks with broad subterminal irregularly crescentic black bands; base of axillaries white, terminally black; bill and legs yellow; irides brown; supercilium white.

Length.—8 to 9·6 inches; wing 4·6; tail 3·6; bill at front 0·75; culmen 1·1.

The female is olive brown above; the supercilium and spots on the wing coverts are fulvous white; throat and breast brownish white.

Hab.—The Himalayas, wintering in the plains of India; southwards as far as Ceylon. Occurs in Southern India on the Neilgherries, also in the Carnatic and Nepaul, the Punjab, and N. W. Provinces (Mussoorie, Nyneetal. At Mussoorie Captain Hutton found the nest early in April. It breeds in June and July, making a pretty nest of green mosses and fibres in the fork of trees. The eggs are usually 4 in number, pale verditer, spotted with sanguine brown Size 1·06 inches in length by 0·76 in breadth. It is very regular, somewhat elongated, oval, only slightly compressed at one end.

367. Geocichla sibirica, (*Pall.*) *Seebohm, Cat. B. Br. Mus.* v. p. 180; *Oates, B. Br. Burm.* i. p. 4. Turdus sibiricus, *Pall., Reis. Russ. Reich*, iii. p. 694; *Gmel. Syst. Nat.* i. p. 815; *Lath. Ind. Orn.* i. p. 333; *Tem. Man. d'Orn.* iii. p. 98; *Gould, B. Eur.* ii. pl. 82; *Seebohm, Ibis.*, 1879, p. 5. Oreocincla inframarginata, *Blyth, J. A. S. B.* xxix. p. 106; *Beavan, Ibis.*, 1868, p. 132; *Ball, Str. F.* 1873, p. 70; *Hume, Str. F.* viii. p. 94. Turdulus davisoni, *Hume, Str. F.* v. pp. 63, 136. Turdulus sibiricus, *Hume and Dav.*, *Str. F.* vi. pp. 255, 513.—The SIBERIAN GROUND-THRUSH.

Male.—The whole upper plumage, with the chin, throat, breast, flanks, sides of the body and sides of the abdomen deep slaty grey, each feather margined paler; centre of the abdomen and vent white; under tail coverts slaty, tipped with white; axillaries white, tipped with slaty; lores and sides of the head almost black; a distinct white supercilium reaching to the nape; quills dark brown, all, except the first two, with a large white patch on the inner web; tail dark brown, the outer feathers tipped with white.

Female.—Has the whole upper plumage olive brown, tinged with slaty and rufescent on the outer webs of the wings and their coverts; tail with the three outer feathers on each side tipped white; supercilium, chin and throat buff; a dark stripe on each side of the chin; sides of the head mixed brown and buff; lower plumage pale buffy white, each feather with a broad tipping of brown; axillaries white, tipped with brown; under tail coverts and vent white, splashed with brown. (Oates.) Bill black; irides brown; legs yellow.

Length.—9 inches; wing 4·8; tail 3·4; tarsus 1·1; bill from gape 1·1.

Hab.—China, Burmah, Sumatra and Java during winter, and, according to Seebohm, has once occurred on the Andaman Islands. It summers in Siberia, breeding in the valleys of the Yenasay and the Lena between lat. 67° and 68°, and also near Yokohama in Japan. In Burmah it was got in Karin at an elevation of 2,500 feet. Davison says it goes about in flocks, as many as sixty being seen together. They generally frequent large trees. Like most of the tribe, the Siberian Ground-Thrush feeds on the ground. It is said, however, to be a very shy bird.

Gen. Turdus.—*Linn.*

The revision of this group of birds by Seebohm in the fifth volume of the British Museum Catalogue includes in it the following genera, some long since obsolete. Of the more familiar ones to Indian naturalists may be mentioned *Ixocossyphus* (Kaup), *Planesticus* (Bonap.), and *Malacocichla* (Gould). Although connected very closely with *Merula*, it was advisible to keep the latter distinct, as, besides geographical range, the large number of species which the two genera comprise is an additional argument for the division. The genus *Turdus* is characterized thus: Bill moderately stout, straight at the base, and gently curving at the tip, somewhat wide at the base, and furnished with short rictal bristles. Wing flat and pointed, the 3rd and 4th primaries nearly equal, the 2nd a little shorter; the bastard primary rarely extends beyond the primary coverts. Tail of 12 feathers nearly even; tarsus short; feet moderate. The males resemble the females in their plumage, and the throat, breast and flanks are more or less spotted at all ages. The young are spotted on the back and breast. Food—insects and berries. The species found in India belong to the palæartic region and are not residents.

Turdus iliacus.

368. Turdus iliacus, *Linn. Syst. Nat.* i. p. 292; *Jerd. B. Ind.* i. p. 332.—The Red-wing Thrush.

Above olive brown, darker, and suffused with russet on the forehead and crown; supercilium whitish; edges of the wing coverts and quills tipped pale; under parts pale buff, fading to white on the belly and ferruginous on the flanks; chin and throat unspotted; cheeks, upper breast, lower throat and upper flanks with dark brown terminal spots; under tail coverts white, the basal half of each feather margined with brown; axillaries and under wing coverts rich chesnut; bill dusky; legs yellow brown; irides brown.

Length.—8·5 to 9 inches; wing 4·75; tail 3·25; culmen 0·7 to 0·85; tarsus 1·25.

Hab.—Atlantic to the Pacific. Winters in the British Isles and Western and Southern Europe, occasionally crossing the Mediterranean into Algeria, and wintering in Persia, Turkestan, and N.-W. India; but is rare in the latter.

Of the habits of this bird nothing need be said, as without its mention no list of British birds would be complete.

369. Turdus viscivorus, *Linn. Syst. Nat.* i. 291; *Scop. Ann.* i. p. 132; *Lath. Gen. Syn. Suppl.* i. p. 285; *Tem. Man. d'Orn.* p. 86; *Sharpe and Dresser, B. Eur.* pt. vi.; *Shelly, B. Egypt,* p. 65; *Blanf. East Pers.* ii. p. 157. Turdus hodgsoni, *Homeyer, Rhea.* ii. p. 150; *Jerd. B. Ind.* i. p. 531; *Hume, Nests and Eggs, Ind. B.* p. 236; *Seebohm, Cat. B. Br. Mus.* v. p. 195.—The Missel Thrush.

Upper parts greyish brown or pale earthy brown, the feathers of the rump edged with ochraceous; lores and the feathers behind the eye greyish white;

ear coverts yellowish white, tipped with dark brown; supercilium none; wings like the back greyish brown or pale earthy brown ochraceous on the outside edges of the secondaries; median wing coverts with conspicuous greyish white tips; greater wing coverts and innermost secondaries with obscure pale tips; tail brown, the outer feathers conspicuously tipped with whitish; under surface of body pale buff, darker on the breast and flanks, each feather with a black terminal spot; under tail coverts margined with brown on the basal half; chin and centre of belly with obscure spots, or wanting them; axillaries and under wing coverts white; inner margins of quills nearly white. Bill dark brown, yellowish at base of under mandible; legs and feet yellowish brown.

The female is like the male, but paler in colour above and below.

Length.—10 6 to 11 inches; wing 6·5 to 6·55; tail 3·9 to 4·75; culmen 0·88 to 1·1; tarsus 1·25.

Hab.—Europe and Africa, extending to the Arctic circle; also Turkestan, the North-West Himalayas, and Southern Persia. Recorded from Kumaon, Almorah, Nepaul, and Koteguгh. Breeds in Central Europe, and in the valleys of the Beas and Sutlej at from 6,000 to 8,000 feet elevation during April, May, and June. Nest, a large deep cup fixed in the fork of a tree. The core is said to be composed of clay and grass stems, founded on a lot of dry leaves, fern, &c., with an external coating of moss and lichen, while internally there is a thick lining of soft grass. Eggs moderately broad ovals, the ground colour varying from pale pink to a pale greenish grey, thickly speckled and spotted with brownish red and pale purplish pink. Size 1·17 to 1·26 inch in length and 0·88 to 0·93 inch in breadth.

370. Turdus pilaris, *Linn.*, *Syst. Nat.* i. p. 291; *Scop. Ann.* i. p. 133; *Lath. Gen. Syn. Suppl.* i. p. 287; *Sharpe and Dresser, B. Eur.* p. 379; *Seebohm*, *Cat. B. Br. Mus.* v. p. 206; *Jerd. B. Ind.* i. p. 530.—The FIELDFARE.

Forehead and crown slate grey, each feather narrowly margined with brown and with concealed dark centres; nape pale slate grey; back and scapulars dark chestnut brown with obseure pale centres to most of the feathers; rump slaty grey; lores and ear coverts blackish; supercilium very faint buffish; wings and wing coverts dark brown with very narrow pale margins; primaries, primary coverts and a few of the outside wing coverts with slate grey on all or part of the outer webs; secondaries and the innermost wing coverts with chestnut brown on all or part of the outer webs, and generally paler and greyer towards the tips; tail dark brown, slightly paler at the tips of the outside feathers; chin, throat and breast buff, each feather having a nearly black fan-shaped terminal spot nearly obsolete on the chin, narrow on the throat, but very conspicuous on the cheeks and breast; the sides of the breast and flanks are nearly black, each feather broadly fringed with white; belly white; under tail coverts white, the basal half margined with brown; axillaries and under wing coverts white; inner margin of quills pale brown; bill yellow in summer, brown in winter.

Length.—11 inches; wing 5·2 to 5·9; tail 3·85 to 4·3; culmen 0·84 to 0·92; tarsus 1·2 to 1·3.

Hab.—Same as the last.

Gen. **Merula.**—*Leach.*

Bill slightly more lengthened generally than in *Turdus*, compressed at tip and notched. Nostrils plumed at base; rictal bristles short and strong; feet strong. Distributed in greater number in the neotropical than in the Australian, oriental, or palæarctic regions.

371. Merula albocincta, (*Royle*) *Blyth, J. A. S. B.* xvi. p. 148; *Gould, B. Asia* ii. pl. 76; *Jerd. B. Ind.* i. p. 526, No. 362; *Godw.-Austen, J. A. S. B.* xiv. pt. 2, p. 196, *Scully, Str. F.* viii. p. 285; *Seebohm, Cat. B. Br. Mus.* v. p. 245. Turdus albocinctus, *Royle, Illustr. Him. Bot.* p. lxxvii. pl. viii. fig. 3.—The White-collared Ouzel.

Male.—Dingy black, slightly glossed above; neck with a nearly white collar; under surface a dark sooty brown; vent feathers white-shafted; bill and orbits deep yellow; legs dingy; irides dark brown.

Female.—Has the white collar pale grey on the hind neck; the upper parts are dusky brown; under parts brown, obscurely barred with grey.

Length.—11 inches; wing 5 to 5·8; tail 4 to 4·55; culmen 1·15; tarsus 1·4.

Hab.—The Himalayas, from Nepaul to Assam, breeding at high elevations, and descending lower in the valleys during winter. It has been obtained in Sikkim and near Darjeeling, also in Bengal, Assam, Nepaul and Simla.

372. Merula boulboul, (*Lath.*) *Blyth, J. A. S. B.* xvi. p. 147; *Gould, B. Asia* ii. pl. 77; *Jerd. B. Ind.* i. p. 525; *Hume, Nests and Eggs, Ind. B.* p. 234; *Seebohm, Cat. B. Br. Mus.* v. p. 248. Lanius boulboul, *Lath. Ind. Orn.* i. p. 80. Turdus pœcilopterus, *Vig. P. Z. S.* 1831, p. 54.—The Grey-winged Ouzel.

Upper parts black; the tips of the median wing coverts, the outer webs of the greater wing coverts and a broad margin to the innermost secondaries greyish white; under surface paler black; the axillaries, under wing coverts, belly, flanks and under tail coverts narrowly margined with greyish white, or the axillaries and under wing coverts, sometimes one or both, greyish white; bill yellow; legs, feet and claws yellow; orbits yellow.

Length.—10·25 to 10·5 inches; wing 5·5; tail 4; culmen 0·9 to 1·1; tarsus 1·25 to 1·4.

The female is olive brown, and the greyish white margins are brownish white.

Hab.—Throughout the Himalayas from Cashmere to Assam and Sikkim; breeds in Kumaon and throughout the outer ranges from Darjeeling to Murree from May to August, and descends to the lower valleys during winter. Jerdon says it is found as high as 7,000 feet elevation. It is tolerably common, but rather shy, and does not show itself in the open or in gardens so much as *M. simillima*. The nest of this species as well as of *M. simillima* is usually placed on the ground, but in some places ledges of rocks, hollow massive roots, or the fork of a tree is selected; in the latter case not very far off the ground. Wattle and dab framework, with an external coating of moss and fern and the same soft internal lining, is the composition of the nest. Eggs, normally 4 in number, ground colour, pale dingy green, but thickly mottled, streaked, and clouded with dull brownish red so closely in some as to entirely obscure the ground colour. Size 1·1 to 1·33 inch in length and 0·83 to 0·92 inch in breadth.

373. Merula nigropileus, (*Lafresnaye*) *Delessert, Voy. de l'Inde*, pt. ii. p. 27; *Seebohm, Cat. B. Br. Mus.* v. p. 250. Turdus nigropileus, (*Lafr*) *Jerd. B. Ind.* i. p. 523.—The BLACK-CAPPED OUZEL.

Head, nape, lores, cheeks and upper part of ear coverts black; back, rump, wings and tail dark blackish or fuscous ashy, tinged with brown on the interscapulars; chin and upper throat darkish brown, shading into dull vinous brown on the breast and into dull slate grey on the axillaries; under wing coverts, belly, flanks and under tail coverts shading into nearly white on the centre of the belly; bill and eyelids orange yellow; legs brownish yellow; irides brown. The female has the head, nape and back an almost uniform brown; the white on the centre of the belly is more developed, and the throat is obscurely streaked with dark brown.

Length.—9·5 inches; wing 4·5 to 5; tail 3·5 to 4; culmen 0·98 to 1; tarsus 1·2 to 1·3.

Hab.—Western, Central and Southern India. Found in Coorg, the Wynaad on the Eastern Ghauts, the higher table-lands of Central India, at Bastar and Jaulnah, also in Nellore in the Carnatic, Tellicherry, Matheran, Madras and the Neilgherries. It feeds on insects and berries. It breeds on the mountains of South India, and descends to the plains a little before winter. Jerdon, says Mr. Ward, obtained the nest in Sirci in North Canara, made of roots, grass, &c., with three eggs, pale blue, spotted with brown.

374. Merula simillima, (*Jerd.*) *Blyth, Cat. B. A. S. Mus.* p. 162; *Seebohm, Cat. B. Br. Mus.* v. p. 251; *Jerd. B. Ind.* i. p. 524, No. 360; *Hume, Nests and Eggs*, p. 232. Turdus simillima, *Jerd. Madr. Journ.* x. p. 253.—The NEILGHERRY OUZEL.

Entirely black, darker on the head and back of neck, lighter beneath, and tinged with dusky; bill orange; legs dusky yellow; irides dark brown. The *female* is dusky olive brown above, lighter beneath.

Length.—10·5 inches; wing 5; tail 4·2; tarsus 1·35; culmen 1·1.

Hab.—Southern India. Confined to the Neilgherries. The nests are similar in structure to those of its congeners, wattle and dab, &c., being used in its composition. Eggs, normally 4 in number, sometimes 5, dingy bluish red. Size from 1·1 to 1·3 inches in length and in breadth 0·82 to 0·93 inches.

375. Merula bourdilloni, *Seebohm, Cat. B. Br. Mus.* v. p. 251; pl. xv. Merula Kinnisi, (*Blyth*) *apud. Hume, Str. F.* vii. p. 35.—BOURDILLON'S TRAVANCORE OUZEL.

Head black, rest of upper parts dull black; under parts very dark brown, with traces of dark slate grey margins to the feathers of the flanks; *below and behind the eye a bare space*; bill orange.

Length.—9·5 to 9·8; wing 4·7; tail 3·94; culmen 1·1; tarsus 1·32.

Hab.—Travancore, breeding at an elevation of 4,000 feet. According to Mr. Bourdillon it is not uncommon in the dense scrub jungle at the extreme summit of the hills.

376. Merula castanea, *Gould, P. Z. S.* 1835, p. 185; *Blyth, J. A. S. B.* xvi. p. 149; *Jerd. B. Ind.* i. p. 526; *Hume, Nests and Eggs, Ind. B.* p. 235; *Seebohm, Cat. B. Br. Mus.* v. p. 259.—The GREY-HEADED OUZEL.

Entire head, neck and throat very pale grey; greyish white on the chin and throat; back and scapulars deep rich chesnut, or chestnut bay, suffused with dark brown on the upper back and olive brown on the longer upper tail coverts; wings, wing coverts and tail dark brown; breast, flanks and belly, also axillaries and under wing coverts, deep rich chestnut, the centre of the belly more or less marked with dark brown and white; under tail coverts dark brown with white tips and shafts; tail dark brown; bill and legs yellow; wings brown.

Length.—10·5 inches; wing 5·5; tail 4·5; culmen 1·1; tarsus 1·4.

The female has the upper parts suffused with olive brown, the chestnut colouring is duller, and there are on the sides of the white throat some obscure streaks.

Hab.—The Himalayas from Cashmere to Assam, breeding at high elevations. Eggs of the type of *M. boulboul.*

377. Merula fuscata, (*Pall.*) *Seebohm, Cat. B. Br. Mus.* v. p. 262. Turdus fuscatus, *Pallas, Zoogr. Rosso Asiat.* i. p. 451; *Gould, B. Asia* i. pl. lxv. Turdus eunomus, *Tem.* pl. col. ii. No. 514. Turdus naumanni, *Tem.*

apud. Gould B. Eur. ii. pl. lxxix. Turdus dubius, *Bechst. apud Jaub.* et *Barth. Lapom. Rich. Orn.* p. 213. Planesticus fuscatus, (*Pall.*) *Jerd. B. Ind.* i. p. 530; *Blyth, Ibis*, 1866, p. 366.—The Dusky Thrush.

Upper parts brown, the feathers centred darker and frequently intermixed with chestnut; lores and ear coverts dark brown; supercilium buffish white reaching to the nape; wings dark brown, the secondaries and wing coverts edged on their outer web with chestnut; tail dark brown, shading into chestnut on the margin of the inner web; chin, cheeks and throat buffish white, in some with traces of a moustachial stripe; breast and flanks dark brown, each feather narrowly edged with buffish white, except on the sides of the breast, which are uniform black; belly and under tail coverts buffish white; axillaries and under wing coverts pale chestnut with obscure white margins; bill dark brown, paler at the base of the lower mandible.

The female is greyish brown in colour, and the feathers of the lower throat and breast have dark brown fan-shaped terminal spots.

Length.—8·5 inches; wing 4·8 to 5·3; tail 3·25 to 4; culmen 0·84 to 0·9; tarsus 1·2 to 1·3.

Hab.—Northern and Central Asia, extending into Japan and China. A rare winter visitor to the Himalayas. Seebohm says it breeds in Siberia, in the valley of the Yenasay, eastward among the willow bushes in the sheltered gorges of the tundra above the limit of forest growth, and in a similar climate on the mountain regions near Lake Baical. On migration it strays westward through north China and winters in Japan, straying as far as Assam and even N.-W. India. It is recorded from Nepaul and Assam.

378. Merula protomomelæna, *Seebohm, Cat. B. Br. Mus.* v. p. 265. Turdus dissimilis, *Blyth, J. A. S. B.* xvi. p. 144. Geocichla dissimilis, (*Blyth*) *Bly. Cat. B. Mus. As. Soc.* p. 163; *Hume, Nests and Eggs, Ind. B.* p. 231; *Hume, Str. F.* ix. p. 103. Turdulus cardis, *Tem. apud Jerd. B. Ind.* i. p. 521. Turdus protomomelas, *Cab. Journ. Orn.* 1867, p. 286.—Cabanis's Ouzel.

Entire head, nape, and throat black, also the breast and upper parts; beneath from the breast brilliant orange chestnut, shading into white on the centre of the belly; under tail coverts white, with slate grey sides; bill yellow; legs yellowish; irides brown.

The *female* is uniform olive brown above; throat nearly white in the centre; the feathers of the sides of the throat and chest with dark brown fan-shaped terminal spots; rest of under surface as in the male.

Length.—8·5 inches; wing 4·5; tail 3; tarsus 1·1; culmen 0·86 to 0·97.

Hab.—Eastern Himalayas, N.-W. Provinces, and Bengal. Has been known to breed at Nynee Tal, where Captain Marshall found a nest during May at about 7,000 feet elevation in a small shrubby tree. The nest was (Hume) placed in a fork about 7 feet from the ground, it was made of moss with a few roots intertwined. The egg (number not given), Hume says, is an elongated oval a good deal compressed towards the smaller end, a delicate pale sea green in colour, profusely speckled and spotted with reddish brown, more dense towards the larger end, where it is almost confluent, and forms a partial cup; size 1·06 × 0·7 inch.

379. Merula atrigularis *Tem. Man. d' Orn.* i. 169; *Gould. B. Eur.* ii. p. 75; *Blyth, Cat. B. Mus. As. Soc.* p. 161; *Seebohm, Cat. Birds B. M.* vol. v. p. 268; *Murray, Vert. Zool., Sind,* p. 131. Turdus atrigularis, (*Tem.*) *Blf. East. Pers.* ii. p. 158; *Seebohm, Ibis,* 1879, p. 6. Planesticus atrigularis, (*Tem.*) *Bp. Cat. Parzud*; *Jerd. B. Ind.* i. p. 529, No. 365; *Hume and Henders., Lahore to Yarkand,* p. 192; *Murray, Hdbk., Zool., &c., Sind,* p. 140. Turdus mystacinus, *Severtz. Turkest. Jevotn.* pp. 64, 115, 119.—The Black-throated Thrush.

Above pale cinereous brown; the feathers of the head, wings and tail darker brown; a black streak from the base of bill to the eyes not very distinct; ear coverts dark brown, tipped paler; chin, throat, breast, and lores black; abdomen, vent and under tail coverts white, the latter with a few brown dashes; axillaries darkish grey; under wing coverts buffy.

The female wants the pectoral gorget; the chin and throat is white; the sides and breast grey brown, with conspicuous dark centres; bill yellow, the tip dusky; orbits yellow; legs horny brown; irides dark brown.

Length.—10·5 inches; wing 5·75; tail 4·75; bill at front 0·91.

Hab.—Beloochistan, Persia, Afghanistan, Western Turkistan, the Himalayas, Nepaul, Punjab, N.-W. Provinces and Sind during winter. Breeds in Siberia and Turkestan.

This Thrush, according to Jerdon, is found throughout the Himalayas, inhabiting the higher ranges in the interior in summer, but descending to the lower ranges in winter. It keeps to the more open woods at a level of from 3,000 to 4,000 feet, and is occasionally seen on roads and pathways. It feeds on insects and berries.

380. Merula ruficollis, *Pall. Reis. Russ. Reichs.* iii. p. 694; *Gmel. Syst. Nat.* i. p. 815; *Pall. Zoogr. Rosso. Asiat.* i. p. 452; *Seebohm, Cat. B. Br. Mus.* v. p. 270. Planesticus ruficollis, (*Pall.*) *Bp. Parzud.* p. 5; *Jerd. B. Ind.* i. p. 528.—The Red-throated Ouzel.

Upper surface and ear coverts grey, the lores darker; supercilium chestnut, scarcely reaching the nape; wings and wing coverts brown, edged with grey;

centre tail feathers brown, the remainder chestnut on inside web and basal portion of outside web; chin, throat, and breast chestnut; under surface pale greyish, white on the flanks, with obscure darker centres; axillaries and under wing coverts buffish chestnut; bill dark brown; lower mandible yellowish at base; legs, feet, and claws brown; irides brown.

The female has very little chestnut on the throat and breast, which have the general colour of the flanks, with black fan-shaped terminal spots to many of the feathers.

Length.—10 inches; wing 5·5; tail 4; tarsus 1·5; culmen 0·85 to 0·9.

Hab.—The Himalayas, where it breeds; Nepaul, Bhootan to China, and Southern Siberia. It winters in Turkestan, India, and China, and occasionally straggles into Europe. It frequents forests, associating in large flocks.

381. Merula unicolor, *Tick. J. A. S. B.* ii. p. 577; *Gould. P. Z. S.* 1837, p. 136; *Gray, Gen. B.* i. p. 220. Geocichla unicolor, (*Tick.*) *Blyth, Cat. B. Mus. As. Soc.* p. 163; *Jerd. B. Ind.* i. p. 519, No. 356; *Murray, Hdbk., Zool., &c., Sind,* p. 140; *Murray, Vert. Zool., Sind,* p. 131.—Tickell's Ouzel.

Above uniform dusky, slaty, or ashy grey; wings and tail dusky brown, their external webs margined with ashy grey; breast, throat, and flanks pale slate grey; chin pale grey, nearly white; abdomen, vent and under tail coverts white; under wing coverts buff; legs and feet pale brown; bill dusky yellow; eyelids and gape yellow; irides brown.

Length.—9 inches; wings 4·5 to 4·75; tail 3·45; bill 0·95.

Female.—Upper parts olive brown; ashy grey on the rump and upper tail coverts; throat and breast paler than in the male, nearly white; the feathers of the throat with some spots.

Hab.—Central, Southern and Western India. Common in the Punjab, N.-W. Provinces, Oudh, Central India, Deccan, Rajputana and Nepaul. Breeds in the Himalayas, and migrates to the plains in winter. In Sind it is rare, and is found in the northern portion only.

382. Merula obscura, (*Gmel.*) *Seebohm, Cat. B. Br. Mus.* v. p. 273; *Oates, B. Br., Burm.* i. p. 1. Turdus obscurus, *Gmel. Syst. Nat.* i. p. 816; *Lath. Ind. Orn.* i. p. 333; *Wald. Tr. Zool. Socy.* ix. p. 187; *Blyth, B. Burm.* p. 99; *Hume and Dav., Str. F.* vi. p. 251; *Dresser, B. Eur.* ii. p. 71 pl.; *Hume, Str. F.* viii. p. 94. Turdus pallens, *Pall. Zoogr. Rosso. Asiat.* i. p. 457. Turdus rufulus, *Drap. dict. Class d'Hist. Nat.* x. p. 443 *Ball, Str. F.* i. p. 69. Turdus modestus, *Eyton, P. Z. S.* 1839, p. 103.—The Dark Ouzel.

Upper plumage olive brown, tinged with slaty on the head, the primaries and the inner webs of the other quills dark brown ; a narrow white supercilium ; lores black ; chin and base of lower mandible white, as also a short line produced downwards from the lower mandible; throat, cheeks, sides of the neck, and ear coverts dusky slaty; breast and sides of the body ochraceous; abdomen, vent, and under tail coverts white; under wing coverts and axillaries pale grey.

The *female* is like the male, but has the lores brown, the supercilium, chin, and a line down the throat buffy white ; the ear coverts are dark brown, striped with buffy ; a buffy white line runs from the bill under the ear coverts, and a brown one between this and the throat ; top of head like the back. *Young birds* have the upper parts striped with ochraceous, and the wing coverts are tipped with the same; the breast feathers are tipped with brown; bill dark brown, the lower mandible yellow, also the gape and inside of mouth; irides olive brown; legs yellowish brown.

Length.—8·6 inches; wing 4·8; tail 3·5 ; tarsus 1·2; bill from gape 1·1.

Hab.—Siberia, passing through China and Mongolia on migration, and wintering in Assam, Malacca, Burmah, North India, and the Islands of the Malay Archipelago. It occasionally strays as far west as Turkestan, Nepaul, and Europe. It has been recorded from Arrakan. Oates got a specimen in Pegu at Kyeikpadein in April. Davison found it common in Tenasserim, both in the hills and plains. Mr. Seebohm found the nest in the valley of the Yenasay in June.

383. Merula pallida, (*Gmel.*) *Seebohm, Cat. B. Br. Mus.* v. p. 274 ; *Oates, B. Br. Burm.* i. p. 274. Turdus pallidus, *Gmel., Syst. Nat.* i. p. 815 ; *Wald, in Bl. B. Burm.* p. 99 ; *Hume and Dav., Str. F.* vi. p. 253 ; *Hume, Str. F.* viii. p. 94. Turdus daulias, *Tem. Pl. Col.* 515.—The PALE OUZEL.

Upper plumage rich russet brown, tinged with grey on the head ; lores very dark brown; ear coverts brown; supercilium none; wings brown; the primaries, primary coverts, and bastard wing feathers with the outer webs slate grey; the outer webs of the secondaries, greater, median, and lesser wing coverts russet brown; tail dark brown, the outer webs margined with olive brown; inner webs of outside tail feathers white for half an inch at the tip, the white being gradually decreased on the inner feathers to the third on each side; throat, cheeks, breast, and flanks slate grey, whiter on the abdomen and centre of the breast, and more or less irregularly shaded with brown on the lower throat, sides of the breast, and flanks; under tail coverts white, the basal half edged with brown; axillaries and under wing coverts pale slate grey, obscurely tipped with white; bill dark brown, yellow at base of lower mandible; irides brown; legs and feet pale yellowish brown.

Length.—8·9 inches; wing 4·8 to 5·1; tail 3·3 to 3·9; culmen 0·9 to 1·0; tarsus 1·15 to 1·2.

Hab.—The hill tracts of Eastern Bengal, Assam, and British Burmah. In Burmah it was procured by Captain Wardlaw-Ramsay in Karin at an elevation of 5,000 feet. In Tenasserim Davison got a specimen on the Mooleyit Mountains.

Gen. **Monticola.**—*Boie.*

This genus is placed by Seebohm in his *Cat. B. Br. Mus.* after *Erithacus.* There are certainly links which Mr. Seebohm may have considered sufficient to establish its position, but, taking both the external and internal structure of the group, there can be little doubt that its systematic position is between the Ouzels and the Chats, instead of after the latter. The genus *Monticola* is shortly characterized as having, like the Ouzels (males), an unspotted under surface; the bill, too, is long and the tail comparatively short; and, as Mr. Seebohm puts it, "never as many as four times the length of the culmen." The bill is long, slender, straight, and moderately hooked at the tip, and either entire or faintly notched; nostrils apert, plumed at the base; rictal bristles small and numerous; wings long, the third quill generally the longest; tail short and even; tarsus moderate, 1 to 1·2 inches in length. All the Indian species have blue chins and throats and chestnut breasts and abdomen. The females have a barred under surface.

384. Monticola saxatilis, (*Linn.*) *Boie, Ibis,* 1822, p. 522; *Seebohm, Cat. B. Br. Mus.* v. p. 314. Turdus saxatilis, *Linn., Syst. Nat.* i. p. 294. Petrocossyphus saxatilis, (*Linn.*) *Boie, Ibis,* 1826, p. 972.—The Rock Thrush.

Entire head and neck cobalt blue; the upper back and scapulars blue black, lower back white; the feathers margined with bluish grey; upper tail coverts and tail chestnut; the two centre tail feathers brown on the terminal half; wing coverts and secondaries dark brown with obscure white tips; under surface of body chestnut.

The female is uniform brown above; the under surface is chestnut, barred with dark brown.

Length.—8·5 to 9 inches; wing 4·7 to 4·8; tail 2·4 to 2·5; culmen 0·94 to 1; tarsus 1 to 1·1.

Hab.—South Europe, Persia, and Siberia, where it breeds. Migrates to Mongolia and North China, North Africa, and Abyssinia, extending its range eastwards in winter to the borders of India and into North Burmah. Occurs, though not commonly, in Cashmere and Afghanistan? (Griffiths), and the North-West Himalayas and North Burmah.

385. Monticola cyanus, *Linn. Syst. Nat.* i. p. 296; *Gmel., Syst. Nat.* i. p. 834; *Lath. Ind. Orn.* i. p. 345. Monticola cyana, (*Linn.*) *Boie, Ibis*, 1822, p. 552; *Shelley, Birds of Egypt*, p. 70; *Blf. Eastern Persia*, ii. p. 155. Petrocossyphus cyaneus, (*Linn.*) *Boie, Ibis*, 1828; *Jerd. B. Ind.* i. p. 511, No. 351; *Ill. Ind. Orn.* p. 20; *Hume and Henders., Lahore to Yarkand*, p. 190; *Heugl., Syst. Uebers.* p. 29; *Sharpe and Dresser, B. Eur.*; *Murray, Hdbk., Zool., &c., Sind.* Cyanocincla cyanus (*Linn.*), *Str. F.* 1874, p. 407; vol. vi. p. 247; *id.* iii. p. 112.—The BLUE ROCK THRUSH.

Male—Head, neck, and back indigo blue, with a faint metallic lustre on the head; lores dusky greyish; wings, their coverts and tail dark brown; the outer webs of the feathers indigo blue; under surface of body cobalt blue; the abdomen and the under tail coverts with faint streaks and spots of whitish.

Female.—Of a dingy brown, scarcely tinged above with indigo or cobalt blue; some of the feathers edged whitish; under parts fulvous with dusky transverse bars, including the under tail coverts; bill black; legs black; irides brown.

Length.—8·5 to 9 inches; wing 4·5 to 5; tail 3·75 to 4; bill at front nearly one inch.

Hab.—Southern Europe, North Africa, Beloochistan, Persia, Afghanistan, wintering throughout the peninsula of India. Recorded from all India, Tenasserim, Cashmere, Nepaul, and North-West Himalayas. Extremely common in the Concan and Deccan, Kutch, Kattiawar, Jodhpore, Sambhur, and North Guzerat, also in South India. Frequents gardens, pagodas, &c. Breeds in the Himalayas, laying 4 eggs, pale blue, spotted with brown; has a fine gloss; size 1·0×0·73 inches.

386. Monticola cinclorhynchus, *Vig. P. Z. S.* 1831, p. 172. Petrophila cinclorhyncha, (*Vig.*) *Jerd. Madr. Journ.* x. p. 252; *Hume, Nests and Eggs, Ind. B.* p. 227. Orocetes cinclorhynchus, (*Vig*). *Bp. Consp.* i. p. 297; *Jerd. B. Ind.* i. p. 515; *Seebohm, Cat. Passerif. B. Museum*, vol. v. p. 320; *Murray, Hdbk., Zool., &c. Sind.*, p. 140; *Str. F.* vol. iv. 398.—The BLUE-HEADED CHAT THRUSH.

Male.—Head, nape, chin, upper throat, and cheeks indigo or cobalt blue, also the lesser wing coverts; lores, ear coverts, sides of neck, back, and scapulars black tinged with dusky blue on the back; primaries, their coverts, and greater and median coverts edged with bluish on their external webs; a white bar on the outer web of the secondaries; rump, upper tail coverts, entire under surface, axillaries, and under wing coverts ferruginous or chestnut; tail black, the external webs of the feathers margined with blue. In the female the colours are less pronounced; bill blackish; legs brown; irides dark brown.

Length.—7 to 7·5 inches; wing 4; tail 2·75 to 3; bill at front 1.

Hab.—The Indian Peninsula, ranging to Nepaul and Cashmere. Occurs sparingly in Sind, Punjab, and N.-W. Provinces, and more abundantly in the Concan, Deccan, Travancore, North Guzerat, and Rajputana in the course of its migration. Breeds in the Himalayas. Eggs 4, pale blue, spotted with brown; size 0·96 × 0·79.

387. Monticola erythrogaster, (*Vig.*) *Dav.* et *Oust. Ois. Chine*, p. 159; *Seebohm, Cat. B. Br. Mus.* v. p. 325. Turdus erythrogaster, (*Vig.*) *P. Z. S.* 1831, p. 171. Orocetes erythrogaster, (*Vig.*) *Jerd. B. Ind.* i. p. 514, No. 352: *Hume and Davison, Str. F.* vi. p. 250. Petrophila erythrogaster, (*Vig.*) *Hume, Nests and Eggs, Ind. B.* p. 227; *Str. F.* viii. p. 94; *Scully, Str. F.* viii, p. 282.—The CHESTNUT-BELLIED ROCK THRUSH.

Whole upper plumage cobalt blue, more or less dusky, and occasionally blackish on the back; wings black, all but the first two primaries blue on the outer web; lores, cheeks, and ear coverts black; chin and throat dusky blue; remainder of lower plumage, including the axillaries and under wing coverts, bright chestnut; tail blue turning to dusky on the inner webs.

The upper plumage of the female is brown; the rump, lower back, and upper tail coverts barred with black; wings brown, each feather edged with dusky white; chin and a line down the throat buff; a spot on the side of the neck fulvous; sides of the head blackish, with pale central streaks; under plumage buffy, barred with black; tail uniform brown. The young are like the female. In the first stage the plumage above is barred with black, which gradually disappears. The variations of colour in the young, however, are very great.

Bill black; irides dark brown; feet vinous brown. In the female the bill is dusky.

Length.—9·4 to 9·5 inches; wing 4·7 to 4·9; tail 4 to 4·2; tarsus 1·1; bill from gape 1·2.

Hab.—The Himalayas from Nepaul to Assam and British Burmah. It is recorded from the N.-W. Himalayas, Kumaon, Nepaul, Darjeeling, and Bhootan, also the Upper Punjab and N.-W. Provinces. Dr. Jerdon procured it in the Khasia Hills and Colonel Godwin-Austen in North Cachar. In Burmah Captain Wardlaw-Ramsay obtained it on the hills east of Tounghoo. Hume says he has only once seen the nest of the Chestnut-bellied Thrush on a journey from Kangra into Kooloo. It was placed at the root of a tree in the forest, and was a large shallow saucer, composed almost entirely of moss and lined with moss roots. The species lay from May to August. Eggs, 4 in number, somewhat buff-coloured and about 1·1 by 0·75 inches in size. The average size is 1 by 0·75 inch.

Gen. **Erithacus**.—*Cuv.*

In this genus, as revised, there are only sixteen known species, six only being found in India. The bill is small or of mean length, generally black above and paler on the under mandible; rictal bristles small or nearly obsolete; wings moderate; tail short, more or less rounded, and of 12 feathers; tarsus long, slender, and not scutellated, except occasionally in young birds. Three species of the six which occur in British India are known to breed in the Himalayas. In habits they closely resemble the Redstarts. They feed mostly on the ground, insects generally being their chief food.

388. Erithacus brunneus, *(Hodgs.) Seebohm, Cat. B. Br. Mus.* v. p. 302. Larvivora brunnea, *Hodgs., J. A. S. B.* vi. p. 102, 1837 (female); *Legge, B. Ceylon*, p. 446. Larvivora cyana, *(Pall.) apud. Hodgs., J. A. S. B.* vi. p. 102, 1837 (male); *apud. Jerd., B. Ind.* ii. p. 145, No. 507; *apud. Hume, Nests and Eggs, Ind. B.* p. 324. Larvivora superciliaris, *(Jerd.) Blyth, Ibis*, 1867, p. 16; *Brooks, Str. F.* 1875, p. 240; *Fairbank, Str. F.* 1876, p. 259.—The Indian Blue Robin or Wood-Chat.

Upper surface dull dark blue; lores, forehead at base of bill, cheeks, and ear coverts black; shading into dull dark blue on the sides of the neck; supercilium white; wing and their coverts brown, their outer webs more or less suffused with dull dark blue; tail brown; the two centre feathers and the outer webs of the others more or less suffused with dull dark blue; under surface of body orange chestnut, shading into white on the centre of the abdomen and under tail coverts; axillaries and under wing coverts grey, more or less suffused with pale blue; bill dark brown, paler at base of under mandible; rictal bristles nearly obsolete.

The female has the upper surface olive brown, slightly suffused with chestnut on the upper tail coverts; the under surface is chestnut brown, paler on the chin and throat and white on the centre of the abdomen and under tail coverts. Birds of the year resemble the female.

Length.—6 to 6·2 inches; wing 2·8 to 3; tail 1·7 to 1·95; culmen 0·5 to 0·6; tarsus 1· to 1·1.

Hab.—The Himalayas from Cashmere to Sikkim, the Neilgherries, Travancore, and Ceylon. Jerdon records it from near Calcutta. At Darjeeling it is said to be common; also about Madras. It frequents open forests in the hills, perching low and descending to the ground to pick up insects. Breeds on the Himalayas and the Neilgherries. Mr. Davison in *Nests and Eggs* says the nest was in a hole in the trunk of a small tree about 5 feet from the ground and was composed chiefly of moss, but mixed with dry leaves and twigs. The egg taken by Mr. Davison was an elongated, slightly pyriform oval, the ground colour a pale slightly greyish green, thickly mottled and streaked with pale brownish red; size 0·98 × 0·67.

389. Erithacus cyaneus, *(Pall.) Seebohm, Cat. B. Br. Mus.* v. p. 303; *Oates, B. Br. Burm.*, i. p. 13. Motacilla cyane, *Pall, Reis Russ. Reichs,* iii. p. 697. Larvivora cyane, *Wald. in Bl.' B. Burm.* p. 101. *Hume and Dav., Str. F.* vi. p. 335; *Hume, Str. F.* viii. p. 100.—The SIBERIAN BLUE ROBIN.

Base of the bill, lores, and a line under the cheeks black; cheeks, ear coverts, and the whole upper plumage blue; wings and tail brown, washed with blue on the outer webs; whole under plumage white, the flanks washed with brown; axillaries and under wing coverts grey, more or less suffused with blue.

The *female* has the whole lower surface white, washed with fulvous on the flanks and breast, the feathers of the latter also tipped slightly with brown; lores, cheeks, and ear coverts mingled fulvous and brown; the whole upper plumage, including the wings and tail, brown. The *young* are like the female, and have the upper tail coverts washed with blue; bill from pale to dark horny brown; lower mandible fleshy white; legs and feet fleshy white; irides deep brown.

Length.—5·5 to 5·6; wing 2·6 to 2·8; tail 1·8; tarsus 1·1; bill from gape 0·7.

Hab.—The Siberian Blue Robin breeds in Eastern Siberia and winters in North India, China, S.-E. Mongolia, and British Burmah, ranging through the Malayan Peninsula. Davison says it occurs in Tenasserim in the better-wooded parts. Oates procured a specimen in Pegu. It keeps entirely to the ground, searching among dead leaves for its food, which is chiefly insects.

390. Erithacus calliope, *(Pall.) Seebohm, Cat. B. Br. Mus.* v. p. 305; *Oates, B. Br. Burm.* i. p. 14. Motacilla calliope, *Pall. Reis. Russ. Reichs,* iii. p. 697. Turdus kamtschatkensis, *Gmel., Syst. Nat.* i. p. 817. Calliope kamschatkensis, *Jerd., B. Ind.* ii. p. 150, No. 512; *Blyth, B. Burm.* p. 101; *Dresser, B. Eur.* ii. p. 341; *Hume and Dav., Str. F.* vi. p. 337; *Hume, Str. F.* viii. p. 100; *Oates, Str. F.* x. p, 213.—The SIBERIAN RUBY-THROATED ROBIN.

Whole upper plumage olive brown, slightly darker on the head and ear coverts; lores black; supercilium white, meeting in a narrow line over the forehead; cheeks white, separated by a narrow dark brown moustachial line from the chin and throat, which are brilliant glossy scarlet; breast ashy grey, shading into nearly white on the centre of the belly and into brown on the flanks and thighs; under tail coverts, axillaries, and under wing coverts very pale buff; bill black; legs, feet, and claws brown; irides brown.

The *female* has the superciliary streak buffy white; lores and in front of the eye dusky brown; no scarlet throat patch, which is replaced by pale brown.

Length.—6 inches; wing 2·9; tail 2·4; tarsus 1·15; bill from gape 0·8.

Hab.—Throughout Siberia, where it breeds, extending southwards as far as the extreme north of China. Winters in the Philippine Islands, British Burmah, and in Northern and Central India and Bengal, also the Western coast, occasionally straying into Europe. It is recorded from Arrakan by Blyth. Abundant in Pegu, rather rare in Tenasserim, also at Thayetmyo and Karin. Jerdon says it is found chiefly in Northern and Central India, also that he saw it south of Bombay. In Bengal he says it is most common, and in the eastern side of India. In its manners it is shy, silent, and solitary; haunts thickets and underwood, and feeds on the ground on various insects. It has a pretty song.

391. Erithacus pectoralis, *Gould, Icones. Avium.* pt. ii. pl. 1; *Blyth, J. A. S. B.* xii. p. 934 (1843); *id.* xvi. p. 135; *Adams, P. Z. S.* 1858, p. 492; *Godwin-Austen, J. A. S. B.* xxix. pt. ii. p. 270; *Jerd. B. Ind.* ii. p. 150, No. 513; *Hume, Nests and Eggs, Ind. B.* p. 325; *Brooks, Str. F.* 1875, p. 241; *Seebohm, Cat. B. Br. Mus.* v. p. 307. Calliope ballioni, *Severtz. Turkest. Jevotn.* pp. 65, 122; *id. Str. F.* 1875, p. 429.—The INDIAN RUBY-THROATED ROBIN.

Upper parts, including the ear coverts and sides of the neck, a uniform dark slate grey, shading into brown on the crown; lores black; eye-stripe white, meeting in a narrow line over the forehead; wings brown, the outer webs of the wing coverts slate grey; tail with sometimes two and sometimes four centre feathers plain brown, the remaining feathers dark brown with more or less white on the base and tips of most feathers; chin and upper throat glossy scarlet; *cheeks*, lower throat, and upper breast dull black; belly and under tail coverts white, shading into slate grey on the flanks, axillaries, and under wing coverts; bill black; rictal bristles almost obsolete; legs and feet brown.

Length.—6 inches; wing 2·7 to 2·9; tail 2·0 to 2·25; culmen 0·65; tarsus 1·25.

The *female* differs from the male in having the general colour of the upper parts a uniform earthy brown; the black on the lores, cheeks, lower throat, and upper breast replaced by greyish brown; the slate grey of the flanks, axillaries, and under wing coverts replaced by brown. Tail feathers brown terminally with a spot of white.

Hab.—Throughout the Himalayas from Cashmere to Sikkim, where and in Turkestan it breeds in the pine districts, and descends into the valleys during the cold season. Frequents thick brushwood or long grass jungle. In the Punjaub and N.-W. Provinces it is less common. In Assam, and probably Upper Bengal, it frequents similar situations. Of its nidification nothing authentic is known. Mr. Hume had a nest and some eggs brought to him in

Native Sikkim during June, found in a deep crevice in a rock at an elevation of about 12,000 feet. The nest was a saucer-shaped pad of very fine moss and fern roots, closely-felted together. The eggs, two in number, were regular ovals, slightly compressed towards the small end. Colour uniform pale salmon buff. Size 0·9 × 0·67 inch.

392. Erithacus tschebaiewi, (*Prejv.*) *Seebohm, Cat. B. Br. Mus.* v. p. 308. Calliope tschebaiewi, *Prejv., Rowley's Orn. Misc.* ii. p. 180; pl. liv. fig l. 1877; *Gould, B. Asia* pt. xxxi. pl. 10, 1879.—The THIBETAN RUBY-THROATED ROBIN.

Upper parts dark slaty-grey, suffused with olive brown on the head and rump; lores black, ear coverts dark brown; supercilium white, quills brown edged with olive brown; lesser wing coverts dark slate grey; median wing coverts edged with dark slate grey; greater wing coverts and innermost secondaries olive brown; tail nearly black, the two centre feathers entirely so; the next on each side tipped with white, the remaining four on each side with the basal half white, except the outside web of the outside feather on each side and a large spot at the tip; cheeks white edged with black; chin and throat glossy scarlet; breast black; axillaries and under wing coverts and flanks slate grey; belly and under tail coverts white, the latter with slate grey bases; bill black; legs and feet dark brown.

Length.- 5·9 inches; wing 2·9 to 3·25; tail 2·4 to 2·5; culmen 0·6; tarsus 1·2 to 1·3.

The female has the upper parts dark olive, a white supercilium, and black lores; the under parts dirty white; the tail dark olive, without the white bases which characterize the male and with the terminal white spots much smaller. (Seebohm.)

Hab.—Sikkim. There is only a single skin of this species in the British Museum.

393. Erithacus cæruleculus, (*Pall.*) *Seebohm, Cat. B. Br. Mus.* v. p. 308; Motacilla cærulecula, *Pall. Zoogr. Rosso Asiat.* i. p. 480; Cyanecula suecica, *Linn. Sys. Nat.* i. p. 336 (*Partim*) *Brehm. Vogt. Deutschl. p.* 350 *Gray, Gen. B.* i. p. 182; *Heugl. Orn. N. O. Afr.* i. p. 336; *Shelly, B. Egypt*; *Blf. East. Persia*, ii p. 169; *Hume and Dav., Str. F.* vi. p. 337; *Legge, Birds of Ceylon*, p. 433; *Murray, S. F.* vii. p. 112; *id. Hdbk., Zool., &c., Sind*, p. 152; *Shelly, Ibis.*, 1881, *Str. F.* ix. p. 330; viii. 304. Cyanecula cæruleculus, (*Pall.*) *Bp. Consp.* i. p. 296; *Gray, Handlist B.* i. p. 223; *Jerd. Birds Ind.* ii. p. 152; No. 514.—The INDIAN BLUE-THROAT.

Head, neck, back, wings, and wing coverts pale brown; the feathers of the head slightly centred darker and the wing coverts and quills edged paler; lores dark brown; supercilium buffy white; chin, cheek, throat, and breast cobalt blue, with a large ferruginous or chestnut spot in the centre of the throat and breast; below the blue of the breast a black band, followed by a chestnut one; rest of under surface buffy white; tail rufous or pale ferruginous, the two centre feathers and the terminal third of the others dark brown, lighter on the outermost; ear-coverts silky rufescent brown; bill dusky; gape yellow; legs dusky brown; irides dark brown.

Length.—5·5 to 6·5 inches; wing 3; tail 2 to 2·25. The female is like the male, but without the pectoral gorget; the throat, chin, and neck buffy white, with a line of dusky brown from the base of the side of the lower mandible continued to, and across the breast; rest of under surface buffy white.

Hab.—Europe, Asia, and North Africa. Winters in the plains of India. Common in Sind, Punjab, N.-W. Provinces, Bengal, and the whole of India, to Nepaul and Cashmere; also in Beloochistan, S.-E. Persia, Afghanistan, and E. Turkistan. It has been recorded from Arrakan, and is found nearly throughout British Burmah. Its habits are quite those of its congeners, frequenting thick brushwood and long grass jungle in the vicinity of water.

Gen. **Sialia.**—*Swainson.*

A small group of birds, the natural position of which is difficult to define. Some authors place the genus among the Saxicolinæ, which is as nearly as possible its true place, being very closely related to the Redstarts.

The single species known in India was characterized by Hodgson under the generic title of *Grandala* (*J. A. S. B.* xii. p. 447), which was admitted by Blyth and subsequently by Jerdon. Seebohm, however, in his *Cat. B. Br. Mus.* v. p. 327, places *Grandala* as a synonym of *Sialia*, which I follow.

The genus is characterized by Jerdon and Seebohm as having a moderate, slender, straight, and black bill, slightly depressed at the base. Nostrils oval; *rictal bristles nearly obsolete*; *legs black*; tarsus not scutellated; tail moderate, of 12 feathers, slightly forked; wings long and pointed; 2nd primary as long or nearly so as the third; tertials half the length of the primaries; colour blue.

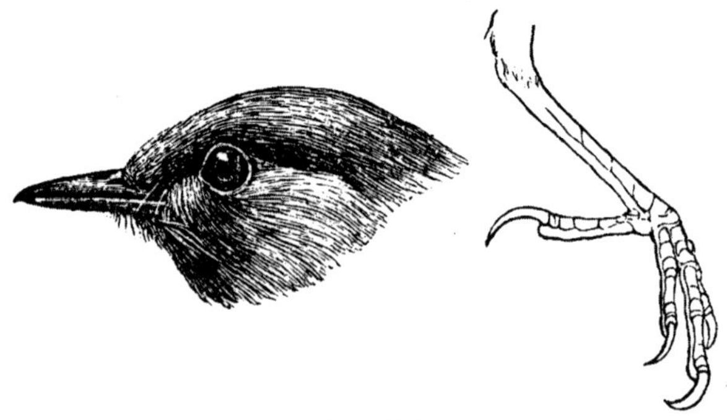

Sialia Cœlicolor.

394. Sialia cælicolor, (*Hodgson*), *Seebohm, Cat. B. Br. Mus.* v. p. 328. Grandala cælicolor, *Hodgs. J. A. S. B.* xii. p. 447. *Blyth, J. A. S. B.* xvi. p. 132; *Gould. B. Asia.* pt. xi. (1862); *Jerd. B. Ind.* ii. p. 119. Grandala schistacea, *Hodgs. J. A. S. B.* xii. p. 447.—The HIMALAYAN LONG-WINGED BLUE-CHAT.

Upper and under surface deep indigo blue, shading into brilliant indigo blue with metallic gloss on the rump and upper tail coverts; lores black; wing coverts, quills, and tail black, margined obscurely with greenish blue; axillaries and under wing coverts dull black, margined with indigo blue.

The female is an almost uniform earthy brown above and below; the feathers of the rump and upper tail coverts broadly tipped with dull brownish blue; secondaries and the primaries next them with a subterminal white bar. (Seebohm.)

Length.—9 to 9·3 inches; wing 5·6 to 5·7; (females 5·2); tail 3·45 to to 3·75; bill 0·7 to 0·8; tarsus 1·15.

Hab.—The Himalayas, breeding at high elevations; eastwards throughout the mountains separating China from Thibet. Jerdon says it inhabits the northern region of Nepaul or Cachar and near the snowy region. According to Hodgson it is solitary in its habits. Insects and gravel were found in the stomach of a specimen examined.

Gen. **Ruticilla**—*C. L. Brehm.*

Bill shorter than in *Sialia*, straight, slender, and black; rictal bristles fairly developed; legs black or nearly always so; tarsus not so long as in *Sialia*, not scutellated; tail of 12 feathers even or slightly rounded; wings moderately long and pointed; 1st primary about one-third the length of the 4th; the 5th and 6th generally equal and longest. Rump and tail (except the two centre) feathers chestnut in most species—the upper plumage generally grey. They have a pleasing song and perch freely on trees, but build in holes of walls, rocks, or tree trunks.

395. Ruticilla phœnicurus, *Linn, Syst. Nat.* i. 335. Sylvia phœnicurus (*Linn.*) *Lath. Gen. Syn. Suppl.*, i. p. 287; *id. Ind. Orn.* ii. p. 11. Phœnicura muraria, *Sws. and Rich, Faun. Bor. Am.* ii. p. 489. Phœnicura ruticilla, (*Eyton*) *Gould. B. Eur.* ii. pl. 95. Ruticilla phœnicura, (*Linn.*) *Jerd. B. Ind.* ii. p. 136, No. 495; *Dresser, B. Eur.* pt. xxvi. (1874); *Blanford, E. Pers.* ii. p. 163; *Seebohm, Ibis*, 1880, p. 191.—The EUROPEAN REDSTART.

A narrow frontal band; lores, cheeks, ear coverts, chin, throat, and upper breast black; a band behind the black frontal band white; upper surface of body brownish ash or slate-grey; rump and upper tail coverts rich chestnut; wings and their coverts dark brown, margined with chestnut exteriorly; lower breast and flanks chestnut; the feathers broadly margined with white, *paling into pure white on the centre of the abdomen* and into pale chestnut on the axillaries and under wing and tail coverts; tail chestnut, except the inner webs of the two central tail feathers, which are dark brown; bill, legs, and feet black; irides brown.

Length.—5·5 to 5·6 inches; wing 2·8 to 3·3; tail 2·1 to 2·5; culmen 0·5; tarsus 0·9 to 0·75.

The *female* resembles the male, except that the under parts are buff and that there are no dark bases to the feathers of the upper surface. *In breeding plumage* the forehead of the male becomes pure white, the head becomes slate grey, and there is a scarcely perceptible pale margin to the wings and their coverts. The breast and flanks have no white margins which, with the feathers of the axillaries, wing coverts, and under tail coverts, become a rich chestnut.

Hab.—Seebohm says it breeds throughout the Palæarctic region as far north as the Arctic circle and as far east as the watershed of the Yenasay and the Lena. It winters in South Persia and Central Africa as far west as Senegal. It is recorded from the N.-W. Provinces of India, the Punjaub, and Afghanistan. It breeds in holes of trees and walls. Eggs verditer blue.

396. Ruticilla mesoleuca (*Hempr.* et *Ehr.*), *Cab. Journ. Orn.* 1854, p. 446; *Seebohm, P. Z. S.* 1879, p 979; *Seebohm, Cat. B. Br. Mus.* v. p. 338; *Murray, Vert. Zool., Sind*, p. x.; Sylvia mesoleuca, *Hempr.* et *Ehr. Symb. Phys., fol. ee.*, 1832. Sylvia phœnicura (*Linn.*) *apud Menetries, Cat. Rais. Cauc.*, p. 35. Ruticilla phœnicura, (*Linn.*) *apud Heugl. Syst. Uebers*, p. 25; *apud Blanford, Geol. and Zool., Abyss.*, p. 358.—Ehrenberg's Redstart.

Differs from *Phœnicurus* by the male having the outer webs of the secondaries more or less broadly margined with white, otherwise it is not unlike the male of *Phœnicurus; 2nd primary between 5th and 7th.* The female, Seebohm says, is slightly darker on the upper and under parts.

Length.—5·5 inches; wing 2·84 to 3·2; tail 2·16 to 2·45; culmen 0·5; tarsus 0·75 to 0·9.

Hab.—The Caucasus, Asia Minor, and Algiers, wintering in Sind (rare), Persia, Western Arabia, Abyssinia, and Senegal.

397. Ruticilla rufiventris, *Jerdon, B. Ind.* ii. p. 137, No. 497; *Gray, Handlist B.* i. p. 221; *Blanf. East. Persia*, ii. p. 163; *Murray, Hdbk. Zool., &c., Sind*, p. 152; *id. Vert. Zool., Sind*, p. 146; *Seebohm, Cat. B. Br. Mus.* vol. v. p. 342. Ruticilla phœnicuroides, *Moore, P. Z. S.* 1854, p. 25, pl. lvii; *Jerd. B. Ind.* ii. p. 136; *Gray, Handlist B.* i. p. 221. Ruticilla erythroprocta, *Gould, apud. Hume and Henders. Lahore to Yarkand*, p. 208; *apud. Severtz. Turkest. Jevotn.*—The Indian Redstart.

Adult Male.—Crown of head ashy grey; throat, neck, lores, ear coverts, breast, back, and wing coverts dark brown or black, the feathers edged greyish; wings dusky brown; the primaries and secondaries margined rufescent on their outer webs; breast, flanks, under wing coverts, belly, rump, upper and lower tail coverts, and tail (except the inner and part of the outer webs of the two central feathers, which are dark brown) uniform chestnut. The female is brownish above. The edge of the wings, belly, and under tail coverts pale rufous; bill and legs dark brown; irides brown.

Length.—6 inches; wing 3·3; tail 2·5; bill at front 0·55.

Hab.—India generally. Breeds in North China, Mongolia, and Eastern Turkestan. Occurs in Sind, Beloochistan, S.-E. Persia, and Afghanistan during winter; also in Nepaul, Kashgar, Behar, N.-W. Himalayas, Kutch, Kattiawar, Jodhpore, North Guzerat, the Concan, and Deccan to South India.

Frequents groves of trees, orchards, gardens, and the vicinity of old buildings, walls, and houses. Feeds on insects. It has a most peculiar quivering motion of its tail on its perch after feeding.

398. Ruticilla hodgsoni, *Moore, P. Z. S.* 1854, p. 26, pl. lviii.; *Jerd. B. Ind.* ii p. 138, No. 498; *Godwin-Austen, J. A. S. Z.*, xlvii. pt. 2, p. 18 (1878). Phœnicura ruticilloides, *Hodgs. MS. Drawings.* Ruticilla erythrogastra, (*Gould*) *apud. Blyth, Cat. B. Mus. As. Soc.*, p. 168.—HODGSON'S REDSTART.

Upper surface of body dull slate-grey, shading into white on the forehead and into bright chestnut on the rump and upper tail coverts; a narrow frontal band at the base of the upper mandible; the lores, feathers behind the eye, ear coverts, cheeks, chin, throat, and upper breast black; lower breast to vent, axillaries, under wing and tail coverts, rump and tail feathers (except the two central tail feathers, the inner and outer margins of which are dusky brown), bright chestnut; hind part of crown, neck, back, wings and their coverts dusky or dark brown; the outer half of the basal half of the secondaries white, forming a wing patch; bill, legs, and feet black; irides brown.

Length.—6·5 inches; wing 3·05 to 3·3; tail 2·6 to 2·85; tarsus 0·9 to 1; culmen 0·6.

The *female* is greyish brown and below the chin is paler, also the axillaries and under wing coverts, shading to albescent or white on the centre of the abdomen; under tail coverts pale chestnut; upper tail coverts rich chestnut.

Hab.—The Himalayas from Nepaul to Assam, where it winters in the valleys. It is recorded from Assam, Bhootan, Darjeeling, Afghanistan, and Nepaul.

399. Ruticilla aurorea, (*Gmel.*) *Jerd. B. Ind.* ii. p. 139, No. 500; *Wald. in Bl. B. Burm.*, p. 201; *Hume Str. F.* iii. p. 135; *Oates, B. Br. Burm.* i. p. 16. Motacilla aurorea, *Gmel., Syst. Nat.* i., p. 976.—The DAURIAN REDSTART.

A narrow line on the forehead, lores, cheeks, chin, ear coverts, and throat black; remainder of lower surface with the axillaries and under wing coverts deep chestnut. Head, nape, and upper back slaty grey; most of the feathers slightly tipped with brown; *back, scapulars and wing coverts black*, sometimes margined with grey; rump and upper tail coverts chestnut; tail chestnut, except the central pair and the terminal half of the outer web of the outer pair of feathers, which are black; wings very dark brown; nearly black on the secondaries, which have a large white patch at the base of each feather.

The *female* differs from the male in having the whole under parts light brown, tinged with rufous on the vent and under tail coverts; head, sides of head and neck, back, and scapulars olive brown; rump and upper tail coverts chestnut; wings and wing coverts brown; each feather margined paler, and the spot on the secondaries smaller than in the male; tail chestnut, the black parts in the male being replaced by brown; bill and legs black; irides brownish.

Length.—5·75 inches; tail 2·5; wing 2·9; tarsus 0·9; culmen 0·6.

Hab.—S.-E. Himalayas, Bhootan, Assam, and Eastern Bengal and Burmah during winter. It summers in S.-E. Siberia, E. Mongolia, North China, and the mountains of Japan. It has also been recorded as occurring during winter in the Malay Peninsula.

400. Ruticilla erythrogastra, (*Gould.*) *Blyth, Cat. B. Mus. As. Soc.* p. 168; *Gould. B. Asia*, i. pl. 49; *Jerd. B. Ind.* ii. p. 139, No. 499; *Hume and Henders., Lahore to Yarkand*, p. 210; *Dresser, B. Eur.* pt. lxvi.; *Blanford, J. A. S. B.* xli., pt. 2, p. 51. Motacilla erythrogastra, *Gould, Nov. Com. Petrop.* xix. p. 469.—The WHITE-WINGED or GULDENSTADT'S REDSTART.

The male in full autumn plumage.—Forehead, crown and nape pale grey, the feathers mesially streaked below with white; a narrow line at base of upper mandible; lores, ear coverts, sides of the neck, cheeks, *chin, throat*, breast, upper and under wing coverts, *back* and scapulars black; quills dark brown, *a white spot on the wing*; rump, upper tail coverts, tail, *axillaries*, belly, flanks and under tail coverts chestnut, slightly darker on the two central tail feathers. Bill, legs, feet and claws black; 3rd, 4th, and 5th primaries sub-equal and longest; 2nd equal to the 7th.

Length.—Wing 4·05 to 4·3 inches; tail 3·01 to 3·3; culmen 0·59 to 0·6; tarsus 1·1.

The female is drab in colour, slightly darker on the lores and ear coverts and much lighter on the margins of the greater wing coverts. The chestnut colouring is duller than that of the male. Axillaries are drab and not chestnut in colour, the under tail coverts only are suffused with chestnut, the belly and flanks being pale drab.

Hab.—The Himalayas, where and in the pine regions of the Caucasus, Turkestan, and the mountain ranges between Thibet and China, Seebohm says, it breeds in the birch and pine regions. It is said to have occurred in the N.-W. Provinces of India, and is known from Nepaul, Cashmere, and Bhootan, also Yarkand. In habits it is not unlike its congeners. Jerdon mentions it from Kumaon, and that a pair was seen by Dr. Stewart near Landour at the side of a stream.

401. Ruticilla erythronota, (*Eversm.*) *Bp. Consp.* i. p. 297; *Blanf. East Pers.* ii. p. 167; *Seebohm, Cat. B. Br. Mus.* v. p. 34. Sylvia erythronota, *Eversm., Add. Pall. Zoogr. Rosso.-Asiat. fasc.* ii. p. 110. Ruticilla rufogularis, *Moore, P. Z. S.* 1854, p. 27, pl. lix; *Hume, Ibis,* 1870, p. 530.—EVERSMANN'S REDSTART.

Adult male in full autumn plumage.—Head and nape grey; a narrow line at the base of the upper mandible; lores, ear coverts and sides of the neck black, each feather more or less conspicuously tipped with brown; back, rump and upper tail coverts bright chestnut, the feathers of the former fringed with brown; scapulars black, also fringed with brown; quills brown; innermost secondaries darker and with their outer webs margined with white; primary coverts white, broadly tipped with dark brown; greater wing coverts dark brown, narrowly tipped with white; median wing coverts white; tail bright chestnut, except the two central feathers and the terminal half of the outer web of the outermost feather on each side, which are black, occasionally mixed with chestnut; *chin and throat,* breast and flanks, bright chestnut, sometimes obscurely tipped with buffish, which is the colour of the belly; under tail coverts shaded with chestnut; axillaries white; bill, legs, feet and claws black; 4th and 5th primaries sub-equal and longest.

Length.—Wing 3·5 inches; tail 2·75 to 2·85; culmen 0·46 to 0·6; tarsus 0·9 to 1·0.

The female is similar to the male, except that the back and under parts (not including the under tail coverts) are greyish brown.

Hab.—Persia, Afghanistan, N.-W. Provinces, Kashgar, and the N.-W. Himalayas generally. Seebohm says it breeds in the pine and birch regions of Turkestan, S.-W. Mongolia, and S.-E. Siberia.

402. Ruticilla frontalis, (*Vigors*) *Gray, Cat. Mam. &c., Nepaul, Coll. Hodgs.*; *Seebohm, Cat. B. Br. Mus.* v. p. 305. Phœnicura frontalis, *Vig. P. Z. S.* 1831, p. 172; *Gould, Cent. Him. B.* pl. xxvi. fig. 1; *Blyth*

J. A. S. B. xi. p. 190 (1842). Ruticilla frontalis (*Vigors*), *Jerd. B. Ind.* ii. p. 141, No. 503; *Godw.-Austen, J. A. S. B.* xxxix. pt. 2, p. 270; *Hume and Henders., Lah. to Yark.* p. 211.—The BLUE-FRONTED REDSTART.

Adult male in full autumn plumage.—Forehead and supercilium cobalt blue; rest of the head, neck and mantle blue black, most of them as if dusted over with chesnut; primaries and secondaries brown, their outer webs margined paler; innermost secondaries dark brown, margined on their outer webs with chestnut; lesser wing coverts dark blue, with narrow pale edges; median and greater coverts black, edged with chestnut; lower back, rump and upper tail coverts rich chestnut; tail rich chestnut, except the two centre feathers which are black, margined on the outer web with chestnut, the terminal half of the outer web of the outermost feather and the tips of the other feathers, which are also black, for about half an inch. Sides of the neck, ear coverts, cheeks, chin, throat and foreneck blue black, dusted over with brownish; rest of under surface rich chestnut, paler in the centre of the belly; axillaries chestnut; thighs sooty brown; bill, legs and claws black.

Length.—6·5 inches; wing 3·4 to 3·6; tail 2·7 to 2·9; culmen 0·5 to 0·6; tarsus 1.

The female is rich sooty brown, the forehead with a shade of chestnut, which deepens on the rump and upper tail coverts. Two centre tail feathers dark brown, with chestnut margins on the basal half of the outside edges; rest of tail feathers rich chestnut, three-fourths of the outside edges of the outermost feather and the tip of the rest brown for about half an inch; under surface pale sooty brown; chin and centre of belly shading into pale chestnut; axillaries and under wing coverts pale chestnut; under tail coverts rich chestnut.

Hab.—The Punjaub, N.-W. Provinces, and Nepaul to Assam. Recorded from Darjeeling, Cashmere, Thibet, Kumaon, Bootan, and near Dhurrumsala, also Sikkim. Jerdon says it is more common in the N.-W. Himalayas, and Seebohm that it breeds in the pine forests of the mountain chains from the Western, Southern, and Eastern boundaries of Thibet, Cashmere, Nepaul, Sikkim, Assam, and Moupin, and that it descends into the valleys during winter.

403. Ruticilla schisticeps, (*Hodgs.*) *Moore, P. Z. S.* 1854, p. 29 pl. lxi.; *Jerd., B. Ind.* ii. p. 140; *Seebohm, Cat. B. Br. Mus.* v. p. 351. Phœnicura schisticeps, *Hodgs. MS. Drawings, B. M. B. Nepaul.* Ruticilla nigrogularis, *Moore, P. Z. S.* 1854, p. 29, pl. lxi; *Jerd. B. Ind.* ii. p. 140; *Hume, Str. F.* iv. p. 497.—The SLATY-HEADED REDSTART.

Adult male in full autumn plumage.—A narrow black line at the base of the bill; forehead and crown cobalt blue, the bases of the feathers on the occiput, nape, and hindneck black; mantle and lower back black; rump and upper tail coverts deep rich chestnut, their bases black; scapulars black, the terminal half rich chestnut; lesser wing coverts black, also the greater and primary coverts; median coverts white; innermost secondaries nearly black, their outer edges margined with white; tail black, chestnut at base, the two centre feathers entirely black; sides of the neck, cheeks, chin, throat, ear coverts and foreneck black; a large white spot on the lower throat; under surface deep rich chestnut; axillaries and under wing coverts black, tipped with white; thighs black; bill, feet, and claws black.

Length.—6 inches; wing 3·1 to 3·2; tail 2·8; tarsus 0·25.

The Adult female is rich sooty brown above the forehead, tinged with cobalt, and the scapulars with pale chestnut; rump and upper tail coverts chestnut; under surface duller sooty brown; base of outer tail feathers chestnut, greater wing coverts white.

Hab.—Nepaul. Seebohm says it breeds in the wooded valleys of Kansu, and winters in Nepaul and Sikkim.

404. Ruticilla cæruleocephala, *Vigors, P. Z. S.* 1830, p. 35; *Gould. Cent. Him. B.* pl. xxv.; *Blyth, Cat. J. A. S. B.* xvi. p. 134; *Bp. Consp.* i. p. 296; *Jerd. B. Ind.* ii. p. 141; *Seebohm, Cat. B. Br. Mus.* v. p. 353.—The Blue-headed Redstart.

Adult Male in full autumn plumage.—A narrow line at base of the upper mandible, lores, feathers round the eye, chin and ear coverts black; head and nape greyish brown; throat, breast, under wing coverts and scapulars black, margined with brown; wings and wing coverts black; median coverts and outer margins of the innermost secondaries white; axillaries, belly and under tail coverts white; bill, legs and feet black.

Length.—6 to 6·25 inches; wing 3 to 3·2; tail 2·3 to 2·7; culmen 0·55; tarsus 0·8 to 0·9.

The female is greyish brown above and below, darker on the wings and tail, and paler on the belly, under tail coverts and axillaries; upper tail coverts dull chestnut; greater and median coverts suffused with chestnut and with white tips.

Hab.—Afghanistan, N.-W. Provinces and Nepaul, also Bhootan and the Himalayas generally.

Distribution Table of the Birds of British India and its Dependencies.

No. in Avifauna.	Jerdon's Nos.	Species.	Sind.	Beloochistan.	Persia.	Afghanistan.	Punjab.	N.-W. Provinces.	Oudh.	Bengal.	Rajputana.	Central India.	Central Prov.	Kutch.	Guzerat.	Concan.	Deccan.	S. India.	British Burmah.	Nepaul.
1	1	Vultur monachus, *Lin.*	×	×	×	×	×	×	×		×	×		×	×					×
2	3*bis.*	Gyps fulvescens, *Hume.*	×	×	×	×	×	×	×	×	×	×		×	×				×	×
3	3*ter.*	Gyps himalayensis, *Hume.*																		×
4	4	Gyps indicus, *Scop.*									×		×			×	×	×	×	×
5	4*bis.*	Gyps pallescens, *Hume.*										×			×		×			
6	5	Pseudogyps bengalensis, *Gm.*	×	×	×	×	×	×	×	×	×	×	×	×	×	×	×	×	×	×
7	2	Otogyps calvus, *Scop.*	×				×	×	×	×	×	×	×	×	×	×		×	×	×
8	6	Neophron ginginianus, *Lath.*	×				×	×	×	×	×	×	×	×	×	×	×	×		×
9	50	Circus cyaneus, *Lin*					×	×	×				×				×			×
10	53	Circus melanoleucus, *Forst.*								×	×	×	×			×	×	×	×	×
11	52	Circus pygargus, *Lin.*	×	×	×		×	×	×	×	×	×	×	×	×	×	×	×	×	×
12	51	Circus macrurus, *S.G. Gm.*	×	×	×	×	×	×	×	×	×	×	×	×	×	×	×	×	×	×
13	54	Circus æruginosus, *Lin.*	×	×	×	×	×	×	×	×	×	×	×	×	×	×	×	×	×	×
14	21	Astur palumbarius, *Lin.*			×													×		×
15	22	Astur trivirgatus, *Tem.*								×			×			×	×	×	×	×
16	23	Astur badius, *Gm.*	×	×	×	×	×	×	×	×	×	×	×	×	×	×	×	×	×	×
17	23*bis.*	Astur poliopsis, *Hume.*								×									×	
18	23*ter.*	Astur soloensis, *Horsf.*																	×	×
19	24	Accipiter nisus, *Lin.*	×	×	×	×	×	×	×	×	×	×	×	×	×	×	×	×	×	×
20	25	Accipiter virgatus, *Temm.*					×	×	×		×	×	×		×	×		×	×	×
21	45	Buteo ferox, *S. G. Gm.*	×	×	×	×	×	×	×	×	×	×	×	×	×	×	×	×		×
22	44*bis.*	Buteo desertorum, *Daud*					×	×	×	×								×		×
23	47	Buteo plumipes, *Hodgs.*						×	×									×	×	×
24	49	Archibuteo strophiatus *Hodgs.*								×										×
25	7	Gypaëtus barbatus, *Lin.*	×	×	×	×	×	×	×											×
26	26	Aquila chrysætus, *Lin.*	×	×	×	×	×	×	×											×
27	27	Aquila heliaca, *Savig.*			×							×					×	×		×
28	27*bis.*	Aquila mogilnik, *S.G. Gm.*	×	×	×	×	×	×	×	×	×	×	×	×	×	×	×		×	×
29	29	Aquila vindhiana, *Frankl.*	×				×	×	×	×	×	×	×	×	×	×	×	×		×
30	30	Aquila hastata, *Less.*					×	×	×	×			×					×	×	×
31	28	Aquila clanga, *Pall.*	×	×	×	×	×	×	×	×	×	×	×	×	×	×	×		×	×
32	33	Nisaëtus fasciatus, *Vieill*	×	×	×	×	×	×	×		×	×	×	×	×	×	×	×		×
33	31	Nisaëtus pennatus, *Gm.*	×	×	×	×	×	×	×		×	×	×	×	×	×	×	×	×	×
34	37	Lophotriorchis kieneri, *Geoff.*										×						×	×	
35	32	Neopus malayensis, *Tem.*						×				×	×			×	×	×	×	×
36	36	Spizaëtus nipalensis, *Hodg.*					×	×	×	×						×	×	×	×	×
37	35	Spizaëtus cirrhatus, *Gm.*								×		×	×			×	×	×		×
38		Spizaetus alboniger, *Bly.*																	×	
39	34	Spizaëtus limnaëtus, *Horsf.*								×						×	×	×	×	
40	38	Circaëtus gallicus, *Gm.*	×		×		×	×	×	×	×	×	×	×	×	×	×	×		×
41	39	Spilornis cheela, *Lath.*					×	×	×	×	×	×	×	×	×	×	×	×	×	×
42	39*bis.*	Spilornis melanotis, *Jerd.*								×			×			×	×	×	×	
43	39*sex.*	Spilornis pallidus																	×	
44	48	Butastur teesa, *Frankl.*	×	×	×		×	×	×	×	×	×	×	×	×	×	×		×	×

No. in Avifauna.	Jerdon's Nos.	Species.	Sind.	Beloochistan.	Persia.	Afghanistan.	Punjab.	N.-W. Provinces.	Oudh.	Bengal.	Rajputana.	Central India.	Central Prov.	Kutch.	Guzerat.	Concan.	Deccan.	S. India.	British Burmah.	Nepaul.
45	48 *ter.*	Butastur liventer, *Tem.*	...	...	...	...	...	...	...	...	...	...	...	...	...	...	...	...	×	×
46	48 *bis.*	Butastur indicus, *Gm.*	...	...	...	...	...	...	...	...	...	...	...	...	...	...	...	...	×	...
47	42*bis.*	Haliaëtus albicillus, *Lin.*	×	×	×	...	×	×	×	×	...	...	...	×	...	×	×	×	×	...
48	43	Haliaëtus leucogaster, *Gm.*	×	...	...	...	×	×	×	×	×	..	×	×	×	×	...	×	×	...
49	42	Haliaëtus leucoryphus, *Pall.*	×	×	×	×	×	×	×	×	×	...	×	×	×	×	...	×	×	×
50	55	Haliastur indus, *Bodd.*	×	×	×	...	×	×	×	×	×	×	×	×	×	×	×	×	×	×
51	56	Milvus govinda, *Sykes*	×	×	×	×	×	×	×	×	×	×	×	×	×	×	×	×	×	×
52	56 *bis.*	Milvus melanotis, *Tem.*	×	...	...	...	×	×	×	×	×	×	×	×	×	×	×	×	×	×
53	56*ter.*	Milvus affinis, *Gould.*	×	...	...	...	×	×	×	×	...	...	×	...	...	...	...	...	×	...
54		Milvus korschum, *Gm.*	×	×	...	×	...	...	...	...	...	...	...	...	...	...	...	...	...	...
55	59	Elanus cæruleus, *Desf.*	×	...	...	...	×	×	×	×	×	×	×	×	×	×	×	×	×	×
56		Machæramphus alcinus, *Westr.*	...	...	...	...	...	...	...	...	...	...	...	...	...	...	...	...	×	...
57	57*ter.*	Pernis ptilorhynchus, *Tem.*	...	...	...	...	×	×	×	×	×	×	×	...	...	×	×	×	×	×
58	58	Baza lophotes, *Cuv.*	...	...	...	...	...	..	...	×	...	...	×	...	...	...	...	×	×	×
59	58 *bis.*	Baza sumatrensis, *Lafr*	...	...	...	...	...	...	...	...	...	...	...	...	...	...	...	...	×	...
60		Baza ceylonensis, *Legge.*	...	...	...	...	...	...	...	...	...	...	...	...	...	...	...	...	...	...
61	20	Microhierax cærulescens, *Lin.*	...	...	...	...	...	...	...	×	...	...	...	..	..	...	..	×	×	×
62	20*ter.*	„ fringillarius, *Drap.*	...	...	...	...	...	...	...	...	...	...	...	...	...	...	...	...	×	...
63	16*bis.*	Poliohierax insignis, *Wald.*	...	...	...	...	...	...	...	...	...	...	...	...	...	...	...	...	×	...
64	8	Falco communis, *Gm.*	×	×	×	×	×	×	×	×	×	×	×	×	×	×	×	×	×	×
65	9	Falco peregrinator, *Sund.*	...	...	×	×	×	×	×	...	...	×	×	...	...	...	×	×	×	×
66	12*bis.*	Falco barbarus, *Lin.*	×	×	×	×	×	×	×	×	...	...	...	...	×	...	...	..	...	×
67	12	Falco babylonicus, *Gurn.*	×	×	×	×	×	×	×	×	...	...	×	...	...	...	...	...	..	×
68	11	Falco jugger, *J. E. Gr.*	×	×	×	×	×	×	×	×	×	×	×	×	×	×	×	×	...	×
69	13	Falco subbuteo, *Lin.*	×	...	×	×	×	×	×	×	...	...	×	...	×	×	×	...	...	×
70	14	Falco severus, *Horsf.*	...	...	...	...	×	×	×	×	...	...	...	...	...	...	...	×	×	×
71	16	Falco chiquera, *Daud.*	×	×	×	×	×	×	×	×	×	×	×	×	×	×	×	×	...	×
72	15	Falco regulus. *Pall.*	×	...	×	×	×	×	×	...	...	...	...	...	...	...	...	...	...	...
73	10	Hierofalco sacer, *Gm.*	×	×	×	×	×	×	×	×	...	...	...	×	...	...	...	...	...	×
74	17	Cerchneis tinnuncula, *Lin.*	×	×	×	×	×	×	×	×	×	×	×	×	×	×	×	×	×	×
75	18	Cerchneis naumanni, *Fleisch*	...	...	×	×	...	...	...	...	...	...	...	...	...	×	×	×	...	×
76	18*bis.*	Cerchneis pekinensis, *Swinh.*	...	...	...	...	×	×	×	×	...	...	...	...	...	×	×	×	...	×
77	19 *bis.*	Cerchneis amurensis, *Radde.*	...	...	...	...	×	×	...	...	...	×	...	...	...	×	×	..	×	×
78	40	Pandion haliaëtus, *Lin.*	×	×	×	...	×	×	×	×	×	×	×	×	×	×	×	×	×	×
79	41	Polioaëtus ichthyaëtus, *Horsf.*	...	..	...	...	×	×	×	×	×	×	×	×	...	×	...	..	×	×
80	41*ter.*	Polioaëtus humilis, *S. Müll. & Schl.*	...	...	...	...	...	...	...	×	...	...	...	...	...	...	...	...	×	×
81	72	Ketupa ceylonensis, *Gm.*	×	×	..	×	×	×	×	×	×	×	×	...	...	×	×	×	×	×
82	73	Ketupa javanensis, *Less.*	...	...	...	...	...	...	...	...	...	...	...	...	...	...	...	...	×	...
83	69	Bubo bengalensis, *Frankl.*	×	×	...	×	×	×	×	×	×	×	×	×	×	×	×	×	×	×
84	70	Bubo coromandus, *Lath.*	×	...	...	...	×	×	×	×	×	×	×	×	×	×	×	×	×	×
85	71	Bubo nipalensis, *Hodgs.*	...	...	...	...	...	...	...	...	...	...	...	...	...	...	...	*	×	×
86		Bubo orientalis, *Horsf.*	...	...	...	...	...	...	...	...	...	...	...	...	...	...	...	...	×	...
87	74	Scops pennatus, *Hodgs.*	×	×	...	×	×	×	×	×	×	×	×	×	×	×	×	×	×	×

* Also the Malabar Coast.

No. in Avifauna.	Jerdon's Nos.	SPECIES.	Sind.	Beloochistan.	Persia.	Afghanistan.	Punjab.	N.-W. Provinces.	Oudh.	Bengal.	Rajputana.	Central India.	Central Prov.	Kutch.	Guzerat.	Concan.	Deccan.	S. India.	British Burmah.	Nepaul.
88	74 *B.*	Scops rufipennis, *Sharpe*	...	...	...	...	...	...	...	...	...	...	...	...	...	...	...	×	...	...
89	74*sept*	Scops brucii, *Hume.*	×	×	...	×	...	...	...	...	...	...	...	...	...	×	×	×	...	...
90		Scops spilocephalus, *Bly.*	...	...	...	...	...	×	×	×	...	...	...	...	...	...	...	...	...	...
91	74 *bis.*	Scops sunia, *Hodgs.*	...	...	...	...	...	×	...	...	...	...	...	...	...	...	...	×	...	×
92	74 *bis.*	Scops plumipes, *Hume*	...	...	...	...	...	×	...	...	...	...	...	...	...	...	...	...	...	×
93	75	Scops lettia, *Hodgs.*	...	...	...	...	...	...	...	×	...	...	...	...	...	×	...	×	×	×
94	75*qnt.*	Scops lempiji, *Horsf.*	...	...	...	...	...	×	×	×	...	...	...	×	...	×	...	...	×	×
95	75 *qt.*	Scops malabaricus, *Jerd.*	×	...	...	×	×	×	×	×	...	×	...	...	×	×	×	×	...	...
96		Scops sagittatus, *Sharpe*	...	...	...	...	...	...	...	...	...	...	...	...	...	...	...	...	×	...
97	74*oct.*	Scops balli, *Hume.*	...	...	...	...	...	...	...	...	...	...	...	...	...	...	...	...	×	×
98	74*qnt.*	Scops modestus, *Wald.*	...	...	...	...	...	...	...	...	...	...	...	...	...	...	...	...	×	×
99	76	Carine brama, *Tem.*	×	×	×	×	×	×	×	×	×	×	×	×	×	×	×	×	×	×
100	76 *qt.*	Carine pulchra, *Hume*	...	...	...	...	...	...	...	...	...	...	...	...	...	...	...	...	×	...
101	76*qnt.*	Heteroglaux blewitti, *Hume.*	...	...	...	...	...	...	...	...	...	×	×	...	...	...	...	...	...	...
102	81	Ninox lugubris, *Tick.*	...	...	...	...	×	×	×	×	...	...	×	...	...	×	×	...	...	×
103	81 *qt.*	Ninox affinis, *Tyt.*	...	...	...	...	...	...	...	...	...	...	...	...	...	...	...	...	×	...
104	81*bis.*	Ninox scutulata, *Raffl*	...	...	...	...	×	×	...	×	×	×	...	...	...	×	×	×	×	×
105	81*qnt.*	Ninox obscura, *Hume.*	...	...	...	...	...	...	...	×	...	...	...	...	...	...	...	...	×	...
106	80	Glaucidium brodiei, *Burt*	...	...	...	...	...	×	...	×	...	...	...	...	...	...	...	...	×	...
107	77	Glaucidium radiatum, *Tick.*	...	...	...	...	...	×	...	×	...	...	×	...	...	×	...	×	×	×
108	78	Glaucidium malabaricum, *Bly*	...	...	...	...	...	...	...	...	...	...	...	...	...	×	...	×	...	...
109	79	Glaucidium cuculoides, *Vig.*	...	...	...	...	×	×	...	×	...	...	×	...	...	...	...	...	×	×
110	67	Asio otus, *Lin.*	×	×	×	×	×	×	×	...	...	...	...	×	...	...	...	...	...	...
111	68	Asio accipitrinus, *Pall.*	×	×	×	×	×	×	×	×	×	×	×	...	×	×	×	×	×	...
112	67*bis.*	Syrnium butleri, *Hume*	...	×	...	...	...	...	...	...	...	...	...	...	...	...	...	...	...	...
113	66	Syrnium nivicolum, *Hodgs.*	...	...	...	...	×	×	...	...	...	...	...	...	...	...	...	...	...	...
114	65*bis.*	Syrnium sinense, *Lath.*	...	...	...	...	...	...	...	...	...	...	...	...	...	...	...	...	×	×
115	65	Syrnium ocellatum, *Less*	...	...	...	...	...	×	×	...	...	×	×	...	×	×	×	×	...	...
116	64	Syrnium newarense, *Hodgs.*	...	...	...	...	×	×	...	...	...	...	...	...	...	...	...	...	×	×
117	63	Syrnium indranee, *Sykes*	...	...	...	...	...	...	...	...	...	...	...	...	...	×	×	×	×	...
118	60	Strix flammea, *Lin.*	×	×	...	×	×	×	×	×	×	×	×	×	×	×	×	×	×	×
119	61	Strix candida, *Tick.*	...	...	...	...	×	×	×	×	...	×	×	...	...	...	×	×	×	...
120	62	Phodilus badius, *Horsf.*	...	...	...	...	...	...	...	×	×	...	...	...	...	...	...	...	×	×
121	664	Trypanocorax frugilegus, *Lin.*	...	...	×	×	×	×	...	...	...	...	...	...	...	...	...	...	...	...
122	657	Corvus corax, *Lin.*	×	...	×	×	×	...	...	...	...	...	...	...	...	...	...	...	...	...
123	660*bis.*	Corvus umbrinus, *Hedenb.*	×	×	×	×	...	...	...	...	...	...	...	...	...	...	...	...	...	...
124	661	Corvus lawrencei, *Hume*	×	×	...	×	×	×	...	×	×	×	...	×	×	...	×	×	...	×
125	665	Colœus monedula, *Lin.*	...	...	×	×	×	...	...	...	...	...	...	...	...	...	...	...	...	...
126	659 *bis.*	Corone cornix, *Lin.*	...	×	×	×	×	...	...	...	...	...	...	...	...	...	...	...	...	...
127	663	Corone splendens, *Vieill.*	×	...	...	...	×	×	×	×	×	×	×	×	×	×	×	×	×	×
128	659	Corone corone, *Lin.*	...	...	...	...	...	×	...	...	...	...	...	...	...	...	...	...	...	...
129	660 *bis.*	Corone macrorhynchus, *Wagl*	×	...	...	...	×	×	×	×	×	×	×	...	...	×	×	×	×	×
130	666	Nucifraga hemispila, *Vig.*	...	...	...	...	...	...	...	×	...	...	...	...	...	...	...	...	...	...
131	668 *bis.*	Pica rustica, *Scop.*	...	×	×	×	...	...	...	...	...	...	...	...	...	...	...	...	×	×
132	671	Urocissa occipitalis, *Bly.*	...	...	...	...	×	×	...	...	...	...	...	...	...	...	...	...	×	...

No. in Avifauna.	Jerdon's Nos.	Species.	Sind.	Beloochistan.	Persia.	Afghanistan.	Punjab.	N.-W. Provinces	Oudh.	Bengal.	Rajputana.	Central India.	Central Prov.	Kutch.	Guzerat.	Concan.	Deccan.	S. India.	British Burmah.	Nepaul.
133	672	Urocissa flavirostris, *Bly.*					×	×		×									×	×
134	674	Dendrocitta rufa, *Scop.*	×				×	×	×	×	×	×	×	×	×	×	×	×	×	×
135	677	,, frontalis. *Mc Clell.*																×		
136	678	,, leucogastra, *Gould.*																×		
137	676	,, himalayensis, *Bly.*						×	×	×								×	×	×
138	678 *bis.*	,, bayleyi, *Tyt.*																	×	×
139	678*qt.*	Crypsirhina varians, *Lath.*																	×	
140	678 *ter.*	Crypsirhina cucullata, *Jerd.*																	×	
141	673	Cissa chinensis, *Bodd.*								×									×	
142	678*qnt.*	Platysmurus leucopterus, *Tem*																	×	
143		Garrulus atricapillus	×	×	×															
144	669 *bis.*	Garrulus leucotis, *Hume*																	×	
145	669	Garrulus bispecularis, *Vig.*						×		×										×
146	670	Garrulus lanceolatus, *Vig.*						×		×										×
147	679	Graculus eremita, *Lin.*		×	×	×	×	×												×
148	680	Pyrrhocorax alpinus, *Koch.*					×	×												×
149	470*bis.*	Oriolus galbula, *Lin*	×		×															
150	470	Oriolus kundoo, *Sykes.*	×			×	×	×	×		×	×	×	×	×	×	×	×	×	×
151	473*bis.*	Oriolus diffusus, *Sharpe*								×						×		×	×	
152	471*ter.*	Oriolus tenuirostris, *Bly.*								×									×	×
153	471*bis.*	Oriolus andamanensis, *Tyt.*																	×	
154		,, xanthonotus, *Horsf.*																	×	
155	472	Oriolus melanocephalus, *Lin*					×	×	×	×		×				×	×	×	×	×
156	474	Oriolus traillii, *Vig.*						×		×									×	×
157	279	Dicrurus annectans, *Hodgs.*								×									×	×
158	286	Chibia hottentottus, *Lin.*						×					×			×		×	×	×
159	282	Chaptia ænea, *Vieill.*								×			×			×	×	×	×	×‡
160	282*bis.*	Chaptia malayensis, *Hay*																	×	
161	278	Buchanga atra, *Herm.*	×	×		×	×	×	×	×	×	×	×	×	×	×	×	×	×	×
162	280	Buchanga longicaudata, *Hay*										×	×					×		×
163	280*bis.*	Buchanga cineracea, *Sharpe*								×			×						×	×
164	280*qnt.*	Buchanga leucogenys, *Wald.*																	×	
165	281	Buchanga cærulescens, *Lin,*						×	×			×						×		×
166	283*ter.*	Dissemuroides andamanensis, *Hume.*																	×	
167	283	Bhringa remifer, *Tem.*																	×	
168	285	Dissemurus paradiseus, *Lin.*						×	×									×		×
169	469	Irena puella, *Lath*																×	×	
170	265	Tephrodornis pondicerianus, *Gm.*	×				×	×	×	×	×	×	×	×	×	×	×	×	×	×
171	263	Tephrodornis pelvica, *Hodgs.*						×	×										×	×
172	264	Tephrodornis sylvicola, *Jerd.*								×								×	×	
173	..	Tephrodornis grisola								×									×	

‡ Also the Malabar Coast.

No. in Avifauna.	Jerdon's Nos.	Species.	Sind.	Beloochistan.	Persia.	Afghanistan.	Punjab.	N.-W. Provinces.	Oudh.	Bengal.	Rajputana.	Central India.	Central Prov.	Kutch.	Guzerat.	Concan.	Deccan.	S. India.	British Burma.	Nepaul.
174	267	Hemipus picatus, *Sykes*	...	...	...	...	×	×	×	×	...	...	×	...	...	...	...	×	×	...
175		Hemipus obscurus, *Horsf.*	...	...	...	...	...	...	...	...	...	...	...	...	...	...	...	...	×	...
176	267 *A.*	Hemipus capitalis, *McClell.*	...	...	...	...	...	×	...	...	...	...	...	...	...	...	...	...	×	×
177	269 *qt.*	Hypocolius ampelinus, *Bp.*	×	...	×	...	...	...	...	...	...	...	...	...	...	...	...	...	...	...
178	668 *ter.*	Platylophus ardesiacus, *Cab.*	...	...	...	...	...	...	...	...	...	...	...	...	...	...	...	...	...	...
179	608	Cochoa viridis, *Hodgs.*	...	...	...	...	...	×	...	...	...	...	...	...	...	...	...	...	...	×
180	607	Cochoa purpurea, *Hodgs.*	...	...	...	...	...	×	...	...	...	...	...	...	...	...	...	...	×	×
181	270 *ter.*	Artamides dobsoni, *Ball.*	...	...	...	...	...	...	...	×†	...	...	...	...	...	...	...	...	×	...
182	270	Graucalus macii, *Less.*	...	...	...	...	×	×	×	...	×	×	×	...	...	...	...	×	×	×
183	269	Campophaga lugubris, *Sund*	...	...	...	...	...	×	×	...	...	×	...	...	...	...	...	...	...	×
184	269 *bis.*	Campophaga intermedia, *Hume.*	...	...	...	...	...	...	...	...	...	...	...	...	...	...	...	...	×	×
185	268 *bis.*	Campophaga melanoptera, *Rupp.*	...	...	...	...	...	...	...	...	...	...	...	...	...	...	...	...	×	...
186	268 *qt*	Campophaga neglecta, *Hume.*	...	...	...	...	...	...	...	...	...	...	...	...	...	...	...	...	×	...
187	271	Pericrocotus speciosus, *Lat.*	...	...	...	...	...	×	×	×	...	×	×	...	...	...	...	...	...	×‡
188	271 *ter.*	Pericrocotus elegans, *Mc Clell.*	...	...	...	...	...	...	×	†	...	...	...	...	...	...	...	...	×	...
189	271 *bis.*	Pericrocotus andamanensis, *Tyt.*	...	...	...	...	...	...	...	×†	...	...	...	...	...	...	...	...	×	...
190	273 *qt*	Pericrocotus flammifer, *Hume.*	...	...	...	...	...	...	...	...	...	...	...	...	...	...	...	...	×	...
191	272	Pericrocotus flammeus, *Forst.*	...	...	...	...	...	...	...	...	...	...	...	...	...	×	...	×‡	...	...
192		Pericrocotus igneus, *Bly*	...	...	...	...	...	...	...	...	...	...	...	...	...	...	...	...	×	...
193		Pericrocotus cinereus, *Laf.*	...	...	...	...	...	...	...	...	...	...	...	...	...	...	...	...	×	...
194	276	Pericrocotus peregrinus, *Lin.*	×	...	.	...	×	×	×	×†	×	×	×	×	×	×	×	×	×	×
195	273	Pericrocotus brevirostris, *Vig.*	×	×	...	...	×	×	×	×	×	×	×	×	×	...	×	...	×	×
196	273 *ter.*	Pericrocotus neglectus, *Hume.*	...	...	...	...	...	...	...	...	...	...	...	...	...	...	...	...	×	...
197	275	Pericrocotus roseus, *Vieill.*	...	...	...	...	×	×§	×	×	...	...	...	...	...	...	...	×	×	×
198	274	Pericrocotus solaris, *Bly.*	...	...	...	...	...	×	...	×	...	...	...	...	...	...	...	...	×	×‡
199	277	Pericrocotus erythropygius, *Jerd.*	...	...	...	...	...	×	×	...	...	×	×	×	×	...	×	×	...	...
200	277 *bis.*	Pericrocotus albifrons, *Jerd.*	...	...	...	...	...	...	...	...	...	...	...	...	...	...	...	...	×	...
201	277 *ter.*	Pericrocotus immodestus, *Hume.*	...	...	...	...	...	...	...	...	...	...	...	...	...	...	...	...	×	...
202	268	Lalage sykesi, *Strickl*	...	...	...	...	...	...	...	×	...	×	...	...	...	×	×	×	×	...
203		Lalage melanothorax, *Sharpe*	...	...	...	...	...	...	...	...	...	...	...	...	...	...	...	×	×	...
204	269 *ter.*	Lalage terat, *Bodd.*	...	...	...	...	...	...	...	...	...	...	...	...	...	...	...	...	...	...
205	296	Hemichelidon sibirica, *Gm.*	...	...	...	...	...	×	×	×	...	...	...	...	...	...	...	...	×	×‡
206	299	Hemichelidon ferruginea, *Hodgs.*	...	...	...	...	...	×	...	...	...	...	...	...	...	...	...	...	×	×‡

† Andamans. § Assam. ‡ Sikkim.

No. in Avifauna.	Jerdon's Nos.	Species.	Sind.	Beloochistan.	Persia.	Afghanistan.	Punjab.	N.-W. Provinces.	Oudh.	Bengal.	Rajputana.	Central India.	Central Prov.	Kutch.	Guzerat.	Concan.	Deccan.	S. India.	British Burmah.	Nepaul.
207	297	Alseonax latirostris, *Raffl.*	...	...	...	...	×	×	×	...	...	×	...	...	...	×*	×	×	×	×
208		Muscicapa grisola, *Lin.*	×	×	×	×	...	×	...	×	×	...	...	×	×	×	×	...	...	...
209		" sordida, *God.-Aust*	...	...	...	...	...	...	...	§	...	...	...	...	...	...	...	...	...	...
210	323*bis.*	Muscicapa parva, *Bechst.*	×	×	×	×	×	×	×	×	×	×	×	×	×	×	×	×	...	×
211	323	Muscicapa albicilla, *Pall.*	...	...	...	...	...	×	×	×	...	×	...	...	...	×	...	...	×	×
212	323*ter.*	Muscicapa hyperythra, *Cab.*	...	...	...	...	...	×	...	...	...	×	...	...	...	...	...	...	...	...
213	485*bis.*	Pratincola macrorhyncha, *Stol.*	×	×	...	×	×	×	×	...	×	...	...	×	×	...	...	×	...	...
214	485	Pratincola insignis, *Hodgs.*	...	...	...	...	...	...	...	×	...	...	...	...	...	...	...	...	...	×
215	483	Pratincola maura, *Pall.*	×	×	×	×	×	×	×	×	×	×	×	×	×	×	×	×	×	×
216	484	Pratincola leucura, *Bly.*	×	...	...	...	×	×	×	×	...	...	...	...	...	...	...	...	×	×
217	481	Pratincola caprata, *Lin.*	×	×	×	×	×	×	×	×	×	×	×	×	×	×	×	×	×	...
218	322	Poliomyias hodgsoni, *Verr.*	...	...	...	...	...	×	...	×	...	...	...	...	...	...	...	...	×	×†
219	310	Muscicapula superciliaris, *Jerd.*	...	...	...	...	×	×	×	×	...	...	×	...	...	...	...	...	×	×
220	311	Muscicapula astigma, *Hodgs*	...	...	...	...	...	×	×	×	...	...	×	...	...	...	...	...	...	×
221	326	Muscicapula maculata, *Tick.*	...	...	...	...	...	×	...	×	...	×	...	...	...	...	...	...	×	×‡
222	312	Muscicapula sapphira, *Tick.*	...	...	...	...	...	×	×	×	...	...	...	...	...	...	...	...	...	×‡
223	508	Tarsiger rufilatus, *Hodgs*	...	...	...	...	...	×	...	...	...	...	...	...	...	...	...	...	...	×‡
224	509	Tarsiger hyperythrus, *Bly.*	...	...	...	...	...	×	...	...	...	...	...	...	...	...	...	...	...	×‡
225	313	Tarsiger hodgsoni, *Moore*	...	...	...	...	...	×	...	...	...	...	...	...	...	...	...	...	...	×‡
226	510	Tarsiger indicus, *Hodgs.*	...	...	...	...	...	×	...	...	...	...	...	...	...	...	...	...	...	×‡
227	511	Tarsiger chrysæus, *Hodgs.*	...	...	...	...	...	×	...	...	...	...	...	...	...	...	...	...	...	×‡
228	290	Hypothymis azurea, *Bodd.*	...	...	...	...	×	×	×	×	...	×	×	...	...	×	×	×	×	×‡
229	290 *bis.*	Hypothymis occipitalis, *Vig*	...	...	...	...	...	...	...	...	...	...	...	...	...	...	...	...	×†	...
230		Xanthopygia fuliginosa, *Vig*	...	...	...	...	...	...	×	×†	...	...	...	...	...	...	...	...	×	...
231	487	Oreicola jerdoni, *Bly.*	...	...	...	...	...	×	×	×	...	...	...	...	...	...	...	...	×	...
232	486	Oreicola ferrea, *Hodgs.*	...	...	...	...	...	×	×	×	...	...	...	...	...	...	...	...	×	×‡
233	294	Chelidorhynx hypoxantha, *Bly.*	...	...	...	...	...	...	...	×	×	...	...	...	...	...	...	...	×	×‡
234	291	Rhipidura albicollis, *Vieill.*	...	...	...	...	×	×	×	×	...	×	...	...	...	.	×	×	×	×‡
235	293 *bis.*	Rhipidura javanica, *Sparrm.*	...	...	...	...	...	...	...	...	...	...	...	...	...	...	...	...	×	...
236	293	Rhipidura pectoralis, *Cuv.*	...	...	...	...	...	...	...	...	...	...	...	...	×	...	×	×	...	...
237	292	Rhipidura albifrontata, *Sharpe*	×	...	...	...	×	×	×	×	×	×	×	×	×	×	×	×	×	...
238	288	Terpsiphone paradisi, *Lin.*	×	×	...	×	×	×	×	×	×	×	×	×	×	×	×	×	...	×
239	289	" affinis, *Hay*	...	...	...	...	...	...	...	...	...	...	...	...	...	...	...	...	×	×
240		Philentoma velatum, *Tem.*	...	...	...	...	...	...	...	...	...	...	...	...	...	...	...	...	×	...
241		" pyrrhopterum, *Tem*	...	...	...	...	...	...	...	...	...	...	...	...	...	...	...	...	×	...
242	295	Culicicapa ceylonensis, *Sws.*	...	...	...	...	...	×	×	×†	...	×	×	...	...	...	...	×	×	×
243	569	Cryptolopha burkii, *Burt.*	...	...	...	...	...	×	×	×	...	...	...	...	...	...	...	...	.	×‡
244	570	" cantatrix, *Tick.*	...	...	...	...	...	...	...	×	...	×	...	...	...	...	...	...	×	×‡
245	576	" affinis, *Hodgs.*	...	...	...	...	...	...	...	×	...	×	...	...	...	...	...	...	×	×‡
246	572*et.* 573	" xanthoschista, *Hodgs*	...	...	...	...	×	×	...	×	...	×	...	...	...	...	...	...	×	×‡
247	571	" schisticeps, *Hodgs*	...	...	...	...	...	×	...	...	...	...	...	...	...	...	...	...	...	×‡

* Malabar Coast. Andamans. ‡ Sikkim. § Assam.

No. in Avifauna.	Jerdon's Nos.	Species.	Sind.	Beloochistan.	Persia.	Afghanistan.	Punjab.	N.-W. Provinces.	Oudh.	Bengal.	Rajputana.	Central India.	Central Prov.	Kutch.	Guzerat.	Concan.	Deccan.	S. India.	British Burmah.	Nepaul.
248	574	Cryptolopha superciliaris, *Tick*	...	...	...	...	...	...	...	×	...	...	...	...	...	...	...	...	×	×‡
249	575	„ poliogenys, *Bly.*	...	...	...	...	...	...	...	×	...	...	...	...	...	...	...	...	...	×‡
250	578	„ castaneoceps, *Hodgs.*	...	...	...	...	...	...	...	×	...	...	...	...	...	...	...	...	...	×‡
251	577	„ albigularis, *Hodgs.*	...	...	...	...	...	...	...	...	...	...	...	...	...	...	...	...	...	×‡
252	579	„ hodgsoni, *Moore*	...	...	...	...	...	...	...	...	...	...	...	...	...	...	...	...	...	‡
253		„ flavigularis, *Godwin-Austen.*	...	...	...	...	...	...	...	×†	...	...	...	...	...	...	...	...	...	...
254	302	Stoporala albicaudata, *Jerd.*	...	...	...	...	...	...	...	...	...	...	...	...	...	...	...	×	...	...
255	301	„ melanops, *Vig.*	...	...	...	...	...	×	...	...	...	×	...	...	...	×	×	×	×	×‡
256	309	Siphia pallidipes, *Sharpe*	...	...	...	...	...	...	...	...	...	...	...	...	...	×	...	×	...	×‡
257	303	„ unicolor, *Bly.*	...	...	...	...	...	...	...	...	...	...	...	...	...	...	...	...	...	‡
258	304	„ rubeculoides, *Vig*	...	...	...	...	×	×	×	×	...	...	...	...	...	...	...	×	×	×‡
259	306 } 305 }	„ tickelliæ, *Bly*	...	...	...	...	...	×	×	×	×	×	×	...	×	×·	×	×	×	...
260	308	„ magnirostris, *Bly*	...	...	...	...	...	...	...	×	...	...	...	...	...	...	...	...	×	‡
261	300	„ nigrorufa, *Jerd.*	...	...	...	...	...	...	...	...	...	...	...	...	...	...	...	×	...	...
262	319	„ strophiata, *Hodgs.*	...	...	...	...	...	×	...	×§	...	...	...	...	...	...	...	...	×	×†
263	307	„ ruficauda, *Sws.*	...	...	...	...	×	×	...	...	...	...	...	...	×	×	×	×	...	...
264	307 *bis.*	„ mandellii, *Hume.*	...	...	...	...	...	...	...	...	...	...	...	...	...	...	...	...	...	×‡
265	307 *ter.*	„ olivacea, *Hume.*	...	...	...	...	...	...	...	...	...	...	...	...	...	...	...	...	×	...
266	320	Digenea leucomelanura, *Hodgs.*	...	...	...	...	...	×	×	...	...	...	...	...	...	...	...	...	...	×‡
267		„ cerviniventris, *Sharpe*	...	...	...	...	...	...	...	†	...	...	...	...	...	...	...	...	...	...
268	317	„ moniliger, *Hodgs.*	...	...	...	...	...	×	...	§	...	...	...	...	...	...	...	...	×	×
269	317*bis.*	„ submoniliger, *Hume*	...	...	...	...	...	...	...	...	...	...	...	...	...	...	...	...	×	...
270	314	Niltava sundara, *Hodgs.*	...	...	...	...	×	×	×	§	...	...	...	...	...	...	...	...	×	×‡
271		„ vivida, *Swinh*	...	...	...	...	...	...	...	...	...	...	...	...	...	...	...	...	×	...
272	316	„ grandis, *Bly.*	...	...	...	...	...	×	×	×†	×	×	×	...	...	...	...	...	×	×‡
273		„ leucoprocta, *Tweed.*	...	...	...	...	...	...	...	...	...	...	...	...	...	...	...	...	×	...
274	315	„ macgrigoriæ, *Burt.*	...	...	...	...	...	×	×	×†	...	...	...	...	...	...	...	...	×	×‡
275		Sylvia cinerea	×	...	×	×	×	×	...	×	...	...	...	×	×	...	×	×	...	...
276	581	„ jerdoni, *Bly.*	×	×	×	×	×	×	×	×	...	×	×	×	×	×	×	×	...	...
277	582	„ affinis, *Bly.*	×	×	×	×	×	×	×	×	×	×	×	×	×	×	×	×	...	...
278	582*ter.*	„ althæa, *Hume.*	×	...	...	...	×	×	×	...	...	×	...	...	×	×	×	...	...	...
279	582*bis.*	„ minuscula, *Hume*	×	×	...	×	×	×	...	...	×	...	...	×	×	...	...	...	...	...
280	583*bis.*	„ nana, *Hemp*	×	×	×	...	×	×	...	...	×	...	...	...	...	...	...	...	...	...
281		„ familiaris, *Mene.*	×	×	×	×	...	...	...	...	×	...	...	×	×	...	...	...	...	...
282	556*bis.*	Phylloscopus borealis, *Blas.*	...	...	...	...	...	...	...	...	...	...	...	...	...	...	...	...	×	...
283	559	„ nitidus, *Bly.*	×	×	...	...	...	×	×	×	...	×	...	...	...	...	...	×	...	×
284	560	„ viridanus, *Bly.*	...	...	...	...	...	×	×	×	...	×	...	...	...	...	...	×	×	×
285	558*bis.*	„ plumbeitarsus, *Swinh.*	...	...	...	...	...	...	...	...	...	...	...	...	...	...	...	...	×	...
286	556 *qt.*	„ tenellipes, *Swinh*	...	...	...	...	...	...	...	...	...	...	...	...	...	...	...	...	×	...
287	556	„ magnirostris, *Bly*	...	...	...	...	×	×	×	×	...	×	×	...	...	×	×	×	×	×

§ Assam. ‡ Sikkim.

No. in Avifauna.	Jerdon's Nos.	Species.	Sind.	Beloochistan.	Persia.	Afghanistan.	Punjab.	N.-W. Provinces.	Oudh.	Bengal.	Rajputana.	Central India.	Central Prov.	Kutch.	Guzerat.	Concan.	Deccan.	S. India.	British Burmah.	Nepaul.
288	558	Phylloscopus lugubris, *Bly.*	...	...	...	...	...	×	...	×§	...	...	...	...	...	...	...	×	×	×‡
289	563	„ occipitalis, *Jerd.*	×	...	...	...	×	×	×	×	...	×	×	...	...	...	...	×	×	×
290	564	„ coronatus, *Tem.*	...	...	...	...	...	...	...	...	...	...	...	...	...	...	...	...	×	...
291	564 } 567	„ reguloides, *Bly.*	...	...	.	...	...	×	×	×	...	...	...	...	...	...	...	...	×	×‡
292		„ viridipennis, *Bly.*	..	...	...	...	...	...	...	×	...	...	...	...	...	...	...	...	×	×
293	554	„ tristis, *Bly.*	×	×	×	×	×	×	×	×	×	×	×	×	×	×	×	×	...	...
294	561	„ affinis, *Tick.*	...	...	...	...	...	×	...	×	...	...	...	...	...	...	...	×	×	×‡
295	560*bis.*	„ tytleri, *Brooks.*	...	...	...	...	...	...	...	...	...	...	...	...	...	...	...	×	...	×‡
296	565*bis.*	„ humii, *Brooks.*	...	...	...	×	×	×	×	×	×	×	×	...	...	...	...	...	...	×
297	565	„ superciliosus, *Gm.*	.	...	...	...	×	×	×	×†	...	×	...	...	...	...	...	*	×	‡
298	566*ter.*	„ maculipennis, *Blyth*	...	...	...	...	...	×	...	...	...	...	...	...	...	...	...	...	...	×‡
299	566	„ proregulus, *Pall.*	...	...	...	...	..	×	...	×	...	...	...	...	...	...	...	...	×	×
300	568	„ pulcher, *Hodgs*	...	...	...	...	...	×	×	...	...	...	...	...	...	...	...	...	×	×‡
301	566*bis.*	„ subviridis, *Brooks*	×	...	...	...	×	×	×	...	...	...	...	...	...	...	...	...		×
302		„ sindianus, *Brooks.*	×	...	...	...	...	...	...	...	...	...	...	...	...	...	...	...	...	...
303	553*ter.*	Hypolais pallida, *Hemp.*	×	×	×	×	...	...	...	...	...	...	...	...	...	...	...	...	...	...
304	553	„ rama, *Sykes.*	×	×	×	×	×	×	×	...	×	×	×	×	×	×	×	×	...	...
305	553*bis.*	„ caligata, *Licht.*	×	×	×	×	×	×	×	...	...	×	×	×	×	×	×	×	...	...
306	517*bis.*	„ obsoleta, *Severtz*	×	...	...	...	...	...	...	...	...	...	...	...	...	...	...	...	...	...
307		Acrocephalus bistrigiceps, *Swinh*	...	...	...	...	...	...	...	...	...	...	...	...	...	...	...	...	×	...
308	515*bis.*	„ orientalis, *Tem.*	...	...	...	...	...	...	...	...	...	...	...	...	...	...	...	...	×	...
309	515	„ stentoreus, *Hemp.*	×	×	×	×	×	×	×	×	×	×	×	×	×	×	×	×	×	×
310	516	„ dumetorum, *Bly*	×	...	...	...	×	×	×	×	×	×	×	×	×	×	×	×	×	×
311	517	„ agricola, *Jerd.*	×	×	...	×	×	×	×	×	...	×	×	×	×	×	×	×	×	×
312	520 } 521	Locustella certhiola, *Pall.*	...	..	...	...	...	×	×	×	..	×	...	...	...	...	...	...	×	...
313		„ traminea, *Severtz.*	...	...	...	...	...	×	...	...	...	...	...	...	...	...	...	...	...	...
314		„ lanceolata, *Tem.*	...	...	...	...	...	...	...	†	...	...	...	...	...	...	...	...	×	...
315	518	Lusciniola ædon, *Pall.*	...	...	...	...	×	×	×	×	...	...	...	...	...	×	...	...	×	×
316	519*bis.*	„ thoracica, *Bly.*	...	...	...	...	...	×	×	...	...	...	...	...	...	...	...	...	...	×
317	522	„ luteiventris, *Hodgs*	...	...	...	...	...	×	...	...	...	...	...	...	...	...	...	...	...	×
318	562	„ indica, *Jerd.*	...	...	...	...	...	×	×	×	...	×	×	...	...	×	...	...	...	..
319	555	„ fuscatus, *Bly.*	...	...	...	...	...	×	×	×	...	...	...	...	...	...	...	...	×	×
320	556*ter.*	„ schwarzi, *Radde.*	...	...	...	...	...	...	...	...	...	...	...	...	...	...	...	...	×	...
321		„ fuliginiventris, *Hodgs.*	...	...	...	...	...	...	...	...	...	...	...	...	...	...	...	...	...	...
322	554*bis.*	„ neglectus, *Hume,*	×	×	×	...	×	×	...	...	...	...	...	...	...	...	...	...	...	...

* Malabar Coast. † Andamans. ‡ Sikkim. § Assam.

No. in Avifauna.	Jerdon's Nos.	Species.	Sind.	Beloochistan.	Persia.	Afghanistan.	Punjab.	N.-W. Provinces.	Oudh.	Bengal.	Rajputana.	Central India.	Central Prov.	Kutch.	Guzerat.	Concan.	Deccan.	S. India.	British Burmah.	Nepaul.
323		Lusciniola melanopogon, *Tem.*	×	×	×	×	×	×	×											
324		Cettia cetti, *Marm.*	×	×	×	×														
325	526	Cettia fortipes, *Hodgs.*								×§									×	×‡
326	552	Cettia flavo-olivacea, *Hodgs.*								§										×
327		Cettia pallidipes, *Blanf.*								§									×	‡
328	527	Cettia brunneifrons, *Hodgs.*																		×‡
329	529	Cettia major, *Hodgs*																		×‡
330	442	Schœnicola platyura, *Jerd.*																×		
331	443	Laticilla burnesi, *Blyth.*	×				×	×	×	×										
332		Laticilla cinerascens, *Wald.*								×										
333	440	Megalurus palustris, *Horsf.*					×	×	×	×§		×	×						×	
334	441	Chætornis locustelloides, *Blyth.*								×		×						×		
335	547	Suya crinigera, *Hodgs.*	×				×	×	×										×	×‡
336	549	Suya atrigularis, *Hodgs.*																		×‡
337		Suya khasiana, *Godw.-Aust.*								‖										
338		Suya albigularis, *Hume.*																	×	
339		Suya superciliaris, *Anderson*																	×	
340	543, 544	Prinia inornata, *Sykes.*	×	×			×	×	×	×§	×	×	×	×	×	×*	×	×	×	×
341	545	Prinia sylvatica, *Jerd.*	×				×	×	×	×§	×	×	×	×	×	×	×	×		×
342	532	Burnesia flaviventris, *Deless.*	×					×	×	×§										
343	534, 535	Burnesia socialis, *Sykes.*					×	×	×	×§	×	×	×			×	×	×		×
344	550	Burnesia lepida, *Blyth.*	×	×	×	×	×	×	×	×	×	×	×	×	×	×	×			
345		Scotocerca inquieta, *Sund.*	×	×	×	×	^	×												
346	530	Sutoria sutoria, *Forst*	×	×		×	×	×	×	×	×	×	×	×	×	×	×	×	×	×
347		Sutoria atrigularis, *Tem.*								×									×	
348		Sutoria ruficeps, *Less.*																	×	
349	531	Phyllergates coronatus, *Jerd. and Blyth.*								×									×	×‡
350	542	Graminicola bengalensis, *Jerd.*								×§										
351	551	Cisticola buchanani, *Blyth.*	×				×	×	×	×	×	×	×	×	×	×	×	×		
352	536	Cisticola gracilis, *Franklin.*								×		×	×			×	×		×	×
353		Cisticola beavani, *Wald.*																	×	×‡
354		Cisticola cinereicapilla, *Moore.*						×												×
355	537	Cisticola poliocephala, *Anderson.*						×												×
356	539	Cisticola cisticola, *Tem.*	×				×	×				×	×	×	×	×	×		×	×
357	540	Cisticola exilis, *Vig. and Horsf.*								×				×			×*	×	×	
358	371	Geocichla dauma, *Lath.*					×	×	×	×		×	×						×	×‡
359	372	Geocichla nilgiriensis, *Bly.*																×		
360	370	Geocichla mollissima, *Bly.*						×												×‡
361		Geocichla dixoni, *Seebh.*										×								×‡
362	350	Geocichla monticola, *Vig*						×		§										×

* Malabar. ‡ Sikkim. § Assam. ‖ Khasia Hills.

No in Avifauna.	Jerdon's Nos.	SPECIES.	Sind	Beloochistan.	Persia.	Afghanistan.	Punjab.	N.W.-Provinces.	Oudh.	Bengal.	Rajputana.	Central India.	Central Prov.	Kutch.	Guzerat.	Concan.	Deccan.	S. India.	British Burmah.	Nepaul.
363		Geocichla marginata, *Bly*				×				§									×	×‡
364	354	Geocichla cyanonotus, *Lath.*								×		×				×	×	×		
365	355	Geocichla citrina, *Bly*								×			×					×	×	×‡
366	357	Geocichla wardi, *Jerd.*					×	×										×		×
367		Geocichla sibirica, *Pall*																	×	
368	369	Turdus iliacus, *Lin.*						×												
369	368	Turdus viscivorus, *Lin*					×	×	×											×
370	367	Turdus pilaris, *Lin*						×												
371	362	Merula albocincta, *Royl.*						×		×§										×‡
372	361	Merula boulboul, *Lath.*						×		§										×‡
373	359	Merula nigropilea, *Lafr.*								×						×		×		
374	360	Merula simillima, *Jerd.*																×		
375		Merula Bourdilloni, *Seebh.*																×		
376	363	Merula castanea, *Gould.*						×												×‡
377		Merula fuscata, *Bechst.*						×		§										×
378		Merula protomomelæna, *Cab.*						×												
379	365	Merula atrigularis, *Tem.*	×	×	×	×	×	×	×	×										×
380	364	Merula ruficollis, *Pall.*						×		§										×
381	356	Merula unicolor, *Tick.*	×				×	×	×		×	×					×	×		×
382		Merula obscurus, *Gmel.*						×		§									×	
383		Merula pallida, *Gmel*								×§									×	×
384		Monticola saxatilis, *Lin.*			×	×		×											×	
385	351	Monticola cyanus, *Lin.*	×	×	×	×	×	×	×	×	×	×	×	×	×	×	×	×	×	×
386	353	Monticola cinclorhynchus, *Vig.*	×				×	×	×	×	×	×	×	×	×	×	×	×	×	×
387	352	Monticola erythrogaster, *Vig.*					×	×		§‖									×	×‡
388	507	Erithacus brunneus, *Jerd.*						×		×								×		×‡
389		Erithacus cyaneus, *Pall*						×											×	
390	512	Erithacus calliope, *Gmel.*								×		×					×		×	×
391	513	Erithacus pectoralis, *Gould.*					×	×		§										×
392		Erithacus tschebaiewi, *Prejv*																		‡
393	514	Erithacus cæruleculus, *Jerd.*	×	×	×	×	×	×	×	×	×	×	×	×	×	×	×	×	×	×
394	478	Sialia cœlicolor, *Hodgs.*						×												×
395	495	Ruticilla phœnicurus, *Lin.*			×	×	×	×												
396		Ruticilla mesoleuca, *Hemp.*	×		×															
397	497	Ruticilla rufiventris, *Vieill.*	×	×	×	×	×	×	×		×	×	×	×	×	×	×	×		×
398	498	Ruticilla Hodgsoni, *Moore.*			×	×				§										×‡
399	500	Ruticilla aurorea, *Gmel.*								×§									×	
400	499	Ruticilla erythrogastra, *Güld.*						×												×
401		Ruticilla erythronota, *Eversm.*			×	×		×												×
402	503	Ruticilla frontalis, *Vig.*					×	×		§										×‡

‡ Sikkim. § Assam. ‖ Khasia Hills.

No. in Avifauna.	Jerdon's Nos.	Species.	Sind.	Beloochistan.	Persia.	Afghanistan.	Punjab.	N.-W. Provinces.	Oudh.	Bengal.	Rajputana.	Central India.	Central Prov.	Kutch.	Guzerat.	Concan.	Deccan.	S. India.	British Burmah.	Nepaul.
403	501	Ruticilla schisticeps, *Hodgs.*	...	...	...	...	...	...	...	...	...	...	...	...	...	...	...	...	...	×‡
404	504	Ruticilla cæruleocephala, *Vig.*	...	...	...	X	...	X	...	...	...	...	...	...	...	...	...	...	...	X
405	494	Myrmecocichla fusca, *Blyth*	...	...	...	...	X	X	X	X	X	X	...	...	...	...	...	...	...	...
406		Saxicola albonigra, *Hume.*	X	X	X	X	...	...	...	...	...	...	...	...	...	...	...	...	...	...
407	489	Saxicola picata, *Bly.*	X	X	X	X	X	X	X	...	X	X	X	X	X	...	...	...	...	...
408		Saxicola capistrata, *Hemp.*	X	X	X	...	...	X	...	...	...	X	...	...	...	...	...	...	...	...
409		Saxicola monacha, *Rüpp.*	X	X	X	X	...	...	...	...	...	...	...	...	...	...	...	...	...	...
410		Saxicola morio, *Hemp. et Ehr.*	X	X	X	X	...	...	...	...	...	...	...	...	...	...	...	...	...	...
411	488	Saxicola opistholeuca, *Strickl.*	X	X	...	X	X	X	X	...	X	X	X	X	X	...	...	...	...	...
412	492	Saxicola deserti, *Rüpp.*	X	X	X	X	X	X	X	...	X	X	X	X	X	X	X	...	...	...
413		Saxicola chrysopygia, *DeF.*	X	X	X	X	X	X	...	...	X	X	X	X	X	...	...	...	...	...
414	491	Saxicola isabellina, *Rüpp.*	X	X	X	X	X	X	X	X	X	X	X	X	X	...	X	...	...	...
415		Ægithina viridissima, *Tem.*	...	...	...	...	...	...	...	...	...	...	...	...	...	...	...	...	X	...
416	468	Ægithina tiphia, *Lin.*	...	...	...	...	...	X	X	X	X	X	X	X	X	X	X	X	X	×‡
417		Ægithina nigrolutea, *Marsh.*	...	...	...	...	X	X	X	X	...	X	X	X	X	...	...	...	...	...
418		Aethorhynchus Lafresnayii, *Hartl.*	...	...	...	...	...	...	...	...	...	...	...	...	...	...	...	...	X	...
419	466	Chloropsis Hardwickii, *Jerd.*	...	...	...	...	...	X	...	§× ‖	...	...	...	...	...	...	...	...	X	×‡
420	465	Chloropsis aurifrons, *Tem.*	...	...	...	...	...	X	...	§× ‖	...	...	...	...	...	...	...	...	X	X
421	464	Chloropsis malabaricus, *Gm.*	...	...	...	...	...	...	...	...	...	X	...	...	...	...	X	X	...	...
422		Chloropsis zosterops, *Vig.*	...	...	...	...	...	...	...	...	...	...	...	...	...	...	...	...	X	...
423	463	Chloropsis Jerdoni, *Bly.*	...	...	...	...	...	...	...	X	...	...	...	...	...	...	...	X	...	...
424		Chloropsis chlorocephala, *Wald.*	...	...	...	...	...	...	...	...	...	...	...	...	...	...	...	...	X	...
425		Chloropis cyanopogon, *Tem.*	...	...	...	...	...	...	...	...	...	...	...	...	...	...	...	...	X	...
426	444	Hypsipetes psaroides, *Vig.*	...	...	...	...	X	X	X	×§	...	...	...	...	...	...	...	...	X	×‡
427		Hypsipetes concolor, *Bly.*	...	...	...	...	...	...	...	‖	...	...	...	...	...	...	...	...	X	...
428	446	Hypsipetes ganeesa, *Sykes.*	...	...	...	...	...	...	...	...	...	...	...	...	...	X	X	X	...	...
429	448	Hemixus flavala, *Hodgs.*	...	...	...	...	...	X	...	×§	...	...	...	...	...	...	...	...	X	×‡
430		Hemixus hildebrandti, *Hume.*	...	...	...	...	...	...	...	...	...	...	...	...	...	...	...	...	X	...
431		Hemixus Davisoni, *Hume.*	...	...	...	...	...	...	...	...	...	...	...	...	...	...	...	...	X	...
432		Hemixus malaccensis, *Blyth*	...	...	...	...	...	...	...	...	...	...	...	...	...	...	...	...	X	...
433		Iole viridescens, *Bly.*	...	...	...	...	...	...	...	‖	...	...	...	...	...	...	...	...	X	...
434	447	Iole MacClellandi, *Horsf.*	...	...	...	...	...	X	X	§‖	...	...	...	...	...	...	...	...	X	×‡
435		Iole Tickelli, *Bly.*	...	...	...	...	...	...	...	...	...	...	...	...	...	...	...	...	X	...
436		Pinarocichla euptilosa, *Jard. & Selb.*	...	...	...	...	...	...	...	...	...	...	...	...	...	...	...	...	X	...
437		Micropus melanocephalus, *Gmel.*	...	...	...	...	...	...	...	...	...	...	...	...	...	...	...	...	X	...
438		Micropus fusciflavescens, *Hume*	...	...	...	...	...	...	...	...	...	...	...	...	...	...	...	...	†	...

† Andamans. ‡ Sikkim. § Assam. ‖ Khasia Hills.

No. in Avifauna.	Jerdon's Nos.	Species.	Sind.	Boloochistan.	Persia.	Afghanistan.	Punjab.	N. W.-Provinces	Oudh.	Bengal.	Rajputana.	Central India.	Central Prov.	Kutch.	Guzerat.	Concan.	Deccan.	S. India.	British Burmah.	Nepaul.
439		Micropus cinereiventris, *Blyth.*																	×	
440	457	Micropus phæocephalus, *Jerd.*														*		×		
441		Criniger phæocephalus, *Hartl.*																	×	
442	451	Criniger flaveolus, *Gould.*								§‖										×‡
443		Criniger griseiceps, *Hume.*																	×	
444		Criniger gutturalis, *Bp.*																	×	
445		Tricholestes criniger, *Bly.*																	×	
446	449	Alcurus striatus, *Bly.*								×‖									×	×‡
447		Trachycomus ochrocephalus, *Gmel.*																	×	
448	450	Xenocichla icterica, *Strickl.*														*		×		
449	462	Pycnonotus hæmorrhous, *Gm.*	×				×	×	×	×	×	×	×	×	×	×	×	×		
450		Pycnonotus burmanicus, *Sharpe.*																	×	
451		Pycnonotus nigripileus, *Bp.*																	×	
452		Pycnonotus atricapillus, *Vieil.*																	×	
453	461	Pycnonotus pygæus, *Hodgs.*				×	×	×	×	×§‖		×								×‡
454	459	Pycnonotus leucotis, *Gould.*	×	×	×	×	×	×	×		×	×	×	×	×	×	×	×		
455		Pycnonotus analis, *Horsf.*																	×	
456		Pycnonotus flavescens, *Bly.*										‖							×	
457	452	Pycnonotus luteolus, *Less.*								×		×				*		×		
458		Pycnonotus Finlaysoni, *Strickl.*																	×	
459		Pycnonotus Davisoni, *Hume*																	×	
460	453	Pycnonotus xantholæmus, *Jerd.*																×		
461		Pycnonotus Blanfordi, *Jerd.*																	×	
462		Pycnonotus plumosus, *Blyth*																	×	
463		Pycnonotus simplex, *Less.*																	×	
464		Pycnonotus salvadorii, *Sharpe*																	×	
465	460	Otocompsa jocosa, *Lin.*					×	×	×	×§‖						×			×†	×‡
466		Otocompsa emeria, *Lin.*													×	×*	×	×		
467	458	Otocompsa leucogenys, *E. Gr.*								×										×‡
468	456	Otocompsa flaviventris, *Tick*						×	×	‖§		×				*			×	×‡
469	455	Rubigula gularis, *Gould*																×		
470		Rubigula cyaniventris, *Bly.*																	×	
471		Spizixus canifrons, *Bly.*								‖										
472	332	Urocichla longicaudata, *Moore*																		

* Malabar. ‡ Sikkim. § Assam. ‖ Khasia Hills.

No. in Avifauna.	Jerdon's Nos.	Species.	Sind.	Beloochistan.	Persia.	Afghanistan.	Punjab.	N.-W. Provinces.	Oudh.	Bengal.	Rajputana.	Central India.	Central Prov.	Kutch.	Guzerat.	Concan.	Deccan.	S. India.	British Burmah.	Nepaul.
473	333	Anorthura nipalensis, *Hodgs.*						×												×‡
474		Anorthura formosa, *Wald*																		
475		Sphenocichla humii, *Mandell*								§										
476	329	Pnoepyga albiventris, *Hodgs*																		‡
477	330	Pnoepyga pusilla, *Hodgs*						×											×	×‡
478	331	Pnoepyga caudata, *Bly.*																	×	×
479	348	Cinclus cashmeriensis, *Gould*						×												×‡
480	347	Cinclus asiaticus, *Swains*			×															×‡
481	343	Myiophoneus Temmincki, *Vig.*				×	×	×	×											×‡
482		Myiophoneus Eugenii, *Hume.*				×		×												×‡
483	342	Myiophoneus Horsfieldi, *Vig.*																	×	
484	440	Callene frontalis, *Blyth*										×	×					×		
485		Callene albiventris, *Blanf*																		‡
486	339	Callene rufiventris, *Jerd.*																×		
487	477	Notodela leucura, *Hodgs*																×		
488	338	Brachypteryx cruralis, *Hodgs.*								‖									×	×‡
489	337	Brachypteryx hyperythra, *Jerd. and Bly*																	×	×‡
490	336	Brachypteryx nipalensis, *Moore*																		‡
491		Brachypteryx stellata, *Gould*								‖									×	×‡
492	506	Chimarrhornis leucocephala, *Vig.*																		‡
493	479	Thamnobia fulicata, *L.*				×	×													×‡
494	480	Thamnobia cambaiensis, *Lath.*										×				×	×	×		
495	475	Copsychus saularis, *L.*	×			×	×	×	×	×	×	×	×	×	×					×
496	613	Lioptila annectens, *Blyth*					×	×		×§		×	×			×	×*	×	×	×‡
497	341	Hodgsonius phœnicuroides, *Hodgs.*								‖									×	‡
498	476	Cittocincla tricolor, *Vieill.*						×	×											×
499		Cittocincla albiventris, *Blyth.*								×§		×				*		×	×	×‡
500		Henicurus leschenaulti, *Vieill.*								†										

* Malabar † Andamans. ‡ Sikkim. § Assam. ‖ Khasia Hills.

No. in Avifauna.	Jerdon's Nos.	Species.	Sind.	Beloochistan.	Persia.	Afghanistan.	Punjab.	N.-W. Provinces.	Oudh.	Bengal.	Rajputana.	Central India.	Central Prov.	Kutch.	Guzerat.	Concan.	Deccan.	S. India.	British Burmah.	Nepaul.
501	585	Henicurus immaculatus, *Hodgs.*	...	...	...	...	...	...	...	‖	§	...	...	...	...	...	...	...	×	×
502	586	Henicurus schistaceus, *Hodgs.*	...	...	...	...	...	...	...	...	...	...	...	...	...	...	...	...	×	×‡
503		Henicurus guttatus, *Gould.*	...	...	...	...	...	...	...	‖	...	...	...	...	...	...	...	...	×	×
504	584	Henicurus maculatus, *Vig.*	...	...	...	...	...	×	...	§	...	...	...	...	...	...	...	...	×	†
505		Hydrocichla ruficapilla, *Temm.*	...	...	...	...	...	...	...	...	...	...	...	...	...	...	...	...	×	...
506		Hydrocichla frontalis, *Blyth.*	...	...	...	...	...	...	...	...	...	...	...	...	...	...	...	...	×	...
507	587, 588	Microcichla scouleri, *Vig.*	...	...	...	...	...	×	...	§	...	...	...	...	...	...	...	...	...	×
508	419	Trochalopterum affine, *Blyth.*	...	...	...	...	...	...	...	§	...	...	...	...	...	...	...	...	...	×‡
509	418	Trochalopterum variegatum, *Vig.*	...	...	...	...	×	×	...	...	...	...	...	...	...	...	...	...	...	×
510	415	Trochalopterum erythrocephalum, *Hodgs.*	...	...	...	...	...	×	...	...	...	...	...	...	...	...	...	...	...	×
511	416	Trochalopterum chrysopterum, *Gould.*	...	...	...	...	...	×	...	...	...	...	...	...	...	...	...	...	...	×‡
512		Trochalopterum ruficapillum, *Blyth.*	...	...	...	...	...	...	...	‖	...	...	...	...	...	...	...	...	...	...
513		Trochalopterum erythrolæma, *Hume.*	...	...	...	...	...	...	...	¶	...	...	...	...	...	...	...	...	...	...
514		Trochalopterum melanostigma, *Blyth.*	...	...	...	...	...	...	...	...	...	...	...	...	...	...	...	...	×	...
515	421	Trochalopterum rufigulare, *Gould.*	...	...	...	...	×	×	...	‖	...	...	...	...	...	...	...	...	...	×‡
516		Trochalopterum cineraceum, *Godw.-Aust.*	...	...	...	...	...	...	...	¶	...	...	...	...	...	...	...	...	...	...
517	420	Trochalopterum squamatum, *Gould.*	...	...	...	...	...	...	...	...	...	...	...	...	...	...	...	...	...	×‡
518	417	Trochalopterum subunicolor, *Blyth.*	...	...	...	...	...	...	...	...	...	...	...	...	...	...	...	...	...	×‡
519		Trochalopterum austeni, *Jerd.*	...	...	...	...	...	...	...	A	...	...	...	...	...	...	...	...	...	...
520	422	Trochalopterum phœniceum, *Gould.*	...	...	...	...	...	...	...	...	...	...	...	...	...	...	...	...	...	×‡
521	423	Trochalopterum cachinans, *Jerdon.*	...	...	...	...	...	...	...	...	...	...	...	...	...	...	...	×	...	...
522	424	Trochalopterum Jerdoni, *Blyth.*	...	...	...	...	...	...	...	...	...	...	...	...	...	...	...	×	...	..
523		Trochalopterum Fairbanki, *Blanf.*	...	...	...	...	...	...	...	...	...	...	...	...	...	...	...	×	...	...
524		Trochalopterum meridionale, *Blanf.*	...	...	...	...	...	...	...	...	...	...	...	...	...	...	...	×	...	...
525	425	Trochalopterum lineatum, *Vig.*	...	...	...	...	...	×	...	...	...	...	...	...	...	...	...	...	...	×

A. N.-E. Bengal Hills. † Andamans. ‡ Sikkim. § Assam. ‖ Khasia Hills. ¶ Munipur Hills.

No. in Avifauna.	Jerdon's Nos.	Species.	Sind.	Beloochistan.	Persia.	Afghanistan.	Punjab.	N.W. Provinces.	Oudh.	Bengal.	Rajputana.	Central India.	Central Prov.	Kutch.	Guzerat.	Concan.	Deccan.	S. India.	British Burmah.	Nepaul.
526	426	Trochalopterum imbricatum, *Blyth.*	...	...	...	...	...	...	...	B	...	...	...	...	...	...	...	...	...	...
527		Trochalopterum virgatum, *Godw.-Aust.*	...	...	...	...	...	...	...	¶	D	...	...	...	...	...	...	...	...	...
528	431	Acanthoptila nipalensis, *Hodgs.*	...	...	...	...	...	×	...	...	...	...	...	...	...	...	...	...	...	×
529	414	Ianthocincla ocellata, *Vig.*	...	...	...	...	...	...	...	...	...	...	...	...	...	...	...	...	...	×‡
530	384	Gampsorhynchus rufulus, *Blyth.*	...	...	...	...	...	...	...	...	...	...	...	...	...	...	...	...	×	×
531		Gampsorhynchus torquatus, *Hume.*	...	...	...	...	...	...	...	...	...	...	...	...	...	...	...	...	×	...
532	437	Argya subrufa, *Jerd.*	...	...	...	...	...	...	...	...	...	...	...	...	...	×	×	×	...	...
533		Argya hyperythra, *Sharpe.*	...	...	...	...	...	...	...	...	...	...	...	...	...	...	...	×	...	...
534	439	Argya earlii, *Blyth*	×	...	...	...	...	...	...	×	...	...	...	...	...	...	...	...	×	×
535	438	Argya caudata, *Drap.*	×	...	...	×	×	×	×	×§	×	×	×	×	×	×	×	×	×	...
536		Argya eclipes, *Hume.*	...	...	...	...	×	...	...	...	...	...	...	...	...	...	...	...	...	...
537		Argya gularis, *Blyth.*	...	...	...	...	...	...	...	...	...	...	...	...	...	...	...	...	×	...
538	436	Argya Malcolmi, *Sykes.*	×	...	...	...	×	×	×	×	×	×	×	×	×	×	×	...	...	...
539	430	Sibia picoides, *Hodgs.*	...	...	...	...	...	...	...	‖	...	...	...	...	...	...	...	...	×	×‡
540	429	Malacias capistrata, *Vig.*	...	...	...	...	...	×	...	...	...	...	...	...	...	...	...	...	...	×‡
541		Malacias melanoleuca, *Blyth.*	...	...	...	...	...	...	...	...	...	...	...	...	...	...	...	...	×	...
542		Malacias gracilis, *McClell.*	...	...	...	...	...	...	...	‖	...	...	...	...	...	...	...	...	...	...
543		Malacias pulchella, *Godw.-Aust.*	...	...	...	...	...	...	...	D	...	...	...	...	...	...	...	...	...	×‡
544	402	Pomatorhinus schisticeps, *Hodgs.*	...	...	...	...	...	...	...	§ B	...	...	...	...	...	...	...	...	×	...
545		Pomatorhinus pinwilli, *Sharpe.*	...	...	...	...	...	×	...	...	...	...	...	...	...	...	...	...	...	...
546	404	Pomatorhinus Horsfieldi, *Sykes.*	...	...	...	...	...	...	...	...	...	...	...	...	...	...	×	...	...	...
547		Pomatorhinus ochraceiceps, *Wald.*	...	...	...	...	...	...	...	...	...	...	...	...	...	...	...	...	×	...
548		Pomatorhinus Austeni, *Hume.*	...	...	...	...	...	...	...	¶	...	...	...	...	...	...	...	...	...	...
549	401	Pomatorhinus ferruginosus, *Hodgs.*	...	...	...	...	...	...	...	...	...	...	...	...	...	...	...	...	...	×‡
550		Pomatorhinus Phayrii, *Blyth*	...	...	...	...	...	...	...	‖ ¶	...	...	...	...	...	...	...	...	...	...
551		Pomatorhinus albigularis, *Blyth.*	...	...	...	...	...	...	...	...	...	...	...	...	...	...	...	...	×	...
552		Pomatorhinus stenorhynchus, *Godw.-Aust.*	...	...	...	...	...	...	...	§	...	...	...	...	...	...	...	...	...	...
553	400	Pomatorhinus ruficollis, *Hodgs.*	...	...	...	...	...	...	...	‖ B	...	...	...	...	...	...	...	...	...	×‡

B. Bhootan. D. Naga Hills. ‡ Sikkim. § Assam. ‖ Khasia Hills. ¶ Munipur Hills.

No. in Avifauna.	Jerdon's Nos.	Species.	Sind.	Beloochistan.	Persia.	Afghanistan.	Punjab.	N.-W. Provinces.	Oudh.	Bengal.	Rajputana.	Central India.	Central Prov.	Kutch.	Guzerat.	Concan.	Deccan.	S. India.	British Burmah.	Nepaul.
554		Pomatorhinus hypoleucus, *Blyth.*								‖									×	
555		Pomatorhinus Tickelli, *Blyth.*																	×	
556	405	Pomatorhinus erythrogenys, *Vig.*					×	×	×	×‖									×	×B
557		Pomatorhinus Maclellandi, *Jerd.*								§										
558	406	Xiphoramphus superciliaris, *Blyth.*																		‡
559	407	Garrulax leucolophus, *Hardw.*						×											×	
560		Garrulax belangeri, *Less.*																	×	
561		Garrulax diardi, *Less.*																	×	
562	411	Garrulax albigularis, *Gould.*						×		B										×‡
563	412	Garrulax pectoralis, *Gould.*								E									×	×‡
564	413	Garrulax moniliger, *Hodgs.*								‖									×	×
565		Garrulax galbanus, *Godw.-Aust.*								¶										
566		Garrulax gularis, *McClell.*								‖§										
567	409	Garrulax delesserti, *Jerd.*																×		
568		Stactocichla merulina, *Blyth.*								‖D										
569	382	Grammatoptila striata, *Vig.*					×	×		‖B										×‡
570	410	Dryonastes ruficollis, *Jard & Selb.*								§									×	×‡
571		Dryonastes chinensis, *Scop.*																	×	
572		Dryonastes nuchalis, *Godw.-Aust.*								D										
573		Dryonastes strepitans, *Tick.*																	×	
574		Dryonastes sannio, *Swinh*								‖										
575	408	Dryonastes cærulatus, *Hodgs.*								D §										×‡
576		Dryonastes subcærulatus, *Hume*								‖D										
577	427	Actinodura Egertoni, *Gould.*								‖										×‡
578		Actinodura Ramsayi, *Wald.*																	×	
579		Actinodura Waldeni, *Godw.-Aust*								¶									×	
580	428	Actinodura nipalensis, *Hodgs.*								§										×‡
581		Actinodura Daflaensis, *Godw.-Aust.*								K										
582		Actinodura Oglei, *Godw.-Aust.*								§								×		
583	432, 434	Crateropus canorus, *Linn.*	×				×	×	×	×								×		
584	433	Crateropus griseus, *Gmel*														×	×			

D. Naga Hills. E. Garo Hills. B. Bhootan. K. Dafla Hills,
‡ Sikkim. § Assam. ‖ Khasia Hills. ¶ Munipur Hills.

No. in Avifauna.	Jerdon's Nos.	SPECIES.	Sind.	Beloochistan.	Persia.	Afghanistan.	Punjab.	N.-W. Provinces.	Oudh.	Bengal.	Rajputana.	Central India.	Central Prov.	Kutch.	Guzerat.	Concan.	Deccan.	S. India.	British Burmah.	Nepaul.
585	435	Crateropus Somervillii, *Sykes.*														×	×			
586	381	Conostoma æmodium, *Hodgs.*																		×‡
587		Suthora Humii, *Sharpe*																		×‡
588	379	Suthora poliotis, *Blyth.*							D	P	K									×‡
589	378	Suthora nipalensis, *Hodgs.*																		×
590	375	Suthora ruficeps, *Blyth.*								B									×	×‡
591	374	Suthora gularis, *Gray*								‖										×‡
592	376	Suthora unicolor, *Hodgs*																		×‡
593	377	Chleuasicus ruficeps, *Blyth.*								§L										‡
594	380	Chleuasicus fulvifrons, *Hodgs.*																		×‡
595	373	Paradoxornis flavirostris, *Gould.*								†L§										×‡
596		Paradoxornis guttaticollis, *David.*								×D	‖§	L								
597	396	Timelia pileata, *Horsf.*								×§	B	‖							×	×‡
598		Timelia longirostris, *Moore.*							×	B	L	P	‖							×
599	385	Pyctorhis sinensis, *Gmel.*	×				×	×	×	×	×	×	×	×	×	×	×	×	×	×
600	386	Pyctorhis altirostris, *Jerd.*								§	B								×	
601	398	Dumetia albigularis, *Blyth.*													×		×	×		
602	397	Dumetia hyperythra, *Frankl.*											×			×				‡
603		Pellorneum nipalense, *Hodgs.*							×	‖B										×‡
604		Pellorneum intermedium, *Sharpe*								L									×	
605	399	Pellorneum ruficeps, *Swains.*														*×	×	×		
606		Pellorneum subochraceum, *Swinh.*																	×	
607		Pellorneum palustre, *Gould.*								§‖										
608	391	Stachyris nigriceps, *Hodgs.*								‖	B								×	×
609		Stachyris guttata, *Blyth*																	×	
610	387	Turdinus Abbotti, *Blyth*								×‖									×	×
611		Turdinus magnirostris, *Moore*																	×	
612		Erythrocichla bicolor, *Less.*																	×	
613		Drymocataphus nigricapitatus, *Eyton*																	×	
614		Drymocataphus ignotus, *Hume.*								×‖										
615		Drymocataphus Assamensis, *Sharpe*								§										
616		Drymocataphus Tickelli, *Blyth.*																	×	

D. Naga Hills. P. K. Dafla Hills. L. Cachar. B. Bhootan.

* Malabar. † Andamans ‡ Sikkim. § Assam. ‖ Khasia Hills.

No. in Avifauna.	Jerdon's Nos.	SPECIES.	Sind.	Beloochistan.	Persia.	Afghanistan.	Punjab.	N.-W. Provinces.	Oudh.	Bengal.	Rajputana.	Central India.	Central Prov.	Kutch.	Guzerat.	Concan.	Deccan.	S. India.	British Burmah.	Nepaul.
617		Drymocataphus rubiginosus, *Wald.*																	×	
618		Gypsophila crispifrons, *Blyth.*																	×	
619		Trichostoma rostratum, *Blyth.*																	×	
620		Malacopterum magnum, *Eyton.*																	×	
621		Mixornis gularis, *Raffles*																	×	
622	395	Mixornis rubricapilla, *Tick.*								B L									×	×
623		Mixornis erythroptera, *Blyth.*																	×	
624		Corythocichla brevicaudata, *Blyth.*																	×	
625		Corythocichla striata, *Wald.*								‖										
626		Turdinulus murinus, *Blyth.*								¶									×	
627	335	Rimator malacoptilus, *Blyth.*																		×‡
628	393	Stachyridopsis ruficeps, *Blyth.*								‖										×‡
629		Stachyridopsis rufifrons, *Hume*								B L									×	
630	392	Stachyridopsis pyrrhops, *Hodgs.*						×												×
631	394	Stachyridopsis chrysea, *Hodgs.*								‖									×	×‡
632		Stachyridopsis assimilis, *Wald.*																	×	
633	327	Oligura castaneocoronata, *Burt.*								‖										×‡
634	328	Oligura cyaniventris, *Hodgs.*								‖										×‡
635	618	Minla igneotincta, *Hodgs.*								‖										×‡
636	619	Minla castaneiceps, *Hodgs.*								‖										×‡
637		Minla brunneicauda, *Sharpe.*								‖										
638	620	Minla cinerea, *Blyth.*																		×‡
639		Minla rufigularis, *Mandelli.*								B										
640		Minla mandelli, *Godwin-Austen*								×										
641		Minla dubia, *Hume*																	×	
642	623	Ixulus flavicollis, *Hodgs.*						×	B	‖										×‡
643	624	Ixulus occipitalis, *Blyth.*								‖										×‡
644		Ixulus humilis, *Hume*																	×	
645		Staphidea castaneiceps, *Moore*								‖										
646		Staphidea rufigenis, *Hume.*																		‡
647	625	Staphidea striata, *Blyth.*						×											×	
648	622	Alcippe vinipectus, *Hodgs.*						×												×‡

B. Bhootan. L. Cachar. ‡ Sikkim. ‖ Khasia Hills. ¶ Munipur Hills.

No. in Avifauna.	Jerdon's Nos.	Species.	Sind.	Beloochistan.	Persia.	Afghanistan.	Punjab.	N.-W. Provinces.	Oudh.	Bengal.	Rajputana.	Central India.	Central Prov.	Kutch.	Guzerat.	Concan.	Deccan.	S. India.	British Burmah.	Nepaul.
649	388	Alcippe nipalensis, *Hodgs.*								‖	L	B							×	
650	389	Alcippe phæocephala, *Jerd.*									×						×	×		
651		Alcippe Phayrii, *Blyth.*																	×	
652	390	Alcippe atriceps, *Jerd.*																×		
653		Alcippe Bourdilloni, *Hume.*																×		
654	621	Alcippe chryseus, *Hodgs.*																		×‡
655	626	Yuhina gularis, *Hodgs.*								‖	B								×	×‡
656	627	Yuhina occipitalis, *Hodgs.*									B									×‡
657	628	Yuhina nigrimentum, *Hodgs.*						×			D									×‡
658	629	Myzornis pyrrhura, *Hodgs.*																		×‡
659	630	Herpornis xantholeuca, *Hodgs.*									‖								×	×‡
660	616	Siva strigula, *Hodgs.*						×												×‡
661		Siva castaneicauda, *Hume.*									B								×	
662	617	Siva cyanuroptera, *Hodgs.*									§									×‡
663		Siva sordida, *Hume*																	×	
664	615	Mesia argentauris, *Hodgs.*									‖								×	×‡
665	614	Liothrix lutea, *Scop.*						×			B								×	×‡
666	612	Cutia nipalensis, *Hodgs.*									B K								×	×‡
667	650	Parus sultaneus, *Hodgs.*								§ ×										×‡
668		Parus cinereus, *Bonn. et Vieil.*				×	×	×	×	§ B		×	×					×	×	×
669	644	Parus monticolus, *Vigors.*					×	×		B	‖									×‡
670	647	Parus xanthogenys, *Vigors.*				×	×					×								×
671	648	Parus haplonotus, *Jerd.*										×						×		
672	649	Parus spilonotus, *Blyth.*								§	B ‖								×	×‡
673	638	Parus melanolophus, *Vigors.*				×	×	×												×‡
674	640	Parus rufonuchalis, *Blyth.*									‖									×‡
675	640	Parus rubidiventer, *Blyth.*																		×
676	637	Parus dichrous, *Hodgs.*						×												×‡
677	632	Parus modestus, *Burton.*										×								‡
678		Parus nuchalis, *Jerd.*																×		
679	642	Parus æmodius, *Hodgs.*																		×‡
680	651	Accentor immaculatus, *Hodgs.*																		×‡
681	655	Accentor atrigularis, *Brandt.*				×	×	×												×‡
682	656	Accentor rubeculoides, *Moore.*																		‡
683	654	Accentor strophiatus, *Hodgs.*																		×‡
684		Accentor Jerdoni, *Brooks.*					×													×
685	653	Accentor altaicus, *Brandt.*					×	×												×
686	652	Accentor nipalensis, *Hodgs.*						×												
687	634	Acredula erythrocephala, *Vigors.*					×	×	×	§‖									×	×‡

B. Bhootan. D. Naga Hills. ‡ Sikkim. § Assam. ‖ Khasia Hills.
L. Cachar. K Dafla Hills.

No. in Avifauna.	Jerdon's Nos.	Species.	Sind.	Beloochistan.	Persia.	Afghanistan.	Punjab.	N.-W. Provinces.	Oudh.	Bengal.	Rajputana.	Central India.	Central Prov.	Kutch.	Guzerat.	Concan.	Deccan.	S. India.	British Burmah.	Nepaul.
688	635	Acredula Jouschistos, *Hodgs.*								B										×‡
689	636	Acredula niveogularis, *Moore*						×												
690	633	Ægithalus flammiceps, *Burton*				×		×												×
691	580	Regulus cristatus, *Koch.*						?												×‡
692	609	Pterythrius erythropterus, *Vigors.*					×	×	§	B										×‡
693		Pterythrius æralatus, *Tickell.*																	×	
694	610	Pterythrius rufiventer, *Blyth.*																		×‡
695		Pterythrius intermedius, *Hume.*																	×	
696	611	Pterythrius melanotis, *Hodgs.*								B ‖									×	×‡
697		Pterythrius xanthochloris, *Hodgs.*								‖ B										×‡
698		Lanius fallax, *Finsch.*	?	×		×														
699		Lanius assimilis, *Brehm.*	×			×	×										×			
700	256	Lanius lahtora, *Sykes.*	×	×	×	×	×	×	×	×	×	×	×	×	×	×	×	×		
701	258	Lanius tephronotus, *Vigors.*								×B	§								×	×‡
702	257	Lanius erythronotus, *Vigors.*	×	×	×	×	×	×	×	×	×	×	×	×	×	×	×	×		×
703	259	Lanius nigriceps, *Frankl.*						×	‖	B×	§	×							×	×‡
704	261	Lanius cristatus, *Lin.*	×	×			×	×	×	×	B	§						×	×	×
705		Lanius lucionensis, *Lin.*										†							×	
706	262	Lanius isabellinus, *Ehrenb.*	×	×	×	×	×	×	×	×	×			×						
707		Lanius phœnicuroides, *Severtz.*	×	×	×	×	×	×	×	×	×									
708	260	Lanius vittatus, *Valenc.*	×	×		×	×	×	×	×	×	×	×	×	×	×	×	×		×
709		Lanius collyrioides, *Less.*																	×	
710	243	Certhia himalayana, *Vigors.*				×	×			§										×
711	245	Certhia discolor, *Blyth.*								B										×‡
712	244	Certhia nipalensis, *Hodgs.*								B	§									×‡
713	246	Salpornis spilonotus, *Frankl.*										×								
714	247	Tichodroma muraria, *Lin.*				×	×	×												×
715		Sitta nagaensis, *Godw-Austen.*								×										
716		Sitta magna, *Wardlaw-Ramsay.*																	×	
717		Sitta himalayensis, *Jard. et Selby.*					×	×												×‡
718		Sitta neglecta, *Wald.*																	×	
719	250	Sitta castaneoventris, *Frankl.*										×	×					* ×		

B. Bhootan. ‡ Sikkim. § Assam. ‖ Khasia Hills. † Andamans. * Malabar.

No. in Avifauna.	Jerdon's Nos.	Species.	Sind.	Beloochistan.	Persia.	Afghanistan.	Punjab.	N.-W. Provinces.	Oudh.	Bengal.	Rajputana.	Central India.	Central Prov.	Kutch.	Guzerat.	Concan.	Deccan.	S. India.	British Burmah.	Nepaul.
720	251	Sitta cinnamomeiventris, *Blyth.*								×									×	×
721	249	Sitta leucopsis, *Gould.*						×												×
722	252	Sitta formosa, *Blyth.*						×		×										
723	253	Sitta frontalis, *Swains.*								×		×	×			×	×	*×	×	
724		Chalcostetha insignis, *Jard.*																	×	
725	231	Æthopyga saturata, *Hodgs.*								§	B									×‡
726	226	Æthopyga Vigorsi, *Sykes.*															×	×		
727	225	Æthopyga seheriæ, *Tickell.*						×		§	B								×	×‡
728	228	Æthopyga ignicauda, *Hodgs.*						×		B										×‡
729	230	Æthopyga nipalensis, *Hodgs.*						×		‖										×‡
730		Æthopyga sanguinipectus, *Wald.*																	×	
731	227	Æthopyga gouldiæ, *Vigors.*						×												×‡
732		Æthopyga dabryi, *J. Verr.*																	×	
733	234	Cinnyris asiatica, *Lath.*	×	×		×	×	×	×	×	×	×	×	×	×	×	×	×	×	×
734		Cinnyris brevirostris, *Blanf.*	×	×																
735	235	Cinnyris lotenia, *Linn.*															×	×		
736	233	Cinnyris minima, *Sykes*															×	×		
737	232	Cinnyris zeylonica, *Lin.*								§×							×	×		
738		Cinnyris Hasseltii, *Temm.*																	×	
739		Cinnyris flammimaxillaris, *Blyth.*								†									×	
740	224	Arachnothera longirostris, *Vieil.*								×	†							*×	×	
741	223	Arachnothera magna, *Hodgs.*								§	‖								×	×‡
742		Arachnothera modesta, *Eyton*																	×	
743		Arachnothera chrysogenys, *Temm.*																	×	
744		Anthothreptes hypogrammica, *S. Mull.*																	×	
745		Anthothreptes simplex, *S. Mull.*																	×	
746		Anthothreptes phœnicotis, *Temm.*																	×	
747		Anthothreptes malaccensis, *Scop.*																	×	
748	631	Zosterops palpebrosa, *Temm.*	×				×	×	×	×	×	×	×			×	×	×	×	×
749		Zosterops aureiventer, *Hume.*																	×	
750		Zosterops siamensis, *Blyth.*																	×	
751	236	Dicæum cruentatum, *Linn.*								×§									×	×
752		Dicæum trigonostigma *Scop.*																	×	

B. Bhootan. * Malabar. † Andamans. ‡ Sikkim. § Assam. ‖ Khasia Hills.

No. in Avifauna.	Jerdon's Nos.	Species.	Sind.	Beloochistan.	Persia.	Afghanistan.	Punjab.	N.-W. Provinces.	Oudh.	Bengal.	Rajputana.	Central India.	Central Prov.	Kutch.	Guzerat.	Concan.	Deccan.	S. India.	British Burmah.	Nepaul.
753	241	Dicæum ignipectus, *Hodgs.*	...	...	...	...	...	×	...	AB‡	...	...	...	...	...	...	...	...	×	×
754	237	Dicæum chrysorrhæum, *Temm.*	...	...	...	...	...	×	...	A×	.	...	...	...	...	...	...	...	×	×
755	239	Dicæum concolor, *Jerd.*	...	...	...	...	...	...	...	..	...	...	...	...	...	...	...	*×	...	...
756		Dicæum inornatum, *Hodgs.*	...	...	...	...	...	...	...	B	...	...	...	...	...	...	...	...	×	×
757	238	Dicæum erythrorhynchum, *Lath*	...	...	...	...	...	...	...	×§	...	×	×	..	...	×	×	×	×	×
758		Prionochilus ignicapillus, *Eyton.*	...	...	...	...	...	...	...	...	...		...	...		...	...	...	×	...
759		Prionochilus maculatus, *Tem.*	..	...	...	...	...	...	...	...	...	...	...	...	...	...	...	...	×	...
760	242	Prionochilus melanoxanthus, *Hodgs.*	...	..	...	...	...	...	...	§	..	...	...	..	...	...	...	...	...	×
761	240	Prionochilus squalidus, *Burton*	...	...	...	...	...	×	...	...	...	...	...	...	...	...	...	...	×	×
762		Prionochilus modestus, *Hume.*	...	...	...	..	..	...	...	...	...	...	...	...	...	...	...	...	×	...
763	92	Chelidon urbica, *Linn.*	...	...	×	...	...	×	...	...	...	..	...	...	...	...	..	×	...	...
764	93	Chelidon cashmiriensis, *Gould.*	...	...	...	...	...	×	...	...	...	...	...	...	...	...	..	..	...	...
765		Chelidon lagopus, *Pallas*	...	...	...	...	...	...	...	..	...	...	...	...	...	...	...	...	×	...
766	94	Chelidon nipalensis, *Hodgs.*	...	...	...	...	...	...	...	‡×	...	...	...	...	...	...	...	...	...	×
767	87	Cotile riparia, *Linn.*	×	×	...	×	×	...	...	...	...	...	..	×	...	...	...	×	×	...
768	88·89	Cotile sinensis, *J. E. Gray.*	×	...	...	...	×	×	...	×	...	...	...	×	×	×	×	...	×	×
769	90	Cotile concolor, *Sykes*	...	...	...	...	×	×	...	×	...	×	×	×	×	×	×	*×	...	...
770	91	Cotile rupestris, *Scop.*	...	...	...	...	×	×	...	B×	§...	×	×	...	..	...	..	*×	...	×
771		Cotile obsoleta, *Cab.*	×	×	...	...	...	...	...	...	...	...	...	×	×	...	...	...	...	...
772	82	Hirundo rustica, *Lin.*	×	×	×	×	×	×	×	§	×	×	×	×	×	×	×	×	×	×
773		Hirundo gutturalis, *Scop.*	...	...	..	...	...	×	..	B §	...	×	...	...	×	..	×	×	×	×
774		Hirundo erythrogastra, *Bodd.*	...	...	...	...	...	...	...	...	...	...	...	...	...	...	...	...	×	...
775		Hirundo tytleri, *Jerd.*	..	...	...	...	...	...	...	‡×	‖...	...	...	...	...	...	...	...	×	...
776	83	Hirundo javanica, *Sparrm.*	..	...	...	...	...	...	...	...	...	...	...	...	...	...	...	×	×	...
777	84	Hirundo smithi, *Leach.*	×	×	×	×	×	×	×	×	×	×	×	?	×	×	×	×	×	×
778		Hirundo nipalensis, *Hodgs.*	...	...	...	...	...	×	...	§×	...	...	...	...	...	..	...	...	×	×
779		Hirundo japonica, *Tem.*	...	...	...	...	...	...	...	...	...	...	...	...	...	...	...	..	×	...
780	85	Hirundo erythropygia, *Sykes.*	×	×	×	×	×	×	×	×	×	×	×	×	×	×	×	×	..	×
781	86	Petrochelidon fluvicola, *Blyth*	...	..	...	...	×	×	×	...	×	×	×	×	×	...	...	...	...	...
782		Motacilla alba, *Linn.*	×	×	×	×	×	×	...	...	...	...	...	...	...	×	×	...	×	...
783		Motacilla ocularis, *Swinh.*	...	...	..	...	...	..	..	×	..	...	...	...	...	...	...	...	×	×
784	591	Motacilla personata, *Gould.*	×	×	×	×	×	×	...	...	×	...	...	..	...	...	...	...	...	...
785	590	Motacilla leucopsis *Gould.*	...	...	...	...	...	...	..	‡×	§...	...	...	...	...	...	...	...	×	×
786		Motacilla hodgsoni, *Blyth.*	...	...	...	...	...	...	...	B §	...	...	...	...	...	...	...	...	×	×
787	589	Motacilla madraspatensis, *Gm.*	×	×	...	...	×	×	...	×‡	×	×	×	×	×	×	×	×	...	×
788	592	Motacilla melanope, *Pall.*	×	×	×	×	×	×	×	×	×	×	×	...	...	...	...	×	×	×

B. Bhootan. * Malabar. † Andamans. ‡ Sikkim. § Assam. ‖ Khasia Hills.

No. in Avifauna.	Jerdon's Nos.	Species.	Sind.	Beloochistan.	Persia.	Afghanistan.	Punjab.	N.-W. Provinces.	Oudh.	Bengal.	Rajputana.	Central India.	Central Prov.	Kutch.	Guzerat.	Concan.	Deccan.	S. India.	British Burmah.	Nepaul.
789		Motacilla citreola, *Pall.*	×	×	×	×	×	×	×	‡×	×	×	×	×	×	...	×	...	×	×
790	594	Motacilla citreoloides, *Hodgs.*	×	×	...	×	...	...	...	§ §×	×	...	...	...	...	...	×	...	...	×
791		Motacilla beema, *Sykes.*	×	×	×	...	...	...	...	‡	...	×	×	...	...	...	...	...	...	×
792	593	Motacilla borealis, *Sundev.*	×	×	...	×	×	×	...	×§	...	×	×	...	...	...	×	×	×	×
793		Motacilla Feldeggi, *Mich.*	×	...	×	×	×	×	×	×	×	×	×	×	×	×	×	×	...	...
794	595	Limonidromus indicus, *Gould.*	...	...	...	...	...	...	...	×§	...	...	...	...	...	...	...	*×	×	...
795	597	Anthus trivialis, *Linn.*	×	×	×	×	×	×	×	×§	×	×	×	×	×	×	×	×	×	×
796	596	Anthus maculatus, *Hodgs.*	...	...	...	...	×	×	×	‖× B	×	×	×	...	...	...	...	×	×	×
797	598	Anthus nilgheriensis, *Sharpe.*	...	...	...	...	...	...	...	...	...	...	...	...	...	...	...	×	...	...
798	604	Anthus sordidus, *Rupp.*	...	...	...	...	...	×	...	...	...	...	...	...	...	...	...	×	...	...
799	603	Anthus Jerdoni, *Finch.*	×	×	×	×	×	×	×	×	...	...	...	...	×	...	×	...	...	...
800	599	Anthus Richardi, *Vieill.*	...	...	×	...	...	...	...	×	...	...	...	...	...	...	...	×	×	×
801	601	Anthus striolatus, *Blyth.*	...	...	...	...	×	×	...	‡	...	×	×	...	...	...	...	×	×	×
802	602	Anthus campestris, *Linn*	×	×	×	×	×	×	×	×§	×	×	×	×	×	×	×	...	×	×
803	600	Anthus rufulus, *Vieill.*	×	×	×	×	×	×	×	×§	...	...	...	...	...	×	×	...	×	×
804		Anthus cervinus, *Pall.*	...	×	×	×	×	×	...	...	...	...	...	...	...	...	...	...	×	...
805	605	Anthus rosaceus, *Hodgs.*	...	...	...	×	×	×	...B	‖×	‡...	...	×	...	...	...	...	...	...	×
806		Anthus spipoletta, *Linn*	×	×	×	×	×	×	...	...	...	...	...	...	...	...	...	...	...	...
807	606	Oreocorys sylvanus, *Hodgs.*	...	...	...	...	...	×	...	...	...	...	...	...	...	...	...	...	...	×
808		Coccothraustes humii, *Sharpe*	...	...	...	...	×	×	...	...	...	...	...	...	...	...	...	...	...	...
809	727	Mycerobas melanoxanthus, *Hodgs.*	...	...	...	...	...	×	...	‡	...	...	...	...	...	...	...	...	...	×
810	725	Pycnoramphus icterioides, *Vigors.*	...	...	...	...	...	×	...	...	...	...	...	...	...	...	...	...	...	×
811	726	Pycnoramphus affinis, *Blyth.*	...	...	...	...	×	×	×	‡	...	...	...	...	...	...	...	...	...	×
812	728	Pycnoramphus carneipes, *Hodgs.*	...	...	...	...	×	×	...	‡	...	...	...	...	...	...	...	...	...	×
813	752	Fringilla montifringilla, *Linn.*	...	...	...	×	×	×	...	...	...	...	...	...	...	...	...	...	...	...
814	746	Procarduelis nipalensis, *Hodgs.*	...	...	...	...	×	×	...	‡ B	...	...	...	...	...	...	...	...	...	×
815		Procarduelis rubescens, *Blanf.*	...	...	...	...	...	...	...	‡	...	...	...	...	...	...	...	...	...	×
816	749	Carduelis caniceps, *Vigors.*	...	...	...	×	×	×	...	...	...	...	...	...	...	...	...	...	...	...
817	750	Chrysomitris spinoides, *Vigors*	...	...	...	...	×	×	...	‡	...	...	...	...	...	...	...	...	...	...
818		Chrysomitris thibetana, *Hume.*	...	...	...	...	...	...	...	‡	...	...	...	...	...	...	...	...	...	...
819	748	Callacanthis Burtoni, *Gould.*	...	...	...	...	?	×	...	...	...	...	...	...	...	...	...	...	...	...
820		Acanthis brevirostris, *Bp.*	...	...	...	...	...	×	...	...	...	...	...	...	...	...	...	...	...	...
821		Acanthis fringillirostris, *Bp.*	×	...	×	...	...	...	...	...	...	...	...	...	...	...	...	...	...	...

B. Bhootan. * Malabar. † Andamans. ‡ Sikkim. § Assam. ‖ Khasia Hills.

No in Avifauna.	Jerdon's Nos.	Species.	Sind.	Beloochistan.	Persia.	Afghanistan.	Punjab.	N.-W. Provinces	Oudh.	Bengal.	Rajputana.	Central India.	Central Prov.	Kutch.	Guzerat.	Concan.	Deccan.	S. India.	British Burmah.	Nepaul.
822		Montifringilla Adamsi, *Moore.*	E	...	...	...	×	×	...	...	...	...	...	...	...	...	...	...	...	...
823		Montifringilla ruficollis, *Blanf.*	...	...	...	...	...	×	...	‡	...	...	...	...	...	...	...	...	...	...
824		Montifringilla blanfordi, *Hume.*	...	...	...	...	...	...	...	‡	...	...	...	...	...	...	...	...	...	...
825	745	Montifringilla sordida, *Stol.*	...	...	...	×	×	×	...	...	...	...	...	...	...	...	...	...	...	...
826	753	Montifringilla nemoricola, *Hodgs.*	...	...	...	...	...	...	...	B ‡	...	...	...	...	...	...	...	...	...	×
827		Montifringilla Brandti, *Bp.*	...	...	...	...	.	×	...	‡	...	...	...	...	...	...	...	...	...	...
828		Rhodopechys sanguinea, *Gould.*	×	...	×	×	.	...	...	...	...	...	...	...	...	...	...	...	...	?
829		Erythrospiza githaginea, *Licht.*	×	×	×	×	×	×	...	...	×	...	...	×	...	...	...	...	...	...
830	711	Petronia flavicollis, *Frankl.*	×	×	×	×	×	×	×	...	×	×	×	×	×	×	×	*×	...	...
831	710	Passer montanus, *Koch.*	×	×	×	×	...	...	...	§‡	...	...	...	...	...	...	×	...	×	×
832	706	Passer domesticus, *Linn.*	×	×	×	×	×	×	×	×	×	×	×	×	×	×	×	×	...	...
833	709	Passer pyrrhonotus, *Blyth.*	×	...	...	...	...	...	...	...	...	...	...	...	...	...	...	...	...	...
834	707	Passer hispaniolensis, *Tem.*	×	×	×	×	×	×	...	...	×	...	...	×	...	...	...	...	...	...
835	708	Passer cinnamomeus, *Gould.*	...	...	...	×	×	×	×	‡§B	...	...	...	...	...	...	...	...	...	×
836		Passer assimilis, *Walden.*	...	...	...	...	...	...	...	...	...	...	...	...	...	...	...	...	×	...
837		Passer flaveolus, *Blyth.*	...	...	...	...	...	...	...	...	...	...	...	...	...	...	...	...	×	...
838		Serinus pectoralis, *Murray.*	×	...	...	...	...	...	...	...	...	...	...	...	...	...	...	...	...	...
839	751	Serinus pusillus, *Pall.*	...	×	×	×	×	×	...	...	...	...	...	...	...	...	...	...	...	...
840	733	Pyrrhoplectus epauletta, *Hodgs.*	...	...	...	...	...	...	...	...	...	...	...	...	...	...	...	...	...	×‡
841	738	Carpodacus erythrinus, *Pall.*	×	×	×	×	×	×	×	§	...	×	...	...	...	...	...	×	×	×‡
842	735	Carpodacus sipahi, *Hodgs.*	...	...	...	...	...	...	...	...	...	...	...	...	...	...	...	...	...	×‡
843	737	Carpodacus rubicilla, *Gould.*	...	...	...	...	×	...	...	...	...	...	...	...	...	...	...	...	...	×
844	741	Carpodacus grandis, *Blyth.*	...	...	...	×	×	...	...	...	...	...	...	...	...	...	...	...	...	‡
845	742	Carpodacus rhodochrous, *Vigors.*	...	...	...	×	...	...	...	...	...	...	...	...	...	...	...	...	...	×
846	739	Carpodacus rhodopeplus, *Vigors.*	...	...	...	×	×	...	...	...	...	...	...	...	...	...	...	...	...	×‡
847		Carpodacus Edwardsi, *Verr.*	...	...	...	...	...	...	...	B	...	...	...	...	...	...	...	...	...	×‡
848	740	Carpodacus thura, *Bp. & Schleg.*	...	...	...	...	...	...	...	...	...	...	...	...	...	...	...	...	...	×‡
849	744	Carpodacus dubius, *Pryr.*	...	...	...	...	...	...	...	...	...	...	...	...	...	...	...	...	...	×‡
850		Carpodacus ambiguus, *Hume.*	...	...	...	...	×	...	...	...	...	...	...	...	...	...	...	...	...	×
851	743	Carpodacus pulcherrimus, *Hodgs.*	...	...	...	...	...	×	...	...	...	...	...	...	...	...	...	...	...	×‡
852	747	Pyrrhospiza punicea, *Hodgs.*	...	...	...	...	...	...	...	...	...	...	...	...	...	...	...	...	...	×‡
853	734	Loxia curvirostra, *Lin.*	...	...	...	...	...	...	...	...	...	...	...	...	...	...	...	...	...	×‡

B. Bhootan. E. Indus Valley. ‡ Sikkim. § Assam. * Malabar.

No. in Avifauna.	Jerdon's Nos.	Species.	Sind.	Beloochistan.	Persia.	Afghanistan.	Punjab.	N.-W. Provinces	Oudh.	Bengal.	Rajputana.	Central India.	Central Prov.	Kutch.	Guzerat.	Concan.	Deccan.	S. India.	British Burmah.	Nepaul.
854	729	Pyrrhula erythrocephala, *Vigors.*	...	...	...	...	×	×	...	...	...	...	...	...	...	...	...	...	...	×‡
855	731	Pyrrhula nipalensis, *Hodgs.*	...	...	...	...	...	...	...	...	...	...	...	...	...	...	...	...	...	×‡
856	730	Pyrrhula erithacus, *Blyth.*	...	...	...	...	...	...	...	...	...	...	...	...	...	...	...	...	...	‡
857	732	Pyrrhula aurantiaca, *Gould.*	...	...	...	...	×	×	...	...	...	...	...	...	...	...	...	...	...	...
858	736	Propyrrhula subhimalayensis, *Hodgs.*	...	...	...	...	...	...	...	...	...	...	...	...	...	...	...	...	...	×‡
859		Emberiza schœniclus, *Lin*	...	...	...	×	×	×	...	...	...	...	...	...	...	...	...	...	...	..
860	720	Emberiza pusilla, *Pall.*	...	...	...	...	...	...	...	‖§	...	...	...	...	...	...	...	...	×	×‡
861	719	Emberiza fucata, *Pall.*	...	...	...	...	×	×	...	...	...	...	...	...	...	...	...	...	×	×
862	721	Emberiza melanocephala, *Scop.*	×	×	×	×	×	×	×	×	×	×	×	×	×	×	×	...	...	...
863	722	Emberiza luteola, *Sparrm.*	×	×	×	×	×	×	×	×	×	×	×	×	×	×	×	×	...	...
864	723	Emberiza aureola, *Pall.*	...	...	...	.	...	...	...	§	...	...	...	...	...	...	...	...	×	×‡
865		Emberiza rutila, *Pall.*	...	...	...	...	.	...	...	B	...	...	...	...	...	...	...	...	×	×‡
866	717	Emberiza spodocephala, *Pall.*	...	...	...	...	...	...	...	§B	...	...	...	...	...	...	...	...	×	×
867	716	Emberiza buchanani, *Blyth.*	×	×	×	×	×	×	×	...	...	×	..	×	×	×	×	...	...	...
868	714	Emberiza Stracheyi, *Moore.*	×	×	...	...	×	×	...	...	...	...	...	...	...	.	...	...	...	...
869	718	Emberiza Stewarti, *Blyth.*	×	×	×	×	×	×	×	...	...	...	...	...	...	...	...	...	...	...
870	712	Emberiza leucocephala, *Gm.*	...	×	...	×	×	×	×	...	...	...	...	...	...	...	...	...	...	...
871		Fringillaria striolata, *Licht.*	×	×	×	×	×	×	×	...	×	...	...	...	×	×	...	...	...	...
872	724	Melophus melanicterus, *Gm.*	×	...	...	...	...	...	...	×	×	×	×	×	×	×	×	×	×	×
873	694	Ploceus phillipinus, *Lin.*	×	×	×	×	×	×	×	×	×	×	×	×	×	×	×	×	×	×
874		Ploceus baya, *Blyth.*	...	...	...	...	...	...	...	×	...	...	...	...	...	...	...	...	×	×
875	695	Ploceus manyar, *Horsf.*	×	...	...	...	×	×	×	×§	..	×	×	×	×	×	...	...	...	...
876		Ploceus bengalensis, *Lin.*	×	...	...	...	?	?	...	§×	...	...	...	...	...	...	...	...	×	...
877	696	Ploceus javanensis, *Less*	...	...	...	...	...	...	...	...	...	...	...	...	...	...	...	...	×	...
878	697	Amadina malacca, *Lin.*	...	...	...	...	.	...	...	×	...	×	...	...	...	*	..	×	...	...
879	698	Amadina atricapilla, *Vieill.*	...	...	...	...	×	×	×	§	...	...	...	...	...	...	...	×	×	...
880	699	Amadina punctulata, *Lin.*	×	...	...	..	×	×	×	§	×	×	×	...	...	×	...	×	×	...
881	700	Amadina pectoralis, *Jerd.*	...	...	...	...	...	...	...	...	...	...	...	...	...	...	...	×	...	...
882		Amadina leucogastra, *Blyth.*	...	...	...	...	...	...	...	...	...	...	...	...	...	...	...	...	×	...
883	702	Amadina acuticauda, *Hodgs.*	...	...	...	...	...	...	...	§	...	...	...	...	...	...	...	...	×	‡
884	701	Amadina striata, *Linn.*	...	...	...	.	...	...	...	×	...	...	×	...	...	*	...	×	×	...
885	703	Amadina malabarica, *Linn.*	×	×	...	...	×	×	×	×	×	×	×	×	×	×	×	×	...	...
886		Erythrura prasina, *Sparrm.*	...	...	...	...	...	...	...	...	.	...	...	...	...	...	...	...	×	...
887		Estrilda punicea, *Horsf.*	...	...	...	...	...	...	...	...	...	...	...	...	...	...	...	...	×	...
888	704	Estrilda amandava, *Linn.*	×	×	×	×	×	×	×	§×	×	×	×	×	×	×	×	×	...	...
889	705	Estrilda formosa, *Lath.*	...	...	...	...	...	...	...	...	...	×	×	...	...	...	...	...	...	...
890	754	Mirafra assamica, *McClell.*	...	...	...	...	...	×	×	×§	..	×	×	...	...	...	...	...	..	...
891	755	Mirafra affinis, *Jerd.*	...	...	...	...	...	...	...	×	...	...	...	...	...	●	...	×	×	..
892	756	Mirafra erythroptera, *Jerd.*	×	×	...	...	×	×	×	×	×	×	×	×	×	×	×	...	...	...
893	757	Mirafra cantillans, *Jerd.*	...	...	...	...	×	×	×	×	...	×	×	...	...	...	...	...	...	...
894	759	Ammomanes lusitania, *Gm.*	×	×	×	×	×	×	×	...	...	...	...	...	...	...	...	...	...	...

• Malabar. ‡ Sikkim. § Assam. ‖ Khasia Hills. B. Bhootan.

No. in Avifauna.	Jerdon's Nos.	Species	Sind.	Beloochistan.	Persia.	Afghanistan.	Punjab.	N.-W. Provinces.	Oudh.	Bengal.	Rajputana.	Central India.	Central Prov.	Kutch.	Guzerat.	Concan.	Deccan.	S. India.	British Burmah.	Nepaul.
895	758	Ammomanes phœnicura, *Frankl.*	...	...	...	...	...	×	×	×	...	×	...	..	...	...	×	×	...	...
896	760	Pyrrhulauda grisea, *Scop,*	×	...	...	..	×	×	×	×	×	×	×	×	×	×	×	×	...	...
897		Pyrrhulauda melanauchen, *Cab.*	×	×	×	..	...	...	...	...	×	..	...	×	...	...	...	...	...	...
898	761	Calandrella brachydactyla, *Leisl.*	×	×	×	×	×	×	×	×	×	×	×	×	×	×	×	×	..	...
899		Melanocorypha bimaculata, *Menetr.*	×	×	×	×	...	...	..	...	...	...	...	...	...	...	.	...	...	...
900	762	Alaudula raytal, *Blyth*	×	..	...	.	...	...	...	§×	.	...	×	..	...	...	...	...	×	...
901		Alaudula Adamsi, *Hume*	×	...	...	...	×	×	×	...	...	...	...	...	...	...	...	...	...	...
902	763	Otocorys penicillata, *Gould.*	.	..	...	.	×	×	...	...	...	...	...	...	...	...	...	...	...	×
903	765	Spizalauda deva, *Sykes.*	...	...	...	...	×	×	×	..	...	×	×	...	...	...	×	×	...	...
904	767	Alauda gulgula, *Frankl.*	×	...	...	..	×	×	×	×	×	×	×	×	×	×	×	×	×	×
905	769	Galerida cristata, *Lin.*	×	×	×	×	×	×	×	×	×	×	×	×	×	×	×	×	...	...
906	770	Certhilauda desertorum, *Stanley.*	×	×	×	×	×	×	×	...	..	...	...	...	...	...	...	...	...	...
907	681	Sturnus vulgaris, *Lin.*	×	×	×	×	×	×	×	×	×	×	×	×	×	×	×	×	...	×
908		Sturnus minor, *Hume.*	×	...	...	...	...	...	..	..	...	...	...	...	...	...	...	...	...	...
909	682	Sturnus unicolor, *Marmora.*	×	×	...	×	×	×	...	...	...	...	...	...	...	..	...	...	...	...
910		Sturnopastor superciliaris. *Blyth.*	...	...	...	...	...	...	...	...	...	...	...	...	...	...	...	...	×	...
911	683	Sturnopastor contra, *Lin.*	...	...	...	...	×	×	×	×	×	×	×	...	...	...	...	...	...	...
912	684	Acridotheres tristis, *Lin*	×	×	×	×	×	×	×	§×	×	×	×	×	×	×	×	×	×	...
913	685	Acridotheres ginginianus, *Lath.*	×	×	×	×	×	×	×	§×	×	×	×	×	×	×	×	×	×	...
914	686	Acridotheres fuscus, *Tem.*	×	...	...	...	×	×	...	§×	×	×	×	×	×	×	×	×	×	×
915		Acridotheres siamensis, *Swinh.*	...	...	..	...	...	...	...	...	...	...	...	...	...	...	...	...	×	...
916	687	Sturnia pagodarum, *Gmel.*	×	...	..	...	×	×	×	§×	...	.	...	...	...	×	×	×	×	...
917		Sturnia sturnina, *Pall.*	...	...	...	...	...	...	...	...	..	...	...	...	...	...	...	...	×	...
918		Sturnia sinensis, *Gmel.*	...	...	...	...	...	...	...	...	...	..	...	...	...	...	...	...	×	...
919		Sturnia Burmannica, *Jerd.*	...	...	...	...	...	...	...	..	..	...	...	...	...	...	...	...	×	...
920		Sturnia leucocephala, *Gigl. & Salv.*	...	...	...	.	...	...	...	...	..	...	...	...	...	...	...	...	×	...
921	688	Sturnia malabarica, *Gmel.*	...	...	..	...	×	×	×	×	§	×	...	...	...	×	×	×	×	...
922	689	Sturnia Blythi, *Jerd.*	...	...	...	.	...	...	...	...	...	...	...	...	...	...	*	×	..	...
923		Sturnia nemoricola, *Jerd.*	...	...	...	...	...	...	...	...	...	...	...	...	...	...	...	...	×	...
924		Calornis chalybea, *Horsf.*	...	...	...	...	...	...	...	×	...	...	...	...	...	...	...	...	×	...
925	690	Pastor roseus, *Lin.*	×	×	×	×	×	×	×	×	§×	×	×	×	×	×	×	×	×	...
926	693	Gracula intermedia, *A. Hay.*	...	...	...	...	...	...	...	...	×	...	×	×	...	...	...	...	×	...
927	692	Gracula religiosa, *Lin*	...	...	...	...	...	...	...	...	...	...	...	...	...	*	...	×	...	...
928	691	Saraglossa spiloptera, *Vigors.*	...	...	...	...	×	×	...	...	...	...	..	...	...	...	...	...	×	...
929		Ampeliceps coronatus, *Blyth.*	...	...	...	...	...	...	...	.	...	...	...	...	...	...	...	...	×	...
930		Gracupica nigricollis, *Payk.*	...	...	...	...	..	...	...	...	...	...	...	...	...	...	...	...	×	...

* Malabar. § Assam.

No. in Avifauna.	Jerdon's Nos.	Species.	Sind.	Beloochistan.	Persia.	Afghanistan.	Punjab.	N.-W. Provinces.	Oudh.	Bengal.	Rajputana.	Central India.	Central Prov.	Kutch.	Guzerat.	Concan.	Deccan.	S. India.	British Burmah.	Nepaul.
931		Anthocincla Phayrii, *Blyth.*	...	...	...	...	...	...	...	...	...	...	...	...	...	...	...	...	×	...
932	344	Pitta nipalensis, *Hodgs.*	...	...	...	...	...	...	...	...	B§‖	...	...	...	...	...	...	...	×	×
933		Pitta Oatesi, *Hume.*	...	...	...	...	...	...	...	...	...	...	...	...	...	...	...	...	×	...
934		Pitta cærulea, *Raffles.*	...	...	...	...	...	...	...	...	...	...	...	...	...	...	...	...	×	...
935		Pitta cyanea, *Blyth.*	...	...	...	...	...	...	...	...	B	...	...	...	...	...	...	...	×	...
936		Pitta cyanoptera, *Tem.*	...	...	...	...	...	...	...	...	...	...	...	...	...	...	...	...	×	...
937		Pitta megarhyncha, *Schl.*	...	...	...	...	...	...	...	...	...	...	...	...	...	...	...	...	×	...
938	345	Pitta brachyura, *Lin.*	...	...	...	...	×	×	×	×	×	×	×	...	×	×	×	•×	×	‡
939		Pitta coccinea, *Eyton.*	...	...	...	...	...	...	...	...	...	...	...	...	...	...	...	...	×	...
940	346	Pitta cucullata, *Hartl.*	...	...	...	...	...	...	...	...	§‖	...	...	...	...	...	...	...	×	‡×
941		Encichla Gurneyi, *Hume.*	...	...	...	...	...	...	...	...	...	...	...	...	...	...	...	...	×	...
942		Calyptomena viridis, *Raffles.*	...	...	...	...	...	...	...	...	...	...	...	...	...	...	...	...	×	...
943	138	Psarisomus Dalhousiæ *Jameson.*	...	...	...	...	×	×	...	B	§	...	...	...	...	...	...	...	×	×‡
944		Serilophus lunatus, *Gould.*	...	...	...	...	...	...	...	...	...	...	...	...	...	...	...	...	×	...
945	139	Serilophus rubropygius, *Hodgs.*	...	...	...	...	...	...	...	B‖§	§	...	...	...	...	...	...	...	...	×‡
946		Eurylæmus javanicus, *Horsf.*	...	...	...	...	...	...	...	...	...	...	...	...	...	...	...	...	×	...
947		Eurylæmus ochromelas, *Raffles.*	...	...	...	...	...	...	...	...	...	...	...	...	...	...	...	...	×	...
948		Corydon sumatranus, *Raffles.*	...	...	...	...	...	...	...	...	...	...	...	...	...	...	...	...	×	...
949		Cimborhynchus macrorhynchus, *Gm.*	...	...	...	...	...	...	...	...	...	...	...	...	...	...	...	...	×	...
950	98	Cypselus melba, *Lin.*	×	×	×	×	×	×	×	...	...	...	...	×	×	×	×	×	...	...
951	99	Cypselus apus, *Lin.*	×	×	×	×	×	×	?	...	×	...	...	×	...	...	...	...	...	...
952	100	Cypselus affinis, *Gray.*	×	×	×	×	×	...	...	...	×	...	...	×	×	×	×	...	...	×
953		Cypselus acuticaudus, *Blyth.*	...	...	...	...	...	×	...	...	...	...	...	...	...	...	...	...	...	...
954		Cypselus pacificus, (*Lath.*)	...	...	...	...	...	...	...	...	...	...	...	...	...	...	...	...	×	...
955		Cypselus subfurcatus, *Blyth.*	...	...	...	...	...	...	...	‖	...	...	...	...	...	...	...	...	×	...
956	101	Cypselus leuconyx, *Blyth.*	...	...	...	...	...	...	...	...	...	...	...	...	...	*	×	...	...	...
957	102	Cypselus batassiensis, *Gray.*	...	...	...	...	...	×	...	×§	...	...	×	...	...	*	×	...	...	...
958		Cypselus infumatus, *Sclater.*	...	...	...	...	...	...	...	§‖	...	...	...	...	...	...	...	...	×	...
959		Hirundinapus giganteus, *Van Hass.*	...	...	...	...	...	...	...	...	...	...	...	...	...	...	...	...	×	...
960	96	Hirundinapus indicus, *Hume.*	...	...	...	...	...	...	...	...	...	...	...	...	...	*	...	×	×	...
961		Hirundinapus leucopygialis, *Blyth.*	...	...	...	...	...	...	...	...	...	...	...	...	...	...	...	...	×	...
962	95	Hirundinapus sylvatica, *Tick.*	...	...	...	...	×	×	...	...	...	×	...	...	...	...	...	×	...	...

* Malabar. ‡ Sikkim. § Assam. ‖ Khasia Hill. B. Bhootan.

No. in Avifauna.	Jerdon's Nos.	Species.	Sind.	Beloochistan.	Persia.	Afghanistan.	Punjab.	N.-W. Provinces	Oudh.	Bengal.	Rajputana.	Central India.	Central Prov.	Kutch.	Guzerat.	Concan.	Deccan	S. India.	British Burmah.	Nepaul.
963	97	Hirundinapus caudacuta, *Lath.*	...	...	...	...	...	...	...	B	...	...	...	...	...	...	...	...	...	×‡
964	103	Collocalia unicolor, *Jerd.*	...	...	...	...	...	...	...	§	...	...	...	...	...	...	*	×	...	‡
965		Collocalia innominata, *Hume.*	...	...	...	...	...	...	...		...	...	...	...	...	...	...	...	×	...
966		Collocalia spodiopygia, *Peale.*	...	...	...	...	...	...	...	...	...	...	...	...	...	...	...	...	×	...
967		Collocalia Linchi, *Horsf. & Moore.*	...	...	...	...	...	...	...	...	...	...	...	...	...	...	...	...	×	...
968		Dendrochelidon coronatus, *Tick.*	...	...	...	...	...	×	...	...	...	×	×	...	...	...	*	×	×	‡
969		Dendrochelidon longipennis, *Rafin.*	...	...	...	...	...	...	...	...	...	...	...	...	...	...	...	...	×	...
970		Dendrochelidon comatus, *Tem.*	...	...	...	...	...	...	...	...	...	...	...	...	...	...	...	...	×	...
971	105	Batrachostomus moniliger, *Blyth.*	...	...	...	...	...	...	...	...	...	...	×	...	...	*	.	×	...	...
972	106	Batrachostomus affinis, *Blyth.*	...	...	...	...	...	...	...	...	...	...	...	...	...	...	...	...	×	‡
973	112	Caprimulgus asiaticus, *Lath.*	×	...	...	...	?	...	...	...	×	...	...	×	×	×	×	...	×	...
974	113	Caprimulgus mahrattensis, *Sykes.*	×	×	...	...	×	×	...	...	×	×	...	×	×	×	×	...	...	...
975	114	Caprimulgus monticolus, *Frankl.*	...	...	...	...	...	...	...	×	...	×	×	...	...	...	...	...	×	...
976	109	Caprimulgus albonotata, *Tick.*		...	...	...	...	×	...	×	...	×	×	...	...	...	...	...	×	‡
977	111	Caprimulgus atripennis, *Jerd.*	...	...	...	...	...	...	...	...	...	...	...	...	...	*	...	×	...	...
978		Caprimulgus Unwini, *Hume.*	×	×	×	×	...	...	...	...	...	...	...	...	...	...	...	...	...	×
979	107	Caprimulgus indicus, *Lath.*	...	...	...	...	...	...	...	...	...	...	...	...	...	...	×	...	...	...
980		Caprimulgus Kelaarti, *Blyth.*	...	...	...	...	...	...	...	...	...	...	×	...	...	...	...	×	...	...
981		Caprimulgus jotaka, *Tem.*	...	...	...	...	...	...	...	...	...	...	...	...	...	...	...	...	×	×
982		Lyncornis cerviniceps, *Gould.*	...	...	...	...	...	...	...	...	...	...	...	...	...	...	...	...	×	...
983	115	Harpactes fasciatus, *Gmel.*	...	...	...	...	...	...	...	...	...	×	...	...	...	...	*	...	...	...
984	116	Harpactes erythrocephalus, *Gould.*	...	...	...	...	...	...	...	§	...	...	...	...	...	...	...	...	×	×‡
985		Harpactes oreskios, *Tem.*	...	...	...	...	...	...	...	...	...	...	...	...	...	...	...	...	×	...
986		Harpactes Duvaucelli, *Temm.*	...	...	...	...	...	...	...	...	...	...	...	...	...	...	...	...	×	...
987	199	Cuculus canorus, *Lin.*	×	×	×	×	×	×	×	×	×	×	×	×	×	×	×	×	×	×
988	200	Cuculus striatus, *Drap.*	...	...	...	...	...	...	...	‖§	...	...	...	...	...	...	...	...	×	×‡
989	201	Cuculus poliocephalus, *Lath.*	...	...	...	...	...	...	...	...	...	...	...	...	...	...	×	×	...	×
990	202	Cuculus sonneratti, *Lath.*	...	...	...	...	...	...	...	...	...	...	...	...	...	...	*	×	×	...

* Malabar. ‡ Sikkim. § Assam. ‖ Khasia Hill. B. Bhootan.

No. in Avifauna.	Jerdon's Nos.	Species.	Sind.	Beloochistan.	Persia.	Afghanistan.	Punjab.	N.-W. Provinces	Oudh.	Bengal.	Rajputana.	Central India.	Central Prov.	Kutch.	Guzerat.	Concan.	Deccan.	S. India.	British Burmah.	Nepaul.
991	203	Cuculus micropterus, *Gould.*	...	...	...	...	...	...	...	×§	...	×	...	...	...	...	*	×	×	...
992	207	Hierococcyx sparverioides, *Vigors.*	...	...	...	...	...	...	...	...	...	...	...	...	...	...	...	×	×	×
993	209	Hierococcyx varius, *Vahl.*	...	...	...	...	...	×	...	×	...	...	...	...	...	...	...	×	...	...
994		Hierococcyx nanus, *Hume.*	...	...	...	...	...	...		...	...	...	...	...	...	...	...	...	×	...
995	206	Hierococcyx nisicolor, *Hodgs.*	...	...	...	...	...	...	...	...	...	...	...	...	...	...	...	...	×	×
996		Cacomantis threnodes, *Cab. et Hein.*	...	...	...	...	...	...	...	×	...	...	...	...	...	...	...	...	×	...
997	208	Cacomantis nigra, *Jerd.*	...	...	...	...	...	...	...	×	...	×	...	...	...	...	...	×	...	...
998	210	Surniculus lugubris, *Horsf.*	...	...	...	...	...	...	...	...	...	×	...	...	...	...	...	*	×	‡
999	211	Chrysococcyx maculatus, *Gm.*	...	...	...	...	...	...	...	...	...	×	...	...	...	...	...	...	×	‡
1000		Chrysococcyx xanthorhynchus, *Horsf.*	...	...	...	...	...	...	...	...	...	...	...	...	...	...	...	...	×	...
1001		Chrysococcyx Limborgi, *Tweed*	...	...	...	...	...	...	...	...	...	...	...	...	...	...	...	...	×	...
1002	212	Coccystes Jacobinus, *Bodd.*	×	...	...	...	×	×	×	×	×	×	×	×	×	×	×	*	...	×
1003	213	Coccystes coromandus, *Linn*	...	...	...	...	...	...	...	×	×	×	×	...	...	...	*	...	×	...
1004	214	Eudynamys honorata, *Linn.*	...	...	...	...	...	...	...	...	...	...	...	×	×	×	×	...	×	×
1005		Eudynamys malayana, *Cab. et Hein*	...	...	...	...	...	...	...	×	...	...	...	...	...	...	...	...	×	...
1006		Rhinortha chlorophæa, *Raffles*	...	...	...	...	...	...	...	...	...	...	...	...	...	...	...	...	×	...
1007	215	Rhopodytes tristis, *Less.*	...	...	...	...	...	...	...	×§	...	×	...	...	...	...	...	...	×	‡
1008		Rhopodytes diardi, *Less*	...	...	...	...	...	...	...	...	...	...	...	...	...	...	...	...	×	...
1009		Rhopodytes sumatranus, *Raffles*	...	...	...	...	...	...	...	...	...	...	...	...	...	...	...	...	×	...
1010	216	Rhopodytes viridirostris, *Jerd*	...	...	...	...	...	...	...	...	...	...	...	...	...	...	×	×	...	...
1011		Rhamphococcyx erythrognathus, *Hartl.*	...	...	...	...	...	...	...	...	...	...	...	...	...	...	...	...	×	...
1012		Zanclostomus Javanicus, *Horsf.*	...	...	...	...	...	...	...	...	...	...	...	...	...	...	...	...	×	...
1013		Centrococcyx maximus, *Hume.*	×	...	...	...	×	×	×	...	...	...	...	...	...	...	...		...	...
1014	217	Centrococcyx rufipennis, *Illigr.*	...	...	...	...	...	...	...	...	×	×	×	×	×	×	×	×	...	...
1015		Centrococcyx intermedius, *Hume.*	...	...	...	...	...	...	...	×	...	...	...	...	...	...	...	...	×	...
1016	218	Centrococcyx bengalensis, *Gmel.*	...	...	...	...	...	...	×	×	...	×	...	...	...	...	...	×	×	...
1017	219	Taccocua Leschenaulti, *Less.*	...	...	...	...	...	...	...	...	...	...	...	...	...	×	×	×	...	...
1018	220	Taccocua sirkeer, *Gray.*	×	...	...	...	×	×	×	×	...	×	...	×	×	×	×	...	...	...
1019	221	Taccocua infuscata, *Blyth.*	...	...	...	...	...	×	...	...	...	...	...	...	...	...	...	...	...	×‡

* Malabar. ‡ Sikkim. § Assam.

No. in Avifauna.	Jerdon's Nos.	Species.	Sind.	Beloochistan.	Persia.	Afghanistan.	Punjab.	N.-W. Provinces.	Oudh.	Bengal.	Rajputana.	Central India.	Central Prov.	Kutch.	Guzerat.	Concan.	Deccan.	S. India.	British Burmah.	Nepaul.
1020		Megalæma marshallorum, *Swinh.*	...	...	...	...	...	...	...	×	...	...	...	...	...	...	...	...	×	...
1021		Megalæma virens, *Bodd*	...	...	...	...		...	...	...	...	...	...	...	...	...		...	×	...
1022		Megalæma mystacophanus, *Tem.*	...	...	...	...	...	...	...	...	...	...	...	...	...	...	...	...	×	...
1023	192	Megalæma Hodgsoni, *Bonap.*	...	...	...	...	...	...	...	×	§	...	...	...	...	...	...	...	×	‡×
1024	193	Megalæma caniceps, *Frankl.*	...	...	...	...	×	×	×	×	...	×	...	×	...	...	...	...	...	...
1025		Megalæma inornata, *Wald.*	...	...	...	...	...	...	...	...	...	×	...	...	...	...	*	×	...	...
1026	194	Megalæma viridis, *Gmel.*	...	...	...	...	...	...	...	...	...	...	...	...	...	...	*	×	...	...
1027	195	Cyanops asiatica, *Lath.*	...	...	...	...	...	×	...	×	§	...	...	...	...	...	...	...	×	‡
1028		Cyanops Davisoni, *Hume*	...	...	...	...	...	...	...	...	...	...	...	...	...	...	...	...	×	...
1029		Cyanops incognita, *Hume.*	...	...	...	...	...	...	...	...	...	...	...	...	...	...	...	...	×	...
1030		Cyanops Ramsayi, *Wald.*	...	...	...	...	...	...	...	...	...	...	...	...	...	...	...	...	×	...
1031	197	Xantholæma hæmacephala, *P. L. S. Mull.*	×	?	...	...	×	×	×	×	×	×	×	×	×	×	×	×	×	×
1032	198	Xantholæma malabarica, *Blyth.*	...	...	...	...	...	...	...	...	...	...		...	...	...	*	×	...	...
1033		Xantholæma cyanotis, *Blyth.*	...	...	...	...	...	...	...	×	§	...	...	...	...	...	...	...	×	...
1034		Caloramphus Hayi, *Gray*	...	...	...	...	...	...	...	...	...	...	...	...	...	...	...	...	×	...
1035	188	Yunx torquilla, *Linn.*	×	×	×	×	×	×	×	×	×	×	×	×	×	×	×	×	×	...
1036	190	Indicator xanthonotus, *Blyth.*	...	...	...	...	...	...	...	...	...	...	...	...	...	...	...	...	...	‡×
1037	186	Vivia innominata, *Burton.*	...	...	...	...	...	...	...	‖	§	...	...	...	...	...	...	×	×	‡×
1038	187	Sasia ochracea, *Hodgs.*	...	...	...	...	...	...	...	‖×	§	...	...	...	...	...	...	...	×	×
1039		Gauropicoides Rafflesi, *Vigors.*	...			...	...	...	...	...	...	...	...	...	...	...	...	...	×	...
1040	177	Gecinulus Grantia, *McClell*	...	...	...	...	...	...	...	...	§	...	...	...	...	...	...	...	...	×
1041		Gecinulus viridis, *Blyth.*	...	...	...	...	...	...	...	...	...	...	...	...	...	...	...	...	×	...
1042	184	Tiga Javanensis, *Ljungh.*	...	...	...	...	...	...	...	...	...	×	...	...	...	...	*	×	×	×
1043	180, 182	Brachypternus aurantias, *Linn.*	×	×	×	×	×	×	×	×	×	×	×	×	×	×	×	×	...	×
1044	181	Brachpyternus chrysonotus, *Less.*	...	...	...	...	...	...	...	...	...	...	...	...	...	×	*	×	...	...
1045	178	Micropternus phæoceps, *Blyth.*	...	...	...	...	...	...	...	×§	...	×	×	...	...	...	...	...	×	‡×
1046		Micropternus brachyurus, *Vieil.*	...	...	...	...	...	...	...	...	...	...	...	...	...	...	...	...	×	...
1047	179	Micropternus gularis, *Jerd.*	...	...	...	...	...	...	...	...	...	...	...	...	...	...	×	*	...	...
1048	176	Venilia pyrrhotis, *Hodgs*	...	...	...	...	...	...	...	×§	...	...	...	...	...	...	...	...	×	‡×
1049		Venilia porphyromelas, *Boie.*	...	...	...	...	...	...	...	...	...	...	...	...	...	...	...	...	×	...
1050		Callolophus mentalis, *Tem.*	...	...	...	...	...	...	...	...	...	...	...	...	...	...	...	...	×	...
1051		Callolophus malaccensis, *Lath.*	...	...	...	...	...	...	...	...	...	...	...	...	...	...	...	...	×	...
1052		Callolophus puniceus, *Horsf.*	...	...	...	...	...	...	...	...	...	...	...	...	...	...	...	...	×	...

* Malabar. ‡ Sikkim. § Assam. ‖ Khasia Hills.

No. in Avifauna.	Jerdon's Nos.	Species.	Sind.	Beloochistan.	Persia.	Afghanistan.	Punjab.	N.-W. Provinces.	Oudh.	Bengal.	Rajputana.	Central India.	Central Prov.	Kutch.	Guzerat.	Concan.	Deccan.	S. India.	British Burmah.	Nepaul.
1053	173	Chrysophlegma flavinucha, *Gould.*								×	§	×§							×	‡×
1054	174	Chrysophlegma chlorolophus, *Vieill.*								×	§	×§							×	‡×
1055	175	Chrysophlegma chlorigaster, *Jerd.*															*	×		
1056	170	Gecinus squamatus, *Vigors*				×	×	×	×											×
1057	171	Gecinus striolatus, *Blyth.*				×	×	×	×	×	§	×§			×			×	×	×
1058	172	Gecinus occipitalis, *Vigors.*				×		×	×	§	B								×	×‡
1059		Gecinus viridanus, *Blyth.*																	×	
1060		Gecinus erythropygius, *Elliot.*																	×	
1061	169	Thriponax hodgsoni, *Jerd.*															*	×		
1062		Thriponax Javensis, *Horsf.*																	×	
1063		Thriponax Feddeni, *Blanf.*																	×	
1064	168	Mulleripicus pulverulentus, *Tem.*						×	×	‖									×	×
1065	166	Chrysocolaptes strictus, *Horsf.*					×	×	×	×	×	§	×	×			*	×	×	×‡
1066	167	Chrysocolaptes festivus, *Bodd.*									×	×					×	×		
1067	165	Hemicercus cordatus, *Jerd.*										×	×			*	×	×	×	
1068		Hemicercus sordidus, *Eyton.*																	×	
1069	154	Picus himalayanus, *Jard. and Selby.*					×	×	×											×‡
1070	155	Picus majoroides, *Hodgs.*																		×‡
1071	156	Picus cathpharius, *Hodgs.*												B						×‡
1072	158	Picus scindianus, *Gould.*	×	×	×	×	×	×	×											
1073	157	Picus macii, *Vieill.*					×	×	×	×									×	
1074		Picus analis, *Tem.*																	×	
1075		Picus atratus, *Blyth.*																	×	
1076	159	Picus brunneifrons, *Vigors.*					×	×	×											×
1077	160	Picus mahrattensis, *Lath.*	×	×			×	×	×		×	×		×	×	×	×		×	
1078		Picus canicapillus, *Blyth.*								×	§								×	
1079		Picus pumilus, *Hargitt.*																	×	
1080	161	Hypopicus hyperythrus, *Vigors.*					×	×												
1081	162	Iyngipicus rubricatus, *Blyth.*																		×‡
1082	163	Iyngipicus pygmæus *Vigors.*					×	×												×
1083	164	Iyngipicus Hardwickii, *Jerd.*					×	×	×			×						×		
1084		Meiglyptes grammithorax, *Mesh.*																	×	
1085		Meiglyptes jugularis, *Blyth.*																	×	

* Malabar. ‡ Sikkim. § Assam. ‖ Khasia Hills. B. Bhootan.

No in Avifauna.	Jerdon's Nos.	Species.	Sind.	Beloochistan.	Persia.	Afghanistan.	Punjab.	N.-W. Provinces	Oudh.	Bengal.	Rajputana.	Central India.	Central Prov.	Kutch.	Guzerat.	Concan.	Deccan.	S. India.	British Burmah.	Nepaul.
1086		Meiglyptes tukki, *Less.* ...	...	...	...	...	...	...	...	...	...	...	...	...	...	...	...	...	X	...
1087		Psittinus incertus, *Shaw.*	...	...	...	...	...	...	...	...	...	...	...	...	...	...	...	...	X	...
1088	153	Loriculus vernalis, *Sparrm*	...	...	...	...	X	X	X	X	§	B	...	...	X	...	*×	X	X	×‡
1089	152	Palæornis fasciatus, *P.L.S. Mull.*	...	..	...	...	X	X	X	X	§	...	...	...	...	...	...		X	...
1090	151	Palæornis columboides, *Vigors*...............	...	...	...	...	...	...	...	...	...	...	...	...	...	...	*	X	...	...
1091	147	Palæornis indoburmannicus *Hume*, ...	...	..	...	..	X	X	X	X	..	...	X	...	...	*	X	X	X	‡
1092	150	Palæornis schisticeps, *Hodgs.*	..	...	...	..	X	X	X	X	§	...	...	...	...	...	...	...	X	...
1093	148	Palæornis torquatus, *Bodd.*	X	...	...	...	X	X	X	X	X	X	X	X	X	X	X	X	X	X
1094		Palæornis cyanocephalus, *Lin.*	..	..	...	...	X	X	X	X	..	...	...	...	...	...	...	...	X	X
1095	149	Palæornis rosa, *Bodd*.......	...	...	..	.	X	X	X	X	X	§×	X	X	X	X	X	X	X	X
1096	254	Upupa epops, *Linn*.........	X	X	X	X	X	X	...	X	X	X	X	X	X	X	X	*×	X	X
1097		Upupa longirostris, *Jerd.*	...	...	...	...	...	...	X	...	...	...	...	...	...	...	...	...	X	...
1098	255	Upupa ceylonensis, *Reich.*	..	...		...	X	X	.	...	...	...	...	...	...	...	...	X	...	...
1099	117	Merops viridis, *Linn.*	X	X	X	X	X	X	X	X	X	X	X	X	X	X	X	X	X	X
1100	118	Merops phillipinus, *Linn.*...	X	X	X	X	X	X	X	X	X	X	X	X	X	X	X	X	X	X
1101	119	Merops Leschenaulti, *Vieill.*	...	...	...	...	...	...	...	X	..	...	...	...	...	..	..	X	X	...
1102	120	Merops persicus, *Pall.*. ...	X	X	X	X	X	?	...	..	...	...	...	...	...	...	...	...	...	...
1103	121	Merops apiaster, *Linn.* ...	X	X	X	X	X	X	...	...	X	...	...	X	...	X	...	...	...	...
1104	122	Nyctiornis Athertoni, *Jard and Selb.*	...	...	...	...	...	X	X	§	..	...	...	...	...	...	...	X	X	...
1105		Nyctiornis amicta, *Tem.* ...	...	..	..	...	...	...	...	...	..	...	...	...	...	...	...	...	X	...
1106	125	Coracias garrula, *Linn.* ...	X	X	X	X	X	X	...	...	...	...	...	...	...	...	...	...	...	...
1107	123	Coracias indica, *Linn.*......	X	X	X	X	X	X	X	X	X	X	X	X	X	X	X	X	X	X
1108		Coracias affinis, *McClell*..	...	...	...	...	...	...	.	X	§	...	...	...	...	...	...	...	X	...
1109	126	Eurystomus orientalis, *Linn*........................	...	.	...	...	...	X	X	X	§	...	...	...	...	...	...	..	X	...
1110	134	Alcedo bengalensis, *Gm.*...	X	X	..	X	X	X	...	...	X	X	X	X	X	X	X	X	...	...
1111		Alcedo grandis, *Blyth*......	...	...	...	...	...	...	...	...	...	...	...	...	...	...	..	...	...	‡
1112		Alcedo ispida, *Linn.*	X	X	X	X	...	...	...	..	...	...	...	...	...	...	...	...	...	...
1113		Alcedo asiatica, *Sws.*	...	...	...	...	...	...	...	..	...	...	...	...	...	...	...	...	X	...
1114		Alcedo euryzona, *Tom*......	...	...	...	...	...	...	...	...	...	...	...	...	...	...	...	...	X	...
1115	137	Ceryle guttata *Vig.*	...	...	...	...	X	X	X	X	×§	...	...	...	...	...	...	...	X	...
1116	136	Ceryle rudis, *Linn.*	X	X	..	...	X	X	X	X	X	X	X	X	X	X	X	X	X	X
1117	131	Halcyon coromanda, *Lath.*	...	...	...	...	...	...	X	X	...	...	...	...	...	...	...	...	X	×‡
1118	129	Halcyon smyrnensis, *Linn,*	X	...	...	...	X	X	X	X	X	X	X	X	X	X	X	X	X	×‡
1119	130	Halcyon pileata, *Bodd.* ...	...	...	...	...	...	...	...	X	...	...	...	...	...	...	*	...	X	...
1120	132	Halcyon chloris, *Bodd.* ...	...	...	...	...	...	...	...	X	...	...	..	...	...	X	...	...	...	...
1121		Halcyon concreta. *Tem.* ...	...	...	...	...	...	...	...	...	...	...	...	...	...	...	...	...	X	...
1122		Carcineutes pulchellus, *Horsf.*	...	...	...	...	...	...	...	...	...	...	...	...	...	...	...	...	X	...
1123	133	Ceyx tridactyla, *Pall*......	...	...	...	...	...	...	...	X	...	...	...	...	...	X	X	X	...	...

* Malabar. ‡ Sikkim. § Assam. B. Bhootan.

No. in Avifauna.	Jerdon's Nos.	Species.	Sind.	Beloochistan.	Persia.	Afghanistan.	Punjab.	N. W. Provinces.	Oudh.	Bengal.	Rajputana.	Central India.	Central Prov.	Kutch.	Guzerat.	Concan.	Deccan.	S. India.	British Burmah.	Nepaul.
1124	127	Pelargopsis gurial, *Pearson.*						×		×		×	×			*		c×		
1125	128	Pelargopsis amauroptera, *Pearson.*								×								c×	×	
1126		Pelargopsis burmanica, *Sharpe.*																	×	
1127	140	Dichoceros bicornis, *Linn.*							§	×						×		•×	×	‡
1128	141	Anthracoceros coronatus, *Bodd.*										×						c •×		
1129	142	Anthracoceros albirostris, *Shaw.*					×		§×	×									×	
1130	143	Anthracoceros affinis, *Hutton.*						×												
1131		Rhinoplax vigil, *J. R. Forst.*																	×	
1132	145	Rhinoplax griseus, *Lath.*													*			×		
1133	144	Ocyceros birostris, *Scop.*														•×		×		
1134		Rhytidoceros subruficollis, *Blyth.*																	×	
1135		Rhytidoceros undulatus, *Shaw.*																	×	
1136		Aceros nipalensis, *Hodgs.*					×	×	?	×									×	†×
1137		Anorrhinus comatus, *Raffles.*																	×	
1138		Anorrhinus galeritus, *Tem.*																	×	
1139		Anorrhinus Tickelli, *Blyth.*																	×	
1140	771	Treron nipalensis, *Hodgs.*								§×									×	×
1141	772	Crocopus phœnicopterus, *Lath.*					×	×	×	×§	×	×								
1142	773	Crocopus chlorigaster, *Blyth.*	×						×	×		×			×		×	×		
1143		Crocopus viridifrons, *Blyth.*																	×	
1144	774	Osmotreron bicincta, *Jerd.*							×	×	§	×	×					C	×	×
1145		Osmotreron vernans, *Linn.*																	×	
1146	775	Osmotreron malabarica, *Jerd.*														×		•×		
1147	776	Osmotreron Phayrii, *Blyth.*								×	§								×	
1148		Osmotreron fulvicollis, *Wagl.*																	×	
1149	777	Osmotreron pompadoura, *Gmel.*																×		
1150	778	Sphenocercus sphenurus, *Vigors.*					×	×		§									×	
1151	779	Sphenocercus apicaudus, *Hodgs.*								×§										×
1152	780	Carpophaga ænea, *Linn.*								×		×	×			*		c×	×	×

E * Malabar. ‡ Sikkim. § Assam C. Ceylon.

No. in Avifauna.	Jerdon's Nos.	Species.	Sind.	Belochistan.	Persia.	Afghanistan.	Punjab.	N.W. Provinces.	Oudh.	Bengal.	Rajputana.	Central India.	Central Prov.	Kutch.	Guzerat.	Concan.	Deccan.	S. India.	British Burmah.	Nepaul.
1153	781	Carpophaga insignis, *Hodgs.*									‖							×		
1154		Carpophaga griseicapilla, *Wald.*																	×	
1155		Carpophaga bicolor, *Scop.*																	A.	
1156	785	Palumbus pulchricollis, *Hodgs.*																		×‡
1157	784	Palumbus casiotis, *Bonap.*	×	×	×	×	×	×												×
1158	786	Palumbus Elphinstonei, *Sykes.*														×	×	×		
1159	787	Palumbæna Eversmanni, *Bp.*	×									×					×			
1160	788	Columba intermedia, *Strickl.*	×	×	×	×	×	×	×	×§	×	×	×	×	×	×	×	c×	×	×‡
1161		Columba livia, *Bonap.*	×	×	×	×													×	
1162	789	Columba rupestris, *Pall.*					×	×	×											
1163	790	Columba leuconota, *Vigors.*					×	×												
1164	782	Alsocomus puniceus, *Tickell.*								×	§	×	×					C.	×	
1165	783	Alsocomus Hodgsoni, *Vigors.*						×												×
1166	791	Macropygia leptogrammica, *Temm.*								×B	‖								×	×‡
1167		Macropygia assimilis, *Hume.*																	×	
1168	792	Turtur pulchratus, *Hodgs.*				×	×	×	×			×	×							×‡
1169	793	Turtur meena, *Sykes.*								×‖	§				×	×	×	c×	×	×
1170	794	Turtur senegalensis, *Linn.*	×	×	×	×	×	×	×		×	×	×	×	×	×	×	×		
1171	795	Turtur suratensis, *Gmel.*	×			×	×	×	×	×	×	×	×	×	×	*×	×	×		
1172		Turtur tigrinus, *Tem.*																	×	
1173	796	Turtur risorius, *Linn.*	×	×		×	×	×	×	×	×	×	×	×	×	×	×	c×	×	
1174	797*bis.*	Turtur humilis, *Tem.*	×	×			×	×	×	×	×	×	×	×	×	×	×	C.	×	
1175	798	Chalcophaps indica, *Linn.*						?		§×	A.	N.					?	c×	×	
1176		Geopelia striata, *Linn.*																	×	
1177		Calœnas nicobarica, *Linn.*										M.	N.							
1178	801*ter.*	Pterocles coronatus, *Licht.*	×	×	×	×	×													
1179	801*bis.*	Pterocles senegallus, *Linn.*	×	×			×				×			×	×					
1180	799	Pterocles arenarius, *Pall.*	×	×	×	×	×	×	×	×	×			×	×					
1181	802	Pterocles exustus, *Tem.*	×	×		×	×	×	×	×	×	×		×	×	×	×		×	
1182	801	Pterocles alchata, *Linn.*	×	×	×	×	×	×			×									
1183	800*bis.*	Pterocles Lichtenstenii, *Tem.*	×	×			×													
1184	800	Pterocles fasciatus, *Scop.*	×				×	×	×		×	×			×		×			
1185		Syrrhaptes thibetanus, *Gould.*						×												×
1186	803	Pavo cristatus, *Linn.*	×				×	×	×	×§	×	×	×	×	×	×	×	c×		
1187		Pavo muticus, *Linn.*																	×	
1188		Argusianus argus, *Linn.*																	×	

* Malabar. ‡ Sikkim. § Assam. ‖ Khasia Hills. C. Ceylon.
M. Mergui Archipel. A. Andamans. N. Nicobars.

No. in Avifauna.	Jerdon's Nos.	Species.	Sind.	Beloochistan.	Persia.	Afghanistan.	Punjab.	N. W. Provinces.	Oudh.	Bengal.	Rajputana.	Central India.	Central Prov.	Kutch.	Guzerat.	Concan.	Deccan.	S. India.	British Burmah.	Nepaul.
1189		Polyplectron thibetanum, *Gm.*	...	...	...	...	...	...	...	B.	‖	...	...	...	...	...	...	...	×	...
1190		Megapodius nicobariensis, *Blyth.*	...	...	...	...	...	...	...	N.	...	...	...	...	...	...	...	...	...	...
1191		Crossoptilon thibetanum, *Hodgs.*	...	...	...	...	...	...	...	...	...	...	...	...	...	...	...	...	...	×
1192	804	Lophophorus Impeyanus, *Lath.*	...	...	...	...	...	×	...	B.	...		...	...	...	...	...	...	...	×‡
1193		Lophophorus Sclateri, *Jerd.*	...	...	...	...	...	...	...	S.	...	...	...	...	...	...	...	...	...	...
1194	805	Ceriornis satyra, *Linn.*	...	...	...	...	×	×	...	B.	...	...	...	...	...	...	...	...	...	×‡
1195	806	Ceriornis melanocephalus, *Gray.*	...	...	...	...	×	×	...	...	...	...	...	...	...	...	...	...	...	×‡
1196	807	Ithaginis cruentus, *Hardw*	...	...	...	...	...	...	...	...	.	...	...	...	...	.		...	...	×‡
1197	808	Pucrasia macrolopha, *Lesson.*	...	...	...	...	...	×	...	B	...	...	...	...	...	.	...	...	...	×
1198	809	Phasianus W a l l i c h i, *Hardw.*	...	...	...	...	×	×	...	...	...	...	...	...	...	...	...	...	...	×
1199	810	Euplocamus albocristatus, *Vigors.*	...	...	...	...	×	×	...	...		...	...	...	...	...	...	...	...	×
1200		Euplocamus leucomelanus, *Lath.*	...	...	...	...	...	...	...	...	...	...	...	...	...	...	...	...	...	×
1201	811	Euplocamus melanonotus, *Blyth.*	...	...	...	...	...	...	...	B.	...	...	...	...	.	...	...	...	...	‡
1202		Euplocamus horsfieldi, *G. R. Gray*	...	...	...	...	...	...	...	‖	§	S.	...	...	...	...	...	...	...	...
1203		Euplocamus l i n e a t u s, *Elliot.*	...	...	...	...	...	...	...	...	...	...	...	...	...	...	...	...	×	...
1204		Euplocamus Cuvieri, *Temm.*	...	...	...	...	...	...	...	H.	...	...	...	...	...	...	...	...	...	...
1205		Euplocamus A n d e r s o n i, *Elliot.*	...	...	...	...	...	...	...	...	...	...	...	...	...	...	...	...	×	...
1206		Euplocamus, V i e i l l o t i, *G. R. Gray.*	...	...	...	...	...	...	...	...	...	...	...	...	...	...	...	...	×	...
1207	812	Gallus ferrugineus, *Gm.*	...	...	...	...	×	×	§×	‖×	×	×	×	...	...	...	...	×	...	
1208	813	Gallus sonnerati, *Tem.*	...	...	...	...	...	...	...	...	...	...	×	...	×	...	...	×	...	..
1209	814	Galloperdix s p a d i c e u s, *Gmel.*	...	...	...	...	...	...	...	...	...	×	×	...	×	×	...	×	...	×
1210	815	Galloperdix l u n u l a t u s, *Valenc.*	...	...	...	...	...	...	...	×	...	...	...	...	...	...	...	×	...	...
1211	816	Tetraogallus Himalayensis, *G. R. Gray.*	...	...	...	...	...	×	...	...	...	...	...	...	...	...	...	...	...	...
1212		Tetrao thibetanus, *Gould.*	...	...	...	...	...	×	...		...	...	...	...	...	...	...	...	...	...
1213	817	Lerwa nivicola, *Hodgs.*	...	...	...	...	...	×	...	...	...	...	...	...	...	...	...	...	.	×‡
1214	818	Francolinus v u l g a r i s, *Steph.*	×	×	×	×	×	×	×	×	×	×	×	×	×	...	...	...	...	...
1215	819	Francolinus pictus, *Jard. and Selby.*	...	...	...	...	...	...	.	...	...	×	×	...	×	...	×	×	...	...
1216		Francolinus chinensis, *Osb.*	...	...	...	...	...	...	.	...	...	...	...	...	...	...	...	...	×	...
1217	820	Caccabis chukor, *Gray.*	×	×	×	×	×	×	...	...	...	...	...	...	...	...	...	...	...	×

‡ Sikkim. § Assam. ‖ Khasia Hills. B. Bhootan. N. Nicobars.
S. Sadya. H. Arracan Hills.

No. in Avifauna.	Jerdon's Nos.	Species.	Sind.	Beloochistan.	Persia.	Afghanistan.	Punjab.	N.W. Provinces.	Oudh.	Bengal	Rajputana.	Central India.	Central Prov.	Kutch	Guzerat.	Concan.	Deccan.	S. India.	British Burmah.	Nepaul.
1218	821	Ammoperdix bonhami, *Gray.*	×	×	×	×	×	×												
1219	822	Ortygornis ponticeriana, *Gmel.*	×	×	×	×	×	×	×		×	×	×	×	×		×	c×		
1220	823	Ortygornis gularis, *Tem.*							×	×	§									
1221	824	Arboricola torqueola, *Valenc.*						×		B.										×‡
1222		Arboricola atrogularis, *Blyth.*									§	Sy.	Ch.	T.	G.					
1223		Arboricola brunneipectus, *Tick.*																	×	
1224		Arboricola chloropus, *Tick.*														×			×	
1225		Arboricola intermedia, *Blyth.*									A.	N.								
1226	825	Arboricola rufogularis, *Blyth.*									§								×	
1227		Arboricola mandelli, *Hume.*									B.									
1228		Bambusicola Fytchi, *Andr.*								§	‖	G.	N.						×	
1229		Caloperdix oculea, *Tem.*																	×	
1230		Rollulus roulroul, *Scop.*																	×	
1231	826	Perdicula asiatica, *Lath.*					×	×	×	×		×	×		×	×	×	c×		
1232	827	Perdicula argoondah, *Sykes.*					×	×	×		×	×	×	×	×	?	×			
1233		Ophrysia superciliosa, *J. E. Gray.*						×												
1234	828	Microperdix erythrorhyncha, *Sykes.*														×	×	×		
1235		Microperdix Blewitti, *Hume.*											×							
1336	829	Coturnix communis, *Linn.*	×	×	×	×	×	×	×	Sy.	×	A.	×	×	×	×	×	×	×	×
1237	830	Coturnix coromandelica, *Gmel.*	×	×	×		×	×	×	×	×	×	×	×	×	×	×	×	×	×
1238		Excalfactoria chinensis *Linn.*								§×	‖	×	×	Sy.				C.	×	×‡
1239	{832 833}	Turnix plumbipes, *Hodgs.*					×	×	×									C.	×	
1240	834	Turnix joudera, *Hodgs.*	×				×	×	×	×	×			×	×	×	×	c×		
1241	835	Turnix Dussumieri, *Tem.*	×				×	×	×	×	×			×	×	×	×	×		
1242		Turnix maculosa, *Tem.*									A.		T.						×	
1243		Turnix albiventris, *Hume.*										Nicobars and Andamans.								
1244		Otis tarda, *Linn.*					Hastnagur.													
1245		Otis tetrax, *Linn.*				?	×	×												
1246	836	Eupodotis Edwardsi, *Gray*	×				×	×			×		×	×	×		×			
1247	837	Houbara Macqueenii, *Gray*	×	×	×	×	×	×	×		×	×	×	×	×					
1248	838	Sypheotides bengalensis, *Gmel.*					×	×	×	×	I.	Sy.	§							
1249	839	Sypheotides auritus, *Lath.*	×				×	×	×	×	×	×	×	×	×	×	×	×		

‡ Sikkim § Assam. ‖ Khasia Hills. A. Arracan. B. Bhootan. C. Ceylon.
Sy. Sylhet. G. Garo Hills. T. Tipperah. Ch. Chittagong.

No. in Avifauna.	Jerdon's Nos.	Species.	Sind.	Beloochistan.	Persia.	Afghanistan.	Punjab.	N.-W. Provinces	Oudh.	Bengal.	Rajputana.	Central India.	Central Prov.	Kutch.	Guzerat.	Concan.	Deccan.	S. India.	British Burmah.	Nepaul.
1250	840	Cursorius coromandelicus, *Gmel.*	×	×	...	...	×	×	×	×	×	...	?	×	×	×	×	×	...	...
1251	840*bis.*	Cursorius gallicus, *Gmel*	×	×	×	×	×	×	×	...	×	...	...	×	×	...	...	...	...	...
1252	841	Rhinoptila bitorquata, *Jerd.*	...	...	...	...	...	...	...	...	...	...	...	...	...	...	...	×	...	...
1253	842	Glareola orientalis, *Leach.*	×	...	...	...	...	...	...	×	...	...	...	...	...	...	×	C.	×	...
1254	842*bis.*	Glareola pratincola, *Linn.*	×	...	×	×	...	...	...	...	...	...	...	...	...	...	×	...	...	...
1255	843	Glareola lactea, *Tem*	×	...	...	...	×	×	...	...	...	...	...	...	...	...	×	...	×	...
1256	844	Squatarola helvetica, *Linn.*	×	×	...	...	...	...	...	×	...	...	...	×	...	...	...	×	×	...
1257	845	Charadrius fulvus, *Gm*	×	...	...	...	×	×	...	?	...	...	...	×	...	...	×	×	×	...
1258	845*bis.*	Charadrius pluvialis, *Linn.*	×	×	...	...	×	...	...	...	...	...	...	...	...	...	...	...	...	...
1259	846	Ægialitis Geoffroyi *Wagl.*	×	×	×	...	...	...	...	×	×	...	...	×	...	×	...	×	×	...
1260	847	Ægialitis mongolica, *Pall.*	×	×	×	×	...	...	...	×	...	...	...	×	...	×	...	×	×	...
1261	848	Ægialitis cantiana, *Lath*	×	×	×	×	×	×	×	×	×	...	...	×	×	×	×	c×	×	...
1262	849	Ægialitis dubia, *Scop*	×	×	×	×	×	×	×	×	×	×	×	×	×	×	...	c×	×	×
1263	850	Ægialitis Jerdoni, *Legge*	×	...	...	...	...	...	...	×	...	...	...	×	×	...	...	C.	×	...
1264	851	Vanellus cristatus, *Meyer*	×	×	×	×	×	×	...	...	...	...	...	...	...	...	×	...	...	×
1265	852	Chettusia gregaria, *Pall.*	×	×	×	×	×	×	×	...	×	×	...	×	...	×	...	...	...	...
1266	853	Chettusia leucura, *Licht*	×	×	×	×	×	×	×	×	×	×	×	×	×	×	?×	...	...	...
1267	854	Chettusia cinerea, *Blyth*	×	...	...	...	×	×	...	...	...	...	...	...	...	...	...	...	×	...
1268	857	Hoplopterus ventralis, *Linn.*	×	...	...	...	×	×	×	×	...	×	...	...	...	...	...	...	×	×
1269	855	Lobivanellus indicus, *Bod.*	×	×	×	×	×	×	×	×	×	×	×	×	×	×	...	×	×	×
1270	855*bis.*	Lobivanellus, atronuchalis, *Blyth*	...	...	...	...	...	...	...	...	...	...	...	...	...	...	...	...	×	...
1271	856	Sarciophorus bilobus, *Gmel*	×	...	...	...	×	×	×	×	×	×	×	×	×	×	×	c×	×	×
1272	858	Æsacus recurvirostris, *Cuv.*	×	...	...	...	×	×	×	×	×	×	×	×	×	×	×	c×	×	...
1273	859	Œdicnemus crepitans, *Tem.*	×	×	×	...	×	×	×	×	×	×	×	×	×	×	×	×	×	...
1274	860	Strepsilas interpres, *Linn.*	×	×	×	...	...	...	...	...	×	...	...	...	...	...	×	c×	...	...
1275	861	Dromas ardeola, *Paykull*	×	×	×	...	...	...	...	...	...	...	...	×	×	×	...	C	...	...
1276	862	Hæmatopus, ostralegus, *Linn.*	×	×	×	×	...	...	...	×	...	...	...	×	...	×	...	c×	...	...
1277	863	Grus antigone, *Linn.*	×	...	...	...	×	×	×	×	×	×	×	×	×	×	×	×	×	...
1278	864	Grus leucogeranus, *Pall*	×	...	...	×	×	×	×	...	...	...	...	...	...	...	...	...	...	...
1279	865	Grus cinerea, *Bechst.*	×	...	...	...	×	×	×	×	×	×	×	×	×	×	×	...	...	...
1280	866	Anthropoides virgo, *Linn.*	×	×	?	×	×	×	×	§	×	×	×	×	×	×	×	×	...	...
1281	867	Scolopax rusticola, *Linn*	×	×	×	×	×	×	×	×	...	...	...	...	...	×	...	×	...	×
1282	868	Gallinago nemoricola, *Hodgs*	...	...	...	...	...	×	...	...	...	...	...	...	...	...	...	c×	...	...
1283	869	Gallinago solitaria, *Hodgs,*	...	...	...	...	...	×	...	...	B.	...	...	...	...	...	...	C.	...	×
1284	870	Gallinago stenura, *Kuhl*	×	×	...	×	×	×	...	×	▲×	▪×	...	×	×	×	×	C.	×	...
1285	871	Gallinago scolopacina, *Bonap.* ....×...	×	×	×	×	×	×	×	×	×	×	×	×	×	×	×	c×	×	...
1286	872	Gallinago gallinula, *Linn.*	×	×	×	×	×	×	×	×	×	×	×	×	×	×	×	×	×	...
1287	873	Rhynchœa capensis, *Linn.*	×	×	×	...	×	×	×	...	×	×	×	×	×	...	...	c×	×	...
1288	886	Limicola platyrhyncha, *Tem.*	×	×	...	...	...	...	...	×	...	...	...	×	×	×	...	×	×	...

Bhootan. C. Ceylon. § Assam.

Note.—Marks in the columns Beloochistan and Persia refer chiefly to the coast and gulf of those countries.

No. in Avifauna.	Jerdon's Nos.	Species.	Sind.	Beloochistan.	Persia.	Afghanistan.	Punjab.	N.-W. Provinces	Oudh.	Bengal.	Bajputana.	Central India.	Central Prov.	Kutch.	Guzerat.	Concan.	Deccan.	S. India.	British Burmah.	Nepaul
1289	887	Eurynorhynchus pygmæus, *Linn.*	...	...	...	...		...	X	...	...	...	...	...	...	...	...	C.	X	...
1290	884	Tringa minuta, *Leisl.*	X	X	X	X	X	X	X	X	X	X	X	X	X	X	X	cx	X	...
1291		Tringa subminuta, *Midd.*	X	...	...	...	...	...	...	X	...	...	...	...	...	...	...	cx	X	...
1292	885	Tringa temmincki, *Leisl.*	X	...	...	...	...	...	...	X	...	...	...	...	...	...	...	cx	X	...
1293		Tringa crassirostris, *Tem. Schleg*	X	X	...	...	...	...	...	...	...	...	...	...	...	...	...	.	X	...
1294	882	Tringa subarquata, *Gould.*	X	X	X	X	X	X	X	X	X	X	X	X	X	X	X	cx	X	X
1295	883	Tringa cinclus, *Linn.*	X	...	...	...	X	X	X	X	X	...	..	X	X	..	...	...	...	...
1296	880	Machetes pugnax, *Linn.*	X	X	X	X	X	X	X	X	X	X	X	X	X	X	X	cx	X	X
1297	888	Calidris arenaria, *Linn.*	X	X	X	X	X	X	X	X	X	X	X	X	X	X	X	cx	X	X
1298	890	Phalaropus hyperboreus, *Linn.*	X	X	X	X	...	...	...	...	...	...	...	...	...	...	...	C.	...	...
1299	889	Phalaropus fulicarius, *Linn.*	..	...	...	...	...	...	..	X	...	...	...	...	...	...	...	C,	...	...
1300	893	Actitis hypoleucos, *Linn.*	X	X	X	X	X	X	X	X	X	X	X	X	X	X	X	cx	X	...
1301	892	Actitis ochropus, *Linn.*	X	X	X	X	X	X	X	X	X	X	X	X	X	X	X	cx	X	...
1302	891	Totanus glareola, *Gmel*	X	X	X	X	X	X	X	X	X	X	X	X	X	X	X	cx	X	...
1303	894	Totanus canescens, *Gmel.*	X	...	...	...	X	X	X	X	X	X	X	X	X	X	X	cx	X	...
1304	895	Totanus stagnatilis, *Bechst.*	X	...	...	...	X	X	X	X	X	X	X	X	X	X	X	cx	...	...
1305	897	Totanus calidris, *Linn.*	X	X	X	X	X	X	X	X	X	X	X	X	X	X	X	cx	X	X
1306	896	Totanus fuscus, *Linn.*	X	X	...	...	...	...	...	X	...	..	..	X	X	X		cx	X	...
1307		Totanus Haughtoni, *Hume.*	...	...	...	...	...	...	...	X	...	...	...	...	...	...	...	...	X	...
1308		Totanus dubius, *Murray*	X	..	...	...	...	...	..	...	...	...	.	...	.	...	...	..	...	...
1309	876	Terekia cinerea, *Gould.*	X	X	...	...	...	X	...	X	...	...	...	X	X	X	...	cx	X	...
1310	874	Pseudoscolopax semipalmatus, *Jerd.*	...	...	...	...	...	...	...	.	...	...	..	...	..	...	.	...	X	...
1311	875	Limosa ægocephala, *Linn.*	X	X	X	X	..	...	...	...	X	...	...	X	X	X	...	cx	X	...
1312		Limosa lapponica, *Linn.*	X	X	X	X	...	.	...	...	...	...	...	X	X	X	...	cx	X	...
1313	878	Numenius phæopus, *Linn.*	X	X	X	...	...	...	...	X	...	...	...	X	X	X	..	cx	X	...
1314	877	Numenius arquatus, *Linn.*	X	X	X	X	X	X	X	X	X	...	...	X	X	X	X	cx	X	...
1315	879	Ibidorhynchus Struthersii, *Vig.*	...	...	...	..	...	...	...	...	.	...	...	...	...	...	...	...	...	X
1316	899	Recurvirostra avocetta, *Linn.*	X	X	X	X	X	X	X	X	X	...	...	X	X	X	X	X	X	...
1317	898	Himantopus candidus, *Linn.*	X	X	X	X	X	X	X	X	X	X	X	X	X	X	X	cx	X	...
1318	900	Metopodius indicus, *Lath.*	...	...	...	...	..	...	..	X	...	X	X	X	X	X	X	X	X	...
1319	901	Hydrophasianus chirurgus, *Scop.*	X	...	...	...	X	X	X	X	X	X	X	X	...	...	...	cx	B.	...
1320	902	Porphyrio poliocephalus, *Lath.*	X	X	X	X	X	X	X	X	X	X	X	X	X	X	X	cx	X	...
1321	903	Fulica atra, *Linn.*	X	X	X	X	X	X	X	X	X	X	X	X	X	X	X	X	X	X
1322		Podica personata, *G.R.Gray*	...	...	...	...	...	...	...	§	...	...	...	...	...	...	...	...	X	...
1323	913	Hypotænidia striata, *Linn.*	...	...	...	...	...	...	§	X	syl	...	‖	...	...	X	*	cx	...	...
1324	914	Rallus indicus, *Blyth.*	...	...	...	...	..	..	§	X	syl	X	...	...	...	...	...	cx	X	X
1325	912	Rallina euryzonoides, *Lafresn.*	...	...	...	...	X	X	‡	X	B	...	...	...	...	...	...	cx	X	X

C. Cashmere.

Note.—Marks in the columns Beloochistan and Persia refer chiefly to the coast and gulf of those countries.

No. in Avifauna.	Jerdon's Nos.	Species.	Sind.	Beloochistan.	Persia.	Afghanistan.	Punjab.	N.-W. Provinces	Oudh.	Bengal.	Rajputana.	Central India.	Central Prov.	Kutch.	Guzerat.	Concan.	Deccan.	S. India.	British Burmah.	Nepaul.
1326		Rallina fasciata, *Raffl.* ...	...	...	...	...	...	...	...	...	...	...	...	...	...	...	...	...	×	...
1327		Rallina Canningi, *Tytler*...	...	...	...	...	...	...	...	A	...	...	...	...	...	...	...	...	?	...
1328	910	Porzana Bailloni, *Vieill.* ...	×	×	×	×	×	×	×	×	×	×	×	×	×	×	×	×c	×	...
1329	906	Porzana maruetta, *Linn.*...	×	×	×	×	×	×	×	×	?	?	×	×	×	×	×	×	×	?
1330	911	Porzana fusca, *Linn.*	.	...	...	...	×	×	...	×	×	×	...	C	...	...	...	×c	...	...
1331		Porzana minuta, *Pall.* ...	×	...	...	...	...	...	...	...	...	...	...	...	...	...	...	...	...	...
1332	908	Porzana akool, *Sykes*	...	...	...	...	×	×	×	×	×	×	×	...	×	...	...	...	...	...
1333	905	Gallinula chloropus, *Linn.*	×	×	×	×	×	×	×	×	×	?	×	×	×	×	×	×	×	×
1334	907	Gallinula phœnicura, *Penn.*	×	×	...	...	×	×	×	×	×	...	...	×	×	×	×	×c	×	...
1335	904	Gallicrex cinereus, *Gm.* ...	×	...	...	...		...	...	×	..	×	...	...	...	...	...	×c	×	...
1336	915	Leptoptilos argala, *Lath*..	×	...	...	...	×	×	×	×	×	×	×	×	×	×	×	×	×	...
1337	916	Leptoptilos javanicus, *Horsf.*	...	...	...	..	×	?	?	×	×	×	×	...	...	..	..	×c	×	...
1338	917	Xenorhynchus asiaticus, *Lat*	×	...	...	.	×	×	×	×	×	×	×	×	×	×	×	×c	×	...
1339	918	Ciconia nigra, *Linn.*.........	×	×	...	×	×	×	×	×	×	×	×	×	×	×	×	..	..	...
1340	919	Ciconia alba, *Belon*........	×	...	...	...	×	×	×	×	×	×	×	×	×	×	×	...	...	...
1341	920	Ciconia leucocephala, *Gm*	×	...	...	...	×	×	×	×	?	×	..	?	×	×	×	×c	×	...
1342	921	Ardea goliath, *Temm.*.....		...	...	...	...	...	...	...	‖	...	...	...	...	...	...	...	...	...
1343		Ardea sumatrana, *Raf.* ...	...	...	...	...	...	...	...	...	...	...	...	...	...	...	...	...	×	...
1344	922	Ardea insignis, *Hodgson*..	.	...	...	...	...	...	...	×	§	...	...	...	...	...	...	...	...	×
1345	923	Ardea cinerea, *Linn.*	×	×	×	×	×	×	×	×	×	×	×	×	×	×	×	×c	×	...
1346	924	Ardea purpurea, *Linn*......	×	×	×	×	×	×	×	×	×	×	×	×	×	×	×	×c	×	...
1347	925	Herodias alba, *Linn.*	×	×	×	×	×	×	×	×	×	×	×	×	×	×	×	×c	×	...
1348	926	Herodias intermedia, *Von Hasselt.*	×	×	×	×	×	×	×	×	×	×	×	×	×	×	×	×c	×	...
1349	927	Herodias garzetta, *Linn.* ...	×	×	×	×	×	×	×	×	×	×	×	×	×	×	×	×c	×	...
1350		Herodias eulophotes, *Swinh.*	...	...	...	...	...	...	...	...	...	...	...	...	...	...	...	..	×	...
1351	928	Demi-egretta gularis, *Bosc.*	×	×	...	...	...	...	...	×	..	...	...	×	...	...	...	×c	...	...
1352		Demi-egretta sacra, *Gmel*	...	...	...	...	...	...	...	N	A	...	...	...	...	...	...	...	×	...
1353	929	Bubulcus coromandus, *Bodd.*	×	×	×	×	×	×	×	×	×	×	×	×	×	×	×	×c	×	...
1354	930	Ardeola grayi, *Sykes*	×	×	×	×	×	×	×	×	×	×	×	×	×	×	×	×c	×	...
1355		Ardeola prasinoceles, *Swinh.*	...	...	...	...	...	...	...	...	...	...	...	...	...	...	...	...	×	...
1356	931	Butorides javanica, *Horsf.*	×	×	×	×	×	×	×	×	×	×	×	×	×	×	×	×c	×	...
1357	932	Ardetta flavicollis, *Lath.* ..	×	...	...	..	×	×	×	×	...	...	...	×	×	×	×	×c	×	...
1358	933	Ardetta cinnamomea, *Gmel.*	×	...	...	...	×	×	×	×	...	...	...	×	×	×	×	×c	×	...
1359	934	Ardetta sinensis, *Gmel*......	×	.	...	...	×	×	×	×	...	...	...	×	×	×	×	×c	×	...
1360	935	Ardetta minuta, *Linn*......	×	×	×		×	×	..	×	...	...	...	...	...	...	...	...	...	...
1361	936	Botaurus stellaris, *Linn*...	×	×	×	×	×	×	×	×	...	...	...	×	..	×	×	×c	×	...
1362	937	Nycticorax griseus, *Linn.*	×	×	×	×	×	×	×	×	×	×	×	×	×	×	×	×c	×	...
1363		Gorsachius melanolophus, *Raf.*	..	...	...	...	...	...	...	N	...	...	...	...	...	...	...	×c	...	...
1364	938	Tantalus leucocephalus, *Penn.*.	×	×	×	×	×	×	×	×	×	×	×	×	×	×	×	×c	×	...
1365	939	Platalea leucorodia, *Linn.*	×	×	×	×	×	×	×	×	×	...	..	×	×	×	×	×c	×	...

Note.—Marks in the columns Beloochistan and Persia refer chiefly to the coast and gulf of those countries.

No. in Avifauna.	Jerdon's Nos.	Species.	Sind.	Beloochistan.	Persia.	Afghanistan.	Punjab.	N.-W. Provinces	Oudh.	Bengal.	Bajputana.	Central India.	Central Prov.	Kutch.	Guzerat.	Concan.	Deccan.	S. India.	British Burmah	Nepaul.
1366	940	Anastomous oscitans, *Bodd.*	×	×	×	..	×	×	×	×	×	×	×	×	×	×	×	×	×	...
1367	938	Threskiornis melanocephalus, *Lath.*	×	×	×	...	×	...	...	×	×	...	..	×	×	×	×	×c	×	...
1368	942	Geronticus papillosus, *Temm.*	×	×	×	...	×	×	×	×	×	×	...	×	×	×	×	×c	×	...
1369		Graptocephalus Davisoni, *Hume.*	...	...	...	...	...	...	...	...	...	...	...	...	..	...	...	...	×	..
1370	943	Falcinellus igneus, *Linn.*	×	×	×	×	×	×	×	×	×	×	×	×	×	...	×	×c	×	...
1371	944	Phœnicopterus antiquorum, *Tem.*	×	×	×	×	×	×	×	×	×	×	×	×	×	×	×	×c	×	...
1372		Phœnicopterus minor, *Geof. St. Hil.*	×	...	×	...	×	×	...	...	×	...	...	...	×	...	×	...	...	...
1373		Cygnus olor, *Gm.*	×	...	..	×	×	...	...	...	...	...	...	×	...	...	...	...	...	...
1374	945	Anser cinereus, *Meyer.*	×	×	×	×	×	×	×	×	×	...	..	×	×	...	...	...	...	...
1375	946	Anser brachyrrhynchus, *Baillon*	...	...	...	...	×	×	...	...	...	...	...	...	...	...	...	...	...	...
1376	947	Anser albifrons, *Gm.*	×	×	×	×	×	×	×	.	...	...	...	...	...	..	...	...	...	...
1377	948	Anser erythropus, *Linn.*	...	...	...	...	...	×	×	..	...	...	..	..	.	...	.	...	...	...
1378	949	Anser indicus, *Lath.*	×	...	...	...	×	×	×	×	...	...	×	...	.	..	...	...	...	...
1379	950	Sarkidiornis melanonotus, *Pen.*	×	...	...	...	×	×	×	×	×	...	...	×	×	×	×	×c	×	...
1380	951	Nettapus coromandelianus, *Gmel.*	×	×	...	...	×	×	×	×	×	×	×	×	×	×	×	×c	×	...
1381	952	Dendrocygna javanica, *Horsf.*	×	...	...	...	×	×	×	×	...	×	×	×	×	×	×	×c	×	...
1382	953	Dendrocygna fulva, *Gmel.*	×	...	...	...	×	×	×	×	...	×	×	×	×	×	×	×c	×	...
1383	954	Casarca rutila, *Pall*	×	×	×	×	×	×	×	×	×	×	×	×	×	×	×	×c	×	×
1384	955	Casarca scutulata, *Mull.*	...	...	...	...	...	...	...	×	§	...	...	...	...	...	...	...	×	...
1385	956	Tadorna cornuta, *Gm.*	×	×	×	×	×	×	×	×	..	...	...	×	×	...	..	...	...	...
1386	957	Spatula clypeata, *Linn.*	×	×	×	×	×	×	×	×	×	×	×	×	×	×	×	×c	...	×
1387	958	Anas boscas, *Linn.*	×	×	×	×	×	×	×	×	×	×	×	×	×	×	×	...	...	...
1388	959	Anas pœcilorhyncha, *Forst.*	×	×	×	×	×	×	×	...	...	...	×	×	×	×	×	×c	×	...
1389	960	Anas caryophyllacea, *Lath.*	...	...	...	...	...	...	...	§	Arr	...	...	...	...	...	...	...	×	...
1390	961	Chaulelasmus streperus *Lin.*	×	×	×	×	×	×	×	×	...	×	×	×	×	×	×	...	×	×
1391		Chaulelasmus rufiventris, *Sp. Nov*	...	×	...	...	...	...	..	Syl	...	...	...	...	..	...	...	...	...	...
1392		Chaulelasmus angustirostris, *Menetries.*	×	×	×	×	×	×	×	×	...	..	..	...	...	...	...	...	.	...
1393	962	Dafila acuta, *Linn.*	×	×	×	×	×	×	×	×	...	×	×	×	×	×	×	×c	×	...
1394	963	Mareca penelope, *Linn.*	×	×	×	×	×	×	×	×	×	×	×	×	×	×	×	×	×	..
1395	964	Querquedula crecca, *Linn.*	×	×	×	×	×	×	×	×	×	×	×	×	×	×	×	×c	×	...
1396	965	Querquedula circia, *Linn.*	×	×	×	×	×	×	×	×	×	×	×	×	×	×	×	×c	×	...
1397	966	Querquedula formosa, *Georgi.*	×	...	...	...	...	×	×	×	...	...	...	...	...	...	...	...	...	...
1398		Querquedula falcata, *Georgi.*	...	...	...	...	×	×	...	×	...	...	...	...	...	..	...	...	...	...
1399	967	Fuligula rufina, *Pall*	×	×	×	×	×	×	×	×	×	×	×	×	×	×	×	...	...	...

Note.—Marks in the columns Beloochistan and Persia refer chiefly to the coast and gulf of those countries.

No. in Avifauna.	Jerdon's Nos.	Species.	Sind.	Beloochistan.	Persia.	Afghanistan.	Punjab.	N.-W. Provinces.	Oudh.	Bengal	Rajputana.	Central India.	Central Prov.	Kutch	Guzerat.	Concan.	Deccan.	S. India.	British Burmah.	Nepaul.
1400	971	Fuligula cristata, *Linn.*	X	X	X	X	X	X	X	X	X	X	X	X	X	X	X	xc	...	...
1401	970	Fuligula marila, *Linn.*	X	...	...	...	...	...	...	...	...	...	...	...	...	...	...	...	...	X
1402	968	Fuligula ferina, *Linn.*	X	X	X	X	X	X	X	X	X	X	X	X	X	X	X	X	...	...
1403	969	Fuligula nyroca, *Gould.*	X	X	X	X	X	X	X	X	X	X	X	X	X	X	X	...	...	X
1404		Clangula glaucion, *Linn*	X	...	...	X	...	X	...	...	...	...	...	...	...	...	...	...	...	...
1405		Erismatura leucocephala, *Scop.*	...	...	...	...	...	X	...	...	...	...	...	...	...	...	...	...	...	...
1406		Mergus serrator, *Linn*	X	...	...	...	...	...	...	...	...	...	...	...	...	...	...	...	...	...
1407	972	Mergus merganser, *Linn*	X	X	X	...	X	X	...	X	...	...	...	...	...	...	...	...	...	...
1408	973	Mergellus albellus, *Linn*	X	X	X	X	X	X	X	...	...	...	...	...	X	...	...	...	...	...
1409	974	Podiceps cristatus *Linn*	X	X	X	...	X	X	X	X	...	...	...	X	X	...	...	...	...	...
1410		Podiceps nigricollis, *Sund*	X	X	...	...	...	...	...	...	...	...	...	...	...	...	...	...	...	...
1411	975	Podiceps minor, *Linn.*	X	X	X	X	X	X	X	X	X	X	X	X	X	X	X	X	X	X
1412	976	Oceanites oceanica, *Kuhl*	X	X	...	...	...	...	...	X	...	...	...	...	...	...	...	...	X	...
1413		Daption capensis, *Linn.*	...	...	...	...	...	...	...	...	...	...	...	...	...	...	...	C	...	...
1414		Puffinus persicus, *Hume*	X	X	...	...	...	...	...	...	...	...	...	...	...	...	...	...	...	...
1415		Puffinus chlororhynchus, *Lesson.*	...	...	...	...	...	...	...	X	...	...	...	...	...	...	...	C	X	...
1416		Stercorarius asiaticus, *Hume.*	X	...	...	...	...	...	...	...	...	...	...	...	...	...	...	...	...	...
1417		Larus cacchinans, *Pall*	X	X	X	...	X	X	...	...	X	...	...	...	...	...	...	...	...	...
1418		Larus affinis, *Reinh.*	X	X	...	...	...	...	...	...	...	...	...	X	X	X	X	...	...	...
1419		Larus gelastes, *Licht.*	X	X	X	...	...	...	...	...	...	...	...	...	...	...	...	...	...	...
1420		Larus hemprichi, *Bp.*	X	X	X	...	...	...	...	...	...	...	...	X	X	X	X	...	...	...
1421	980	Larus brunneicephalus *Jerdon*	X	X	X	...	...	...	...	X	...	...	...	X	X	...	X	C	X	...
1422	979	Larus ichthyætus, *Pall.*	X	X	X	...	X	X	...	X	...	...	...	...	...	X	...	X	...	...
1423	981	Larus ridibundus, *Linn.*	X	X	X	...	X	...	...	X	...	...	...	...	...	X	...	...	...	...
1424	984	Hydrochelidon hybrida, *Pall.*	X	X	X	X	X	X	X	X	X	X	X	X	X	X	X	xc	X	...
1425		Hydrochelidon leucoptera, *Meisn and Schinz.*	X	X	X	X	X	X	X	X	X	X	X	X	X	X	X	xc	X	...
1426		Hydrochelidon nigra, *Lin.*	X	...	X	...	...	...	...	...	...	...	...	...	...	...	...	...	...	...
1427	983	Gelochelidon anglica, *Mont.*	X	X	X	...	...	...	...	X	X	...	...	X	...	X	X	...	X	...
1428	982	Sterna caspia, *Pall*	X	X	X	...	X	X	X	...	...	...	...	...	...	...	...	C	...	...
1429	989	Sterna Bergii, *Licht.*	X	X	X	...	...	...	...	X	...	...	...	X	...	X	...	cx	X	...
1430		Sterna cantiaca, *Gm.*	X	X	X	...	...	...	...	...	...	...	...	...	...	...	...	...	...	...
1431	990	Sterna media, *Horsf.*	X	X	...	...	...	...	...	X	...	...	...	...	...	X	...	xc	X	...
1432	991	Sterna melanauchen, *Temm.*	...	...	...	...	...	...	...	...	...	...	...	...	...	...	...	...	X	...
1433	985	Sterna seena, *Sykes*	X	X	X	X	X	X	X	X	X	X	X	X	X	X	X	xc	X	...
1434	987	Sterna melanogastra, *Temm.*	X	X	X	X	X	X	X	X	X	X	X	X	X	X	X	xc	X	...
1435		Sterna Dougalli, *Mont.*	...	...	...	...	...	...	...	X	...	...	...	...	...	...	...	C	X	...
1436	986	Sterna hirundo, *Linn.*	X	...	...	...	X	...	...	...	...	...	...	...	...	...	...	cx	...	...
1437		Sterna albigena, *Licht*	X	X	...	...	...	...	...	...	...	...	...	...	...	...	...	...	...	...
1438		Sterna Saundersii, *Hume*	X	...	...	...	...	...	...	...	...	...	...	...	...	...	...	...	...	...
1439	988	Sterna sinensis, *Gm.*	X	...	...	...	...	...	...	X	...	...	...	...	...	...	...	C	X	...
1440	992	Sterna anæsthetus, *Scop*	X	X	X	...	...	...	...	...	...	...	...	...	...	X	...	C	X	...

Note.—Marks in the columns Beloochistan and Persia refer chiefly to the coast and gulf of those countries.

No. in Avifauna.	Jerdon's Nos.	Species.	Sind.	Beloochistan.	Persia.	Afghanistan.	Punjab.	N.W. Provinces.	Oudh.	Bengal.	Rajputana.	Central India	Central Prov.	Kutch.	Guzerat.	Concan.	Deccan	S. India.	British Burmah.	Nepaul.
1441		Sterna fuliginosa, *Gm.*	×	×	×	...	...	...	...	...	...	...	...	...	...	*	...	C	...	...
1442	993	Anous stolida, *Linn.*	×	×	...	...	...	...	...	×	...	...	...	...	...	...	...	.	...	...
144	994	Anous tenuirostris, *Tem.*	...	...	...	...	...	...	...	×	...	...	...	...	...	...	...	...	...	...
1444		Anous leucocapillus, *Gould.*	...	...	...	...	...	...	...	×	...	...	...	...	...	...	...	...	...	...
1445	995	Rhynchops albicollis. *Swains.*	×	×	×	...	...	...	...	×	...	...	...	×	...	×	...	×	×	...
1446	996	Phæton rubricauda, *Bodd.*	...	...	...	...	...	...	...	×	...	...	...	...	...	...	...	...	...	...
1447	997	Phæton flavirostris, *Brand.*	...	...	...	...	...	...	...	×	...	...	...	...	...	...	...	...	...	...
1448		Phæton indicus, *Hume.*	×	×	...	...	...	...	...	×	...	...	...	...	...	...	...	...	×	...
1449	1000	Fregata aquila, *Linn*	...	...	...	...	...	...	...	×	...	...	...	...	...	*	...	C	...	...
1450		Sula cyanops, *Sundev.*	×	×	...	...	...	...	...	×	...	...	...	...	...	×	...	C	...	...
1451	998	Sula australis, *Steph.*	...	...	...	...	...	...	...	×	...	...	...	...	...	...	...	...	×	...
1452	999	Sula piscator, *Linn.*	...	...	...	...	...	...	...	×	...	...	...	...	...	...	...	...	...	...
1453		Pelicanus crispus, *Bruch.*	×	×	...	...	×	×	×	...	...	...	...	...	...	...	...	...	...	...
1454	1004	Pelicanus manillensis, *Gm.*	×	...	×	...	...	...	...	×	×	...	...	×	×	...	×	×c	×	...
1455	1001 } 1003 }	Pelicanus roseus, *Gm.*	×	...	×	...	...	...	...	×	×	...	...	×	×	...	×	×c	×	...
1456	1005	Phalacrocorax carbo, *Linn.*	×	×	×	×	×	×	×	×	×	×	×	×	×	×	×	×c	×	×
1457	1006	Phalacrocorax fuscicollis *Steph.*	×	...	...	...	...	...	...	...	×	...	...	×	×	...	×	C	×	...
1458	1007	Phalacrocorax pygmæus *Pall.*	×	...	...	...	...	...	...	...	×	...	...	×	×	...	×	C	×	...
1459	1008	Plotus melanogaster, *Penn.*	×	...	...	...	...	...	...	×	×	...	...	×	×	×	×	C	×	...

Note.—Marks in the columns Beloochistan and Persia refer chiefly to the coast and gulf of those countries.